ENVIRONMENTAL ECONOMICS AND POLICY

The Addison-Wesley Series in Economics

ENVIRONMENTAL ECONOMICS AND POLICY

Jonathan A. Lesser
School of Business Administration
University of Vermont

Daniel E. Dodds
Washington State Department of
Transportation

Richard O. Zerbe, Jr.
Graduate School of Public Affairs
University of Washington

 **ADDISON-WESLEY**

An imprint of Addison Wesley Longman, Inc.

Reading, Massachusetts • Menlo Park, California • New York • Harlow, England
Dan Mills, Ontario • Sydney • Mexico City • Madrid • Amsterdam

Acquisitions Editor: Bruce Kaplan
Project Editor: Ellen MacElree
Design Manager: John Callahan
Cover and Text Designer: John Callahan
Cover Photo: Keren Su, FPG International
Art Studio: ElectraGraphics, Inc.
Electronic Production Manager: Su Levine
Desktop Administrator: Laura Leever
Electronic Page Makeup: Interactive Composition Corporation
Printer and Binder: R. R. Donnelley & Sons Company
Cover Printer: Lehigh Press

Library of Congress Cataloging-in-Publication Data

Lesser, Jonathan A.
    Environmental economics and policy / Jonathan A. Lesser, Daniel E. Dodds,
  Richard O. Zerbe, Jr.
      p. cm.
  Includes bibliographical references and index.
  ISBN 0-673-98210-6
  1. Environmental economics.   I. Dodds, Daniel.   II. Zerbe,
  Richard O.   III. Title
  HC79.E5L465   1997
  330--dc20   96-44798
                                                 CIP

2345678910— DOC —   9900

*To Donna and Ellen, for their patience,
support, and inspiration.*

*To Richard Zerbe, Sr. for his devotion to
his children's intellectual development.*

BRIEF CONTENTS

DETAILED CONTENTS

*†NOTE: Sections marked with a dagger refer to material that is
more advanced.*

PART IV   SELECTED POLICY TOPICS   437

15 Exhaustible Resources   439

18 Energy Resources   552

CASE STUDIES

PREFACE

In writing this book, we have had two goals: first, to show how economics can, and should, contribute to the formation of environmental policy, and second, to explain the tools that allow environmental economists to make that contribution.

A book on environmental *policy* needs little justification. Every day, the media are full of stories about environmental problems and governments' attempts to deal with them. Often the news is bad. Another species is endangered; another chemical has been found to cause cancer. Less frequently, the news is good. Air and water quality has improved in many developed countries, and several species of animals have been brought back from the edge of extinction. Sometimes it is hard to tell whether the news is good or bad. Governments promise to do something about a particular environmental problem and then bicker about who will do what, who will pay for it, and who will get the credit during the reelection campaign.

A book on environmental *economics* needs little justification to economists but may need much justification to noneconomists. Ours is simple. Many environmental problems have an economic problem at their core, and *all* environmental policies have an economic component—they involve allocating scarce means to competing ends. The success or failure of environmental policies can turn on whether they exploit or ignore economic aspects of human behavior. The importance of economics for understanding environmental problems and for solving them is the first theme we repeat throughout this book.

Environmental economists frequently become discouraged when policymakers ignore the simple and elegant theoretical solutions we offer them. This is not the result of stupidity. Few environmental problems are *strictly* economic problems. In many cases, other aspects of environmental problems are more important to everyone except professional economists. Where economists see an externality, environmental activists may see evil: wealthy corporations poisoning innocent people and wildlife, violating their rights to clean air and water, and generally behaving like thugs. In these cases, it is more fruitful, we believe, to show how economics can help solve problems as they are defined by the parties involved than to try to change people's worldview. We also believe that it is better to use economics to make incremental improvements in messy public policies than to rail against the imperfections of the public policy process. This is the second theme we repeat throughout the book—the importance of understanding *all* aspects of a problem and then tailoring a solution to the problem, rather than trying to redefine the problem to fit a predetermined solution.

Although environmental economists are occasionally asked to declaim on the great issues of our time and to recommend appropriate policies, most of what we do is more prosaic. We are asked to estimate the costs of an oil spill, the value of water for fishing and boating, or the possible costs of global warming. However, prosaic does not mean unimportant. Few, if any, environmental policy questions can be answered with theory alone. They must be answered with facts and with analysis that applies appropriate models to appropriate data. This is the third theme we stress. Any recommendations and pronouncements we make should be backed up by solid applied research.

There are quite a few good books on environmental economics. Most of the ones we like—they are cited in our chapter references—are fairly narrowly focused, fairly abstract, or both. They are aimed at working professionals or advanced graduate students. They go into one or more areas of environmental economics in depth but assume a thorough grounding in economic theory and in environmental policy issues. Undergraduate textbooks seem to fall into two groups. Some are aimed at students with little or no previous experience with economics. Others read like compendia of canned answers to simplified policy questions. A major motivation for writing this book was our experience that there never seemed to be a canned answer to the problems we encountered in our professional work and that the canned answers we found all too often turned out to apply only in special cases or to be politically infeasible.

We have aimed this book at students in upper-level undergraduate and graduate classes in environmental economics, public policy, and environmental studies. For undergraduate classes in environmental economics, this book has more than enough material and topics to serve as the main text, with supplementary readings on topics the instructor wants to stress. For graduate classes in environmental economics, it can serve as the core text, providing the general framework and context for topics to be covered in greater depth by more specialized texts and journal articles. For classes in environmental studies and public policy, where several aspects of environmental issues are covered, this book can serve as the main source for the environmental economics portion of the course.

STRUCTURE OF THE BOOK

The book is divided into four sections. Part I introduces the major concepts to be discussed. Chapter 1 provides a tour of the book by using global climate change as a case study. We discuss how environmental policies affect the economy in Chapter 2, then provide a review of basic economic concepts such as willingness to pay in Chapter 3. Chapter 4 reviews the basic ethical concepts that lurk behind various policy suggestions and pronouncements, and Chapter 5 provides a method students can use to develop sound environmental policies.

Part II presents the most fundamental economic concepts and policy issues. Chapter 6 defines externalities and their effect on economic efficiency. Chapter 7 develops the policies that can be used to address externalities. Chapter 8 then discusses how externalities affect other important policy goals, such as equity and rights. Chapter 9 reviews key U.S. environmental legislation. Chapter 10 is unique among environmental economics textbooks in that it presents a methodology that can be used to balance different, and often competing, policy goals.

Part III focuses on measuring environmental costs and benefits and applying those measurements to policy decisions. Chapter 11 presents the empirical techniques used by economists to measure environmental costs and benefits, and Chapter 12 applies these techniques to a difficult and controversial issue, the value of human lives. Chapter 13 discusses the importance of time and discounting and the controversy that surrounds it. And Chapter 14 addresses how environmental policies can be developed in the presence of uncertainty.

In Part IV, we turn our attention to a smorgasbord of applied topics that are at the forefront of many environmental policy issues, beginning with a discussion of exhaustible and renewable resource use. The first two chapters in this part, 15 and 16, are designed to provide a solid footing in the principles of natural resource use while addressing some of the key policies that have grown up around the management (and mismanagement) of such resources, including the world's fisheries and forests. Chapter 17 discusses water resource development and use. Chapter 18 discusses energy use and related policies. Chapter 19 is devoted to the popular but ethereal concept of sustainability; we review definitions of sustainability and then devote most of the chapter to asking how it can be measured. Chapters 20 and 21 are devoted to international issues: Chapter 20 discusses localized international issues such as acid rain and water pollution that cross international borders, and Chapter 21 looks at global issues, including ozone depletion and global climate change. Chapter 22 provides a brief summation of how environmental policymakers can develop good environmental policies using the tools presented in the book.

PEDAGOGY

Each chapter starts with a case study to frame the issues. These issues are drawn from the real world and are often the subject of continual and sometimes rancorous debate. In each chapter, we tie the economic concepts and tools to real-world policy issues. Throughout, we stress processes that can lead to better environmental policies, rather than pushing a single "correct" outcome. Each chapter ends with a summary of the economic concepts and tools and policy issues covered in the chapter. Each chapter also has a list of discussion questions and problems and a reference list.

We expect students to be able to follow rigorous economic arguments. We have included a review of relevant topics from microeconomic theory, but students with no previous economic background will have some catching up to do. We have used mathematics where it helps to explain the economics. Most of the time we stick to algebra and geometry, but where calculus is the best tool for making a point, we have not been afraid to use it. However, we have put the heaviest mathematics in optional sections that are highlighted with a dagger (†) and in the appendices.

Students can skip this material without missing the main points, but students who work through it will be rewarded with a deeper and broader understanding.

ACKNOWLEDGMENTS

We want to thank the many students, friends, and colleagues who encouraged us to produce an accessible book that focused on actual environmental policy implementation. We were fortunate to have the skills of numerous reviewers who devoted much time and effort to improving the content and presentation of material. We thank the following: Renatte Adler, San Diego State University; Donald Cocheba, Central Washington University; A. Myrick Freeman, Bowdoin College; David Jacques, California State Polytechnic University, Pomona; Akbar Marvasti, University of Houston; Fred Menz, Clarkson University; Jim Moncur, University of Hawaii, Manoa; and Richard Rosenberg, Pennsylvania State University. Special thanks go to Walt Hecox, Colorado College, and Geoff Black, Marist College, for their painstaking reviews of the entire manuscript and their many valuable suggestions. Of course, the errors and omissions that remain are ours, not theirs.

Special thanks also go to Rick Hammonds, for his initial faith in the manuscript, and Bruce Kaplan, economics editor at Addison-Wesley, for his tireless advice and guidance in shepherding the book through production. Addison-Wesley's production staff also displayed patience, assistance, and professionalism far beyond the call of duty. To all of them, we are indebted.

Last, we extend special thanks to our families, for their patience and support. This book would not have been possible without their understanding and encouragement.

Jonathan A. Lesser
Daniel E. Dodds
Richard O. Zerbe, Jr.

PART I

BUILDING

BLOCKS

We interact with the environment around us. Throughout most of our history, we have taken the environment for granted; it provided us with all of the food, fuel, and shelter we needed, with little or no complaint. Over the past century, however, this one-way relationship has changed. The environment can no longer satisfy our growing demands. Consequently, we have begun to feel the pain of scarcity. Many of us are forced to breathe dirty air and drink fouled water; we notice too that nature's abundance, from fisheries to forests, has become far less abundant. The environment has changed the rules.

This change has elevated the importance of developing sound environmental policies. Without them, economic growth is damaging; industry, urbanization, and development in many countries have brought with them alarming declines in environmental quality. The need for policies that can preserve the benefits of economic growth *and* the environment has taken on new priority.

In Part I, we begin our exploration for such policies. We begin in Chapter 1 by describing environmental economics and its importance to this exploration and explaining how it differs from other branches of economics. Then we provide a brief "guided tour" of the critical issues that must be addressed to develop sound environmental policies and where in the book those issues are confronted.

Chapter 2 discusses the relationship between economic growth and environmental quality. We do this by first introducing the concept of an input-output framework and then showing how the environment provides necessary inputs to an economy, whether raw materials or as a waste sink, and outputs that consumers demand, such as clean air and beautiful views, free-flowing rivers for recreation, and species preservation to maintain global biodiversity.

Chapter 3 reviews the economic foundations of public policy decisions. We start by looking at individual decisions, for two reasons. First, the concepts of economic welfare and equity that we use throughout this book are based on individuals' preferences reflected through their choices. Second, we start with individual choices because all choices are ultimately individual choices. The chapter defines

1

a variety of basic economic concepts that are critical to environmental policymaking, including willingness to pay and willingness to accept, consumers' and producers' surplus, and Pareto efficiency.

Chapter 4 then introduces another critical facet of many environmental policy debates: the role of ethics. As we will discuss in later chapters, many environmental policies are not based solely on the fundamental concepts discussed in Chapter 3. Rather, they incorporate a variety of philosophical concepts about fairness and justice. Though we are not philosophers, we believe that a little philosophical background is useful in understanding many environmental policy debates, some of which have little to do with basic economics. As we shall see, the development of public policies often requires weighing and balancing competing values and sometimes choosing between them.

Chapter 5 is devoted to the general process of policy development: both as it should be and as it usually is. We examine the five steps necessary to develop and implement good public policy: defining the problem, setting goals, choosing a preferred policy instrument, implementing the policy, and evaluating the results and, if necessary, revising the policy. We then look at some of the reasons why these steps are often not followed in the real world.

CHAPTER 1

INTRODUCTION TO ENVIRONMENTAL ECONOMICS

More Heat than Light? The Challenge of Global Climate Change

Unless you are a hermit, you have probably heard or read about global climate change. In an introduction to a 1993 symposium on the subject, economist William Nordhaus stated that "Albert Einstein's reaction to quantum mechanics was 'God does not play dice with the universe.' Yet, mankind is playing dice with the natural environment through a multitude of interventions" (p. 11).

Climate change, per se, is nothing new. The earth's climate has changed throughout its history, varying between tropical periods warmer than today and ice ages far cooler. Instead, it is the potential for sudden and possibly avoidable changes in rainfall patterns, sea level increases, extremes of drought or freezes, and losses of forests and species that is causing concern. Over the past century, climatologists have observed a significant increase in levels of carbon dioxide (CO_2), corresponding to the burning of fossil fuels, such as coal and petroleum, and significant deforestation of the earth. CO_2 traps heat in the earth's atmosphere. Too little CO_2, and the earth would be inhospitably cold; too much, and the earth would resemble its nearby cousin Venus. Other gases besides CO_2, including methane, oxides of nitrogen, and chlorofluorocarbons like freon, trap heat in the atmosphere. Collectively, these are known as greenhouse gases, or GHGs. Although CO_2 gets the most attention, other GHGs have better insulating properties than CO_2 but occur in much smaller concentrations. Many scientists and environmentalists fear that the observed increase in concentrations of these so-called anthropogenic (human-caused) GHGs will overwhelm the natural variability of

3

the earth's climate, cause catastrophic changes in the climate, and ultimately lead to the extinction of many species, including humans (IPCC 1996).

The rate of change and the overall impacts are still unknown. They are also the subjects of much speculation. Although computers can model global climate changes, they can do so only on a large-scale basis. And because no one yet understands precisely how the climate works or what all of the relevant variables are, none of these computer models is guaranteed to produce accurate predictions. Indeed, when run using past (and therefore already known) data, many of these climate models have done a poor job of duplicating observed climate changes. As a result of this uncertainty, some scientists and other analysts either discount the theory of global climate change or even welcome some of its predicted impacts, such as moderating northern climates and lengthening growing seasons.

Nevertheless, the concern about GHGs and global climate change has led to proposals to drastically reduce anthropogenic emissions of greenhouse gases. In 1992, a series of global meetings took place in Rio de Janeiro; these came to be known as the Rio Summit. One outcome of these meetings was an international agreement to stabilize emissions of greenhouse gases at 1990 levels. In 1993, President Clinton produced the Climate Change Initiative, which outlined how the United States would reduce its CO_2 emissions to 1990 levels by the year 2000. However, little has been done since then. Many nations have either quietly backed away from the Rio Summit goals or ignored them altogether.

Given the frightening prospects of global climate change, why has so little been done? Simply put, significantly reducing global GHG emissions today will be costly, and the future benefits remain uncertain. Almost every form of energy humans use—whether burning gasoline to power cars, natural gas to heat homes, or coal to generate electricity—produces CO_2. Unfortunately, energy technologies that produce little or no CO_2, like solar cells and wind turbines, are still more expensive and less reliable than existing technologies. Or they have other adverse environmental impacts, such as with hydroelectric plants that can inundate wilderness areas and eliminate fisheries such as those for salmon. CO_2 emissions will probably increase as developing nations continue to grow economically and their citizens demand more of the "conveniences" (e.g., refrigeration, automobiles, computers) that citizens in developed nations take for granted.

Addressing global climate change can be thought of as a massive insurance problem, with some twists. First, the insurance policy has to cover a multitude of GHGs simultaneously. Second, GHG control requires international cooperation; a large country like China, for example, could thumb its nose at the rest of the world and make other efforts to reduce CO_2 emissions moot. Third, there is still uncertainty about what is being insured against and when the impacts might occur. Fourth, who pays for the insurance today, how much should be paid, and who will receive any "payouts" are disputed; there are critical equity issues across generations and across countries that must be dealt with.

Given the uncertainties and the costs, what should be done? How should an environmental policymaker, who has little more than a basic understanding of climatology but a solid understanding of economic principles, wrestle with the complexities and competing concerns? Should the policymaker recommend wait-and-

see policies that encourage collection of additional scientific data so as better to determine the magnitude and the scope of the problem? What if wait-and-see policies reveal a problem far worse (and far more costly to solve) than originally thought? Perhaps the policymaker should recommend significant greenhouse gas reductions today, regardless of the cost. But if these policies reduce wealth significantly, where will the resources needed to combat other environmental and social problems—poverty, disease, and overpopulation, to name just three—be found? Will global climate change policies that "invest" in the welfare of future generations require too much sacrifice of the present generation? How can societies weigh the uncertainty of saving lives in the future against increasing the misery of those living in poverty today?

And what if the costs and benefits of global climate change are uneven among countries and individuals? Suppose that climate models predict increases in rainfall and agricultural production in areas of Africa that now suffer through years of drought and crop failures but decreases in production in North America? Would policies that reduced the magnitude of global climate change, and hence potentially deny many countries that are in desperate need of more food, be unfair? Would such policies be "racist"?

All of these questions raise complex economic, scientific, moral, and even political issues. Though the answers may not be forthcoming with any ease, the worst approach would be to remain ignorant of the issues themselves. Ultimately, in the case of global climate change, the adage may be "If you can't stand the heat, stay in the kitchen."

INTRODUCTION

Thankfully, not all environmental issues are as difficult as global climate change. Yet most involve similar sets of concepts, often at odds with one another. All environmental problems can be traced to the fundamental economic problem of *scarcity:* we cannot have everything we want because our resources are limited. Although everyone would prefer a world of pristine air and water, abundant old-growth forests, and free-flowing rivers, we have made trade-offs for the other goods and services we want. Determining the most reasonable trade-offs is where the study of environmental economics is important.

Solving environmental problems requires an understanding of fundamental economic concepts such as scarcity. More fundamentally still, solutions require identification of and agreement on the problems to be solved. Unfortunately, that step is too often ignored. By developing the necessary tools to understand and address environmental policy issues, we can increase the likelihood that the best policies will be enacted.

The rest of this chapter provides a brief introduction to and tour of this book. As we will discuss, many environmental policy debates are the result of different sets of values: different *economic* values, in terms of our willingness to pay for a variety of goods and services, including environmental ones; different *moral* values, in terms of human rights and the rights of nature; even even different *spiritual* values, in terms of the propriety of limiting human populations and, presumably, human-caused environmental degradation. Although environmental policymakers will never be able to determine the "right" set of values, they can understand and separate different types of values and use them to develop better policies.

What Is "Environmental Economics," and How Does It Relate to Environmental Policy?

We interact with the environment around us. That environment encompasses the entire natural world in which we live: air, land, oceans, plants, and animals. Without our environment, none of us would be here. We have gained increasing control over the environment around us, and this has raised the question of whether the environment exists solely for our species's benefit. That question is a source of debate that weaves through much of the ecological and philosophical literature. Yet even as our ability to alter the environment in which we live has increased, the capacity of the environment to absorb those alterations is limited.[1] Global climate change is one such manifestation. We have also made great progress in understanding the environment. Natural sciences such as biology, zoology, chemistry, and ecology, to name a few, have provided significant insights into how the environment "works." But these sciences do not explain interactions between ourselves and our environment.

Traditional economics, by contrast, while unable to explain how the environment works, can explain how limited or scarce resources are allocated. It can explain (with arguable degrees of success) everything from why countries trade to why some individuals drive BMWs and others Fords.

In many cases, traditional economics begins with the interaction of supply and demand, such as the market for apples shown in Figure 1.1(a). Economists often use such supply and demand diagrams to explain how well-established markets function. The market for apples has many buyers and sellers, and there are few market barriers to prevent transactions. Ownership of the goods in question is always clear. In short, the market for apples is a good "textbook case" of how a market functions, one that you have probably seen in an introductory economics textbook.

If you look at Figure 1.1(b), you will see the same sort of supply and demand diagram for "clean air." You may object to defining the "market" for clean air the same way we define the market for apples. After all, one cannot go down to the local grocery store and purchase clean air. There is not a *direct* market for clean air that can support exchanges between buyers and sellers; no one has distinct ownership of clean air supplies. All of us—and none of us—own the atmosphere. No one has an explicit right to use the atmosphere, but we all have implicit rights to do so. That lack of ownership, which economists sometimes refer to as a *market failure,* is a key reason why the air is polluted, whether with wood smoke from the neighbors' fireplaces or greenhouse gases from all of us.

It turns out, however, that the same economic principles that determine the price of apples at the grocery store can apply equally well to nonmarket goods like clean air. Clean air, like apples, is a desired and scarce good. Clean air, like apples,

---

[1]This is sometimes called the *carrying capacity* of the environment.

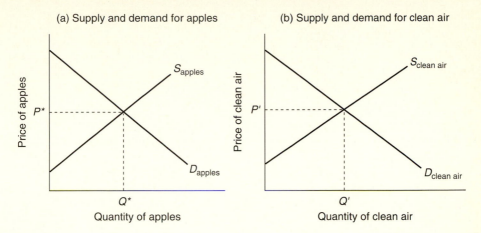

Figure 1.1   Supply and Demand for Consumer and Environmental Goods

requires resources to produce. In the case of apples, those resources are land, labor, water, fertilizer, and other inputs, one of which is clean air. "Producing" clean air requires that the atmosphere not be used as a waste dump, or at least used less so. That means that wastes must be diverted elsewhere, which also requires scarce resources. One solution, at least for some environmental problems, is to introduce the same market interactions where none had existed previously. That is one of the key goals of environmental economics.

Environmental economics links broad concepts of how the environment "works" with fundamental economic concepts like supply and demand. Because humans interact with the environment and because humans allocate scarce resources, applying economic concepts to the study of the environment can lead to greater insights about why environmental "problems" exist and what the "best" solutions to those problems are. Why is the air polluted? How "clean" should the air be? Why is global climate change an issue? What is the "right" amount of carbon dioxide in the atmosphere? How much should society spend to prevent oil spills like the one involving the Exxon *Valdez*? And if a spill does occur, how much should the firm responsible have to pay in damages, and to whom? These insights can, in turn, serve as the basis for sound policies that can eliminate or at least lessen the severity of environmental problems.

Of course, natural science and economics are not the only factors that enter into the development of environmental policy. Ethical and religious values, as well as social and political traditions, also play a role—often a dominant one. That is one reason why economists are sometimes frustrated by environmental policies. However, *all* environmental policy questions involve important economic components like scarcity and economic efficiency. Regardless of the other issues involved, environmental policymakers need to be concerned with the *economic* aspects of both environmental problems and policies to remedy them. Environmental economics cannot answer all environmental policy questions, but it will be the *only* source of answers for many.

How Does Environmental Economics Differ from Other Branches of Economics?

Environmental economics uses the same *microeconomic* and *macroeconomic* tools as other branches of applied economics. However, it uses them to address issues that do not arise in other fields, and in a unique context.

Consider again the similarities and the differences between the market for apples and the market for clean air. One difference between environmental economics and other branches of economics arises from the differences between environmental "goods" (e.g., clean air, clean water, diverse species, healthy forests) and traditional economic goods (e.g., cars, television sets, books). Whereas there is a well-defined market for apples, in many cases there are no markets for environmental goods. You cannot revive an extinct species the way you might revive hula hoops.

The first key difference is that environmental goods are often *public goods,* in that they can be enjoyed ("consumed") by many individuals simultaneously without affecting individual consumption.[2] The public-good aspects of many (not all) environmental goods frequently involve breakdowns in the way markets work or a complete absence of markets. Even so, your purchasing decisions of consumer goods like compact discs or apples *can* affect the demand and the supply of environmental goods. If the demand for apples increases, apple growers will want to increase supplies. Perhaps growers will want to buy more land to plant apple orchards. But if that land lies downwind of an oil refinery, apple growth may be stunted because of the pollution emitted from the refinery.

In most markets, your consumption decisions do not materially affect my consumption decisions. If you purchase this environmental economics textbook, so can I. But if you burn your trash next to my house and foul the air I breathe, I have little recourse; I cannot go to the store and purchase new clean air to breathe. Your actions will have affected my well-being and *created* an environmental problem. Economists call such effects *externalities.*

A second difference is that time often plays a crucial, sometimes defining, role in environmental economics. Traditional economics can determine the most efficient way to allocate resources for producing goods and services and determine the most profitable mix of goods and services to produce. Traditional economics can also demonstrate the linkages between different sectors of the economy—why manufacturing steel affects the electric industry or why the consumption of more television sets affects wheat production.[3] If you wish to manufacture compact discs, economics can tell you the most efficient mix of electricity, labor, plastic, and metal that should be combined to produce a compact disc at the lowest cost. Economics can also determine the relative quantities of compact discs and television

---

[2]More specifically, public goods are defined by two major characteristics: *nonrivalry* and *nonexcludability.* We will discuss these concepts formally in Chapter 6.
[3]These concepts are reviewed in Chapters 2 and 3.

sets to produce. Those allocations are simplified because producing an additional compact disc or television set today does not preclude producing one tomorrow.

For many environmental goods and services, however, allocation of resources over time is critical. If we burn fossil fuels today and release GHGs, we may be creating an environmental problem for our descendants hundreds of years from now. If we harvest and eat all of the world's salmon today, the salmon will be gone forever; science fiction notwithstanding, we still lack the ability to re-create extinct species. Thus our consumption decisions of some environmental goods may be *irreversible* and may have profound effects on the well-being of future generations.

A third difference is that other branches of economics often ignore environmental resource constraints. For example, in Figure 1.2(a), if we were to use traditional microeconomic principles, we would conclude that an increased demand for apples from D to D' would increase the equilibrium price and the quantity of apples supplied from (P^*, Q^*) to (P', Q'). But traditional economics might not consider that if apple growers expand production by purchasing land downwind of a factory spewing out pollution, the costs of growing more apples will increase more than assumed. Perhaps pollution from the factory will slow apple growth and productivity per tree, requiring growers to use more fertilizer. Or perhaps bees used to pollinate the new trees will get sick in the polluted air and not pollinate either new or old orchards as effectively. If these impacts occur, the supply curve for apples will shift upward from S to S', reflecting the *external* costs imposed on apple growers. Instead of seeing a new equilibrium supply of Q' apples at a price P', the new equilibrium in the apple market will be (P'', Q''), as in Figure 1.2(b).

Environmental economics addresses these sorts of "nonmarket" issues and a general concern about the environment. Older branches of economics developed when there was less interest in environmental issues. Few, if any, economists studied global climate change in the 1970s. Instead, many focused on the issues raised

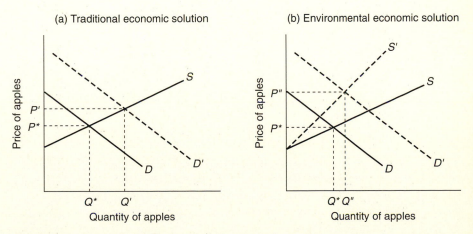

Figure 1.2   Market Equilibrium Changes Caused by an Increase in the Demand for Apples

by the creation of the Organization of Petroleum Exporting Countries (OPEC) and its subsequent 1974 oil embargo.

One reason for the relatively new emergence of environmental economics is the change in our society's attitude toward the environment over time. Before the American Revolution, there was a colonial tradition of social control that provided a great deal of environmental protection (Horwitz 1977). Common law at that time imposed significant legal restrictions on the ability of landowners to pollute streams used by their neighbors. By about 1820, however, the whole landscape of common law had been changed into one that had all the appearances of a free-market, or *laissez-faire,* economic system. Under this new system, the economic development sentiments of New England entrepreneurs were emphasized above all else. No one questioned whether trees should be cut down, prairies plowed up, or rivers dammed, as long as it was in the interest of economic growth.

Until the 1960s, in the United States, as in many other nations, the view prevailed that the world was capable of absorbing all of the unwanted by-products of the human pursuit of economic well-being. Economists concentrated on the allocation of scarce capital and labor; none recognized the *environment* as a scarce resource. There then began a widespread shift in values and expectations, which represented almost a return to the pre-Revolutionary colonial tradition of social control (Hughes 1970). We began to notice the effects of our economic actions on the environment. We discovered that the air above our cities was polluted and that many of our water supplies were fouled and unfit to drink. As if to highlight the degree to which we had misjudged the capability of the world to absorb our wastes, we even witnessed the bizarre spectacle of the Cuyahoga River catching fire where it ran through Cleveland, Ohio. Our society then began its hurly-burly response toward environmental protection, combining everything from legislation mandating improvements in water and air quality, to sit-ins protesting what some believed to be our "profligate" existence as a capitalist society. Economists responded by studying the allocation of environmental quality.

With the end of the Cold War and the collapse of communism, the world discovered that environmental degradation was not a unique attribute of the "capitalist" Western world. Quite the contrary. In many formerly communist countries, including Poland, Russia, and the Czech Republic, pollution existed at levels unimaginable in the West. Decades of heavy industrialization had led to crippling declines in air and water quality. Water pollution levels in some rivers and lakes in eastern Europe made the Cuyahoga River fire seem benign by comparison. Unfortunately, these environmental problems were compounded by an overarching silence, in the belief that no physical price was too great to pay to seek economic and military parity with the West.

In many developing countries today, pollution is still seen as a necessary price for economic growth. As a result, some cities such as Mexico City and São Paulo regularly suffer air pollution levels that are far more severe than those in the United States. Worst of all, many of the poorest nations seem stuck in an unending cycle of poverty and economic degradation; they are unable to devote the necessary resources to secure tomorrow's economic interests because they are too focused on survival today. No more do these nations have the resources to combat major environmental concerns like global climate change than they have to launch probes to distant planets. Theirs is a daily struggle to provide enough arable land and uncontaminated water, all the while watching their populations burgeon and the strain on their limited natural resources increase.

Cuba, for example, which remains a "holdout" communist state still subject to a U.S. economic embargo as this is being written, struggles with the development of several resort islands to promote tourism versus concerns about disrupting the fragile ecosystems on those islands. But many Cubans ask, if they cannot develop these resources to provide income and jobs, what are they to do, knowing that switching to a market system will not resolve the dilemma immediately?

HOW TO APPROACH ENVIRONMENTAL ISSUES

We have discussed why the study of environmental economics is important and how it differs from other branches of economics. Now we turn to the subject of most of this book: how to study environmental issues. Generally, economists will not *identify* environmental issues like global climate change. They can, however, help environmental policymakers confront the complexities of the issues involved. Developing *effective* environmental policies (it is easy to develop an ineffective policy!) requires that policymakers go through a series of steps:

1. They must understand economic concepts, such as supply and demand, and also understand the broader linkages between the economy and the environment.
2. They must understand the economic concepts of scarcity, value, and efficiency, as well as often conflicting philosophical concepts such as equity, fairness, rights, and justice.
3. They must determine the most important economic, environmental, and philosophical issues to be addressed for the environmental problem under consideration.
4. They must be familiar with the contents of the economist's "toolbox" and how those tools can be used to make necessary trade-offs and resource allocations among worthy goals.
5. They must be able to measure and value trade-offs, in monetary terms or otherwise.
6. They must understand the critical role of time because environmental problems (and the policies that address them) can have impacts for years, centuries, even forever.
7. They must know how to deal with uncertainty, risk, and the unknowable.

The Linkage Between the Economy and the Environment

The first step is for policymakers to understand how market economies work and how actions in one part of the economy can reverberate throughout. Policymakers must understand, for example, that implementing policies to combat global climate change will affect *all* sectors of the economy, not just the sectors their policies target.

These sorts of macroeconomic environmental interactions are the subject of Chapter 2, which explains why economic and environmental well-being are closely linked. Ultimately, successful environmental policies will be the ones that improve the economic well-being of the world's inhabitants so as to provide the means with which to clean up basic environmental hazards, all the while guarding against the degradation of the environmental resources that remain the final arbiters of our quality of life. This is no easy task. It continues to be complicated by ignorance of basic economic behavior and by addressing environmental issues on a piecemeal basis, rather than in a more comprehensive framework.

Economic and Environmental Values

Policymakers must also have a knowledge of economic and philosophical concepts. They must understand what *scarcity* and *efficiency* mean. They must understand the meaning of *value, fairness,* and *rights.* At the very least, they must define what *they* mean by those terms. The reason is that as human beings, we compete with other species for many resources, such as land, forests, water, and wetlands. We also extract and deplete mineral and other nonrenewable resources, transform them into usable products, and create wastes in the process. The goods and services we desire require environmental inputs and often create undesirable environmental outputs that affect other individuals, cultures, and species. Yet without environmental resources, we would be unable to produce the economic goods and services we desire. Thus it would appear that our *economic* values conflict with our *environmental* values.

However, as most philosophers and many economists know, *value* is a difficult term to define and consequently is often the subject of conflicting definitions. It is also a term you will see often in this text. Most economists focus on monetary measures of value, expressed through the preferences of individual (human) consumers. Those preferences form the basis of consumer theory in microeconomics and concepts of economic efficiency that we review in Chapter 3. For some economists, unless *consumers* expresses a preference for certain environmental attributes or objects (e.g., clean water, pristine views, old-growth forests), those attributes have no *intrinsic* value. These economists argue that environmental values *are* economic values, based on a willingness to pay to obtain them, much as an individual is willing to pay a certain dollar amount for a new car, house, or apple.

By contrast, ecologists, environmentalists, and some economists often focus on two other types of values: the values reflecting the environmental preferences of society as a whole[4] and the intrinsic values of ecosystems, including the entire earth. They believe that individual plant and animal species and the environment

---

[4]Sen (1995) discusses whether the environmental preferences of society can be defined meaningfully.

as a whole have certain *unmeasurable* values that cannot be expressed in monetary terms or other *metrics*.[5] In this view, whether or not individual humans share those values is irrelevant because environmental preservation will be a *moral imperative*. Unfortunately, these latter values can conflict with the notion of economic value and are often the source of bitter debates in environmental policy development. Therefore, policymakers need to understand those other types of environmental values and the different *ethical* concepts on which they are based. We do this in Chapter 4.

In many cases, different types of values cannot be compared easily (Sunstein 1994); some environmental values (e.g., hectares of old-growth forest) cannot be compared directly with other environmental values (e.g., number of species) or other social values (e.g., preservation of human rights). Yet these sorts of "apples and oranges" problems also can wreak havoc when resource allocation questions arise. They require different approaches to make rational policy decisions because trade-offs will still be required. Rather than making such trade-offs blindly, we present one possible approach to making them in Chapter 10.

Determining Key Environmental, Economic, and Philosophical Issues

Once an environmental problem, such as global climate change is identified, and assuming that environmental policymakers understand the various economic and philosophical concepts involved, they must determine the key policy issues and understand why the problem raises those issues. (This task is discussed in Chapter 5.) For example, suppose that a policymaker decides that global climate change is primarily an issue about economic efficiency. Knowing that, the policymaker can compare how increased emissions of GHGs will affect economic efficiency and well-being over time (Chapter 6) and look at the ongoing economic impacts that alternative policies will have (Chapter 7). Nordhaus (1994), for example, developed a model to do just this.

Alternatively, a policymaker may decide that global climate change is primarily an ethical issue. That policymaker may decide that because the actions of human beings today may irreparably harm future generations as well as lead to the extinction of many animal and plant species, potential future impacts must be mitigated, regardless of their impact on economic well-being. If so, that policymaker must understand how alternative environmental policies can affect ethical concepts, such as equity and human rights (Chapter 8). With that understanding, the policymaker can then examine policies to improve equity and rights (Chapter 9) and select those that achieve the desired goals at the lowest cost.

For complex environmental issues such as global climate change, a policymaker will probably be concerned with *both* efficiency and equity issues. The policymaker will want to improve economic well-being in the future but will also want to do what he or she believes to be fair and just. Unfortunately, in many cases, what

---

[5]These values also are called *nonmonetary* values.

is the most efficient can be the most unfair. So the policymaker will have to balance worthy but competing goals and will need a method of doing so (Chapter 10).

Measuring and Valuing Trade-Offs

Regardless of what environmental policymakers decide about global climate change, which ethical concepts of value they embrace, how they balance competing goals, and what policies they select, they will need a way to measure different values. For example, what trade-off exists between improving the quality of life for individuals today and increasing GHG emissions that may harm future generations? How do individuals decide what nonmarket goods and services to consume? How do they choose between spending money to preserve old-growth forests and spending it to save whales?

Economists have developed sophisticated empirical techniques with which to elicit monetary estimates of environmental values based on the preferences of individuals. We examine these techniques in detail in Chapter 11 and provide several examples of how they have been used. Economists even have developed techniques to value the *human* part of intrinsic environmental values, which are called *existence values*. Existence values are defined as the value humans place on the existence of other species and environmental attributes that they will never "consume." None of these techniques is without controversy, nor can they derive "exact" values for such things as cleaner air, pristine views, and preservation of endangered species. Nevertheless, such techniques are important to environmental policy development; without them, there is no way of knowing how individuals value different aspects of the environment.

Chapter 12 follows with a discussion of how economists estimate one of the most controversial components in determining environmental policies: the "value of life." By this economists do not mean the value of any specific individual's life, such as Grandma, the president of the United States, or a child who has fallen down a well. Instead, estimates of the "value of life" are designed to determine how much individuals are willing to pay for small changes in the risks they face in their daily lives, whether from air pollution, faster cars, or safety hazards. Value-of-life calculations can play an important role in developing policies that are designed to reduce environmental risks where society must decide how much to pay to reduce certain risks and to what level to reduce those risks.

The Problems of Time and Risk

The effects of global climate change, if any, may not be realized for centuries, but they may change the climate forever. Water pollution today can kill fish for decades. Nuclear wastes can remain dangerously radioactive for thousands of years. Environmental policy issues often focus on the importance of time and an ability to compare future environmental costs and benefits with costs and benefits incurred today. As we show in Chapter 13, how time should be addressed in environmental policy decisions is often misunderstood, resulting in poorly designed policies.

Economists treat time through a process called *discounting*.[6] Future benefits and costs are "brought back" or discounted to the present to compare those benefits and costs with current ones. In general, this results in future benefits and costs having *less* weight than those in the present. Intuitively, this makes sense; for most people, a dollar today is worth more than a dollar ten years from now. Perhaps you have seen one of those sweepstakes advertising that "you may win $10 million." If you look at the fine print, however, you will discover that you will not receive your $10 million right away. Instead, it will be paid to you in $50,000 increments for 20 years. There is nothing wrong with that, but you probably would prefer the whole $10 million right now.

Discounting is a standard technique used to improve economic efficiency by comparing alternative environmental (and other) projects in a consistent manner. The *discount rate* reflects the strength of preferences for current consumption over future consumption. Society as a whole is often said to have an aggregate or *social discount rate*. This discount rate depends on numerous factors, including productivity and growth of the economy, the amount of the capital stock that is "inherited," and the level of "impatience" in a society. Not surprisingly, different societies can have different social discount rates.

Even though discounting is a straightforward empirical technique, the choice of appropriate discount rates for environmental policy decisions remains controversial. Because the discount rate used will often determine whether certain resources are developed and what environmental policies are chosen, selecting an appropriate discount rate is crucial for many environmental policy analyses, for it will affect the allocation of current and future resources. Much of the controversy centers around arguments that market interest rates are inappropriate for use as the discount rate and should be "adjusted" in various ways. For example, some environmentalists and economists argue that future environmental costs and benefits not be discounted at all. As we suggest in Chapter 13, however, adjusting discount rates in this manner results from a mistaken desire to address equity and rights goals by adjusting future prices. It is not that such goals are unimportant, but they can, and should, be addressed in more straightforward ways.

In part, controversy over the choice of discount rate also reflects different attitudes toward risk and uncertainty. That is why, in Chapter 14, we define the concepts of risk and uncertainty and explore how the value of reducing uncertainty can be determined. Then we examine how policymakers' attitudes toward risk can affect environmental policy choices.

SOME SPECIAL ISSUES

With the necessary expertise, environmental policymakers can tackle a variety of issues. These issues change over time. In the 1970s, petroleum supply, population growth, and food supplies were debated fervently. More recently, the concept of

---

[6]If you are unfamiliar with discounting, an introduction to the concept appears at the beginning of Chapter 13.

sustainability, which encompasses numerous economic, ethical, and environmental concepts, has been in the forefront of environmental economics. Yet policymakers must understand more than just today's hot environmental issue. Often solutions to new environmental problems will be found by examining past issues. And in other cases, the issues will remain the same, but new tools will be developed to address them.

The final chapters of this book are devoted to a variety of topics, encompassing different subjects. Some are old and some are new; all are relevant, especially in the context of environmental policy development. Specific issues of importance or interest to you may not be covered. No slight is intended. Covering all environmental issues would be impossible without creating a book of encyclopedic proportion.

Natural Resources

Environmental and natural resource issues are closely linked. Nature provides the resources that humans use. Mining copper from the ground can have environmental impacts. Extracting that copper today means that it cannot be extracted in the future, and its price may change. Given the interactions in the economy, that may lead to greater use of substitutes for copper and different sorts of environmental impacts. Whereas some resources, like copper and oil, are finite and *exhaustible,* others can renew themselves. Fish can be harvested today while leaving fish to be harvested next year. If trees cut today are replanted, there will be trees to cut tomorrow—at least up to a point. Often the same market breakdowns or lack of well-defined markets that lead to environmental impacts lead to inefficient use of these *renewable* resources and sometimes to their irreversible depletion.

Chapter 15 looks at the economics of exhaustible resources. This is a well-established subject with implications throughout the economy and the environment. Decisions on how to develop and use exhaustible resources today affect the supply of those resources in the future and can lead to significant environmental impacts. Were it not for the 1974 OPEC oil embargo, for example, the Alaska pipeline might not have been built, and the Exxon *Valdez* would not have run aground in Prince William Sound.

Chapter 16 looks at the economics of renewable resources such as fish and trees. Poor harvesting decisions can have significant economic and environmental impacts. At the limit, overharvesting leads to the extinction of species, which is an important environmental issue. But overharvesting need not be severe to have environmental impacts. Logging trees in the Amazon may affect the earth's climate by destroying rain forests and increasing emissions of GHGs. Overfishing can lead to a loss of a major protein source throughout the food chain and encourage overuse of agricultural lands. Together, Chapters 15 and 16 examine how resource prices are set, whether markets allocate natural resources efficiently, and whether we are in danger of running out of essential resources.

Sustainability and Sustainable Development

For many ecologists, the intrinsic value of the environment and the existence of species forms the core of their beliefs about sustainability, which we discuss in

Chapter 19. Although the interest in sustainability and sustainable development was probably spurred most by the publication of the 1987 World Commission on Environment and Development report *Our Common Future,* the concept itself bears a strong resemblance to themes of conservation that were discussed as early as the beginning of the twentieth century. As Brown (1991) notes, conservationists argued long ago for the "wise use" of natural resources and for the reuse of irreplaceable resources. Gray (1913), for example, wrote an important article in which he argued that the central issue of the conservation movement was the "conflict between the present and the future." Although these authors did not use the term *sustainability* or *sustainable development* specifically, their aims were similar.

The WCED report (usually referred to as the Bruntland Commission report) defined sustainable development as "development that meets the needs of the future without compromising the ability of present generations to meet their own needs" (p. 43). The Bruntland Commission report focused primarily on large-scale development that could have irreversible environmental consequences, such as construction of major hydroelectric projects. Essentially, the report raised two issues. First, it questioned the degree of substitutability between "natural capital" assets (e.g., forests, plant and animal species, clean air) and human-made capital, in the form of physical investment and investment in knowledge and institutions (Toman 1994). Second, the report raised the issue of the present generation's responsibility to future generations in a way similar to Gray's development of the conservation issue.

How sustainability and sustainable development are incorporated into workable environmental policies is not always clear. As Toman and others point out, there are different and conflicting definitions of sustainability. As we discuss in Chapter 19, forming workable policies to achieve sustainable development goals cannot be designed if there is no agreed definition. Nor, as we also discuss in that chapter, are there uniform *measures* of sustainable development. In other words, there is no single *unit of account,* like money, that can measure whether or not a country's development is sustainable. Advocates of sustainability often argue that we should limit our use of all natural resources and that economic development should be based on the use of renewable rather than exhaustible resources. Yet how much the current generation should limit its own use of resources is not clear. As we will discuss, one of the most difficult issues with sustainable development is the necessity to confront the need to allocate scarce resources. Choosing between saving whales and saving salmon from extinction, for example, still requires that scarce resources be allocated (Lesser and Zerbe 1995).

Earth, Air, Fire, and Water

Environmental problems in the United States (and many other countries) affect the water we drink and the air we breathe. Few resources are as important as water. Adequate supplies of water for drinking, agricultural production, and sanitation have enabled civilizations to flourish. Lack of water can create immeasurable hardship and suffering and has brought nations to blows, as in the Middle East. In Chapter 17, we look at a variety of water resource issues that affect how water supplies are allocated and the quality of those supplies. Water quality has been affected by the development of water resources, such as large hydroelectric and irrigation dams, as well as by economic development.

Determining the "right" amount of water quality requires valuing what that quality is worth. Using the techniques we develop in Chapter 11, we explore in Chapter 17 how clean water has been valued and how distortions in water allocation policies, such as subsidized water for agriculture, affect overall water quality.

The production and use of energy also raise environmental quality issues that affect water, air, and soil quality. What types of new power plants should be built to meet increasing electricity demands? Where should they be located? How should air pollution from these plants be regulated? Should exploratory drilling for oil be allowed in "sensitive" environments, such as marine estuaries and remote arctic tundra? Should fuel efficiency standards for cars be increased or eliminated? Should a developing country like China not build the massive Three Gorges hydroelectric project to meet its citizens' increasing need for electricity? If not, should China be allowed to exploit its large reserves of "dirty" coal? What is the trade-off between water and air pollution? Because energy use is ubiquitous, in Chapter 18 we focus on two specific areas of energy use that affect the environment: transportation and electricity production.

International Environmental Issues

What one country finds an unacceptably poor degree of environmental quality, another cannot hope to attain. In the United States, in between doses of political rhetoric, we have placed great importance on environmental quality, as evidenced by numerous federal, state, and local environmental laws and the environmental attitudes of our citizens. Strong concern for the environment also is observed in other countries, especially in western Europe. In some countries, however, much less attention has been paid to environmental quality. In part, this reflects different attitudes and beliefs; more fundamentally, it is a function of different levels of wealth. In many poor countries, such as those in Africa and Asia, individuals struggle merely to survive. They don't worry about the effects of global climate change 100 years hence because they are too busy worrying about whether they will find food or clean water today. Many of these countries lack the basic infrastructure—clean water, sewage treatment, electricity for refrigeration, and so on—that we in the West take for granted (World Bank 1992). As a result, the demand for environmental quality differs between countries and wealth levels.

Some of these differences lead to environmental decisions that appear "unfair." Poorer countries may actively seek "dirty" industries, even though the environmental toll is high, because those industries offer the prospect of jobs and new wealth for their people. Richer countries may be criticized for "exporting" pollution to these poorer countries, raising issues of equity and fairness. Developing sound environmental policies requires that these issues be understood and separated, which we do in Chapter 20. In some cases, it may make economic sense for richer countries to export polluting industries to poorer countries; in other cases, stronger international regulation may be needed to prevent "unjust" actions.

Sometimes international pollution issues are localized. For example, Chapter 20 contains a discussion of the issues raised because of the saline water flowing into Mexico from the Colorado River. Though an international environmental issue, it does not materially affect other nations. We also discuss water pollution in the Great Lakes and the policy solutions that have required cooperation between the United States and Canada. By contrast, some international pollution issues, such as global climate change and atmospheric ozone depletion, require far more cooperation because the pollution has global implications. We discuss these more diffuse international issues in Chapter 21.

CHAPTER SUMMARY

The world faces many significant environmental problems. Maintaining and improving environmental quality and ensuring that economic development does not impose unacceptable costs on future generations will require appropriate government policies. Environmental economics has much to tell us about how environmental problems arise and how to correct them. To us, environmental economics is exciting partly because of its practical importance.

Although this is a book about environmental policy, it is not a cookbook of policy prescriptions with economic justifications. It is a how-to book for people who want to use the theoretical and the empirical tools of environmental economics in developing environmental policy prescriptions. Environmental economics is also exciting because the field of environmental policy is full of controversies. These controversies have many sources. The basic values behind environmental policies are the focus of unresolved philosophical debates. In many cases, environmental policy must be made with limited information. Policymakers often have conflicting goals and are often unclear about their goals. Lastly, environmental economics is a relatively new field, and there are still controversies among environmental economists about empirical and theoretical questions.

In general terms, we have four goals for this book. First, we clarify the concepts and the values that form the bases for environmental policies and the questions that need to be answered to develop appropriate policies. This is necessary to guarantee that we are using economics to answer economic questions and that we are answering noneconomic questions in appropriate ways. Second, we clarify the role of economic forces in creating environmental problems. If we understand *why* we have a problem, we are more likely to be able to solve it. Third, we show how the tools of economics and economic forces can be used in solving environmental problems. Many environmental problems are problems of inefficient resource use, which means that they are essentially economic problems with economic solutions. Other environmental problems revolve around issues of equity, human rights, or rights of nature. In these cases, economics has much to tell us about how to minimize the cost of solving these problems. Finally, we clarify the trade-offs environmental policymakers face and provide some tools to use in making hard choices. With this approach, we hope that you will come to share some of our excitement about environmental economics and environmental policy.

CHAPTER REVIEW

Economic Concepts and Tools

- The fundamental concept of scarcity is central to the study of environmental economics and the development of sound environmental policies.
- Environmental economics uses the same *microeconomic* and *macroeconomic* tools as other branches of applied economics.
- Many environmental goods are *public goods* in that they can be consumed by many individuals simultaneously without affecting individual consumption.
- Time often plays a crucial and sometimes defining role in environmental economics.
- Most economists focus on monetary measures of value, expressed through the preferences of individual (human) consumers. Those preferences form the basis of consumer theory in microeconomics and concepts of economic efficiency
- Economists have even developed techniques to value the *human* part of intrinsic environmental values, which are called *existence values.*

Policy Issues

- Developing *effective* environmental policies requires a series of steps:
  1. Understand economic concepts, such as supply and demand, and also understand the broader linkages between the economy and the environment.
  2. Understand economic concepts of scarcity, value, and efficiency, as well as often conflicting philosophical concepts such as equity, fairness, rights, and justice.
  3. Determine the most important economic, environmental, and philosophical issues to be addressed for the environmental problem under consideration.
  4. Use the tools of economics to make necessary trade-offs and resource allocations between worthy goals.
  5. Measure and value trade-offs, in monetary terms or in some other way.
  6. Understand the critical role of time because environmental problems (and the policies that address them) can have impacts for years, centuries, even forever.
  7. Deal with uncertainty, risk, and the unknowable.

DISCUSSION QUESTIONS

1. What do you think are the three most pressing environmental problems in the world today? Why? How would you go about addressing them?
2. What is "value"? When is something valuable? Do you think it is possible to place a value on improved environmental quality? Is it possible to place a value on the environment? If so, what is the value of whales? If it is impossi-

ble to place a value on the environment itself, how do we allocate environmental resources?

3. Should environmental regulations always be based on an analysis of their costs and benefits, as some members of Congress have recently proposed? If not, what criteria should form the basis for environmental regulations? Should a factory be allowed to emit any pollution at all if that pollution is harmful?

4. What is the "value of life"? Can a life be defined in dollar terms? Would such valuation mean that society might choose not to rescue a small child who had fallen down a well if the cost were "too high"? Are young people "worth" more than old people? Suppose that the president of the United States and a child have both fallen down wells but we have only the resources to rescue one at a time. Who should be rescued first?

5. Comment on this statement: "Nuclear waste may remain radioactive for thousands of years. Therefore, nuclear power is unfair to future generations."

6. Suppose that a majority of humans decide that as a species, they are too harmful to the environment and therefore all human beings should be sterilized immediately so as to cause the extinction of the species over a period of around 100 years. (This has actually been proposed!) Would such an action be unfair to future generations who, as a result of this policy action, would be denied the opportunity ever to exist?

7. The president of the United States announces that "the quality of our environment must be sacrificed if we are to create more jobs for our people." Outline an analysis to either support or refute this hypothesis. What data would you need? What would be the scope of your study?

8. Countries that have more lax environmental standards than the United States have an unfair competitive advantage. Therefore, the United States should force these countries to raise their environmental standards. Do you agree? How would you analyze this proposition?

9. How and by whom are environmental laws fashioned? Which environmental law are you familiar with? What are the major goals of these laws? Have these environmental laws achieved their goals? How can you tell? How should environmental policymakers balance competing goals? How should environmental priorities be set?

10. In the 1970s, it was estimated that we would run out of natural gas within 20 years. In the mid-1990s, natural gas was plentiful and cheap. What happened?

REFERENCES

Brown, G. 1991. "Can the Sustainable Development Criterion Adequately Rank Alternative Equilibria?" Department of Economics, University of Washington, Seattle.

Gray, L. 1913. "Economic Possibilities of Conservation." *Quarterly Journal of Economics* 27(4): 499–510.

Horwitz, M. 1977. *The Transformation of American Law, 1780–1860.* Cambridge, Mass.: Harvard University Press.

Hughes, J. 1970. *Social Control in the Colonial Economy.* Charlottesville: University Press of Virginia.

Intergovernment Panel on Climate Change (IPCC). 1996. *1996 IPPC Report.* Cambridge: Cambridge University Press.

Lesser, J., and R. Zerbe. 1995. "What Can Economic Analysis Contribute to the Sustainability Debate?" *Contemporary Economic Policy* 13(3): 88–100.

Nordhaus, W. 1993. "Reflections on the Economics of Climate Change." *Journal of Economic Perspectives* 7(4): 11–25.

————. 1994. *Managing the Global Commons: The Economics of Climate Change.* Cambridge, Mass.: The MIT Press.

Sen, A. 1995. "Rationality and Social Choice." Presidential Address to the American Economic Association. *American Economic Review* 85(1): 1–24.

Sunstein, C. 1994. "Incommensurability and Valuation in Law." *Michigan Law Review* 92: 779–861.

Toman, M. 1994. "Economics and 'Sustainability': Balancing Trade-offs and Imperatives." *Land Economics* 70(4): 399–412.

World Bank. 1992. *World Development Report 1992: Development and the Environment.* New York: Oxford University Press.

World Commission on Environment and Development (WCED). 1987. *Our Common Future.* New York: Oxford University Press.

CHAPTER 2

ECONOMIC ACTIVITY AND THE ENVIRONMENT

Taxing Times

In his first State of the Union address in January 1993, President Clinton proposed a broad-based energy tax as part of his administration's economic recovery plan and budget proposal. The energy tax was to serve several purposes. First, it was designed to collect revenues for reducing the budget deficit, providing around $70 billion its first five years and over $20 billion each year thereafter. Second, it was supposed to conserve energy and improve the environment by increasing the price of energy, reducing the amount used, and thereby reducing related environmental impacts such as air pollution.

The energy tax was to be based on the energy content of fuels, measured in British thermal units (Btu). (One Btu is the amount of energy required to raise the temperature of 1 pound of water by 1 degree Fahrenheit.) There was also to be an additional surcharge on petroleum. The "Btu tax" was introduced into Congress, but by the fall of 1993, it had been neutered by hordes of special interests.

Energy-intensive industries, such as aluminum smelting, feared for their "competitiveness" against foreign producers. Electric utilities complained that the tax would raise electricity rates. Even automobile associations lamented the tax's potential for crippling the mobility of millions of contented but fuel-thirsty U.S. motorists. And most Republicans in Congress vehemently opposed the tax because, well, it was a tax and a Democrat was in the White House.

One of many vociferous critics of the Btu tax was William Dahlberg, then president and CEO of Georgia Power Company. In testimony before the U.S. Senate Finance Committee in April 1993, Dahlberg stated that the Btu tax would increase inflation, wound big industries, and have a ripple effect throughout the economy as the cost of all products and services increased. Dahlberg claimed that the tax would destroy as many as 600,000 jobs because of the ripple effect. He also argued that because many foreign competitors purchased subsidized energy from their governments, the Btu tax would subsidize foreign imports and make them cheaper relative to American-made goods.

Gradually, the different interest groups received the exemptions they sought. Eventually the tax, Swiss cheese–like with its myriad exemptions, was abandoned completely. Though the budget passed by Congress in 1993 raised income taxes and increased the gasoline tax by 4.3 cents nowhere were broad-based energy taxes to be found. And none has since been considered.

What would be the economic impacts of an energy tax? How would the effects ripple through the economy? What would be the incidence of an energy tax on different areas of the economy? Would the Btu tax have caused the economic devastation testified to by Dahlberg? Would it have had the favorable environmental impacts that had been touted? How can policymakers even estimate such widespread impacts?

Clearly, the size of any ripple effect would depend on the size of the tax. As the price of energy increased, the cost of producing goods and services requiring energy as an input (just about everything in the economy) would also increase. This would seem to argue for the devastation forecast by Dahlberg. But the economy is already full of distortions that sap its strength. One purpose of the Btu tax, for example, was to reduce the budget deficit because a large and growing budget deficit can lead to higher interest rates, less economic growth, reduced income, and fewer jobs. By reducing the budget deficit, the Btu tax could have reduced this existing distortion. The Btu tax was also designed to improve environmental quality. Again, if successful, the tax could reduce environment-related costs, such as those associated with increased cases of respiratory disease. If the Btu tax led to healthier workers, productivity would increase. That would increase economic growth, income, and jobs.

So would Dahlberg's company have been better off with a Btu tax? Perhaps, but not immediately, which probably explained his opposition. But the dire predictions made for any policy that fingers some parties should always be compared with the status quo of doing nothing. In other words, always ask, "Compared to what?"

INTRODUCTION

It is easy to observe that human economic activity affects the environment. Whatever else humans may be, we are biological organisms like all other species. We take in food, water, and air from our environment, use these inputs in chemical reactions within our bodies, and return carbon dioxide and other waste products back to the environment. Even the act of breathing can be thought of as a form of "pollution."

Unlike most other species, however, we are also technological organisms. We are adept at using some parts of our environment as tools to manipulate other parts. Sometimes we do this indirectly, as when we use tools to make tools that make other tools that may be used to provide consumer goods or services. Even our most sophisticated production processes, however, draw their raw materials and energy ultimately from the natural environment and return by-products to the environment.

We are also social organisms. Our interactions with the environment are heavily influenced by our interactions with each other. Most of our behavior is learned, and our need to establish and maintain social relations causes us to interact with our environment in many ways: we build highways and cars to drive over them; we build electric generating plants to power television sets so we can "see" what the rest of us are doing; we set aside land for parks and recreation. All of these interactions do not seem absolutely necessary to maintain our biological existence.

Because most of our interactions with the environment, whether biological, technical, or social, constitute some form of economic activity, almost all environmental "problems" have an economic aspect. As a result, *environmental* problems are *economic* problems.

For most of our species' existence, we did not have the environmental problems we think of today. Certainly we had problems with our environment. No doubt the odd Neanderthal or Cro-Magnon muttered about feeling too hot or too cold or about the scarcity of food to eat. No doubt, too, parts of the environment viewed us as food. But as long as there were relatively few humans on the planet, the adverse impacts the environment inflicted on humans were generally *not* the result of humans inflicting adverse impacts on the environment.

This is no longer the case. Our modern environmental problems arise when one person's use of his or her environment degrades others' environments, whether the others are humans, animals, or plants. We have environmental problems because the environment, like copper, electricity, and steel, is a scarce resource. There are more people with more potential uses for the environment than the environment can provide while remaining essentially unchanged. We can no longer treat the environment as a *free* good, with a natural supply exceeding our demands on it.

The Role of Scarcity

Scarcity is the defining element of economics. Because all modern environmental problems involve scarcity of some aspect of the environment, environmental problems are economic problems even when caused by human activity that we think of as noneconomic.

The environment has become scarce for two reasons. There are more of us than in the past, and each of us places greater demands on the environment than our predecessors. Some people believe that a Western lifestyle has contributed to environmental degradation, which has led some environmental advocates to urge us to "live more with less." We are exhorted to have fewer children, not to drive cars, use less electricity, and live in smaller houses. Yet as we mentioned in Chapter 1, many individuals in less developed countries, who struggle to meet the daily needs of survival, dream of one day attaining our lifestyle. Some environmentalists question whether the earth's resources can support an improved lifestyle for these less fortunate individuals, pointing out that to do so would require massive increases in the use of resources and lead to much higher levels of pollution. They are concerned whether significant improvements in lifestyles are *sustainable*.

Economic Growth and the Environment

It is easy to be pessimistic about our collective economic and environmental future, and such pessimism is not new. In 1798, economist Thomas Malthus wrote *An Essay on the Principle of Population.* He predicted a time when growth in the number of people would outstrip the growth of food supplies. Malthus argued that agricultural productivity could increase only linearly while population would grow exponentially. This, he argued, would lead eventually to mass starvation and death and constrain the population to the available food supply. Malthus predicted also that survivors in this dismal world would have just sufficient food to avoid starvation.

Although there is much hunger and deprivation in the world, Malthus's predictions did not come true. Malthus did not foresee the productivity benefits of mechanized agriculture, fertilizers, and modern irrigation. In essence, Malthus saw a world where there were only two available inputs—land and labor—which could be used only in fixed proportions. Malthus could not have imagined the benefits of using capital, increased knowledge, and renewable resources to improve productivity (Barnett and Morse 1963).

Nevertheless, a number of individuals (e.g., Meadows, Meadows, and Randers 1972; McKibben 1989) continue to believe that the world is on a path to self-destruction. Biologist Paul Ehrlich, most famous for his 1968 book *The Population Bomb,* predicted a world of misery and starvation by the end of the 1970s because of overpopulation and extremely high energy prices arising from dwindling supplies of crude oil and natural gas. His predictions did not come true.

Even though environmental limits have not yet stifled economic growth, there remains the question of whether economic growth *necessarily* harms the environment. Increasing scarcity of environmental resources because of increasing numbers of human beings and individually higher demands would seem to imply that growth and environmental quality must be at odds. If so, how can we reduce the harm from economic growth yet raise the standard of living for so many of the world's people? What environmental policies can be used, if any, to preserve and improve environmental quality while at the same time improving the quality of life for so many people? Answers to these questions are part philosophy and part economics. The answers are neither simple nor without controversy.

As the world's population continues to grow, so too will the demands for economic goods and services (e.g., food, shelter, clothing, transportation). If historic practices are any guide, these greater demands for goods and services will also increase the pressures on scarce natural resources and environmental quality. Larger populations place greater demand on land for agricultural production, water for drinking and industrial processes, and forest products for shelter and fuel. They increase the need for new sources of employment and increase pressures on urban areas as more people migrate in search of work.

But environmental degradation is also caused by poverty, uncertainty, and ignorance (World Bank 1992). Addressing these three elements is the first step required for effective environmental policies. Accomplishing this requires policies that make *economic* sense, ones that allocate scarce resources efficiently, even in the absence of environmental benefits. Improving sanitation and water supplies, investing in soil conservation, and improving the health and education levels of the populace, especially women, will be key priorities (World Bank 1992). Providing greater access to health care resources, especially family planning, will help ease the environmental pressures wrought by a rapidly expanding population. A better-educated populace will also adapt more easily to complex environmental management tools. Individuals who are healthy and better fed will be more productive workers and make for a more competitive economy.

Promoting macroeconomic stability (e.g., low inflation rates, a stable and exchangeable currency, a climate conducive to investment) also provides a foundation for environmental improvements. Integration into the global economy can provide greater economic and social benefits. For example, policies that promote free trade can improve productivity, introduce new technologies, and increase economic efficiency by promoting comparative advantage. Open trade policies are somewhat controversial, however, because they can increase environmental pressures. Nevertheless, if history provides any guidance, it is probably better to maintain open trade policies in conjunction with environmental protection policies than to restrict trade and its accompanying economic benefits.

Ignoring the potential for human ingenuity to address some environmental issues will lead to the adoption of policies that create much misery for all concerned. If we assume that fundamental economic principles, such as the potential benefits from trade, are incompatible with environmental improvement and equity, we risk adoption of policies that do indeed limit growth but also *reduce* environmental quality. Economic growth may be a source of environmental problems, but it also appears to be a prerequisite for solving many of them.

TRACING ECONOMIC INTERACTIONS

Designing effective environmental policies requires an understanding of how the environment and the economy are related. Methods of tracing the ripple impacts of different economic and environmental policies are needed, as minor policy changes can reverberate throughout the economy.

The environment provides the raw materials for existence: air to breathe, food to eat, water to drink, and materials for shelter. As human beings, however, we have developed a unique adaptation strategy: rather than adapting gradually to the environment, we have adapted the environment to us. If we are too cold, we construct shelters and use sources of heat. If we are too hot, we use mechanical methods of air conditioning. If we have too little to eat, we increase the productivity of land so

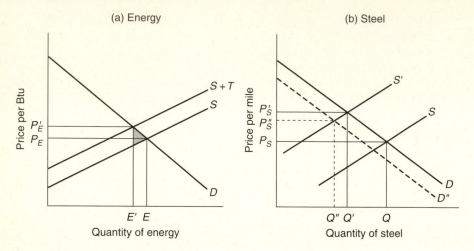

Figure 2.1   Economic Impacts of a Btu Tax

as to produce greater quantities of food. Essentially, we have transformed the raw materials available in our environment into forms more to our liking. The environment is one of many *inputs,* in the same way an automobile manufacturer uses steel, rubber, and assembly workers to produce cars or other economic *outputs.*

Over the past few centuries, this transformation of raw materials has permitted an explosion of economic growth. Industries that could transform raw materials into useful products, such as steel from iron ore, gave rise to other industries, such as automobiles, that used these intermediate products to produce goods and services ultimately purchased by consumers. Wealth was created, which led to additional investment and technological improvement. That investment created and increased the demand for the goods and the products that have improved the length and the quality of our lives.[1]

Growth in demand for goods and services has continued to increase the demand for raw materials that provide "fuel" for a growing economic "engine." Thus inputs and outputs are dependent on one another in what economists usually refer to as the *circular flow.* Firms purchase inputs from other firms and purchase the services of labor and capital to create new products, which are then used by still other firms or purchased by individual consumers.

To see these interactions, let's consider the Btu tax again. In Figure 2.1, we show demand and supply curves for "energy" and for steel. A Btu tax on energy will increase the cost of supplying energy to consumers. In the case of Georgia Power, for example, a tax on the energy content of coal would increase the cost of coal used to generate electricity and shift the supply curve for energy upward and to the

---

[1]Some people may question whether our lives are truly of higher quality than in the past. We avoid that philosophical debate for now, although we touch on it in Chapter 19 in our discussion of sustainability and sustainable development.

TABLE 2.1   INPUT-OUTPUT REPRESENTATION OF A THREE-SECTOR ECONOMY.

	Outputs				
Inputs	Utility (1)	Manufacturing (2)	Mining (3)	Final Demand (4)	Totals (5)
(1) Electric Utility	X_{11}	X_{12}	X_{13}	Y_1	F_1
(2) Manufacturing	X_{21}	X_{22}	X_{23}	Y_2	F_2
(3) Mining	X_{31}	X_{32}	X_{33}	Y_3	F_3
(4) Labor, Capital, and Other Value Added	C_1	C_2	C_3	D	J
(5) Totals	F_1	F_2	F_3	G	T

left. The price of energy increases from P_E per Btu to P_E' per Btu, and the quantity of energy demanded falls from E Btu to E' Btu. As a result, the Btu tax causes a *deadweight loss* of economic welfare, which is shown as the small shaded triangle in Figure 2.1(a).[2]

Next consider Figure 2.1(b), which shows the demand and supply curves for steel. The quantity of steel demanded depends on the price of steel. That price will depend partly on the price of energy because energy is used to manufacture steel. Since energy has become more expensive, the supply curve for steel shifts upward from S to S'. As a result, the quantity of steel purchased will fall from Q to Q', while the equilibrium price increases from P_S to P_S'. So even though the tax was placed on energy only, it has affected the steel market.

There are still other impacts to consider. Both steel and electricity are inputs used to manufacture automobiles. Increases in the price of steel and energy will increase the cost of manufacturing automobiles. Manufacturers will adjust by changing the mix of inputs used, perhaps using less steel and more aluminum and using less energy-intensive processes. Yet manufacturers still will be worse off. Because higher manufacturing costs will reduce the quantity of automobiles demanded, there will be less need for autoworkers. As autoworkers are laid off, their incomes will decrease. Thus the demand for other goods and services (many of which use steel as an input) will also fall, leading to further layoffs, and so on. Ultimately, assuming that demand for steel changes in relation to income levels, the demand for steel will decline from D to D''. This process is the *ripple effect* referred to by William Dahlberg. Conversely, higher energy prices will cause consumers to buy more of goods that use less energy in their production, with resulting positive ripple effects.

To trace the flow of these different inputs and outputs, picture the economy as a large box, as shown in Table 2.1. Table 2.1 is called an *input-output (I/O) table*. It is broken down into different sectors of the economy and shows purchases and sales from one sector to another. In this hypothetical economy, we assume there are only three industries. Each industry purchases some amount of inputs, valued

---

[2]Deadweight losses are covered in all of the references shown in Chapter 3, footnote 1, if you require a review of the concept.

in dollars, from the other two industries, as well as from itself. These purchases are read *down* the column as X_{1i}, X_{2i}, X_{3i}, where X_{ji} represents purchases of industry i from industry j. Industries also purchase the services of labor and capital in order to produce goods and services. The total value of the goods and services produced equals the sum of the value of the material inputs, labor and capital, taxes, and profit. The latter three often are lumped together under the heading *value added*.

The goods and the services produced by each industry are sold to other industries to produce their own set of goods and services; they are also purchased directly by consumers. In our economy, for example, industry 1 is the electric utility industry, industry 2 is manufacturing, and industry 3 is mining. Reading down column 1, we see that the electric industry purchases X_{11} inputs from itself, X_{21} from the manufacturing sector, and X_{31} from the mining sector and purchases labor, capital, and other value added worth C_1. F_1, which is the sum of X_{11}, X_{21}, X_{31}, and C_1, equals the total value of production of the electric utility industry. Sales of the electric utility industry's output are read across each row of the matrix. It sells output to itself, to the other remaining two industries, and directly to consumers. Thus total electricity sales are X_{11} to the electricity industry, X_{12} to the manufacturing sector, X_{13} to the mining sector, and Y_1 to final consumers. The total value of the output sold is *by definition* identical to the total value of production. Thus, $\Sigma X_{1i} + Y_1 = \Sigma X_{i1} + C_1$. By adding up the values from all industries, as well as all final demands, we arrive at the total value of output produced in the entire economy, which in Table 2.1 equals T.

Now let's take a numerical example, as shown in Table 2.2. Here we use dollar values for the inputs and outputs in our three industries. Reading down column 1, for example, we see that the electric utility industry purchases $50 million of electricity from itself, $400 million worth of manufactured equipment, and $500 million worth of mined fuels, such as coal. Together with $450 million worth of value added, the electric industry uses a total of $1.4 billion worth of inputs. Because the value of output must equal the value of input, total sales by the electric utility industry will also equal $1.4 billion. We can read across row 1 to see that the industry sells $50 million of electricity to itself, $200 million to the manufacturing sector, $150 million to the mining industry, and $1 billion to consumers.

TABLE 2.2   THREE-SECTOR INPUT-OUTPUT MODEL (MILLIONS OF DOLLARS)

Inputs	Outputs				
	Utility (1)	Manufacturing (2)	Mining (3)	Final Demand (4)	Totals (5)
(1) Electric utility	50	200	150	1,000	1,400
(2) Manufacturing	400	300	250	600	1,550
(3) Mining	500	350	50	100	1,000
(4) Value added	450	700	550	200	1,900
(5) Totals	1,400	1,550	1,000	1,900	4,850

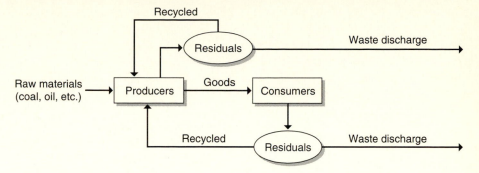

Figure 2.2   Environmental Effects of Production

We can trace similar patterns for the other two industries and compute the overall value of our economy, which is the $4.85 billion figure shown in the bottom right hand corner of Table 2.2.

ADDING THE ENVIRONMENT TO THE INPUT-OUTPUT FRAMEWORK

The environment and policies that affect its quality can be fit into the input-output framework by noting that the environment is used both as a source of resources to use as *inputs* and as a sink for waste *outputs*. In 1990, for example, coal was used to generate about 45 percent of the electricity produced in the United States. The mining industry does not create coal from capital, labor, and electricity. It uses those inputs to remove coal from the ground. In effect, it uses inputs of capital, labor, electricity, and coal in the ground to produce the output of mined coal. In the process, the industry exhausts part of our natural reserves of coal.

In general, the transformation of materials creates waste by-products. The factory producing steel for cars also produces smoke in the smelting process. The iron ore mined to make the steel may have caused water pollution near the mine site. The cars produced from the steel cause water and air pollution. Thus the raw material inputs used to produce the goods and the services people want also produces wastes, which sometimes are called *residuals*. Some of these wastes are recycled for further use, such as scrap metal made from old cars or aluminum beverage cans. Other wastes are returned to the environment: dispersed into the air, dumped into the water, and buried in landfills. This process is shown in Figure 2.2.

In general, environmental policies will affect the inputs required to produce goods and services and thereby change their costs. For example, because coal is a relatively "dirty" fuel (burning coal is one cause of "acid rain"),[3] the 1970 U.S. Clean Air Act required that coal-fired electric power plants have special pollution

---

[3]We discuss "acid rain" in Chapter 20.

control devices called scrubbers and precipitators. These devices are expensive to install and require lots of electricity to operate. Outfitting coal-fired plants with these devices increased the price of electricity generated with coal and increased the demand for substitutes, both substitute forms of electric generation and substitute forms of energy.

The effects of environmental policies such as those in the Clean Air Act can reverberate throughout an economy. After 1970, industries that relied heavily on electricity began to use less of it and more of other inputs such as natural gas and fuel oil. As a result, the demand for natural gas and fuel oil increased. That increased the demand for drilling rigs, pipelines, and refineries—produced in the manufacturing sector—as well as increased the demand for workers in those industries.

Unfortunately, oil and gas also release harmful pollutants when burned, including hydrocarbons, particulates, and carbon dioxide. Furthermore, drilling and transporting oil and natural gas can cause damage to land and water, as several notorious oil tanker spills, such as the Exxon *Valdez* and Amoco *Cadiz,* demonstrated. Lastly, if the prices of oil and gas are *distorted* because of *inefficient* environmental or other policies, reserves may be depleted at a nonoptimal rate.[4] Using an input-output framework, we can trace these economic and environmental reverberations throughout an economy and predict the ultimate impacts on the demand for all goods and services produced, including environmental ones. Thus we could estimate the overall economic and environmental impacts from a requirement for scrubbers on coal-fired power plants.[5]

The input-output framework can also be used to determine which groups in society bear the largest burden of certain environmental policies.[6] This has been done by some authors, such as Robison (1985). For example, using an input-output framework, we could determine whether environmental controls on coal-fired electric generation benefit primarily the poor or the rich. Answering questions related to the equity and the fairness of environmental policies are often important, sometimes more so than answering questions about whether the environmental policies considered improve economic efficiency. That may distress some economists, but it is a reality of most nations' political and bureaucratic processes that should be understood.

The effects of economic activity on the environment can also be traced directly, without converting everything to dollars or another standard. This can be useful when examining the *physical* impacts of alternative environmental policies. For example, would a tax on coal reduce emissions of carbon dioxide, or would it lead to substitutions and other impacts that actually increased emissions? Would a Btu

---

[4]We take up optimal extraction of natural resources in Chapter 15.

[5]A more detailed discussion of this topic can be found in Chapter 7 of Miller and Blair (1985) and the references cited therein.

[6]Simple input-output models are usually *static,* that is, they do not account for adjustments that occur over time. However, analytical techniques are available to transform static input-output models into *dynamic* ones.

tax reduce greenhouse gas emissions and, if so, by how much? Answering these sorts of questions may be important in the context of developing effective policies to address global climate change.

To see how the environment can be included directly in the input-output framework, the environment can be added to the standard input-output table as another sector, turning it into an *augmented* input-output table. Environmental inputs include land (including mineral resources), water, and air. A coal-fired electric power plant, for example, requires not only large quantities of coal but also water to generate steam that is subsequently run through an electric generator.

Waste products discharged into the environment are outputs. Coal-fired power plants emit sulfur dioxide, oxides of nitrogen, heavy metals, and carbon dioxide, among other things. Coal plants also discharge contaminated water. And they produce solid waste in the form of ash. All of these wastes can be thought of as additional outputs to the economy. Those wastes, and the policies that apply to them, will affect the mix of inputs used by other sectors of the economy. A laundry located downwind of a coal plant, for example, may need less detergent per load of wash after scrubbers are installed on the plant. Conversely, the price of the electricity used by the laundry may increase.

With the addition of environmental inputs and outputs, we can modify Table 2.1, as shown in Table 2.3, where we have added an additional row and column. EX_1, EX_2, and EX_3 represent the quantities of environmental inputs used to produce goods and services by each of the three industries. For example, EX_1 might equal the amount of clean water used by the coal-fired power plant. ED_1, ED_2, and ED_3 represent the quantities of waste products discharged into the environment. Thus ED_1 would equal the coal plants' emissions to the air and water and solid wastes.

EX_C represents the environmental inputs used by consumers. These will include potable water, land, and fresh air. Similarly, consumers' environmental outputs will be ED_C. These will include disposal of litter, pollution from automobiles,

TABLE 2.3 INPUT-OUTPUT TABLE INCORPORATING ENVIRONMENTAL GOODS

| | Outputs | | | | | |
Inputs	Utility (1)	Manufacturing (2)	Mining (3)	Final Demand (4)	Totals (5)	Waste Discharge (6)
(1) Electric utility	X_{11}	X_{12}	X_{13}	Y_1	F_1	ED_1
(2) Manufacturing	X_{21}	X_{22}	X_{23}	Y_2	F_2	ED_2
(3) Mining	X_{31}	X_{32}	X_{33}	Y_3	F_3	ED_3
(4) Value added	C_1	C_2	C_3	D	J	ED_C
(5) Totals	F_1	F_2	F_3	G	T	ED
(6) Environmental inputs	EX_1	EX_2	EX_3	EX_C	EX	—

TABLE 2.4   THREE-SECTOR ECONOMY WITH PHYSICAL ENVIRONMENTAL FLOWS

	Outputs (millions of dollars)					Waste Discharge (tons)
Inputs	Utility (1)	Manufacturing (2)	Mining (3)	Final Demand (4)	Totals (5)	(6)
(1) Electric utility	50	200	150	1,000	1,400	1,000
(2) Manufacturing	400	300	250	600	1,550	2,000
(3) Mining	500	350	50	100	1,000	1,500
(4) Value added	450	700	550	200	1,900	800
(5) Totals	1,400	1,550	1,000	1,900	4,850	5,300
(6) Environmental inputs (tons)	1,200	500	600	2,100	4,400	—

and wastewater. *EX* represents the total of all environmental inputs, and *ED* represents total discharges of waste products. But unlike the dollar totals, the environmental inputs and outputs are expressed in physical quantities.[7] (There are many ways to *value* such inputs and outputs, as we discuss in Chapter 11. For now, however, we can see the interactions between the economy and the environment despite the dichotomy.) Unlike the dollar totals in the standard I/O table, total environmental inputs may not equal total environmental outputs. Consider Table 2.4, in which we augment the dollar flow of Table 2.2 with environmental flows. We assume that these environmental flows are measured in "tons of stuff."

Thus the electric utility industry uses 1,200 tons of environmental inputs while discharging 1,000 tons of waste. The manufacturing sector uses 500 tons of environmental inputs while discharging 2,000 tons of environmental waste. Consumers use 2,100 tons of environmental inputs and discharge 800 tons. Of course, in an actual input-output model, there could be many different forms of environmental inputs and outputs, covering water, air, and mineral resources and various forms of pollutants.

Environmental Regulation and "Competitiveness"

The input-output tables show that environmental regulations can ripple through an economy. What they do not show, however, is that environmental regulations can themselves stimulate or retard new industries and economic growth. This can complicate the macroeconomic evaluation of environmental regulations and policies.

The "conventional wisdom" is that environmental regulation imposes significant costs, reduces productivity growth, and generally hinders the ability of firms to compete in international markets not subject to such stringent environmental

---

[7]Of course, some environmental inputs will be priced. An industry may purchase water from the local water utility. Such purchases would be accounted for in the industry by the industry portion of the I/O matrix.

regulations (Jaffe et al. 1995). The result is economic weakness of the sort described by William Dahlberg and movement of pollution-intensive industries to other countries.

Recently, however, the economic impacts of environmental regulations have been reexamined and found to provide net economic benefits because the regulations create new industries that provide environmental services. Examples include industries that dispose of toxic wastes, recyclers, and firms that develop less polluting equipment and industrial processes. Some economists believe that environmental regulations encourage innovation and technical progress (Porter and van der Linde 1995; Porter 1990). Thus they believe that environmental regulations can be a sort of "free lunch," where one gets both a better environment and greater economic growth. Other economists take strong issue with this view, insisting that the benefits of environmental improvements must be compared to their costs (Palmer, Oates, and Portney 1995).

Which view is correct is complicated by disagreements over definitions.[8] For example, what does *competitiveness* mean? What should be considered *benefits*, and what should be considered *costs*? The creation of jobs, for example, is seen as a sign of economic strength. Under this view, environmental regulations that create new industries and jobs are beneficial. But jobs are also viewed as costs. Many industries demonstrate their competitive strength and productivity by reducing employment, and societal "make work" policies are viewed unfavorably. Thus job creation may impose costs on society.

Jaffe and colleagues (1995) examine the linkages between environmental regulations and competitiveness. After reviewing a number of empirical studies, they conclude that there is little evidence to support the view that environmental regulations damage competitiveness, however defined. The authors acknowledge that there are numerous costs associated with environmental regulations. However, they find these effects to be small or statistically insignificant. They also note that if U.S. environmental regulations are stringent, the same is true in other Western nations. And even in countries where environmental regulations are lax, many U.S. companies are reluctant to build "dirty" industries.[9] However, the authors find no evidence that environmental regulations benefit the economy. They note, "Given the large direct and indirect costs that regulation imposes, economists' natural skepticism regarding this free regulatory lunch is appropriate" (p. 159).

Does this mean that environmental laws should be passed with no regard to their overall economic impacts? Hardly. Even if overall macroeconomic impacts of environmental regulations are small or negligible, *local* macroeconomic impacts may be significant. Requiring a copper smelter to close because of its adverse environmental affects on the local community will not affect worldwide copper markets significantly, but it will affect the economy of the local community.

---

[8]A good overview of this debate is provided by Stewart (1993).
[9]Jaffe and colleagues note that the 1985 accident at the Union Carbide plant in Bhopal, India, may have contributed to this reluctance.

The Environment as a Good in Itself

The environment does not just serve as an input to produce other goods and services or as a receptacle for waste products. The environment can *itself* be a final good purchased by individuals who enjoy "consuming" environmental amenities. They like to see clear mountain vistas, trek through ancient forests, and sail in unpolluted lakes. The values that individuals place on using such environmental amenities are called *use values*. As we discussed briefly in Chapter 1, however, individuals may also have existence values for environmental amenities that they do not intend to themselves "consume."[10] Thus the environment, in addition to providing physical inputs and outputs, can provide sensory and aesthetic output.[11] These, too, can be affected by the consumption of environmental resources. A coal plant whose pollution reduces the view of the Grand Canyon not only discharges wastes into the environment but also reduces the amount of a desirable environmental amenity, the view.[12]

Factoring the value of environmental amenities into the economic framework is difficult and must be done indirectly. For example, increased pollution at the Grand Canyon may lead to reductions in tourism and to a shrinking of tourism-related industries. Destruction of old-growth forests may reduce the number of individuals interested in backpacking trips, reducing the demand for backpacks. That reduction in demand would then ripple through the economy backward to industries supplying inputs for manufacturing backpacks and forward to industries and consumers that purchased backpacks.

CHAPTER SUMMARY

One chapter cannot provide a comprehensive and detailed picture of the interactions between the economy and the environment. Clearly, these interactions are many. Environmental policymakers must be aware of the static and dynamic interactions between environmental policies and the economy. Resources are required as inputs to the system of production in the economy, which then supplies consumer goods, as well as goods that are used in other production processes. Use of resources generates wastes that are discharged into the environment. These wastes can themselves affect both the production process (e.g., an industry may see its costs rise if the quality of the water it uses declines) as well as consumption (e.g., consumers who are unable to enjoy a pretty view due to high levels of air pollu-

---

[10]We discuss how to determine and estimate existence values in Chapter 11.

[11]It can also be argued that environmental amenities provide inputs to the production of some goods and services. A provider of a recreational fishing trip, for example, will likely want an unpolluted river or lake so as to enhance the value to the customer.

[12]See Chapter 11 for a discussion of the estimated value of the view across the Grand Canyon.

tion). Some waste products can be recycled and used again. The majority of aluminum cans in this country, for example, are recycled and used to produce still more cans. However, many waste products cannot be recycled, either because of the expense involved or the lack of usability of the waste products.

The flow between inputs and outputs will change over time as the flow of resources into production and final consumption, as well as the direct consumption of environmental amenities, changes in response to numerous factors (population, economic well-being, technological improvements, even weather patterns). How all of these will change will depend on the rate of discharge into the environment and the pace of resource depletion. A *sustainable* economy could be defined as one that maintains constant resource balances over time. An *unsustainable* economy might cause the level of resources to decline over time and possibly increase the magnitude of the waste sink. Conversely, using a little more of a resource might lead to technological breakthroughs that would improve the wealth of future generations.

As you read this book, we will often focus on individual markets to make the concepts and policy implications more straightforward to follow. Nevertheless, you should keep in mind that economic interactions will invariably occur. These interactions can make the analysis and implementation of "good" environmental policies more difficult. However, ignoring the interactions may result in unintended impacts and wasted resources.

CHAPTER REVIEW

Economic Concepts and Tools

- Most economic activity involves the environment either directly or indirectly.
- Almost all production processes use natural resources or their derivatives as inputs. The environment also is a sink for waste products.
- The natural environment provides some final consumer goods and services.
- All environmental problems are economic problems because they involve a scarce resource, the environment.
- Input-output analysis can be augmented by including the environment as an input row and output column. Such an augmented I/O table can be used to show the effects of changes in economic activity on the demands for raw materials and the creation of wastes. It can also demonstrate the effects of different environmental policies on economic activity.

Policy Issues

- Environmental policies directed at one industry or economic activity will affect other parts of the economy. Environmental policies that either increase or decrease the costs of goods will affect the demands for substitutes and complements and change the allocation of resources throughout the economy. Environmental policies directed at a given industry will also affect *upstream* industries that sell inputs to that industry and *downstream* industries that purchase the outputs of that industry.

- Limited resources or limited environmental capacity to absorb wastes may limit economic growth. However, wealthier societies can and do spend more on environmental quality.

DISCUSSION QUESTIONS

1. How would population growth affect the input-output framework in Table 2.4?
2. As we use the most readily available resources, the cost of finding and extracting other resources usually increases. This should reduce economic growth because what was once easy to use becomes more expensive to use, raising production costs. Yet the world's economy has grown tremendously and continues to do so. How is this possible?
3. Suppose that to protect the northwestern spotted owl, the government institutes a complete ban on all logging activities in the states of Washington and Oregon. How would you trace the effects of this environmental policy using an I/O model? Suppose instead that the government reduced logging activities by only 50 percent. Could the input-output framework be used to determine whether this was a "better" policy? Why or why not? Why do actual studies of these impacts differ so much?
4. Because of a concern for diminishing landfill space and deforestation, President Clinton ordered all government agencies to begin purchasing recycled office paper products. Using an I/O framework, trace the impacts of this action on the economy, assuming that recycled products are more expensive than traditional products. Repeat the exercise for the case where recycled products are less costly.
5. A scientist discovers a new battery technology that will make electric cars cheaper to buy and to operate than existing internal-combustion cars. The technology will greatly reduce the demand for gasoline and reduce pollution from automobiles. However, the production process for this battery will release large quantities of a new ozone-depleting chemical, which will subsequently increase skin cancer rates. The new technology will also lead to a large, though probably temporary, increase in unemployment due to layoffs of oil refinery workers and automobile mechanics. What are the benefits and the costs of this new technology? How could it be evaluated? Should this new technology be used?
6. In 1985, the United States spent a little less than 2 percent of its gross domestic product (GDP) for pollution control measures. Suppose that as a result of new environmental legislation, spending for pollution control measures increases to 5 percent of GDP by the turn of the century. Will the

economy have "grown"? What will happen to the "competitiveness" of the U.S. economy relative to that of, say, China?

7. The state of Vermont requires that major new business developments or expansions receive a "certificate of public good" before approval. What criteria should such a certificate include?

8. How has the North American Free Trade Act (NAFTA) affected environmental quality along the U.S.-Mexico border? Is there evidence that *maquiladoras* (U.S. industries that locate just south of the U.S.-Mexico border) are flouting U.S. environmental laws?

REFERENCES

Barnett, H., and C. Morse. 1963. *Scarcity and Growth.* Baltimore: Johns Hopkins University Press.

Ehrlich, P. 1968. *The Population Bomb.* New York: Ballantine Books.

Jaffe, A., S. Peterson, P. Portney, and R. Stavins. 1995. "Environmental Regulation and the Competitiveness of U.S. Manufacturing: What Does the Evidence Tell Us?" *Journal of Economic Literature* 23(1): 132–163.

Malthus, T. 1975. "An Essay on the Principle of Population." In *An Essay on the Principle of Population: Text, Sources and Background: Criticism,* ed. P. Appleman. New York: Norton. (Originally published 1798)

McKibben, W. 1989. *The End of Nature.* New York: Random House.

Meadows, D.H., D. L. Meadows, and J. Randers. 1972. *The Limits to Growth.* New York: Universe Books.

Miller, R., and P. Blair. 1985. *Input-Output Analysis: Foundations and Extensions.* Upper Saddle River, N.J.: Prentice Hall.

Palmer. K., W. Oates, and P. Portney. 1995. "Tightening Environmental Standards: The Benefit-Cost or the No-Cost Paradigm?" *Journal of Economic Perspectives* 9(4): 119–132.

Porter, M. 1990. *The Competitive Advantage of Nations.* New York: Free Press.

———, and C. van der Linde. 1995. "Toward a New Conception of the Environment Competitiveness Relationship." *Journal of Economic Perspectives* 9(4): 97–118.

Robison, H. 1985. "Who Pays for Industrial Pollution Abatement?" *Review of Economics and Statistics* 57: 702–706.

Stewart, R. 1993. "Environmental Regulation and International Competitiveness." *Yale Law Journal* 102(8): 2039–2106.

World Bank. 1992. *World Development Report, 1992: Development and the Environment.* New York: Oxford University Press.

CHAPTER 3

FOUNDATIONS OF ECONOMIC EFFICIENCY AND EQUITY

Catalyst of Consistency?

*One of the policies instituted with passage of the 1970 Clean Air Act was a require-
ment that catalytic converters be installed on all new automobiles. The converters
were expected to add about $400 to the price of a new car. This policy affected
many individuals, rich and poor, including two friends of ours living in Chicago in
the 1970s. Howard was an economics professor who had invested successfully in
the stock market and was relatively wealthy. Carol, who was not at all wealthy, had
recently earned a Ph.D. in political science at a time when there was an excess supply of teachers in that field.*

*Howard was a strong advocate of the catalytic converter requirement. He said
that he would be willing to pay $600 more for a car with a catalytic converter, as
long as converters were required for all new cars. After all, he said, preserving air
quality and controlling air pollution benefits everyone. Based on his own willingness to pay, Howard expected that most Chicagoans would be willing to pay more
than $400 for converters because of the cleaner air that would result in the Chica-
go area. He therefore concluded that the regulation requiring the converters was
economically efficient; he presumed that individuals' willingness to pay for converters would exceed the price.*

*Carol, by contrast, said that while paying more for cleaner air was fine for
Howard, who had the money to do so, she was unwilling to pay $400 more for a car
regardless of how clean the air became. She said that even if most Chicagoans were
willing to pay the $400 cost of a converter, it would be inequitable to require her to
pay $400 for something she did not value so highly. Carol did say, however, that
she might be willing to pay $100 for a catalytic converter.*

At this same time, Carol owned a cabin near the small town of Morton Grove, Illinois. The cabin was not far from where Commonwealth Edison Company proposed to build a new coal-fired electric generating plant. Carol opposed construction of the plant because of its potential effect on air quality near Morton Grove. She stated that she would be unwilling *to accept even as much as $1,000 to agree to allow the plant to be built.*

Why was Carol willing to pay only $100 for a catalytic converter to clean the air in Chicago but unwilling to accept even $1,000 in exchange for dirtying the air around Morton Grove? Was her response consistent with economic theory? What about Howard? Was his willingness to pay more for a catalytic converter than the estimated cost consistent with an economically efficient regulation? Did Carol's unwillingness to pay the $400 cost mean that it was an inefficient regulation? Or were both avoiding Emerson's admonition that "foolish consistency is the hobgoblin of little minds, adored by little statesmen and philosophers and divines"?

INTRODUCTION

The differences between Carol and Howard illustrate a variety of economic concepts, all crucial to the study of environmental economics, and the importance of understanding the differences between them. There is an implicit assumption that all of us know what we mean by "value." Yet what is value, particularly as it relates to environmental "objects" that might be as small as a snail, as large as the earth itself, or as elusive as human cultures? And assuming that we know what value is, how can we best measure it?

Throughout this book, we focus on two broad concepts: economic efficiency and equity.[1] These concepts are important in the study of environmental and natural resource economics and the development of their related policies. Paradoxically, policies supposedly implemented to improve economic efficiency (including those designed to reduce air pollution) have often focused on equity effects, while policies whose goals have been to improve equity have sometimes focused on economic efficiency. Often the result has been costly policies that do not achieve what is intended.

This chapter reviews concepts of economic efficiency and equity. We focus first on individual decisions and preferences and then move on to collective choice and preferences, which are more difficult to clarify but more important in the context of many environmental policy decisions. In doing so, we address key concepts, including willingness to pay, willingness to accept, externalities, public goods, and the social welfare function.

---

[1]Although this chapter provides a brief review of important economic concepts, it is not intended to substitute for a course in microeconomics. If you wish to know more about the subject, see Layard and Walters (1978), Varian (1992), Browning and Browning (1989) and Just, Hueth, and Schmitz (1982).

We recommend a three-part strategy for reading this chapter. First, we recommend that you skim the whole chapter to see if all the topics look at least vaguely familiar. Second, if you find any topics you are unfamiliar with or unsure about, take some time to study them now before we apply them in later chapters. Third, turn back to this chapter, and to the books and articles referenced in it, when these concepts come up later in the book.

INDIVIDUAL DECISIONS AND PREFERENCES

Our ultimate goal in this chapter is to review the economic foundations for public policy decisions, but we will start by looking at individual decisions. We do this for two reasons. First, the concepts of economic welfare and equity that we use throughout this book are based on individuals' preferences reflected through their choices. Second, we start with individual choices because all choices are ultimately individual ones. Although group choices reflect group dynamics, they come down to the choices of the individuals who make up the group.

Everyone makes choices. At this instant, you are choosing to read this chapter, even though you might well prefer to be engaged in some other activity. In fact, your decision to read this chapter involves some complex calculations. You have weighed implicitly the potential future benefits and costs associated with reading the chapter against the benefits and costs of other choices available to you now. Presumably, you will continue to read this chapter and beyond until the *marginal value* of continued reading (e.g., the value of greater understanding of environmental economics) equals the *marginal cost* (e.g., lost time with friends, excessive sleepiness, delayed shopping).

As we discuss in later chapters, determining such matters as how much individuals value improvements to the environment, how much society could benefit from controlling overfishing, or whether environmental amenities are distributed fairly all involve valuing choices and preferences.

The Concept of Utility

Economists attempt to model, predict, and explain consumer choice. They approach this task by assuming that consumers have *preferences* for different goods and services. Economists often use the concept of *utility* to help model consumer preferences and choices. Although utility is sometimes treated as an absolute measure of happiness or pleasure, a normative economic theory based on the use of utility as a hedonistic measure is open to many criticisms (Zerbe 1991). Therefore, most economists limit utility to the role of an *indicator* of preferences (Broome 1978; Zerbe and Dively 1994). This means that if you prefer going to the beach to going to the mountains, we can assign a higher utility index to your going to the beach than to your going to the mountains. Using utility to measure preferences can be applied quite generally. Utility or preference exists for any activity in which choice is involved, although the choices may themselves involve truth, justice, or beauty just as easily as the consumption of goods and services. So you can derive utility from looking at a beautiful apple tree in full bloom in the spring as well as by eating an apple harvested from that tree in the fall.

Economists find it convenient to represent preferences for an individual in the form of a *utility function*. In its general form, a utility function for an individual can be written:

$$U = U(X_1, X_2, \ldots, X_N) \tag{3.1}$$

where $X_1, X_2, \ldots, X_N$ represents the mix of goods and services that are available to the individual and make up total utility U. Equation 3.1 states that an individual's utility is a function of the goods and services he or she consumes. The individual's preferences and income, along with market prices, will determine the mix of goods and services chosen. In welfare economics, the mix of goods and services an individual chooses implicitly maximizes Equation 3.1. In other words, if I see you choosing a particular basket of goods and services, I can assume that you prefer it to any other available basket (subject to your income). Otherwise, your choice would violate a fundamental postulate of welfare economics: that individuals make rational choices.

If utility were actually *measurable* in the same way as temperature or humidity, we would call it *cardinal utility*. Cardinal utility might be useful as a measure of happiness or pleasure. However, economists use utility as an *ordinal* rather than a cardinal measure; they use it to rank preferences and choices rather than the intensity of the preferences themselves. For example, we could assign a utility index of 400 to your going to the beach and 300 to your going to the mountains. But we could assign any other index with the same ranking, such as 2 million and 1 million or 60 and 59.9.[2] Regardless of the index chosen, all would show that you preferred going to the beach over going to the mountains.

Indifference Curves

Suppose that your utility was determined by your level of consumption of just two goods, X_1 and X_2. If we could measure utility, your total utility function might look something like Figure 3.1. By "slicing" the surface in Figure 3.1 at different heights, we can examine the different combinations of X_1 and X_2 that would provide you with equal levels of utility. For example, suppose that we made three horizontal slices at utility levels U_1, U_2, and U_3. We could plot the combinations of X_1 and X_2 for each of these utility levels, as shown in Figure 3.2. Thus along U_1, for example, you are indifferent between combinations such as point A (X_1', X_2') and point B (X_1'', X_2''). Because

---

[2]Mathematically, if a person's preferences can be represented with the utility function U and g is any *monotonically increasing* function—that is, $g(X + \epsilon) > g(X)$ for any $\epsilon > 0$—then $g(U)$ is a utility function representing the same preferences. The relative magnitude of utility contains information about preferences, but neither the value nor the slope does. We will see later that the *curvature* of the utility function can contain information about attitudes toward risk.

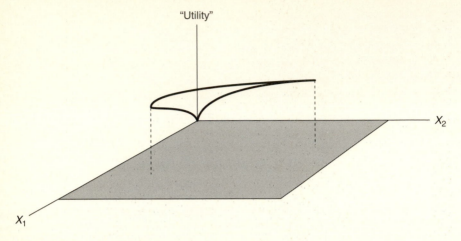

Figure 3.1   A Total Utility Function

you are assumed to get increased satisfaction from consuming additional amounts of X_1 and X_2, the indifference curves U_2 and U_3 are above and to the right of U_1.

A crucial concept when we deal with individual preferences is *marginal utility* (MU). The marginal utility of a good, X_1, is the additional utility associated with one additional unit of the good.[3] Note also that the indifference curves become less negatively sloped as the amount of X_1 increases relative to the amount of X_2. The slope at any point along the indifference curve reflects the *marginal rate of substitution* between X_1 and X_2, that is, the amount of X_2 you will forgo to obtain an additional unit of X_1. Also, the slope of indifference curve U_1 at point B is greater than the slope of U_2 at point C. This is a result of *diminishing marginal utility*. What this means is that the increase in satisfaction you derive from consuming additional quantities of X_1 decreases as you consume greater quantities of it. Thus for a given quantity of X_2, the *more* of X_1 you have, the *less* you will value it. Intuitively, this is a reasonable concept. That first piece of chocolate cake will be quite satisfying, the next less so, and still another may provide no utility whatsoever.

Determining Optimum Levels of Consumption

Given the indifference curves in Figure 3.2, the next question is how your individual consumption choices will be made. The first thing to remember is that your consumption will be governed by your available income. If your income is $10,000, you can consume only $10,000 worth of goods and services. (We will ignore the possibility of borrowing money to increase your consumption until Chapter 13. It turns out that such intertemporal consumption decisions are a critical component of environmental and natural resource policy debates.)

---

[3]In symbols, marginal utility of X_1 is written $\partial U/\partial X_1$, where ∂ is a partial derivative sign designating a small change, holding other things constant. In this case, we are dealing with the change of utility associated with a small change in good X_1.

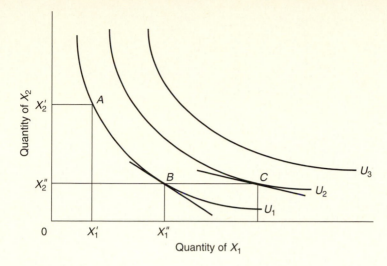

Figure 3.2 Indifference Curves (direction of preference is away from the origin)

Suppose that your income is $10,000 and that the price of X_1 and X_2 is given by P_1 and P_2, respectively. Then it must be the case that your expenditures are no greater than $10,000. Thus we can write

$$P_1X_1 + P_2X_2 \leq \$10,000 \qquad (3.2)$$

Where Equation 3.2 is an equality, it traces out a *budget line*. Along this line, consumption fully exhausts income. Graphically, the set of all affordable consumption possibilities is shown by the shaded area 0YY in Figure 3.3. Both points A and B are feasible consumption possibilities, which give a total level of satisfaction equal to U_1. However, given an income of $10,000, point C is also a feasible consumption possibility, and the utility associated with it is greater. In fact, it turns out that since indifference curve U_2 is tangent to the budget line at point C, the combination (X_1^*, X_2^*) will be the optimal consumption combination.

In addition to the income constraint, the choice of the optimal consumption bundle will be influenced by the relative prices of X_1 and X_2. To see this, recognize that if we replace the inequality with an equal sign, Equation 3.2 represents the equation for a straight line. Solving Equation 3.2 for X_2, we have

$$X_2 = \frac{10,000}{P_2} - \frac{P_1}{P_2} X_1 \qquad (3.3)$$

The slope of the budget line therefore equals $-(P_1/P_2)$. As the price of X_1 increases relative to X_2, the budget line will be sloped more negatively, and the set of feasible consumption possibilities will diminish to the area 0YY'. Similarly, if the price of X_1 decreases relative to X_2, the budget line will become less negatively sloped, and the set of feasible consumption possibilities will increase to area 0YY'''. At the optimal (utility-maximizing) consumption choice, it turns out that the ratio of the

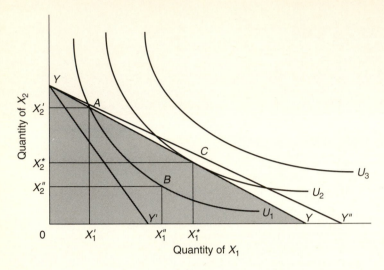

Figure 3.3 Consumption Possibilities and the Optimal Consumption Choice (direction of preference is away from the origin)

marginal utilities of X_1 and X_2 will just equal the negative of the slope of the budget line. This occurs where the budget line is tangent to (just touches) an indifference curve. If the budget line cuts an indifference curve rather than just touching it, it must touch another indifference curve with higher utility. At such a point of tangency, the marginal utility per dollar spent on good X_1 will equal the marginal utility per dollar spent on good X_2. If that were not the case, the consumer could select a different feasible consumption point that would be at a higher overall level of utility.

Indifference curves are also used to trace out individual demand curves. From Figure 3.3 we can see that as the relative price of a good or service changes, the preferred level of consumption will change. By examining a variety of changes, we can trace out an individual's ordinary demand curve for the good or service, as shown in Figure 3.4. Initially, the relative prices of goods 1 and 2 are given by the slope of the budget line, $-(P_1/P_2)$. This results in the quantity X_1 of good 1 to be selected by the consumer, as shown in both the top and the bottom graphs of the figure. As the price of good 1 is reduced to P_1', it becomes relatively cheaper. The consumer selects a different combination of the two goods and increases consumption of good 1 to X_1'.

WILLINGNESS TO PAY AND WILLINGNESS TO ACCEPT

At this point, you may be wondering what all of this has to do with environmental economics and policies. After all, you cannot go to the store and buy a free-flowing river, a pristine view of the Grand Canyon, or biodiversity. Nevertheless, policy-

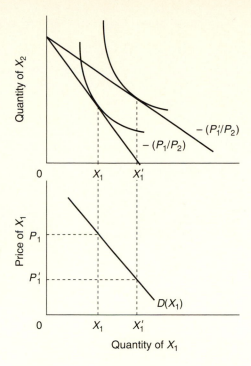

Figure 3.4   Indifference Curves and the Derivation of an
Individual Demand Curve

makers will often want to know the value of certain environmental goods. How
much, for example, do people value pristine views of the Grand Canyon or an ability to kayak down a free-flowing river? How do they value small changes in the
risks they face, perhaps from greater amounts of air pollution or more congested
highways?

Many environmental "goods" are what economists call *nonmarket goods,*
meaning that they are not bought and sold in the same way that you might buy a
pair of shoes or purchase groceries. Nevertheless, determining good environmental policies will often (but not always) hinge on measuring the value of environmental goods and services. Because we believe measurement of the value of environmental impacts and policies to be such a critical issue, we devote all of Part III
to the topic. Here we merely define the basic concepts used in such valuations.

Attempts to measure the value of environmental projects and policies often
center around the concepts of *willingness to pay,* or *WTP,* and *willingness to accept
payment,* or *WTA.*[4] *WTP* is the maximum amount of money one would give up to
buy some good or service. Thus the *WTP* for an additional unit of a good can be

---

[4]For an exhaustive development of these concepts, see Just, Hueth, and Schmitz (1982) or Freeman
(1993).

thought of as the price of the good times the marginal rate of substitution between it and other goods and services.

WTA is the minimum amount of money one would accept to forgo some good or to bear some harm. For any normal good (i.e., one for which the demand increases with income), WTA always exceeds WTP. WTP reflects the price that someone who does not have a good would be willing to pay to buy it. WTA reflects the price that someone who has the good, and therefore has greater wealth, would accept to sell it.

Compensating and Equivalent Variations

WTP and WTA are related to the concepts of *compensating variation* and *equivalent variation.* These are money measures of a change in utility. For a single individual, they are known as exact utility indicators and give an exact measure of the ranking of choices. Consider Figure 3.5. Money is on the vertical axis, and an environmental good such as clean water is on the horizontal axis.

Suppose that we wish to have a measure of welfare change from point 1 on indifference curve U_1 to point 2 on indifference curve U_2. We can't use utility, since it is only ordinal. The original budget line is AA, and the consumer's optimal consumption mix (the one with the highest attainable utility) is point 1. The slope of budget line AA shows the relative price of clean water. Next suppose that the relative price of clean water declines, perhaps as a result of a technological innovation in water purification technology. The new budget line will shift outward to AA'. The individual is better off, for he or she now pays a lower price for the same good.

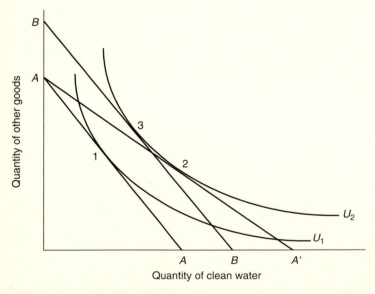

Figure 3.5   The Equivalent Variation (*EV*)

To determine the consumer's equivalent variation (*EV*) for this price decrease, draw a line, *BB*, parallel to line *AA* but tangent to U_2. Along this line, the individual's welfare will be the same as with the price decrease, but the relative price of clean water will be its old value. The income difference measured on the vertical axis between points *B* and *A* is an income measure of difference between the indifference curves U_1 and U_2. This difference is the *EV*: it is *the amount of money one would accept to forgo a benefit such as a price decrease or the amount of income one would pay to avoid a harm such as a price increase.*

The compensating variation (*CV*) can be determined in a similar way. This is shown in Figure 3.6. *CV* will equal the income difference between points 1 and 2 by using the new prices and new budget line *AA'* tangent to indifference curve U_2. In this case, line *BB* is drawn to be parallel to *AA'* but tangent to U_1. The income difference between *AA* and *BB'* along the vertical axis is the *CV*. Thus the CV is *the amount of money one would pay to gain a benefit such as a price decrease or the amount one would accept to agree to the imposition of a harm such as a price increase.* Table 3.1 summarizes the measures of value represented by the *CV* and the *EV*. CV is the willingness to pay for a welfare gain or the willingness to accept a welfare loss. *EV* is the willingness to accept forgoing a welfare gain or the willingness to pay to avoid a welfare loss.

CV and *EV* measures play an important role in environmental valuation issues because of the assignment of rights to the environment. Carol's unwillingness to pay more than $100 for improved air quality by purchasing a catalytic converter is a *CV* measure. Her refusal to accept $1,000 for diminished air quality because of the coal-fired power plant near Morton Grove is an example of *EV*. *Both* measures are relevant to environmental policy decisions, and both lie at the heart of many

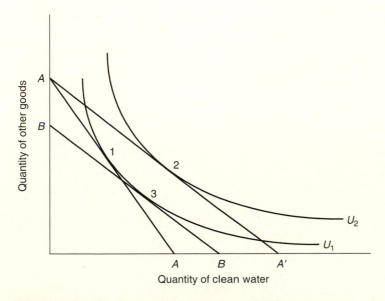

Figure 3.6   The Compensating Variation (*CV*)

TABLE 3.1   COMPENSATING VARIATION AND EQUIVALENT VARIATION

	Compensating Variation	Equivalent Variation
Definition	Money that can be taken or given to leave an individual as well off as before the economic change.	Money taken or given that leaves an individual as well off as after the economic change.
Welfare gain (benefit)	Amount an individual would be willing to pay (*WTP*) for the change (finite—limited by income).	Amount an individual would be willing to accept (*WTA*) to forgo the change (could be infinite).
Welfare loss (cost)	Amount an individual would be willing to accept (*WTA*) as compensation for the change (could be infinite).	Amount an individual would be willing to pay (*WTP*) to avert the change (finite—limited by income).

Source: After Layard and Walters (1978), pp. 150–152.

environmental policy disputes. To see this in a general context, consider Figure 3.7, which addresses the initial allocation of environmental rights.

In Figure 3.7, the amount of environmental good Q allocated to individual A equals the horizontal distance to the right of Q_A. Similarly, the amount of Q allocated to individual B equals the horizontal distance to the left of Q_B. The line denoted WTP_A equals A's demand curve for Q. As expected, A's willingness to pay

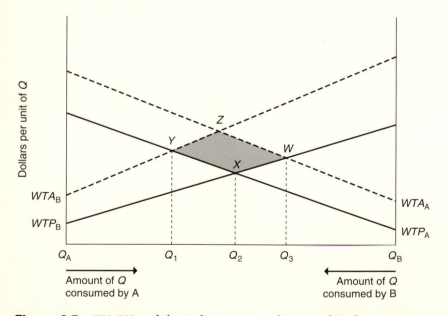

Figure 3.7   *EV, CV,* and the Indeterminacy of Marginal Rights

Source: Zerbe and Dively (1994), p. 106.

for additional units of Q declines as the total quantity of Q allocated to that individual increases. WTA_A shows the minimum the person would accept to forgo successive units of good Q. WTP_B and WTA_B illustrate the same concepts for individual B.

If individual A were initially assigned a right to all of good Q, the final allocation would be Q_AQ_3 units for A and Q_BQ_3 units for B. This allocation is shown by point W. At point W, A's WTA compensation to forgo an additional unit of Q is equal to B's WTP for an additional unit. Similarly, if B were initially assigned a right to all of good Q, the final allocation would be Q_AQ_1 units for A and Q_BQ_1 units for B. This allocation is shown by point Y. If none of the units of Q were given to A or B but instead were offered for sale, the final market allocation would occur at point X, where $WTP_A = WTP_B$.

If society wished to minimize the transactions costs of allocating previously unallocated units of Q to A and B, then A should receive at least Q_AQ_1 units and B should receive at least Q_BQ_3 units. This is because, regardless of the initial ownership assignment to A or B, A would always be willing to purchase at least Q_AQ_1 units of Q and B would always be willing to purchase at least Q_BQ_3 units from A. Unfortunately, the question of *how* to allocate the units between Q_1 and Q_3 is far more difficult, since there is no unique efficient allocation. Any allocation within the shaded quadrilateral $WXYZ$ is consistent with an economically efficient allocation.

Consumer and Producer Surplus

The major policy problem associated with either the EV or the CV is that neither is measurable directly because we cannot measure indifference curves directly.[5] In applied benefit-cost analysis work, therefore, economists have used *consumer surplus (CS)* as an approximation of CV or EV because CS can be estimated from observable information.

Consumer surplus is (approximately) *the amount the consumer is willing to pay over what the consumer is required to pay*. Graphically, consumer surplus is the area above the price line and below the demand curve. In Figure 3.8, D_{Wi} is an individual's demand curve for clean water and P is the equilibrium price. At this price, the individual will consume Q_i gallons. The individual's total willingness to pay for clean water equals the area under the demand curve between 0 and Q_i gallons, or $CS_i + A_i$. The shaded area labeled CS_i equals the *excess* of the individual's willingness to pay for clean water over the price that the individual is required to pay. This is the individual's consumer surplus.

---

[5]Strictly speaking, the EV and the CV measure welfare changes for Hicksian, or income-compensated, demand curves. These hold real income (measured as an ability to purchase a consumption bundle of equal utility) constant. Ordinary observed demand curves, however, are Marshalian. As the price of the good changes, real income changes as well because the consumer will no longer be on an indifference curve with an equivalent level of utility. See Layard and Walters (1978) for further explanation.

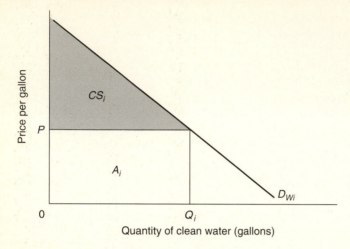

Figure 3.8   An Individual's Consumer Surplus

The same sort of exercise is done when we look at the overall market for clean water. Suppose that there are N individuals who demand clean water. We can sum the N separate demand curves to derive the overall market demand curve for water, as shown in Figure 3.9. The overall consumer surplus, CS, just equals the sum of the various individual CS_i figures.

In Figure 3.9, there is now a supply curve for clean water, S_W. P remains the equilibrium price. At this equilibrium, total WTP for clean water is approximately the area under the market demand curve D_W between 0 and Q gallons, or area $CS + PS + C$. The amount actually paid by consumers will be area $B + C$. Thus the consumer surplus associated with the supply of Q gallons of clean

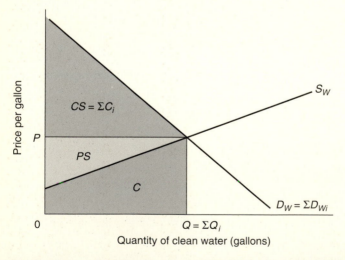

Figure 3.9   Aggregate Consumer Surplus and Producer Surplus

water equals area A. In this example, the consumer surplus associated with the demand curve for clean water represents the sum of the various individual CV measures.

The area PS also has special significance. It is called the *producer surplus*. Producer surplus is *the amount that could be taken from the producer in the form of a lump sum without affecting the amount the producer supplies*. Graphically, producer surplus is the area below the price line and above the supply or marginal cost curve. Producer surplus will usually equal profits plus rents (i.e., payments above the minimum needed to induce an economic agent to do what the agent does). In Figure 3.9, area $PS + C$ equals the total paid to suppliers of clean water. The area under the supply curve, area C, represents the cost of supplying that water. The difference between them just equals PS.

The *usual* decision criterion in applied analyses is that a change is acceptable when the sum of PS and aggregate CS is positive. Consumer surplus, like the EV and the CV, is an income measure of the change in welfare. Because it measures a change in income, aggregate CS represents a welfare *change if all incomes are given equal weight*.[6] In many benefit-cost analyses, the economic welfare associated with a market (i.e., the value of having the market) is measured by the sum of producer and consumer surplus. This will be areas $A + B$.

Why *EV* and *CV* Differ—and Does It Matter?

It turns out that, for a normal good, the consumer or producer surplus will lie between the CV and the EV.[7] To gauge whether consumer surplus and producer surplus are reasonable approximations of the EV and the CV, we need to understand why EV and CV differ and how much they can differ. This has been a pressing empirical issue in environmental economics because the larger the difference between the EV and the CV, the larger the difference between WTP and WTA. If this difference is small, it would matter little which of the two measures were chosen to represent "value." But if the difference is large, the choice of EV or CV as the appropriate welfare measure may be critical.

In an important paper, Willig (1976) showed that the difference between WTP and WTA would be small for many private market goods. Willig developed mathematical relationships between EV, CV, and consumer surplus, showing that the differences are a function of prices, quantities demanded, and income levels (Freeman 1993). He showed that the differences related to the income elasticity of demand for a good, that is, the responsiveness of the demand curve for a good to changes in income, and the magnitude of consumer surplus relative to total income. As those parameters decrease, the percentage difference between CV, EV,

---

[6]The importance of the weight given to all incomes is discussed later in this chapter.
[7]Proofs can be found in Willig (1976), Just, Hueth, and Schmitz (1982), and Freeman (1993). See also Silberberg (1972).

and *CS* declines. Thus for a good like salt, for which the amount of consumer surplus is likely to be very small, as will the income elasticity of demand, the difference between *CV* and *EV* will be extremely small, and *CS* will be a good approximation of either. The *CS* associated with a new car, by contrast, may differ significantly from both *EV* and *CV*.

Initially, it was thought that the Willig results always would apply to nonmarket goods, such as environmental amenities (Randall and Stoll 1980). Unfortunately, empirical work using various types of interview procedures produced evidence of significant differences between *WTP* and *WTA*.[8] More recent theory shows that *WTP* and *WTA* can also differ significantly because of substitution effects and because indifference curves may be "kinked."

Goods in Fixed Supply   Hanemann (1991) showed that for goods available only in fixed supply or outside the control of the purchaser (e.g., Yosemite National Park), the divergence between *WTP* and *WTA* depends not only on income effects but also on *substitution* effects. Holding income constant, the smaller the substitution effect (i.e., the fewer substitutes available for a good), the larger will be the divergence between *WTP* and *WTA*. This will be especially true for public goods, since many will have few substitutes (again, think of Yosemite National Park). In fact, Hanemann showed that the difference between *WTP* and *WTA* can be infinite. Thus an individual may accept no level of compensation to forgo a good that is unique. As we will see in later chapters the implications of Hanemann's findings on the valuation of environmental goods may be considerable.

Loss Aversion and Kinked Indifference Curves   Recent theories and experimental evidence have challenged some of the underlying postulates of standard utility theory (Knetsch 1990, 1995). These, too, may have significant implications for environmental policy development and environmental attribute valuation. The new theory postulates that indifference curves may be "kinked," with the location of the kinks corresponding to an individual's *endowment* of goods. An example is shown in Figure 3.10.

In essence, this theory suggests that an individual will value a loss much more highly than an equivalent gain. Suppose that an individual's initial or endowment point corresponds to A, with quantities of a good E and all other goods of (E_0, X_0). To forgo Δ units of E, the individual would require compensation equal to $X_2 - X_0$. But the individual would be willing to pay only $X_0 - X_1$ to acquire an additional Δ units of E. Thus the individual appears to place a significantly higher value on units of the good already possessed than on acquiring additional units of the same good. Think back to Carol's unwillingness to pay more than $100 for a catalytic converter for cleaner air and her unwillingness to accept even $1,000 to give it up and allow the coal-fired power plant to be built near her cabin. In standard utility the-

---

[8]These procedures, which fall under the category of *contingent valuation studies*, are discussed in detail in Chapter 11.

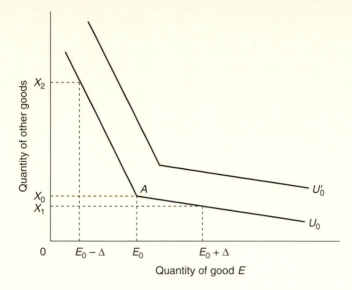

Figure 3.10   Kinked Indifference Curves

ory, this large disparity should not exist. Yet many empirical studies, as well as anecdotal evidence like ours, show that it does (Knetsch 1990). As we will discuss in Chapter 11, this disparity can have significant impacts on empirical measures of environmental values and therefore on the formation of environmental policies.

COLLECTIVE CHOICE AND PREFERENCES

Until now, we have focused on individual choice and preferences. Many environmental goods, however, have characteristics of what economists call *public goods.* (We define public goods more formally in Chapter 6.) Because of those characteristics, individual choices may not be sufficient to ensure that the "right" choices, *from the perspective of society,* are made.[9] For example, suppose that you value a pristine view of the Grand Canyon, but I do not, and I build a coal-fired power plant nearby whose pollution obscures your view. In such a case, my individual choice has affected yours. Ideally, we would want some way of knowing whose choices to "value" more: yours or mine.

This sort of complication arises in economics because we often consider the analysis of both *normative* and *positive* issues. *A positive analysis is a description*

---

[9]A well-known result in economics is Arrow's "impossibility theorem" (Arrow 1963), which states that social choices cannot be made solely on the basis of individual preferences. However, that does not mean that social choices cannot be made at all. They can and are. To do so, however, requires additional assumptions about how society should aggregate preferences. We discuss this shortly.

or prediction about what is or what will be; a normative analysis considers questions about what should be. The concept of economic efficiency is used in the economic analysis of normative issues. The branch of economics that considers normative analysis is welfare economics. The central concepts of welfare economics are those of economic efficiency, equity, and fairness.[10] One way to approach these concepts, and the problem of collective choice and preferences, is through what economists call the *social welfare function.* In introducing this concept, we use a little bit of descriptive calculus, although the argument can be followed without it.

The Social Welfare Function

A social welfare function is a function that aggregates individual welfares to give a measure of social welfare. A social welfare function is not a tool that can be applied directly to public policy decisions, but we study it because many decision tools, such as benefit-cost analysis, implicitly embody a particular social welfare function. Assume that a society has N individuals, each with a utility function U_i, for $i = 1$ to N. We can write a social welfare function for this society as

$$W = W(U_1, U_2, \ldots, U_N) \tag{3.4}$$

Equation 3.4 states that collective welfare is a function of the utility of all of the individuals in society.[11] Suppose that we ask what happens to overall social welfare when the utility of one or more individuals changes in response to an external factor such as a price change. We can determine this change by totally differentiating[12] Equation 3.4 to give

$$dW = \sum \frac{\partial W}{\partial U_i} dU_i \tag{3.5}$$

Equation 3.5 states that a change in social welfare (dW) equals the change in the utility of the ith person (dU_i), multiplied by the weight $\partial W/\partial U_i$ given to the ith person's utility by society. The weight given to the ith person's utility is called the person's *marginal social utility.* If we incorporate the information that utility is a function of goods and services as expressed in Equation 3.2, we can rewrite Equation 3.5 as

$$dW = \sum_{i=1}^{n} \sum_{j=1}^{N} \frac{\partial W}{\partial U_i} \frac{\partial U_i}{\partial X_{ij}} dX_{ij} \tag{3.6}$$

---

[10]Note that equity and fairness are not always the same thing. It may be equitable for everyone to have one dollar. But it may not be fair to take away a dollar from someone who, through hard work, has earned two dollars.

[11]Some would argue that the welfare of society should also include the welfare of all life on earth. This can be an important issue when sustainability issues arise.

[12]An explanation of the total differential is provided in Appendix A.1.

Thus a change in social welfare reflects the changes in each individual's change in his utility, which will be reflected through changes in the amounts of goods and services (including such "goods" as truth, justice, or preservation of species) they consume.

As we discussed earlier, any individual will maximize utility if she arranges her choice of goods so that her marginal utility of income (the value of an additional dollar) times the price of the good equals the marginal utility of the good. For example, she will maximize her utility when the utility value of a unit of nonpolluting detergent is equal to the price of a unit of the detergent times the value to her of an additional dollar (the marginal utility of income). Suppose that this condition was not met so that the marginal utility of a unit of the detergent was greater than the price of the unit times the marginal utility of a dollar. Then the individual could increase her utility by purchasing another unit of the detergent. In symbols, this condition for maximization of utility is

$$\frac{\partial U_i}{\partial X_{ij}} = \frac{\partial U_i}{\partial Y_j} P_j \tag{3.7}$$

Substituting this condition into Equation 3.6, we obtain

$$dW = \sum_{i=1}^{n} \sum_{j=1}^{N} \frac{\partial W}{\partial U_i} \frac{\partial U_i}{\partial Y_j} P_j dX_{ij} \tag{3.8}$$

Equation 3.8 states that the change in social welfare is determined by the change in goods and services going to the ith person times the prices of those goods and services. This yields an income change for the ith person. This income change is then weighted by the ith person's marginal utility of income to give an expression for the utility change of the ith person. Finally, this utility change is in turn weighted by the marginal social utility of that person.

Equation 3.8 can also be expressed as an income change and a *distributional* change as follows:

$$dW = \sum_{i=1}^{n} \sum_{j=1}^{N} P_j dX_{ij} + \sum_{i=1}^{n} \sum_{j=1}^{N} (\alpha_j - 1) P_j dX_{ij} \tag{3.9}$$

where the term α_j is the *marginal social utility of income* $(\partial W/\partial U_i)(\partial U_i/\partial Y_i)$.[13] The marginal social utility of income is the weight society gives to a change in person i's income. The weight is made up of the importance of income to the person herself, that is, her marginal utility of income, and the weight society places on that person's utility, her marginal social utility. The term dX_{ij} is the change in the quantity of the jth good going to the ith individual, and the term P_j is the price of the jth good.

---

[13]Notice that choosing α_i can be conceptualized in two steps: choice of one of the infinite number of utility functions that can describe the individual's preferences (choice of $\partial U_i/\partial Y_i$) and choice of the weight to give the individual's preferences (choice of $\partial W/\partial U_i$).

The first expression on the right-hand side of Equation 3.9 says that a change in welfare is equal to the sum of the changes in goods going to the various individuals times their price. This is called the *income change* measure, or the *efficiency effect.* The second term on the right-hand side of the equation is the income change *weighted by the marginal social utility of income.* This is called the *distribution effect.* In general, society will care about the particular distribution of gains and losses. If, for example, a change in the income of a poorer person is given more weight than that of a richer person, this would show up in the second expression on the right-hand side of Equation 3.9.

An Example

The Environmental Protection Agency's catalytic converter policy might lower the cost of producing some goods and thus increase the quantities of these goods. But the change might lower incomes for certain individuals (like Carol) and result in their consuming less of certain goods. All of these changes in the quantities times the price are summed in the first expression and will affect rich and poor. If there is to be a difference in the weight given to income changes affecting the rich and the poor, however, this will be accounted for in the second expression. Thus if society wanted to "count" Carol's loss more than Howard's gain, it would assign a larger marginal social utility of income to Carol.

DEFINING ECONOMIC EFFICIENCY

A fully defined social welfare function would always tell us whether a policy action increased or decreased overall welfare. In practice, we have to settle for less precise and less complete measures of welfare change. This has led economists to depend heavily on the concept of efficiency, which does not require us to know, or define, the social marginal utility of each individual's income.

Pareto Efficiency

The concept of economic efficiency was first formalized by Vilfredo Pareto toward the end of the nineteenth century and it is often called *Pareto efficiency.* Pareto efficiency applies to states of the economy. It judges states according to whether it is possible to improve the welfare of at least one person at no cost to anyone else. An economy where there remain unexploited ways to make someone better off while making no one else worse off is inefficient. An economy is efficient when all free ways of increasing welfare have been used.

Pareto efficiency has three components: consumption efficiency, production efficiency, and exchange efficiency. Consumption efficiency requires that, of the combinations of goods and services they can afford, all persons are consuming the ones they value most highly. This means that there are no opportunities to make people better off by changing how they spend a fixed amount of wealth. Production efficiency requires that the total cost of producing any given set of final goods and services is minimized. This means that there are no unexploited opportunities to increase wealth by reducing production costs. Exchange efficiency requires that everyone place the same relative values on goods, that is, that everyone make consumption and production decisions based on the same relative prices. This means that there are no unexploited opportunities to increase wealth through trade.

When an economy is Pareto-efficient, any possible increase in one person's welfare reduces someone else's; in other words, it involves redistributions of wealth. However, the state resulting from such a redistribution may itself be Pareto-efficient. In fact, Pareto efficiency defines a frontier, not a single point. This *Pareto frontier* is the set of efficient allocations of goods corresponding to different distributions of wealth.

Few experts would object to using Pareto efficiency as one of several normative criteria. Its political analogue is the requirement of unanimity in voting. An action that satisfies the Pareto efficient test would be eminently supportable. The difficulty, of course, is that it has limited application. There are few actions that satisfy the Pareto criterion of hurting no one while helping someone. The requirement that all cars have catalytic converters would have benefited Howard but hurt Carol. It is difficult to imagine a presidential election in the United States in which one candidate would receive every single vote cast.

Alternatively, imagine that the Sierra Club has paid $10 million to the Tiger Creek Timber Company to preserve a section of privately held old-growth forest in the Pacific Northwest. Sierra Club members are better off, as is the lumber company that previously owned the forest. Yet as a result, lumber prices will be higher. Somewhere there will be a builder who does not care about preserving old-growth forests who will be hurt by the higher lumber prices. Thus even this transaction does not satisfy Pareto optimality.[14]

Pareto Improvements

If an economy is inefficient, it is possible to make at least one person better off at no cost to anyone else. Such a change is called a *Pareto improvement* or a *Pareto superior move*. A Pareto improvement is a move from a *Pareto inferior* state to a *Pareto superior* state.

In terms of the social welfare function, a Pareto superior move is a move that increases total welfare *regardless* of the weights assigned to individuals because individual levels of welfare all either increase or do not decrease. A public policy resulting in a Pareto improvement should have universal approval. It would seem, therefore, that policymakers should spend their time looking for Pareto improvements. To some extent, they do. Politics is often the art of cooperation for mutual advantage. But politics is often the art of compromise, precisely because there are

---

[14]This is an example of a pecuniary externality, which will be discussed in Chapter 6.

frequently no Pareto improvements available to policymakers. This is largely because people take advantage of most opportunities for gains from trade or from cutting costs on their own. Policymakers are often in a situation where all of their options involve some redistribution and net losses for some of the parties. This is an important point to remember, and it is one reason that policies aimed at promoting efficiency sometimes face stiff opposition: a move from the status quo to the Pareto frontier is not necessarily a Pareto superior move.

Potential Pareto Improvements and the Kaldor-Hicks Criteria

The scarcity of Pareto improvements available to policymakers led economists to search for ways to judge whether the gains from a policy outweigh the losses. Kaldor (1939) and Hicks (1939) simultaneously developed complementary tests for comparing gains and losses. The Kaldor-Hicks criteria are often used in applied benefit-cost analysis work. The Kaldor criterion states that *a project is an improvement when the winners from a project could, in principle, compensate the losers from the project.* More formally, under the Kaldor criterion, state 1 is preferable to state 2 if state 1 could, in principle, be changed solely by costless lump-sum transfers into state 1′, which is Pareto superior to state 2. In terms of the catalytic converter example, we would ask, could Howard have bribed Carol to agree to the EPA rule requiring catalytic converters?

Hicks developed a slightly different criterion: *a project is an improvement when the potential losers could not bribe the potential winners not to undertake the project.* More formally, state 1 is preferable to state 2 if it is not, even in principle, possible to make lump-sum redistributions changing state 2 to state 2′ so that everyone would be as well off in state 2′ as in state 1. Thus under the Hicks criterion, we would ask whether Carol could have bribed Howard not to require catalytic converters.

Although they appear similar, the Kaldor and Hicks criteria do differ. Suppose that in state of the world 1 a park exists that does not exist in state of the world 2. Suppose that the gain to the winners from creating the park—that is, in moving from state 2 to state 1—is $200, while the loss to the losers is $160. The losers in the move could not bribe the winners not to undertake the project as long as the mix of goods available in the two states is such that the winners prefer state 1 more than the losers prefer state 2. The move from state 2 to state 1 would then satisfy the Hicks test.

Suppose instead that the losers, in moving from state 2 to state 1, could be costlessly compensated with $165 and that a mix of goods is available to them in state 1 so that with the $165 they could be at least as well off in state 1 as they were in state 2. The winners would now have a surplus of $35 after compensating the losers. As a result they can buy a set of goods that is more valuable to them than they could in state 2. Thus the winners are unambiguously better off in state 1 than in state 2. In this situation the move from state 2 to state 1 would satisfy the Kaldor test. If the compensation were actually carried out and no party was worse off while someone was better off, the move would also meet the Pareto test.[15]

In terms of our example of EPA-mandated catalytic converters, we can say that the practice used by the EPA of mandating the technology does not satisfy a Pareto efficiency test. Insofar as the critics are correct that the EPA practice increases the cost of technology, consumers and producers will lose, as will investors in some potential new technology. We can also say, however, that the abandonment of the EPA procedure would also not be a Pareto superior move. This is because an abandonment of the practice would clearly hurt investors in the currently mandated (or about to be mandated) technology and those who valued cleaner air more than the cost of the converters.

It is a different story with the potential Pareto or Kaldor-Hicks test. A superior technology will generate gains that exceed the losses to the losers. If the technology affects only the mix of goods on the margin and does not have major impacts on the losers' wealth, one can be confident in saying that the winners could in principle compensate the losers with a surplus remaining for the winners and that the losers could not bribe the winners not to develop the new technology.

In terms of Equation 3.9, the potential Pareto test assumes that the social marginal utility of income is the same for all, that is, that $(\partial W/\partial U_i)(\partial U_i/\partial Y_i) = 1$. This means that the distributional part of the equation disappears and we are left with a change in welfare:

$$dW = \sum_{i=1}^{n} \sum_{j=1}^{N} P_j dX_{ij} \qquad (3.10)$$

The change in welfare is just the sum of the income changes for individuals. Note that this definition of efficiency, while a great deal more usable than the Pareto criteria, may be harder to defend. To see this, suppose that a project cost a very poor person $100, and its result was to increase the income of a very rich person by $101. Such a project would pass the test but might not appear very attractive to many people.

A Justification for Using Kaldor-Hicks

If used as the only criterion for judging a single policy, the Kaldor-Hicks test might lead to an unattractive decision. However, when it is used as one of the criteria for judging all policies, it is very attractive. Other criteria can be used to screen out policies that have undesirable distributional or human rights effects. The Kaldor-Hicks test is a screen for policies that have undesirable economic effects. Most

---

[15]It is possible that using only one of the tests will result in *cycling*, in which a move from state B to A is desirable but then a move back from A to B is also desirable. For a fuller explanation, see Zerbe and Dively (1994) or Broadway and Bruce (1986). See also Zerbe (1997).

policies change the mix of goods and services and redistribute wealth. If a policy fails the Kaldor-Hicks test, it means that the change in the mix of goods and services is a net loss to society. Everyone would be better off if policymakers just redistributed wealth and left the mix of goods and services alone. A policy that fails the Kaldor-Hicks test should be adopted only if there are compelling noneconomic reasons to adopt it and there are no policies that will accomplish the same ends and pass the Kaldor-Hicks test.

With many policy decisions, the gainers from some decisions are likely to be the losers from others. The distributional effects are unlikely to net out exactly, but policymakers have many tax and spending tools to make further redistributions. Thus policymakers can justify actions as part of a package that would have unacceptable distributional consequences if considered alone.

The Harberger Criterion

In reality, transferring income is not costless.[16] Recognizing this, Harberger (1976) and later Zerbe (1991) proposed a test that takes policymakers' overall distributional goals and the costs of redistribution into account. The *Harberger criterion* assumes that policymakers want the combined effects of all their actions to make the distribution of income more equal. When a policy has the opposite effect—that is, if the losers are poorer than the winners—the Harberger criterion subtracts the costs of an offsetting income transfer from the net benefits of the policy.

Consider an environmental project that reduces automobile pollution and improves the quality of the air. Cleaner air is more valuable to the rich than to the poor. The people affected are made up of 1,000 rich people and 1,000 poor people. The rich people each value the cleaner air at $175; the poor people, at $30 each. The air will be improved through the use of a catalytic converter that will cost each person $100. Each rich person will have a net gain of $75, for a total gain of $75,000. Each poor person will lose $70, for a total loss of $70,000. This project would satisfy a potential Pareto test because the sum of the gains and losses, not counting distributional effects, is $5,000.

Suppose now that the administrative costs of transferring money to the poor is 20 percent of the amount of money transferred. That is, these costs would be 20 percent of $70,000, or $14,000. We add the $14,000 in costs to the $70,000 for a total of $84,000, which exceeds the net benefits of the richer group by $9,000. Thus the Harberger criterion would lead to rejection of the project. Table 3.2 summarizes these figures. The first row shows the analysis when no additional weight is given to the fact that the policy has adverse distributional effects on the poor. The second row includes the administrative costs required to compensate the poor. When this cost is taken into account, the result is a negative net social

---

[16]In most cases, there will be both administrative costs and losses due to inefficiencies introduced by the transfer mechanism, known as deadweight losses.

TABLE 3.2 EVALUATION OF PROJECTS UNDER DIFFERENT BENEFIT-COST CRITERIA (DOLLARS)

Criterion	Richer Group Gross Gain	Cost to Richer Group	Poorer Group Gross Gain	Poorer Group Cost	Transfer Cost (Distribution Effect)	Total Benefits Minus Costs
Potential Pareto	175,000	100,000	30,000	100,000	0	5,000
Harberger	175,000	100,000	30,000	100,000	−14,000	−9,000

benefit. This says that although the project has a positive welfare effect of $5,000 using the potential Pareto criterion, it is nevertheless a poor project, because the poor lose enough from it that the inclusion of the administrative costs of their compensation render the project not worthwhile.

The Harberger criterion could be used instead of the Kaldor-Hicks criteria in benefit-cost analysis of environmental policies as long as the costs of determining the distributional effects are not too great or there is a strong presupposition that the distributional effects are liable to be small.

BENEFIT-COST ANALYSIS OF ENVIRONMENTAL POLICIES

Benefit-cost analysis is a technique that we will consider in more detail later. Its application to environmental policy issues is often controversial because of concerns about both the ability to measure benefits and costs and the moral defensibility of weighing benefits and costs in environmental contexts. (We discuss some of these arguments in later chapters.)

Assuming that one has no moral objections, benefit-cost analysis involves a summation of either the *CV*s or the *EV*s for a project to see if it is worthwhile. Consider again Figures 3.5 and 3.6. If the sum of the *CV*s or the *EV*s is positive for a move from *A* to *B*, it is said that the project is worthwhile. Thus the *EV* and the *CV* can be used as measures of value. Note that these measures *include* the redistribution of income as a good so that distributional effects would be considered as part of any benefit-cost analysis that used the *CV* or *EV*.

To see how these measures work, suppose that we are considering a policy toward an old-growth forest in the Pacific Northwest. First, consider a proposal that does not take account of distributional effects. Suppose that Tiger Creek Timber Company owns the forest. The Sierra Club would pay $10 million for its preservation. Tiger Creek Timber would accept no less than $8 million to give up its harvest. The $10 million would be the *CV* for the Sierra Club. The $8 million would be the *CV* for Tiger Creek Timber, but because it represents a cost of preservation, it would be a negative figure. The sum of the *CV*s would be a positive

$2 million. Therefore, a benefit-cost analysis would indicate net benefits of $2 million for preservation, and the analysis would suggest that the old-growth forest should be preserved. The *EV*s, by contrast, would be the amount that the Sierra Club would accept and the amount that Tiger Creek Timber would pay. The Sierra Club may require (accept) $100 million before it would accept that the forest could be cut. Suppose that Tiger Creek Timber would pay $8 million to avoid having the forest taken away. These *EV* amounts would be the cost or value of preservation.[17] The sum of the *EV*s would be a positive $92 million. Now the benefit-cost analysis suggests that the value of preservation is $92 million. Whether the *CV* or the *EV* measure is used, the benefit-cost conclusion would be that the forest should be preserved.

An analysis may also determine consumer and producer surplus instead of *CV*s and *EV*s. Assume that the consumer surplus of the Sierra Club for preservation of the old-growth forest is $12 million. This figure is greater than its *CV* but less than its *EV*. The producer surplus for Tiger Creek Timber, if allowed to exploit the forest for lumber, would be the net value of the income the company would receive from it. This would be just $8 million as we determined for the *CV* previously; the *CV* for Tiger Creek Timber doesn't change because there is no income effect for a firm. In this example, the sum of the consumer surplus and producer surplus would be a positive $4 million for preservation.

As part of this analysis, we also might determine the income distributional consequences of the proposed preservation. Suppose that we estimate that the poor will lose $3 million and the rich will gain $5 million so that the Kaldor-Hicks measure remains a positive $2 million, as in the case in which the Sierra Club must buy the forest. If the costs of transferring income to the poor are 20 percent of the amount transferred, we would add a transfer loss of $600,000. The Harberger measure of welfare gain from preservation would now be $1.4 million. Note that this assumes that there is a *WTP* for income redistribution and that such a redistribution is treated simply as one of the goods in question whose price is determined by the most efficient alternative.[18]

Rights and the Measurement of Benefits and Costs

How is it that the benefit-cost analysis gave us such different answers according to whether we used the sum of the *CV*s or the *EV*s? Notice that in the case of the *CV*s, we assume that Tiger Creek Timber owns the forest now and that it will be preserved only if the Sierra Club can buy it from Tiger Creek Timber. The amount the Sierra Club can pay limits its measure of value of the forest. In the second case, using *EV*s, it is as if we were using the *CV*s again but changing our assumption about ownership of the forest. In this case, we implicitly assume that the Sierra

---

[17]In this example, the amount that Tiger Creek would pay or would accept is the same and is the value of the forest for timber.

[18]The social weight given to any person's change in income is the weight reflected by the willingness to pay to transfer money to that person.

Club owns the forest or at least the rights to its preservation. Now the Sierra Club is not limited to what it can pay. The use of the *CV* and the *EV* is equivalent to using only the *CV* but assuming a change in ownership. For policy purposes, it appears more useful to use just the *CV* but to explicitly consider the change that results if one assumes a different ownership. If we assume that the Sierra Club had a right to preserve the old-growth forest, the correct measure of benefit from preservation would be the $100 million the Sierra Club would require to sell the right. The costs would be the $8 million Tiger Creek Timber would pay to harvest the forest. As we have seen, this would be a measure of preservation using the sum of the *EV*s and would be $92 million. If we considered the project as harvesting the forest but still assumed that the Sierra Club had the right to the forest, the measure of value would be the same but with a negative sign. The benefits would be the *WTP* of Tiger Creek Timber of $8 million, and the costs would be the *WTA* of $100 million by the Sierra Club. This would be the sum of the *CV*s and would be −$92 million.[19]

We discussed previously that the difference between *CV* and *EV* will depend on income effects, substitution effects, and whether losses are valued more than gains. Where the good in question is a small part of the budget and where there are good substitutes, the *CV* and the *EV* will give similar measures of value. This is true for many ordinary goods and services. For many environmental goods, such as environmental preservation, the values will vary greatly on the basis of what is assumed about rights. Think about how differently you would measure the value of your life if we asked how much you would be willing to pay to preserve it as compared to how much you are willing to accept to give it up.

CHAPTER SUMMARY

This chapter presented some basic foundations of welfare economics that are often used in environmental policy analysis. Conceptually, a social welfare function would give precise measures of aggregate welfare changes, but its use is almost entirely limited to theory. A Pareto improvement is a change that makes at least one person better off while harming no one. A potential Pareto improvement is a change where the gains exceed the losses. The Kaldor-Hicks test provides two criteria for determining whether a change is a potential Pareto improvement. They differ in their assignment of property rights: the Kaldor criterion requires that the gainers from a change be able to compensate the losers, whereas the Hicks criterion requires that the losers not be able to bribe the gainers not to make the change. The Harberger criterion accounts for the costs of redistribution in deciding whether such compensation is possible.

Empirical measurement of the benefits and the costs of environmental impacts and policies has focused on measures of willingness to pay and willingness

---

[19]The sum of the *CV*s for a move from *A* to *B* is the same as the negative of the sum of the *EV*s for a move from *B* to *A*.

to accept, which are embodied in the *EV* and *CV* measures of welfare changes and approximated by measuring consumer surplus and producer surplus. Such approximations, however, may not always be valid. Furthermore, whether an environmental impact or policy should be evaluated using *WTP* or *WTA* will depend on the structure of property rights.

CHAPTER REVIEW

Economic Concepts and Tools

- Utility theory postulates indifference curves that reflect consumer preferences.
- Kinked indifference curves can reflect individuals' greater valuation of losing something they already have versus gaining that same thing. This is sometimes called *loss aversion*. Theorists have postulated kinked indifference curves to explain experimental results that pose paradoxes for conventional utility theory.
- The compensating variation (*CV*) is the amount of money an individual would be willing to pay to gain a benefit such as a price decrease. It is also the amount an individual would be willing to accept to suffer imposition of a harm such as a price increase.
- The equivalent variation (*EV*) is the amount of money an individual would be willing to accept to forgo a benefit such as a price decrease or the amount of income an individual would be willing to pay to avoid a harm such as a price increase.
- *CV* and *EV* can be approximated by consumer surplus and producer surplus. Consumer surplus is (approximately) the amount the consumer is willing to pay over what he or she is required to pay. For goods with few substitutes and those that represent a large fraction of income, *CV* and *EV* may differ significantly, making the use of *CS* as an approximation problematic. Producer surplus is the amount that could be taken from the producer as a lump sum without affecting the amount the producer supplies.
- The central concepts of welfare economics are those of economic efficiency, equity, and fairness. One way to approach these concepts is through consideration of what economists call the social welfare function.
- An individual's marginal utility of income is the importance that individual places on additional income.
- The marginal social utility of income is the weight society gives to a change in an individual's income. The weight is made up of the individual's marginal utility of income and the weight society places on that person's utility, the individual's marginal social utility.
- A state of Pareto efficiency is attained when there is no action or decision that would improve the well-being of someone without harming someone else. In this state, it is not possible to rearrange the existing supply of goods so as to make someone better off or to increase production by rearranging existing inputs. Furthermore, people's subjective relative valuation of goods at the margin corresponds with the relative cost of the goods so that there are no unexploited gains from trade between individuals or firms.

- A change satisfies the Kaldor-Hicks criteria when the beneficiaries of a policy or an action can *potentially* (not actually) compensate the losers yet still be better off than without the policy or action.
- The Harberger criterion takes the costs of transferring income into account in judging whether the gainers from a policy could compensate the losers.

Policy Issues

- Valuation of environmental damages can take place using either *WTP* or *WTA* estimates. The correct policy application will depend, in part, on the initial assignment of property rights.
- Loss aversion may be especially important in determining environmental policy valuations because of the critical nature of the initial assignment of property rights.
- Policymakers seldom have the opportunity to implement a Pareto improvement.
- The Kaldor-Hicks criteria provide a way to judge whether the benefits of a policy exceed the costs. Since most policies have both winners and losers, such criteria are necessary in most cases. A policy that fails the Kaldor-Hicks tests is undesirable because the changes in the mix of goods and services from the policy makes everyone worse off. The gains from the policy could be accomplished entirely through redistribution while leaving the losers better off than if the policy were implemented.
- The magnitude of distributional (equity) impacts can be assessed using the Harberger criterion.

DISCUSSION QUESTIONS

1. Do you think that the *EV* and *CV* measures of the value of an apple would differ much for a single individual? Why or why not?
2. What if the good in question is not an apple but the right to preserve a wild salmon run? Now do you think the *EV* and *CV* measures would differ much? Why or why not?
3. Suppose that the president proposes a new Btu tax to help preserve salmon runs in the Pacific Northwest. For convenience, assume that each income group has the same number of people. This tax will have costs among income groups as follows:

	Rich Income Group	Middle Income Group	Poor Income Group
Tax costs	$2,000	$1,800	$1,600
Benefits as measured by *WTP*	$1,000	$1,900	$2,500

This might seem a peculiar distribution of benefits and costs by income class until we realize that the salmon are an important commercial source for relatively poor Indians who have fishing rights along the Columbia and elsewhere.

    a. What will be the result of a benefit-cost analysis that uses a potential Pareto test?

    b. What will be the result of a benefit-cost analysis that uses a Harberger test? Explain the different results.

4. Explain how you as an analyst would compare efficiency and equity considerations in practice. What is your justification for your method?

5. Because of population pressure on national parks, suppose that the government considers two alternative plans. One would impose a market-clearing price on use of the parks. The other would limit admission to the parks on a first-come, first-served basis. Who will benefit and which will be harmed by the alternative policies? Explain.

6. Bob values an extra dollar of income more than Alice. Is it efficient to transfer money from Alice to Bob? Does the answer depend on your definition of efficiency?

7. A consumer spends his entire income on clean water and books. Draw the budget line under the following conditions:

    a. The price of clean water is $10 and income is $1,000.

    b. The price of clean water is $10 and income is $2,000.

    c. Income is $1,000 and the price of clean water is $2.

8. Draw an indifference curve for an economic good that is desirable up to five units and then gives negative utility.

9. Draw an indifference curve for Dick between his and Don's income on the assumption that Dick cares as much for Don's income as Dick cares for his own.

10. A tax of 10 cents per quart is levied on all backpacks. No other taxes exist in the economy. Which of the marginal efficiency conditions are violated by the tax?

11. "Since 1900, real income has increased tremendously, yet the average number of children per family has decreased." Consider the following possible explanations, and illustrate in terms of market opportunity sets and family indifference curves between the number of children (X) and all other goods.

    a. Children are an inferior good: since we're richer now, we want fewer of them.

    b. Children are not an inferior good: however, it has become more expensive to raise children.

    c. Children are not an inferior good, nor have they become relatively more expensive. What has happened is that tastes have changed: couples today want smaller families than couples in 1900.

    d. The shift from farming to urban life has meant that children are less valuable to the family than they were in 1900.

REFERENCES

Arrow, K. 1963. *Social Choice and Individual Values*. 2d ed. New York: Wiley.

Broadway, R., and N. Bruce. 1986. *Welfare Economics*. London: Blackwell.

Broome, J. 1978. "Trying to Value a Life." *Journal of Public Economics* 9(1): 91–100.

Browning, E., and J. Browning. 1989. *Microeconomic Theory and Applications*. 3d ed. Glenview, Ill.: Scott, Foresman.

Freeman, A. 1993. *The Measurement of Environmental and Resource Values: Theory and Methods*. Washington, D.C.: Resources for the Future.

Friedman, L. 1984. *Microeconomic Policy Analysis*. New York: McGraw-Hill.

Hanemann, W. 1991. "Willingness to Pay and Willingness to Accept: How Much Can They Differ?" *American Economic Review* 81(2): 635–647.

Harberger, A. 1976. "On Measuring the Social Opportunity Cost of Public Funds." In *Project Evaluation: Collected Papers*. Chicago: University of Chicago Press.

Hicks, J. 1939. "The Foundations of Welfare Economics." *Economic Journal* 49(4):696–712.

Just, R., D. Hueth, and A. Schmitz. 1982. *Applied Welfare Economics and Public Policy*. Upper Saddle River, N.J.: Prentice Hall.

Kaldor, N. 1939. "Welfare Propositions in Economics and Interpersonal Comparison of Utility." *Economic Journal* 49(4): 549–552.

Knetsch, J. 1990. "Environmental Policy Implications of Disparities Between Willingness to Pay and Compensation Demanded Measures of Values." *Journal of Environmental Economics and Management* 18(2): 227–237.

———. 1995. "Asymmetric Valuation of Gains and Losses in Preference Orderings." *Economic Inquiry* 33(1): 134–141.

Layard, P., and A. Walters. 1978. *Microeconomic Theory*. New York: McGraw-Hill.

Randall, A., and J. Stoll. 1980. "Consumer's Surplus in Commodity Space." *American Economic Review* 71(2): 449–457.

Silberberg, E. 1972. "Duality and the Many Consumers' Surpluses." *American Economic Review* 62(4): 942–956.

Varian, H. 1992. *Microeconomic Analysis*. 3d ed. New York: Norton.

Willig, R. 1976. "Consumers' Surplus Without Apology." *American Economic Review* 66(4): 589–597.

Zerbe, R. 1991. "Comment: Does Benefit-Cost Analysis Stand Alone? Rights and Standing." *Journal of Policy Analysis and Management* 10(1): 96–104.

———. 1997. "Is Benefit-Cost Analysis Legal?" *Journal of Policy Analysis and Management* 16, forthcoming.

———, and D. Dively. 1994. *Benefit-Cost Analysis in Theory and Practice*. New York: Harper Collins.

CHAPTER 4

ETHICS, PUBLIC POLICY, AND THE ENVIRONMENT

Heavy Metal: Lead, Poverty, and Discrimination

Lead has been an environmental threat for thousands of years. The ancient Romans may have weathered the short-run effects of their bacchanalias, but there is much evidence that over the long run, they poisoned themselves with lead. It leached into their wine from the glazes on wine goblets and was absorbed from many other sources. Centuries of mining, smelting, and use of lead in a variety of human activities have increased the background concentration of lead in the environment.

With the dawn of the industrial age and, in the twentieth century, the use of lead as a gasoline additive, lead became a pervasive environmental threat, found in almost every medium with which humans came into contact—food, water, air, soil, dust, and paint, each a potential pathway for human exposure. The widespread presence of lead in the environment posed a significant health risk: in sufficient concentrations, it damages the blood, the kidneys, and the central nervous system; over time, exposure to high lead concentrations can cause anemia, kidney damage, severe brain damage, and death.

Prior to its regulation under the Clean Air Act in 1970, exposure to lead in the United States generally was highest among low-income groups and racial minorities. The poorest members of society, especially poor and minority children, were at the highest risk of exposure. They tended to live in older, decaying houses that had peeling lead-based paint. They tended to live nearer industries that put high concentrations of lead in the air. But by far the largest source of lead emissions was the exhaust from motor vehicles: the U.S. Environmental Protection Agency (EPA) estimated that vehicle exhaust accounted for 88 percent of total atmospheric lead emissions.

Under the Clean Air Act, the administrator of the EPA was responsible for setting standards for airborne lead concentrations. Setting these standards focused on two key questions: what is the maximum safe *blood lead level for children, and what percentage of the target population should be kept below this blood lead level? Ultimately, the maximum safe individual blood lead level for children was set at 30 micrograms of lead per deciliter (μg Pb/dl).[1]*

This choice was based on three grounds. First, it is at this blood lead level that the adverse health effects of lead exposure were observed in children. Second, it was thought that a maximum safe individual blood lead level of 30 μg Pb/dl would allow an adequate margin of safety *in protecting children against more serious effects of lead exposure that were observed to appear in children at blood lead levels of 40 μg Pb/dl and central nervous system deficits that were observed at blood lead levels of 50 μg Pb/dl. Third, the EPA administrator reasoned that the maximum safe individual blood lead level should be no higher than the 30 μg Pb/dl blood lead level used by the Centers for Disease Control to screen children for lead poisoning.*

Having set the maximum allowable individual blood lead level for the target population, the administrator next focused on the question of what percentage of children between the ages of 1 and 5 years the standard should attempt to keep below this blood lead level. According to the 1970 census, there were approximately 20 million children under the age of 5 years in the United States. Of those, 12 million lived in urban areas and 5 million lived in inner cities where lead exposure was thought to be especially high. The administrator concluded that to provide an adequate margin of safety and to protect special high-risk subgroups, the standards should aim at keeping 99.5 percent of the target population below the maximum safe individual blood lead level of 30 μg Pb/dl. The last step in the EPA analysis was to determine what target mean exposure would ensure that this target population would be kept below that maximum safe individual blood lead level. Ultimately, the result was an ambient air quality standard of 1.5 μg Pb/m³ of air.

Since the regulations were enacted, lead concentrations in the air have declined significantly. By 1994, over 90 percent of all gasoline sold in the United States was unleaded; in many states, no leaded gasoline is sold whatsoever. Between 1970 and 1992, total lead emissions fell by almost 98 percent. Thus the EPA standards have succeeded in reducing lead emissions and exposure.

While the standards were being debated, all parties agreed that exposure to high levels of lead was especially dangerous to children. But because the highest levels of exposure had been observed in minority groups, setting the standard became more of a question of a right to be free from the adverse health effects of lead rather than a standard that was based solely on the benefits and the costs of exposure. That impetus for policy setting raised numerous challenges from industries that were forced to change their production methods.

In the case of lead, as with many other pollutants, the "safe" level of exposure was questioned. Some observers argued that the only safe level of exposure would

---

[1]Subsequently, the EPA lowered the level to 10 μg Pb/dl for Superfund cleanups (see Chapter 9).

be no *exposure whatsoever.*[2] *Others argued that the sensitivity of individuals would vary and raised questions of whether standards should be directed to protect the most sensitive individuals (children in the case of lead) or the population as a whole. Still others, while not disputing the safety of no exposure whatsoever or the laudability of protecting the most sensitive groups, pointed out the impossibly high costs of achieving such goals. Thus in setting standards for maximum "safe" levels of exposure to hazardous pollutants, the EPA confronted numerous conflicting goals and a great deal of uncertainty.*

The much higher exposure levels of minority children and the poor raised still more difficult issues. Was exposure to lead "discriminatory" or, even worse, openly "racist"? If so, what should be done about it? What about exposure to other pollutants? Were there also discriminatory and racist overtones associated with them?

No one denied that there was a problem, but there were disagreements about the best solutions, and even what a "solution" implied. One party's complaints that its rights to life and health were being trampled would be answered by a second party's arguments about the costs of various lead control measures, and a third party would respond that it was being asked to bear too large a share of those costs. As in most policy debates, what is often called the "economic problem" played an important role—how to allocate scarce resources to meet competing ends. As in most policy debates, many other questions were important. What kinds of ends should count? Ends that can be measured in monetary terms, the rights of poor children, social justice, or freedom of choice and individual responsibility? Whose ends should count, and how should they be weighted? Should public health benefits be given greater weight than costs to consumers from removing lead from gasoline? How can values and interests that cannot be put in the same units be weighed? The EPA did not resolve most of these issues. Yet as policymakers do every day, the EPA did make decisions and take action.

INTRODUCTION

As we stated in Chapter 1, this book is about the use of economics in developing environmental policies. We concentrate on policy questions that economics provides answers for and on obtaining answers to those questions. We try also to show how those questions fit into the overall context of environmental policymaking. The specific policymaking context this book assumes is a pluralistic democracy with a largely market economy (i.e., a large fraction of economic activity takes place through markets, and citizens can participate in the governmental processes that lead to public policy). This describes the context for environmental policy in a growing portion of the world today. This description also rules out some parts of the world. Much of what we have to say can be applied in societies with nondemocratic governments or nonmarket economies, but we will have little to say about how to do so.

---

[2]This is sometimes called a *zero-tolerance* policy.

Pluralism and diversity have been hotly debated topics in the United States; we take that as evidence that they actually exist. We live in a society made up of people with different backgrounds, beliefs, values, and interests. One result of this is that there are many topics on which we have no moral consensus. Not only do we disagree on the specific actions we believe individuals and governments should take, but we also have fundamental disagreements on how we believe such questions should be decided.[3] At the same time, we use ethical terms such as *good* and *bad*, *right* and *wrong*, and *should* and *should not* that implicitly or explicitly appeal to impersonal and objective, or at least intersubjective, standards.[4]

The Role of Philosophy

Although this is not a philosophy textbook, a little philosophical background is useful to understand environmental policy debates such as lead exposure. Philosophers have spent millennia wrestling with the question of the proper foundation of ethical judgments and are no closer to agreeing on an answer than the rest of us. Western philosophers fall roughly into two camps, tracing back to Plato and Aristotle. The Aristotelian position is that X is better than Y if it is better for people and that we can know this from our knowledge of human nature. The Platonic position is that there are *objective* standards of good *independent* of human beings.

Eastern philosophy can also be divided roughly into two camps. Confucian philosophy holds that either what is good is embodied in tradition or that tradition is good for its own sake. Hinduism and Buddhism hold that good and evil, like everything else, are illusory. While Eastern philosophy has tended toward either authoritarian foundations for ethics or a denial of ethics, Western philosophy has concentrated on rational justifications. Unfortunately, no philosopher has produced a set of fundamental principles for an ethical system that has proved immune to other philosophers' attacks.

For public policy, including environmental policy, this means that many debates *cannot* be reduced to issues of fact and logic. If two parties disagree on a policy question, it is not true that one of them is necessarily mistaken about the facts or has made faulty inferences from them. People can agree on facts and logic and yet disagree *because they have different values*. Thus *setting public policy requires weighing and balancing competing values and sometimes choosing between them*.

---

[3]For an exposition of this thesis, see MacIntyre (1981).

[4]Some modern philosophers have claimed that when we make statements of ethical value, we are really only making disguised statements about our personal preferences. For example, Hare (1952) argued that "X is good" really means "I approve of X, and I want you to do likewise" and that "A should be done" really means "I want A done and I want you to want it too." A moment's reflection is all that is needed to disprove this position. Normal English speakers mean more by "X is good" than by "I approve of X." However, we may not be able to agree on what additional meaning the first statement has.

Even if everyone agrees on the facts and their implications, people can disagree because they have different interests. All of us may agree on what will be the effects of building a new sewage treatment plant, which of those effects are "good" and which are "bad," and that the good effects outweigh the bad. But we could still disagree on where the plant should be built. This could be true even if *everyone* valued the shared benefits more than the shared costs. Everyone may want the plant built, but no one may want it in their neighborhood. Setting public policy often requires weighing and balancing, and sometimes choosing between, individual's interests.

ETHICAL CONCEPTS IN ENVIRONMENTAL POLICY DEBATES

Public policy can involve a number of ethical concepts. We will encounter seven distinct concepts at various points in this book. Some will have a central role to play; others will arise only in passing. In general, we will be concerned with showing what economic analysis and economic solutions have to tell us about various policy questions. Generally, we will neither promote nor attack any particular point of view. We are presenting these seven ethical concepts because they arise in actual discussions about environmental policy, not because we wish to promote any one of them.

Table 4.1 summarizes these seven ethical concepts and indicates areas where they can be relevant to environmental policy development.

Human Welfare

This concept (actually a group of related concepts) has been given a number of names including "happiness" and "utility." The concept may have originated with Aristotle (1946, 1962), who used the term *eudaimonia*, which is probably best translated as "blessedness." As we discussed in Chapter 3, economists generally use

TABLE 4.1   ETHICAL CONCEPTS IN ENVIRONMENTAL POLICY DEBATES

Concept	Selected Environmental Applications
Human welfare or "utility"	Promoting economic efficiency, measuring the value of environmental goods
Human rights and property rights	Common property resources, rights not to be exposed to certain pollutants
Rights of nature	Preservation of endangered species, biodiversity
Obligations	Intergenerational equity
Distributive justice	Environmental "racism"
Procedural justice	Development and structure of environmental laws
Character	Putting monetary values on environmental goods

the term *welfare* for this broad concept of well-being. Philosophers often use the term *utility* to describe a broad conception of welfare, whereas, as we discussed in Chapter 3, economists have a more technical and narrower definition for *utility.*

Welfare is a concept that is difficult to define and measure, partly because different things make different people happy. There are many questions that can be raised about welfare. Is it a state or a process? Does happiness consist of being happy or of living well? Is welfare objective or subjective? Can it be measured? If so, how? If not, can we at least rank people as better off and worse off? Can we rank states of the world according to people's welfare in them? Is welfare individual or social? If we can talk legitimately about a society's welfare, is it an aggregate of the individual welfare of the society's members? If so, how do we aggregate individual welfare?

Economists are generally vague about defining welfare. Yet much of this book consists of applied welfare economics—techniques for measuring whether one situation produces more welfare than another. Although we do not claim to know precisely what welfare is, we do claim generally to "know it when we see it." The way we make that claim is by observing the *choices* people make. When someone who can have either A or B chooses A, we assume that having A makes that person better off than having B would. It is this assumption that lets us claim to be able to measure changes in welfare in monetary terms. If someone suffers an environmental impact that he or she would have sacrificed goods, services, and time worth up to $100 to avoid, we use that $100 as one measure of the loss in welfare resulting from the impact.

Generally, we will proceed as if all of the questions about welfare have been answered. However, all of these questions must be considered open to some extent. Though the answers to some of them may seem obvious to any one person, no answer to any of them will gain universal assent. This may be an inconvenience that is often ignored in the course of economic analysis, but it can be critically important to remember when applying economic analysis to environmental policy issues.

Human Rights and Property Rights

A nation's constitution, if it has one, generally specifies that citizens have certain rights. It is often asserted that people have certain rights by virtue of the fact that they are human (or perhaps sentient or even alive). These can be divided into *positive rights* and *negative rights.* A positive right is a right to do something (e.g., the right to vote, the right to express one's opinions in public or private, or the right to engage in certain forms of business). A negative right is a right not to be interfered with (e.g., the right not to be fined or imprisoned without a fair trial, the right not to participate in or support a state religion).

Human rights in the environment often, but not always, take the form of *property rights.* Property rights define a three-way relationship between the person or persons owning the property, the property itself, and the rest of society. This three-way relationship can take a wide variety of forms, but all of those forms have three common aspects. First, property rights define the ways in which the owner may use (or refrain from using) the property. Second, property rights define the ways in which the owner can prevent others from using the property and, in some cases, who may and may not be excluded. Third, property rights define how these rights to use and to exclude may be transferred to others.[5] These three aspects of the property relationship are often called *use rights, exclusion rights,* and *transfer rights.*

Rights in the environment can also be classified as either *positive* or *negative.* Positive rights in the environment may be associated with property or persons and generally consist of a right to "consume" an environmental good, such as pristine views and clean air. Negative rights in the environment consist generally of a right to be free from risk or harm without consent. Thus in the case of lead exposure, the EPA assigned a negative right to children when it developed the rules we discussed at the beginning of this chapter.

As we discuss in Chapter 6, externalities exist when legal rights, either property rights or personal rights, are ambiguous or unenforceable. Deciding which environmental impacts to allow and which to prohibit implicitly takes one side or another. The ambiguity of rights that leads to an externality often exists because of the public-good nature of parts of the environment.[6] Large numbers of people may be affected by a change in air quality, and all of them experience the same air quality. With large numbers of people involved, each of whom will benefit from actions that others take to improve air quality, it can be prohibitively expensive to obtain the consent and cooperation of everyone affected. Some externalities with small numbers of people involved arise when legal rights are unenforced or unenforceable. In some cases, individuals affect their neighbors because they and their neighbors are unaware of the consequences of their actions. In other cases, such as the illegal dumping of toxic materials, individuals push costs off onto others deliberately because they expect not to be caught.

Some rights have thresholds. A treaty between the United States and a Native American tribe may specify a number of acre-feet of water or a fraction of a salmon run that belongs to the tribe. As long as the threshold is met or exceeded, the tribe's rights are fulfilled. Other rights are a matter of degree. A right to clean air may be violated by any pollution, but the violation becomes worse with more pollution.

Many arguments about the environment are best seen in terms of rights rather than benefits and costs. Arguments that no one has a right to pollute or that people have a right to clean air and clean water are about people being affected adversely without their consent, not about the value of the impacts. Many environmental regulations are best understood as a response to such arguments. In the United States, environmental laws and regulations are often based on considerations of public health and safety, and air and water quality standards are often based on the avoidance of health risks. If people cannot choose whether to breathe air contaminated with lead and particulates or whether to drink water laced with heavy metals, allowing these emissions exposes people to health risks without their

---

[5]*Primogeniture,* the exclusive right of the firstborn to inherit property, is an example of a rule for transferring property that gives the owner little flexibility.
[6]A classic description can be found in Hardin (1968).

consent. Whether such emissions are to be allowed, and if so, how they are to be regulated, is a matter of the rights of those exposed and the rights of those whose activities might cause emissions.

Arguments about whether the costs of an environmental regulation are justified may be about whether the benefits of that regulation exceed its costs. Such arguments are at least as likely to be about who has rights in the environment.

Policies based on human rights may look very different from policies intended to maximize benefits less costs. This may have been the case with the EPA's lead regulations. In many cases where human rights are the issue, no mechanisms exists for people to exchange or waive the rights in question. Suppose that people show by their choices of occupations and activities that on average they would be willing to pay up to $100 per year to avoid a one-in-a-million risk of premature death. If cleaning up air pollution to the point where it poses a risk of premature death no greater than one in a million costs more than $100 per person, a comparison of total benefits and costs would lead to a lower level of pollution control. However, if there is a right to be free from this risk, if there is no mechanism for waiving or selling that right, and if some people would pay more than $100 to avoid the risk, a policy based on human rights would lead to a higher level of pollution control.

Rights of Nature

Some people extend the concept of rights to nonhumans or even to inanimate nature. This is a controversial idea, but it is one that plays a role in many environmental policy debates, such as preserving endangered species and maintaining biodiversity. Attempting to place a value on nature, or even defining what "nature" is, is difficult and controversial (Booth 1994).

The concept of the rights of nature is problematic because it is not clear that nonhuman nature, in part or as a whole, can be considered to be a *moral agent,* and only moral agents can have rights.[7] This difficulty can be circumvented by talking about nature as being *morally considerable.* If something or someone is morally considerable, I have a duty to consider the *consequences* of my actions for that person or thing. This could imply, for example, that killing the last members of a species is wrong because of what it does to the species or the ecosystem, regardless of what people want. Whether people are willing to pay more to have the last whales as stuffed trophies or as a living population is irrelevant from the standpoint of the whale's rights. Economics has little to offer policymakers deciding whether nonhuman nature is morally considerable or what specific obligations to nature we might have. However difficult it may be, questions of the rights of nature must be dealt with on their own terms, not in terms of human welfare.

As with human rights, policies based on the rights of nature may look very different from policies based on benefits and costs to people. Nonhuman nature has

---

[7]Moral agents take deliberate actions for which they are responsible. Philosophers argue about whether people are really moral agents, but there is general agreement that rocks and trees are not. See Goodpaster (1978).

no way of expressing consent with or dissent from actions we take and therefore has no way to waive its rights. Policies based solely on protecting rights of nature must therefore have an absolute character.

Obligations

An *obligation* is a legal or ethical requirement to do something or to refrain from doing something. Obligations can arise from moral or governmental laws. Obligations can also arise from others' rights or moral considerability. Rights generally imply corresponding obligations on the part of others. A positive right implies that others have obligations not to interfere with the exercise of that right and may imply obligations to help in its exercise. A negative right generally implies only an obligation not to interfere. Moral considerability entails an obligation to consider the impact of our actions on someone or something else but may not entail an obligation to act in any specific way or refrain from any specific action as a right generally does. Sometimes we speak of obligations to oneself, generally in terms of pursuing one's genuine long-term interests rather than short-term advantages that may have bad consequences in the long run.

Most of the obligations we will consider are those arising from others' rights or from laws, and our discussion will generally be in terms of the rights or laws that give rise to the obligation. The one exception will be obligations the present generation may have to future generations, which is sometimes called *intergenerational equity.* Philosophers disagree strongly over whether nonexistent, potential, future persons (who may not even be conceived for centuries or millennia) have rights. However, there seems to be more agreement that if we have obligations to anyone, some of those obligations may extend to future generations.

Distributive Justice

Distributive justice is concerned with the fairness of the distribution of goods (or bads). It is concerned with whether individuals have, or receive, more or less than their "fair" share. Whether minority children received more than their fair share of lead exposure is a question of distributive justice. Philosophers and others have advanced a number of conceptions of distributional justice. We will not argue for or against any of them here. Where we deal with specific distributional issues, we will try to use minimal principles of justice that are supported by, or at least acceptable to, most schools of thought, but we cannot pretend to decide what is just.

The distribution of environmental impacts from economic activity is part of the overall distribution of benefits and costs of that activity. Ignoring environmental impacts may give a misleading picture of the distribution of total benefits and costs. Environmental impacts may affect only a few people or may be spread over the entire population. The same impact may also be valued differently by different people.

Many environmental impacts are the result of ambiguities in property rights. Does the atmosphere belong to people who want to breath clean air or to people who want to pollute it with automobile exhaust? Allowing pollution reduces the wealth of breathers. Requiring clean air reduces the wealth of potential polluters.

Environmental impacts can raise distributional issues even with no ambiguity of ownership. We may have reduced emissions of a pollutant so far that the costs of reducing them further are greater than anyone is willing and able to pay. At the same time, the remaining impacts may be distributed unfairly, falling disproportionately on some and less than proportionately on others.

It is possible to look at distributional issues either globally or incrementally. Global, or overall, distributional justice is concerned with the totality of benefits received by and costs inflicted on different individuals. Incremental distributional justice is concerned with the distribution of benefits and costs from a specific action or change of circumstances. Whether income and wealth are distributed justly between different groups in society is a question of global distributional justice. Whether the benefits and costs of building a factory or a recreation facility, including the environmental impacts, are distributed justly is a question of incremental distributional justice.

In *A Theory of Justice* (1971), John Rawls argues that justice should be based on the idea of a *social contract* that people would be willing to agree to if they did not know who they would be or their own particular interests. He concludes that such a social contract would allow inequality only to the extent that inequality benefits the worst off. Rawls's principles, for example, would permit differences in incomes if it resulted in more goods and services being available at lower prices and this benefited the worst off in society. Thus Rawls was concerned primarily with global distributional justice.

Utilitarians argue that benefits and costs should be distributed to maximize total welfare. Some utilitarians argue that this requires approximate equality. The basis of this argument is the idea of diminishing marginal utility of income (i.e., an additional dollar is worth more to a homeless person living under a bridge than to a billionaire). Others argue that utilitarianism justifies inequality. People differ in their capacities to derive well-being from any given situation, and a greater share of society's resources should be given to those with greater abilities to enjoy it. Utilitarians have been concerned primarily with global, rather than incremental, distributional justice.

More recently, a number of writers, including Baumol (1986) and Varian (1975, 1984), have espoused a theory of distributive justice based on a "commonsense" idea of fairness. In their view, a distribution is "fair" if no one would want to trade places with someone else. This takes into account the fact that people may have different preferences and therefore everyone may prefer an unequal distribution that gives people more of what they want and less of things they don't care about.

A common conception of distributional justice is that goods and services should be distributed according to merit. This idea is sometimes supported on utilitarian grounds. People should be rewarded in proportion to their contribution to society because doing so encourages people to supply more goods and services to others. Other conceptions of merit are also possible.

None of these conceptions of distributive justice requires, or even makes use of, a monetary measure of justice or injustice. Quantitative measures of inequality may be useful to some of them, but these measures tell how much inequality there is, not how much it is worth. It is possible to infer values people place on justice from the sacrifices they are willing to make to achieve it, but this measures the importance people place on justice relative to other goals. It does not give a monetary measure of justice or injustice. *Trying to measure justice in monetary terms is not particularly useful or even meaningful.*

However, it is impossible to know whether the distribution of benefits and costs is just without knowing what those benefits and costs are. This will generally require knowing their monetary value. Estimating the monetary value of the benefits and the costs of a factory or a ski resort is a prerequisite for knowing whether they are distributed justly, but it is *only* a prerequisite.

Procedural Justice

Procedural justice is concerned with the fairness of procedures. To some extent, concepts of procedural justice are tied to concepts of individual rights. A procedure for setting public policies may be unfair if it violates anyone's rights. For example, suppose that the EPA administrator had developed the policy on lead exposure without allowing any public comment or review whatsoever. Regardless of whether the policy itself was "fair," its development would have violated the rights of U.S. citizens to have their views heard on such matters.

Procedural justice is also concerned with decision mechanisms. The outcomes of voting procedures depend on whether alternatives are voted on one at a time, in pairs, or all together, on the order in which different votes are taken, and on whether people vote for options they want or against options they do not want. In a market, different auction procedures can produce different prices. It is possible for a procedure to be biased without violating any formal rights.

The relationship between distributive justice and procedural justice is controversial. At one extreme, it is possible to claim that the outcome of a just procedure is always just. This position subsumes distributive justice under procedural justice (see Nozick 1974). The other extreme is the claim that the justice of a procedure is determined by the justice of the outcome. It is also possible to view the two types of justice as related but separate. On this view, a just or unjust procedure can produce a just or unjust outcome.

Although economists have written a great deal about procedural justice, little of it is related specifically to environmental issues (see Arrow 1963 or Sen 1970). Instead, procedural justice may place limits on the mechanisms that may be used to pursue environmental policies.

Character

A person's character consists of his or her tendencies to behave in certain ways and to decide in certain ways when facing certain choices. It can be argued that the effects on citizens' characters should be a consideration in public policy decisions. We will encounter this argument when we consider whether it is appropriate to place monetary values on the environment or on human life and health in Chapters 11 and 12. Opponents of monetization sometimes argue that people's common moral sense is that placing monetary values on certain things is wrong but that repeated exposure to the idea can corrode people's moral sense, damaging their character.

ENVIRONMENTAL LAWS AND THE ROLE OF GOVERNMENT

In addition to questions posed by the ethical concepts discussed in this chapter, there is always another question to be answered when we are dealing with public policy: what is the proper role of government? Even if everyone agreed on the facts, on what moral concepts applied and how they should be applied, and on whose interests should be taken into account and how, there still could be disagreement about the proper public policy because people disagree about the proper role of government. Americans tend to view the proper role of government as being more restricted than citizens of other countries, but even in the United States there are diverse views on this subject.

At one extreme is the view that government exists to solve any and all problems and the proper sphere of government action is restricted only by the particular problems that government is unable to solve. This is the *interventionist* school of thought. At the other extreme is the view that government has few, if any, legitimate functions: government should be limited to maintaining order and enforcing the law, including property law, and even those functions might be better left to the private sector. This view represents the *laissez-faire* approach. Obviously, many gradations between these extremes also exist.

Different views of the proper role of government imply different types and scope of government actions on environmental policy. Governments have a range of actions they can conceivably take. Governments can regulate behavior directly, creating new legal obligations to act or refrain from acting. For example, in the United States and some other countries, it is now illegal to make and sell cars that require leaded gasoline. Governments may seek to develop markets where none had existed before. Prior to passage of the 1990 Clean Air Act Amendments, for example, there were no "markets" for trading emissions of sulfur dioxide between firms. Instead, there were specific technological requirements that limited emissions from different firms. In this case, the federal government played a *market-enhancing* role. Governments may also seek to define and enforce rights other than property rights. Historically, you might have had the "right" to emit unlimited amounts of lead into the air. But as we discussed, the government may determine that the right of some groups of citizens, minority children in this case, to be free from harmful exposure to pollutants takes precedence over the right of industries to use the atmosphere as a waste receptacle.

Governments can also do nothing. It is possible to believe that an environmental problem exists and that there are certain potential solutions to that problem but that the problem and its solutions are outside the sphere of legitimate government action. However, we must draw a line around the economics of environmental policy somewhere, and therefore we leave questions of the legitimacy of government action to texts devoted to politics and political philosophy.

Why Is Law Relevant to Environmental Economics?

Environmental policy will generally be encoded into law or administrative rules. This can take many forms. It can be "command and control" regulation of behavior. It can be the creation and enhancement of markets. It can be the creation, clarification, or redefinition of property rights. Whatever form it takes, environmental policy must be made within an existing constitutional and legal framework. It must be consistent with that framework, and it may be limited by that framework. There will be cases where what looks like an ideal environmental policy instrument simply cannot be implemented within a given legal framework. There may be other cases where the existing legal framework already contains all the mechanisms necessary to implement environmental policy.

In some cases, legal structures that evolved for other purposes have been applied to environmental problems. In the United States, *tort law,* which deals with damage one party inflicts on another, and *nuisance law* have been used to deal with local environmental problems. Zoning and land use laws also have environmental aspects and have been used to deal with environmental issues.

Whatever form it takes, environmental law is a small part of the overall legal and regulatory system. Environmental policymakers need to keep this in mind for at least three reasons. First, environmental policymakers need to make sure that their policies are consistent with existing laws and the national constitution. For example, in the United States, state policymakers cannot take certain actions because they conflict with the U.S. Constitution or have been preempted by federal law. Second, environmental policymakers need to take the effects of other laws and regulations into account in estimating the impacts of their own actions. This applies directly to the environmental goals that policymakers may be pursuing. Whether environmental policies are successful in reducing lead emissions, for example, will depend on whether there are other government actions encouraging or discouraging activities that emit lead. It also applies to other goals that policymakers may want environmental policy to satisfy. An environmental policy that is seen as inequitable may be more acceptable if it is part of a package including other government actions that are seen as increasing equity.

The third reason that environmental policymakers need to be aware of other laws and regulations is that choosing the environmental policy that is most efficient, in the sense of having the greatest net benefits, may depend on what other laws and regulations are in place. This is known as the problem of the *second best,* some of whose implications and seemingly paradoxical results we will discuss in Chapters 6 and 7. For example, it is usually the case that reducing the production of a good that causes environmental problems will increase economic efficiency and welfare. However, if other regulations cause the good to be priced far above its marginal cost and hence too little of it is produced, reducing output further may reduce welfare, not increase it.

CHAPTER SUMMARY

The ethical concepts introduced here all enter into the development of environmental policies. We all have our own biases, and our purpose in this chapter and this book is not to create a manifesto of specific policy positions or a simple cookbook for developing positions. In a society whose members have a constantly changing range of ethical views about the environment, a manifesto or cookbook could only present our own personal positions, not universally acceptable dogma.

Although we do not have answers to all environmental policy questions, we do provide some general guidelines about the use of economics in the search for such answers. The first guideline, which we take up in the next chapter, is to be clear about the issues and the questions that must be answered. This may seem obvious, but it is not always easy. For many people, environmental policy issues are emotionally charged; they see environmental issues primarily as a matter of character and motives. For example, they may see pollution as the result of greedy people acting with no regard for other people's health or for nature. Others may see environmentalists as selfish elitists who are more concerned with their own aesthetic experience of nature than with other people's ability to earn a living.

This sort of emotional focus on others' motives can make it difficult for people to make fine logical distinctions between issues and approaches for solving problems. It can be difficult to get someone whose primary concerns are achieving an absolute moral victory and punishing the "wicked" to consider the proper role of benefit-cost analysis in setting emissions limits or timber harvest levels or to recognize the role economic incentives might play in achieving environmental goals.

Difficult as it may be, being clear about the issues is a prerequisite for effective policy analysis. If the primary issue is human rights, economics may have little to tell us. If the primary issue is which of two policies will have more economic benefits, economic analysis obviously provides us with the tools to come up with an answer. If the primary issue is the distribution of the benefits and costs of a policy, economics will be important, but we may use different economic tools to answer different questions. Ultimately, we must use ethical concepts to determine the questions we need to answer and whether and how to apply the tools of economics to those questions.

CHAPTER REVIEW

Economic Concepts and Tools

- Welfare economics provides tools for measuring and comparing human well-being. Measuring changes in human welfare is essential for developing policies to increase that welfare.
- Welfare economics does not measure human rights, the rights of nature, obligations, distributive or procedural justice, or human character.

- The measurement of welfare is important for policies designed to correct or avoid distributive injustices. Knowing whether an individual's gains from a policy and costs are proportionate to the costs they pay requires measuring both.

Policy Issues

- Environmental policy debates may center on facts and logic; more often they will center on conflicting values and interests. Environmental policymakers must weigh and balance competing values and interests.
- Environmental policy debates may also hinge on opinions about the proper role of government: whether governments should actively intervene in markets or merely enforce property rights and contracts.
- Many environmental policies deal with changes in human welfare.
- Human rights are central to many environmental policy issues. These may be positive rights to use of the environment or negative rights—rights to be free from harm or interference.
- Some people argue that nonhuman nature has rights that must be considered by humans in setting environmental policies.
- Some environmental policy issues center around our obligations to others, particularly our obligations to future generations.
- Distributive justice is central to some environmental policy issues, particularly when the environmental costs of an action are borne by people who do not receive the benefits of the action.
- Whereas distributive justice is concerned with the fairness of outcomes, procedural justice is concerned with the fairness of decision processes themselves. Concerns about procedural justice may limit the mechanisms that can be used to pursue environmental goals.
- Sometimes it is argued that certain types of policies should be avoided because of their effects on people's character.
- Environmental laws enforced by governments are the mechanisms through which environmental policies are most often carried out.

DISCUSSION QUESTIONS

1. A study determines that exposure levels to sulfur dioxide are higher on the East Coast of the United States than on the West Coast. Is this pattern of exposure discriminatory?
2. Another study shows that people living within 5 miles of landfills are more likely to be poor and nonwhite than the population as a whole. Does this reveal discrimination? If so, why? If not, what other reasons could explain the findings?
3. How can we measure human rights? How can we measure nonhuman rights?
4. Suppose that a particular environmental policy will reduce the exposure of an endangered species of bird to a harmful pollutant. The policy involves relocating a manufacturing facility to an urban center farther away from the bird's natural habitat and installing special controls that can reduce emissions by 90 percent. Unfortunately, even with the reduction, exposure levels to

humans in the area will increase slightly, raising the possibility of harmful health impacts on the local population. As the chief environmental policy-maker, do you recommend that the policy be implemented?

5. In general, how should environmental policymakers balance competing poli-cy goals? Can you suggest any methods for doing so?

6. Which do you believe is more important, procedural justice or distributive justice? Why?

7. Benefit-cost analysis is not appropriate for environmental policy decisions because a dollar value cannot be placed on the environment. Do you agree? Why or why not?

8. Under what circumstances is there a need for environmental laws? Under what circumstances do you think individuals could work out environmental differences without government intervention?

REFERENCES

Aristotle. 1946. *The Politics of Aristotle*, trans. E. Barker. London: Oxford University Press.

———. 1962. *The Nichomachean Ethics*, trans. M. Ostwald. Indianapolis: Bobbs-Merrill.

Arrow, K. 1963. *Social Choice and Individual Values*. 2d ed. New York: Wiley.

Baumol. W. 1986. *Superfairness: Applications and Theory*. Cambridge, Mass.: MIT Press.

Booth, D. 1994. *Valuing Nature: The Decline and Preservation of Old-Growth Forests*. Lanham, Md.: Rowman and Littlefield.

Goodpaster, K. 1978. "On Being Morally Considerable." *Journal of Philosophy* 75(6): 308–25.

Hardin, G. 1968. "The Tragedy of the Commons." *Science* 162: 1243–1248.

Hare, R.M. 1952. *The Language of Morals*. New York: Oxford University Press.

MacIntyre, A. 1981. *After Virtue: A Study in Moral Theory*. Notre Dame, Ind.: University of Notre Dame Press.

Nozick, R. 1974. *Anarchy, State, and Utopia*. New York: Basic Books.

Rawls, J. 1971. *A Theory of Justice*. Cambridge, Mass.: Harvard University Press.

Sen, A. 1970. *Collective Choice and Social Welfare*. Boca Raton, Fla.: Holden-Day.

Varian, H. 1975. "Distributive Justice, Welfare Economics, and the Theory of Fairness." *Philosophy and Public Affairs* 4: 223–247.

———. 1984. "Equity, Envy, and Efficiency." *Journal of Economic Theory* 9: 63–91.

CHAPTER 5

DEFINING
POLICY GOALS

Trash or Treasure? The Goals of Urban Recycling

When did you last throw out an aluminum can or a newspaper? What about a plastic jug or a tire? How about the remains of last night's dinner? In our "throwaway" society, it seems we spend a lot of time dealing with trash. Since the 1970s, many cities have developed recycling programs for much residential and commercial waste. Some cities provide residents with special containers to sort garbage into various components: glass, metals, newspaper, other paper, and plastics. Gasoline service stations and other automobile repair shops are required to recycle used motor oil. Germany is even moving toward regulations that will ultimately require all cars to be recycled completely.

Many environmental issues surround garbage: How much is really created and where? What are the benefits and limitations of recycling? What issues does disposal raise?[1] Proponents of recycling argue that it reduces overall waste management costs—siting and maintaining new landfills, purchasing and operating garbage trucks, and so on—and conserves depletable natural resources that would otherwise be used. Some proponents also point out that humans have no right to "trash" the earth. Critics argue otherwise; they insist that the costs of recycling programs far outweigh their savings and that concerns about running out of landfill space are nonsense.

Both sides' arguments are compelling, depending on whose data are believed. Regardless of the data, however, there are deeper issues separating proponents and opponents of recycling. In terms of recycling's costs and benefits, Scarlett (1993) reports that figures are available to substantiate both the positive and the negative claims about recycling. Some reports have pegged recycling costs as high as $1,000 per ton of material collected. Other studies show that recycling can save munici-

---

[1]Cairncross (1993) provides an excellent and readable summary of these issues.

palities over $150 per ton. Scarlett collected data from more than 30 community recycling programs. Of those, she verified a breakdown of the overall costs, including material collection, processing, and marketing, for seven programs. Her results indicated that recycling programs for these seven communities cost between $98 and $138 per ton of material collected. In all seven cases, actual material collection accounted for about 75 percent of the total cost. Revenues from the sale of recycled materials averaged between $28 and $39 per ton, enough to pay at least a significant portion of the processing and marketing costs.

Why such disparate estimates? As Scarlett notes, one reason arises from using different bases for measurement, leading to "apples and oranges" comparisons. For example, the city of Chicago pays private haulers $50 per ton for a curbside recycling program; this reflects the cost of recycling to Chicago but certainly not to society. The societal cost will equal the market cost of hauling plus the costs of processing and marketing the materials collected. In addition, there may be environmental costs arising from processing the materials. From those costs can be subtracted the revenues from the sale of recycled materials, the avoided costs of otherwise disposing of the waste materials, the avoided environmental costs, such as avoided water and air pollution, and the benefit of delaying development of new landfills. Developing monetary estimates of all of these costs and benefits is not an easy exercise. And that is only the beginning.

Another issue to consider is the cost of processing recycled materials versus production from virgin materials. For example, one could compare the total cost of recycling an aluminum beverage can to the cost of the entire production process of mining alumina, smelting, and rolling. Similar analyses could be done for various recycled materials, including glass, plastics, newsprint, and various metals. To this also would be added various environmental costs (e.g., pollution from the electricity generated and used in the alumina ore smelting process or to de-ink old newspaper).[2] Ultimately, the overall benefit-cost calculations associated with recycling may be complex.

Though the economics of recycling is important, there are other policy considerations. First, policymakers may wish to investigate the feasibility of recycling. That may require a variety of experimental programs to determine the most efficient collection, processing, and marketing methods. Because markets for recycled materials may not be well established, policies that require market development (e.g., requirements that some fraction of government paper supplies be composed of recycled materials) may be needed to convince the users of recycled products of their quality. Third, there may be equity and rights issues associated with acquiring additional space for landfills or siting waste-to-energy facilities that burn garbage. Often such "locally undesirable land uses," or LULUs, will be found near neighborhoods that have high concentrations of minorities and the poor.[3] Or there may be concerns about the unknown risks

---

[2] For a detailed examination of the costs of virgin versus recycled materials, see SRMG (1993).

[3] We discuss LULUs and whether their siting represents a form of "environmental racism" in Chapter 9.

posed by burning waste materials and the risk that landfills will contaminate water supplies in the future.

Some advocates of recycling see it as a form of sustainable development to be promoted regardless of the monetary cost. They see it as a way to prevent the "wasteful" use of natural resources by present generations and thereby preserve a greater natural resource legacy for future ones. Though such arguments may lack economic merit, they may address legitimate moral concerns over the well-being of future generations. Ultimately, the development of policies that promote recycling, like the development of all environmental policies, must begin with identifying goals. To do otherwise is to make treasure into trash.

INTRODUCTION

In the first four chapters, we looked at some of the environmental problems facing us and their economic aspects, we reviewed the basic concepts of welfare economics, and we looked at some of the other normative criteria that enter into deliberations about environmental policy. In the chapters following this one, we address the specific tools of environmental economics and apply them to a number of issues. Before we do that, however, we devote this one, short chapter to the general process of policy development, both as it should be and as it usually is.

We begin by examining the five steps necessary to develop and implement good public policy: identifying the problem, setting goals, choosing a preferred policy instrument, implementing the policy, and evaluating the results (and, if necessary, revising the policy). For the remainder of the chapter, we look at some of the reasons why these steps are often not followed in the real world.

In the past several decades, economists have written volumes about the process of government, much of it arguing that governments do not, and perhaps cannot, produce economically rational policies. Even if we accepted that position, we would argue that economists should, and will, participate in policy formation. Economics has much to contribute to the debate, and even if economists cannot perfect environmental policy, they can hope to improve it.

NECESSARY STEPS IN DEVELOPING ENVIRONMENTAL POLICIES

Ideally, the public policy process would go through five steps: (1) *identifying* the problem based on the relevant normative criteria (societal values), (2) weighing alternative solutions and evaluating their consequences relative to the criteria identified in step 1, (3) *selecting* an appropriate policy instrument or instruments, (4) *implementing* the policy instruments, and (5) *evaluating* the results. A rational public policy process would incorporate all of these steps, but they do not necessarily form a linear sequence. Even the best public policy process is likely to involve some iteration. The process of defining alternative solutions and selecting policy instruments may shed new light on the definition of the problem. An evaluation of the results may show that the policy instrument chosen was not appropriate or was implemented poorly. Poor environmental policy decisions are more likely to be the result of leaving out one or more steps than of repeating the steps too many times. All too often, environmental policymakers succumb to the urge to "do something—anything" in response to what they see as a pressing problem or constituent pressure.

Identifying the Problem

The first step toward environmental policy development is identifying the problem on the basis of relevant normative criteria. This does not mean just identifying that there is a problem, such as polluted air. It means identifying the type of problem it is. For example, is the problem that poor air quality is reducing overall economic well-being? Are human rights being violated because people are being exposed involuntarily to risks to their lives or their health? Are individuals bearing certain external environmental costs without receiving concomitant benefits, such as pollution from a power plant falling downwind onto people who do not consume the electricity generated? Are the rights of nature in jeopardy, such as the loss of species or ecosystems? Or, as is more likely, are several criteria involved?

Identifying the problem is important because different types of problems require different solutions. For example, in the case of policies to promote recycling, is the problem primarily the economic cost of new landfill space, environmental issues associated with landfills (e.g., groundwater pollution, methane, visual or olfactory pollution), or concerns about natural resource use and depletion that preclude sustainable development? Does recycling promote human rights because it is immoral for rich, developed countries to ship their wastes to poor, less developed ones in need of capital? The "correct" policy to address the rights of the poor is almost certainly different from the correct policy to address scarce landfill space because of siting restrictions.

Unfortunately, this step of the policy process is most often skipped. There are many reasons for this. One is that policymakers often are confronted by constituents claiming that "the situation is intolerable and something must be done about it *now!*" Another reason is that problems are often brought to policymakers' attention by interest groups who have ready-made solutions, either for this problem or for all problems, and who present the problem as the absence of their solutions.[4]

Weighing Alternative Solutions and Consequences

Once the problems to be addressed are identified, the second step is to examine alternative solutions to see which best address the problems identified in step 1. This requires establishing targets and objectives to measure "success." Identifying

---

[4]As Groucho Marx said, "Politics is the art of looking for trouble, finding it everywhere, diagnosing it incorrectly, and applying the wrong remedies" (Eigen and Siegel 1993).

the problem means determining what the world looks like now and what is wrong with it according to the criteria chosen. Determining alternative solutions means visualizing what the world should look like and how that differs from the current situation. Part of this process is defining measures of success to determine whether a problem has been solved.

Suppose that the problem has been identified as excessive costs for municipal waste disposal. A solution to this problem must lower waste disposal costs, and its success would be measured by the amount of the cost reduction. If the problem were identified as groundwater pollution from landfills that was exposing people to toxic chemicals, however, any solutions must improve groundwater quality or at least prevent its deterioration. Success would be measured by reductions in pollutant concentrations in the groundwater and exposure levels in the affected populations. Now, if the problem is identified as limited landfill space, solutions would require methods of handling future generations' waste products. A simple measure of success might be difficult to devise for this problem; that would be an indication that the problem had not been well defined. Waste disposal is not a final good that people want for its own sake. It is closer to an intermediate good (like steel for buildings and cars) that people demand because it contributes to the production of final goods and services. In this case, the problem may need to be redefined as maintaining future generations' standard of living with reduced waste disposal in landfills.

Some measures of success are obviously economic, such as the dollar savings from lower-cost waste disposal. In other cases, success may be measured in nonmonetary terms. In those cases, however, there should always be a secondary goal of accomplishing the primary goal at the lowest possible cost. Success in achieving this secondary goal will generally be measured in monetary terms.

It is important to remember that defining alternative solutions means focusing on results, not on how they are achieved. With a municipal waste problem, the solution may be lower-cost waste disposal, cleaner groundwater, or continued prosperity. A recycling program may be a way to achieve any or all of these solutions, but it is not the solution itself, any more than the absence of a recycling program defines the problem to be solved. A recycling program is one of many alternative policy instruments that could be used to provide a solution.

Selecting the Policy Instruments

Once goals and measures of success are determined, the appropriate policy instruments can be chosen. A policy instrument is a tool for solving a problem. It may be regulation of individual or business behavior, it may be a tax or subsidy, it may be running a program to provide services, or it may take any of a hundred other forms. In choosing a policy instrument, policymakers need to have examined the alternative policies available, their costs of implementation, monitoring and enforcement, and their likely effectiveness in achieving the desired targets.

Consider the case of lead emissions we discussed in Chapter 4. The main sources of atmospheric lead were identified as automobile exhaust and paint. Using medical data correlating lead concentrations in the bloodstream with physical and mental disorders and social data identifying the most affected populations (poor, minority children), the EPA decided that an atmospheric lead standard should aim at keeping 99.5 percent of the target population below the maximum "safe" individual blood lead level of 30 μg Pb/dl. The EPA decided that an atmospheric lead target level of 1.5 μg Pb/m^3 would accomplish this policy goal.

Once that was done, the EPA still had to decide *how* to achieve the atmospheric lead standard. Banning the use of leaded gasoline would reduce lead in automobile exhaust, but would it be too costly? Would a tax on lead emissions from automobiles result in lower overall emissions? How would the administrative and the enforcement costs compare with an outright ban on leaded gasoline? How would programs reducing lead in automobile exhaust affect poor people living in older houses with lead paint? Would they still be vulnerable? If so, what sort of program would best solve this problem? Should *all* houses first be tested for lead paint and, if lead paint were found, be stripped and repainted at taxpayer cost? Should only low-income housing be targeted, and if so, how should "low-income" be defined? Finally, what would be the political ramifications, specifically on industries such as oil refiners and smelters that contributed to atmospheric lead concentrations?[5]

In general, the choice of policy instruments should depend on five attributes of the instruments: (1) effectiveness in achieving the policy goals, (2) the cost to achieve the identified targets with each instrument, (3) the value of achieving the targets and the certainty with which policymakers know this value, (4) the associated enforcement, monitoring, and other administrative costs, and (5) the risks of unforeseen results and the willingness of policymakers to deal with those risks.

Choosing a policy instrument requires comparing many options and may take several iterations. For example, whether recycling is the best instrument for dealing with a city's waste disposal problem may depend on how recycling is implemented (e.g., higher disposal fees or a taxpayer-funded recycling program). Policymakers cannot always know in advance what the deciding factors will be, and even the criteria for choosing between policies may change during the policymaking process.

Implementing and Evaluating Policy

Once appropriate policy instruments are chosen and implemented, the final step of the policy process should be evaluation. Are the policies actually achieving their targets? For example, is a curbside recycling program collecting the predicted amount and mix of materials? Are the enforcement and the monitoring costs near predicted levels? In the case of recycling and higher disposal fees, for example, has illicit dumping increased significantly, and if so, where? Are any *unanticipated* impacts reducing the desirability of the target or its achievement using the chosen policy?

---

[5]In fact, the EPA's atmospheric lead standards were challenged all the way to the U.S. Supreme Court. See *Lead Industries* v. *EPA*, 647 F.2d 1130, 10 ELR 20643 (D.C. Circuit, 1980), cert. denied 101 S. CT. 621.

IT'S EXPENSIVE, BUT IS IT GOOD?

Sometimes, the "value" and effectiveness of environmental policies have been defined by their cost. Arguments over preferred policies to restore salmon runs in the Pacific Northwest, for example, have at times focused on the costs of specific programs. Thus the expenditure of $2 billion towards fisheries habitat restoration must be preferable to the expenditure of $1 billion. The fallaciousness of such logic seems obvious: *cost* is not the same thing as *value*. Why, then, does this measure of "success" persist?

There are several reasons. First, estimating *costs* is sometimes easy, often much easier than estimating *benefits*. Rather than having to focus on how to achieve what is to be accomplished most efficiently, throwing money at problems can act like an enveloping fog, obscuring the measurement of the value of righting environmental "wrongs." Second, proponents of particular environmental goals may scoff at measures of value. They may see willingness-to-pay or willingness-to-accept estimates that determine value as inaccurate or even immoral. Third, proponents may highlight their favorite environmental problem in terms of the cost of correcting it. If repair of fisheries habitat A will cost $2 billion and repair of fisheries habitat B will cost only $1 billion, surely restoration of A should take priority.

Unfortunately, combating such twisted logic can be difficult but will be made easier by arguing forcefully for clear definitions of a policy's goals. It does seem odd to define the "value" of human rights, for example, in terms of money. If one child has a defined legal right not to be exposed to a toxic pollutant, then that right ought not to be half as important as reducing the exposure of two children to another toxic pollutant.

Similarly, people who distrust empirical measures of value may actually be arguing either for better empirical research or that the problems to be addressed, such as human rights or the rights of nature, not be based on monetary decisions. Someone who rejects pollution taxes, for example, by arguing that such taxes allow polluters to "pay for the right to pollute" may actually be voicing concern over the importance of goals other than economic efficiency, such as a moral crusade to "punish" wicked polluters.

Whatever policy instruments are contemplated, policymakers should avoid the temptation to use expenditure levels as a measure of program success. The level of expenditures may be an easy proxy, but rarely, if ever, will it reflect whether policy goals are achieved at the lowest cost or even achieved at all.

If a policy appears not to be working as expected, policymakers need to go back to one of the previous steps to see what they did wrong. Perhaps they chose the wrong instrument. Perhaps they did not implement it well. Perhaps they even misdiagnosed the problem. However, once a policy instrument is in place, policymakers should be careful to examine the burdens that changes will impose on the affected groups. Consider the example of a petroleum refinery that installed millions of dollars' worth of required equipment to reduce lead emissions at the behest of the EPA. Suppose that two years later, the EPA decides that actions taken so far will not meet lead reduction targets and orders the industry to install newer equipment at a cost of additional millions of dollars. The total cost will probably be much higher than if the stricter controls had been imposed to begin with. In the worst case, the original control equipment will be useless and the original expense will have been a waste.

Regulators should try to minimize the burdens they impose by changing regulations. They should also be aware of this possibility when they are designing regulations and try to avoid creating situations where they will be forced to change regulations in the future. Even uncertainty about future regulatory changes can impose burdens by making it difficult for companies to make investment decisions or obtain financing.

WHY ENVIRONMENTAL POLICYMAKING FALLS SHORT OF THE IDEAL

There are many reasons why environmental policymaking in the real world does not always follow the steps just outlined. In the rest of this chapter, we will discuss some of those reasons. Unfortunately, space precludes presenting an exhaustive list of reasons, nor can we give in-depth coverage of the ones we do present. Instead, our purpose here is to provide a flavor for the complexity and the messiness of real-world policymaking.

Values and Problem Definition

Defining problems is the step of the policy process that is most often skipped or done poorly. Sometimes this is because policymakers do not see the need for it. More often it is because it is difficult and controversial.

Defining problems and solutions are both value-based activities, and as we noted in Chapter 4, values are often difficult to define. Something is a problem only if people think that things are worse than they could be. But judgments of "better" and "worse" are value judgments. Consider the example of water vapor as an environmental problem. Many human activities emit water vapor into the atmosphere. There is water vapor in our exhalations and in the exhaust of all combustion processes. Thus we all breathe and live in air "polluted" with anthropogenic water vapor.

Apparently, water vapor meets all of the criteria for an environmental problem except one. People are affected by water vapor without their consent. There is no market for water vapor where the right to emit or be free from exposure can be bought and sold. And no mechanism forces "emitters" to consider the costs of their emissions. However, none of this matters because *no one cares.* No one objects to being exposed to water vapor (except perhaps in localized situations such as next to the exhaust fan from a laundry), and hence *there is no problem.* Under exactly the same physical and institutional circumstances, emissions of oxides of nitrogen and carbon dioxide are problems solely because people place a higher value on a world with less of these gases in the atmosphere.

Defining problems is difficult because people have different values and interests and therefore see different problems in the same circumstances. In fact, it is common for people to disagree about whether a set of circumstances is a problem. For example, suppose that a group of rich citizens in the United States opposes development of a nuclear waste depository on a poor Indian reservation in New Mexico, but the majority of the Indians welcome the depository as a source of much-needed jobs. What if the rich citizens' group counters that the government should offer the Indians other jobs or provide them with cash grants? Whose values should "count"?[6] And if both groups' beliefs count, how should they be weighed against one another?

Not only do people value things differently, but they value things in different ways (Sunstein 1994; Anderson 1993). The New Mexico Indians may see nuclear waste disposal as an economic issue, while the outside citizens' group sees it as an issue of justice. This is one facet of what is called the *incommensurability* problem. It poses a particular challenge for economists who are used to comparing many alternatives using a single metric: money. Without such a metric, choosing between different alternatives can be difficult and controversial.

Many differences in values are apparent in debates about environmental policy (Sunstein 1994). Some regard any pollution as immoral (Kelman 1981); others (e.g., Ruff 1970) see no such moral issue.[7] Some argue that these conflicts should be settled within the normal democratic process; others believe that the moral principles involved override the values of a democratic process.

There can also be conflicts of values between societies. Should one society impose its environmental values on another, even if the former is not affected materially by the actions of the latter? And if it is affected, what then? The United States, for example, produces far more carbon dioxide emissions than other countries relative to its population. If carbon dioxide is causing global climate change and if global climate change will impose environmental costs on the earth, should the United States be forced to reduce its emissions? If so, by how much?

In the United States, we often recognize human "rights" that are not recognized in other countries. The punishments for certain crimes, for example, differ in many countries; in some, punishment is swift and severe, and in others, less so. The same is true for environmental "crimes." As we discuss in Chapters 6 through 9, the United States has a myriad of environmental laws, some of which exact severe punishment for offenders. Many other countries have fewer such laws. The United States favors a ban on commercial whaling; Japan and Norway do not. The

---

[6]The legal term for having values that count is known as *standing*. Thus we would say that the burglar who steals your television set has no standing in that he cannot justify his action in court on the basis that he values watching television more than you do. See Zerbe (1991) or Lesser and Zerbe (1995) for further discussion.

[7]See, for example, Page (1977, 1992) and Sagoff (1988, 1993). See also the response to Sagoff by Kopp (1993).

United States requires extensive treatment of sewage; other countries, either for lack of capital or lack of desire, allow raw sewage to pollute streams, lakes, and oceans.[8]

All of these considerations pose enormous problems for policymakers. In fact, the problem they face is greater than the sum of all the problems defined by various interested parties because they must consider and weigh the views of all these parties.[9] Part of the policymaker's problem is reconciling or choosing between a multiplicity of problem definitions. The policymaker who tries to develop a societal view of the issue that takes all interests into account will be alone in doing so. Economists are continually being disappointed by the fact that no one else seems to care about the idea of economic efficiency except when it can be used to argue for positions that are based on self-interest. Yet this is exactly what economics predicts! People put their efforts into working for outcomes that they personally value highly in situations where their efforts will be rewarded by appreciable personal rewards, even if those rewards are nonmonetary (e.g., a sense of well-being about helping one's fellow man). They put much less effort into working for outcomes in which the gains, though possibly large, are widely dispersed and their personal gains are small.

This can apply to policymakers themselves. They come to the process with their own values and interests. One of their primary interests is often resolving problems in such a way that a majority of their constituents will be willing to entrust them with future problems.

New Information, New Problems

In some cases, environmental policymakers attempt to fix long-standing problems. In others, however, they must deal with an issue because it has been newly identified as a problem. Advances in technology have allowed us to measure smaller and smaller quantities of pollutants. Technology has also created new pollutants. Chlorofluorocarbons, which have been linked to the destruction of the earth's ozone layer (see Chapter 21), were first hailed as an important advance in refrigeration and led to cheaper, more efficient refrigerators. Thus chlorofluorocarbons provided important social benefits. For many years, asbestos was used in schools to retard the spread of fires to protect schoolchildren. Unfortunately, it is a potent carcinogen,

---

[8]This has been a controversial issue in Washington State. Port Angeles, which lies on the south side of the Strait of Juan de Fuca (the entrance to Puget Sound), has invested millions of dollars in secondary treatment plants. Across the Strait, however, Victoria, British Columbia, pumps raw sewage directly into the strait. That sewage is migrating toward Port Angeles. In 1992, voters in British Columbia rejected a proposal that would have raised their taxes to build treatment facilities. As a result, many Washington residents boycotted Victoria, which derives much of its income from Washington tourists. The government of British Columbia has promised a solution, but the issue remains unresolved. We discuss this issue in greater detail in Chapter 20.

[9]We discuss empirical techniques to do just this in Chapter 10.

causing lung cancer when inhaled. Automobiles reduced the health effects of horse dung that once blew around cities but are a significant source of other pollutants.

Epidemiological research, such as that on the effects of atmospheric lead, continues to identify new relationships between various environmental pollutants and risks to our health and well-being. No doubt certain substances considered safe today will be tomorrow's environmental hazards. Unfortunately, much epidemiological research, even when preliminary, can be reported in near hysteria so that it can seem that nothing is "safe" to eat or drink.[10]

Even changing morals and philosophies have identified environmental problems that were not previously perceived. One hundred years ago, few people were concerned about hunting species to extinction. Recently, however, some individuals have recognized animal species' "rights," such as those of salmon, which has led to restrictions on harvesting. More people are concerned about the use of animals for research purposes, even when the results of that research save human lives. New approaches to the global environment and ecosystems are also recent developments. And concern about environmental "racism" is more recent still.

By itself, the fact that we are discovering new environmental problems does not imply poor policymaking. However, in most cases, we discover new environmental problems after they have become problems that people want corrected, not while they can still be averted. For example, we discovered that DDT was harmful to bird populations as we tried to explain observed population declines. When a problem has been identified after the fact, both the public and policymakers are likely to be in a hurry to find a solution, which works against a thoughtful, deliberative policy process.

Pressure from Interested Parties

Newly identified environmental problems often are identified and brought to policymakers' attention by interest groups, who often demand an immediate solution and often advance their own preferred solution. This poses several problems for policymakers. They are put in the position of reacting to someone else's problem definition rather than simply developing their own. Citizens demanding that a problem be solved *now* may have little patience with policymakers who want to start at the beginning of the process rather than rush to the end. This can put policymakers under pressure to take immediate action instead of waiting for the evidence and making a balanced assessment.

Once an interest group has defined a problem and proposed a solution, it has a vested interest in those positions. Any compromise or change of position can be seen as a defeat. Although interest groups often do recognize superior solutions or the need to face up to political reality, they can and do cling tenaciously to their positions, once stated. This can be as true for groups that enter the process in

---

[10]As we reduce the risks of death and sickness from exposure to some environmental hazards, the risks from others will increase. The reason is simple: the probability of eventual death remains absolutely certain.

PRUDENCE OR HYSTERIA? THE CASE OF ALAR*

Washington State is known for its apples, which are one of the state's largest agricultural exports. Most people enjoy a cold, crisp apple, so growers strive for ways to provide them. One substance that helps is called Alar. Alar is a chemical that has been sprayed on apples to enhance their "shelf life." The Alar scare, little of which is heard today, provides a good example of the difference in perceived versus actuarial risk.

In 1989, the Natural Resources Defense Council, a large environmental organization in the United States, raised the concerns of people by announcing that Alar was a known carcinogen. The television show *60 Minutes* ran a frightening exposé on Alar (including a backdrop of an apple marked with a skull and crossbones!), which the NRDC had labeled the most dangerous chemical in children's food. The justification for the NRDC's conclusions were laboratory tests, called *toxicology* tests, in which large amounts of Alar were fed to mice. The Alar was metabolized into another chemical that proved to cause cancerous tumors in the mice. Similar studies with rats, however, did not produce tumors. Nevertheless, the NRDC raised the specter of Alar-tainted apples as a major public health risk, especially for small children who drink lots of apple juice. (Since children have less body weight than adults, large doses of apple juice meant that children had higher consumption of apple products than most adults. In addition, because children's cells divide rapidly as they grow, they would be more vulnerable to the carcinogenic effects.)

Besides the *60 Minutes* exposé, stories appeared in the popular press about the dangers of Alar. Even Hollywood got into the act, with actress Meryl Streep testifying before Congress about Alar. Not surprisingly, biting into a cold, crisp, *cancer-causing* apple was not relished by a lot of people. Schools stopped buying apples, and people stopped eating them. As a result, the demand for Washington apples fell, causing prices to fall with them and making apple growers an unhappy lot. In fact, apple growers themselves asked the U.S. Environmental Protection Agency to ban the use of the chemical to ease the panic that had set in. Finally, the EPA announced that Alar ought to be banned from food. As a result, the Uniroyal Company, the manufacturer of Alar, voluntarily removed Alar for use on all foods. Thus the NRDC won its battle. Fortunately, for Washington's apple growers, apple demand rebounded, and people seem to be eating lots of apples once again.

It turns out, however, that the NRDC may have been somewhat extreme in its views, so much so that in 1990, Washington apple growers sued the NRDC and CBS News for spreading "false, misleading, and scientifically unreliable statements about apples." The toxicology tests that the NRDC used to make its claims were limited in scope. Tests completed in 1991 showed that Alar, though indeed carcinogenic, was only half as potent as had been estimated in 1989 and as used by the NRDC. And that value was only one-tenth as high as the value estimated in 1987.

No doubt many individuals drove their automobiles to their local grocery stores to return potentially Alar-tainted apples, exposing themselves to far

(continued)

higher personal risks from automobile travel than from eating the apples. And by reducing their consumption of apples, individuals may have increased other health risks, owing to the well-known health benefits of fruit consumption.

Of course, we cannot determine precisely the increased risk of cancer, if any, from eating one Alar-coated apple or from drinking a glass of apple juice. But the perception of risk was almost certainly far greater than the actual risk. As technology allows us to measure suspected carcinogens more precisely in ever more minute quantities, the controversy over the safety of our food will undoubtedly continue. Whether such risks will be compared rationally with other risks we take is less certain.

*A more complete discussion of this case can be found in Marshall (1991).

response to another group's actions as for the group that initially raised the issue. When many parties weigh in on an issue, the dynamics of policy development can be driven as much by the antagonists' desires to win a victory over their opponents as by the way the possible outcomes address their concerns.

These problems do not always arise. There are amicable policymaking processes in which all parties are willing to compromise and policymakers do their best to define and reflect the broad public interest while protecting all parties. However, there are many cases where the dynamics of interest group behavior work against that end.

Inadequate Enforcement and Monitoring

Too often, environmental laws are passed by a legislative body with little or no thought as to actual enforcement of the law. Enforcement may require the creation of new institutions to ensure compliance: ones that monitor performance, perhaps through complex measurements of air emissions and water effluents from industrial facilities; ones that evaluate facility siting impacts; ones that provide legal sanctions for noncompliance, such as levying fines; and ones that themselves perform environmental services, such as emergency environmental response teams who clean up toxic waste spills.

Enforcement can require significant resources that are not always accounted for. A 1986 survey undertaken by Resources for the Future, for example, showed that the average cost of measuring air pollution emissions by source was over $1,700 (Russell, Harrington, and Vaughn 1986). This survey also revealed that the average state environmental agency assigned to measure air pollution was responsible for measuring emissions from over 4,500 sites. If all sites were measured each year, a typical state might spend around $8 million just for monitoring pollution, to say nothing of enforcing standards.

Divided Policymaking Authority

In many cases, an environmental problem will fall within the authority of more than one policymaking body. This can result in a lack of coordination where different

COMMON SENSE RUN AGROUND?

Why do some environmental policies appear to violate common sense? In part, the lack of common sense arises from the presence of multiple goals, including political ones. Rare is the politician unwilling to crow about a popular "victory," especially one that may translate into future votes. But politicians are not alone. Common sense will be embraced by any group whose particular goals it advances. Unfortunately, common sense is often the last thing on anyone's mind.

Consider the Shell Oil Company's plan to sink a huge, aging oil storage buoy, the *Brent Spar,* in the North Atlantic Ocean. Shell's decision to scuttle the buoy in water 2,000 meters deep was greeted by howls of outrage by environmental groups in Europe, such as Greenpeace, and many politicians. Greenpeace argued that sinking the buoy would release hundreds of tons of toxic and radioactive wastes and would also set a precedent for other oil companies to dispose of their platforms in the same way. Greenpeace organized a flotilla of vessels to accompany the buoy as it was towed from the North Sea, as well as a massive boycott of Shell's gasoline stations in Germany. Politicians of every bent, especially in Germany, weighed in on the side of Greenpeace, to the cheers of most of their constituents. Ultimately, Shell capitulated, and the rig was towed to the mainland to be dismantled, cut up, and recycled.

Was Shell's decision "a victory for everybody, a victory for common sense, and a victory for the environment," as Greenpeace crowed? It's doubtful. Initially, Shell proposed to sink the waste sludge from the *Brent Spar* in shallow waters. But this proposal had been opposed by British scientists as potentially too harmful to marine life. At the cold depths of 2,000 meters, however, there is little sea life. And although the *Brent Spar* still retained some 100 tons of residual sludge, as well as small quantities of heavy metals and radioactive salts, the pollutants would have leaked out slowly. Instead, all of these pollutants must now be dealt with on land, where workers will be exposed to the wastes and where the environment is far more sensitive. Not only that, but the land dismantling is estimated to cost $50 million more than the original deep-sea scuttling. Common sense indeed.

Source: Adapted from "Hollow Shell," *Economist,* June 24, 1995, pp. 76–77.

laws and regulations work at cross-purposes. In the 1990 Clean Air Act Amendments, for example, Congress instituted an emissions trading program for sulfur dioxide allowing electric utilities to buy and sell emissions rights among themselves so as to reduce emissions at the lowest possible cost.[11] At the same time, some state electric utility regulators issued orders banning such trades or eliminating all financial incentives to engage in them, defeating the purpose of the regulations.

---

[11]See Chapter 7 for a discussion of tradable emissions permits.

Even when policymakers are not acting at cross-purposes, they can run afoul of one another. In some cases, policymakers working on different problems can take contradictory actions. In many cities in the United States, programs to reduce automobile emissions are working to reduce parking at new commercial developments. Local zoning boards, however, are requiring more parking to ensure that there is no spillover into neighboring residential areas or offering free parking as an economic development incentive for downtown business districts. In other cases, policymakers take redundant actions. The EPA has required states that violate air quality standards to develop programs to reduce drive-alone commuting. These programs are being implemented in cities that already have similar programs initially developed to reduce traffic congestion.

DO ENVIRONMENTAL REGULATORS' PREFERENCES CORRESPOND TO PUBLIC PREFERENCES?

Sometimes the argument is made that the choice of environmental policy goals and instruments reflects the preferences of the public and in fact provides us with a measure of society's willingness to pay for environmental quality. On the surface, such a statement may seem to make sense; after all, if regulators and elected officials do not reflect the views of the public they represent, they are unlikely to stay in their positions long. There are two major problem with such thinking. First, as we have just seen, there are many reasons associated with the policymaking process to expect that policymakers' decisions will not reflect the public interest, however it is defined.

Second, even if environmental legislation and regulation reflect the public interest, this is often not the same as reflecting society's willingness to pay for a specific environmental good. If we had an environmental problem that was defined strictly in economic efficiency terms, the best solution would be one that equated the marginal cost of correcting the problem with society's marginal willingness to pay. However, most of the time, policymakers must address several policy goals simultaneously. Other factors besides willingness to pay will affect decisions and may even dominate decisions. Generally, this will produce a different solution than would a consideration of economic efficiency alone. Thus the costs of regulation will generally *not* be equal to the willingness to pay to avoid environmental damages. The economic cost of policies that were set on the basis of both economic and noneconomic values will not give an accurate measure of the economic values that contributed to the decision.

CHAPTER SUMMARY

This chapter provided an introduction to the process of developing environmental policy. The first step in developing any environmental policy should be to determine the problems and goals on the basis of society's environmental values.

Of course, environmental values that ultimately shape environmental policies can raise many moral and legal questions because of the different values individuals and societies hold. Next, policymakers should determine which of alternative solutions are preferred and which policy instruments are appropriate. Once a policy has been implemented, the results should be evaluated to decide whether changes are desirable. Lastly, we noted that the practical identification of environmental problems and the policies selected to combat them can be the result of changing public preferences, changing information, the dynamics of interest group behavior, and broad interpretations of the public's environmental views by regulators and legislators.

CHAPTER REVIEW

Economic Concepts and Tools

- Incommensurability is the inability to compare different goods using a single metric.

Policy Issues

- The formation of environmental policies should follow five steps:
    1. Identification of the problem based on normative criteria
    2. Identification of alternative solutions and their impacts
    3. Selection of appropriate policy instruments
    4. Implementation of policy instruments
    5. Evaluation and revision, if necessary
- One reason for unsatisfactory policies is a desire by some policymakers to do something quickly without thinking about what is to be accomplished or why.
- Value judgments about the environment will differ within individual societies, between societies, and over time.
- A society's environmental values can affect the environment through individual actions, through behavior reflected through markets, through group actions, and through government actions.
- The actions of environmental policymakers will not always reflect their constituents' willingness to pay for environmental goods and services. Environmental legislation and regulation will frequently address several goals simultaneously. Students of environmental policy should not expect to be able to infer willingness to pay from public policy decisions.
- Politics can interfere with "commonsense" environmental decisions, especially when only incomplete pictures of environmental benefits and costs are presented.
- Enforcement and monitoring costs are often overlooked in developing and implementing environmental policies.

DISCUSSION QUESTIONS

1. Should other forms of life, as well as inanimate objects, have environmental standing? If so, what sort of standing should they have? How can their rights be valued? How should these rights be presented? [*Hint:* See Stone (1974) for a discussion.]

2. Suppose that the California condor, which is extremely rare, is the only known species producing a certain hormone that can cure 1,000 poor children dying of a newly discovered and extremely virulent disease. There is no known way of producing the hormone in a laboratory, and the only way to extract the hormone is by killing a condor. Curing all 1,000 children would require killing all of the condors in order to extract enough of the hormone. You have been asked to make the decision. What do you do? Why?

3. An environmental regulator in the state of Hypochondria adamantly opposes continued operation of a nuclear power plant because she believes it is immoral to dispose of the waste generated outside her state. However, all of the electricity produced by the plant is exported to meet the demand for electricity in other states. Thus she also believes it immoral to make the citizens of Hypochondria live with the waste stored within the boundaries of Hypochondria. A Native American tribe outside the state has offered to construct and operate a storage facility because it will provide high-paying jobs for tribal members. If the waste is not correctly stored, however, all of the tribal members will perish. What should the regulator do?

4. Suppose that a ban has been imposed on the use of a certain pesticide by wheat farmers. At first, the farmers argued vehemently against the ban because it would reduce crop yields per acre and total wheat production. After talking with a renowned agricultural economist about the demand for wheat, however, farmers now support the ban wholeheartedly. What could the economist have told the farmers to make the farmers change their views?

5. You may live in a city or town that has a recycling program or is considering one. Evaluate the pros and cons of such programs. How clear are the goals? How are the goals measured? What policy instruments are in use? How consistent are the policy instruments with the stated goals? Do you believe there may be other, unstated goals? If so, why?

6. Traffic congestion creates environmental and other social problems. What are they? Identify four policy alternatives that would reduce traffic congestion and these environmental and social problems. Discuss the likely impacts of your policy choices, if any, on economic efficiency, equity, and human rights. How do you balance competing goals? [*Hint:* See Arnott and Small (1994) for a discussion of traffic congestion.]

7. Bovine growth hormone (BGH) is a naturally occurring hormone that encourages milk production in cows. A synthetic version of this hormone has been developed by a chemical manufacturer. Injection of this synthetic hor-

mone is said to increase milk production around 10 percent. Some farmers use BGH. Others oppose it because increased production will lower market prices. Many consumers are fearful that synthetic BGH will cause birth defects, cancer, and other health problems. Other consumers object to its use because of its alleged effects on cows themselves, such as increased mastitis. Still others oppose its use because they believe it will lead to the demise of "family farms." The Food and Drug Agency (FDA) has approved the sale and use of BGH, saying that there are no health effects associated with it. Despite this, in the state of Vermont legislation was passed (later overturned) that required *all* food products containing BGH to be labeled as such. As a policymaker, outline a study of BGH. Discuss the various policy issues, likely solutions, and policy instruments. Discuss the reasons for the labeling law. How would you have "solved" the BGH controversy?

REFERENCES

Anderson, E. 1993. *Value in Ethics and Economics.* Cambridge, Mass.: Harvard University Press.

Arnott, R., and K. Small. 1994. "The Economics of Traffic Congestion." *American Scientist,* September-October, pp. 446–455.

Cairncross, F. 1993. "All That Remains: A Survey of Waste and the Environment." *Economist,* May 29, 1993, pp. W1–W18.

Eigen, L., and J. Siegel (Eds.). *The MacMillan Dictionary of Political Quotations.* New York: Macmillan, 1993.

Kelman, S. 1981. *What Price Incentives? Economists and the Environment.* Westport, Conn.: Auburn House.

Kopp, R. 1993. "Environmental Economics: Not Dead but Thriving." *Resources* 111: 7–12.

Lesser, J., and R. Zerbe. 1995. "What Can Economic Analysis Contribute to the Sustainability Debate?" *Contemporary Economic Policy* 13(3): 88–100.

Marshall, E. 1991. "A Is for Apple, Alar, and . . . Alarmist?" *Science* 208: 20–22.

Page, T. 1977. *Conservation and Economic Efficiency.* Baltimore: Johns Hopkins University Press.

———. 1992. "Environmental Existentialism." In *Ecosystem Health: New Goals for Environmental Management,* ed. R. Costanza et al. Washington, D.C.: Island Press.

Ruff, L. 1970. "The Economic Common Sense of Pollution." *Public Interest* 19: 69–85.

Russell, C., W. Harrington, and W. Vaugh. 1986. "Enforcing Pollution Control Laws." Resources for the Future, Washington, D.C.

Sagoff, M. 1988. *The Economy of the Earth.* New York: Cambridge University Press.

———. 1993. "Environmental Economics: An Epitaph." *Resources* 111: 2–5.

Scarlett, L. 1993. "Recycling Costs: Clearing Away Some Smoke." *Solid Waste and Power* 10: 12–17.

Sound Resource Management Group (SRMG). 1993. "The Economics of Recycling and Recycled Materials." Revised final report for the Clean Washington Center, Seattle.

Stone, C. 1974. *Should Trees Have Standing? Toward Legal Rights for Natural Objects.* Los Altos, Calif.: Kaufman.

Sunstein, C. 1994. "Incommensurability and Valuation in Law." *Michigan Law Review* 92: 779–861.

Zerbe, R. 1991. "Comment: Does Benefit-Cost Analysis Stand Alone? Rights and Standing." *Journal of Policy Analysis and Management* 10(1): 96–105.

PART II

ECONOMIC WELFARE, EQUITY, AND RIGHTS

We now begin our exploration of environmental economics and policy in earnest. We defined the concept of economic efficiency in Chapter 3, discussed different equity and rights issues in Chapter 4, and highlighted the problem of defining policy goals in Chapter 5. We are now ready to begin the process of addressing environmental problems and the policies used to correct them. We begin in Chapter 6 by carefully defining environmental externalities and exploring their relationship between externalities and economic inefficiency. We then consider open-access externalities, which are often found with fisheries and other biological resources, and then move on to a discussion of public goods, which are often what environmental goods are.

Chapter 7 examines eight different policies that can address the economic inefficiencies associated with environmental externalities. We also examine the efficiency of the policies themselves, as that can be a major consideration in determining which policies should be adopted. Specifically, we examine three categories of environmental policy instruments: taxes and fees, subsidies to reduce environmental damages, and "command and control" policies. We look at the broader effects of environmental policies, building on the discussion of the interactions within the economy discussed in Chapter 2.

Chapter 8 examines environmental externalities and their effect on equity, human rights, and the rights of nature. We discuss how externalities can affect the distribution of wealth in a society and between societies, as well as how wealth influences the demand for environmental quality.

Chapter 9 then examines policy alternatives that can address equity and rights goals. We look at a variety of U.S. environmental laws and the ways they consider equity and rights goals. We also examine the relatively new concept of "environmental racism." We then discuss the importance of incorporating economic efficiency into all environmental policies so that, regardless of the primary purpose of an environmental policy, it is achieved as efficiently as possible.

Because policymakers often have a variety of environmental goals, Chapter 10 concludes Part II with a discussion of a methodology for addressing and balancing multiple goals. This methodology, called multiattribute analysis, can be useful in reducing the number of policy alternatives to be considered and exploring the implications of different goals on preferred environmental policies. The chapter then looks at how politics and bureaucracy can interfere with setting policy goals and the ways in which different environmental laws have balanced competing goals.

CHAPTER 6

EXTERNALITIES AND ECONOMIC INEFFICIENCY

By Land, by Sea, and by Air

One of the authors once lived in an isolated valley in the western United States. The dry summers were punctuated by occasional thunderstorms, which often brought lightning but no rain. Several times each summer, lightning would start a grass fire. If the fire were not controlled, it could sweep through the valley, burning thousands of acres of pasture and hayfields and any houses and barns that were in the way. A fire could start anywhere and move in any direction. Everyone in the valley was at risk, and a single fire could damage several families' property.

To protect themselves from this danger, the residents formed a volunteer fire department. To raise money, they held dances, garage sales, and poker rides (a local tradition that consists of a daylong gambling game played while riding horseback between the local bars). The fire department purchased a used fire truck, protective gear, and other equipment. Every Thursday night, the volunteers met to maintain the equipment and practice. Whenever someone spotted a fire, the person would call the fire department telephone number, which would ring all of the volunteers' phones. Everyone who could do so then rushed to help put out the fire.

Today, there are still fires in that valley. Sometimes up to 100 acres burn before a fire is brought under control. Occasionally, a house or barn burns. However, since the fire department has been organized, there has not been a catastrophic fire, and the average annual fire damage is much lower.

Lake Washington is a large freshwater lake extending for many miles that was created thousands of years ago by glaciation. It is located in the Seattle metropolitan area of western Washington State and connected to Puget Sound, which is part of the Pacific Ocean, by the Lake Washington Ship Canal. This canal contains a series of locks allowing boats, primarily fishing and pleasure craft, to travel between Puget Sound and the lake. From the air, Lake Washington is one of the "crown jewels" of Puget Sound. Its aesthetic value, noticeable by the dollar premium that homes and offices with lake views can command, is significant. More directly, the lake is used by swimmers, boaters, and anglers. And it has been used as a waste dump.

In the mid-1950s, however, there were no swimmers and few fishermen. Lake Washington was dying, polluted heavily by raw sewage and other materials. Under the leadership of active citizens, a new local government entity, called METRO, was created to deal with the pollution. METRO was governed by a council of political representatives from the various affected municipalities and by King County. METRO succeeded in reducing pollution levels in the lake significantly. Laws were passed prohibiting the dumping of raw sewage into the lake, and state-of-the-art treatment facilities were built using tax dollars. Curiously, in 1994, the METRO form of government was declared illegal, and in 1996, METRO was folded into the King County government.

In many large urban areas, there are fairly serious air pollution problems. In the Seattle area, for example, by the mid-1980s, atmospheric concentrations of ozone and other pollutants had reached levels that caused health problems for some people several times a year. People complained about the situation to each other; they complained also to the local, state, and federal governments. The Environmental Protection Agency declared that the area was not in compliance with the air quality standards of the federal Clean Air Act.

The largest single source of air pollution in the area, as in most cities in the United States, is motor vehicles. Although industries pollute too, by the 1980s most large industrial point source emissions were already regulated. Each such source is significant, but there are relatively few of them. By contrast, automobiles and other sources of pollution, including lawn mowers and backyard barbecues, are more difficult to regulate. These pollution sources are individually small but are widespread.

Where air quality standards are violated, the U.S. Clean Air Act requires states to develop plans that reduce pollution and comply with federal standards. These state plans require reductions in industrial emissions. They require also that motor vehicles be tested for their emissions and that vehicles with excessive emissions be repaired. To address air pollution in the Puget Sound region, the Washington State legislature passed its own Clean Air Act, with additional requirements. These included a requirement that employers develop programs to get their employees to carpool or use transit. As a result of these actions, air quality has improved in the region, but it is not clear yet whether it has improved enough to meet federal standards. Unfortunately, even if air quality meets federal standards now, it may not meet them in the future as the population continues to grow.

Three different environmental problems, three very different solutions.

INTRODUCTION: THE EXTERNALITY PROBLEM

The neighbors concerned about grass fires solved their environmental problem voluntarily. The residents of King County organized a new local governmental entity to address pollution in Lake Washington. The citizens of large cities like Seattle have relied on federal and state government action to solve their air pollution problems. Why were the outcomes so different? In the first case, the neighbors came to a voluntary agreement. In essence, their agreement was a *market-based* solution. In the second and the third cases, citizens were unable to develop voluntary solutions. Instead, they relied on government to develop *market-substituting* solutions to correct the environmental problems. In the latter two cases, an *externality* existed because a market solution did not.

This chapter provides an introduction to externalities. First, we introduce the concept of an externality carefully, suggesting that it means looking at the costs of setting up or operating an exchange system. In this regard, the issues posed by the existence of externalities are not different from those confronting entrepreneurs who wish to reduce market transactions costs. Thus the existence of an externality is not reason *in itself* for government or any other kind of action. Rather, it is an invitation to think about how activities are organized.

We begin by defining the term *externality*. Then we examine why externalities exist (and why they don't) and how externalities reduce economic efficiency. Next we look at two concepts often related to externalities: public goods and open access. We finish the chapter with a brief look at some general principles for policies to correct externalities.

EXTERNALITIES DEFINED

Although there are different definitions of externalities, the one used by most economists (e.g., Baumol and Oates 1988) is this:

> An externality is present when one person's consumption or production relationships contain real (nonmonetary) variables chosen by someone else (persons, corporations, governments) without deliberately choosing the real variable with the one person in mind.[1]

The idea is that externalities arise when costs are borne without benefits received or benefits are received without any costs borne. This definition excludes *interactive* effects transmitted through the market system (hence the use of the term *nonmonetary*), as well as acts toward another that are *deliberate*. The term *exter-*

---

[1] In a simple form, an externality can be expressed by considering two firms producing goods X and Z. The production of Z is said to have an external effect on the production of X if the production of X depends in part on Z. Suppose that the production of X depends on labor and on the production of Z. We can write $X = f(L_X:Z)$. The symbol L_X denotes the amount of labor used in producing good X. Good Z appears to the right of the semicolon, denoting that it is not under the control of the producer of good X. For example, firm X may be in the business of cleaning clothes and firm Z may pollute the air as a by-product of producing Z, thereby increasing cleaning costs for firm X.

nality includes both of what Marshall (1920) called *external economies* and *external diseconomies,* and these terms are often used to differentiate harmful and beneficial effects. The term *externality* is often used incorrectly as a synonym for any environmental impact. Many environmental impacts are externalities, but not all are, and not all externalities involve the natural environment.

Externalities in Consumption and Production

Externalities can occur in either the consumption or the production of goods and services. The recipients of an unintended side effect can be either consumers or producers. Some externalities affect consumers directly. Your neighbor can affect the view from your living room window by planting flowers or storing garbage cans. Emissions from cars and industrial plants affect the quality of the air you breathe and possibly your health. In these cases, one party's actions directly affect another party's utility. Other externalities affect firms' production processes and therefore their production costs. Airborne particulates or turbid water may increase the operating costs incurred by a laundry to produce clean clothes. Externalities can affect both production and consumption activities, and can arise from both of these activities.

Externalities as Unintentional Side Effects

A situation where one party's actions affects another does not necessarily involve an externality. The world is full of situations where one party affects another with no externality involved. Employers and employees, a store and its customers, and a retailer and its wholesale suppliers are all examples of economic interdependences that are not externalities.

Yet the world is also full of externalities. A factory causing acid rain downwind, airport noise disturbing nearby residents, and motorists getting in one another's way are all examples of externalities. The key to distinguishing interactions involving externalities is whether or not the interactions are taken into account in decision processes. That can be done directly or through market prices.

Suppose that your neighbor accidentally spilled a pesticide into your yard and the fumes made you ill. Using our definition, this would be an externality. But what if your neighbor spilled the poison *on purpose,* hoping to make you ill? Is that an externality? The two situations have identical outcomes (your illness) but differ from both legal and ethical standpoints. The first situation is simple negligence; the second is criminal assault. While some economists have proposed that criminal acts be considered externalities, the most common view is that deliberate acts are best analyzed in a class by themselves, since they have different causes and different remedies (Mishan 1969; Baumol and Oates 1988). With an externality, the harm is usually economic and a remedy can be sought through regulation, civil law, or even private negotiations. Assault is dealt with through the criminal law because the harm, although it may have economic aspects, is primarily personal.

Externalities Are External to Markets

The price system is a market mechanism that accounts for what individuals want. When the effects of a decision are transmitted fully through the price system, all of the effects will be taken into account. For example, suppose that a large computer chip manufacturer intends to expand its operations and hires several hundred additional engineers. To lure engineers from other local firms, the chip manufacturer offers higher wages, excellent benefits, lush offices, and free ice cream every Friday. Other local firms must decide to respond in kind or offer similar benefits. In any case, those firms' costs will increase. It is the price system that is acting as the "contract" in which different, competing interests are considered. This does not mean that no one is hurt by market decisions (firms needing to pay more for engineers are) but simply that the consequences are taken fully into account.[2]

A Definition Again

We can now reiterate in slightly different language our earlier definition of an externality:

> A (technological) externality exists when an unintended side effect of one or more parties' actions affect the utility or production possibilities of one or more other parties, and there is no contract between the parties or price system governing the impact.

WHY EXTERNALITIES EXIST AND WHERE WE FIND THEM

Before we can examine policies to correct externalities, we need to understand why they exist, be able to recognize one when we see one, and not see an externality where none exists. In this section, we look at the causes of externalities and the conditions where they do and do not exist.

Conditions for the Absence of Externalities

Before considering why externalities exist, we should ask why they so often do *not* exist. Why do people ever take their impacts on others into account? In many cases, the answer is obvious: people take the impacts of their activities on others

---

[2]In this example, we have defined what economists call *pecuniary externalities.* For example, one of the side effects of the use of catalytic converters on cars was an increased demand for the rare metals used as catalysts and a decreased demand for tetraethyl lead used in leaded gasoline. The price of rare metals rose, and the price of lead fell. Rare metal producers were made better off, and tetraethyl lead producers were made worse off. These sorts of side effects are strictly distributional and do not reduce economic efficiency. The externalities we will address are called *technological externalities.* Those have side effects that directly affect economic efficiency.

into account because those impacts are the whole reason for the activity. People produce and sell goods and services because other people want them and are willing to pay for them. When the amount others are willing to pay exceeds the cost of providing a good or service, there are gains from trade to be realized.

For market goods, additional units will be produced only if the production costs of the good *plus* the costs of using the existing market exchange mechanism are less than the willingness to pay for the good. This is why effects transmitted through market mechanisms are not externalities. By definition, externalities are not transmitted through market mechanisms. For example, I cannot go to the store and purchase clean air. The reason I cannot is that the costs of *creating* a market mechanism for buying and selling clean air exceeds the gains.

We have defined externalities as unintentional side effects, not actions that people take for their own sake. Can there be gains from trade involving side effects? Yes. But we must ask why the good associated with the externality, in this case clean air, is not produced. The answer is the same as that for an unproduced market good—the costs of producing and delivering clean air exceed the market's willingness to pay for clean air, when all of the costs necessary to complete the transaction are included.

That an externality exists does not indicate if the good should be produced. It simply calls attention to the costs that are preventing the good from being produced. If people find reasons to change the level of an activity, it becomes an intentional activity, not a side effect, and will no longer be an externality. In such a case, we say that the externality has become *internalized* because it will have become part of a market mechanism.

Suppose that we have a duplex with upstairs and downstairs apartments that are heated separately. Both are inhabited by students, who keep the thermostats lower than they would really like because they are on limited budgets. They each set their thermostats at the point where the value they place on additional heat is just equal to its marginal cost. However, the downstairs heater warms the downstairs ceiling, which warms the upstairs floor, which warms the entire upstairs slightly. The marginal dollar the downstairs residents spend on heat is worth a dollar to them and some fraction of a dollar (say, 25 cents) to the upstairs residents. There is an unintentional side effect here, and there are also potential gains from trade.

An externality exists. There are gains from trade if there is a mechanism to realize them. For example, if the upstairs residents paid the downstairs residents less than 25 cents—say, 20 cents—to spend an extra dollar on heat, both would be better off. The upstairs residents would get additional heat they valued at 25 cents for only 20 cents and thereby gain 5 cents. The downstairs residents would get additional heat they valued at a dollar but would pay only 80 cents for that heat because the upstairs residents were paying the additional 20 cents. Thus the downstairs residents would gain 20 cents.

If both parties would gain, why might this arrangement not take place? One reason is that the negotiating costs between the upstairs and the downstairs residents might be too high to make such negotiations worthwhile. What might change to make the negotiations worthwhile? Perhaps the landlord sends a letter to each tenant suggesting the amount of payment from upstairs to downstairs tenants. This would reduce the costs of negotiations. If the landlord's letter reduces the transactions costs sufficiently, the transaction will take place. The downstairs residents will turn the heat up, and the upstairs residents will pay some portion of the additional heating cost. If this occurs, the unintentional side effect will have become part of a transaction, and gains from exchange will have been realized. The students will have *internalized* the externality.

If neither the landlord nor the students can find a sufficiently inexpensive mechanism by which they can internalize the externality, what should be done? Should there be some form of government action that mandates negotiation? Should the government pass a law that requires the downstairs residents to raise the heat in the apartment? Certainly, government intervention is always a possibility. However, it is likely that any mechanism the government could suggest would be more expensive than the gains realized. If the property owner and the tenants could not find a sufficiently inexpensive mechanism, the government is unlikely to find one. Government action may be warranted in some cases, but probably not in this one. These are the sorts of questions posed by the existence of externalities.

Internalizing Externalities

Internalizing an externality through private transactions will take place when three conditions are met. First, there must be *technically feasible* gains from trade. Each party must be able to provide something the others want at a lower cost than the others could provide it on their own. This condition will always be met when we encounter an externality. For example, in theory, store owners could sell clean air that I could purchase. One of the attributes of an externality is that it causes potentially feasible gains from trade *not* to be realized.

Second, a transaction must be *institutionally feasible*. There must be a way for the parties to agree on a formal or informal contract within the existing legal and institutional structure. It must be possible for them to define the terms of an agreement—to define the rights and obligations of each party, to set forth their mutual expectations, and to specify recourse if obligations are not met. In short, there must be well-defined property rights in whatever is to be traded, and there must not be institutional and legal structures that prohibit the particular type of trade. Slave trading, for example, may be technically feasible, but in most countries it is not institutionally feasible.

Third, the affected parties must be able to capture at least some of the gains from trade or at least not be harmed by the trade. The exchange must be a Pareto superior one, as no party will enter voluntarily into an agreement that harms that party.

In sum, the costs of negotiating and enforcing an agreement, the *transactions costs,* must be less than the gains from trade for each of the parties. Thus the existence of an externality should be considered as the *efficient result given the existing institutional arrangement.* The key public policy question that the existence of an externality raises is whether or not there are institutional changes that will improve the situation. This may at first seem startling because it leads us to consider "optimal" amounts of pollution. That concept troubles many individuals (e.g., Kelman 1981) because, as we discussed in Chapter 4, many individuals have goals other than improving economic efficiency.

When all potential gains from trade have been realized, there is no externality. The conditions for this to be realized are stated formally by what has come to be known as the *Coase theorem* (Coase 1960; Zerbe 1980):

> If there are well-defined property rights for all goods and services and zero transactions costs, the equilibrium allocation of goods and services will be efficient and there will be no externalities.

The importance of the Coase theorem is that it raises an identical question to that raised by the existence of the externality—are there institutional changes that will lower transactions costs and thereby promote economic efficiency?

The Coase theorem can teach us many lessons and has spawned many controversies. We will discuss three, but there are others.[3] The lesson Coase himself seemed most anxious to impart is that *the mere existence of economic interdependence does not mean that there is an externality, nor, even if there is an externality, does this imply that corrective action is needed.* Coase stated that an action would be efficient only if it lowered transactions costs. If there were well-defined property rights and minimal transactions costs, the affected parties could reach a mutually beneficial resolution and turn interdependence into an opportunity rather than a problem.

A second lesson can be stated as a corollary of the Coase theorem: *Where an externality exists, property rights must be ill-defined and/or transactions costs must exceed the potential gains from trade.* Another corollary is this: *Where the affected parties could reach a solution through negotiation but choose litigation or regulation, the real issue is: Who is to be assigned property rights rather than how to realize gains from trade.*

Externalities and Property Rights

Ownership of property can be thought to involve the right to exclude others from its use, the ability to sell the property, and the right to use the property. The degree of ownership can be defined by the strength of these qualities. Allen (1991) defines transactions costs as *resources used to establish and maintain property rights.* Externalities often involve incomplete property rights or ownership. In our earlier examples, no one owned the urban air or owned Lake Washington. More to the point, no one owned the right to clean air or water in the sense that they could charge or restrict polluters.

When markets for the exchange of well-defined property rights do not exist, there is a reason. In some cases, the absence of property rights may be a matter of public policy. For example, Ault and Rutman (1989) note that private property in land arose only as land became scarce, whereas previously the costs of defining private property in land had exceeded the benefits. In other cases, many societies have placed restrictions on the buying and the selling of land, requiring that ancestral land be kept in a family or limiting the amount that one person could own. Historically, in the United States, incomplete property rights were developed for

---

[3]See, for example, Medema and Zerbe (1995) for a more detailed discussion.

water resources. But as water has become more scarce, it has become more worthwhile to develop a private property rights system.

Property rights may be ill-defined because they are *unenforceable* or *untradable*. If I can neither prevent others from using my property nor collect payment for its use, people who want to use my property will have no reason other than altruism to enter into a mutually beneficial contract with me. In many cases, this may be because there are social or legal restrictions on certain trades. In the United States, for example, many western states have tied ownership of water to ownership of land and placed restrictions on the sale of water for use off the associated land. In other cases, property may not be tradable because of inconsistencies between formal property rights and physical reality. This is often the case where property rights are defined in a way that ignores the impacts on third parties.

Some western states have experimented with defining water rights in terms of *consumptive use,* the amount of water that is diverted from a stream less the amount that returns downstream.[4] For irrigation, this is the sum of water that is used by plants, that is lost to evaporation, and that percolates into deep aquifers. Defining ownership of water this way makes it a tradable commodity, but water sales based on consumptive use rights can have major impacts on third parties downstream. This is because return flows from irrigation typically travel through shallow aquifers and reemerge downstream over a period of several months, and selling upstream rights to consumptive use can change the timing of water availability downstream.

Before two or more people can negotiate any new arrangement of rights and obligations, they need an initial set of rights and obligations, and they need a framework of behavioral norms and expectations, including sanctions for violating the norms. If those do not exist (i.e., if there are no property rights), they must be invented as part of the negotiations. Thus when property rights are undefined, the costs of negotiation will be high.

Externalities and Transactions Costs

Arrow (1969) defines transactions costs as *the costs of running the economic system.* Transactions costs are the costs of gathering information (as opposed to discovering new information), making decisions, negotiating agreements, seeing that agreements are carried out, and enforcing sanctions when they are not. Transactions costs are often divided into *information costs, contracting costs,* and *enforcement costs.* Information costs are the costs of discovering what options are available and who is available to trade with. Contracting costs are the costs of reaching an agreement with one or more trading partners. Enforcement costs are the costs of making sure that the other side carries out its part of the bargain. Some transactions costs are themselves explicit parts of a transaction and are easily quantified, such as brokers' fees and legal fees. Most transactions costs are not so obvious but are just as real. Many transactions costs involve expenditures of time

---

[4]We discuss water resource development and markets in the western United States in Chapter 17.

rather than money. Time spent comparison-shopping and haggling over price are examples of transactions costs.

In the example of neighbors concerned about grass fires, all three types of transactions costs are low. By contrast, transactions costs are high in the case of urban air pollution or in the case of users of Lake Washington. For the residents of the small valley, the source of fire danger is easy to see, and there are few parties involved. The parties to a potential agreement will not need to expend many resources gathering information. For someone whose eyes sting from pollution or who finds the Lake too dirty to use for swimming, the source of the pollution and even the type of pollution are unlikely to be obvious because there are many sources. Someone wanting to initiate a private agreement to reduce pollution would face a long and expensive period of gathering information. For the small group of neighbors, however, the contracting costs are likely to be small unless some neighbors are uncooperative. They can all get together some evening and agree to form a fire department in a few hours.

Getting several million people together at once to solve an air pollution problem is as impractical as getting several million people to agree on anything is unlikely. Contracting costs for a private solution to air pollution would be astronomical. The problem is not just the number of people involved but a combination of the number of people and the type of agreement required. There are many markets with thousands or millions of participants, but the actions in these markets generally consist of many simple bilateral trades (direct trades between buyers and sellers). Fully internalizing air pollution would require a single multilateral agreement involving everyone who wants cleaner air and everyone who emits anything into the air. For the neighbors putting out grass fires, enforcement will be simple and informal. The community can bring informal but enormous social pressure to bear on residents who do not do their share. If a private contract regulating air or water pollution could be worked out, the costs of enforcing it would be extremely high. Once again, it is not just the large number of parties involved; it is the combination of a large number of parties and the fact that anyone who does not live up to his or her part of the agreement will still benefit from all the actions of others who do their part to clean up the air or water. This is known as the *free-rider problem,* and it provides a strong incentive for people to cheat on agreements. We do not have well-defined property rights in air quality largely because transactions costs for market trades involving such rights would be prohibitive. No one has found it worthwhile to expend the resources necessary to create a legal right that would have no practical value.

Free-rider problems can be seen in terms of ill-defined property rights as well as large transactions costs. A free-rider problem exists when significant gains from trade can be captured by people who are not parties to the transaction. This will occur when the exclusionary aspect of property rights is weak or nonexistent.

The presence of transactions costs leads to a general converse of the Coase theorem: *An externality will exist when property rights and transactions costs are such that transactions costs exceed the gains from trade that would be captured by the parties to a contract internalizing the externality.* When the transactions costs for each party are greater than the gains from trade capturable by that party, there will be no agreement. When the net gains from trade from bringing an additional party into the contract are less than the transactions costs of including the additional party, some parties will be left out of any contract.

THE COSTS OF ALTERNATIVE ARRANGEMENTS

The discussion of externalities in an economic efficiency policy context is just a discussion of the best way to organize economic activity. So far, we have been discussing the transactions costs associated with markets. In the United States, for example, there are few private roads. In other countries, however, there are many. Either institutional arrangement can provide transportation. Government-provided roads may be more efficient if the administrative costs and the costs in terms of traffic delays associated with private ownership of roads are sufficiently high. Markets are only one of many possible ways of organizing economic activity. All institutions for organizing economic activity have costs. None of them is free. In particular, government actions involve institutional costs—the costs of running government.

In the case of Lake Washington, it took a great measure of public concern, goodwill, and creative and exceptional civic leadership to bring about the formation of METRO. It was necessary for the state to write enabling legislation, but also it required a vote of the people. In fact, a vote of metropolitan residents failed at first to approve METRO's formation. After redrafting the plan, and with a tremendous effort by the League of Women Voters, a door-to-door campaign involving over 5,000 volunteers, and substantial contributions from others, the vote creating METRO passed. By 1968, the phosphorus levels in Lake Washington had fallen from 70 parts per million (ppm) to 29 ppm. Raw sewage discharges into Puget Sound were eliminated around 1969. Another approach would have been to create a market for rights to use the lake. Was METRO the lowest-transactions-cost solution? Perhaps. It was certainly a lower-cost solution than private action.

Government and markets may be substitutes or complements. Government is often an ingredient—an input into the creation or the operation of private markets. Laws governing contracts and fraud, for example, can be regarded as market-enhancing mechanisms because both types reduce transactions costs by providing an efficient mechanism for enforcement (Williamson 1985).

In terms of economic efficiency, markets can fail, but so can government. Government actions involve many of the same kinds of information costs as market transactions. Government actions can be powerful, but they can also be coercive or despotic. Governments may sacrifice efficient actions for distributional ones. Government actions can fail because governments are not good at getting the right information or because they fail to predict the consequences of their actions. People wanting to use government effectively to solve a problem must gather information to identify the source of their problem and possible solutions. They must also convey that information to others, including political decision makers. Legislative and regulatory proceedings have costs that are equivalent to contracting costs. Lastly, enforcement costs for government actions include the administrative costs of government agencies, which can be considerable.

Government actions often have another category of costs that are not present in market transactions. Many government actions are implemented through taxes, and those that are not are often financed using taxes. Most taxes change the relative prices of goods and services, and except when a tax is offsetting a preexisting price distortion, this causes people to make inefficient changes in consumption or production decisions. This results in an efficiency loss to taxpayers that is greater than the tax revenue—what economists call a *deadweight loss.*

In sum, it is difficult to generalize about the most efficient economic arrangements. The most important generalization is that there is a great deal of accumulated evidence to the effect that where markets can be reasonably created or where government action can lower the costs of market operation, this is the best approach to internalizing externalities. Beyond this, the benefits and the costs of alternative arrangements must be examined in particular cases.

EXTERNALITIES AND INEFFICIENCY

It has become popular to talk about correcting environmental problems by making polluters pay the full costs of their actions. This makes externalities sound primarily like a distributional issue—polluters are getting something for nothing and others are paying. Although externalities do have distributional implications (which we explore in Chapters 8 and 9), they are not the reason that economists have devoted so much attention to externalities. Economists are interested in externalities primarily because they lead to inefficiency. And externalities lead to inefficiency because they cause people to make inefficient decisions, not because people pay more or less than they deserve to.

In this section, we look at the ways that externalities distort choices made by producers and consumers and the gains in welfare that result from reducing or eliminating those distortions. The economic inefficiencies resulting from externalities are at the core of the economic aspect of many environmental problems. The policy question as far as economic efficiency is concerned is whether the costs of reducing or eliminating the distortions are less than the benefits to be gained.

When we have economic efficiency, the marginal rate of substitution between two goods equals the marginal rate of transformation between them, for all goods and for all people. That is, the relative value of two goods in consumption is equal to the relative cost of producing them. When these conditions exist, there are no remaining gains from trade to be exploited. Markets work to produce economic efficiency through the intermediary of the price system. Firms maximize profits by setting the marginal rate of transformation between goods (i.e., the relative costs of producing two goods) equal to the ratio of their prices.

Consumers maximize utility by setting the marginal rate of substitution between two goods equal to the price ratio between those goods.[5] Competitive markets create efficiency by forcing everyone to face the same price ratio. Another way of saying this is that competitive markets equate the price buyers pay for a good to its marginal social cost.[6]

When there is an externality, part of this mechanism is missing. Firms still try to maximize profits and consumers still try to maximize utility, but there are one or more markets missing. Not everyone faces the same prices, and the resulting decisions are inconsistent. The price that buyers pay no longer reflects marginal social cost because some of the costs (or benefits) have not been internalized into the market transaction.

An Illustration of Inefficiency

Consider the case of urban air pollution in which pollution is being produced by steel mills. There are no restrictions on use of the atmosphere as a sink for pollution. Suppose that the only way to control such pollution is by curtailing the production of steel. Figure 6.1 illustrates the situation. The demand for steel is given by the curve D. The marginal private cost is given by the curve MPC. The curve MSC shows the marginal social cost of producing steel, including the cost of using

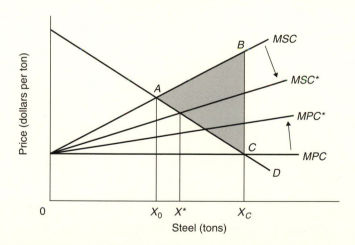

Figure 6.1   Inefficiency in Private Production

---

[6]The marginal rate of transformation between one good and another good with a price of 1 is its marginal social cost. The conditions for economic efficiency are a set of n equations in $n + 1$ variables. The value of any one variable can be set arbitrarily. If we make one good our unit of account by setting its price to 1, we have n equations in n variables, and they reduce to the n equilibrium conditions for n markets.

the atmosphere to dispose of waste. Without restrictions on production, output occurs at X_C. However, society will be better off with less steel produced. In fact, the optimal amount of steel production will be X_0 tons. The size of these gains is shown by the shaded triangle ABC in Figure 6.1, which is the amount by which the social cost of producing units from X_0 to X_C exceeds the willingness to pay for these units.

Now suppose that there were a less expensive way of reducing pollution than by simply cutting back production. For example, suppose that steel mills could be outfitted with special precipitators to reduce air pollution. In that case, there would be a new marginal private cost of producing steel, MPC^*, that would exceed MPC. However, the new MSC for production of steel, MSC^*, would be less than MSC and would include the optimal treatment of the pollutant. In this case, optimal output would exceed X_0. (Many texts fail to note this and assert optimal production is at X_0 even though there are cheaper methods of curtailing the pollution than cutting back on production.) Thus the "optimal" output of steel and hence steel-related pollution can be found by looking at the damage from pollution as compared with its control costs.

Externalities and Producers' Input Choices

Now let's examine the situation from the standpoint of an individual firm producing steel. The steel firm uses the atmosphere as a disposal dump. Thus the atmosphere is an input into the production of steel, just like iron ore, coke, and electricity. A profit-maximizing steel firm will choose the mix of inputs where the value of the marginal product (VMP) of each input just equals its price (or its marginal factor cost, if an input is not purchased).[7] A competitive firm producing steel will use the atmosphere as a waste dump as long as the value of doing so exceeds the cost of doing so—in this case, zero. The equilibrium price for any input will be determined where the industry demand curve for that input intersects the supply curve for the input.

If there are no externalities, the industry demand will capture all of the value from using the input in the production of the product, and the supply will capture all of the relevant social costs. The outcome for the industry and the firm is then shown in Figure 6.2. The figure shows the demand for the atmosphere as an input, measured by its VMP, and the marginal social cost (MSC) of this use. The optimal use of the atmosphere as an input for steel production will be X^*. As long as use of the atmosphere is free, however, it will be used to the higher level X_0. The gains to firms from using the additional amount of atmosphere are again shown by the shaded triangle ABC, which is exactly the same size as that in Figure 6.1 when the cheapest method of reducing pollution is to cut back on production of the good.

---

[7]A unit of input produces a marginal product, and the value of this marginal product is found by multiplying it by its price, which for the competitive firm is exogenous.

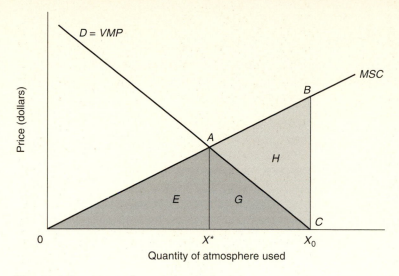

Figure 6.2   Input Choice of an Industry

What would happen if there were a cheap method of curtailing pollution from the steel manufacturing plants? Suppose that all of the air pollution from the steel manufacturers could be eliminated for $1 using a simple mechanical device. In that case, the potential gains from reducing use of the atmosphere would equal the additional horizontal shaded areas $E + G + H - \$1$, which essentially represents the entire area under the MSC curve. As long as someone was willing to pay the steel manufacturers $1, there would be almost no demand for use of the atmosphere as a dump. If the conditions of the general Coase theorem hold, the marginal factor cost will equal the input's marginal social cost; that is, the marginal cost to the firm will equal the marginal cost to society.

If the conditions for efficiency are satisfied in all other markets, marginal social cost can be derived from the production possibilities frontier (*PPF*), as shown in Figure 6.3.[8] The absolute value of the slope of the production possibilities frontier at any point is the amount of good X_2 that must be given up to provide an additional unit of good X_1. This is the marginal rate of transformation between X_1 and X_2, MRT_{12}, and is the opportunity cost of producing additional quantities of good X_1 in terms of forgone quantities of good X_2. At point A, for example, the slope of the tangent point equals dX_2/dX_1 (which is the limit of $\Delta X_2/\Delta X_1$ as $\Delta \to 0$). Multiplying by the monetary price of X_2 gives the opportunity cost of X_1 in monetary terms, $P_2 \cdot MRT_{12}$, which is the marginal social cost.[9]

---

[8]We examine marginal social cost when some other efficiency conditions are not satisfied in Chapter 7.
[9]With more than two goods, the *PPF* is an n-dimensional surface. If the conditions for efficiency are satisfied in all other markets, then $|\Delta X_i/\Delta X_1| = P_2/P_i$ or $P_i = P_2|\Delta X_2/\Delta X_i|$. Multiplying the marginal social cost of X_1 by $P_i/(P_2|\Delta X_2/\Delta X_i|) = 1$ and canceling gives $MSC = -P_i|\Delta X_i/\Delta X_1|$. Marginal social cost is the same regardless of which marginal rate of transformation we base it on.

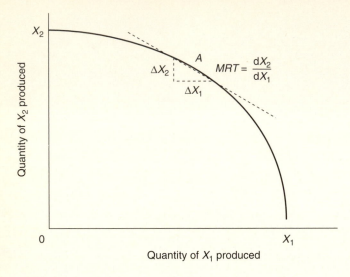

Figure 6.3   Marginal Social Cost and the Production Possibilities Frontier

If a firm's production process has external costs, this can be viewed as using *unpriced* inputs. If steel firms are emitting pollutants into the atmosphere that impose costs on others and for which it makes no payments, it will use these free waste disposal services as an input into the production process. A profit-maximizing steel firm will use the atmosphere to the point where the value of the marginal product equals its zero price. This is shown as point X_0 in Figure 6.2. The firm will use relatively too much of the unpriced input and relatively too little of the other, priced inputs.

Another way of seeing this is to examine a production isoquant showing combinations of a priced input, X_1, and the unpriced atmospheric input, X_2, that yield a given amount of steel, as shown in Figure 6.4. If both inputs were priced, the lowest cost combination of X_1 and X_2 would be a point like W, where the marginal rate of transformation equals the slope of the *isocost* line, which is $-P_1/P_2$.[10] Since X_2 is unpriced, $-P_1/P_2$ is infinite and the isocost line is vertical. The firm will use the free disposal service of atmospheric emissions up to the point where more emissions do not allow it to reduce its inputs of X_1. This occurs at point Z.

The firm will not emit an infinite amount of pollution into the air just because doing so is free. Emissions do not produce any revenue; they just allow a firm to reduce other costs up to a point. A firm will set its emissions at the point where the value of additional atmospheric waste disposal is zero. Past that point, increasing emissions would take deliberate effort and would increase the firm's costs rather than reduce them.

---

[10]The isocost line is defined as the combinations of X_1 and X_2 along which $P_1X_1 + P_2X_2$ is the same.

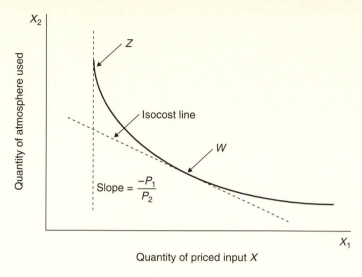

Figure 6.4   Production Isoquants and Relative Prices Inputs

The aggregate gain in welfare that could result from internalizing this externality has been shown in Figures 6.1 and 6.2. Because atmospheric disposal is unpriced, the firm will emit X_0 instead of X^*, the amount where the marginal value of atmospheric waste disposal just equals its marginal social cost. In Figure 6.2, the value to the firm of the additional waste disposal is the area under the demand curve between X^* and X_0: AX^*X_0, or G. The cost of this additional pollution is the area under the MSC curve between X^* and X_0: AX^*X_0B, or $G + H$. Therefore, finding a way to internalize atmospheric waste disposal and reducing emissions to X^* would have a net benefit of H. The trick is to determine whether there are ways of achieving this gain that cost less than H. If there are, internalizing the externality will improve economic efficiency; if there are not, then the "optimal" level of pollution will have been achieved.

When a firm's production process has external benefits, it is equivalent to the firm's receiving a price of zero for one of a set of joint products. The firm will produce too little of the joint product with a zero price. Owners of a commercial forest may produce many goods besides timber. The forest may filter water, clean the air, and provide recreational opportunities. If the only product the forest owners are paid for is timber, they will not consider the value of these other products when they make decisions. A firm will not necessarily produce none of the unpriced good. It will produce at the point where producing either more or less would increase its costs, that is, the output where the marginal cost of the unpriced good (holding other outputs constant) is zero. This is shown in Figure 6.5, where the efficient output is Y^* and the actual output is Y_0.

Figure 6.5 also shows the potential gain from internalizing the supply of this unpriced output. The value of the additional output is the area under the demand

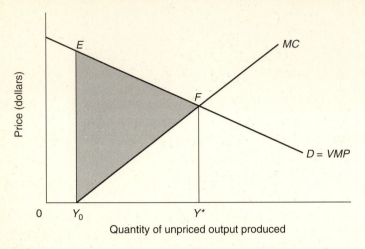

Figure 6.5　Gains from Internalization of an Unpriced Output

curve between Y_0 and Y^*, $Y_0 E F Y^*$, while the cost of the additional output is the area under the marginal cost curve, $Y_0 Y^* F$. The net gain from internalization is the difference, $E Y_0 F$.

Externalities and a Firm's Supply Function

The supply curve of a profit-maximizing firm is the upward-sloping portion of its marginal cost curve. When a firm's production process creates external costs or benefits, the firm will base its supply decision on the costs that it pays, not on the social opportunity cost of its output. The marginal cost paid by the firm is called its *marginal private cost* to distinguish it from marginal social cost.

When a firm's production process has external costs but no external benefits, marginal private cost will be greater than marginal social cost. One reason for this is obvious: the firm is not paying some of the costs of its production. Marginal cost is defined as the change in input cost with a change in output:

$$MC = \frac{\Delta TC}{\Delta Y} = \frac{\sum_{i=1}^{n} P_i \Delta X_i}{\Delta Y} \tag{6.1}$$

where $X_1, \ldots, X_n$ are the inputs used in producing the output Y. If X_n is an unpriced input such as atmospheric waste disposal, it will be left out of marginal private cost:

$$MPC = \frac{\Delta TPC}{\Delta Y} = \frac{\sum_{i=1}^{n-1} P_i \Delta X_i}{\Delta Y} \tag{6.2}$$

We have just seen that externalities in production will distort a firm's input choices. Thus the input quantities X_i in Equation 6.2 are not the socially optimal quantities X_i^*. Marginal social cost, as defined by the production possibilities frontier, is

$$MSC^* = \frac{\Delta TSC}{\Delta Y} = \frac{\sum_{i=1}^{n} \pi_i \Delta X_i^*}{\Delta Y} \qquad (6.3)$$

where each π_i is the marginal social costs of the ith input. However, with the firm making nonoptimal input choices, the cost actually paid by society is

$$MSC' = \frac{\sum_{i=1}^{n} \pi_i \Delta \overline{X}_i}{\Delta Y} \qquad (6.4)$$

where the $\overline{X}_i$ are the firm's actual inputs. Usually, $MSC' > MSC^*$, but this is not always the case. It is *always* true that the total cost of any given output is greater with nonoptimal inputs, but the cost of some increments of output may be lower. Suppose that contaminated water discharged from an industrial plant damages a fishery. MSC^* reflects the damage to the fishery that would occur with an optimal water treatment system. This damage may not be zero, but it will be lower than the damage with untreated effluent. MSC' reflects the damage to the fishery with untreated effluent. Now suppose that at some pollution level, the fishery is wiped out. Increases in production and pollution beyond this point will have no additional costs on the fishery. However, with optimal water treatment, there would still be a fishery to damage, and MSC^* would be greater than MSC'.

The result of these differences between MPC and MSC is that a firm whose production process has external costs will supply more than the optimal amount of its output at every price. This is shown in Figure 6.6. Q_0 is the quantity the firm supplies at the market price P. Q^* is the optimal quantity at that price, and Q is the quantity where marginal social cost with nonoptimal inputs equals the price.

Figure 6.6 also shows the potential gains from correcting the firm's supply decision. Reducing output from Q_0 to Q^* will reduce the value of output supplied by the area Q^*adQ_0 while reducing costs by Q^*bfQ_0. Thus there is a net gain of the shaded area *abfd* from reducing output. If we can correct the firm's input mix at the same time, there will be an additional welfare gain of shaded area *hgba*.

If a firm's production process has external benefits, similar distortions occur. Marginal private cost will be greater than marginal social cost because the firm does not take the value of the unpriced joint product into account. Marginal social cost will be greater than is technically possible because the firm produces too little of the unpriced joint product at each level of output of its primary product.

Externalities and the Market Supply Curve

The market supply curve is the horizontal summation of individual firm's marginal cost curves. At each price, it shows the sum of quantities supplied by all firms in the industry. When all the firms in the industry have the same production process

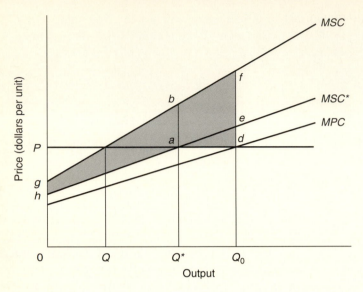

Figure 6.6 Supply of a Good in the Presence of External Costs

with the same external costs or benefits, the industry supply curve will reflect marginal private cost rather than marginal social cost in exactly the same way as the supply curves for the individual firms.

When firms have different production processes with different side effects, there can be another distortion of the industry supply curve. Because each firm makes its supply decision on the basis of its marginal private cost rather than marginal social cost, production is likely to take place at the wrong mix of plants. Figure 6.7 shows how this occurs. Plant 1 in panel (a) causes positive externali-

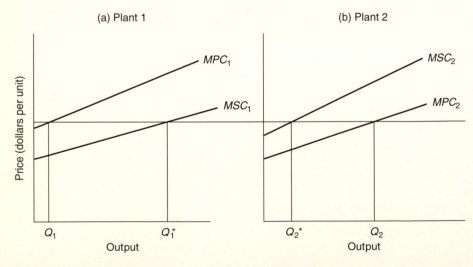

Figure 6.7 Externalities and the Production Mix at Plants

ties but is privately more expensive, while plant 2 in panel (b) causes negative externalities. The optimal output from each plant is where marginal social costs equal price—at Q_1^* and Q_2^*. The actual output will be where marginal private costs equals price, Q_1 and Q_2. The plant causing external costs produces too much, and the plant causing external benefits produces too little. Even if both plants cause external costs, the division of production between them will be inefficient if the marginal external costs are different. Too much will be produced at the plant with the higher marginal external costs, and too little will be produced at the plant with the lower marginal external cost.

Externalities and Social Production Possibilities

Most of the time, economists assume that when more of a given input is used in the production process, eventually the marginal product of that input will begin to decrease, holding constant the supply of other inputs. When applied to a single production process, holding constant the quantity of other inputs, this is termed *diminishing marginal productivity*.[11] When it is applied to an economy as a whole, it is referred to as the *convexity* of the production possibilities frontier or production set. This simply means that as more and more of society's resources are devoted to the production of any one good, the additional production of that good that is made possible by taking resources away from the production of other goods declines. This is normally true because most productive resources are specialized. If, for example, the economy were to produce nothing but wheat, there would be many resources being used in wheat production that made little or no contribution. This might include electrical engineers, hydroelectric dams, and transmission lines. Using some of these resources to produce additional electricity would likely cause little or no loss in the production of wheat but would result in large increases in electricity production. A further increase in electricity production would require the use of some resources that were slightly less specialized, and each additional kilowatt-hour would require giving up more and more wheat production. This would continue until, when society produced mostly electricity and little wheat, most of the resources used in wheat production would be highly specialized to wheat production and not at all useful for producing electricity.

This is shown graphically in Figure 6.8. The outer curve shows the combinations of wheat and electricity that could be produced if there were no externalities. At point W, only wheat is produced. At point E, only electricity is produced. The curve is very flat at W, showing that increasing electricity production requires only a small sacrifice of wheat. Moving from W through C toward E, the slope becomes steeper, until at point E the very steep slope shows that giving up the last bit of wheat production gains little electricity.

---

[11]Diminishing marginal productivity is sometimes confused with *decreasing returns to scale*. Returns to scale refer to changing the scale of the entire production process, using, say, twice as much of all inputs, and determining the change in output.

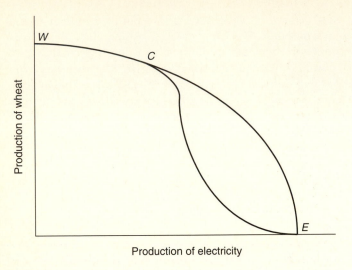

Figure 6.8   Nonconvexities and Externalities

The inner curve shows the effects that the external costs of the power plant's emissions impose on wheat production. If no electricity is produced, wheat production is unaffected. Therefore, point *W* must lie on both curves. Increasing electricity production affects wheat production in two ways. First, it requires taking some resources out of wheat production so that they can be used to produce electricity. Second, the side effects of electricity production reduce the productivity of the resources used to produce wheat. If only small amounts of electricity are produced, the technologies used will impose only small external costs on wheat production. This is shown as the inner curve from point *W* to point *C*. As long as the external costs are small, the curve reflecting external costs will be inside the curve with no externalities, but it will still become steeper as more electricity is produced.

As long as we are in this region of the production frontier, equating the marginal benefits of pollution controls with marginal costs of those controls will lead to a maximum of net social benefits. However, suppose that increasing electricity production beyond point *C* requires the use of technologies that devastate wheat production. The pollution from a small increase in electricity production beyond point *C* causes a large decrease in wheat production, and the curve suddenly becomes very steep. Further increases in electricity production create even more pollution and further devastate wheat production. Eventually, however, the *total* damage begins to fall. When then is no longer any wheat production, there can be no damage to the crop, and point *E* must lie on both curves. The section of the curve from point *C* to point *E* therefore becomes flatter, rather than steeper, as electricity production is increased. The gain in electricity production from each ton of wheat given up is increasing in this region. This is because the pollution has reduced wheat production so much that taking more resources out of wheat production has little effect on total wheat production. As a result, the production possibilities frontier becomes concave, and it will appear that the marginal productivity of resources devoted to electricity production is increasing rather than decreasing. The problem with nonconvexities is that traditional policies can lead to inferior solutions where *too little* of the offending good is produced.

The problem of nonconvexities can also be seen in the context of the Coase theorem, which implies that bargaining will eliminate all externalities if transactions costs are zero. Suppose that the initial level of pollution is greater than the level that eliminates wheat production entirely. At this point, eliminating a unit of pollution has no effect on wheat production. Thus if the electricity generator has a right to pollute, and if bargaining is just over marginal units, the wheat farmer will not offer any positive bribe to reduce pollution. But if the nonconvexity did not exist, the farmer could offer a bribe to reduce the electricity generator's pollution, as long as the value of the gain in wheat production was less than the cost of controlling that pollution. From a policy standpoint, the nonconvexity does not mean that it is optimal to have pollution levels so high that wheat production is eliminated. Instead, it means that bargaining must consider reducing pollution in large blocks rather than by marginal amounts. This is a counterintuitive result that we shall explore further in the next chapter, when we discuss alternative policy instruments to address externalities.

Externalities and Consumers' Choices

When consumers buy a good whose production has external costs or benefits, the market price they pay will equal the marginal private cost of production (assuming that it is supplied by a competitive industry). If there are external costs of production, this price will be less than the marginal social cost, and consumers will buy more than they would if the price equaled marginal social cost. As a result, consumers must be consuming less than optimal amounts of some other goods because the external costs of production must show up either in higher costs for other market goods or in lower quantities of nonmarket goods like environmental quality.

Figure 6.9 shows this distortion of consumer choices. Y^* is the efficient level of consumption, and Y_0 is the market level. The figure also shows the gains from

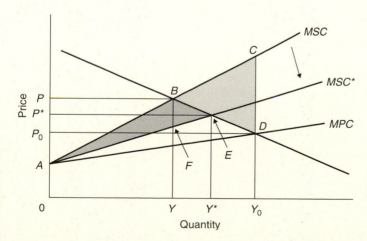

Figure 6.9   Consumer Choice in the Presence of External Costs

internalizing the externality. There are two parts to this gain. There is a gain from correcting the pricing distortion in the final good market, and there is a gain from correcting the input mix and reducing the social cost of the good. Raising the price to reflect the internal and external costs of incremental production *without* correcting the input mix would give new equilibrium price and quantity of P and Y, corresponding to point B. The net gain to society would be the difference between the reduction in total social costs, $YBCY_0$, and the total loss of product value to consumers, $YBDY_0$, which just equals the shaded area BCD.

If the input mix were corrected, the total social cost of producing any level of output would be reduced and would reduce the marginal social cost. This is shown as the downward shift in the marginal social curve from MSC to MSC^*. Both corrections would lead to the optimal price and quantity combination of P^* and Y^*. Consumers would value the gain in consumption by the area under the demand curve between Y and Y^*, $YBEY^*$, while the cost of the additional consumption would be the area under MSC^* between Y and Y^*, $YFEY^*$. Total social cost would be reduced by the area between MSC and MSC^* to the left of Y. This gives a net gain from correcting the input mix equal to the darker shaded area ABE.

When production of a good has external benefits, consumers will generally consume too little of the good because the price is greater than the marginal social cost. However, total social cost will still be greater than total private cost. Again, there will be two potential gains from correcting the externality: a net gain from increasing consumption of the output to the optimal level and a gain from reducing the total social cost, this time by increasing the output of the desirable side effect.

Consumers can also experience external costs and benefits directly. When this occurs, there is a good (or bad) that affects an individual's utility but over which the person has no influence. The consumer does not determine the quantity of the good or bad directly and does not have a contractual relationship with the party who does determine the quantity. The good is in fixed supply, and since the good is being supplied as a side effect of some other activity, the supply is fixed at the quantity that minimizes costs for the party creating the side effect. This can be visualized as the point where the supply price is zero. Someone who would be willing to pay to obtain more experiences an external benefit, and someone who would be willing to pay to have less experiences an external cost.

Figure 6.10 illustrates the case of an external benefit, and Figure 6.11 shows the case of an external cost. In both cases, the quantity of the side effect supplied is Q_0. In Figure 6.10, consumers are willing to pay to obtain more of the good, as is shown by the demand curve D_B. Q_B^* is the efficient level of output. Increasing output from Q_0 to Q_B^* would increase costs by $Q_0Q_B^*a$, while the value of the additional output is $Q_0Q_B^*ab$. The net gain from finding a way to change this side effect into an intentionally supplied good and inducing the optimal quantity is the shaded area Q_0ab.

In Figure 6.11, consumers are willing to pay to have less of the good, as is shown by the upward sloping "demand" curve D_C. This curve shows consumers' willingness to pay to avoid a bad they would rather have less of, in contrast to a true demand curve, which shows willingness to pay for a good consumers want. The efficient level of this bad is Q_C^*. Reducing output from Q_0 to Q_C^* will cost $Q_C^*Q_0d$.

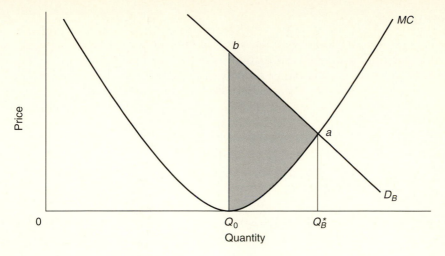

Figure 6.10   Willingness to Pay for a "Good"

The value of that reduction to consumers is $Q_C^* Q_0 bd$. The net gain from finding a way to reduce output to the optimal level is the shaded area $Q_0 bd$.

Consumers can also cause external costs and benefits directly through their consumption activities rather than indirectly through the goods they buy. Their choices between consumer goods are distorted by such externalities in exactly the same way that firms' input choices are distorted.

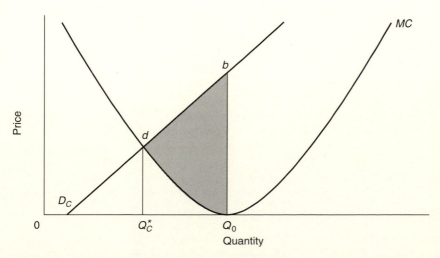

Figure 6.11   Willingness to Pay to Avoid a "Bad"

Summary

This section has shown the ways that externalities reduce economic efficiency and the *potential* gains from correcting them. All externalities lead to distortions of consumer choices, either directly because the externality affects consumers directly or indirectly because externalities in production cause prices to diverge from marginal social cost. Externalities originating in production also distort firms' input choices and the allocation of production between plants. This causes the actual social cost of production to be higher than is technically necessary.

When we consider policies to correct externalities in the next chapter, it will be important to keep in mind all of the distortions that externalities can cause. Few policies address them all, and different policies may address different sets of distortions. Lastly, it will be important to consider the costs associated with correcting externalities, since no policies will be costless.

RELATED PHENOMENA: OPEN ACCESS AND PUBLIC GOODS

When there is an externality, there is *nonexclusive* use of an economic resource. One party's use of a resource affects other parties, with the impact not being mediated by a market. Two or more parties are trying to make allocation decisions about the same resource simultaneously with no mechanism to coordinate those decisions. This causes problems. Exactly what kinds of problems it causes depends on how different parties' uses interact. Specifically, it depends on whether that use is *rivalrous* or *nonrivalrous*.

Rivalrous resource use is just what it sounds like: two or more people want to use the same resource, but they cannot. Two people can share an apple only if each of them eats part and lets the other eat part. Nonrivalrous use occurs when two people can share the same resource, when both of them can use it without either of them depleting the amount available to the other. Two people, or 2 billion people, can look at the Milky Way in the night sky at the same time. It looks the same to me no matter how few or how many other people are looking up at it. The Milky Way does not become dimmer or less beautiful when other people look at it.

Nonexclusive nonrivalrous use defines a *public good*. With nonexclusive but rivalrous use, we have what is known in the natural resource literature as *open access*. In both cases, we have an externality and the resulting inefficiency. However, the inefficiency occurs differently in the two cases, and the two problems require different kinds of solutions.

Open Access: Nonexclusive Rivalrous Use

A simple example will serve to introduce the problems resulting from open access. Table 6.1 shows the kind of relationship often found between number of fishing boats and the fish catch in a typical fishery. The number of fish caught per boat

TABLE 6.1 NUMBER OF FISHING BOATS AND CATCH OF FISH

Number of Fishing Boats	Catch per Boat per Season (pounds)	Total Catch per Season (millions of pounds)	Marginal Catch per Season per 100 Boats (millions of pounds)
100	22,000	2.2	2.2
200	20,000	4.0	1.8
300	16,000	4.8	0.8
400	12,750	6.1	0.3
500	10,600	6.3	0.2
600	8,050	4.8	−0.4

declines as the number of boats increases, and the maximum total catch occurs with around 500 boats.

Suppose that the costs, including a normal rate of return on capital, of running a fishing boat amount to about $16,500 per season. Table 6.2 shows the profits of the boats on the assumption that the price declines by 3 percent for each 10 percent increase in total catch and that the price with only 100 boats is $2.50 per pound. With no restrictions on entry or on the size of catch per boat—that is, with no property rights in the fishery or the fish—boats will enter as long as they cover their opportunity cost. This cost will consist of the cost of labor and fuel and the lost opportunity to use the boat in another use. Thus the short-run equilibrium size of the fleet will be 600 boats. No boat will be making any economic profit; each will be breaking even. Yet the fleet level that maximizes total net revenues and total profit is only 200 boats.

This simplified example does not account for increases in costs as fishermen attempt to capture rents with equipment improvements, by sailing in bad weather, or by fishing longer each day. With a larger number of boats, the size of the catch and of the stock of fish may be declining each year. The species could even be driven to extinction if the equilibrium catch rate stays above the net reproductive rate as the stocks decline.

TABLE 6.2 FISHERY COSTS AND REVENUES

Number of Fishing Boats	Cost per Boat Per Season (Opportunity Cost) (dollars)	Gross Revenues per Boat per Season (dollars)	Net Revenues per Boat (dollars)	Total Fleet Net Revenues (millions of dollars)
100	$16,500	$55,000	$38,500	3.85
200	$16,500	41,800	25,300	6.06
300	$16,500	32,160	15,660	4.70
400	$16,500	25,245	8,745	3.50
500	$16,500	20,776	4,276	2.14
600	$16,500	16,500	0	0

The absence of institutions that govern property rights results in overuse of resources for two reasons. First, individual users of the resource are unable to prevent others from using any of the resource that they leave unused. Individual users are therefore unable to capture any potential gains from saving resources for future use. Therefore, each user has an incentive to push his or her resource use to the point where the marginal value of resource use equals marginal cost, *ignoring user cost and any costs to other users.*[12] Second, with no restrictions on who may use a resource, potential users have an incentive to enter as long as there are any rents that can be earned by using the resource. This results in too many users each using the resource too intensively. A fisherman who forgoes taking a fish today may lose that fish to another fisherman tomorrow. A fisherman who decides to take a fish today imposes a cost on other fisherman because they must search harder for a fish tomorrow. The individual incentive to refrain from fishing to conserve the stock is very small in the absence of a mechanism to ensure that all refrain from fishing. Everyone has an incentive to fish as long as there is money to be made in the effort. The result has often been depletion of fisheries.[13]

Governments have tried many types of regulations to prevent overfishing.[14] Most have failed because they have failed to address the causes of overfishing. Many types of fishery regulations have relied on limiting one or more inputs, such as length of season, size of nets, or size of boats. When there is a shorter season, fishermen respond by fishing for longer hours with bigger boats and bigger gear. When the size of gear is limited, more boats appear. When the type of gear is limited, fishermen respond with improved technology. None of these get at the root of the problem—the incentive for too many boats to enter the industry and for each to catch too much fish. Attacking the root of the problem requires some kind of property rights. Ideally, there should be rights to catch a limited number of fish, but limitations on the right to fish would also help.

Figure 6.12 compares the marginal cost of fishing when fishermen have property rights in the fishery and when they do not. Where there are no property rights in the fishery, the costs will consist of such things as manpower, the cost of running a fishing vessel, and wear and tear on the nets. This will produce an equilibrium harvest rate of H_1. Where there are property rights in the fishery, there are the additional costs that a fish taken today will not be available to catch tomorrow or to reproduce and maintain or increase stocks for future fishing.

Open access is often erroneously called *common property.* Open access is an *absence* of property rights, whereas common property is an institution whereby a resource is owned in common by a well-defined group and each member of the group has well-defined rights to use the resource. Garrett Hardin, in his famous article "The Tragedy of the Commons" (1968), presents the same type of scenario

---

[12]The concept of *user cost* is developed formally in Chapter 15.
[13]The classic article that developed the analytics of common-property resources is Gordon (1954).
[14]For some examples, see Dept. of Fisheries and Oceans (1993a, 1993b). See also McEvoy (1986).

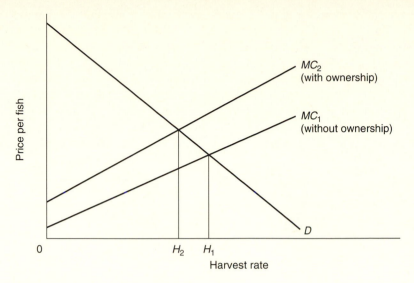

Figure 6.12   Effects of Ownership on Harvest Rates

as we presented in the box for a fishery using the example of a "commons," or common pasture, of a medieval European village. Although he makes an important point, his example is inaccurate historically. In fact, the medieval commons was *not* an open-access resource. Its use was limited to certain residents of the village who used it subject to historical rules. (This is the origin of the term *commoner*.) Both outsiders and village residents who did not have rights to the commons were excluded, and each commoner had well-specified rights in the commons, such as the right to graze a defined number of livestock. In essence, common-property resources are exclusive but also nonrivalrous.

Stevenson (1991) has studied grazing commons as they exist today in Switzerland and has argued that they may be efficient, or at least not very inefficient. These commons limit entry to the resource and limit each user's use, but they do not remove the incentive for each user to try to use the resource first before others do. However, in this case, common property reduces the need for fencing and allows one or a few employees to watch cattle owned by many farmers.

Any number of institutional arrangements could be, and have been, devised to correct open-access problems. Stevenson (1991) distinguishes three such arrangements: sole ownership, common property, and limited-user open access. Table 6.3

TABLE 6.3   COMPARISONS OF OWNERSHIP STRUCTURES

Type of Limitation	Sole Owner	Corporate Ownership	Common Property	Open Access Limited User	Open Access Unlimited User
Access limitation	One person	Corporation only	Group members only	Group members only	Anyone
Use limitation	Use limited by owner's decision	Use limited by management's decision	Use limited by rules	Use unlimited	Use unlimited

SHELL GAME: OYSTERS IN CHESAPEAKE BAY

In the 1890s, roughly 20 million bushels of oysters were harvested from the waters of Chesapeake Bay each year. By 1992, the harvest had fallen to 168,000 bushels, less than 1 percent of the harvest a century earlier. Chesapeake Bay oysters have fallen victim to the ravages of three separate assaults. First, increasing pollution levels from industrial and farm runoff, which is funneled into the bay by several rivers, including the Potomac, the James, and the Susquehanna, have wrecked spawning grounds. This loss of spawning grounds has been compounded by locating heavy industries and numerous housing developments along the shores of the bay. Second, two small parasites new to the bay, called *dermo* and *MSX,* have been killing off the oysters. The third is the oldest assault of all: greed. Overharvesting has devastated oyster stocks. As a result, beginning in the early 1990s, the states of Virginia and Maryland significantly curtailed the length of the harvesting season and restricted total harvests. Virginia, for example, limited the 1993 harvest to just 6,000 bushels.

It is not clear whether the oyster fishery will ever recover, but there are some glimmers of hope. Like the oysters, stocks of striped bass living in the bay were also depleted severely. But owing to stringent harvest limits, their numbers have begun to recover. Pollution is also slowly being cleaned up through tighter restrictions on polluted runoff. And scientists are gaining a better understanding of the parasites.

The oyster fishery in Chesapeake Bay has attracted much attention from economists and policymakers. Unlike many other fisheries, especially ocean fisheries for tuna and mackerel, establishing private property rights for oysters is feasible because oysters don't move. When they are young, oysters settle onto the bottom of the bay on hard, clean surfaces, such as old oyster shells. There they remain for about three years, which is the time it takes for them to reach the minimum harvest size in the bay. By establishing property rights to the beds where the oysters settle, property owners have an incentive to manage their "crops" carefully. Private owners also improve production in the beds by using old oyster shells and "seeding" the areas with oyster larvae. The success of the privately managed beds has become a textbook case for the establishment of private property rights (Santopietro and Shabman 1992).

Things are not quite so simple in Chesapeake Bay, however. There private property rights can be established only in locations that are not natural oyster beds. The natural beds are reserved as public oyster grounds and are managed by the states that border the bay. Since the 1950s, the state-owned oyster beds have been carefully controlled. Maryland and Virginia, like private owners, seed the public beds and improve them with old oyster shells. These states have undertaken such activities in part to preserve a way of life. Santopietro and Shabman question whether or not it is worthwhile to establish private property in these beds. They point out that if all of the oyster beds were converted to private property, there would be two effects: oyster harvesters (called *watermen*) would become farm production managers instead of traditional fishermen, and capital would be substituted for labor as newer harvest technologies were introduced. This would result in higher unemployment rates for the watermen and effectively eradicate a "traditional" industry, its associated lifestyles, and many small fishing villages that have existed for two centuries.

Santopietro and Shabman classify all of these effects of privatization under the rubric of economic efficiency. They ask whether a standard benefit-cost welfare test could be satisfied if all of the public oyster beds were privatized.* And they wonder whether the standard definitions of economic efficiency ignore the value of the *political* consensus established to manage this particular fishery. The types of lifestyle and cultural "benefits" addressed by Santopietro and Shabman are not commonly considered in a benefit-cost analysis but may be no less legitimate for consideration, depending on society's goals.

Of course, the value of a "traditional" lifestyle is relative and raises questions of society's willingness to pay to preserve such lifestyles. No doubt the arrival of the watermen two centuries past affected the "traditional" lifestyles of Native Americans, who may have fished the waters of Chesapeake Bay for thousands of years. Technological change almost always imposes costs and alters lifestyles. Automobiles and computers, for example, have profoundly affected the lifestyles of millions of people. For some of them, such as past employees in the carriage and slide rule industries, that change has exacted a cost. But for many others it has provided great benefit.

Ultimately, though overharvesting can be managed under public ownership, the problems of other forms of pollution may not be so easily controlled. These problems can also arise because of a lack of property rights. However, such problems are often far more difficult to correct through the establishment of property rights than merely marking off boundaries of oyster beds.

*Recall from Chapter 3 that these tests are the Kaldor-Hicks or potential Pareto compensation rules.

compares these three arrangements with corporate ownership and with pure open access with unlimited users.

Public Goods: Nonexclusive Nonrivalrous Use

With a public good, one person's use does not interfere with another person's use, and we do not have the kind of conflict we see with open-access resources. Instead, the problem arises in reaching agreement on how to provide the good that all consume. Several people can watch the same TV show without interfering with one another. However, they must agree on what show to watch. With nonrivalrous use of a public good, people do not just consume a good simultaneously; they consume the *same* good. People watching a movie or listening to a lecture consume the same good. Everyone in a small enough area experiences the same air quality, and everyone in a country gets the same national defense. Improving air quality for me also improves it for you. Improving national defense for you also improves it for me.

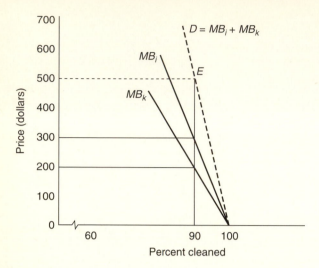

Figure 6.13   Total Demand for Cleaner Air

When consumption is rivalrous, the total amount consumed is the sum of the amounts consumed by each individual. The market demand curve is therefore the horizontal summation of individual demand curves. It tells the sum of the quantities demanded at each price. The demand curve for a nonrivalrous good is found by summing individuals' demands vertically, rather than horizontally. It shows the total amount that all consumers together would pay to have each quantity supplied. This is shown in Figure 6.13. The curves MB_i and MB_k are individual demand curves for air quality for two people; let's call them Ingrid and Karen. For convenience, we will say that completely unpolluted air is 100 percent clean air. Air that is just barely tolerable for most people is 60 percent clean. Suppose that Ingrid would be willing to pay $300 for 90 percent clean air and Karen would be willing to pay $200. If the air is 90 percent clean, both get 90 percent clean air. The total amount the two together would be willing to pay for 90 percent clean air is $500.

As with a private good, efficiency requires that the quantity of the good be supplied (and consumed) where the marginal social value of the good equals the marginal social cost. This is the point at which the sum of individual willingness to pay equals the marginal social cost. This is shown in Figure 6.14, where point E is the efficient outcome.[15]

Reaching this efficient solution is difficult for public goods, for many reasons. One is the free-rider problem. With a pure public good, use is nonrivalrous and exclusion is expensive or impossible. Everyone consumes whatever amount of the good is provided, including people who do not help pay for it. This is a strong incentive for people to avoid paying for public goods. It also creates very high con-

---

[15] Charging Ingrid $300 and Karen $200 for 90 percent clean air is an example of Lindahl prices or Lindahl taxes (Lindahl 1958).

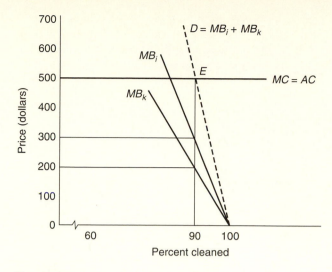

Figure 6.14   Market Demand for Clean Air

tracting costs because with most mechanisms for paying for public goods, people have an incentive to misrepresent their willingness to pay. If individuals think that the amount of the good provided, but not what they pay individually, depends on the values they express to decision makers, people will tend to overstate those values. Conversely, if individuals think that the values they express to decision makers will affect what they will pay but not the amount provided, they will tend to understate their values.

Many externalities that pose significant environmental policy issues involve goods that have both nonrivalrous and rivalrous uses. For example, use of air for breathing and for viewing scenery is nonrivalrous, but use of air for waste disposal is generally rivalrous with other uses. The rivalrous use, waste disposal, determines the quantity or, in this case, quality available for nonrivalrous uses. The efficient level of air quality is the level where the marginal value of air for waste disposal (which equals the marginal cost of controlling emissions) equals the sum of marginal willingness to pay for cleaner air.

The relationship among ownership, exclusivity, and nonrivalry can be considered in the context of our example of Lake Washington. Imagine a situation in which there were many lakes in an area, all of which were privately owned, and all the conditions for the Coase theorem were satisfied. As a result, all users of the lakes would be charged for their use, and the optimal mix of activities would result. For this to work, the owners of the lake would need to be able to keep nonpayers (free riders) from using the lake, or at least those nonpayers who interfered with others' use. In the case of Lake Washington, however, monitoring the different uses of the lake would be difficult. The power to require all users around the lake to hook up to a sewage service seems crucial. Thus the solution proposed involved a new government entity.

Another important class of public policy problems arises from *congestible public goods.* These goods are nonrivalrous, but only up to the point where congestion begins. Beyond this point, each additional user contributes to greater congestion for the other users. Beaches, parks, and highways are examples of congestible public goods.

EXTERNALITIES, ENVIRONMENTAL PROBLEMS, AND ENVIRONMENTAL POLICY

In the next chapter, we will examine policies to correct externalities in detail. We will close this chapter with some questions that should be answered before rushing to propose any particular type of policy.

Is There an Externality?

The first step to take before rushing to correct an externality is to be certain that there really is an externality. An externality is an impact without a contract. The fact that there is an impact does not indicate that there is an externality or any kind of problem. If the impact is already covered by an agreement between the affected parties, there is no externality. Even if there is no explicit agreement, there may be an implicit agreement. This will be the case if the potential buyer's willingness to pay is less than the potential seller's willingness to sell. The fact that I do not like the way my neighbors are using their property does not necessarily mean that there is an externality. It may just mean that I am not bothered enough by their land use to pay their price for changing it.

When few parties are involved and property rights are well defined, externalities will be rare. (This is just the Coase theorem.) An impact is more likely to be an externality when large numbers of people are affected or the impact has the characteristics of a public good.

In short, many environmental problems involve externalities, but not all do. Identifying whether a problem is an externality or some other type of problem is the first step toward developing an appropriate solution.

Why Is There an Externality?

Policies to correct externalities can target the cause of the externality or its effects. Which is more appropriate depends on why the externality exists. Generally, an externality exists because property rights are ill-defined or because transactions costs are prohibitive. If property rights do not exist or are ill-defined, is it because defining property rights is technically infeasible, or are there other reasons? If property rights could be defined appropriately but are not, why have they not been? Is it because there never has been a reason to define property rights in the past? Is it because property rights once were well defined, given conditions that existed in the past, but technical or social conditions have changed? Is it because society has prohibited or discouraged certain types of transactions for reasons unrelated to economic efficiency? Or could it be that imperfectly defined property rights are the best that we can do and may even be better than perfectly defined pure private property if the costs of defining and enforcing property rights are high?

If the problem is that market transactions costs are greater than the potential gains from trade, is it because the gains from trade are trivial and no problem really exists, or is it because transactions costs are enormous? If the problem is high transactions costs, why are they high? Is it because a market is technically infeasible or because there are institutional barriers to a market's functioning? Or is the problem that the costs of setting up a market are high? In this case, the total gains from trade may exceed the total transactions costs, but the parties who take the initiative to start trading cannot hope to recoup their costs.

What Type of Policy Response Is Needed?

The best type of policy response depends on the type of problem. In some cases, the best response is to attack the cause of an externality. This will generally require institutional change. It may require defining, redefining, or clarifying property rights. It may require removing institutional barriers to a market solution. Or it may require taking steps to set up a market. In other cases, the best response is to attack the effects of an externality through nonmarket solutions. This may take the form of direct regulation. It may mean taxes, fees, or subsidies. It may also mean government supply of goods and services. In some cases, there will be no solution with benefits greater than its costs or even no solution at all. In those cases, the best response may be to do nothing.

CHAPTER SUMMARY

Externalities are effects that are not taken into account in the decision-making process because there is no market where the party causing an impact can make arrangements with the parties experiencing the impact. Thus externalities are impacts without contracts. Externalities may be technological or pecuniary, positive or negative. Important environmental externalities are often associated with open access to resources, that is, the absence of property rights. Other externalities involve public goods for which exclusion costs are high and for which consumption is nonrivalrous. Externalities point to the existence of a situation where public or private action *may* improve the situation. However, what type of action and whether any action is appropriate depend on the circumstances.

CHAPTER REVIEW

Economic Concepts and Tools

- Externalities are impacts without agreements. When one party's actions affect another's, and the parties have not agreed on the level of impacts allowed, an externality exists. An externality may make the affected party better or worse off.

- A technological externality affects the relation between inputs and outputs and reduces Kaldor-Hicks welfare. (These are sometimes called Pareto-relevant externalities.)
- An effect often called a pecuniary externality occurs when one party's actions change prices and these price changes affect other parties' welfare. Pecuniary externalities are not externalities as we have defined them and do not produce economic inefficiency.
- The Coase theorem states that when there are well-defined property rights in all goods and zero transactions costs, a competitive general equilibrium will be efficient and there will be no externalities. A corollary of the Coase theorem is that when an externality exists, either property rights are ill-defined or transactions costs are prohibitive.
- Externalities point to the relationship between economic efficiency and the way economic activity is organized. Compared with a zero-transactions-cost world,
   1. An externality can cause consumers to select a suboptimal mix of goods and services because the prices of consumer goods do not equal their marginal social costs.
   2. An externality can cause producers to use a suboptimal mix of inputs, using too much of inputs that are not priced or are priced below their marginal social costs or too little of inputs that are priced above their marginal social costs.
   3. An externality can cause output to be produced by a suboptimal mix of plants or firms, with too much produced by plants with external costs and too little produced by plants with external benefits.
- A strong negative externality can lead to nonconvexity of the production set. In these cases, economic efficiency may be achieved where the externality is eliminated by eliminating one of the conflicting activities.
- Externalities can exist because of ambiguous or nonexistent property rights, high transactions costs, or government actions that prevent internalization. Externalities are also closely tied to legal concepts, such as tort law.

Policy Issues

- The presence of externalities can result in economic inefficiency and welfare loss. Many, but not all, environmental "problems" are the result of externalities. Few environmental problems, however, can be defined solely as problems of economic inefficiency, for other issues will often be more important to policymakers and the public.
- The existence of an externality does not necessarily mean that a policy action is warranted. This is because externalities are usually defined against the standard of costless markets. In reality, correcting an externality will have costs, which must be compared to the gains from internalizing the externality.

DISCUSSION QUESTIONS

1. Suppose that a farmer who receives subsidized water to irrigate a subsidized crop suffers environmental damages from a nearby electric generating plant that emits sulfur dioxide. Is there an externality present? If so, how should society internalize the externality? How would you evaluate graphically the change in economic efficiency arising from the sulfur dioxide? Would consumers be better off with the generating plant? Why or why not?
2. Suppose that nonconvexities in production between electricity producers and nearby farmers are observed. What is the most efficient solution that can be obtained?
3. How could we measure exclusion costs in practice?
4. How would you evaluate the solutions developed by the states of Maryland and Virginia for increasing the Chesapeake Bay oyster population? Do you believe that this solution was based solely on economic efficiency criterion?
5. If a government seeks to limit fishing licenses, what is the most efficient way of allocating them? How should considerations of efficiency and equity be weighed? What do you think about proposals to issue quotas to fishermen regulating the amount of fish they may catch? What would be your position if you were a fisherman?
6. Is a classroom discussion an example of a nonrivalrous good? Why or why not? What about seeing a movie inside a movie theater?

REFERENCES

Allen, D. 1991. "What Are Transactions Costs?" *Research in Law and Economics* 14: 1–18.

Arrow, K. 1969. "The Organization of Economic Activity: Issues Pertinent to the Choice of Market Versus Nonmarket Allocation." In *The Analysis and Evaluation of Public Expenditure: The PPB System,* issued by the Joint Economic Committee of the U.S. Congress. Washington, D.C.: U.S. Government Printing Office.

Ault, D. E., and G. L. Rutman. 1989. "Land Scarcity, Economic Efficiency, and African Common Law." *Research in Law and Economics* 12: 33–54.

Baumol, W., and W. Oates. 1988. *The Theory of Environmental Policy.* New York: Cambridge University Press.

Coase, R. 1960. "The Problem of Social Cost." *Journal of Law and Economics* 3: 1–44.

Department of Fisheries and Oceans. 1993a. *Draft Report, Executive Summary: An Evaluation of Individual Quota Management in the Halibut Fishery.* Vancouver, B. C.: Fisheries Pacific Region.

———. 1993b. *Draft Report, Executive Summary: An Evaluation of Individual Quota Management in the Sablefish Fishery.* Vancouver, B.C.: Fisheries Pacific Region.

Gordon, H. 1954. "The Economic Theory of a Common Property Resource: The Fishery." *Journal of Political Economy* 62: 124–142.

Hardin, G. 1968. "The Tragedy of the Commons." *Science* 162: 1243–1248.

Lindahl, E. 1958. "Just Taxation: A Positive Solution." In *Classics in the Theory of Public Finance*, ed. R. Musgrave and A. Peacock. New York: Crowell-Collier.

Kelman, S. 1981. *What Price Incentives? Economists and the Environment.* Westport, Conn.: Auburn House.

Marshall, A. 1920. *Principles of Economics.* 8th ed. London: Macmillan.

McEvoy, A. 1986. *The Fisherman's Problem.* New York: Cambridge University Press.

Medema, S., and R. Zerbe. 1995. "Ronald Coase, the British Tradition, and the Future of the Economic Method." Working Paper 95-3, Graduate School of Public Affairs, University of Washington, Seattle.

Mishan, E. 1969. "The Relationship Between Joint Products, Collective Goods, and External Effects." *Journal of Political Economy* 77(2): 329–348.

Santopietro, G., and L. Shabman. 1992. "Can Privatization Be Inefficient? The Case of the Chesapeake Bay Oyster Fishery." *Journal of Economic Issues* 26(2): 407–419.

Stevenson, G. 1991. *Common Property Economics: A General Theory and Land Use Applications.* New York: Cambridge University Press.

Williamson, O. 1985. *The Economic Institutions of Capitalism.* New York: Free Press.

Zerbe, R. 1980. "The Problem of Social Cost in Retrospect." *Research in Law and Economics* 2: 83–102.

CHAPTER 7

POLICIES TO ADDRESS EFFICIENCY GOALS

Blowing Smoke? Policies to Control Sulfur Dioxide Emissions

Sulfur dioxide emissions have long been recognized as a principal cause of acidification, or "acid rain," as it is usually (and somewhat incorrectly) called.[1] In the United States, the main sources of sulfur dioxide are older electric generating plants that burn high-sulfur coal and oil. These plants are concentrated in the midwestern and eastern parts of the nation.

The first response to "control" emissions of sulfur dioxide at these plants was to construct tall emissions stacks, many of them hundreds of feet high. These tall stacks reduced atmospheric sulfur dioxide concentrations in the regions near the plants, as required under the original Clean Air Act regulations. However, by building the stacks so high, sulfur dioxide particles were dispersed in much larger downwind areas, primarily in the eastern United States and Canada. Not surprisingly, the increasing acidification of lakes, streams, and forests in these areas was met with disdain by those in the East and denial by those in the Midwest. It seemed that the generating-plant owners had simply transferred their pollution problem onto someone else, a classic externality situation.

Further amendments to the Clean Air Act imposed more stringent "command and control" regulations on new generating plants. Under these regulations, actual emissions from the plants were restricted by requiring specific pollution control technology requirements. Yet because of the "grandfathering" allowed under the

---

[1]We discuss the policy implications of acid rain in more detail in Chapter 21.

act, some of the most highly polluting plants were exempted from the regulations owing to economic "hardship."

The 1990 Clean Air Act Amendments significantly revised the previous regulations. First, the amendments imposed more stringent controls on the allowable emissions from plants in two phases. The dirtiest plants were required to clean up in phase 1, which began in 1995. Second, the amendments established a series of tradable emissions permits or allowances, each conferring the right to release one ton of sulfur dioxide annually into the atmosphere, and an overall limit on total allowable emissions nationwide. By the year 2000, when phase 2 is fully in effect, every power plant in the United States will have received an initial allowance of emissions permits. Under this approach, plant owners will be able to determine for themselves the cheapest and most flexible ways of reducing emissions. Plants that are able to reduce emissions cheaply will have excess allowances that they can sell. Plants facing the highest costs of controlling emissions, principally those burning high-sulfur coal, may find it cheaper to buy allowances rather than install expensive new scrubbing equipment.

Though the goal behind tradable emissions permits—control of pollution at the lowest possible cost—is straightforward, political and parochial interests have intruded. First, state regulatory commissions, which now regulate private electric utilities, can disregard the federal laws. Some state regulatory commissions determine how revenues from any allowance sales are treated and to whom allowances can be sold. In 1994, for example, New York State regulators decreed that allowances could be sold only to utilities downwind so as to ensure that air quality in New York State would not be affected adversely because of greater amounts of pollution emitted by upwind plants. In other states, especially those in the Midwest, regulators concerned about the health of their states' coal-mining industries and their associated jobs initially forced utilities in those states to use only locally produced high-sulfur coal.[2]

Still other threats to an efficient emissions trading market arise from the byzantine practices of utility regulation. Under these rules, utilities may be required to pass through revenues from selling allowances to consumers through lower rates. Unfortunately, while doing so allows a utility's customers to benefit, it reduces the utility's incentive to engage in such trades. Yet investments in costly scrubbing equipment can be treated as "prudent" investments, which the utility's ratepayers must repay through higher rates.[3]

It is possible that the meddling by state regulators and politicians, however well intentioned, may provide a clear case of how not to reduce pollution. Long-standing regulations, designed (rightly or wrongly) with other policy goals in mind such as creating jobs and reducing the threat of monopolistic behavior by utilities, are clashing with policies designed to promote efficient reductions in pollutant emissions. New policies to increase overall utility industry competition at the wholesale level are in place, in the form of the Energy Policy Act of 1992, and com-

---

[2]Federal courts have ruled that such restrictions are violations of interstate commerce.
[3]As the electric industry is restructured, generation is likely to be deregulated entirely.

petition at the retail level is being debated in many states. Depending on how it is implemented, such retail competition could have far-reaching consequences on the ease of attaining the Clean Air Act's goals.

INTRODUCTION

If you have read Chapter 6, you should have a good idea of what an externality is and why externalities are a problem. For policymakers, identifying whether they are dealing with an externality or some other type of problem is a critical (and sometimes overlooked) first step. The second step is knowing which tools and policies are available to correct the problem. Of course, whether a problem is *worth* correcting may depend on measuring the associated environmental costs and benefits, but we leave that issue to Chapter 11.[4] A variety of tools and policies have been used to address environmental externalities. In this chapter, we examine these tools from the standpoint of their impact on overall economic efficiency.

Common-Law Remedies

All policy tools designed to improve environmental quality are legal tools, in the sense that their operation depends on laws and regulations. These rules, including federal legislation such as the Clean Air Act and the Clean Water Act, are in the regulatory tradition of the law. In addition to such rules, there are tools associated with the *common law,* the law made by judges. These tools include private and public nuisance suits, as well as applications of what is called the *trespass doctrine.*

A *private nuisance* is an unreasonable interference with the use and the enjoyment of private land. For example, suppose that a suit is brought against a socially useful activity, such as a factory that has polluted a private lake. In that case, the factory owner's conduct must be "unreasonable" and cause "substantial" harm for a private nuisance to exist. A *public nuisance* is an unreasonable interference with the interest of the community or the general public. Normally a public nuisance is dealt with through actions taken by public authorities. As with a private nuisance, the offending action must be found "unreasonable." For both private and public nuisance actions, courts decide first whether or not a nuisance has occurred. They do this by engaging in a *balancing* process that weighs the harm caused by the action against the social utility of the defendant's conduct. In economic language, the courts perform a benefit-cost test.

Trespass suits, like nuisance suits, relate to interference with the land. *Trespass* involves interference with *exclusive possession* of land, whereas *nuisance* involves interference with a right to use and enjoy land. In the case of pollution, trespass would normally be invoked if the pollution caused substantial damage by accumulating on land (e.g., acidification of farmland because of sulfur dioxide emissions or polluted water that flows into a private lake).

---

[4]As we discussed at the end of Chapter 6, correcting an externality also depends on the cost of the corrective policy itself.

In addition to nuisance and trespass suits, courts may determine *strict liability* for damages. With strict liability, it is not necessary to show fault. In other words, actions may be reasonable yet still cause damage. This doctrine is sometimes applied to actions that are abnormally dangerous. In determining whether or not an action is unreasonably dangerous and therefore subject to strict liability, the courts balance the risks of the activity and the harm it causes against the utility of the activity.

The problem with common-law remedies is their high administrative cost. Nuisance and trespass actions are almost always applied to single individuals or firms. They are of little value to address large-scale environmental problems. Imagine if the millions of automobile owners in this country were sued by their neighbors (and sued their neighbors themselves) for polluting the air. The legal costs would be staggering, and there would be little likelihood of reaching any sort of efficient solution. Thus for larger-scale issues, approaches that are more parsimonious must be used if environmental problems are to be addressed successfully. Two other approaches—establishing property rights or markets and the use of regulatory solutions—are the subject of the next sections.

Establishing Property Rights and Markets

In some cases, establishing private property rights can mitigate environmental problems. Although at times it falls under the heading of regulatory remedies, establishing private property rights extends beyond government regulation.

Some government policies are designed to prevent the development of well-defined private property rights. For example, most societies no longer sanction slave trading, which allowed some human beings to claim property rights over others. Nor does our society allow parents to sell their children to childless couples. (But laws do allow surrogate mothers to "incubate" babies for other couples.)

Government policies can also establish private property rights where none had existed previously. Many formerly communist nations, for example, now allow their citizens the right to own land, where previously ownership was the exclusive privilege of the state. Establishing private property rights to land can prevent, at least in some cases, the problems associated with open access, such as those we discussed in Chapter 6. And as we discuss later in this chapter, the U.S. Clean Air Act created limited forms of property rights to the atmosphere by allowing polluters the right to emit certain quantities of those pollutants and to exchange those rights in a market.

Establishing property rights also allows other remedies to be applied. Common-law remedies, such as trespass and nuisance, cannot be applied if there are no established private property rights. Legally, I cannot be accused of hunting on your land if you don't own it. Some regulatory remedies can also be applied more effectively when private property rights exist. Regulatory restrictions on killing endangered species or destroying tropical rain forests can be enforced more effectively if specific owners, even common property owners, are granted exclusive use. In that way, the rewards of careful stewardship and management of resources accrue directly to the owners, providing a powerful incentive to avoid "exploitation" of resources.

In some cases, establishing a system of property rights may be infeasible. It is hard to imagine a system of enforceable private property rights to the air we breathe. Nor will the establishment of property rights always correct a given externality because the property rights established may not be relevant to the particular externality. For example, charging a toll on a crowded freeway may reduce traffic congestion, but it may not reduce air pollution emitted by those cars efficiently. Lastly, establishing private property rights will not work for pure public goods.

Regulatory Remedies

The last, and most common, category of remedies is regulatory remedies. In many cases, private remedies will be insufficient to control pollution and environmental damage. That is why a variety of regulatory tools and policies have been developed to address environmental externalities and achieve certain environmental goals and why, in this chapter, we examine these regulatory tools from the standpoint of their impact on overall economic efficiency.

We consider eight alternative regulatory policy instruments. These instruments can be grouped into two broad categories: market-enhancing mechanisms and market-substituting mechanisms. Table 7.1 lists these eight instruments and shows into which category they fall. As we discuss in the sections that follow, these eight policy instruments differ in the degree of their effectiveness to achieve economic efficiency. After discussing the mechanics of these policy instruments, we examine policies that combine several instruments. We also examine these instruments' impacts on other markets, focusing on *second-best* issues and complications arising when a *general-equilibrium* approach to environmental policy is taken versus a more straightforward *partial-equilibrium* approach.

TAXES ON POLLUTING ACTIVITIES

In Chapter 6, we showed how externalities can lead to the production of the wrong mix of goods. If production of a good has external costs, its competitive market price will not reflect the full social cost of its production. For example, prior to regulation under the U.S. Clean Air Act, owners of coal-fired power plants could use

TABLE 7.1   TYPES OF ENVIRONMENTAL POLICY INSTRUMENTS

Market-Enhancing Mechanisms	Market-Substituting Mechanisms
Taxes on polluting activities	Subsidies for pollution control
Direct taxes on pollutants	Payments to reduce pollutants
Tradable emissions permits	Imposition of prescribed technology
	Limits on the quantity of pollutants
	Emergency restrictions

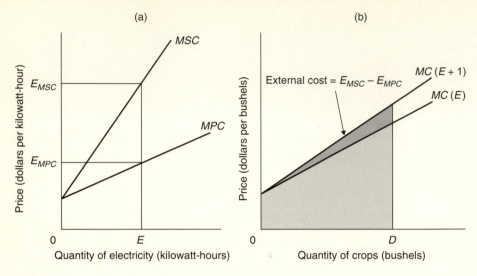

Figure 7.1   External Costs of Electricity Production

the atmosphere as a receptacle for sulfur dioxide disposal at zero cost to them-selves.[5] If the price of the polluting good is too low, people will buy more of it and less of other goods. One way to correct this inefficiency is to levy a tax on the good whose production has external costs.[6]

A tax on a good whose production has external costs should be set at the equi-librium marginal external cost per unit of output. This marginal external cost is shown in two ways in Figure 7.1. Suppose that we consider the effects of electricity generation on crop production at farms downwind from a nearby coal-fired power plant: specifically, that the plant's emissions reduce crop yields per acre. In Figure 7.1(a), the marginal external cost for E kilowatt-hours (kWh) of electricity production is the difference between the marginal social cost (MSC) of E kWh and the margin-al private cost (MPC) of E kWh. This difference equals the vertical $E_{MSC} - E_{MPC}$.

Figure 7.1(b) shows the MPC curves for crops associated with E and $E +$ 1 kWh of electricity production. The shaded area below the curve $MC(E)$ is the total variable cost of producing D bushels when E kWh of electricity are produced. The crosshatched area between the $MC(E + 1)$ curve and the $MC(E)$ curve is the *increase* in the total variable production cost of the *same* amount of crops that results from a marginal increase in *electricity* production. It is therefore equal to the marginal external cost of electricity production.

---

[5]Interestingly, some scientists believe that sulfur dioxide may lessen the effects of global climate change by reflecting light back into space. Thus efforts to reduce sulfur dioxide emissions may exacerbate glob-al climate change. See Chapter 21 for further discussion.

[6]Use of the word *tax* may be confusing. Unlike "conventional" taxes, such as sales and income taxes, the purpose of an output or emissions tax is to impose a price on something that was previously unpriced: the environment.

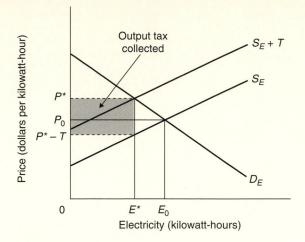

Figure 7.2   Effect of an Output Tax on Production

If E kWh are produced, the "correct" level of the output tax on electricity will equal $E_{MSC} - E_{MPC}$. Unfortunately, imposing this tax provides no incentive to the owners of the coal plant to reduce *emissions*. Instead, emissions will be reduced only to the extent that the tax leads to a reduction in electricity output. An output tax does not eliminate the waste from producers choosing the wrong mix of inputs, since the firm's internal costs of producing any given level of output are still lowest with no emissions controls. Instead, an output tax imposed on an industry will reduce the total amount of output (in this case, electricity) produced, as shown in Figure 7.2, by raising the equilibrium market-clearing price and reducing the equilibrium return to electricity producers.

In the figure, the initial supply curve for electricity is S_E, and the demand curve is D_E. The initial market-clearing price is $\$P_0$/kWh, and the equilibrium quantity of electricity sold is Q_0 kWh. After imposition of the per-unit tax on electricity output, however, the supply curve shifts upward to $S_E + T$. At the new equilibrium, however, producers receive only $(\$P^* - T)$/kWh. Output is reduced, therefore, to Q^* kWh, and the equilibrium price paid by consumers will equal $\$P^*$/kWh.[7]

The total amount of tax collected will equal the tax rate times the amount of electricity produced. Thus total tax collections will equal $\$T \cdot E^*$, which corresponds to the crosshatched area in Figure 7.2. Also, in our example, the amount of the tax collected exceeds the overall external damages. The reason is that although the marginal damages of the Eth kWh of electricity produced is set to the tax, damages from intramarginal electricity production (i.e., production of kWh 1 to $E - 1$) are less.

---

[7]The relative changes in the price paid by consumers and the net after-tax price received by producers depend on the price elasticities of demand and supply. These elasticities determine the *incidence* of the tax on producers and consumers. For further explanation, see any intermediate microeconomics text (e.g., Browning and Browning 1989).

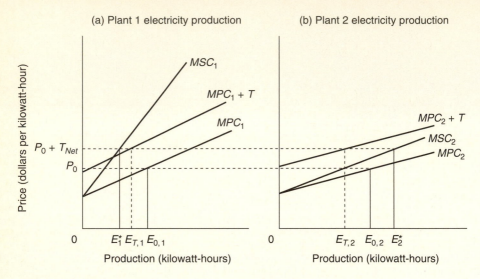

Figure 7.3   Effects of an Output Tax: Multiple Plants

These taxes represent a transfer of wealth from the private sector (both producers and consumers) to the public sector—the tax collector. It turns out that how the taxes collected are used can have a significant impact on the overall economic impacts associated with such a tax. In terms of the input-output model we described in Chapter 2, the ripple effects throughout the economy can be changed, possibly to a significant extent, if taxes are *recycled,* that is, if they are used to reduce other taxes in the economy.[8]

Output Taxes and Multiple Plants

Next, suppose that there are several coal-fired power plants that, because of their different ages and types of coal they use, each have a different MPC. If a uniform output tax is levied on electricity, production between these plants will not be allocated optimally. If different plants have different levels of emissions, the marginal social cost of output from dirtier plants will be greater than the marginal private cost plus the tax, and the marginal social cost of output from cleaner plants will be less than the marginal private cost plus the tax. Thus a uniform tax will result in too much output from dirty plants and too little from clean plants. Achieving the optimal allocation of production between plants would require a separate output tax for each plant, set equal to the damage from an increment of the particular plant's output. This is shown in Figure 7.3 for the case of two plants. Plant 1 is assumed to have a higher MPC than plant 2. Plant 1 is also assumed to be "dirtier," emitting more pollution per kilowatt-hour of electricity produced than plant 2 does.

---

[8]We will take this issue up in Chapter 21, when we discuss carbon taxes as a means to reduce the future impacts of global climate change,

Initially, the market price for electricity is P_0/kWh. Output at plant 1 and plant 2 equals $E_{0,1}$ and $E_{0,2}$ kWh, respectively. Next the government imposes a tax of T/kWh on both plants' output. Because consumers and producers will both bear a portion of the tax,[9] the new equilibrium price will equal $P_0 + T_{Net}$. The marginal private cost curves increase for both plants to $MPC_1 + T$ and $MPC_2 + T$, respectively, leading to a decrease in output from both plants to E_{T1} and E_{T2} kWh, respectively. Are these outputs optimal? The answer is no. Output at plant 2 is overly restricted, while plant 1 continues to produce excessively. The optimal output for plant 2 with this output tax is E_2^* kWh. The optimal output for plant 1 is only E_1^* kWh. The uniform per-unit tax does not allocate production optimally between plants that have different private and social cost characteristics.

Thus a tax on output can eliminate one of the sources of waste arising from an externality. Output taxes can force buyers and sellers to pay the full marginal social cost and thereby eliminate overproduction. In terms of the results achieved, it will not matter whether the tax is imposed on producers or consumers; each group will bear some share of the tax burden. A tax on a good whose production has external costs will have relatively low administrative and enforcement costs. It will not require monitoring of emissions levels and can be administered much like any other tax. However, if there are multiple plants with different external costs, a uniform output tax will not achieve an economically efficient result.

EMISSIONS TAXES

The effects of an emissions tax differ from those of an output tax. Charging specific emissions taxes can substitute for market prices. First, it forces producers to pay the costs associated with their waste disposal. Producers will therefore have an incentive to control emissions, as long as the costs of emissions controls are less than the tax. Second, because a profit-maximizing or cost-minimizing firm will set its marginal pollution control cost equal to the tax rate, a correctly set emissions tax will lead to an optimal input mix because the waste disposal services provided by the environment will be considered as an input. Third, an emissions tax will increase the cost of production, which will be reflected in the price of the final good produced. This will reduce the amount of the good purchased by consumers and eliminate overproduction. An emissions tax should be set at the marginal external cost per unit of emissions. Thus unlike a tax on output, an emissions tax can correct all three kinds of waste caused by an externality.

We examine the effects of an emissions tax in Figures 7.4 through 7.6. Suppose we consider sulfur dioxide pollution from a coal-fired electric-generating plant. As with Figure 7.1, Figure 7.4 shows that without any sort of tax, the coal plant produces E kWh at a price of P_{MPC}/kWh, where market price equals MPC. The marginal social cost again is the curve labeled MSC. The marginal social cost of E kWh of electricity production equals P_{MSC}/kWh. Too much electricity is produced, and too low a price is charged.

---

[9] See note 7.

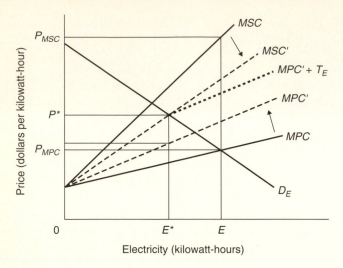

Figure 7.4   Effects of an Emissions Tax on the Electricity Market

By imposing an emissions tax, the plant owner will have an incentive to adopt technologies that reduce emissions. For example, the plant owner may install a scrubber on the coal plant to reduce air pollutant emissions. Because a scrubber requires electricity to operate, the marginal private cost of operating the plant will increase, in this case from MPC to MPC'. With the scrubber, however, there will be less environmental damage per kilowatt-hour of electricity produced. Thus marginal social cost per kilowatt-hour will decline from MSC to MSC'.

The emissions tax T_E is set where the marginal benefit of pollution reductions (or *abatement*) equals the marginal cost of pollution abatement, as shown in Figure 7.5. As the total amount of pollution abated increases, the marginal benefits of additional abatement falls, eventually reaching zero. (How we measure the marginal benefit and marginal cost curves is the subject of Chapters 11 through 14.)

Now let's examine the effects of the emissions tax on the crop market, much as we did in Figure 7.1. As in Figure 7.1, Figure 7.6 shows the marginal external cost imposed on farmers when total electricity production increases by 1 kWh. First, suppose that the coal plant again reduces crop yields at nearby farms. In Figure 7.6, the initial external costs, in the form of higher production costs, equals the total of the two shaded areas. (This is the same as the shaded area in Figure 7.1, which equals the difference in variable production costs of $E + 1$ and E kWh.)

Because the owner of the coal plant will adopt pollution control measures (e.g., scrubbers, precipitators) whose marginal cost per kilowatt-hour is less than the emissions tax, MPC is increased to MPC' and MSC is reduced to MSC'. In Figure 7.6, this means that an additional kilowatt-hour of electricity production causes a *smaller* reduction in crop yields and therefore imposes a smaller external cost.

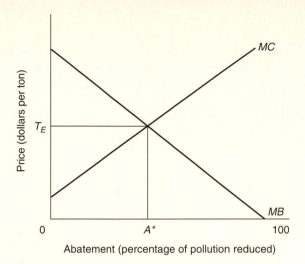

Figure 7.5 Determination of the Optimal Emissions Tax

This new external cost will equal the crosshatched shaded area between $MC'(E + 1)$ and $MC(E)$.

Even after installing the pollution control measures, the coal plant owner still will pay a tax of T_E on any remaining emissions. Therefore, the coal plant's MPC eventually increases to $MPC' + T_E$, as shown in Figure 7.4. Total tax payments will equal the crosshatched area in Figure 7.4. Because the owner of the plant now sees a direct relationship between production and emissions, output will be reduced to E^* kWh, and the new market price will be P^*.

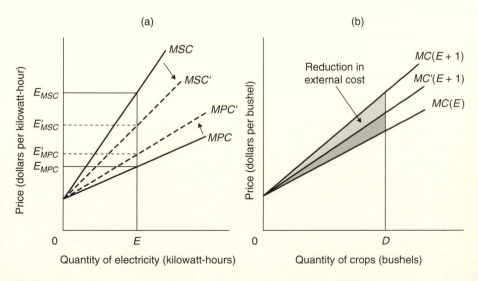

Figure 7.6 Changes in MPC and MSC Because of an Emissions Tax

It is important to understand the *simultaneous* nature of the tax, marginal private cost, and marginal social cost. In Figure 7.4, the equilibrium level of the emissions tax T_E corresponds to the equilibrium social and private cost curves MSC' and MPC', *not* the initial curves MSC and MPC. Setting the tax as the difference between the initial private and social cost curves will impose too high a tax and result in too much pollution abatement.

Also, unlike an output tax, an emissions tax will also result in the optimal allocation of production between multiple plants because the emissions tax will equate marginal private cost and marginal social cost for each plant automatically. Therefore, plants facing a uniform price will divide output between them so that all produce where marginal social cost equals price.

It would appear that emissions taxes are an ideal policy instrument to achieve economic efficiency. Why, then, are they rarely used in practice? One reason is their high cost of implementation and monitoring. Taxing emissions from mobile emissions sources such as motor vehicles is now prohibitively expensive because of the large number of vehicles that would have to be measured and the difficulty of accurate measurement.[10] Measuring stationary-source emissions such as those from coal-fired power plants is easier but can still be expensive.

TRADABLE EMISSIONS PERMITS

So far, we have discussed output and emissions taxes, both of which are market-enhancing policy instruments for addressing environmental costs. The third market instrument we discuss is called the *tradable emissions permit*. As the name implies, this is a permit allowing polluters to pollute (for a price) that can be bought and sold in a well-defined market.

We have shown that if different polluters have different cleanup costs, uniform output taxes will not achieve an economically efficient outcome. This is because it would be possible to achieve the same total emissions reduction at a lower cost. If firm A's marginal cleanup cost is $5 at the emissions limit and firm B's is $10, society can have the same total emissions and save $5 by letting B emit one unit more and making A emit one unit less. One way to do this is to allow polluters to buy and sell rights to pollute and let them exchange those rights among themselves. This is rationale behind tradable pollution permits.[11]

In a system of tradable permits, such as the one that exists for sulfur dioxide emissions in the United States, policymakers first determine the total amount of pollution that will be permitted. This is often called an emissions *ceiling*. Ideally, the total amount of pollution permits will be set at the optimal level, such as that shown in Figure 7.5. Thus if nationwide emissions of sulfur dioxide total 16 million tons today and the optimal amount had been determined to be 8 million, the

---

[10]Numerous efforts are under way in the United States and abroad to design technologies that will measure mobile source emissions cost-effectively.

[11]See Tietenberg (1980, 1985) for detailed discussions of tradable emissions permits in theory and in practice. See also Hahn (1989) for a discussion of the actual experience with emissions taxes and marketable permits in the United States and Europe.

optimal percentage abatement would be 50 percent. The government would issue permits for 8 million tons of sulfur dioxide, with each permit granting the owner the "right" to emit 1 ton of sulfur dioxide. (We will discuss how the number of permits is determined a little later in the chapter.)

Polluters with high control costs will have an incentive to purchase permits from polluters with low control costs, and vice versa. This trading of permits should lead to a point where all polluters have the same marginal control cost and total control cost is minimized. The administrative costs of tradable permits are not excessive because trades are made in observed markets.

A number of jurisdictions in the United States require new polluters to purchase existing permits totaling more than the amount they will emit. This is known as the degree of *offset*. For example, a regulator may require that a polluter selling 100 tons' worth of permits reduce its emissions by 150 tons. Offsets are a way of limiting trades where uniform trade prices may not be efficient, as in the case where pollution reductions in certain areas (e.g., the downtown area of a large city) are more valuable than in other areas (e.g., an unpopulated area). If regulators know that the initial amount of permits is too high, this can provide a mechanism to lower total pollution over time. It will lead to minimum cost for each level of emissions because each polluter will control emissions up to the point where marginal control cost equals the cost of additional permits, and new polluters will start up only if they can outbid current polluters. To do so, a firm would need to have lower control cost or more valuable output than existing polluters.

NO$_X$ AROUND THE CLOCK

In June 1995, New England Power sold 65 tons of excess emissions of oxides of nitrogen (NO$_X$) to Montaup Electric Company for use at its Somerset, Massachusetts, combustion turbines. The sale allowed Montaup to avoid the installation of reasonably available control technology (RACT) equipment on the small units, which have a total generating capacity of only 47 megawatts (MW).

New England Power created a total of 1,350 tons of NO$_X$ credits when it installed pollution controls on its coal-fired Brayton Point plant ahead of the deadline imposed by the Clean Air Act. The total cost of these controls was $15 million. By purchasing the emissions credits, Montaup was able to avoid about $450,000 worth of RACT compliance costs. While the price Montaup actually paid was confidential, 1995 prices for NO$_X$ emissions were between $500 and $1,500 per ton in New England. Montaup's generating units are expected to emit only about 15 tons of NO$_X$ each year, and Montaup will donate some of its newly purchased emissions credits to the state of Massachusetts. The net result will be fewer NO$_X$ emissions in the region and cleaner air.

Source: Adapted from *The Electricity Daily*, June 26, 1995.

SMOG FOR SALE—CHEAP!

Southern California, especially the four counties surrounding Los Angeles, has some of the highest pollution levels in the United States, although much progress has been made.* In January 1994, an emissions trading program was introduced by the South Coast Air Quality Management District (SCAQMD). This program, known as the Regional Clear Air Act Incentive Market (RECLAIM), focuses on the 390 companies in the region that emit more than 4 tons of nitrogen oxides and sulfur dioxide each year. These two pollutants are the biggest contributors to the region's air pollution problems.

By 2003, each firm will have to reduce its emissions of nitrogen oxides by about 75 percent and emissions of sulfur dioxide by about 60 percent. The idea behind RECLAIM is for the firms to determine themselves how to achieve these reductions most efficiently. Some firms may reduce their pollution emissions more aggressively and sell air pollution credits; others will find it cheaper to purchase those credits and postpone investments in new technologies.

At the end of July 1994, the first RECLAIM air credits auction was run. In that first auction, companies in the Los Angeles area purchased about 10.5 million pounds of NO_x offsets (allowing them to emit more NO_x) and received 2.2 million pounds' worth of offers to buy. Polluters bought and sold credits for the years 1994 through 2003. The prices for NO_x credits ranged from $2 per ton for 1994 credits to $2,090 per ton for 2003 credits. For sulfur dioxide (SO_2), prices were $1,500 per ton for 1995 and $1,900 per ton for 1996. This first RECLAIM auction resulted in prices that were significantly lower than initially predicted by SCAQMD, indicating that the agency overestimated marginal cost curves for emissions control. (Prices in the 1995 auction were even lower, leading some critics to wonder whether the market-trading mechanism was working properly.)

RECLAIM's proponents claim that the emissions trading program will save $90 million per year. Critics of the program, however, abound. Some firms, such as Southern California Gas, fear that some of their customers will reduce their pollution by fuel-switching (forgoing natural gas for "cleaner" electricity) or abandoning the region altogether. Other firms will be able to earn credits by scrapping older, smog-belching automobiles and replacing antiquated equipment that would have been replaced anyway. Environmentalists are concerned that RECLAIM will delay new federal government pollution control programs and that "big" polluters will somehow escape the regulations entirely. Thus the acrimony seems less directed toward *whether* the program will reduce pollution and more toward *who* will do the reducing. Time, and the region's air quality, will ultimately determine RECLAIM's success.

Sources: "Right to Pollute," *Economist,* October 30, 1993; *California Energy Markets,* August 5, 1994.

*See Lents and Kelly (1993) for a detailed description on air quality improvements in the city of Los Angeles.

SUBSIDIES FOR POLLUTION CONTROL

So far we have discussed market-enhancing policy instruments that can improve economic efficiency. Now we turn to market-substituting mechanisms, which remain far more prevalent as actual policy instruments.

Incentives can change people's behavior in two ways: they can make activities less attractive through taxes, or they can make activities more attractive through subsidies. This argument has led to proposals to encourage environmental cleanup through subsidies under the reasoning that if a system of taxes can reduce pollution, a mirror-image set of subsidy payments can achieve the same thing. Subsidies for environmental cleanup fall into two categories: those that subsidize the cost to firms of installing necessary pollution control equipment and those that pay firms directly for the amount of pollution they reduce.

Subsidizing Pollution Control Equipment

Providing firms with tax breaks for pollution control measures is an ineffective and inefficient policy for reducing pollution. Suppose that taxpayers provide the money for installing sulfur dioxide–reducing equipment, instead of owners of the coal-fired power plants. With the new equipment, the marginal and average private cost of producing electricity *must* increase; otherwise the plant's owners would install the equipment themselves. (In fact, equipment such as electrostatic precipitators consume a fair portion of the electricity generated at a coal-fired power plant.) Unless the subsidy is 100 percent, the firm's marginal and average costs will increase with the equipment installed. Thus it is unlikely that a partial subsidy for purchasing pollution control equipment will induce firms to reduce pollution by themselves. Subsidies can reduce the economic impact on firms of mandatory emissions controls, but then it is the mandate, not the subsidy, that changes behavior (Kneese and Bower 1984).

Paying Firms Not to Pollute

Paying a firm to reduce pollution can induce it to change its behavior. However, if there are not significant barriers to entry, subsidies may induce new firms to enter the industry and therefore *increase* the overall amount of pollution (Baumol and Oates 1988). To see this more clearly, consider Figure 7.7, which depicts the equilibrium positions of a given firm and the industry as a whole. Initially, in the absence of any tax or subsidy, the firm's output level will be q_c, with the corresponding industry equilibrium output and price equal to (Q_c, P_c).

Next, suppose that a per-unit tax on output of $\$t$ per unit is imposed. The effect will be to shift both the firm's average and marginal cost curves upward by an amount t equal to the level of the tax. Thus the new marginal cost curve will be $MC_t = MC_c + t$, and the new average cost curve will be $AC_t = AC_c + t$. In the short run, the firm's production will decrease, because the market price P_c is below the new average cost AC_t. As a result, some firms will exit the industry, shifting the

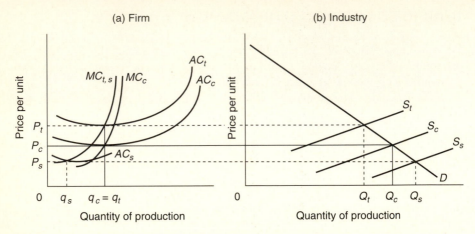

Figure 7.7 Taxes Versus Subsidies for Individual Firms and for an Industry as a Whole

industry supply curve S_c to the left, until a new long-term equilibrium supply S_t is reached. The new equilibrium price will increase to P_t, and the individual firm's output will remain *unchanged* at $q_t = q_c$. Total industry output will decrease, however, to Q_t.

Now suppose that we provide the firm with a per-unit subsidy, s, where $s = t$. The firm receives the subsidy if it reduces emissions below some benchmark level. Initially, we might expect that the firm's marginal cost would decrease. This is not the case. Consider again Figure 7.7, where the subsidy is set to the same level as the tax. It turns out that just as with the imposition of an emissions tax, the firm's new marginal cost curve will shift *upward* to MC_s, where $MC_s = MC_t$.

The explanation for this upward shift is as follows: as the firm increases its output, it *forgoes* a subsidy that it would receive if it reduced pollution. Thus just as with the per-unit tax, there is an increase in the *opportunity cost* associated with higher levels of output, only in the case of a subsidy, the increased opportunity cost is in the form of forgone subsidy payments. Although the firm's marginal cost curve shifts upward, its average cost does shift downward because the firm receives a per-unit payment for reducing output that lowers its average cost. Thus $AC_t = AC_c - s$. In the short run, the initial price P_c will be greater than average cost. This will encourage new firms to enter the market, shifting the supply curve outward from S_c to S_s. The new long-run equilibrium output and price will equal (Q_s, P_s).

The overall impact on pollution levels from a subsidy is unclear. Although an *individual firm* receiving a subsidy will indeed emit less pollution, the number of firms may increase. Thus the *entire industry* may pollute more. Whether or not this occurs will depend on the elasticity of demand and of supply. The less elastic either is, the less likely that a subsidy will increase overall levels of pollution.

Why Subsidies Are Not Mirror Images of Taxes

Why should the effects of subsidies differ from those of taxes? The reason is that the overall change in pollution is linked inextricably to the public-good nature of environmental quality. With a private good, it is well known that trading between individuals can result in an efficient outcome regardless of the initial ownership pattern. If person 1 owns all of good X, person 2 has to buy any that he wants to consume. If person 2 initially owns all of good X, person 1 has to buy any she wants. Bargaining between the two can produce efficiency in either case, but the distribution of wealth will generally be different.

With a public good (or bad), it is impossible to assign exclusive property rights. Everyone in an airshed experiences the same air quality. Taxing air polluters implicitly assigns a *pseudo* property right to air breathers but does not create exclusive private property in air. (We say *pseudo* property right because air breathers cannot buy and sell the air they breathe, nor can they claim quantities of air for their exclusive use.) It defines a baseline level of air quality, which any polluter must pay to reduce. However, efficiency requires that no payments be made to breathers for allowing emissions. Paying breathers reduces their incentive to take action to avoid damage from pollution. If air pollution ruins some kinds of house paint but not others, compensating homeowners for damage to their paint removes the incentive to buy pollution-resistant paint, even if that is the cheapest way to avoid the damage.[12]

An efficient outcome could be produced by reversing the assignment of pseudo property rights. This would require establishing a baseline level of dirty air and requiring breathers to pay to get higher air quality. The optimal improvement in air quality would be determined by equating the sum of all breathers' marginal values for cleaner air and the marginal emissions control cost. This is the same condition that must hold when breathers are assigned the pseudo property right, but since breathers have lower wealth in this case, the efficient outcome will be different. In this case, efficiency requires that no payments be made to polluters because paying polluters reduces the incentive to produce their products with less pollution.

So far, the two cases are symmetric. Efficiency requires the party without the initial pseudo property right to pay for a change in air quality and prohibits payment to the party with initial pseudo ownership. This is the source of the asymmetry. From the breathers' point of view, air quality is a public good. Everyone consumes the same air quality, and no one can be excluded from consuming it. From the polluters' point of view, however, once an allowable level of pollution is established, air quality is not a pure public good. Each polluter's emissions leaves fewer of the allowable emissions for other polluters. Air quality is a pure public good from the consumer's point of view but a private good from the provider's point of view. Some mechanism is necessary to allocate the allowable emissions level among

---

[12]There can also be a common-law context. The law generally requires compensation net of efficient *mitigation*. Thus the rancher who owns a herd of cattle that trespass and trample a nearby farmer's crops may be required to pay damages to the farmer net of the cost of an "efficient" fence.

potential polluters. This could be a market for pollution permits or even an emissions tax. But paying individual polluters for emissions reductions without mandating and allocating a level of total industry pollution will not result in efficiency.

COMMAND-AND-CONTROL POLICIES

In the United States, the most common form of environmental policy instruments are known collectively as *command-and-control instruments*. Curiously, in most cases, such policies are the *least* likely policy instruments to improve economic efficiency, although there is no doubt that they can reduce pollution levels. Command-and-control policies fall into three main categories. The most common are *prescribed-technology* policies, which regulate the types of pollution control measures that must be used. The second group of policies regulates emission quantities themselves, restricting emissions either *per unit of output* (e.g., tons of sulfur dioxide per kilowatt-hour) or *per unit of time* (e.g., maximum allowable carbon monoxide concentrations in a 24-hour period). The last and least common category is *emergency restrictions,* which can ban certain operations (e.g., limits on industries, bans on woodstove use) during periods of extremely high levels of pollution.

Prescribed Technologies

In areas that do not meet air quality standards, the Clean Air Act forces new polluters to use the best available control technology (BACT), as determined by the U.S. Environmental Protection Agency (EPA). BACT does not consider the actual damage costs from pollution or the costs of controlling pollution. Also, BACT does not address a new polluter's emissions directly. In general, this type of command-and-control policy will yield an economically efficient outcome only by accident.

Command-and-control policies like BACT require that polluters adopt the same technological solutions, regardless of whether such technologies are the most efficient technologies available, regardless of whether polluters have equal costs of reducing pollution, and regardless of whether the costs of the reductions exceed the benefits. To see this more clearly, suppose that regulators have adopted an inferior pollution control technology. This means that the marginal cost of pollution abatement can be reduced through the use of newer, better technologies. By requiring polluters to use the old technology, expenditures to reduce pollution will be higher than necessary and overall pollution levels may be higher than optimal. This is shown in Figure 7.8.

In this figure, MC_1 represents the marginal cost of controlling pollution using the prescribed technology. MC_2 represents the marginal cost of controlling pollution using the new technology. Because the old technology is more costly, regulators selected an abatement target of A_1 percent. In doing so, they imposed excess costs on society equal to the shaded triangle *ABC*. Furthermore, with the new technology, further pollution reductions would be warranted to the level $A*$ of abatement. As a result, there is an additional social cost from too much pollution equal to the shaded triangle *BCD*. Of course, there are many variants of this diagram. It

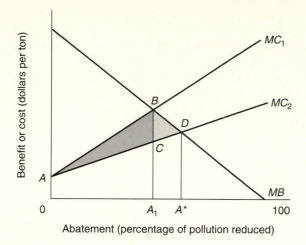

Figure 7.8 Excess Costs of Inefficient Regulations

may be that regulators have imposed overly stringent pollution reductions that are not warranted by the marginal benefits of those reductions. Thus even with a new, lower-cost technology, too much pollution may still be emitted.

There is one situation where controls can result in an efficient outcome. This is the case where all known control technologies have technical limits, but marginal control cost is less than marginal damage cost up to this limit. This is shown in Figure 7.9. MB shows the marginal benefit from pollution control. With existing technology, it is possible to remove up to S^* percent of potential emissions at a cost less than the benefits of doing so, but no more can be removed at any cost. Thus the marginal control cost, MCC, becomes a vertical line at S^*. In this case, BACT will produce economic efficiency. However, BACT poses two problems. First, if

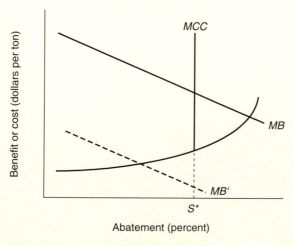

Figure 7.9 Application of BACT in a Limiting Case

the benefits of abatement are unknown, regulators do not know that marginal benefits exceed marginal cost at S^*. If, however, the marginal benefit curve is actually MB', imposing BACT may improve welfare from a situation of no pollution control. However, it will reduce pollution too much and produce a smaller welfare gain than is possible. Second, BACT does not give polluters any incentive to develop new control technologies. As with other policies that do not charge polluters for their emissions, there is no reward for firms that find a way to reduce emissions even further. In addition, with BACT, there is an incentive not to look for new control technologies because firms fear that they will be forced to adopt any new technology that works, regardless of cost.

Emissions Limits

Taxes and subsidies are intended to induce polluters to change their behavior. Emissions limits try to get to the same result by prescribing behavior. Direct con-

---

COMMAND AND CONTROL BELOW THE SURFACE: THE CLEAN WATER ACT

U.S. policy toward control of water pollution has focused on large *point* sources of pollution, which are analogous to stationary sources of air pollution. Point sources include industries and sewage plants. *Nonpoint* pollution, whose major sources include agricultural and urban runoff, is much harder to address. In 1972, Congress passed the Water Pollution Act, which primarily subsidized improvements in municipal sewage treatment plants. In 1977, Congress passed the Clean Water Act and its amendments. Both of these acts were based on command-and-control policies. All untreated pollution discharges were made illegal, and dischargers of water pollutants were required to use best practical technology (BPT) and best available technology (BAT). BAT, like best available control technology (BACT) for air pollutants, does not consider cost, whereas BPT does.

Unlike sources of air pollution, which arise primarily from private sources, the Clean Water Act imposed the majority of its costs on local governments. Thus, one set of regulators was affecting the actions of public officials. The act has generated much controversy, primarily because of the significant costs it has imposed on local municipalities through its requirements that sewage be treated using advanced techniques. Even though the federal government subsidized 75 percent of the total cost of these treatment facilities, many municipalities were forced to raise local taxes. The Clean Water Act has not differentiated between sources of pollution or their environmental costs. As such, it seems to have focused on requiring equitable cleanup of point sources, rather than efficient cleanup.*

*As this is being written, Congress is considering major changes in the Clean Water Act, including not reauthorizing it.

trols can limit emissions either per unit of time or per unit of output. The results are not the same.

An emissions limit per unit of time can achieve the same emissions as an emissions tax. Output will be reduced because its price will include the pollution control costs. However, output will be greater than optimal because the price does not include the cost of environmental damage. This is shown in Figure 7.10. The curve labeled MPC is the marginal private cost with no controls. The curve labeled $MPC + C$ is the marginal private cost with emissions set at some level E^*. For output below Q_0, emissions are lower than E^* with no controls, and the two curves are the same. As output is increased above this point, more and more must be spent to keep emissions the same, and the difference between the curves grows. The curve $MPC + D_0$ is the marginal social cost without controls, which is the sum of MPC and marginal damages without controls. The curve $MPC + D_1$ is the marginal social cost with controls and is the sum of MPC, control costs, and the lower level of marginal damages with controls. The efficient level of output is Q^*, but the equilibrium level of output is $\overline{Q}$.

The equilibrium with emissions restrictions may differ from the equilibrium with an emissions tax because the emissions tax transfers wealth from producers and consumers of the offending good, while the emissions restriction does not. This will result in a change in these individuals' consumption spending, including spending on this good.

Uniform emissions restrictions, like uniform emissions taxes per unit of output, may not allocate production between plants optimally. The total cost of achieving any level of emissions will be lowest if plants with lower control costs are required to clean up more and less is required from plants with higher control costs. Uniform emissions restrictions will result in costs that are higher than necessary by requiring the same emissions from all plants, regardless of the cost at

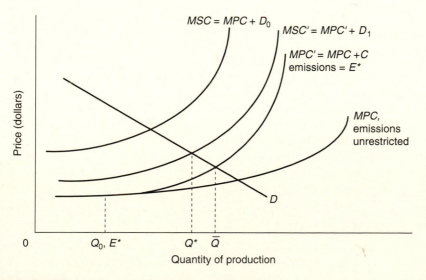

Figure 7.10   Emissions Limits per Unit of Time

each plant. Allocating production efficiently between plants would require a separate emissions limit for each plant, set at the point where that plant's marginal control cost equals the marginal damage cost.

If they are set correctly, limits on emissions per unit of output can force producers to use the right mix of inputs, including environmental waste disposal, because firms will want to minimize their costs regardless of whether emissions limits are prescribed or freely chosen. Emissions limits per unit of output will not produce an efficient level of output, however, because they do not force consumers to pay the full marginal social cost of their purchases. Uniform emissions limits per unit of output will allocate production between plants efficiently. All plants will produce up to the point where marginal private cost, including control costs, equals the price. Since the emissions accompanying a change in output will be the same for all plants, the marginal external cost is the same for all plants. Therefore, the marginal social cost is the same for all plants, and the social cost of producing this level of output cannot be reduced by shifting output between plants.

Direct controls have a disadvantage relative to taxes or fees. They force polluters to take the same actions now and in the immediate future, but they do not give polluters an incentive to develop new technologies that would make it cost-effective to reduce emissions further (Kneese and Bower 1984). Direct controls also require monitoring of emissions and enforcement of penalties for violators. However, they do not require tax collections and may therefore have lower administrative costs than emissions taxes do.

Emergency Restrictions

The damage from environmental pollution often depends on environmental conditions. During a temperature inversion over a city, air pollution is not dispersed by the wind. Pollutants remain in a populated area, and the concentrations of pollutants rise. This increases the damage from incremental emissions. This could be handled by having emissions fees or permit levels that depend on existing pollution levels or weather conditions. However, such programs would be costly to administer and enforce, and polluters may not respond quickly to temporary changes in fees. Temporary bans on specific polluting activities can reduce emissions levels during emergency conditions with much lower administration and enforcement costs.

This is the approach many jurisdictions in the western United States have taken with wood stoves. When air quality is below a predetermined level, the use of wood stoves is prohibited. Administration consists of monitoring overall air quality and issuing daily statements to news media. Enforcement generally depends heavily on people tattling on their neighbors.

PRICES OR QUANTITIES?

One vexing issue when deciding on a policy approach to controlling pollution is whether to focus on prices, as by imposing emissions taxes, or on quantities, as through tradable permits or command-and-control policies. Until now, we have ignored issues such as how an emissions tax would be calculated, how many trad-able permits should be created in total, and which specific emissions control tech-nologies should be imposed on firms.

The problem is one of uncertainty in the actual control cost and damage cost functions, such as those shown in Figure 7.5. Although we do not discuss empirical issues associated with measuring environmental costs and benefits until Part III, here we provide a brief overview of the problems involved with uncertain mea-surement. These uncertainties can, in part, determine how regulations are devel-oped and implemented.

Suppose that the marginal control costs of abatement are known with certain-ty, but the marginal benefits are not. Instead, the marginal benefits are estimated to be within a certain range, as shown in Figure 7.11. In this figure, marginal ben-efits range between MB_L and MB_H.

The true but unobservable marginal benefits schedule is MB^*. In this case, the optimal emissions tax will be T^* with a level of abatement A^*. This is shown as point Z in the figure. Unfortunately, regulators don't know this and therefore must decide a tax-abatement combination somewhere between (T_L, A_L) (point Y) and (T_H, A_H) (point X). The question is, how should they make their choice? Further-more, should regulators even use a price-based policy instrument, or would a quantity-based policy instrument be less likely to differ significantly from the "optimal" solution?

Weitzman (1974) showed that the choice of price-based or quantity-based instrument should depend on the slopes of the marginal cost and marginal benefit functions. Weitzman showed that the steeper (less elastic) the marginal benefit function and the flatter (more elastic) the marginal cost function, the greater will be the social losses from choosing the "wrong" tax level.

Unless regulators serendipitously choose the tax level T^*, there will be a social loss associated with either allowing too much pollution or levying too high a tax and

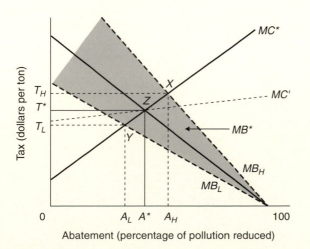

Figure 7.11   Choosing an Emissions Tax when Marginal Benefits are Unknown

reducing pollution unnecessarily. If the true marginal cost curve is flatter (MC'), the errors will be compounded. This will make command-and-control policies that regulate quantities of pollution reductions more appealing, for regulators will be better able to achieve the desired pollution reductions with quantity restrictions.

Of course, it may be that regulators have little knowledge about the actual costs of controlling pollution but an accurate assessment of the benefits from control. In that case, it will be the marginal cost curve that is uncertain, as shown in Figure 7.12. The analysis of price versus quantity restrictions in this case will be similar, and we leave it as an exercise.

COORDINATED POLICIES

Why would a single agency want to adopt two types of policies to achieve the same goal? Why would it ever be appropriate for two agencies to coordinate environmental policies? None of the policies we have discussed is perfect. Thus it may be desirable to combine policies because they are complementary; one policy's strengths may compensate for another's weak points. It may also be desirable to combine policies when the effects of any one policy are uncertain.

Emissions taxes or fees set equal to marginal external cost are by far the best policy if external costs are known and administrative costs can be kept low. However, with many pollutants, the costs of pollution depend on ambient conditions and can vary widely over time. Keeping an emissions tax at marginal external cost would require changing it every time conditions changed. This could be unmanageable for regulators and polluters alike. Combining emissions taxes that are based on typical conditions with emergency restrictions would give increased flexibility for dealing with times when external costs were unusually high without having prohibitive administrative costs.

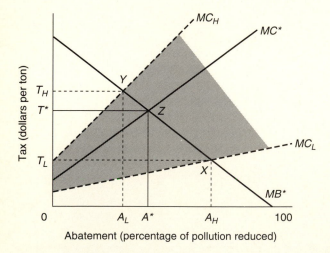

Figure 7.12   Choosing an Emissions Tax when Marginal Costs are Unknown

Direct regulations of emissions do not give polluters any incentive to reduce emissions beyond the target level. Regulators may be uncertain of the pollution reduction that will result from a set of emissions charges. Combining emissions charges with absolute emissions limits or auctioning off a set number of annual permits would reduce these problems. Every polluter would have incentives to adopt existing control technologies that were cheaper than the fees and to develop new ones. However, there would be an upper limit on the uncertain emission levels that would result from the fee.

GENERAL EQUILIBRIUM ISSUES AND THE PROBLEM OF THE SECOND BEST

So far, we have restricted our attention to setting a tax in a single market, thus focusing on partial equilibrium solutions. Also, we have ignored nonconvexities in the production set (previously discussed in Chapter 6) and ignored the complications introduced when multiple sets of policymakers, each of whom has jurisdiction over only certain aspects of markets, can affect the choice of policy instruments.

Nonconvexity

In Chapter 6, we discussed the problem of nonconvexity in the production possibilities frontier. To recap that discussion, we assumed that increasing electricity production beyond some level would require the use of technologies that were devastating to wheat production. The pollution from a small increase in electricity production would then cause a large decrease in wheat production, and the production possibilities frontier would suddenly become very steep. Further increases in power production would create still more pollution, increasing the production loss on each wheat field. However, there would also be fewer and fewer wheat fields. Eventually the total damage would decline. Ultimately, when there is no wheat production, there can be no damage to the crop, and there is no external cost associated with electricity production from the coal-fired plant. As a result, at some point it may appear that the returns to scale from resources devoted to electricity production are *increasing* rather than decreasing. This means that the tax and control policies outlined in this chapter may not yield the greatest net economic benefits.

Figure 7.13 shows how nonconvexity complicates the choice between two goods. Initially, in Figure 7.13(a) (which is similar to Figure 7.4), suppose that electricity production currently has no external costs. However, increasing electricity production requires using a new technology that will adversely affect wheat production. If the new electricity generation technology were not used, there would be no externality. Similarly, there would be no externality if the new generation technology were used and wheat production stopped. With no wheat production, the curve MPC would show both the private and the social marginal cost for electricity. The sum of additional producer and consumer surplus in the electricity market would be the area of the triangle ABC.

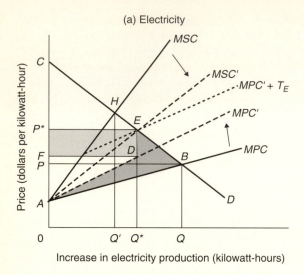

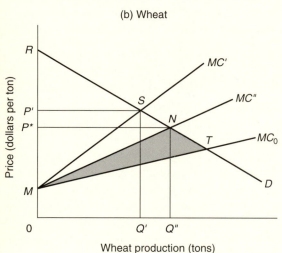

Figure 7.13   Effects of an Emissions Tax on Consumer's and Producer's Surplus

If the new technology is used and there is wheat production, the externality exists but can be corrected by imposing a tax on emissions. With the tax on emissions, electricity producers would pay a positive price for their use of the atmosphere and would emit less pollutants. As we discussed earlier, this would reduce the marginal social cost of electricity from MSC to MSC'. Because reducing emissions will require using more of some other inputs, the marginal private cost of additional electricity will increase from MPC to MPC'. If the tax is set correctly, it will raise the price of electricity to its marginal social cost. Consumer's surplus will therefore be reduced to triangle CEP^*. The lightly shaded area $FDEP^*$ will equal the total tax collections. This leaves producer's surplus equal to the area of triangle ADF. If no tax is imposed because there is no wheat production and hence no externality, the sum of consumer and producer surplus (equal to triangle ABC) will exceed the sum of consumer surplus (CEP^*), tax revenues ($FDEP^*$), and producer surplus (CEP^*) with wheat production and the optimal tax by the area of the shaded irregular polygon $ABED$. Thus electricity consumers and producers will be worse off.

Now let's examine the impacts in the wheat market, as shown in Figure 7.13(b). MC_0 is the marginal cost curve for wheat without the externality. MC' is the marginal cost curve for wheat with the full externality. MC'' shows the marginal cost of wheat when the power plant's emissions are controlled optimally. The sum of consumer and producer surplus is triangle MTR without the power plant, triangle MSR with the power plant and no pollution controls, and triangle MNR with emission controls on the power plant.

Unfortunately, the area of polygon ABED in Figure 7.13(a) may be greater than the area of triangle MSR in Figure 7.13(b). Thus it is possible that the *gain* to electricity consumers and producers from doing away with wheat production will be greater than the net value of the entire wheat crop. Of course, the reverse is also possible. Forgoing the new generation technology and restoring additional electricity production to Q' would produce a gain of MTN in the wheat market and a loss equal to the area of the quadrilateral $ADEH$ in the electricity market, and triangle MTN may be larger than $ADEH$.

What this means is that society may be better off adopting the new electricity technology and doing without wheat than adopting the new technology with pollution controls and emissions taxes. Or society may be better off to keep its current low-cost wheat production and do without the new technology than adopting it with controls and still losing some wheat production. It is even possible that both are true. Of the three options, adopting the new technology with the optimal level of controls may provide the lowest net benefits to society.

This is a counterintuitive result with important policy implications. The most important is that an unregulated market may produce *too little* of a good that has undesirable side effects. While it may be true that a small reduction in pollution from the new power plant is an improvement, it may also be true that allowing the power plant to pollute unchecked and doing away with wheat would be a bigger improvement. If the assumption of decreasing returns to scale is correct, there is too much pollution and correcting it through controls or taxes is the solution. If the assumption of decreasing returns to scale is incorrect, policymakers need to compare three discrete options: (1) allowing but optimally regulating the new polluting technology, (2) allowing the new technology with no regulation while doing away with affected activities, and (3) prohibiting the new polluting activity.

WHO REGULATES WHAT?

Another vexing issue that arises in environmental policy settings is the presence of multiple regulators. Sometimes different regulators will want to address market failures in the areas they control. This can create conflicts when they must take other regulations as given. These conflicts, most of which fall under the general

PUNISHING THE INNOCENT? HOW SOME PUBLIC UTILITY REGULATORS HAVE ADDRESSED THE ENVIRONMENTAL COSTS OF ELECTRIC POWER GENERATION

The issue of primary versus secondary regulators can be a crucial one. In the late 1980s, in response to what they believed to be inadequate consideration of the environmental cost of new power plants, many state public utility commissions (PUCs) began examining ways of reducing those costs further without having to amend environmental legislation such as the Clean Air Act. A variety of methods were developed and, in some states, adopted. Some were sensible, some less so.

Unfortunately, the first and most common method was to use the *highest* marginal costs of controlling pollution emissions as a proxy for marginal damage costs in comparing the social costs of electricity produced by different sources. Many regulators (e.g., Wiel 1991) favored this approach because, unlike environmental damage costs, control costs are measured easily.* The cost of installing and operating a scrubber for a coal plant, for example, is easily determined. Arguments for the use of control costs as a proxy have generally run as follows: marginal control cost is determined by environmental laws and regulations; environmental laws and regulations are set by legislators who have weighed the evidence and taken the interests and values of their constituents into account; environmental laws and regulations show the costs that society is willing to pay to reduce pollution; therefore, marginal control cost equals marginal damage cost.

There are at least three major problems with this reasoning, and therefore this approach. First, in most cases, control costs have no particular relationship to damage costs. Environmental laws and regulations may tell us a great deal about the costs that legislators and regulators are willing to impose on society to reduce pollution. In some cases, individuals' willingness to pay to avoid pollution may have entered into legislators' deliberations. But most environmental regulations are based partly or largely on other grounds. In the United States, air and water quality laws and regulations are generally based on avoiding involuntary health risks.† Legislators' primary concerns seem not to have been overall economic welfare but rather equity and individual rights. American air and water quality laws generally presume that there is a right not to be involuntarily exposed to significant, avoidable health risks because of others' actions and that no mechanism exists to waive or sell that right. Air and water pollution control costs tell us a great deal about the trade-offs legislators and regulators are willing to make between protecting this right and other goals they may have. They tell us nothing about the trade-offs the directly affected parties would be willing to make between electricity and pollution. Thus the argument that control costs represent "the costs that society is willing to pay to reduce pollution" is invalid because they are not the same as pollution victims' willingness to pay to avoid pollution.

The second problem is that PUCs can "correct" environmental regulations only if marginal damage costs and marginal social costs are not equal. In that case, any secondary regulation by PUCs should be based on the *difference* between the external cost and the control costs resulting from production of an increment of electricity.‡

The third problem is that the choice between alternative electric production technologies should be based on total social costs, not marginal costs. Total emissions control costs and total remaining damage will be equal when marginal control cost and marginal damage cost are equal only by chance. PUCs using control costs may improve welfare by accident but cannot know whether they are increasing or decreasing welfare without using damage costs to estimate the changes in welfare because of their actions.

Finally, just as environmental regulators may have made decisions for reasons other than strict welfare maximization, PUCs will often have additional social goals they are required to address. PUCs may wish to reduce risks to future ratepayers out of concerns for equity. Differing degrees of risk aversion may, of course, lead to different sorts of decisions. There may be concerns over whether the utilities they oversee have the right to impose environmental costs on certain groups of ratepayers or other consumers. Thus decisions that appear to be unjustified on strict efficiency grounds may be justified on equity or human rights grounds. Concerns about "exporting pollution," for example, may make sense when viewed from such a perspective.

*See Chapter 11 for a thorough discussion of measuring environmental damages.

†We discuss these regulations in more detail in Chapter 9.

‡See the Appendix to Chapter 7 for a more detailed discussion of the implications of this statement.

---

area of the *second best,* can result in lower welfare from environmental policy instruments that might improve overall welfare if implemented by themselves.

As we discussed earlier, the U.S. Clean Air Act required the EPA to set emissions limits and prescribe technologies for many pollutants. One area that received much attention from the EPA was electric power generation. Owners of generating plants were required to install different technologies such as scrubbers and precipitators for control of air pollution and were also required to dispose of solid wastes in prescribed ways and control water pollution. Many, but not all, of these generating plants are owned by private electric utilities. Historically, these utilities have been regulated by state public utility commissions (PUCs), which set the prices at which the power generated by these plants is sold to consumers.[13]

In the late 1980s, many utility regulators became interested in promoting environmental quality and ensuring that demand-side resources (i.e., conservation and energy efficiency measures) were evaluated equivalently to traditional generating

---

[13]As this is being written, the electric utility industry is engaged in restructuring and deregulation that may eventually lead to electric prices established in competitive spot and futures markets. Some utility regulators are concerned that this restructuring will weaken environmental protection.

resources. Utility regulators reasoned that utilities were not accounting adequately for the environmental impacts of their generating facilities. As a result, these facilities would be favored over demand-side resources, even though the latter had minimal, if any, environmental impacts. Thus utility regulators required that the external costs of generating plants be added to their marginal costs and the total be compared to the marginal cost of demand-side resource alternatives. As revealed in the box, on pp. 172–173, however, in most cases utility regulators didn't understand the economic theory behind externalities and their internalization (Joskow 1992; Freeman et al. 1992). As a result, regulators' analyses and basis for environmental costs were almost always flawed.

CHAPTER SUMMARY

In this chapter, we discussed various environmental policy instruments from the perspective of achieving greater economic efficiency. We have shown that, all other things being equal, taxes on emissions or systems of tradable emissions permits can best achieve economic efficiency because they will promote both the correct input mix and the correct level of output. We have also shown that in general, direct restrictions on emissions per unit of output or unit of time, which are the most common form of environmental policy, are unlikely to achieve economic efficiency, even if restrictions are set at the correct level. We discussed the possibility of nonconvexities in the production sets of different commodities, which could lead to an optimal solution of eliminating the activities affected by polluting activities rather than limiting the polluting activities themselves. Finally, we discussed the implementation of policies from a second-best framework, showing that if environmental regulations are taken as given, subsequent policies that attempt to "fix" deficiencies in the environmental regulations may either be limited in scope or have perverse consequences.

CHAPTER REVIEW

Economic Concepts and Tools

- Taxes on polluting activities, usually called *output taxes,* can lead consumers to choose the correct mix of goods but will not cause producers to use the correct mix of inputs. However, the administrative costs of such taxes are usually lower than those associated with emissions taxes.
- Emissions taxes can correct all three forms of inefficiency caused by externalities. Emissions taxes can be difficult to administer owing to their measurement cost, especially for mobile sources of pollution such as that from motor vehicles.
- A system of tradable permits is similar to an emissions tax in that it can correct all three types of economic inefficiencies.
- In theory, prescribed technologies can force producers to use the right mix of inputs, including environmental waste disposal, but will not produce an effi-

cient level of output because they do not force consumers to pay the full marginal social cost of their output. Uniform prescribed technology requirements also fail to equate marginal social costs across different plants. And such requirements are unlikely to anticipate technological innovation and increased information about the effects of different pollutants.

- Subsidies for pollution control equipment rarely produce desired results and can, in fact, exacerbate environmental problems by reducing the costs of production for goods having external costs.

Policy Issues

- The choice of policy instrument to improve economic efficiency will depend on the type of environmental problem to be addressed. Market-enhancing mechanisms to improve economic inefficiency by internalizing externalities will generally be preferred to market-substituting mechanisms. In some cases, however, market-enhancing mechanisms will not be forthcoming because the costs of measurement and enforcement are prohibitive.
- Coordination of a variety of policies may often be needed to correct an externality effectively. Policymakers must also determine whether they are operating in a second-best framework. This is especially important for policymakers who are not primarily environmental regulators.
- Policies that improve economic efficiency may conflict with other policy goals, requiring policymakers to develop methods for balancing desired outcomes.

DISCUSSION QUESTIONS

1. How could nonconvexities in a production set be determined empirically?
2. If damages from pollution emissions are site-specific, how would policymakers design a set of emissions taxes? What about output taxes? Would there be any equity impacts?
3. Assuming site-specific damages, how could a system of tradable emissions permits be designed? What should its ultimate goals be? Would there be any equity impacts associated with a system of such emissions permits? If so, how could they be addressed? What sorts of enforcement costs would likely arise?
4. "Industries should not be allowed to purchase air pollution permits because they have no right to pollute in the first place." Evaluate this statement. Is it consistent with economic efficiency? Is it consistent with equity considerations?
5. Why are command-and-control measures so popular with regulators?
6. Assume that wheat farmers are paid a minimum guaranteed price per bushel by the government. How will this affect the optimal emissions tax for electricity if the minimum wheat price is greater than the competitive market price?
7. What rules should govern how tradable emissions permit can be exchanged? Should there be geographic limitations on exchanging parties? Should there be minimum prices? Should there be required offsets, such as having to reduce pollution by 1.1 tons for each 1-ton permit purchased? How would

uncertainty enter into a determination of a reasonable offset? Should the rules vary by pollutant or be uniform?

8. Using Figure 7.12, determine when price-based regulations will be preferred to quantity-based regulations when marginal control costs are uncertain. How would you determine a preferred solution if both the marginal benefit and marginal cost curves were uncertain?

REFERENCES

Baumol, W., and W. Oates. 1988. *The Theory of Environmental Policy.* New York: Cambridge University Press.

Browning, E., and J. Browning. 1989. *Microeconomic Theory and Applications.* Glenview, Ill.: Scott, Foresman.

Dodds, D., and J. Lesser. 1994. "Can Utility Commissions Improve on Environmental Regulations?" *Land Economics* 70(1): 63–76.

Freeman, A., D. Burtraw, W. Harrington, and A. Krupnick. 1992b. "Weighing Environmental Externalities: *How* to Do It Right." *Electricity Journal* 5(7): 17–25.

Hahn, R. 1989. "Economic Prescriptions for Environmental Problems: How the Patient Followed the Doctor's Orders." *Journal of Economic Perspectives* 3(1): 95–114.

Joskow, P. 1992. "Weighing Environmental Externalities: Let's Do It Right!" *Electricity Journal* 5(3): 53–67.

Kneese, A., and B. Bower. 1984. *Managing Water Quality.* 2d ed. Baltimore: Johns Hopkins University Press.

Lents, J., and W. Kelly. 1993. "Clearing the Air in Los Angeles." *Scientific American* 269(4): 32–41.

Tietenberg, T. 1980. "Transferable Discharge Permits and the Control of Stationary Source Air Pollution." *Land Economics* 55(3): 391–416.

———. 1985. *Emissions Trading: An Exercise in Reforming Pollution Policy.* Washington, D.C.: Resources for the Future.

Weitzman, M. 1974. "Prices vs. Quantities." *Review of Economic Studies* 41(3): 477–499.

Wiel, S. 1991. "The New Environmental Accounting: A Status Report." *Electricity Journal* 4(10): 46–53.

APPENDIX TO CHAPTER 7

Constrained Marginal Costs and the Second Best

To consider environmental regulations determined in a second-best situation, we construct a simple, but fairly general, mathematical model.[1] We also assume a partial-equilibrium framework. To frame the discussion, suppose that the design and operation of an industrial facility is subject to environmental regulations set by the EPA. The plant also produces output for a regulated marketplace, such as the market for electricity.

Assume that in the absence of any environmental controls required by an environmental regulator, emissions, E_u, are proportional to output, Q, so that $E_u(Q) = \alpha Q$. Also assume that emissions are assumed to be the only source of environmental costs. Thus there are no "fixed" environmental costs, such as might be present with, say, a dam that eliminates a salmon fishery and whitewater recreation benefits from a previously free-flowing river.[2] The production costs associated with the plant are given by $C_1(Q)$.

Now, in response to environmental regulations, such as emissions control requirements, the owners of the plant are assumed to install emissions control equipment that reduces emissions to E_c, where $E_c < E_u$. The cost of using these control measures is given by C_2, which is assumed to increase with the required level of emissions *reduction* $E_u - E_c$ and also increase as total output increases. Thus

$$C_2 = C_2(E_u - E_c, Q) = C_2(\alpha Q - E_c, Q) \tag{7A.1}$$

Of course, it may be the case that there are pollutants, such as carbon dioxide, for which there are no regulations that require controls to be installed. In these cases, C_2 will be zero.

The damage from pollution emitted by the plant will be denoted $D(E)$, where $D(E)$ is assumed to be an increasing function of E. We know that, absent nonconvexities in the production frontier, full efficiency with an efficient level of output and an efficient level of emissions requires that marginal private cost (MPC) equal marginal social cost (MSC), that both equal marginal willingness to pay, and that marginal control cost equal marginal damage cost.

The total private cost (TPC) associated with production will equal the sum of the internal production costs and the costs of any control measures. Thus

$$TPC = C_1(Q) + C_2(\alpha Q - E_c, Q) \tag{7A.2}$$

Now, MPC is just the *derivative* of total private cost. Therefore, MPC will equal the marginal cost of increasing production, MC_1, plus the marginal cost of controlling the additional emissions, MC_2. Thus

$$MPC = MC_1 + MC_2 \tag{7A.3}$$

---

[1]A more detailed derivation of this model can be found in Dodds and Lesser (1994).
[2]This assumption is made for ease of exposition and does not fundamentally alter the results.

Next, we examine the total and marginal social costs associated with production. The total social cost (*TSC*) is just *TPC* plus any residual environmental damages. Thus

$$TSC = C_1(Q) + C_2(\alpha Q - E_c, Q) + D(E) \tag{7A.4}$$

It then follows that *MSC* equals *MPC* plus marginal damages, *MD*. Thus

$$MSC = MC_1 + MC_2 + MD \tag{7A.5}$$

If the level of control has been previously set, regulators whose focus is only on the market for the plant's output will see these costs as constraints. In other words, they will be unable to require different control levels because that is not in their jurisdiction. A PUC, for example, cannot tell the EPA to change the Clean Air Act requirements. Instead, the PUC must operate within those requirements.

We can examine the second-best impacts by considering the primary environmental regulators' actions and their effects on any secondary regulation. We will do this for output taxes and emissions limits per unit of output and leave the cases of emissions taxes and tradable permits as exercises. In each case, the secondary regulators take the primary regulators' actions as given. Thus secondary regulators will deal with total and marginal costs that are *constrained* by the actions of the primary regulators.

AN OUTPUT TAX

Recall from the chapter that an output tax does not affect the inputs used in the production process. In this case, we determine constrained marginal social cost, $CMSC_q$, and constrained marginal private cost, *CMPC*, as follows:

$$CMSC_q = MC_1 + \alpha MD \tag{7A.6}$$

which means that

$$CMPC_q = MC_1 + \tau_q \tag{7A.7}$$

because an increment of output creates α units of emissions. Thus

$$CMSC_q - MPC_q = \alpha MD - \tau_q \tag{7A.8}$$

If the output tax is set at its optimal value of αMD, which, as pointed out in the chapter, still would not ensure the correct input mix, secondary regulators should not change the output tax. However, the correct secondary tax would be positive at lower tax rates and negative at higher tax rates.

EMISSIONS LIMITS PER UNIT OF OUTPUT

This case is likely to be the most common one. In this case, the primary environmental regulator has imposed emissions limits requiring the installation of various pollution control measures, such as scrubbers. Suppose that the emissions limit per unit of output is given by β, where β is less than the unconstrained emissions rate α. With an emissions limit per unit of output, we determine constrained marginal private cost, $CMPC_0$, and constrained marginal social cost, $CMSC_0$, as follows:

$$MPC_0 = MC_1 + (\alpha - \beta)MC_2 \tag{7A.9}$$

$$CMSC_0 = MC_1 + (\alpha - \beta)MC_2 + \beta MD \tag{7A.10}$$

In this case, $CMSC$ will *always* exceed marginal private cost by the amount βMD. What this means is that no matter how stringent an emissions limit is, a secondary regulator will want to impose a positive emissions tax on the remaining emissions. This is a counterintuitive result but is explained by considering the difference between first-best and second-best solutions.

We know that an unconstrained first-best optimum could be achieved through the imposition of an emissions tax, say τ^*. With this emissions tax, there is no further action that should be taken by secondary regulators.

Now suppose that environmental regulators have imposed too high an emissions tax τ', where $\tau' > \tau^*$. In this case, the plant owners would add more stringent emissions controls, resulting in a new, higher overall MPC equal to $MC_1 + MC_2' + \tau'\beta'$, where β' equals the new emissions per unit of output. In this case, $CMSC$ equals $MC_1 + MC_2' + MD'$, where D' equals the remaining marginal damages after the overly stringent controls are incorporated into the plant. As we discussed in the chapter, secondary regulators can achieve a second-best equilibrium by reducing the price of the output.

Next suppose that environmental regulators have imposed an emissions limit per unit of output. This leads to a new MPC equal to $MC_1 + MC_2'$ and a new $CMSC$ equal to $MC_1 + MC_2' + MD'$. Thus $CMSC$ in this case is identical to the previous $CMSC$ arising from the too high emissions tax.

Unlike the previous case, however, to achieve the second-best equilibrium, the secondary regulator must *raise* the price because from a second-best viewpoint, $MPC < CMSC$. Therefore, in this latter case, the secondary regulator will impose a higher price, even though the control measures are already too high. The difference is that with the emissions tax, marginal environmental damage is already overcounted in the energy price, whereas with the emissions constraint, it is not included in price at all.

PROBLEMS

1. Using Equation (7A.4) determine the impacts associated with an emissions tax of $\$P$ per unit of emissions.
2. Do the same for a system of tradable permits with permit price $\$P$.
3. How would you modify the analysis presented in the chapter to account for the effects on unregulated substitutes for electricity? For example, suppose the use of heating oil, which is unregulated, emits more pollutants per Btu

than the use of electricity. If utility regulators nevertheless impose an additional tax on electricity, there will be additional substitution to heating oil use, and higher levels of pollution. [*Hint:* Will the definition of marginal damages change?]

REFERENCE

Dodds, D., and J. Lesser. 1994. "Can Utility Commissions Improve on Environmental Regulations?" *Land Economics* 70(1): 63–76.

EXTERNALITIES, EQUITY, AND FAIRNESS

Fish Story: Salmon and the Columbia River

In the early 1930s, harnessing of the Columbia River began in earnest. By 1935, in the depths of the Great Depression, construction was well under way on Grand Coulee Dam, which at the time could have supplied the power needs of just about everyone living west of the Mississippi River (Reisner 1993). Grand Coulee was to be the largest hydroelectric dam in the world. It would create thousands of construction jobs, provide electricity, divert water for irrigating the desert in eastern Washington, and lay a foundation for economic and agricultural development in the entire Pacific Northwest.

As Reisner points out, the construction of Grand Coulee involved much more than economic and agricultural development. The Columbia River had the greatest spawning run of salmon in the world. Millions of salmon migrated upriver each year. During the Depression, salmon represented a cheap, nutritious source of protein: a can of salmon cost only 10 cents per pound. Unfortunately for the salmon, Grand Coulee Dam was almost 600 feet tall when it was completed. No matter how adept salmon were at navigating rapids and small waterfalls, they were unable to get past Grand Coulee. The salmon's spawning runs ended at the dam, eventually destroying a once vibrant industry. But completion of Grand Coulee helped the United States win World War II. The electricity generated at the dam provided power to smelters that produced aluminum to build thousands of aircraft and hundreds of ships. Without the dam, Reisner (1993) avers, "the war would have been seriously prolonged" (p. 162).

Today, several species of Columbia River salmon are listed under the Endangered Species Act. Some runs into tributaries of the Columbia today consist of only a few hundreds or even dozens of fish. Hundreds of millions of dollars have been spent building extensive fish ladders, barging juvenile salmon downstream, and building hatcheries. The success of these efforts has been limited. At the same time, the price of electricity has risen to pay for these expenditures, which has hurt electric-intensive industries in the region and led to the loss of manufacturing jobs.

In its developed state today, the Columbia River supports numerous valuable activities. Besides the production of electricity, the river is second only to the Mississippi in terms of shipping, with over one-third of all U.S. wheat exports traveling on it. The value of commercial and sport fishing and related industries for salmon is estimated to be in the hundreds of millions of dollars. Other recreation, such as windsurfing, provides much value to thousands of people who use the river and its tributaries each year. And the value of the agricultural output made possible by the Columbia Basin Irrigation Project has been placed at over $5 billion.

Under the rules of the Endangered Species Act, protection of the salmon must be achieved without regard to cost. As a result, water in the Columbia is increasingly being used to help migrating fish rather than to produce electricity when it is needed most. Further mitigation expenditures are likely as many environmental and Native American groups seek to protect and enhance what was once a bountiful natural resource. Whatever the expenditure, the past grandeur of the salmon has almost surely been lost forever.

Should Grand Coulee and the other dams on the Columbia River have been built? In retrospect, were the trade-offs worthwhile? Was the loss of salmon forever a necessary sacrifice to reduce the loss of human life in World War II? What about the loss of a cheap food source? Should that have been considered? And what about the "rights" of the salmon themselves? Do they have any?

None of these are easy questions to answer, and it is likely that reasoned arguments can be made that cover a wide spectrum of views. Yet environmental policymakers often confront such difficult and divisive issues. Today, with the Endangered Species Act and the quest for "sustainability," questions of the "rights" of nonhuman species have taken on new importance. Yet the costs of restoration must be paid by humans, who have their own needs.

There are also the issues of who should pay for restoration and how.[1] Should it be only people living and working in the Pacific Northwest? Should a general tax be levied on all U.S. taxpayers to pay for what has been a national resource? Should restoration costs be paid more by the rich than by the poor, especially if the rich value improvements in environmental quality more highly?

The designs of many environmental policies must take these and other equity and rights questions into account. On top of all that, those policies must somehow survive the almost inevitable distraction of political and parochial interests.

---

[1]For a discussion of some of the payment options and the specific strategies envisioned to restore salmon runs, see NPPC (1992).

INTRODUCTION

Suppose that, having studied the material in Chapter 7 carefully, an intrepid environmental policymaker recommends imposing a tax of 2 cents per kilowatt-hour of electricity to pay for salmon restoration. The recommendation sets off a great hue and cry. Advocates for low-income groups complain that the tax will punish their constituents, who cannot afford further increases in the price of electricity. Manufacturers complain that the tax will increase their production costs, raising the price of everything from cans to cars, and lead to the loss of thousands of jobs, not only in the Pacific Northwest but in other parts of the country as well. The input-output framework discussed in Chapter 2 and the political framework of Chapter 5 rear their heads. Instead of being congratulated for developing a cogent solution, the policymaker is run out of town on a rail. What went wrong?

In Chapter 7, we showed how externalities affect economic efficiency. But there are many other issues relating to the *distributional* impacts of externalities and environmental policies. In this chapter, we begin by addressing how distributional impacts can affect policies developed to promote economic efficiency. We then examine how the demand for environmental quality changes as a function of income. Clearly, the sensitivity of the demand for environmental quality to income will also bear on the distribution of the benefits and the costs of environmental policies by income class. The poor may have little demand for environmental quality because they receive few of its benefits.

Next we turn to compensation issues. In Chapter 6, we saw how a "polluter pays" policy for external environmental costs can increase economic efficiency. In this chapter, we examine the flipside of that issue: whether *victims* of pollution should be compensated. Finally, we consider environmental issues in the context of human rights and the rights of nature, as these may raise additional concerns beyond those raised by issues of equity. All of these distributional and rights issues can arise when environmental policies are under development.

EQUITY VERSUS EFFICIENCY IN ENVIRONMENTAL POLICIES

In Chapter 6, we discussed the Coase theorem, which states that in the absence of transactions costs, market failures will be self-correcting regardless of the initial assignment of property rights. Coase showed that an efficient outcome could be arrived at without government intervention. One often-used example is known as the "fable of the bees" (Cheung 1973), which involves orchard owners and beekeepers. Orchard owners require bees to pollinate their trees. For a long time, it was thought that this was a classic externality because orchard owners would have their fruit trees pollinated at no cost because the beekeepers' bees were collecting nectar to make honey. It turns out that the Coase theorem came into practice in this case. Cheung discovered that the orchard owners did *not* receive the services of bees free of charge. In fact, beekeepers charged orchard owners to have the bees put in the orchards for pollinating services. The externality was internalized through a market mechanism with no government intervention. Beekeepers were better off because they were paid for the services provided by their bees. Orchard owners were better off because the value of the bees' pollination services exceeded the payments to the beekeepers. All was right with the world.

Suppose, however, that orchard owners enjoyed a right not to have bees "trespass" in their orchards. In that case, beekeepers, whose bees required nectar, would pay orchard owners a fee allowing the bees to collect nectar. The ultimate outcome would be the same: bees would have their nectar and orchard owners would have pollinated fruit trees. An efficient outcome would result, and economists would congratulate themselves for their theoretical acumen.

Unfortunately, as we discussed in Chapter 6, the Coase theorem requires transactions costs to be small relative to the potential benefits of internalization. So the fable of the bees might not work as well if one hive of bees wandered off to pollinate hundreds of orchards simultaneously. In that case, beekeepers would have a difficult time contracting with all of the orchard owners for pollination services.

In Chapter 7, we discussed the different policy instruments that could achieve efficient outcomes when there were many affected parties and sources of an externality. Thus pollution taxes or tradable permits can work, even though there are thousands of polluters and millions of affected people.

We also discussed examples where a divergence of private and social costs have created common property problems because ownership was not well defined. Unlike the case of the orchard owners and the bees, where ownership was clear but there were still external impacts, ownership rights are incomplete or nonexistent in many cases. For example, we discussed fishermen who would expend fishing effort without regard to the effort expended by other fishermen, resulting in overfishing and fishery stock depletion.[2]

In their zeal to promote efficiency, economists sometimes ignore equity impacts of different policies. Few policies result in Pareto superior moves where everyone is made better off. Far more often, a move from an inefficient situation to an efficient one results in losses for some individuals or firms. Think of the situation where a monopolist is forced to produce at a competitive equilibrium. The competitive equilibrium is Pareto-optimal but is not a Pareto improvement for the monopolist! These distributional consequences are often at least as important as efficiency goals, especially when policies are developed and debated in the context of political settings. As a result, efficient policies are sometimes opposed bitterly by parties who will be affected adversely by the policies.

Consider the case of mushroom hunters in the Pacific Northwest. Mushroom hunting has grown rapidly in popularity as more people have discovered that many species of delicious mushrooms grow wild in forests. The number of mushroom hunters has grown significantly, and as a result, finding wild mushrooms has

---

[2]See Chapter 16 for a thorough discussion of fisheries.

become more difficult. Hunters must go farther into forests to find new supplies, and stocks have become depleted. Some mushroom hunters have taken to establishing property rights using extralegal methods: guarding "their" areas of the forest and threatening to shoot individuals who trespass. Although this is one way of establishing property rights and an "efficient" harvest, we do not recommend it as a policy instrument.

Suppose that selling forests lands to private owners is not a politically viable solution. To solve the mushroom problem, suppose that officials require all mushroom hunters to pay a fixed licensing fee and a tax on each pound of mushrooms they harvest. The policy will reduce the number of mushroom hunters and the amount of mushrooms harvested. Marginal would-be mushroom hunters will choose not to get licensed if they believe that the benefits from the mushrooms they expect to collect will be less than the license fee and taxes they expect to pay, based on choosing to participate and their expected harvest. Hunters who choose to purchase licenses will not have to compete with so many other hunters. On average, they will harvest fewer mushrooms, continuing to harvest only until the marginal value of additional mushrooms exceeds the cost (time, fuel, etc.), plus the marginal tax paid.

Who benefits from this policy? Former mushroom hunters who choose not to buy a license are unambiguously worse off. Instead of harvesting tasty wild mushrooms, they must now be content with ordinary store-bought ones. Mushroom hunters who do buy licenses will also be worse off, depending on the size of the tax. Although on average they will expend less effort per pound of mushrooms harvested, the savings may exceed the taxes and the license fees they pay. This is a surprising result that we show graphically in Figure 8.1.

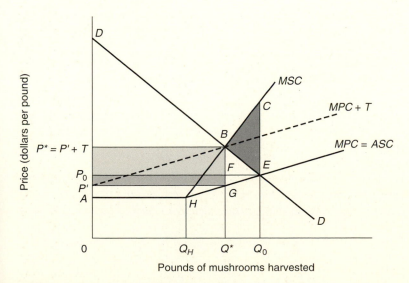

Figure 8.1   Equity Impacts of Mushroom Taxes and License Fees

In Figure 8.1, curve DD represents the demand for mushrooms. Initially, access to the forest is free, but hunters pay the costs associated with their trips, including the costs of driving into the forest and the value of their time. The line MPC is the marginal private cost and average social cost associated with mushroom hunting. As long as fewer than Q_H pounds are harvested, there is no common-property problem. Supplies of mushrooms are not depleted, nor do hunters run into or threaten to shoot one another. As more hunters enter the forest and more mushrooms are harvested, however, private and social costs diverge, as shown by the line labeled MSC. (It would even be possible to have so many hunters in the forest that the total harvest fell because the hunters were on top of one another.)

With unregulated access to the forest (i.e., no license fees or taxes), assume there are a total of Q_0 pounds of mushrooms collected by N hunters. At that point, the average cost per hunter equals $\$P_0$ per pound. With a harvest of Q_0 pounds (point E), the marginal social costs of hunting exceed the marginal private benefits. The efficient harvest level will be at point B, where MSC intersects the demand curve. This corresponds to a total harvest of Q^* pounds. To achieve this efficient level, suppose that regulators set the tax at $\$T$ per pound (equal to the vertical distance BG), reflecting the marginal external cost each hunter imposes on the others. In addition, they impose a license fee of $\$F$ per hunter.

With the tax and license fee system imposed, some hunters will stop hunting, leaving only N' hunters ($N' < N$). If Q^* pounds are harvested by these remaining hunters, the average hunter will pay an additional $\$TQ^*/N' + \$F$, where the average hunter harvests Q^*/N' pounds of mushrooms. Unfortunately, the average hunter's private costs will fall only by the amount ($\$P_0 - P')Q^*/N - \$F$. Thus, on average, remaining hunters will be worse off.

How can everyone involved be worse off from a move that improves efficiency? The answer is that they cannot. *Someone* must gain. In this case, the only parties who experience a direct gain are the recipients of the taxes. The taxes collected exceed the net societal gains from reducing mushroom hunters. Of course, gains may also be experienced by users of the forest who are not mushroom hunters. For example, hikers may benefit because they are less likely to accidentally run into an irate and armed mushroom hunter.

This example illustrates one of the potential conflicts between efficiency and equity goals. Often the benefits from efficient solutions are *diffuse,* but the costs are borne by a focused set of players. Think of a factory whose output is taxed as a means of reducing the pollution that rains down on thousands of nearby residents. The tax will exceed the social costs imposed, but the benefits to each individual resident will be small.

The lesson of the Coase theorem and policies that seek economically efficient solutions is that the ultimate results can have significant distributional and equity consequences. Forcing residents living near a factory to pay the factory to reduce its pollution may achieve the same efficient solution (in terms of the amount of pollution reduced) as levying a tax on pollution emitted by the factory. Economists often talk of the "polluter pays" principle as a guideline for economic efficiency. That guideline is not strictly correct, at least as far as the Coase theorem is concerned, because the efficient solution can be achieved (at least in theory) regardless of whether the polluter or the polluted pay. But the distribution of wealth and the policy consequences will be far different.[3]

Environmental policymakers seeking efficient outcomes will have to address these sorts of equity issues. This fact explains, as we will discuss in Chapter 9, why many environmental policies have focused on equity and fairness goals rather than on economic efficiency.

DISTRIBUTIONAL CONSEQUENCES OF EXTERNALITIES AND EXTERNALITY POLICIES

Most people, when asked whether a factory owner should pay a tax on pollution emitted by the factory or whether nearby downwind residents should pay the factory owner to reduce pollution levels, will choose the former. The "polluter pays" principle aligns itself nicely with "common sense" and our intrinsic definition of fairness. Unfortunately, things are not always so simple, which is why externalities can have significant distributional consequences.

Suppose that the factory was built 40 years ago. At that time, there were no nearby residents. Perhaps the land downwind of the factory was used to graze cattle, which were unaffected by the pollution. Or perhaps the land lay fallow. So when the factory first began operations, there was no environmental externality; pollution was emitted, but no one was affected adversely by it. Suppose that 30 years later, the land was sold to a developer, who built a residential neighborhood. Residents moved in and soon began to complain that the pollution from the factory was soiling their clothes and wilting their flowers. As more residents moved into the neighborhood, an increasingly large externality was created. Or was it?

Recall from Chapter 6 that environmental externalities often arise because of ambiguities in property rights. As a result, externalities almost always raise distributional issues because *all* externalities imply an ambiguity in the distribution of wealth. Initially, the impact on the distribution of wealth in our example appears obvious: homeowners move into the neighborhood and experience economic losses. But what if the price paid by homeowners was less than the prices of similar houses not near the factory. And what if the homeowners were told about the factory before they moved in? In that case, the distribution of wealth would have been affected *in expectation of the pollution.* However, the externality would still exist, as long as the polluter did not account for the impacts of the pollution. Does that mean it is appropriate to internalize the externality? As we discussed in

---

[3]Knetsch (1995) discusses fairness issues from the standpoint of the "reference point." The reference point refers to a "natural" assignment of initial property rights. For example, in the case of the startup of a factory that will pollute the air, the reference point would be the state when there was no air pollution. Determining an acceptable reference point obviously may be contentious.

Chapter 6, the answer is "not necessarily." To force the factory owner to pay a tax on the pollution emitted by the factory would reduce the pollution and indirectly distribute wealth to the homeowners. However, the costs of the remedy could be greater than the benefits.

In a market economy, people's wealth is determined by the assets they own and the prices of those assets. People earn income by selling assets they own or the services of their assets, including their labor. While the people living downwind of a factory see the factory owners as polluting "their" air and reducing the value of their assets (the homes they live in), the factory owner sees the neighbors as objecting to a legitimate right to dispose of waste products. If a tax is levied on the factory's pollution, that tax will reduce the wealth of the factory owner. Depending on the initial conditions (who was there first), each side can legitimately view the externality as arising because others are using or controlling something (in this case, air) that each believes it has a right to without the other's consent. And both sides will have a point.

If the other party were not there, no externality would exist. If the asset in question is the atmosphere, the wealth of both the factory owners and their neighbors is ambiguous. If the owner increases the factory's output and hence emissions, the neighbors' wealth decreases. This effect can actually be observed in real estate values in some neighborhoods: homes and apartments in more heavily polluted areas tend to have lower prices for the same quality of dwelling.

How Externality Policies Redistribute Wealth

The presence of externalities can affect the distribution of wealth, and so can policies to correct them. If the neighbors band together and get government action limiting pollution emitted by the factory, the factory owners' wealth will be reduced, while the neighbors' will be increased.[4] Unfortunately, as in the case with an emissions tax paid by the factory owner when the residents of the neighborhood were aware of the emissions prior to moving, policies designed to correct externalities may achieve efficient outcomes while further "skewing" distributions of wealth.

Correcting an externality *always* redistributes wealth, whether that redistribution is direct, such as the mushroom hunters paying license fees and taxes, or indirect, such as the value gained from reducing pollution from a factory. It turns out, however, that the redistribution effect can exceed the value of the economic damages themselves. For example, the loss to the factory owner from imposition of a tax may exceed the market value of the entire neighborhood downwind.

An even more curious impact of some environmental policies is that firms will sometimes seek to have such policies imposed on *themselves*. Some firms in Germany, for example, have lobbied to create stringent recycling and packaging

---

[4]Note that these wealth effects will not necessarily cancel each other out.

requirements. And in the United States, some large refuse disposal firms have lobbied for strict regulations on landfills and mandatory recycling programs. If environmental policies raise costs for these industries, why should they propose such regulations?

The reason is that such policies can create wealth for incumbent firms by increasing barriers to market entry. In doing so, potential entrants to the industry are deterred, and the incumbent can earn higher profits. A firm that has developed (and patented) a specialized process, for example, in anticipation of a new environmental regulation will have an incentive to require all firms to use the same

ENVIRONMENTAL DETERRENCE IN THE ELECTRIC INDUSTRY

As states such as California and Massachusetts deregulate their electric utility industries, one concern is that deregulation will lead to greater imports of cheap but dirty electricity, principally electricity generated from coal-fired power plants. This is an especially sensitive issue for Massachusetts and other New England states because most of that coal-fired generation takes place in the Midwest, and the prevailing winds blow toward the Northeast.

The regulatory problem is that electrons are not choosy where they travel. They follow the laws of physics, not the laws of contracts. Thus "banning" the direct importation of "dirty" midwestern electricity is impossible. Furthermore, power contracts can be written in series so that buyers may believe they are purchasing "clean" power, such as hydroelectric power from Canada, rather than the nasty stuff. Compounding the difficulties is the commerce clause in the U.S. Constitution, which takes a dim view of states' restricting trade from other states. (For example, Illinois tried to legislate that its electric utilities purchase only coal mined in Illinois in order to protect its coal-mining industry, even though cheaper coal was available from other states. That law was struck down as unconstitutional.)

One response has been to demand that generator owners wishing to peddle their wares in New England clean up their plants to meet the latest Clean Air Act requirements. These requirements, called the New Source Performance Standards (NSPS), are a form of command-and-control regulation that specifies how much pollution a plant can emit per ton of coal burned. In essence, the requirement would be a quid pro quo to sell electricity in a competitive retail market in the northeastern states. Whether this deterrent strategy works is another matter, for it will still have to overcome the ease with which transactions can be designed to appear "clean" and no doubt will be challenged in court by those midwestern utilities (and other owners of such generators) who see a chance to profit. Of course, northeastern states can abandon their plans to introduce retail competition into the industry, but such a "head in the sand" approach may only make things worse in the long run. Stay tuned.

process. Potential market entrants are deterred, or they enter and are forced to license the process from the incumbent. Either way, the incumbent benefits.

The Problem of Multiple Goods   Wealth redistributions caused by environmental policies can be complicated when multiple goods are produced. In a classic article, Turvey (1963) described the case of two producers, one of whom produces multiple goods. Suppose that producer B is a laundry and producer A is a factory that can produce either cheese or ice cream. A standard microeconomics result is that A would determine the level of production of cheese and ice cream on the basis of the marginal costs and market prices of each. In this case, A would decide which of the two goods to produce and devote all of its resources to producing that good.

We assume also that production of cheese releases more air pollution than production of ice cream. The pollution drifts downwind to the laundry and requires that the laundry add more deodorizers to each load of wash to remove the smell of the pollution from the clothes. The external cost imposed on the laundry depends on which good A produces. We assume that the losses to B (in the form of additional deodorizer required) per pound of cheese produced is greater than the loss per pound of ice cream. As shown in Figure 8.2, in the absence of any negotiations or restrictions, we assume that A would produce C_{max} pounds of cheese, where the marginal gain of additional production falls to zero, because its total gain will equal $0EC_{max}$, which we assume is larger than A's total gains from producing ice cream, $0XI_{max}$. (This is the same as saying that A will produce where the marginal benefit just equals its marginal cost.)

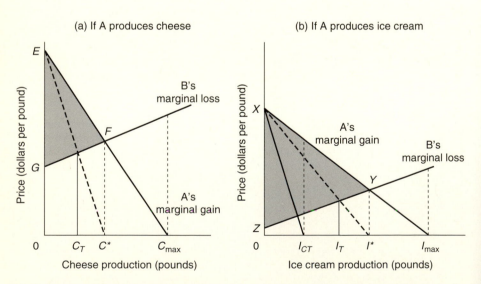

Figure 8.2   Distributions of Gains and Losses from an Externality Policy

Source: Adapted from Turvey (1963), p. 311.

If A and B are both profit maximizers, know the available production alternatives, and are willing and able to negotiate, the Coase theorem tells us that an optimal solution will be reached, regardless of to whom the law grants rights. With negotiations only, A will switch production from cheese to ice cream, regardless of who has rights. The reason for this is that the *total* social gain from A's producing the optimal amount of ice cream, shown as the shaded triangle XYZ, is larger than the total social gain from A's producing the optimal amount of cheese, shown as the shaded triangle ABC, and total losses to B are less if A produces ice cream than if A produces cheese. The amount of ice cream produced will equal I^*. Of course, the distribution of wealth will differ, depending on who must compensate whom.

Now assume that in addition to the possibility of direct negotiations between A and B, the government levies a tax on A, with the tax set equal to the amount of marginal damages to B. We want to know whether this tax will achieve the same optimum as negotiation and how the tax will affect the distribution of wealth. The tax effectively reduces A's marginal gains from production. These new marginal gains are shown as the dashed lines in Figure 8.2. There are several possible outcomes.[5]

Suppose that the government observes A producing cheese and levies the "correct" cheese tax equal to FC^*. Either A will continue to produce cheese, although a smaller amount, C^*, or it will switch to producing ice cream. A will continue to produce cheese if its new total gains, $0EC^*$, are greater than the total gains from producing ice cream. The level of those latter gains will depend on how the tax would be levied on A's ice cream production. If A switched to producing ice cream but the tax continued to be at a level FC^*, A's ice cream production will be only I_{CT}, which is lower than the optimal level of ice cream production. If the tax amount fell to YI^*, A would produce the optimal amount of ice cream, *but only if A's new total gains, $0XI^*$, were greater than $0EC^*$.*

The "correct" tax would be set to adjust A's level of ice cream production to the Coase result of I^* pounds. Suppose that that happens. From B's standpoint, there will *still* be an incentive to negotiate to reduce output further to levels C_T and I_T. The reason is that from its standpoint, B's marginal losses exceed A's marginal gains. Only if A and B cannot negotiate, perhaps because there are large numbers of factories or many laundries, will the tax achieve the optimum solution, and then only if all of the relevant marginal gain and loss curves have been measured correctly. Finally, measuring the relevant gains and losses and the administration of the tax will be costly. (An emissions tax, though more efficient, could be even more costly to administer than the output tax.) The essence of Turvey's argument is that these policy costs may be significant in themselves, perhaps even higher than the costs of negotiation. And this example further reveals that policies levied "at the margin," such as taxes, may not achieve an optimal result when nonmarginal changes are required.

There are two lessons to be gleaned from Turvey's presentation: (1) no single externality policy can guarantee a socially optimal result in all cases, and (2) every externality policy will have distributional consequences. Furthermore, the choice

---

[5]This is another example of the nonconvexity problem we discussed in Chapter 6. See also Baumol and Oates (1988).

of a preferred policy may be influenced by whether the "victims" are compensated. This is the subject of the next section.

Compensating for Environmental Damages

In an earlier example we discussed a combination of license fees and harvest taxes on mushroom hunters to reduce the overharvesting of mushrooms. We showed that *all* of the affected parties—both former and remaining mushroom hunters—on average would be harmed; their wealth would be reduced from the tax and fee payments more than it would be increased because of fewer hunters and more mushrooms. Only the receipients of the tax revenues would benefit directly.

We also considered a case where individuals in a neighborhood suddenly found themselves living downwind from a newly built factory that spewed pollution. In that case, we saw how the factory caused a reduction in the wealth of the homeowners and how an emissions tax levied on pollution emitted by the factory would reduce emissions and increase the homeowners' wealth by increasing the value of their homes. However, the homeowners would still be less wealthy than if the factory had not been built. Both of these examples raise an important policy issue: should victims of environmental damage be compensated, and if so, what is the appropriate amount of compensation?

Assessing compensation for parties bearing environmental damages raises many complex legal, economic, and moral questions. Rather than presenting a voluminous discussion of these questions, we will look at three key issues for environmental policy consideration: the efficiency effects of compensation, the types of harm for which compensation can be expected, and the appropriate level of compensation. The policy relevance of these issues should not be disputed; several legislative proposals are pending before Congress requiring compensation for a wide range of government regulations.

Compensation and Efficiency   We must first distinguish compensation in a Coasian sense from compensation in an administrative sense. In the case of the factory and the laundry, the Coase theorem suggested that the ultimate outcome would be the same regardless of the initial assignment of rights. Thus the outcome would be the same whether the factory owner paid the laundry owner for the right to pollute or whether the laundry owner paid the factory owner to pollute less. In this simple example, the two affected parties negotiated among themselves to reach the optimal solution. There was no administrative rule requiring compensation by one party or the other.

Administrative policies that require compensation differ from Coasian compensation. For example, policies that promise full compensation of environmental damages weaken incentives to avoid such damages.[6] Suppose that an administrative rule required the factory owner to compensate all laundries for the full extent of pollution damages. First, that compensation would not be the same amount as the

---

[6]Compensation will also depend on common-law remedies, as was discussed in Chapter 6.

laundry and factory would otherwise negotiate among themselves. Second, such a rule would reduce the incentive for laundry owners to avoid pollution damages.

As another example, suppose that the factory is surrounded by agricultural land and that emissions from the factory reduce certain crop yields when they are carried back to earth by rain. However, it rains only when the wind is from the west. It may be possible to shift crop production to farms west of the power plant and to grow a crop that is not harmed by the pollution on farms to the east of the power plant. This may be a much cheaper way to avoid the damage than reducing emissions, but if farmers are fully compensated for their pollution damage, they have no incentive to make such a change. In other words, the social costs of changing farmers' practices may be less than the social costs of controlling the factory's emissions. Thus *compensation for pollution victims may conflict with the goal of economic efficiency when the impact is a public good (or public bad).* This conflict arises because of an "impurity" in the public-good aspect of environmental quality. Although it may be impossible to exclude anyone from the benefits of some environmental policies, individuals may be able to affect the environmental quality they consume personally by their own actions.[7]

What Is Compensated?   Many of the impacts of environmental externalities and externality policies are the result of price changes. This is particularly true for more indirect impacts, such as to the suppliers of businesses that are harmed by an externality. In general, our society does not require compensation for harms inflicted through the market. This is true even when the harm is fairly direct. A firm that switches from fuel oil to natural gas is not required to compensate its oil supplier unless it breaks a contract in doing so.[8] Neither can the fuel oil supplier expect compensation from the natural gas marketer whose lower prices lured the customer away or from the gas producers whose new discoveries led to lower gas prices.

Our society generally does not require government to compensate private parties for losses because of regulatory changes, although the exact extent of when compensation is required continues to be a matter of legal debate in the courts.[9] Engaging in business is somewhere between a legal right and a legal privilege. The

---

[7]This problem can be mitigated if compensation is defined as net of *efficient* mitigation. For example, suppose that a laundry claimed that emissions from a nearby factory caused $500 worth of damage to its washing machines. However, the laundry could have installed a simple filter for $50 that would have eliminated the pollution and prevented the damage. Then the efficient level of compensation would be only $50.

[8]This is where common-law remedies can come in.

[9]Arguments for compensation are generally made under the U.S. Constitution's "takings clause," contained in the Fifth Amendment. What this means is that the government cannot arbitrarily take or restrict the use of an individual's property and in doing so cause that individual economic harm. For example, I might own a piece of land that I intend to build a house on. If the government prevents me from building a house, the economic value of my land may be reduced. The question is whether the government should compensate me for that loss.

United States treats it as much closer to a right than most societies but still regards regulation as imposing legitimate limits within which that right may be exercised. A change in regulation is a change of the scope for the exercise of private property rights, not a taking of those rights. Thus governments may be required to consider the impacts of regulations on private property but are not required to pay compensation for any resulting harm.

ENDANGERED PROPERTY OWNERS?

In June 1995, the U.S. Supreme Court addressed the issue of to what the Endangered Species Act (ESA) applied. The law had been under attack for years by loggers, farmers, developers, and other property rights advocates, who claimed it prevented them from making the most economic use of their land. The particular challenge in this case was brought by a coalition of individuals, communities, and companies in the Pacific Northwest and Southeast engaged in or dependent on the timber industry.* They alleged that they were adversely affected by the ESA because of its application to the northern spotted owl, which was listed as a threatened species in 1990, and the endangered red-cockaded woodpecker. The coalition argued that the language of the ESA, which makes it unlawful for any person to "take endangered or threatened species" and defines *take* as "harass," "harm," "pursue," "wound," or "kill," was never intended to encompass habitat modification. They argued that the ESA prohibits only *direct* harm of endangered species (shooting, trapping, squashing, etc.) on private land but does not impose restrictions on the use of private land, *even if that use may inherently harm an endangered species.* They argued that preventing private property owners from using their land as they saw fit amounted to illegal takings under the Fifth Amendment of the U.S. Constitution and that the government was therefore required to fully compensate landowners for prohibiting any specific uses, such as logging.

Environmentalists argued that habitat protection was a critical part of the ESA; otherwise, endangered species would have little real protection. Bruce Babbitt, then secretary of the interior, agreed with the environmentalists that "taking" or "harming" an endangered species did include habitat modification.

Though a federal court of appeals sided with the coalition, the U.S. Supreme Court rejected the property rights argument. In a 6–3 decision, the Court reversed the court of appeals, stating that the Endangered Species Act did apply to protection of habitat as well because destruction of habitat could harm the species in question. After the decision, property rights advocates approached Congress, where the ESA was not popular, to alter the act significantly. Who or what will ultimately be the endangered species remains to be seen.

Babbitt et al. v. *Sweet Home Chapter of Communities for a Great Oregon et al.* (17 F.3d 1463, rev.).

Despite the Supreme Court decision described in the box on p. 194, our society generally *does* require compensation for property damage or confiscation. If A inflicts damage on B's property without B's permission and without a legal right to do so, A is generally required to pay compensation. This is true whether A is a private or a public party. Thus if a factory owner has no right to emit pollution that harms a laundry owner but does so anyway, the laundry owner is entitled to some form of compensation. Unfortunately, as we discussed in Chapter 6, externalities generally involve poorly defined or ambiguous property rights. Whether compensation is required for past, present, or future pollution is an issue that can be decided only on a case-by-case basis.

These points can be summarized as a tentative empirical observation: in the United States, the right to enjoy private property, within legally defined limits, is protected, *but the value of property is not.* Following this principle, only compensation for direct property damage will be considered. Indirect damage mediated through a market and damage caused by regulatory changes will not be considered.

The Level of Compensation   If compensation is to be based on the damage inflicted, that damage must be valued. For real estate or personal property, the damages from pollution exposure will equal the reduction in the market value of the property. As we discuss in Chapter 11, this is simple in concept but may be difficult to measure. For example, measuring damages from air pollution may be complicated by the fact that the pollution's impacts on property values may occur concurrently with other impacts. Property values close to a new power plant may be driven down because of pollution, but they may be increased by an influx of new workers at the power plant.

For businesses adversely affected by pollution, the damage is the reduction in the value of the business. This is a more difficult concept. The value of a successful business is generally greater than the value of the business's tangible assets (equipment, land, inventory, etc.). The value of the business is based on the stream of net income it is expected to provide its owners into the future. In this context, this means that even if the impact of pollution on the market price of each of the firm's assets were known, summing these impacts would not necessarily give the impact on the value of the firm.

An industry as a whole may be able to shift part of the costs of pollution controls forward to its customers or backward to its suppliers, but this is not so for an individual business in a competitive industry.[10] Thus to estimate a business's loss, it is necessary to estimate output, price, and total costs with and without the pollution, stretching into the fairly remote future.

Two simple measures of this loss, both of which have been used or recommended, are wrong. The first is lost output multiplied by price.[11] At best, this is a measure of lost revenue, not lost profit. While the pollution increases the cost of producing any given level of output, a firm adversely affected by the pollution will

---

[10]This is discussed further later in this chapter.
[11]See, for example, Ottinger, et al. (1990), p. 72.

cut output and thereby avoid some costs. For firms that do not face an infinitely elastic demand for their product, this will not be even a measure of lost revenue. While the firm loses revenue from selling less at the old price, it gains revenue from selling its remaining supply at a higher price. The second measure is the increase in unit cost. Again, this does not measure lost profit. It ignores the part of the change in average cost that arises because of reduced output and not because of the pollution. It also ignores changes in revenue because of higher price and lower output.

A third simple candidate for an amount to use in compensation is the revenue raised by a pollution tax. But as we have discussed previously, this tax revenue not only exceeds the compensation that property owners might reasonably expect to receive under U.S. law and tradition but also exceeds the total external cost imposed by the pollution.

Wealth and the Demand for Environmental Quality

The demand for environmental quality is influenced by income and wealth. In debates over preservation versus development, one often hears arguments that development will create jobs for local residents. Preservationists, for their part, wish to enjoy aesthetic and recreational activities and sometimes point to the jobs created through tourism. These sorts of debates have been evident in the Pacific Northwest, among other places, not only in regard to preservation and restoration of salmon runs in the Columbia River but also to preservation of old-growth forests and habitat for the northern spotted owl. Unfortunately, too often such debates are portrayed simplistically as jobs versus the object of the preservation effort.

Policymakers will often want to consider the impact of pollution and environmental policies on different income groups within society, even though doing so requires complex analysis. In the case of hydroelectric power versus salmon, electricity consumers, power plant owners, and their suppliers all would benefit from having part of the costs of electricity production shifted to others. Salmon harvesters would be worse off unless the demand for salmon is sufficiently inelastic. Salmon consumers and suppliers of equipment for salmon harvesters (boats, netting, etc.) would also suffer losses.

An output tax on electricity would hurt electricity consumers, power plant owners, and their suppliers. It would benefit salmon harvesters, consumers, and their suppliers.[12] It would also raise tax revenues that could be used to lower other taxes or to provide additional government services or transfer payments. However, any one individual may consume both electricity and salmon or may be an electric company stockholder or both a salmon harvester and an electricity consumer. Thus examining the net impacts to any individual, much less all groups of individuals, would be difficult.

---

[12]This assumes that changes in electricity output can increase salmon runs. Although the physical structure of a dam cannot be altered (easily), the output tax could be set to encourage downstream releases of water, construction of fish ladders, and other mitigation efforts.

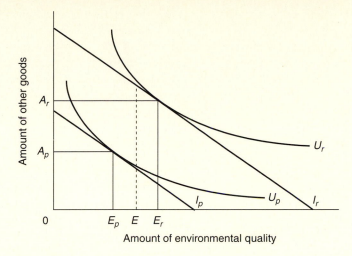

Figure 8.3   Demand for Environmental Quality as a Function of Income

Examining the net impacts on the poor, or any other specific socioeconomic group in society, requires measuring the characteristics of the affected individuals (e.g., who is classified as "poor" or "disadvantaged"), estimating the gain or loss to each functional group identified, and then allocating those gains and losses to the groups in question in proportion to their participation in the functional groups.[13] For example, the poorest 5 percent of the population is unlikely to own utility stock or salmon farms. These people probably consume electricity but may eat little salmon. They are unlikely to sell anything, including their labor, to an electric utility, but many workers in salmon canneries will be poor. They probably pay at least certain kinds of taxes, but also consume government services and receive transfer payments (e.g., social security, food stamps). Determining the impacts on specific groups of individuals will be a time-consuming task. However, given sufficient resources, such impacts can be determined, and several empirical studies have in fact addressed the issue.

If environmental quality is a "normal" good, then an individual's demand for environmental quality will increase with the level of income. This can lead to social policy issues if environmental quality is a public good. To see this, consider Figure 8.3.

Figure 8.3 shows how the demand for environmental quality depends on income, even if everyone has the same preferences. Poor individuals are assumed to have preferences U_p and a budget of I_p. The slope of this budget line is determined by the societal opportunity cost of environmental quality. The poor wish to consume E_p of environmental quality and A_p of all other goods. The rich have preferences U_r

---

[13]There is also the problem of *defining* the segment itself, such as setting the criteria for being "poor" or "rich."

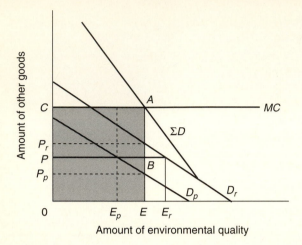

Figure 8.4   Demand for a Public Good by Income Class

and a budget equal to I_r and wish to consume E_r worth of environmental quality and A_r of all other goods. However, if environmental quality is a public good, both rich and poor must consume the same amount.

The efficient level of supply for a public good was discussed in Chapter 6. If society cannot charge different people different prices for environmental quality, then the efficient amount supplied will exceed the amount desired by the poor and be less than that desired by the rich. This is shown in Figure 8.3, where society ends up with an amount E of environmental quality supplied. This level is less than that preferred by the rich but more than that preferred by the poor. Therefore, it would not be surprising to see higher-income groups favor policies that will increase the supply of environmental quality and lower-income groups favor policies with fewer expenditures on environmental quality.[14] To see this explicitly, consider Figure 8.4.

Figure 8.4 shows the demand curves for environmental quality by income class, D_r and D_p, and the overall public demand for environmental quality, ΣD. (Again, recall from Chapter 6 that total demand for a public good is derived by *vertically* summing the individual demand curves.) The marginal cost of environmental quality is given by the curve MC. The efficient level of environmental quality equals E, which is derived from the intersection of the total social demand curve and MC at point A. The total cost of supplying this level of environmental quality is given by area $0CAE$. The efficient prices to charge are P_r and P_p for rich and

---

[14]As we will discuss in Chapter 20, this issue has implications for international trade, development, and the "exporting" of pollution.

poor, respectively (Lindahl 1958). With this set of prices, total revenues will match the total cost of supplying environmental quality exactly.

Suppose, however, that it is impossible for the government to charge the rich and the poor different prices for environmental quality. Instead, the government chooses a uniform price that will still ensure that revenues precisely match the total cost $0CAE$. Thus the government chooses the price P such that $P = \frac{1}{2}0C$. Seeing that environmental quality is a public good, both income classes will still consume E units of environmental quality. However, at the price P, the rich will prefer to consume $E_r > E$ units of environmental quality, while the poor will prefer to consume $E_p < E$ units.[15] Thus the rich will favor policies that increase the supply of the environmental amenity while the poor will not.

Distributional Policy Issues   Although our example assumed that environmental quality was a pure public good, the real world is very impure. Air and water quality can vary substantially even within a single community. Thus in many cases, individuals do have some choice of the level of environmental quality they wish to consume, subject to their budget constraint. Suppose that the rich and the poor could each consume their desired levels of environmental quality. What would happen?

Individuals in each income class would consume environmental quality until the price of environmental quality just equaled their marginal value. Thus in Figure 8.4, if the rich and the poor could consume the amounts of environmental quality they desired, supplied at price P, then even though the rich would consume more than the poor, *at the margin* both would equally value an additional unit of environmental quality (Tiebout 1956). In other words, the marginal rate of substitution between environmental quality and other goods would be equal across income classes. Thus we would observe that the rich enjoyed greater environmental amenities than the poor, even though their respective marginal valuation of those amenities was identical.

Next suppose that to redress a perceived inequity in environmental quality, the government undertakes programs that will provide additional environmental quality to the poor. Say that the poorest neighborhoods of a city are those nearest to an abandoned factory site, which is adjacent to the downtown central business district. The government begins an urban renewal program that cleans up the site. In addition, the government provides other amenities, such as parks, better streets, and refurbishment of abandoned houses. Ultimately, the neighborhoods nearest the factory are transformed into livable areas that offer convenience to downtown workers. To the extent that the poor were formerly renters in the area, rents will be bid up as the demand for housing in the newly improved area increases. The neighborhood will experience "gentrification." Many of the original residents will

---

[15]In technical terms, at price P, the marginal rate of substitution between environmental quality and other goods will be less than P for the poor and greater than P for the rich.

find themselves unable to afford the higher rents and be forced to move to other neighborhoods that have fewer amenities. Even though the urban renewal program was designed to help the poor, it will ultimately have benefited the rich.[16]

Empirical Studies of the Demand for and Distribution of Environmental Quality   There have been relatively few empirical studies of the demand for environmental quality. We review three of the major ones. Freeman (1972) examined the distribution of various aspects of environmental services, including use of the environment as a waste receptacle, the demand for air quality, and recreational use of water resources. He found that the demand for environmental quality was positively correlated to income levels. His results were particularly striking for the relationship between exposure to air pollutants and both income and race. In Washington, D.C., for example, Freeman found that exposure of nonwhites to suspended particulates was almost double that of whites. And wealthier individuals, regardless of race, were exposed to pollution levels one-third lower than low-income individuals. Similarly, the demand for water-based recreation was positively correlated to income levels. This was not a surprising result; the poor are less likely than the rich to be able to afford boats and vacations at recreational facilities.

In a later study, Gianessi, Peskin, and Wolff (1979) examined the distribution of air quality benefits associated with the U.S. Clean Air Act. They found that the majority of the benefits were concentrated in eastern U.S cities. Again, this result was not surprising because many of these cities were heavily industrialized and historically suffered from the highest pollution levels. Pittsburgh, Pennsylvania, and Gary, Indiana, for example, were once major centers for steel production. These two cities experienced some of the highest pollution levels in the nation. (Today they are far cleaner, because of both environmental legislation and the restructuring of the steel industry.)[17]

Robison (1985) used a complex input-output model to examine the distribution of the costs of federal regulations that required industries to reduce their levels of pollution. His model suggested that the costs of required pollution control technologies (e.g., scrubbers, precipitators, water treatment facilities) would be passed forward in the form of higher prices to customers who purchased the output of these industries. Those customers were both final consumers and other industries. For example, an electric utility building a coal-fired power plant would need steel to construct the plant. To the extent that steel companies were required to pay for pollution control measures, the price of the steel would increase. As a result, the cost of building the coal-fired power plant would increase. The coal plant would also be subject to environmental regulations, such as scrubbers to reduce sulfur dioxide emissions. Those scrubbers would increase the cost of oper-

---

[16]This is an argument used by Silverberg (1994).

[17]Gianessi and Peskin (1980) found similar results for U.S. water pollution policy, notably the Clean Water Act.

ating the coal plant, raising the cost of producing electricity. Of course, because the steel companies use electricity, their costs would increase further.

Robison examined these types of interactions throughout the economy until he determined the ultimate increase in prices of consumer goods and services. Then he examined the consumption patterns of these goods and services by income class. He found that the lowest income classes spent about 0.75 percent of their income for pollution control costs, while the highest income groups spent less than 0.25 percent of their income on pollution control costs. This indicated that the costs of the industrial pollution control programs were regressive, made more so because the demand for environmental quality increases with income. Thus, he argued, the rich were paying relatively less for environmental quality than the poor, even though the rich place a higher value on environmental quality.

HUMAN RIGHTS TO THE ENVIRONMENT

Individuals or groups may have rights relating to their environment. If so, environmental regulators must decide several issues when they face claims of human rights in the environment. The first, and probably hardest, is deciding who has what rights. Is there a right to clean air? If so, how clean? Is there a right to clean water? If so, for whom? For anyone who happens to come across any stream? For property owners with their own wells? For customers of municipal water utilities?

A second issue is whether the goal of environmental policy is *preventing violations* of human rights or *limiting impacts* that violate people's rights. This can be seen as deciding whether any specific human right in the environment has a primary or secondary ethical status. Is a right to clean air, if there is one, a fundamental human right, or is it derived from a more fundamental right not to be involuntarily exposed to health risks generally? If a right to clean air or water is a fundamental right, then the appropriate policy goal should be no impacts whatsoever. If the fundamental right is not to be exposed to risks without consent, then the appropriate policy goal would be to keep impacts below some safe level.

Whether we view environmental issues as human rights issues matters greatly for our perception of polluters. Buying environmental services for waste disposal is an ethically neutral action. Violating human rights by deliberately poisoning children with lead is not.[18] People will react differently to the same action, depending on how it is portrayed. Environmental regulators must temper the emotional response that goes with viewing pollution in moral terms with reasonableness about achieving desired goals. If a society's goal is to prevent an impact, encouraging moral outrage against polluters may be useful. If the goal is to limit an impact to a safe level, however, moral outrage could be counterproductive. The effectiveness of any environmental policy depends on the costs of enforcing it and the costs

---

[18]Of course, doing so would not be classified as an externality.

of complying with it. The most effective policies for limiting impacts to acceptable levels may not be the best at satisfying the moral sensibilities of environmentalists.

Distributional Justice: Exporting Pollution

One of the most controversial aspects of human rights to environmental quality is the problem of "exporting" pollution.[19] This is sometimes deemed "environmental racism," but not always. In many cases, the social costs of a polluting industry are lower the fewer people are affected by the pollution.[20] This means that for efficiency, polluting industries should be located away from residential areas and possibly away from urban areas. Some people object to this conclusion because it will result in the "exporting" of pollution. For example, coal-fired power plants built in Wyoming help meet California's demand for electricity. The benefits of the plants accrue to California customers and the power plant's owners. The external costs from the air pollution emissions are imposed on residents in Wyoming and other areas downwind.

Objections to exporting pollution in this way may be based on distributional justice and equity. The costs of the pollution are borne by people who get few or no benefits from the project. Objections may be based also on noneconomic considerations.[21]

Distributional objections often focus on the fact that the parties harmed by the pollution are not compensated, rather than on exporting pollution per se. To decide whether this is a real issue and what should be done about it, it is necessary to know who bears the external costs. With external costs imposed on individuals, it is straightforward. Health impacts, reduced visibility, increased griminess, and similar impacts are all borne by the people who receive them. Current residents of an area where a new pollution source is located will be harmed unless they are somehow compensated. However, some of them may be compensated automatically. To the extent that the area becomes less pleasant to live in, the demand for housing should fall. The costs that new pollution imposes on people living in the formerly clean area will be at least partly capitalized into lower property values. Homeowners will see the pollution they suffer reflected in losses on their houses. Renters may see their rents go down by enough to compensate them for the new pollution. The costs of the new pollution will therefore be passed on to landlords.

The ultimate incidence of external costs imposed on businesses is more complex. Businesses facing an increase in costs will raise their prices if they can. This makes the businesses's customers worse off. Part of the external cost is therefore

---

[19]A discussion of pollution that crosses international boundaries, called *transboundary pollution*, is contained in Chapters 20 and 21. Here we focus on impacts that are distributional, but on a more local scale.

[20]Of course, the impacts to nonhuman nature may be greater. We discuss the rights of nature in the next section.

[21]We take up the issue of environmental "racism" in Chapter 9.

passed through to them. Customers will generally respond to higher prices by buying less. With lower sales, the affected businesses will probably need less of some inputs, such as labor and raw materials. Workers who are laid off but who can find other work at the same wage are no worse off. Laid-off workers who can find only lower-paying jobs and workers who take a pay cut to keep their current jobs are worse off. Part of the external cost is therefore passed back to them. Part of the external cost may be passed back to suppliers of other inputs, who may pass part back to their suppliers, and so on. Even with reduced sales, businesses may need more of other inputs to offset the effects of the new pollution. If this raises the prices of these inputs, their suppliers will be better off, though they may pass part of their gains back to their suppliers, and so on.

How much, if any, of a new external cost a business can pass on to its customers depends on the elasticity of demand. Businesses facing very inelastic demand for their products will be able to pass at least 100 percent of the external cost through to their customers. They will raise prices to reflect their new marginal costs, but the resulting fall in sales will be so small that both revenue and profit increase. This is an exceptional case that is not likely to be very relevant.

Businesses facing demand that is inelastic, but not to such an extreme degree, will see their revenues go up when they raise prices in response to higher costs. However, revenues will not increase as much as costs. Businesses facing elastic demand will see revenues go down as their costs go up. Part of the external cost falling on these businesses will be passed through to customers, part will be absorbed by the business owners, and part may be passed back to the firms' suppliers and employees. Most local retail businesses and many manufacturing, wholesale, and service businesses will fall in these categories. Some of these firms may be forced out of business. Others may stay in business with the owners absorbing a capital loss.

Firms facing completely elastic demand are unable to raise prices and cannot pass through any of the costs of new pollution to their customers. They may pass some costs back to employees, suppliers, and landlords. Many manufacturing businesses and most farms will be in this situation.

How much of a new external cost a business passes back to its suppliers depends on the elasticity of supply of its inputs. If a firm is such a small part of the market for an input that its purchases do not affect the price, it faces perfectly elastic supply for that input. None of the new external cost will be passed back to the suppliers of such an input. This will be true, or close to true, of many inputs used by most businesses.

Inputs that are in fixed supply have completely inelastic supply. If a firm used only one input, and that input were in fixed supply, the external cost would be shifted back completely to suppliers of that input through lower prices. Few, if any, firms use only one input, but some inputs are at least approximately in fixed supply. These include agricultural and recreation land, the labor and management skills of self-employed farmers, and existing buildings.

The distributional aspect of exporting pollution is very complex. Exporting pollution means uncompensated costs to property owners and owners of businesses whose production processes are affected. Part of the external costs may be shifted forward to the customers of affected businesses, and part may be shifted back to their suppliers. The impacts may or may not be felt as external costs by current residents of the affected area. People who move in after the impact starts will experience the pollution but may be fully compensated by lower housing costs.

Any simple compensation scheme is likely to compensate people who are not harmed, miss many who are harmed, and either overcompensate or undercompensate almost everyone. Yet identifying who gains and loses and the magnitude of individuals' gains and losses would be a task of enormous magnitude.

THE RIGHTS OF NATURE

The policies we have discussed for protecting human rights in the environment also are available for protecting the rights of nature. The same considerations for choosing between policies also apply. Unfortunately, protecting the rights of nature involves one additional complication: it is much more difficult to decide what rights nature has or what moral consideration we owe to nonhuman nature.

People can tell us what they want. They can claim their rights or have a representative do it for them. Even when people do not or cannot claim their rights against us, we can have a pretty good idea of what their interests and claims are. We know our own interests and the rights we are prepared to claim for ourselves and grant to others. We can easily and safely assume that other people have broadly similar interests. The rights other people are prepared to claim and grant may differ from ours, but we can still extrapolate from our own experience to the behavior we can expect from others.

This is not the case with nonhuman nature. Nature acts on us and reacts to us, but other than in the case of some domestic animals, it is difficult or impossible to find anything that can reasonably be interpreted as urging a claim against us. This is not to say that people do not feel that nature has claims on them, only that that those feelings are generally not in response to acts of nature that nature could have internalized to affect our feelings. Nature may still have claims against us, but nature rarely sends us a bill directly. We can generalize our interests and rights claims to other species to some extent. However, it is difficult to see how our insights about human interests can be extended to insects, colonial microbes, rocks, the oceans, or other planets. This does not mean that nonhuman nature is not morally considerable. It does mean that it will be difficult, and controversial, to decide what particular duties, if any, we have as a result of the moral considerability of nature. It can also lead to controversies over how resource development projects should be evaluated.[22]

---

[22]For example, a great deal of the sustainability literature is concerned with discounting and discount rates. We shall explore the role of discounting and discount rates in Chapter 13.

The literature on sustainability illustrates some of the controversies associated with defining the rights of nonhuman nature. As we discussed briefly in Chapter 1, Toman (1994) discerned three distinct and mutually exclusive definitions in a review of the existing literature on the concept of *sustainability*.[23] The most radical of these definitions, which Toman refers to as the *organicist* position, argues that humans have a responsibility to maintaining the earth's biological and institutional integrity. How this is done is less clear.

To the extent that resource allocation decisions involve choices between competing objectives (e.g., how do we trade off actions that increase wealth and well-being with those that may have adverse consequences on nature),[24] distributional consequences of externalities that affect human rights and the rights of nature may be disputed bitterly, in terms of both their very existence and the remedies required to restore those distributions to something considered "fair." In the United States, a variety of environmental policies that affect human rights to the environment have been enacted, and the rights of nature have been incorporated into the Endangered Species Act. These policies, which remain the source of much debate, are discussed in Chapter 9.

CHAPTER SUMMARY

In this chapter, we discussed the linkages among externalities, equity, and fairness. Equity and fairness issues can raise far different concerns than those affecting economic efficiency. In some cases, policies that appear to be efficient may be unfair. The most efficient policy with which to address an externality may cause unacceptable harm to certain groups or individuals. Or economically efficient policies may affect nonhuman nature. It may also happen that there are several policies that could be used to promote efficiency with far different distributional consequences.

We also have seen that the demand for environmental quality is a function of wealth. Poorer individuals and societies tend to be willing to pay less for environmental quality than their wealthier counterparts. This does not mean that the poor do not value environmental quality; it simply means that they may value other things more.

We have also shown that direct compensation schemes for environmental harms are generally inappropriate because they reduce or eliminate incentives not to be harmed. Whereas correcting externalities will redistribute wealth, direct compensation will lead to inefficiency. Of course, compensation schemes may be implemented to address equity and rights concerns. In such cases, policymakers will have to decide which goals—equity, efficiency, or rights—are more important to achieve.

---

[23]Chapter 19 discusses sustainability in more detail.
[24]We discuss a methodology for making such trade-offs in Chapter 10. See also Lesser and Zerbe (1995).

CHAPTER REVIEW

Economic Concepts and Tools

- Externalities and policies to internalize them affect the distribution of wealth.
- If environmental amenities are normal goods, the demand for them will increase with income levels.
- External costs and benefits often are borne indirectly by third parties. The parties who directly bear external costs (or receive external benefits) may pass them forward or backward to others through changes in prices and corresponding changes in supply and demand.
- The welfare gains from correcting an externality, if any, can be transferred by taxes or can be passed forward or backward through price changes. The parties who bear an external cost may not receive these welfare gains and may even be made worse off.
- Compensation paid to victims of an external cost reduces their incentive to avoid the cost.
- Simple measures of external costs and benefits, such as the value of lost output, may be far higher or lower than actual costs and benefits as measured by changes in consumer and producer surpluses.

Policy Issues

- Reducing environmental damage to efficient levels may mean imposing costs on poorer members of societies, who have a lower willingness to pay for environmental amenities, or imposing costs on individuals who receive no benefits from the projects that result in those costs.
- The demand for environmental quality has been observed to be an increasing function of wealth. Sometimes policies designed to improve environmental quality mainly benefit the parties who are relatively well off.
- There is no agreement on whether nonhuman nature has rights or what those rights may be. Views range from a rejection of the concept of rights of nature through views of negative rights for nature and corresponding human duties not to cause certain types of harm to views of positive human obligations to be stewards of nature, even at a higher cost to ourselves. Balancing the rights of different aspects of nature, such as one species or another, is particularly difficult.
- Compensation of damages may be required as a specific remedy for past "wrongs," especially criminal acts. In general, however, compensation of damages reduces the incentive to avoid being damaged and may lead to greater inefficiency and inequity. Furthermore, compensation requires a determination of the correct amount to be compensated.
- Because externalities can encompass both human rights and efficiency issues, environmental policies are sometimes more concerned with protecting the rights of one or more parties than with achieving economic efficiency.

DISCUSSION QUESTIONS

1. Why might policies designed to correct economic inefficiencies lead to different outcomes than policies to address inequities?
2. Economic efficiency can usually be measured using willingness-to-pay or willingness-to-accept criteria. How might equity be measured? What would be the "benefits" and "costs" of measuring equity?
3. Suppose that a poor country in Africa, which has suffered repeated famines, expresses a desire to be the disposal site for all of the world's nuclear waste because of the jobs and the income it will bring its people. The country proposes to build a waste dump that will not meet strict U.S. disposal standards and will likely lead to increased cancer deaths for the inhabitants. Is this fair?
4. Suppose that an empirical study shows that African Americans are exposed, on average, to higher levels of air pollutants than Hispanic Americans. Is this an example of environmental racism?
5. The government is considering several alternative environmental programs. The first would remove lead paint from homes occupied by low-income individuals with young children because exposure to lead can lead to severe mental impairment. Another program would remove asbestos from schools because breathing asbestos can lead to lung cancer. A third program would save several species of salmon from extinction. Each program would cost $50 billion. The government has only $50 billion to spend. The president has called you for your advice. Which program would you recommend? Why?
6. In the *Sweet Home Communities* case, do you think the property rights coalition should have argued that its members' way of life was endangered by habitat protection and therefore deserved recognition and protection?
7. Under what conditions do you think the government could charge the rich and the poor different prices for a public good and so achieve a Lindahl equilibrium?
8. In Figure 8.2, how would the analysis change if the laundry imposed external costs on the factory, as in the form of dirty water that required the factory to install water treatment facilities?

REFERENCES

Baumol, W., and W. Oates. 1988. *The Theory of Environmental Policy.* 2d ed. New York: Cambridge University Press.

Cheung, S. 1973. "The Fable of the Bees: An Economic Investigation." *Journal of Law and Economics* 16(1): 11–33.

Freeman, A. 1972. "The Distribution of Environmental Quality." In *Environmental Quality Analysis: Theory and Method in the Social Sciences,* ed. A. Kneese and B. Bower. Baltimore: Johns Hopkins University Press.

Gianessi, L., and H. Peskin. 1980. "The Distribution of the Costs of Federal Water Pollution Policy." *Land Economics* 56(1): 85–102.

————, and E. Wolff. 1979. "The Distributional Effects of Uniform Air Pollution Policy in the United States." *Quarterly Journal of Economics* 43(2): 281–301.

Knetsch, J. 1995. "Asymmetric Valuation of Gains and Losses in Preference Orderings." *Economic Inquiry* 33(1): 134–141.

Lesser, J., and R. Zerbe. 1995. "What Can Economic Analysis Contribute to the Sustainability Debate?" *Contemporary Economic Policy* 13(3): 88–100.

Lindahl, E. 1958. "Just Taxation: A Positive Solution." In *Classics in the Theory of Public Finance,* ed. R. Musgrave and A. Peacock. New York: Crowell-Collier.

Northwest Power Planning Council (NPPC). 1992. *Columbia River Basin Fish and Wildlife Program: Strategy for Salmon,* Vol. I. Issue Paper No. 92-21. Portland, Ore.: NPPC.

Ottinger, R., et al. 1990. *The Environmental Costs of Electricity.* Dobbs Ferry, N.Y.: Oceana.

Reisner, M. 1993. *Cadillac Desert: The American West and Its Disappearing Water.* Rev. ed. New York: Viking Penguin.

Robison, H. 1985. "Who Pays for Industrial Pollution Abatement?" *Review of Economics and Statistics* 57(4): 702–708.

Silverberg, S. 1994. *The Armchair Economist: Economics and Everyday Life.* New York: The Free Press.

Tiebout, C. 1956. "A Pure Theory of Public Expenditure." *Journal of Political Economy* 64(3): 416–424.

Toman, M. 1994. "Economics and 'Sustainability': Balancing Trade-offs and Imperatives." *Land Economics* 70(4): 399–412.

Turvey, R. 1963. "On Divergences Between Social Cost and Private Cost." *Economica* 30(3): 309–313.

CHAPTER 9

POLICIES THAT ADDRESS NONECONOMIC GOALS

That Old-Time Religion: Salmon and Native American Rights

In Chapter 8, we discussed the trade-offs between obtaining the benefits of hydro-electric power from Grand Coulee Dam on the Columbia River and the resulting decimation of the largest salmon runs in North America. We focused on equity and rights issues associated with providing needed jobs during the Depression, as well as the benefits in terms of lives saved that were achieved by shortening the duration of World War II (Reisner 1993).

The decimation of the salmon runs affected not only commercial and sport fisheries; it also inflicted harm on several Native American tribes. These tribes have lived in the Pacific Northwest for thousands of years, and the salmon have played an integral role of their lives, from providing needed protein for their diets to figuring prominently in their religious ceremonies. In 1855, the U.S. government and several of the tribes signed a treaty decreeing that "the right of taking fish at usual and accustomed grounds . . . is further secured to said Indians."

In the effort to restore historical salmon runs on the Columbia River and its tributaries, Native American rights have figured prominently. Tribal representatives have argued that no price can compensate them for the loss of salmon, that the loss has fundamentally altered their religion, their culture, and their economic survival. The interests of many other users of the Columbia River—agriculture, industry, navigation, and recreation—also insist on representation. Although the Endangered Species Act prohibits economic considerations from entering the restoration debate, political realities may derail restoration plans by making them prohibitively expensive for various political constituencies.

In addressing the salmon situation from the standpoint of Native American rights, there are three important policy issues. First, should Native Americans be compensated for the loss of their right to salmon, as specified in the treaty of 1855, owing to the development of the Columbia River system? Second, since everyone wants the salmon to be restored, who should pay for the restoration and compensation, if any? Third, what considerations will be made between Native American rights and the rights of the salmon themselves? After all, the Endangered Species Act does not state that species restoration and preservation will occur only to allow further exploitation by humans.

Answering the first question is a matter of judicial interpretation. Only lawyers can provide any sort of guidance on that issue. There appears to be legal precedent for compensation, although determining the "correct" amount of compensation would ultimately be a political exercise. In essence, society would have to determine just compensation for the loss of culture and religion, as well as economic well-being.

In 1992, the Northwest Power Planning Council (NPPC) issued a long-term plan for increasing the number of salmon in the Columbia River and its tributaries. That plan called for doubling the size of the current salmon runs by improving fish transportation past the many dams, eradicating salmon predators (principally squawfish), conserving water used for agriculture and diverting that water for increased river flows, reducing commercial and sport fishing, and improving salmon spawning habitats along streams on private and public lands. The NPPC strategy will require a great deal of cooperation among a diverse set of individuals, regulators, and industries. Wood products industries, for example, will need to refrain from logging near streambeds, which destroys habitat by silting. Agricultural interests will have to adjust livestock grazing to reduce runoff into streams and rivers and adjust water-intensive farming practices. Industries will have to pay more for the electricity they use as more water is diverted for fish.

None of these measures will restore salmon runs to their former size when the Treaty of 1855 was signed. The NPPC established a goal of doubling the existing salmon runs to about 2 million fish, far less than the 10 to 16 million estimated to have existed in 1855. Thus none of the NPPC's proposed actions will restore the runs guaranteed to those Native Americans. Does this mean that the policy is of no value and should be rejected by Native Americans? Not necessarily. In pursuit of the NPPC goal, new restoration techniques may be learned that reduce the cost of further enhancements.

As to the last issue, balancing the rights of nature versus the rights of Native Americans, this too may be debated. If the NPPC goal is met, or even exceeded, there will be prohibitions against excessive "takings" by Native Americans that would once again endanger the survival of any of the salmon runs.

INTRODUCTION

Are environmental policies designed to improve economic efficiency doomed to failure because they may have adverse effects on some individual or interest group? Must environmental policies clear a Pareto superiority hurdle, or can they be judged on a more relaxed potential Pareto criterion? How should "noneconomic" goals be incorporated in public decision processes? Just how important such goals are can be gleaned from a review of some of the major environmental legislation that has been enacted. Does that mean that there is no place for economic efficiency in environmental policies? Hardly.

In Chapter 7, we discussed a variety of policies to reduce economic inefficiencies from externalities, including doing nothing when the costs of internalization exceed the potential gains. Economists have made such recommendations often; more often still their advice has been ignored. Some economists take this as evidence of the irrationality of the political process, if not the abject irrationality on the part of anyone who dares ignore their advice. Based on the material in Chapter 8, however, there are clear differences in the demand for environmental quality among different groups, as well as significant distributional impacts associated with "efficient" environmental policies. Thus many economically "irrational" environmental regulations can be explained as attempts to address considerations of distributional equity, human rights, or moral obligations to nonhuman nature than as failed attempts to deal with economic inefficiency.

To understand this point, in the first part of this chapter we examine a selection of U.S. environmental laws that contain such "noneconomic" motivations.[1] Some of these regulations *explicitly* reject the use of benefit-cost analysis as a basis for regulating specific environmental problems. Instead, those regulations assert that certain goals must be achieved, regardless of the cost, and often specify how those goals will be achieved. This first part of the chapter is descriptive; we discuss the considerations that have motivated some U.S. environmental laws and the types of regulations that have resulted.

The importance of noneconomic goals in much legislation, however, does not mean those laws have been well thought out. In the second part of the chapter, we argue that economic efficiency should always be at least a second-order goal of *any* environmental law. This just means that whatever society's environmental policy goals may be, society ought not to waste resources achieving them; environmental goals should be achieved at the lowest possible cost. As a result, economics has a great deal to say about environmental policies designed to achieve noneconomic goals.

---

[1]Use of the term *noneconomic* may itself be controversial in that some economists argue that *all* goals are economic ones. We prefer to separate "traditional" economic goals emphasizing efficiency from goals that emphasize equity and rights.

A REVIEW OF SELECTED U.S. ENVIRONMENTAL LAWS WITH NONECONOMIC GOALS

Over the years, Congress has passed many environmental laws having diverse policy goals. Here we describe some of the most important ones.

Many of the most expensive environmental laws have dealt with the disposal of waste, be it solid, liquid, or gaseous. This should not be surprising. For hundreds of years, the environment has served as a "free" disposal site. However, the costs associated with disposal have increased significantly over time and raised many complex issues concerning how best to dispose of the wastes our society generates. Furthermore, as Portney (1990) points out, the fundamental choices made by environmental regulators who have addressed waste disposal issues have not always been clear. In some cases, economic efficiency has played a key role; in other cases, it has been explicitly prohibited from doing so.

Anytime society must address environmental risks, trade-offs must be made. But in many cases, U.S. environmental laws have mandated "zero risk" to citizens, even though the practical possibility of achieving such a goal is virtually impossible. That zero-risk requirement is just one aspect of how many environmental laws have been designed with "fairness" in mind. Unfortunately, what is defined as "fair" may in fact be grossly unfair. Requiring all polluters to reduce their emissions by 50 percent, for example, does not consider that the costs of achieving those reductions may vary greatly owing to the diversity of sources. Imposing the same technological requirements on dry cleaners and bakeries as on steel mills and oil refineries may mean that one source can reduce emissions at a relatively small cost while another may endure severe financial hardship. Thus requirements for equal-percentage reductions may mean unequal financial burdens. Even basing compliance on the ability to pay can be unfair by penalizing well-managed firms at the expense of poorly managed ones (Portney 1990).

Some environmental laws, such as the Endangered Species Act, have focused on single-minded goals without considering the consequences. The goals may themselves be reasonable (e.g., "to prevent species extinctions") with respect to the choices society makes but unreasonable if the consequences are not considered first. Undoubtedly, that leads to even greater controversy later on and, as may be the ultimate fate of the Columbia River salmon fishery, a failure to attain even the primary goal.

The Resource Conservation and Recovery Act

Because of increased public concern about the effect of toxic substances and hazardous wastes on the environment, Congress passed a series of laws to regulate the disposal of these products and clean up contaminated sites. It is arguable whether these laws have worked effectively at reducing risks. There is less argument that they have not done so efficiently. Toxic substance and hazardous waste laws have been the subject of much controversy because of concerns that the most hazardous substances were not addressed adequately, the regulations arising from these laws have not been cost-effective, and the regulations have created undue burdens on businesses and, in some cases, individuals. One thing is clear, however: these laws have not been designed with economic efficiency as a primary or even secondary goal.

One particularly frightening aspect was the specter of hazardous wastes dumped illegally by unscrupulous businesses. Many such sites were found. Leaking and rusting drums filled with unknown wastes and dumped alongside roadways frightened people, who did not know what they were being exposed to and what the dangers were. Passed in 1976, the Resource Conservation and Recovery Act (RCRA) was designed to combat this problem, among a variety of other waste disposal issues.[2]

The RCRA regulates hazardous wastes "from cradle to grave," including their production, storage, transportation, and disposal. The act has four major parts. First, it defines *hazardous waste*. Because determining the potential damages from any and every substance would be prohibitively expensive, the Environmental Protection Agency (EPA), which administers the law, developed definitions of hazardous wastes based on physical properties. For example, substances that are corrosive, like acids, are considered toxic under the RCRA. Any substance that meets the criteria established by the EPA in any of the property groups is considered hazardous. The second part of the RCRA creates a system, called a "manifest," that tracks hazardous wastes: How much waste was generated? Where was it stored? How was it transported? Third, the RCRA establishes standards for treatment, storage, and disposal facilities. For example, landfills that accept hazardous wastes must be constructed with liners that reduce the risk of groundwater contamination. Last, the RCRA establishes a permit system to enforce standards.

In 1984, the RCRA was amended significantly in order to shift its emphasis away from effective land disposal to treatment alternatives. Ironically, the increasing stringency of regulations designed to reduce air and water pollution created an incentive to dispose of wastes on land. At the same time, however, there was increasing concern about these wastes contaminating groundwater supplies, even at sites such as landfills that had met the previous standards.

The 1984 amendments severely restricted land disposal of hazardous wastes without bothering about the cost effectiveness of the supposed reductions in contamination risks or of the availability of alternatives. These costs are not trivial; Russell, Colglazier, and Tonn (1992) estimated the cleanup costs associated with the RCRA to be at least $200 billion, and possibly over $400 billion, between 1990 and 2020. The RCRA mandated advanced disposal techniques without considering that such technologies might not be available by the time that waste generators were banned from disposing their wastes in landfills, effectively closing all legal disposal options for some generators (Russell 1988).

Nor did the amendments consider the trade-offs that might occur because of different technologies, something that a regulation designed with economic efficiency in mind would do. An industry that used resource inputs efficiently might

_____

[2]Russell (1988) provides an excellent analysis of the RCRA and why, as designed, it will not work well.

face with higher costs of disposing of the remaining residues than inefficient users did. For example, wood-fired electric generating plants create a residue of ash, much like fireplaces and wood stoves. The more efficiently the wood is burned, which incidentally means less air pollution, the more "concentrated" will be the residual ash. In some actual cases, that residual ash has been so concentrated that it has been classified as a hazardous waste. This has raised disposal costs for the owner of the generating unit significantly, increasing the cost of the power supplied. That sort of perverse penalty for operating efficiently can lead to several other impacts: it can encourage the use of substitute forms of generation that are more polluting, but whose pollution falls outside the scope of the RCRA, and there can be an incentive to burn wood *inefficiently* if the costs of meeting air pollution regulations are lower than the costs of meeting hazardous waste disposal rules.

The Comprehensive Environmental Response, Compensation, and Liability Act

The Comprehensive Environmental Response, Compensation, and Liability Act (CERCLA), better known as "Superfund," was enacted in 1980 as an extension of the RCRA.[3] Waste disposal sites that had been identified under the RCRA had been the subject of increasing public concern in the late 1970s. The most famous of these occurred in 1978 at Love Canal, New York, where individuals were exposed directly to wastes that had migrated through the soil, creating panic about the possibilities of thousands of other "time bombs" around the country. Superfund was designed to assign financial responsibility for cleaning up hazardous waste sites, ensuring that what was identified under the RCRA would, in fact, be cleaned up.

Despite the obvious appeal of removing toxic substance and hazardous waste sites, Superfund has been the focus of much controversy. Critics of Superfund contend that it has spent too much money to achieve too few results, perhaps owing to political interests taking precedence over public interest (Hird 1990). Critics also express concern over the manner in which Superfund determines who shall pay for cleaning up identified sites and the expense of litigation to determine responsible parties (Cairncross 1993). Proponents of Superfund point to the law's success at improving the care with which wastes are handled and how the law has prompted private cleanup efforts.

Superfund Components Superfund has several major components. First, it establishes a method for identifying and ranking contaminated sites, called the National Contingency Plan (NCP). The most egregious sites are placed on the National Priorities List (NPL). It is these sites (which numbered around 1,300 by

---

[3]An excellent summary and analysis of the Superfund controversy can be found in Portney and Probst (1994). An empirical study of the distribution of Superfund cleanup costs can be found in Hird (1990). Grigalunas and Opaluch (1988) discuss the method Superfund uses to measure environmental damage.

CREATING WASTE TO CLEAN THE ENVIRONMENT

For some years, the Electric Power Research Institute (EPRI) has researched new methods of destroying harmful substances in drinking water. Since the beginning of this century, the methods used to disinfect water, primarily chlorination, have changed little. It was only in the 1970s that scientists discovered that chlorine could react with organic waste material in water to form certain toxic compounds. In the 1980s, concerns about the safety of water supplies increased, as people wondered whether chlorine could remove parasites and viruses, as well as bacteria. New regulations governing water treatment were passed in 1986 as part of the Safe Drinking Water Act, all of which have increased the costs of water treatment significantly, without considering whether the increased costs of compliance were worth the reduction in risk.

EPRI has been working with the American Water Works Association to develop advanced wastewater treatments, many of which use electricity. For example, ozone is now being used in selected areas in the United States to disinfect water. The ozone, which is produced by an electric corona discharge (imagine small lightning bolts in water), is bubbled through water to kill bacteria and destroy organic materials and herbicide residues. The main drawback of ozone treatment is that its capital and operating costs are higher than those of chlorination.

Another, less expensive treatment is the use of ultraviolet (UV) light. Since UV involves no moving parts, capital investment is lower. And, unlike chlorination, UV eliminates the need to transport or store hazardous chemicals for the treatment process. UV treatment is effective in killing bacteria and viruses quickly. A third, and still experimental, treatment method is the use of electron beams. Fast-moving beams of electrons are directed through wastewater, both disinfecting and eliminating toxic compounds that are often found in industrial waste.

Changing the technologies used to purify drinking water and clean waste water is not a simple task, however, especially if environmental laws mandate specific technologies. Furthermore, all three technologies developed by EPRI require the use of additional electricity, which can itself generate various types of waste. In addition to the air pollutants generated by burning fossil fuels, some generating technologies, especially coal, can leave their own set of liquid and solid wastes.

Ultimately, the question in need of answering is "Which approach is best?" Individuals whose drinking water is just fine may object to the need for more electric generating plants nearby. They may reason that they are unfairly bearing the costs of clean-up without receiving the benefits. Or, skeptics may see the new technology as unproven, and worry that it will not work and therefore expose individuals to unnecessary risks.

Determining an answer may be complex and controversial. It almost certainly will involve questions not only of costs, but also of treatment effectiveness, comparisons of pollutants generated, their impacts on the environment, and the equity impacts on affected individuals and groups. As a result, policymakers will need to develop comprehensive methods to make such comparisons, and identify their most important goals.

Source: Douglas (1993), pp. 4–13.

1995) that can be cleaned up with federal money. The NCP also establishes a process to determine feasible response actions (cleanup approaches) for sites listed on the NPL and selection of the preferred approach.

Second, the act creates a trust fund for emergency cleanups of sites posing immediate health and environmental risks and to finance nonemergency cleanups at sites where no responsible (guilty) parties can be identified. The trust fund is fed by several taxes: one on chemical and petroleum feedstocks used by manufacturing industries and the other a more general corporate income tax.

The third, and most controversial, aspect of Superfund is the mechanism that was created to identify responsible parties. Under this section of the law, the EPA can identify the responsible parties and sue for cleanup costs, dividing these costs among the parties. The definition of a responsible party is quite broad; it can include any party who ever owned or operated, contributed waste to, or transported waste to the site. It can also include the buyers of sites where wastes had been dumped in the past. Thus, under Superfund, if you bought land that was subsequently found to have been used for dumping, you could be liable for the entire cleanup cost, even though you were not responsible for the original dumping.

Policy Issues Associated with Superfund   Superfund has generated much controversy.[4] Why? Portney and Probst (1994) argue that although controversy surrounds all of Superfund's provisions, the heart of the controversy focuses on the assignment of liability and the appropriate extent of cleanup at identified sites. These issues encompass not only economic efficiency issues but also issues of equity and human rights.

When Superfund was passed in 1980, Congress did not want to pay for another potentially large environmental program.[5] So Congress created a system to assign liability to different parties. This liability system is called "retroactive, strict, and joint-and-several." In plain English, *retroactive liability* means that Superfund laws apply to activities that took place before Superfund was enacted. Thus, to take a hypothetical example, in the early 1940s, BigNasty Industries may have dumped wastes legally next to its factory, which was producing bombers for the government's war effort. Now BigNasty can be sued to clean up the site to the specifications dictated by Superfund, even though at the time its activities were legal.

Strict liability means that you can be on the hook regardless of your actions in the past. Suppose that BigNasty was purchased in the 1960s by NiceGuys, which

---

[4] Portions of this discussion are based on a more detailed treatment by Portney and Probst (1992, 1994).
[5] How large is large? The average cleanup cost per site is around $30 million. With just under 1,300 sites in 1993, that represents a total outlay of just under $40 billion. However, the EPA has been adding an average of 50 sites per year to the NPL, for an additional cost of $1.5 billion per year.

was unaware of the wastes that had been dumped. Under strict liability, NiceGuys would be treated as if it had dumped the wastes itself.

Joint-and-several liability means that any one party can be required by the government to pay for all of the cleanup costs. Suppose that in addition to BigNasty having dumped waste next to its plant, ten other companies that were manufacturing material for the government's war effort had done the same. All of these companies are long since bankrupt. Under joint-and-several liability, NiceGuys is liable for the *entire* cleanup bill. If those ten other industries were still in business, under joint-and-several liability, NiceGuys could still be assigned full liability, but it could sue (at its expense) the other companies for their shares of the cleanup costs.

Not surprisingly, the assignment of liability under Superfund has generated much controversy, and many efforts to revise the liability standard.[6] The existing web of liability now snares many firms: banks that lent money to owners subsequently found liable; municipal officials, since many Superfund sites are landfills; private firms, who do not want to be held liable for actions they did not commit or for actions they committed that were perfectly legal at the time; and insurance companies, who have been sued by their policyholders to cover cleanup costs.

It seems clear that the existing liability standards are inequitable to some extent. Several remedies have been proposed to fix the inequities. One would eliminate retroactive liability. No party would be responsible for wastes dumped prior to 1981. This would benefit responsible parties and insurance companies. Another proposal would let insurers avoid responsibility for paying for reimbursing their clients for cleanup costs. Instead, under both proposals, Congress would create a separate fund, financed in part by a general tax on insurance companies, to help pay for cleanup costs at sites where liability had been eliminated.

Although the changes in liability would address one type of inequity, they could create others. Suppose that NiceGuys is off the hook for paying for cleanup at the waste site next door. Instead, the cleanup is paid for by the government, from funds raised by taxing insurance companies. Where do the insurance companies get the money to pay? In part, from everyone they insure. Just as a portion of a tax on suppliers will be paid by consumers, so would a tax on insurers be paid in part by its clients, many of whom will also have had nothing to do with the waste sites.[7]

A second equity issue, which also addresses human rights concerns, is the proper degree of cleanup at sites. Section 121 of the Superfund law calls for cleanup "to the maximum extent practicable." The determination of what that

---

[6]The issue of liability for past dumping practices is not limited to the United States. In Great Britain, for example, under the 1990 Environmental Protection Act, a list of contaminated sites throughout the country will be developed. Under the act, British authorities appear to have the power to recover the costs of cleanups from the "original" landowner. See "Paying for the Past" (1992).

[7]Recall that the distribution of taxes paid between consumers and suppliers is called the *incidence* of the tax. Any good microeconomics text will explain how the incidence is calculated.

phrase means has also been the subject of intense controversy. To see this more clearly, consider again the saga of BigNasty's dump site. Suppose that the site, which is now owned by NiceGuys, is neither leaking wastes into any aquifers nor emitting wastes into the air and is fenced off to prevent contamination of individuals wandering into the site. One cleanup solution would be to place some sort of concrete cap over the site and continue to monitor it carefully to ensure that no wastes begin leaking beyond the site or into any aquifers. This approach is based on the tenets of economic efficiency. The site would be cleaned to the extent that the marginal cost of additional cleanup just equaled the marginal benefit from reducing the risk of future exposure to the wastes. To extend the cleanup beyond that point would be to waste scarce economic resources.

Some people, including many members of Congress, would say that this is not cleaning up to the maximum extent practicable and would not be "fair." Suppose that the wastes were migrating slowly toward a nearby low-income neighborhood. Now there are fears that the residents will be exposed to the wastes, much as at Love Canal. Here the issue becomes one of involuntary exposure to an environmental risk. Suppose that the waste can be contained completely at a cost of $100 million. However, suppose that a reduced control effort, which would lower exposure risks to "safe" levels and relocate the residents to other neighborhoods, would cost $50 million. Which approach should be undertaken? Economic efficiency suggests the latter approach. However, from equity and human rights perspectives, the former may be preferred. Recent research indicates that the presence of a waste site that lowers property values may provide more affordable housing to low-income residents. Thus it may not be necessarily the sites themselves but the dynamics of housing markets that create adverse impacts (Been 1994).

Portney and Probst (1994) discuss a possible hybrid approach to cleanup. Under this approach, the EPA would set cleanup standards based on the intended future uses of cleanup sites. Thus a Superfund site on which a new industrial park is to be developed would be subject to less stringent standards than, say, a site for a new school or housing development. How feasible such a change in the existing Superfund law would be is unclear. As Hird (1990) suggests in his research, cleanup priorities seem to be based as much on politics and publicity as environmental priority. Yet Portney and Probst suggest that these very discrepancies already mean that remedies are not based on strict adherence to the "permanence" requirements of Superfund.[8] It may be that developing a policy of flexible standards may be feasible politically after all.

The Nuclear Waste Policy Act

If the issues surrounding toxic and hazardous waste cleanup under Superfund have proved difficult, the issues surrounding nuclear waste disposal seem intractable.

---

[8]Gupta, Van Houten, and Cropper (1993) suggest that the EPA has balanced benefits and costs of cleanup to the extent possible but that it has also preferred strategies that met the Superfund "permanence" guidelines.

No type of waste engenders more fear from the public than radioactive waste. This fear has been focused by events at Three Mile Island in 1977 and the far more serious nuclear plant accident at Chernobyl, Ukraine. In general, when people think of nuclear wastes, they think of the wastes from nuclear weapons and nuclear power plants. These wastes will remain dangerously radioactive for thousands of years and must be thoroughly isolated from human beings. Such waste is known as high-level radioactive waste (HLW).

Policy Issues Associated with Storage of HLW   Disposal of HLW creates policy issues of almost immeasurable complexity. These encompass economic efficiency, equity among different members of society today, intergenerational equity between individuals today and those who will live far in the future, human rights, and even the rights of nature. One issue, for example, is whether any nuclear power facilities should be allowed to operate. Indeed, in some European countries, such as Sweden, voters have elected to phase out their reliance on nuclear-generated electricity. Other countries, such as France and Japan, continue to promote reliance on nuclear power. As the 1987 Chernobyl accident demonstrated, however, radioactive fallout does not respect international boundaries. Thus policies initiated by one country may have devastating effects on others.

In part as a response to public concerns over nuclear power in general, which were galvanized by the Three Mile Island accident, the U.S. Congress passed the Nuclear Waste Policy Act in 1982. Initially, the act required the U.S. Department of Energy to find a *permanent* and safe storage location for high-level nuclear wastes by the year 1998. The standards for radiation exposure from such wastes were set by the EPA and cover a period of 10,000 years. The entire waste-siting effort is funded by a tax of $\frac{1}{10}$ cent per kilowatt-hour of electricity generated at nuclear power plants, although wastes arising from nuclear weapons would also be stored at the repository.

When candidate sites first were announced, local opposition became intense. In 1987, Congress postponed the deadline to 2010 at the earliest. The search for suitable geological sites was narrowed to just one: Yucca Mountain in Nevada. With the choice of this site, the opposition has grown still more intense. Many uncertainties have been raised by opponents, including political, legal, procedural, and, perhaps most important, technical ones ("Radioactive Waste" 1991).

Critics have complained that federal and state laws concerning transportation of these wastes conflict. For example, Idaho has banned shipments of radioactive wastes from Colorado to a federal depository in Idaho Falls. Other states, fearing catastrophic releases of radiation should an accident occur, also oppose transportation of wastes on highways. And there are questions about the actual stability of the site itself: Will it be immune to all geological and volcanic activity for 10,000 years? Is there any way to prove such stability?

Prior to beginning the search for a permanent nuclear waste depository, the Department of Energy undertook construction in 1981 of an experimental depository in southeastern New Mexico, near Carlsbad Caverns. The repository is located in salt caves, which run throughout the region. The Waste Isolation Pilot Project (WIPP) was scheduled to receive its first shipment of waste in 1988. As with its permanent cousin at Yucca Mountain, opposition and delay have been the norm. Critics have raised numerous transportation and geological issues, although many local residents favor completion of WIPP for the jobs it promises.

Despite the critical issues of waste site selection and operation and waste transportation, one immutable fact remains: HLW is now stored aboveground at nuclear plant and defense facilities. Thus policymakers and the public must determine whether it is better to leave the waste where it lies or to proceed with development of a centralized, and likely imperfect, storage site.

Given the opposition to transportation and siting a repository, the major policy issues involve equity, both between generations and between members of the current generation. Resolution of these issues remains difficult because of an inability to assess the risks of pronouncing a site geologically "safe" for 10,000 years, which is beyond our predictive capacity, and mistrust of the agencies responsible for constructing and operating the facilities, including ancillary transport.

There is empirical evidence that, at least for the real and perceived risks associated with siting a nuclear waste storage facility, the question may be moot. A study by Kunreuther and Easterling (1990) relied on interviews of 1,001 residents of Nevada to determine whether those residents would be more willing to accept the Yucca Mountain repository if they were given promises of annual compensation. Respondents were asked whether or not they would approve of the facility for different levels of compensation and different degrees of riskiness associated with the project. The authors' study revealed that increasing compensation to nearby residents would be unlikely to affect their views. In other words, the benefits from nearby siting (an annual payment) was usually rejected out of hand unless the safety of the facility was assured.

A "solution" to the issue of storing HLW remains elusive, although if the Kunreuther and Easterling study is valid, the issue will ultimately hinge on citizens' trust of government officials, elected or otherwise. Unfortunately, that level of trust seems to be decreasing rather than increasing. It will continue to make an extremely complex technical issue a politically irresolvable one.

Policy Issues Associated with Disposal of LLW   Although the storage of HLW continues to be the high-profile radioactive waste issue, the majority (by volume) of the radioactive waste created today is much less virulent. This latter category of nuclear waste is called low-level radioactive waste (LLW) and is composed primarily of medical and industrial wastes that can be disposed of in approved landfills or incinerated.

For the most part, low-level radioactive wastes are disposed of in approved landfills in several states. Prior to 1980, there were three of these landfills, located in South Carolina, Washington, and Nevada. Because the amount of this type of waste has grown rapidly, these three states have raised objections to being the sole available depositories. Of course, no other states wanted to open their own LLW sites, for fear of having to accept waste from other states. In 1980, Congress passed the Low Level Radioactive Waste Policy Act to encourage states to form interstate compacts to open new sites that would accept LLW from all states. States did not pursue this objective, so in 1985 Congress amended the law allowing the three states with sites to charge increasingly high fees. After 1990, there was to be a complete ban on the acceptance of interstate wastes.

The law has not produced its intended results. As at many nuclear power plants, many generators of LLW are storing it on-site. This may be the least desirable alternative, since these storage facilities are temporary. Some states have reached new agreements with others. In 1994, for example, Vermont reached an agreement with the state of Texas in which the former agreed to pay the latter $750,000 to accept LLW at a new storage site in the southwestern part of Texas. But in late 1995, the agreement was stalled in Congress. The Texas representative objected to the site, even though the area is sparsely populated, because the residents are almost all poor and Hispanic. Thus policy issues of both equity and human rights will have to be addressed.

Biodiversity and the Endangered Species Act

In the past few decades, we have developed a greater appreciation for the benefits of biodiversity. Broadly speaking, biodiversity covers both species and whole ecosystems.[9] Biodiversity promotes environmental resilience and productivity, much as a diverse portfolio of investments can prevent catastrophic financial losses. Thus biodiversity can, in one sense, be thought of as a form of ecological insurance.

Enacted in 1973, the Endangered Species Act (ESA) seeks to protect individual species from extinction. Declining species are categorized as either "endangered" or "threatened," depending on the risk of their extinction. Once a species is listed as endangered or threatened, the ESA generally prohibits any governmental action or approval of private action that would negatively affect that species, including the killing (sometimes called "takings") of any individual of that species. (The law does allow small or incidental takings of a listed species in specific circumstances, such as for religious purposes.) The ESA not only protects species from direct harm but also protects endangered species's habitats. This latter restriction is quite broad and has been the focus of most of the controversy surrounding the ESA. Habitat restrictions can have a major effect on human utilization of land because essentially any human intrusion or exploitation may affect a species's habitat.

Once it is determined that a species requires protection, the cost to humans of that protection is not taken into consideration. Thus the ESA is devoted almost wholly to the rights of nature, rather than economic efficiency, equity, or human rights. In passing the ESA, Congress determined that the survival of a species is more important than any other governmental policy or goal. The act is designed to protect species from extinction regardless of the cost. Nor does it take into account

---

[9]Biodiversity can also be applied to genetic diversity, that is, diversity within the gene pool of one or more species. This is important because insufficient genetic diversity may lead to eventual extinction. See Wilson (1986) for a thorough discussion.

any differences in the public's willingness to pay (*WTP*) to preserve particular species. For example, the public's *WTP* to preserve bald eagles, which are a symbol of the United States, probably would be higher than the *WTP* to preserve the snail darter, a fish that was almost unknown until the controversy about Tellico Dam (see accompanying box).

The ESA continues to generate much controversy, especially when species protection is perceived to interfere with economic growth and job creation or job preservation. That explains why we have witnessed numerous debates of "owls versus jobs" or "salmon versus jobs."[10]

Endangered Species and Safe Minimum Standards   Determining the value of a species is obviously difficult. First, there is a question of perspective, which is similar to the issue of standing we discussed briefly in Chapter 5. Is the value of a species its value to humans, or do species have their own intrinsic value? Asking what I might be willing to pay to preserve a species of salmon, for example, is not the same as asking the salmon themselves. Presumably, we are still unable to communicate with salmon, so humans must necessarily act on behalf of salmon and all other species.

In light of the difficulties in determining when a species is "adequately" protected, Ciriacy-Wantrup (1964, 1968) developed a policy approach known as the "safe minimum standard," or SMS.[11] The SMS approach to species preservation states that in light of the uncertain and irreversible costs of extinction, species should be preserved unless the social costs of doing so are "unacceptably large." How large is "unacceptably large" depends on the weight given to future generations, as well as the affected species themselves. Thus an SMS approach goes beyond strict guidelines of economic efficiency.[12]

Castle and Berrens (1993) provide a graphical illustration of the SMS approach, shown in Figure 9.1. Consider the marginal cost of protecting a particular species when the costs are defined in terms of opportunity costs. Castle and Berrens argue that the MC of protecting a species will decline first, then increase gradually. With very small populations, the marginal cost of maintaining and increasing population size will be high. (One example might be the expenditures spent to preserve the California condor, whose numbers had fallen to well below 100, and reintroduce it to the wilds. With so few condors, the incremental costs per additional bird are high.)

---

[10]As we discuss in Chapter 18, such either-or polarizations generally miss key points. You might wish to review the discussion in Chapter 3 of the 1995 Supreme Court case *Babbitt et al.* v. *Sweet Home Chapter of Communities* (17 F.3d 1463, rev.) concerning the meaning of *take* and *harm* in the ESA.

[11]Ciriacy-Wantrup did not limit application of the SMS approach to endangered species. For example, he proposed applying the SMS approach to the problem of urbanization of prime agricultural lands in California. See also Bishop (1978, 1979) and Smith and Krutilla (1979).

[12]Of course, once a preservation decision has been made, the most efficient preservation policies should be enacted.

CATCHING A SMALL FISH WITH A BIG STICK?

In 1967, Congress authorized construction of a dam on the Little Tennessee River, known as the Tellico Dam. In 1973, a Tennessee ichthyologist, Dr. David Etnier, Jr., discovered a previously unknown species of fish, called the snail darter, in the Little Tennessee River, whose habitat would have been adversely affected by the dam. Following Etnier's discovery, the U.S. Fish and Wildlife Service listed it as an endangered species in 1975. Under the Endangered Species Act, this was sufficient to halt construction on the dam, which was by then 75 percent complete, to the great displeasure of the Tennessee Valley Authority. In 1976, the Little Tennessee River was declared a critical habitat for the snail darter.

The snail darter was not considered a particularly valuable fish. It was not sought after by sport fishermen, nor did it have any commercial value. When the U.S. Supreme Court in 1978 allowed construction of the dam to be halted permanently, it stated that "the plain language of the Act, buttressed by its legislative history, shows clearly that Congress viewed the value of endangered species as incalculable."*

At about the same time that the Supreme Court upheld the Endangered Species Act and the halting of construction at Tellico, the Department of the Interior's Office of Policy Analysis released a benefit-cost study of the dam. This study showed that the TVA's claimed benefits were insupportable and that the costs of the project exceeded its expected benefits. This should have been the end of Tellico. It was not.

The value of the snail darter may have been economically incalculable, but the same could not be said of the political value of the dam. In 1979, with the nation's economy suffering from the effects of a second OPEC oil embargo and subsequent promotion of energy independence by President Carter, Tennessee Senator Howard Baker was able to exert heavy political pressure to amend the Endangered Species Act so as specifically to exempt Tellico Dam from any federal law impeding its completion. President Carter reluctantly signed the legislation, having limited political capital with which to use for other initiatives. The next day, construction on the dam resumed.

Was that the death knell for the snail darter? Surprisingly not. Within six years after the dam's completion, the snail darter was found in other habitats downstream from Tellico. In 1984, the Fish and Wildlife Service downgraded the status of the snail darter from "endangered" to "threatened." Since then, the snail darter has been found in still other rivers in Tennessee. Ironically, the battle turned out to be between a fish that did not need protection and a dam that should never have been built. Not all species are so fortunate.

Tennessee Valley Authority v. *Hill* (437 U.S. 153 at 180).

Sources: Zerbe and Dively (1994), chap. 23; U.S. Department of the Interior 1979; Davis 1988.

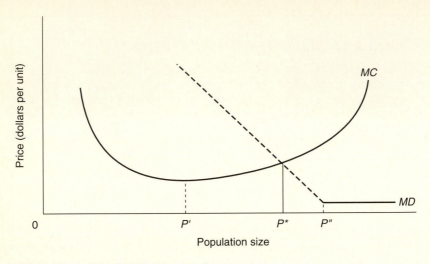

Figure 9.1 The SMS Approach

Source: Adapted from Castle and Berrens (1993), p. 120.

Beyond some population size P', the marginal opportunity cost of preservation will increase. More productive lands, for example, may have to be made off limits to human activities. Economically valuable resources, such as forests, may no longer be harvested or even open to recreationists. Similarly, the marginal benefits from increased population size can be thought of as a reduced risk of extinction and forgone "benefits," however defined. Destruction of all yew trees, for example, which were once thought of as "garbage" trees, would have precluded the discovery of the substance taxol, which is now used to treat certain cancers. Castle and Berrens assume that the risk of extinction falls as population size increases up to population P''. Thus the marginal damage curve MD is shown as increasing as species population falls below P''. Beyond that population, they assume that the risk of extinction is constant and very low.

A strict policy of economic efficiency would lead to the choice of population size P^*, where marginal benefits equal marginal cost. Of course, as the authors argue, it is unlikely that such a point can be located accurately, owing to uncertainty about the location of the MD curve. (That is why the curve is drawn as a dashed line.) Instead, the biological threshold occurs at point P''. The minimum-opportunity-cost solution is P'. Thus the "critical zone" for a species is at population levels between P' and P''. According to the authors, point P' provides an economic signal that a threshold has been reached, and point P'' provides a biological signal. Under the SMS, the species population would not be allowed to fall below P''. (Of course, it may be that the intersection of MC and MD occurs at a population below P'. In that case, it is unclear as to what the SMS would be.)

Castle and Berrens apply the SMS to preservation of the northern spotted owl, which has been listed under the ESA. They do this to illustrate the differences between the SMS approach and the legislative requirements for preservation under the ESA. While they note that an *MC* curve of survival has been estimated (Montgomery and Brown 1992), they point out that no empirical estimate of the *MD* curve exists. Thus Castle and Berrens argue for the use of *existence values* as a measure of marginal benefits.[13] The difference between the ESA and SMS approaches to preservation boil down to the burden of proof each requires. The ESA determines endangered status biologically. Under the ESA, the attempt would be made to estimate the dashed portion of the *MD* curve. With the SMS approach, however, biological thresholds would be identified so as to prevent irreversible species loss. Thus it can be thought of as a preservation-cost-plus approach, which is more flexible than the ESA.

The Clean Air Act

One major piece of environmental legislation that affects all of our lives on a daily basis is the Clean Air Act (CAA) and its many amendments. The CAA regulates the types of cars we drive, the location and types of industries in our communities, the plants that generate our electricity—anything, in fact, whose production and use affects the air we breathe. The original CAA was passed in the 1950s and modified slightly in 1963. But it said little. It was not until the debate and passage of the 1970 and 1977 CAA amendments that significant, costly, and controversial provisions were included.

To give a flavor for the influence that political dialogue can exert in actual environmental policy development, it is useful to consider some background material to the 1970 and 1977 CAA amendments, which were the focus of intense debate. Much of the substance of that debate, if not the spirit, is captured in the House-Senate Conference Report that accompanied the 1970 CAA amendments prior to their passage (U.S. Code 1970). Different versions of the CAA amendments had been developed by the U.S. Senate and House, requiring establishment of a House-Senate conference committee to develop an acceptable compromise. Section 202 of the 1970 CAA amendments established various emission standards for different pollutants. The conference report noted:

> The Senate Amendments deleted the requirements that such standards be based on a test of technical and economic feasibility, and provided statutory standards for passenger cars and required that such standards be achieved by a certain date. . . . The conference substitute follows substantially the Senate amendments. The Administrator is directed to establish emission standards for pollutants . . . which are likely to endanger the public health or welfare.

What this statement means is that the Senate *deleted* a provision that would have set emissions standards based on economic efficiency and substituted a provision

---

[13]We address existence values in Chapter 11. A more thorough explanation can be found in Freeman (1993). Measurement of existence values, however, presupposes that humans accurately represent the interests of the species affected.

to set standards based on *public health or welfare*.[14] Either the Senate had broader goals than economic efficiency in mind, or even if economic efficiency were the sole criterion, the Senate was not going to bother with determinations of both the benefits and the costs associated with the regulations.[15]

This same sort of language was used in the amendments affecting emissions of hazardous pollutants, one of which, lead, we discussed in Chapter 4. The conference committee report stated that "emission levels must provide *an ample margin of safety to assure public health protection*" (emphasis added). Again, this argued for standards set on the basis of something other than economic efficiency, such as a right not to be exposed to certain pollutants deemed hazardous or at the very least standards that did not consider the benefits side of an economic efficiency calculation.

The 1977 CAA amendments made substantial modifications to the 1970 law. In the 1977 amendments, the *multiple* goals of cleaner air were recognized explicitly. For example, when referring to emissions from stationary sources, the 1977 amendments state:

> The plan provisions required by subsection (a) shall ... (9) evidence public, local government, and State legislative involvement and consultation in accordance with section 174 [relating to planning procedures] and include (A) *an identification of and analysis of the air quality, health, welfare, economic, energy, and social effects of the plan provisions* (P.L. 95-95, 91 Stat 747, emphasis added).

The 1977 House-Senate committee report also stated that "state and local governments (not federal agencies) will determine appropriate policy after considering the *multiple objectives* of minimizing air pollution increases in clean air regions, and permitting stable, long-term commercial, industrial, and energy developments." The report went on to state that

> the committee purposely chose not to dictate a federal response to balancing sometimes conflicting goals. ... The committee carefully balanced State and national interests ... in which State and local governments and the people they represent will be free to carry out the reasoned *weighting of environmental and economic goals and needs* (emphasis added).

It seems clear from this language that Congress was concerned with numerous effects, only one of which was economic efficiency. It also seems clear that Congress recognized that sometimes different policy goals could conflict with

---

[14]As mentioned, even under the 1990 CAA amendments, the market-enhancing tradable permit system does not necessarily provide the "correct" level of allowances.

[15]It is perhaps ironic that in 1995 the Republican-controlled U.S. House of Representatives debated a requirement that all new federal regulations pass a cost-benefit test. This was vigorously opposed by House Democrats.

one another. And it seems reasonable to conclude from this language that Congress's definition of "welfare" or "public welfare" was far broader than just economic efficiency.

Even if one argues that Congress had only economic efficiency in mind when it drafted this legislation, there is no evidence whatsoever that comprehensive benefit-cost analyses of different rules were performed. And in some instances, such as the *Lead Industries* case,[16] the U.S. Court of Appeals set legal precedent by stating that benefit-cost analyses were specifically *prohibited* for certain regulations promulgated by the Clean Air Act.

The Lead Industries Association (LIA) argued that the stringent emissions standards called for in the CAA amendments were not based on benefit-cost analyses. Essentially, the LIA argued that imposition of the standards would lead to severe economic hardships for its members, hardships whose costs would exceed the benefits from imposing the strict regulations. The industries argued that the EPA had set standards that were "too low," in the sense that the standards were set below exposure levels that, at the time, had been shown to have any clinical effects.[17] For example, prior to passage of the 1977 CAA amendments, an executive for the Dow Chemical Company suggested that

> to avoid the undesirable strangulation of reasonable economic development within major contributing sections of American society . . . the Clean Air Act be amended to incorporate several concepts as follows . . . Revise Section 109 to include allowance for the consideration of social and economic factors in the definition of "health" and "welfare."

The federal appeals court rejected the arguments of the LIA. The court stated:

> The legislative history of the Act also shows the Administrator may not consider economic and technological feasibility in setting air quality standards; the absence of any provision requiring consideration of these factors was no accident; it was the result of a deliberate decision by Congress to subordinate such concerns to the achievement of health goals.

Thus the statement by the court of appeals seemed clear: other goals are embedded in the setting of air quality standards, and these goals take precedence over considerations of economic efficiency.

---

[16]*Lead Industries Association, Inc.* v. *EPA* (647 F.2d 1130, 10 ELR 20643; D.C. Circuit, 1980, cert. denied 101 S. Ct. 621), summarized in Chapter 4.

[17]We should note that the industries did not argue that breathing and ingesting lead was safe, which was the approach taken by the tobacco industry for many years when responding to claims that smoking caused cancer. Rather, the issue was what threshold level of exposure should be set. (There was also a side issue over whether the EPA had the authority to set standards at all, although that will not concern us in the discussion that follows.)

The Executive Order on "Environmental Racism"

The term *racism* conjures up explosive images of segregation and subjugation. There are concerns, however, of a more subtle type of racism, including that based on the quality of the environment enjoyed by different groups of individuals. In February 1994, President Clinton signed an executive order designed to combat this form of racism. In it, he called for federal agencies to ensure that their policies did not have "disproportionate" environmental impacts on minorities or low-income groups.[18] Yet, as we discussed in Chapter 8, there is empirical evidence that the demand for environmental quality varies by income class. Lower-income groups tend to value improvements in environmental quality less than higher-income groups. This does not mean that the poor are less environmentally conscious than the rich. It does mean that the poor may be unwilling to trade off other goods and services for improvements in environmental quality as easily as the rich.

Charges of "environmental racism" raise potential policy conflicts. First, should society protect certain minority groups, who may value increases in environmental quality less than others, from absorbing more environmental costs? For example, suppose that I am willing to pay you $20 to take my garbage and you are willing to accept it for $10. One efficient solution is for me to pay you some amount between $10 and $20 to take my garbage. But does society have an interest in *preventing* that market transaction? Is there a greater societal "good" served by protecting you from yourself? This question is relevant to several major environmental issues. For example, some minority groups, notably certain Indian tribes, have expressed a desire to locate nuclear waste dumps on their reservations because of the well-paid jobs that would go along with doing so. Ignoring for the moment the fact that accidents at such dumps might have effects far beyond reservation boundaries, should the majority society let the Indians proceed? Would allowing the siting of a nuclear waste dump on the reservation be more or less environmentally racist than preventing it, even if any potential impacts were limited solely to the reservation and its inhabitants?

Second, the specter of environmental racism raises many definitional issues. How is a "disproportionate" environmental impact to be defined and measured? Will policies correct for past "injustices" or merely seek to prevent future ones? How can impacts on different groups be compared? Suppose that there are two options for siting a low-level nuclear waste dump. The first potential site is the aforementioned Texas county that is sparsely populated and whose residents are almost entirely poor Hispanics. The second potential site is a Louisiana county that is also sparsely populated and whose residents are almost entirely poor African

---

[18]Prior to President Clinton's executive order, several bills were brought for consideration by Congress to "correct" racial issues associated with the siting of environmentally damaging industries, including the Environmental Justice Act of 1992 and the Environmental Equal Rights Act of 1993. None has become law.

Americans. Assuming that both options had been found to be equally safe geologically, which option would have more disproportionate minority impacts?

Although overt acts of environmental racism may occur, more often what appears to be racist may be the result of the complex workings of markets. For example, as we will discuss further in Chapter 18, energy resources, such as waste-to-energy facilities, are often surrounded by neighborhoods that are poorer and have higher percentages of minorities than do local populations as a whole.[19] It may be that once-middle-class neighborhoods become poorer and have a higher proportion of minorities because wealthier inhabitants are able to move. Thus siting undesirable land uses may not be intentionally racist but may lead to racial impacts through the workings of markets.[20]

TOXIC IMPERIALISM?

For many decades, developed nations have exported hazardous wastes to poor countries to escape more stringent domestic environmental regulations. The environmental advocacy group Greenpeace has described this practice as "toxic imperialism" and, along with many poor countries, campaigned to ban this sort of trade. In 1994, Greenpeace succeeded. The 1994 Basel Convention made such environmental dumping illegal. More than 100 countries signed on.

Unfortunately, the benefits and costs of this ban now appear less clear. In September 1995, at a meeting of the third-world signatories to the ban, business leaders from those countries complained that the ban may cost them dearly, especially when a provision banning the export of wastes for recycling takes effect in 1997.

The problem lies not with the ban on hazardous waste exports in theory. Instead, problems arise because many poor countries rely on exports of these wastes as sources of raw materials. Many poor countries rely on scrap materials that are classified as hazardous waste for their supplies of aluminum, lead, zinc, steel, and paper, because those materials are far cheaper than virgin ones. Third-world firms that recycle scrap materials are concerned that the ban on exports for recycling will put them out of business. For example, India relies on imports of scrap for almost half the copper it uses.

The overall economic consequences of the ban will depend on what will be classified as "hazardous." For example, a shipment of scrap paper might be deemed hazardous if it contained tiny quantities of lead. Unfortunately, the convention left such questions unanswered; what would constitute hazardous wastes was never defined. And environmental groups like Greenpeace vow that they will fight attempts to weaken definitions, even though they admit

(continued)

---

[19]A discussion can be found in Been (1994).
[20]O'Reilly (1994) discusses the case of siting hazardous waste facilities in Indiana and its deleterious effects on inner cities and job creation.

that the bans might damage some third-world industries. For environmentalists like Greenpeace, those damages will be far less than the environmental and health benefits arising from a strict ban.

What's the answer to this dilemma? Unfortunately, no one is sure yet. Clearly, the ban has benefits and costs. Just as clearly, these benefits and costs will encompass not only economic welfare and growth but also issues of equity and rights. Poor countries will have to decide whether the environmental pain of relaxing the ban is worth the economic gain. Interestingly, some of the most vocal calls for relaxing the ban come from individuals in third-world countries, some of whom argue that the ban is a "conspiracy by the developed world."

Source: Adapted from "Muck and Morals" (1995).

ECONOMIC EFFICIENCY AS A SECOND-ORDER GOAL

Although there is nothing intrinsically wrong with any of the environmental policies we have discussed, little attention was paid to achieving those goals efficiently. This is what we mean when we state that economic efficiency should be a *second-order goal*. Consider again the Northwest Power Planning Council's proposal to increase runs of Columbia River salmon and thus partially restore the rights granted to Native Americans under the Treaty of 1855. There has been much controversy over the way the council's goal of doubling salmon runs should be achieved. One way would be simply to destroy all of the dams along the Columbia River and let nature eventually restore the river and the runs to what they once were. But that is not realistic. The dams serve too many other valuable purposes.

With the dams in place, restoring the runs requires getting adult fish upstream to spawn and getting smolts downstream. Two basic alternative methods have been proposed. The first involves transporting smolts in barges, and the second involves increasing water flows in the river to "flush" the fish downstream more quickly. Proponents of both approaches are equally vocal. Barging fish has the advantage that they do not perish while going through the dams and avoid predators (mostly squawfish) that find them easy prey in the slow waters behind the dams. Unfortunately, barging also may be traumatic for the fish, which lessens their survival rate in the open sea.

Another debate is the "quality" of the fish that survive. Many fish are raised in and released from hatcheries. Critics of this approach, while acknowledging that it increases the overall number of fish, lament that hatchery fish are "dumb," in that they lack the survival instincts and toughness of wild fish. These critics do not want hatchery fish to spawn with wild fish because they fear that the overall gene pool of salmon will be weakened, leading to eventual extinction anyway.

Economics cannot determine what methods are biologically most sound, but it can evaluate the trade-offs between the different approaches and determine the most cost-effective means of achieving the desired goals. This is why economic efficiency should always be a second-order goal of policies that address equity and rights. Unfortunately, as we discussed earlier in this chapter, that has not always been the case with U.S. environmental laws.

Liability and Economic Efficiency

Distributional and human rights considerations have been paramount when considering policies that address toxic and hazardous wastes, yet in some cases the creation and disposal of these wastes may be free from externalities. Legal liability for damages or cleanup may induce a company creating toxic wastes to reduce the risk of exposure up to the point where the cost of reducing the risk further is greater than the value that people place on additional risk reductions. The primary issue is that the escape of wastes into the environment exposes people to risks to life, health, and property without their consent. (Of course, there may also be rights-of-nature implications, if toxic waste decimates populations or destroys habitats.)

The selection of an appropriate policy tool in this example will hinge on compliance and enforcement costs. If enforcement costs are low, policies that would be useful if this were an externality problem (taxes, quotas, etc.) can be employed. If, as appears to be true in some cases, enforcement is extremely costly and illegal disposal is much cheaper than complying with standards or paying disposal fees, these tools will probably be ineffective (Sullivan 1987).

In the latter case, regulators have two other approaches open to them. They can treat toxic waste disposal as a matter of criminal law and impose strict criminal penalties for illegal dumping or even for excessively risky waste-handling procedures. If the costs of legal disposal are high, the penalties for illegal disposal will have to be higher to serve as a deterrent. The other approach is to provide for disposal at public expense, either through subsidies or public disposal. It may even be necessary to purchase waste and dispose of it at public expense to guarantee a satisfactory rate of participation in the program.

Regulators will have to determine which of their options is most likely to work and which will impose the lowest costs on society. They may also have to be concerned about additional distortions that regulations introduce into the economy. Policymakers considering publicly funded disposal will also have to consider whether taxpayers are willing to pay for solving what they may see as someone else's problem.

Equity and Tradable Emissions Permits Under the 1990 Clean Air Act Amendments

In Chapter 7, we discussed the use of tradable emissions permits to reduce pollution to an efficient level. We showed how a system of tradable permits could correct all three of the distortions (by creating a market for a previously unpriced good, correcting the input mix, and correcting the level of output) caused by externalities. After years of command-and-control regulations that addressed emissions of sulfur dioxide from electric-generating plants, the 1990 CAA amendments created a market for emissions of sulfur dioxide. The change from a market-substituting approach to a market-enhancing one represented quite an innovation in pollution control, one that had been advocated for years by many economists and opposed by many environmentalists. The CAA amendments created sulfur dioxide "allowances," with one allowance equal to 1 ton of sulfur dioxide, that can be traded between utilities and other parties at an agreed price.

The permit system has two phases. Phase 1 began in 1995 and continues through the year 2000. Phase 1 affects 110 electric utility generating plants located in 21 midwestern and eastern states. The plants involved in this phase are older and dirtier coal-fired plants.[21] Phase 1 allocates about 5.5 million allowances, with over half of these going to plants located in just five states: Georgia, Indiana, Ohio, Pennsylvania, and West Virginia. In addition, selected plants in Illinois, Ohio, and Indiana received a "special" allocation of phase 1 allowances. Another 3.5 million allowances have been held in reserve by the EPA to accommodate growth in electricity demand. Utilities that need allowances can purchase them from EPA.

In phase 2, the trading program will be expanded to cover all coal-, oil-, and natural gas–fired power plants in the country. In this phase, the formula for the initial allocation of permits will be more restrictive.[22] The number of permits will be capped at 8.95 million; no additional sulfur dioxide emissions will be allowed. Trades will not be limited between utilities. Anyone can buy and sell the permits. One utility, for example, donated some of its permits to the American Lung Association. The utility was able to write off the value of these permits to reduce its tax bill, and the lung association "bought" cleaner air.

Two obvious questions arise: How was the total number of permits determined, and how were those permits allocated? Did Congress rely on studies of marginal damage from sulfur dioxide emissions, measured through surveys of individuals' willingness to pay to avoid damage, and the marginal cost of controlling emissions to determine the economically efficient level of permits? Hardly. The determination of allowances and their initial allocation was a *political* decision, designed to gain acceptance for the tradable-permit approach. Nevertheless, even if the actual number of allowances is not efficient, the permit system is, in the sense that, given a determination of the total number of allowances, the system will redistribute those allowances in the most efficient, least-cost manner.

A further equity concern is the area in which permits can be traded. One of the arguments against tradable allowances is that they can lead to poorer air quality in already affected areas. For example, an electric generator in Massachusetts could purchase allowances from generators in New Hampshire, leading to exposure of higher sulfur dioxide pollution levels by residents in Massachusetts. If the area where the pollution will be deposited is heavily populated, regulators in

---

[21]The standard for a plant to be included in phase 1 is emission of more than 2.5 pounds of sulfur dioxide per million Btu of fuel used.

[22]The standard will drop to 1.2 pounds of sulfur dioxide per million Btu.

Massachusetts may disapprove of such trades. In fact, this is a weakness of the 1990 Clean Air Act Amendments, for while they allow pollution trading, there are no geographic distinctions made between locations. Pollution is traded on a ton-for-ton basis.

This sort of limitation can be overcome, but compromises must be made. Trades can be limited to certain subregions, for example, or trades can occur on other than a one-for-one basis between certain areas. For example, a generator wishing to purchase permits from an upwind generator might have to buy 2 tons' worth of allowances for each additional ton it would be allowed to emit. The problem, of course, is identifying the "correct" set of geographic trade-offs, something that, given political sensitivities, will not be easy.[23]

CHAPTER SUMMARY

We have seen that policies addressing equity and rights concerns often look different from policies addressing economic efficiency. In some cases, as with the preservation of endangered species or the protection of human rights to a clean environment, this is likely always to be the case. Placing a specific value on rights makes little sense; they are simply rights. In other cases, however, policies designed to achieve other policy goals can resemble those addressing efficiency. The development of a tradable-emissions-permit system for sulfur dioxide may not have set the level of allowances at the optimally efficient level, but once fully in place, it should achieve the desired reduction in emissions in the most efficient way possible.

When policy goals extend beyond economic efficiency, policymakers must often grapple with complex moral and legal issues. Regulations requiring the "safe" disposal of nuclear waste for 10,000 years in order to protect future generations call up mind-boggling complexities: How will future visitors be warned away, since we cannot presuppose that they will understand any language spoken or written today? How can we test whether a structure will last 10,000 years? How can we test whether warning markers will even last that long?

None of this is to suggest that policies addressing goals besides economic efficiency are any less important. But environmental policymakers need to be cognizant of their goals and express those goals clearly. As we shall discuss in later chapters, attempting to achieve nonefficiency goals by altering the tools of economic efficiency makes little sense, much as pounding a nail with a sewing machine is ill-advised. Equity and rights considerations will require far different approaches and will often be more difficult to address. As we discussed in Chapter 4, defining what we mean by "fair" or "just" is nontrivial. Neither will be applying such definitions in practice. Policymakers may have to weigh distributional issues against human rights and the rights of nature, even when there is no social consensus on the meaning of the individual goals, let alone how to

---

[23]See Krupnick, Oates, and Van de Verg (1983) for another compromise system.

choose between them. The fact that a public policy decision cannot be justified on economic grounds does not necessarily mean that it is a bad decision or that it cannot be justified at all. It simply means that if it can be justified, it must be on some other basis.

CHAPTER REVIEW

Economic Concepts and Tools

- Externalities can cause distributional, human rights, and rights-of-nature problems as well as economic inefficiency. An external cost exists when one party bears costs imposed by another without the affected party's consent.
- Minimizing the costs of meeting a constraint imposed by distributional or rights values is an example of a second-best solution.
- If environmental quality is a normal good and empirical evidence bears this out, the demand for environmental quality will be positively correlated with income.
- Even with no market failures and no government intervention, people with a higher (lower) willingness to pay for environmental quality would tend to experience fewer (more) environmental problems because of the choices they make.

Policy Issues

- People with a higher willingness to pay for environmental quality are more likely to try to use the political process to provide additional environmental amenities, particularly the ones they consume.
- Many environmental laws in the United States appear to be motivated by considerations other than economic efficiency. The Clean Air Act, for example, bases limits for pollutant concentrations and exposure levels on a standard of no measurable health impacts. This can be interpreted as legislative recognition of a right not to be exposed involuntarily to health risks.
- Many environmental conflicts have distributional aspects. The issue may be that different groups reap the benefits and bear the costs of a project, as in cases of exporting pollution. The issue may be that some groups bear more than a perceived "fair" share of costs, as in the case with charges of environmental racism. However, in the absence of evidence of overt actions, defining environmentally racist behavior will require separating normal differences in the demand for environmental quality.
- The fact that a public policy decision cannot be justified on economic grounds does not necessarily mean that it is a bad decision or that it cannot be justified at all. It simply means that if it can be justified, it must be on some other basis.

DISCUSSION QUESTIONS

1. As discussed at the beginning of the chapter, several Native American tribes catch salmon for use in their religious rites. Now that several of these species of salmon have been listed as endangered, should the tribes be forbidden from taking any salmon? Would that violate their human rights? How can human rights and the rights of nature be weighed against one another?

2. Why do you think the EPA set a standard for nuclear waste storage of 10,000 years, even though some HLW still will be dangerously radioactive?

3. Suppose that farmers will be disadvantaged by the banning of a certain pesticide because substitutes are more expensive. Is this a human rights issue? What about loggers who lose their jobs because forest lands are preserved for spotted owl habitat?

4. How would you design a conceptual framework to evaluate whether or not a policy of generating additional electricity, which causes pollution, to power a new technology that destroys toxic wastes will provide net environmental benefits?

5. What would have happened to the snail darter and Tellico Dam if a safe minimum standard approach had been used? Do you think the outcome would have been different?

6. Is there any way to determine whether economic efficiency should be a primary or a secondary policy goal? Did the Lead Industries Association have a case for arguing that complete elimination of airborne lead emissions, besides being prohibitively costly, was not justified on a health basis?

7. Many pollution exposure standards are determined on the basis of increased cancer incidence. For example, the standard for exposure to carbon monoxide is based on one additional cancer death per million people. Is this a reasonable standard? Can you think of any alternatives?

8. Suppose that residents of Nevada had agreed to compensation for siting the Yucca Mountain nuclear waste repository. Where should the money come from: taxpayers in general? individuals who receive power generated by nuclear power plants? What objections to different revenue raising mechanisms are likely to be raised? How valid do you think such objections would be?

REFERENCES

Been, V. 1994. "Locally Undesirable Land Uses in Minority Neighborhoods: Disproportionate Siting or Market Dynamics?" *Yale Law Journal* 103(2): 1383–1422.

Bishop, R. 1978. "Endangered Species and Uncertainty: The Economics of a Safe Minimum Standard." *American Journal of Agricultural Economics* 57(1): 10–18.

————. 1979. "Endangered Species, Irreversibility, and Uncertainty: A Reply." *American Journal of Agricultural Economics* 58(2): 376–379.

Cairncross, F. 1993. "All That Remains: A Survey of Waste and the Environment." *Economist,* May 29, 1993, pp. W1–W18.

Castle, E., and R. Berrens. 1993. "Endangered Species, Economic Analysis, and the Safe Minimum Standard." *Northwest Environmental Journal* 9(1): 108–130.

Ciriacy-Wantrup, S. 1964. "The 'New' Competition for Land and Some Implications for Public Policy." *Natural Resources Journal* 4: 252–267.

————. 1968. *Resource Conservation: Economics and Policies.* 3d ed. Berkeley: University of California Press.

Coloquette, K., and E. Robertson. 1991. "Environmental Racism: The Causes, Consequences, and Commendations." *Tulane Environmental Law Journal* 5(1): 153–207.

Davis, R. 1988. "Lessons in Politics and Economics from the Snail Darter." In *Environmental Resources and Applied Economics: Essays in Honor of John V. Krutilla,* ed. V. Smith. Washington, D.C.: Resources for the Future.

Douglas, J. 1993. "Electrotechnologies for Water Treatment." *EPRI Journal* 18(2): 4–13.

Freeman, A. 1993. *The Measurement of Environmental and Resource Values: Theory and Methods.* Washington, D.C.: Resources for the Future.

Grigalunas, T., and J. Opaluch. 1988. "Assessing Liability for Damages Under CERCLA: A New Approach for Providing Incentives for Pollution Avoidance." *Natural Resources Journal* 28(3): 509–533.

Gupta, S., G. Van Houten, and M. Cropper. 1993. "Cleanup Decisions Under Superfund: Do Benefits and Costs Matter?" *Resources* 111: 11–17.

Hird, J. 1990. "Superfund Expenditures and Cleanup Priorities: Distributive Politics and the Public Interest." *Journal of Policy Analysis and Management* 9(4): 455–483.

Krupnick, A., W. Oates, and E. Van de Verg. 1983. "On Marketable Pollution Permits: The Case for a System of Pollution Offsets." *Journal of Environmental Economics and Management* 10(2): 233–247.

Kunreuther, H., and D. Easterling. 1990. "Are Risk-Benefit Trade-offs Possible in Siting Hazardous Facilities?" *American Economic Review* 80(2): 252–256.

Montgomery, C., and G. Brown. 1992. "Economics of Species Preservation." *Contemporary Policy Issues* 10(1): 1–12.

"Muck and Morals." 1995. *Economist,* September 2, pp. 61.

Northwest Power Planning Council (NPPC). 1992. *Columbia River Basin Fish and Wildlife Program: Strategy for Salmon,* Vol. 1. Issue Paper No. 92-21. Portland, Ore.: NPPC.

O'Reilly, J. 1994. "Environmental Racism, Site Cleanup, and Inner-City Jobs: Indiana's Urban In-fill Incentives." *Yale Journal on Regulation* 11(1): 43–73.

"Paying for the Past." 1992. *Economist,* February 29, p. 80.

Portney, P. 1990. "EPA and the Evolution of Federal Regulation." In *Public Policies for Environmental Protection,* ed. P. Portney. Washington, D.C.: Resources for the Future.

————, and K. Probst. 1992. *Assigning Liability for Superfund Cleanup: An Analysis of Policy Options.* Washington, D.C.: Resources for the Future.

————. 1994. "Cleaning Up Superfund." *Resources* 114: 2–5.

"Radioactive Waste: Finding a Safe Place." 1991. *Civil Engineering News,* July, pp. 48–51.

Reisner, M. 1993. *Cadillac Desert: The American West and Its Disappearing Water.* Rev. ed. New York: Viking Penguin.

Russell, C. 1988. "Economic Incentives in the Management of Hazardous Wastes." *Columbia Journal of Environmental Law* 13(1): 257–274.

Russell, M., E. Colglazier, and B. Tonn. 1992. "The U.S. Hazardous Waste Legacy." *Environment* 34(1): 12–39.

Smith, V., and J. Krutilla. 1979. "Endangered Species, Irreversibilities, and Uncertainty: A Comment." *American Journal of Agricultural Economics* 58(2): 371–375.

Sullivan, A. 1987. "Policy Options for Toxics Disposal: Laissez-Faire and Riskless Choice: A Reference Dependent Model." *Journal of Environmental Economics and Management* 14(1): 58–71.

U.S. Code Congressional and Administrative News. 1970. Conference Report No. 91-1783. Washington, D.C.: U.S. Government Printing Office.

U.S. Department of the Interior. 1979. *Tellico Dam and Reservoir.* Staff Report to the Endangered Species Committee. Washington, D.C.: U.S. Government Printing Office.

Wilson, E. 1986. *Biodiversity.* Washington, D.C.: National Academy Press.

Zerbe, R., and D. Dively. 1994. *Benefit-Cost Analysis in Theory and Practice.* New York: HarperCollins.

CHAPTER 10

BALANCING
POLICY GOALS

How Clean Is My Valley? Siting Wind Turbines in Rural Vermont

Wind turbines are often pointed to as "clean" sources of electricity because they do not pollute air or water. Many public utility regulators are encouraging electric utilities to develop wind turbines and other sources of "renewable" energy, including solar power and biomass. These renewable energy sources are seen as an alternative to coal, oil, and nuclear-generated electricity, which may be monetarily less costly but whose environmental problems are well known and potentially significant.

Unfortunately, although wind turbines emit no pollutants like their fossil- and nuclear-fueled brethren, they are not entirely without environmental impacts. First, whirring turbine blades can be noisy, and the noise can disturb wildlife in remote areas or humans near population sites. Second, wind turbines can be unsightly, although perhaps less so than many generating plants. Nevertheless, turbines are often located on hilltops or mountain peaks to maximize the amount of wind, and that siting creates visual pollution, much as air pollution reduces the quality of vistas. Third, for reasons that are still not understood entirely, birds sometimes fly into spinning turbine blades. This concerns many environmentalists, especially if the turbines are located near nesting sites for endangered bird species. Fourth, some environmentalists fear that development of wind turbines in remote locations such as wilderness areas will harm native wildlife and allow increased access by humans, leading to further local environmental damage.

In 1995, an electric utility in the state of Vermont, with the backing of the Electric Power Research Institute and the U.S. Department of Energy, applied for a permit to build a wind turbine facility on a remote mountaintop in southeastern Vermont in order to study the ability of wind turbine technology to withstand extremely cold and harsh climates. Ultimately, if the test is successful, it will prove that wind turbines can be operated effectively in other areas with harsh climates, such as Wyoming and the Dakotas, where there is the potential for wind power to generate much electricity.

The particular site chosen in Vermont is adjacent to a wilderness area managed by the United States Forest Service (USFS). Some environmental groups fear that construction of the necessary roads to the site will adversely affect wildlife, such as black bears, in the nearby wilderness area.[1] These groups wanted an exhaustive and costly environmental impact statement (EIS) prepared, tying together the development of the wind turbine with the USFS's land management techniques. Other environmental groups favor development so as to demonstrate the feasibility of wind turbines and thus the availability of practical alternatives to fossil-fueled electric generation. Some residents do not want to see the site developed because there is no need for the electricity it would generate. And some residents are concerned that they will lose some of their views. Finally, many local residents favor development because of the potential jobs it would create. The utility, although keen to develop the project, is loath to become caught up in a bitter and expensive environmental battle.

The dispute over the development of this site points to the potential conflicts between different but laudable environmental and social goals. Which is more important: research to assess the feasibility of a new, clean electricity source or ensuring that various species in wilderness habitat are protected from all forms of human activity? Should residents who built homes in the area to enjoy the views be made to suffer "damages" because those views will be marred? There are no easy answers, but in early 1996, the state of Vermont approved the project. Barring other delays, the project should be producing electricity sometime in 1997.

Two broad policy issues are evident. First, it is not clear whether there are absolute restrictions to development. Initially, an environmental impact assessment was performed for the proposed site itself.[2] It was found acceptable, as the site does not itself lie in a wilderness area. But the potential for damage from development near a wilderness area is less clear. Should there be a "buffer zone" around wilderness areas, in which no development can take place? If so, how large should such zones be?

Second, it is not clear how to make the trade-off between the rights of nature at the location in question and the potential efficiency, equity, human rights, and rights of nature gains from reduced pollution elsewhere, should the research prove successful. There is always an element of risk and uncertainty associated with research; potential costs today must somehow be weighed against potential future benefits. But how much risk should be taken, and who should decide? The arguments over developing wind power in Vermont and elsewhere go beyond standard private-versus-social-cost debates and extend into more difficult moral and philosophical territory. It may be that an ill wind does blow no good.

---

[1]Curiously, Vermont allows black bears to be hunted at certain times of the year.

[2]An environmental impact assessment (EIA) is a less thorough environmental review than the more rigorous and better-known environmental impact statement (EIS) as described in the National Environmental Policy Act (NEPA).

INTRODUCTION

As we have seen in Chapters 7, 8, and 9, policymakers and regulators will usually have multiple goals. In making decisions, they may need to compromise in order to accommodate different goals, including those that improve environmental quality. Doing so will be difficult; policymakers and regulators will always face a variety of interest groups, well meaning and otherwise, who will stress their own desired subsets of goals. Avoiding difficult policy decisions, or masking them under the guise of poor descision methodology, will ultimately create more problems. Thus, as we argued in Chapter 5, it is imperative that policymakers first clarify their goals. In this chapter, we assume that policymakers have taken that first crucial step: through some process, they have identified the goals they wish to achieve. We focus, therefore, on methods that can evaluate different options satisfying multiple goals *in a consistent manner.*

These methods fall into the general category of *decision analysis.* And although we cannot offer a complete course in decision analysis,[3] in this chapter we introduce one method for balancing competing goals that we have found useful in our own applied environmental policy work: *multiattribute decision analysis.* Though no one methodology can determine a uniquely "correct" balance between competing goals, we believe that multiattribute decision analysis can provide a useful framework for policymakers because it has the virtue of providing a clear understanding of *what* the alternative goals are and *how* they are balanced.

One possible objection to discussing these methods is that policymakers don't employ them. After all, there is no evidence that policymakers, such as those at the Environmental Protection Agency (EPA), used multiattribute analysis to develop standards for lead exposure in children or other air toxics covered under the Clean Air Act. Nor do regulators who oversee the siting of generating facilities, such as wind turbines, tend to incorporate multiattribute analysis in any formal way. Instead, policymakers often conduct their own "informal" multiattribute analyses, using attributes that may or may not be obvious. For example, one attribute that may be considered is political viability. A regulator or policymaker may consider the political ramifications of making an unpopular decision, such as siting a waste-to-energy facility or a wind turbine, even though the public opposes the decision. A formal multiattribute analysis could include those sort of attributes, too. However, because policymakers sometimes wish to hide "political" attributes, they may be reluctant to include such attributes in any formal analysis.

We do not pretend that multiattribute analysis is in common use, but we believe that it should be used more often to clarify multiple policy goals for the public. People will always disagree about the importance of different goals. Multiattribute analysis is one way of determining whether those differences are critical to specific decisions and, if so, how changing the importance of specific goals affects preferred decisions.

---

[3] There are many texts on decision and policy analysis. Two excellent ones are Stokey and Zeckhauser (1978) and Kleindorfer, Kunruether, and Schoemaker (1993).

QUALITATIVE AND QUANTITATIVE GOALS

Before different, and possibly competing, goals can be balanced, there must be a way to measure them. After all, if we cannot measure a goal, we cannot determine whether we have met it. As we discussed in previous chapters, the goals of increasing economic efficiency, improving equity, ensuring human rights, and protecting the rights of nature are fundamentally different types of goals.

Some policy goals are *qualitative.* Either they are satisfied or they are not. For example, if preventing species extinctions is a policy goal, it will be satisfied if a policy action does not increase the likelihood of any species' becoming extinct. It is not satisfied if the likelihood of a species' becoming extinct is increased. Goals directed toward human rights and the rights of nature are often qualitative: it makes little sense to say, for example, that there has been a "15 percent increase in human rights." Vegetarians who oppose eating meat on moral grounds are unlikely to state that eating fish is "50 percent less immoral than eating pork" because fish have less intelligence than pigs.

Conversely, some policy goals are *quantitative.* They can be satisfied in varying degrees and can be measured numerically, sometimes with monetary measures. All other things being equal, an action with greater net benefits will be preferred (Pareto superior) to one with fewer net benefits. However, determining whether a policy improves the distribution of income between the richest and the poorest members of society requires defining the affected groups and measuring their incomes.

Finally, some policy goals will have both quantitative and qualitative elements. They may have thresholds, below which they are not satisfied and above which they are satisfied, but may also be satisfied to varying degrees. For example, a given distribution of benefits and costs below some threshold may be unacceptably unfair, but above that acceptable threshold, some distributions may be perceived as more fair than others. A policy goal or preserving forest habitat for endangered species may be quantitative, in that it can be measured in terms of hectares of habitat preserved, but it may also be qualitative if endangered species require that a minimum number of hectares be preserved to survive.

In at least some cases, the four overall policy goals we have considered in previous chapters all fall into the latter category. Improving economic efficiency is quantitative, but it can have a threshold. Ideally, no action should be taken if its costs exceed its benefits. Actions can be ranked by the fairness of their consequences, but there may be a line, albeit fuzzy, separating the acceptably fair and the unacceptably unfair. Human rights and the rights of nature involve thresholds between respect and violation, but rights can be violated to varying degrees.

The easiest decisions for policymakers to make are ones where only one option is acceptable. If all options but one have negative net benefits or are unfair or violate human rights or the rights of nature, that one option is the unambiguous choice. Cases where several options are acceptable are harder. Policymakers must rank options or at least choose a single best option. Deciding whether to build a wind turbine poses conflicts between the desire to develop "clean" renewable sources of energy and the desire to protect pristine views and species. Ranking on the basis of benefits and costs is easy, at least conceptually. Ranking options in terms of their fairness or respect for rights is more difficult. With several acceptable options, policymakers may have to make trade-offs between goals. When every option violates at least one goal, policymakers cannot avoid trade-offs between goals. These are the hardest decisions to make and, unfortunately, probably the most common.

Developing quantitative goals will not always reveal how to make difficult decisions, but it can help policymakers clarify and explore different trade-offs, such as those involved in siting the wind turbines described at the beginning of this chapter. In the case of the wind turbines, for example, policymakers may wish to explore the benefits and the costs of granting an absolute right in the environment in cases where no mechanism exists for people to sell or waive that right. They may wish to determine the "cost" of habitat preservation or the implicit cost of producing less air pollution from fossil-fired generation. Policymakers still will have to make the decisions themselves but will not be forced (or permitted to) make such decisions blindly.

Limitations of Quantitative Goals

In Chapter 11, we discuss the how-tos of quantifying environmental values, primarily in monetary terms. However, though quantitative measurements and goals can provide useful information, they have important limitations. First, quantitative goals can tell us the effects on people's welfare of having one arrangement of rights rather than another. If the rights in question have only a secondary moral status—if, say, they exist because having them promotes economic well-being—this is an important piece of information. For example, in the United States we believe that a system of private property rights promotes economic growth. But rights may have a *primary* moral status—they are basic human rights that everyone has as a consequence of being human. For example, most people believe that no one has the right to enslave someone else. Finally, rights may have a *secondary* moral status that has some basis other than economic well-being, such as distributive justice. In those cases, using quantitative goals to compare welfare with different systems of rights (e.g., "young children protected from working in factories are 50 percent better off than children who are not so protected") is neither informative nor appropriate.

Proponents of the rights of nature, including the right of a species not to be extinguished because of the actions of humans, often argue that *any* monetary valuation of environmental impacts is undesirable because it assumes that everything can and should be compared on the same basis, even though some things are or should be incommensurable. There is some validity in this belief, for some choices *are* qualitatively different from others. Choosing religious beliefs is qualitatively different from choosing what to eat for breakfast. Such choices should be made on different grounds and therefore cannot be compared. Thinking that they can be compared involves a fundamental confusion between *preferences* and *values*.

When moral or ethical values and preferences conflict, values should take precedence. For example, I can want a eagle over my mantle while knowing that killing the last eagle would be wrong. If I am moral, I will follow my values and forgo my eagle trophy. The conflict over measuring and monetizing environmental costs and benefits (placing a dollar value on them) arises from this basic philosophical difference. Determining monetary values of different attributes is based on the premises that human welfare is the basis for moral value and that people usually choose more rather than less welfare. Rights of nature, however, must be based on other premises. Rights of nature can arise only within an ethical system that bases right and wrong, rights and duties, on something other than human welfare as measured by people's preferences.

Sometimes it is argued that forcing people to make inappropriate comparisons is bad because it can damage their perceptions of the difference between moral and nonmoral values. These arguments suggest that comparing eagles to cornflakes demeans both us and eagles. The worst consequence of this thinking is not that such comparisons may cause us to make wrong decisions but rather that it may change the *way* we think about such questions.[4] In this view, it is our ethics that should determine our preferences. Thus forcing individuals to take actions because of an existing system of laws, even when those actions are viewed as morally reprehensible, substitutes law for morality.

This argument assumes that there is one correct moral system. Whether that is true, we do not have any moral system that commands universal assent. The best that someone confronted with a variety of conflicting ethical theories can hope for is what Rawls (1971) called *reflective equilibrium*. If, after openly and honestly considering arguments for and against my moral beliefs, I continue to hold them and believe that I am justified in holding them, I am in reflective equilibrium. Someone whose ethical beliefs about nature are modified after being told that an economist can measure the strength of a person's convictions in monetary terms on the basis of that person's behavior does not have strongly held or well-founded beliefs.

These arguments may be resolvable. Many ethical systems hold that things other than individuals' preferences have moral weight. However, with the possible exception of some religious systems, they do not deny that individuals' preferences do or may have moral weight. Similarly, most ethical systems based on human welfare have been willing to admit that people may not always act in their own best interest and that other considerations besides individual human welfare may have moral weight.

Thus there are many points of view that can agree that monetary measurement of people's valuations of environmental impacts has a place in public decision making but are not the only thing that is relevant. This is a very general principle that may be difficult to apply to specific situations. In rather blunt terms, any argument for basing a decision on the rights of nature rather than human welfare comes down to an assertion that (other) people have the wrong preferences. It may be very difficult to distinguish between a good-faith argument that the rights of nature are being violated and an attack on monetization that results from assigning

---

[4] See Kelman (1981) or Sagoff (1988).

a low value to someone's personal favorite part of nature. All sides of the environmental spectrum have been fairly cynical about adopting economics when it is convenient and rejecting it when it is not.

Limitations of Qualitative Goals

Regardless of the arguments, environmental policymakers will still have to examine trade-offs because even absolutes have consequences. But if all goals are qualitative, there may be no way of trading off goals that meet acceptable qualitative thresholds. Alternatively, policymakers may be forced to make the best of a bad set of options, all of which violate one or more qualitative goals. In such cases, policymakers will need some method of comparing and ranking alternative qualitative goals, even if doing so is deemed morally repugnant.

Suppose that all potential sites for building wind turbines are located near critical habitats for various species. An absolute moral protection granted to those species would preclude the development of wind turbines, even if development of nonpolluting, renewable energy sources were a desirable policy goal. Such an absolute protection might increase children's exposure to air pollutants (another policy goal expressed in the Clean Air Act).[5] Thus a policy based on this absolute moral protection could impose costs on society, either by requiring the development of alternative, more expensive forms of energy or by relying more on "dirtier" resources. Thus development of some method to quantify goals, even those that are qualitative, appears to be necessary for environmental policymakers.

AN INTRODUCTION TO MULTIATTRIBUTE DECISION ANALYSIS

Within the four broad categories of impacts we have discussed in earlier chapters—economic efficiency, equity, human rights, and the rights of nature—there will be trade-offs. Environmental policymakers can benefit by using empirical techniques that help clarify potentially complex trade-offs. Multiattribute decision analysis is one such technique.[6] It allows different goals to be weighed and traded off against one another, *regardless of whether those goals are qualitative, quantitative, or mixed.* This technique takes the axioms of utility maximization we discussed in Chapter 3 and applies them to "bundles" of attributes, much as traditional utility maximization techniques determine the optimal bundle of goods and services for a consumer.

---

[5]Note that these arguments assume a variety of normative goals. As we discussed in Chapter 9, for example, one of the goals of the Clean Air Act was to limit children's exposure to lead. Nothing in that act said the same about limiting the exposure of the aged to lead.

[6]There is an exhaustive literature on multiattribute decision analysis. Our discussion draws primarily on Keeney and Raiffa (1993). A less mathematical but also less comprehensive discussion can be found in Kleindorfer, Kunruether, and Schoemaker (1993).

Steps in Performing a Multiattribute Decision Analysis

There are three major steps in performing a multiattribute analysis. First, the goals must be determined. It is difficult to determine whether a "good" decision has been made until we have clearly defined what it is we wish to achieve. Goals may take specific forms, such as increasing profits or reducing mortality and morbidity, or may be as vague as "improving overall well-being." A goal simply illustrates the direction in which the decision is supposed to lead us. Thus a goal to reduce mortality means that we seek to reduce premature deaths for whatever reason.

Once goals have been determined, next we have to determine the best way of measuring success by selecting the attributes most appropriate to the objectives chosen. The last, and most difficult, step is to weigh all of the attributes for all of the decisions under consideration so as to reach a final decision. This step, especially in the presence of uncertainty and risk, will almost always be open to attack as "arbitrary." Despite that criticism, however, keep in mind that the *ultimate* goal of decision analysis is the decisions themselves. If environmental policymakers can define their selection criteria more clearly, they are less likely to be criticized for arbitrariness than if their decisions are made in private.

Selecting Attributes

Once goals have been defined, the next step is to determine the *attributes* that will measure whether we are moving in the right direction. Suppose that one goal of an environmental policy limiting particulate emissions from coal-fired power plants is to reduce mortality rates, based on the causal relationships established by epidemiologists between pollutant emissions and mortality rates. In that case, one possible attribute to measure would be particulate emissions per kilowatt-hour of electricity generated. Another might be ambient concentrations of particulates downwind of coal-fired power plants.

The more that goals can be *subdivided,* the easier it will be to define measurable attributes. To see this, suppose that an environmental policymaker's ultimate goal is to achieve "the good life."[7] Unfortunately, defining easily measurable attributes associated with "the good life" is probably difficult and controversial. Someone may decide that wealth and possessions are the best determinants of the good life; someone else may argue that knowledge is the best determinant. To address the controversy, it helps to subdivide, or reduce, "the good life" into separate subgoals. If necessary, these subgoals can be further broken down until a level is reached where the different attributes can be measured. This process is shown in Figure 10.1.

In Figure 10.1, "the good life" is divided into three subgoals: "health," "wealth," and "beauty." Unfortunately, at this level, it is still difficult to determine measurable attributes for "health" and "beauty." (Even "wealth" will be difficult to measure.) Therefore, we subdivide the three further subgoals. "Health" is divided

---

[7] This objective was used by Manheim and Hall (1967).

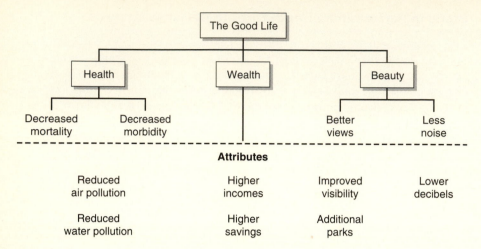

Figure 10.1   Diagrammatic Representation of Objectives and Attributes

into goals of decreased mortality and decreased morbidity. These goals are relatively straightforward, as are attributes that may be associated with them, such as air and water pollution levels.

A similar procedure is followed with the subgoal "beauty." It is broken down into the subgoals of "better views" and "lower noise." Measurable attributes for "better views" are assumed to be visibility levels and the number of national parks, and the measurable attribute for reduced noise is assumed to be the ambient decibel level.

This step should not be trivialized. Selecting attributes can be controversial. For example, better views may include fewer billboards along highways or simply fewer highways. Visibility levels may compete with fewer mountain peaks with antennas and wind turbines at their summits. Wealth may include "spiritual" wealth and charitable contributions.

Characteristics of "Good" Attributes

Assuming that we can subdivide goals into a measurable set of associated attributes, we must next determine whether the attributes identified are appropriate to the decision analysis. If the ultimate goal is "the good life," does the list of attributes in Figure 10.1 truly capture all aspects of that goal? Are any of the attributes redundant? For example, savings levels generally rise with income levels. By including attributes for both income and savings, will we "double-count" because savings rates depend on income?

Keeney and Raiffa (1993) list five desirable characteristics for the chosen set of attributes. These characteristics are *completeness*, so that the set of attributes covers all of the important aspects of the decision problem; *operational ease*, so that the set of attributes can be used meaningfully; *decomposability*, meaning that the set of attributes can be broken down into smaller independent sets; *nonredundancy*, so that, taken together, attributes do not double-count impacts; and *simplicity*, meaning that the attribute set is as small as possible while still being complete.

For example, suppose that environmental policymakers must determine an appropriate level of research funding for renewable generation. The policymakers' ultimate goal is to maximize net social benefits (i.e., social benefits less social costs). Because social costs and benefits will include environmental costs and benefits, a desirable set of attributes should be good proxies for the presence of environmental costs and benefits, as well as more traditional market cost and benefit values.

Evaluating Trade-Offs

The crux of multiattribute decision analysis is the ability to visualize trade-offs between different attributes, much as indifference curves show different combinations of goods and services that are preferred equally by an individual. Once a set of attributes is identified, each separate decision (or action) alternative can be evaluated on each of the attributes. For example, suppose that energy policymakers wish to decide on funding levels for ten alternative renewable generation projects, including wind turbines. A total of $35 million has been appropriated by Congress for this research, but the total cost if all of the projects were funded would be $150 million. The policymakers must choose which projects to fund.[8]

Suppose that policymakers have decided to focus on four measurable attributes: total monetary cost (A_1), plant reliability (A_2), net emissions of greenhouse gases (A_3), and noise impacts (A_4). Let the ten alternative renewable generating plants be represented as X_1 ($A_{1,1}, \ldots, A_{1,4}$), $\ldots, X_{10}$ ($A_{10,1}, \ldots, A_{10,4}$). Associated with each plant are a set of values for the four attributes. Thus each plant can be thought of as representing a point in space, called *attribute space*. This is shown in Figure 10.2, where we have graphed alternatives X_1 and X_5 into the three-dimensional attribute space (A_1, A_2, A_3). For example, a hydroelectric plant may be less costly and more reliable other alternatives (i.e., low value for A_1 and high value for A_2) but may be quite noisy and cause emissions of methane when inundated vegetation decays (i.e., high values for both A_3 and A_4). The decision maker's problem is to determine the preferred choice among the alternative actions, based on how those actions map into attribute space. The first step in doing this is to construct the *efficient frontier*.

The Efficient Frontier   Once all of the resource alternatives have been mapped into attribute space, the process of selecting the "best" resources begins. To do this, alternatives that are *dominated* by others can be eliminated. For example, suppose that a particular biomass project would be more costly, less reliable, noisier, and produce more greenhouse gases than all of the other nine options. The policymakers can eliminate the biomass project from consideration because no matter which plants they decide to fund, the biomass project will always rank at the

---

[8]You may ask how Congress determined the $35 million budget limit in the first place. For this example, however, we must assume that environmental policymakers are operating in a second-best framework, taking the amount of funding as given.

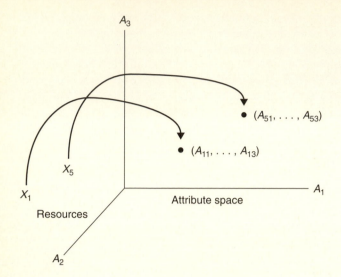

Figure 10.2   Mapping of Decision Alternatives into Attribute Space

Source: Adapted from Keeney and Raiffa (1993), p. 67.

bottom. The biomass plant is a dominated alternative. Formally, an alternative X_i is said to *dominate* alternative X_k if, for every attribute A_i, X_i is preferred to X_k. Figure 10.3 illustrates this condition for the case of two attributes.

In Figure 10.3(a), decision makers are assumed to prefer greater amounts of attributes A_1 and A_2. Since alternative X_k provides greater amounts of both of those attributes than X_i, X_k dominates X_i (written $X_i > X_k$). Alternative X_i can be eliminated from consideration.

In some cases, of course, policymakers will prefer *less* of certain attributes: they will want the lowest-cost resource portfolio, fewer emissions of pollutants, and so on. This can also be represented easily, as shown in Figure 10.3(b). Here again, all resource alternatives that lie within the shaded areas are dominated by portfolios lying outside the shaded areas.

By eliminating dominated alternatives, policymakers are left with a set of alternatives that require trade-offs to be made. These alternatives are not dominated by one another and are said to lie along the *efficient frontier* in attribute space. This is illustrated in Figure 10.4 on p. 250 for both increasing and decreasing attribute preferences. Paths EE and $E'E'$ in panels (a) and (b), respectively, trace efficient frontiers. Along either EE or $E'E'$, no alternative is dominated by any other alternative. One obvious benefit of this approach is that it allows decision makers to visualize the choices under consideration. The efficient frontier illustrates the trade-offs that exist between alternatives.

With more than three attributes, of course, the efficient frontier cannot be visualized. Yet the policymaker's problem remains the same: selecting the preferred alternative along the efficient frontier. One technique is to examine "slices" of the efficient frontier in two dimensions by holding the other attributes constant. (This is exactly the same sort of approach we showed in Figures 3.1 and 3.2 in

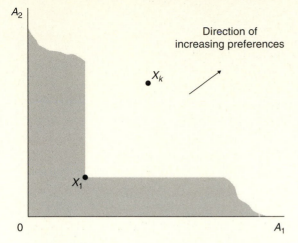

(a) Preferences for increasing attribute levels

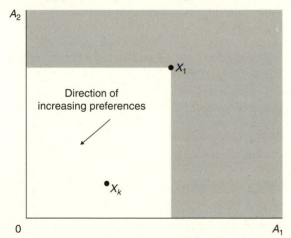

(b) Preferences for decreasing attribute levels

Figure 10.3   Dominance with Two Attributes

Source: Adapted from Keeney and Raiffa (1993), p. 70.

Chapter 3, where we took slices of a total utility function to derive different indifference curves.) Suppose that policymakers wish to examine the shape of the efficient frontier between greenhouse gas emissions and dollar costs, holding noise levels and reliability constant. This is shown in Figure 10.5(a).

In panel (a) of the figure, it is important to note that the shapes of the efficient frontier "slices" will be different depending on the direction we do the slicing. As a result, the resource alternatives lying along the different frontiers may change. Policymakers are assumed to prefer resources that are less costly and that have the least amount of greenhouse gas (GHG) emissions. Thus the preference directions

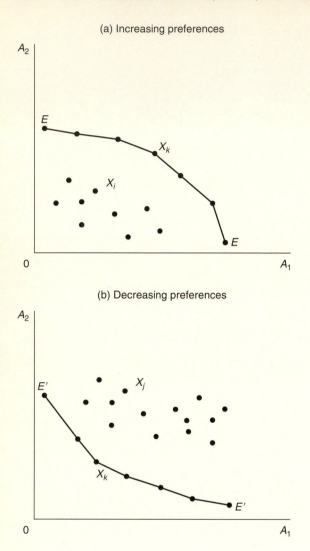

Figure 10.4 An Efficient Frontier with Two Attributes

are down and to the left. Because four of the five resources lie on the frontier, there is no uniquely dominant resource choice. For example, the hydroelectric resource is the least costly but results in the highest net GHG emissions (because of inundation of trees). The solar resource has the least GHG emissions but is the most expensive.

In panel (b) of Figure 10.5, we show a different slice along the dimensions of cost and reliability. The preference directions are up and to the left because in addition to their preference for low-cost resources, we assume also that they prefer the most reliable resources. In our example, the hydroelectric, wind, biomass, and solar resources lie on the efficient frontier of GHG emissions and cost. How-

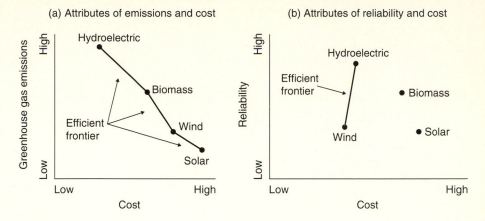

Figure 10.5   Alternative Two-Attribute Efficient Frontiers, Holding Other Attributes Constant

ever, the biomass and solar resources are dominated by the hydroelectric resource along the frontier of reliability and cost because they are *both* more costly and less reliable. Does this mean that we can eliminate biomass and solar entirely from the decision? Unfortunately, no. The reason is that although establishing dominance can simplify the decision making process, dominance must be established along *all* of the attribute dimensions before a resource can be eliminated entirely.

Shadow Prices   The slopes of the different segments of the efficient frontiers have a special meaning. They are called *shadow prices*.[9] Unlike market prices, which are observed, shadow prices are implicit prices. The shadow prices associated with a move from one point on the frontier to another reflect the relative trade-offs between attributes. For example, in Figure 10.5(a), suppose that the cost and GHG attribute levels of the biomass facility are $1,000 and 100 tons, respectively, while those of the wind facility are $1,500 and 20 tons. The shadow price of GHG emissions associated with moving between wind and biomass equals $- (\$1,500 - \$1,000)/(20 - 100) = \$6.25$ per ton.

There is no reason why shadow prices must be expressed in monetary terms. We could as easily determine shadow prices in terms of increased GHG emissions per unit of reliability. As we will discuss shortly, shadow prices can be useful when evaluating moves along an efficient frontier and the choices of policymakers. For example, if policymakers make a choice that implicitly requires the expenditure of

---

[9]Readers familiar with linear programming concepts will notice a slight difference between the definition of shadow prices in that context and the definition we use here. See, for example, Stokey and Zeckhauser (1978) for a very readable introduction.

$10,000 per ton of sulfur dioxide reduced (based on the shadow price along an efficient frontier), but those same reductions can be achieved using an existing tradable emissions system at a cost of only $200 per ton, policymakers may be weighing attributes incorrectly. This is the subject of the next section.

Weighing Different Attributes   At this point, we assume that policymakers have selected their various goals, have derived measurable attributes that satisfy Keeney and Raiffa's conditions for "good" attributes, and have created an efficient frontier of alternatives. In doing so, policymakers will ideally have reduced the number of alternatives under consideration. For example, perhaps the number of renewable resource projects has been reduced by half to just five. Unfortunately, the total cost of these five projects is over $60 million, still far more than the $35 million allocated for research. Thus policymakers must now weigh the competing attributes against one another until they have an acceptable list of projects that are within the overall budget.

The final selection of the preferred renewable projects will depend on how the four different attributes are weighed. This is where multiattribute analysis becomes more difficult and controversial, as there are innumerable ways to select weights. There may also be arguments against weighing certain attributes against others in any way, perhaps for some of the philosophical or the moral reasons we discussed earlier. Unfortunately, such arguments do little to address the fundamental scarcity of economic resources. What they do suggest is a particular weighting scheme in which one attribute receives infinite weight.[10]

One of the most straightforward ways of weighing different attributes is the use of linear weights. In our example, we have identified our four attributes as reliability, cost, GHG emissions, and noise. We define a set of weights ω_i, where $\sum \omega_i = 1$, and multiply each renewable resources attributes $(A_{k,1}, \ldots, A_{k,4})$ by the associated weights $(\omega_1, \ldots, \omega_4)$. Thus the overall "score" for each of the five remaining renewable resources will be $X_k(\omega_1 A_{k,1}, \ldots, \omega_4 A_{k,4})$ for $k = 1$ to 5. With these weights, the optimal choice is shown in Figure 10.6 to be resource alternative X_4, where the dashed line ($\omega_1 = 0.4$, $\omega_3 = 0.2$) is tangent to the efficient frontier. Once this resource is chosen, a new frontier can be drawn among the remaining four resources to determine the next most desirable resource, and so on, until the $35 million budget is exhausted.

Of course, if a different set of weights is chosen, the resources chosen may also differ. For example, by reducing the dollar cost weight ω_1 to 0.2 and increasing the GHG weight ω_3 to 0.4, tangency with the efficient frontier occurs for resource portfolio X_2.[11] The *sensitivity* of the choice of preferred alternative to different weights is also important to examine and will be discussed shortly. But before

---

[10]We consider an example of this dilemma later in this chapter.

[11]To be strictly precise, the reduction of the original four-attribute problem into the two attributes is relying on a condition called *preferential independence,* which is discussed in the next section. A complete discussion of preferential independence can be found in Keeney and Raiffa (1993).

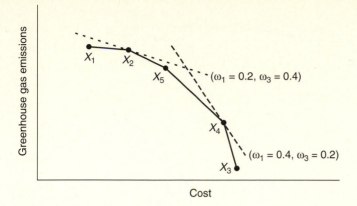

Figure 10.6   Optimal Choice with Alternative Linear Weights

doing so, we need to develop a method for comparing the different alternatives, especially when the efficient frontier cannot be visualized.

Transforming Attribute Values   One question that can arise is whether weighing attributes induces "apples and oranges" comparisons. In other words, how can we weigh costs in dollars, noise in decibels, and GHG emissions in tons if it makes no sense to add them up directly? Fortunately, there are techniques that allow weightings to be developed. One of the most straightforward of these techniques is to *normalize* the attribute values. To see this, consider the five remaining renewable resource portfolios with the measured attribute levels shown in Table 10.1. The normalization process begins with the selection of a *value function*, $V(A_1, \ldots, A_j)$, for each of the attributes A_j. The value function can be thought of as an ordering mechanism. Thus if alternative X_n is preferred to alternative X_k, it must be the case that $V(A_{n,1}, \ldots, A_{n,4}) > V(A_{k,1}, \ldots, A_{k,4})$. The actual numeric value doesn't matter as much as the ranking of the different alternatives.

TABLE 10.1   PERFORMANCE ATTRIBUTES FOR ALTERNATIVE GENERATING RESOURCE PORTFOLIOS

Resource	Type	Cost (millions of dollars)	Reliability Index (0–100)	GHG Emissions (10^3 tons)	Ambient Noise (decibels)
(1)	(2)	(3)	(4)	(5)	(6)
X_1	Hydro 1	9	76	76	70
X_2	Wind 1	16	42	8	80
X_3	Solar 1	18	53	5	60
X_4	Hydro 2	8	88	100	80
X_5	Biomass 1	17	66	45	100
	Minimum value:	8	42	5	60
	Maximum value:	18	88	100	100

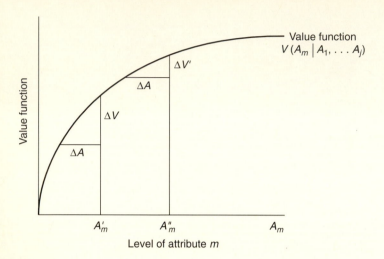

Figure 10.7   Value Function Exhibiting Diminishing Marginal Substitution

A "good" value function will incorporate some basic economic theory. One component of a value function may therefore be *diminishing marginal substitution*. If we prefer lower noise levels, the value we place on a 10-decibel drop from 110 to 100 will likely be valued more than a drop from 60 to 50 because that low a noise level is barely perceptible to humans. (This reflects the familiar diagram of a downward-sloping demand function or declining marginal benefit function associated with pollution reduction.) A value function exhibiting diminishing marginal substitution would look something like that shown in Figure 10.7. In this figure, the value of an alternative increases with the amount of attribute A_m associated with it. However, as the absolute level of attribute A_m increases, the increase in value ΔV for a given increase in the amount of attribute ΔA *decreases*. Thus in Figure 10.7, $\Delta V' < \Delta V$ because $A''_m > A'_m$.

Another useful assumption in defining value functions is known as *preferential independence*. This means that the preference ordering for one attribute is independent of the other attributes. For example, in Table 10.1, suppose that the hydro 2 plant (alternative X_4) is ultimately chosen over the wind project (alternative X_2). The ambient noise level of each is the same at 80 decibels. Preferential independence means that as long as the two resources have the same noise levels (though not necessarily 80 decibels), hydro 2 will always be preferred to wind 1.

If attributes are preferentially independent, the structure of the value function can be simplified. It turns out that preferential independence allows the value function to be written in an *additive* form.[12] In general, with m attributes, the value function V can be written as

$$V(A_1, \ldots, A_m) = \omega_1 V(A_1) + \omega_2 V(A_2) + \cdots + \omega_m V(A_m) \qquad (10.1)$$

---

[12] A proof can be found in Keeney and Raiffa (1993).

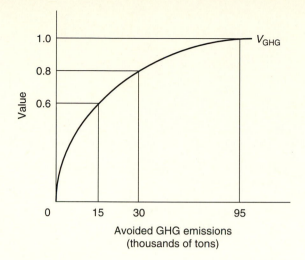

Figure 10.8   A Value Function for Avoided GHG Emissions

With this structure, we can define value functions for each of the attributes independently, then "add up" those values to determine the preferred resource alternative.

Empirically, the determination of such a value function would begin by arbitrarily setting endpoint values for the particular attribute of interest. In Table 10.1, for example, estimated GHG emissions range between 5,000 and 100,000 tons. Because policymakers prefer lower GHG emissions, we can restate the GHG goal as maximizing *avoided* GHG emissions. Because hydro 2 has the maximum GHG emissions (100,000 tons), by definition it *avoids* no GHG emissions. Thus we set $V_{GHG}(0) = 0.0$, as shown in Figure 10.8. Solar 1 has the fewest GHG emissions with 5,000 tons. It therefore avoids 95,000 tons when measured against hydro 2. Thus we can define $V_{GHG}(95) = 1.0$.

As Figure 10.8 shows, the initial avoided GHG emissions are valued most. In other words, avoiding the first 15 million tons is assigned a value of, say, 0.6, while avoiding twice as much CO_2 (30 million tons) is assigned a value of only, say, 0.8. This value function therefore exhibits *diminishing marginal substitution*. Diminishing marginal substitution may be appropriate for some attributes but inappropriate for others. Some may have thresholds, such as survival of an endangered species or meeting the salmon harvest stipulations of a treaty. Others may be continuous, such as reductions in GHGs. And some may be "yes or no," such as providing human rights. Thus incorporation of diminishing marginal substitution in value functions must be done in consideration of the attributes to be valued.

One good proxy function that displays diminishing marginal substitution is called a *flexible functional form*.[13] With this functional form, we can define a general value function V_m for each attribute A_m as:

---

[13]This is only one of many possible functional forms. See Keeney and Raiffa (1993) for a discussion of others.

$$V_m(A_m) = \left(\frac{A_{jm} - A_{jm}^{\min}}{A_{jm}^{\max} - A_{jm}^{\min}} \right)^{1/\lambda_m} \qquad \lambda_m \geq 1 \qquad (10.2)$$

The quantity $(A_{jm} - A_{jm}^{\min})/(A_{jm}^{\max} - A_{jm}^{\min})$ *normalizes* the attribute values by restricting them to between 0 and 1 for all values of the attribute A_m. Raising the entire quantity to the $1/\lambda_m$ power changes the *curvature* of the function. This is shown in Figure 10.9. With $\lambda_m = 1$, for example, the value function is a straight line, which does not exhibit diminishing marginal substitution. As λ_m increases, the value function becomes more convex.

The weights used by policymakers, as well as the value of λ_m, can affect the ultimate ranking of the different resource options. To see this, we can use the data in Table 10.1 to determine values for each of the five resource alternatives. Suppose that we first weigh each of the four attributes equally (25 percent each) and set $\lambda_m = 1$. Using Equation 10.2, we can derive the ranking of alternatives as shown in column 7 of Table 10.2. (As an exercise, you should try to derive the values shown in this table.)

The results show that hydro 1 is the highest-scoring renewable resource option, followed by Hydro 2 and Solar 1. The total cost for the three projects equals $35 million, exactly equal to the research budget allocation from Congress.

Suppose, however, that policymakers decide to place a much larger importance on reducing GHG emissions. Assume, therefore, that policymakers assign a weight of 75 percent to GHG emissions. They also decide that cost is the next most important attribute and assign it a weight of 15 percent. Reliability and noise are

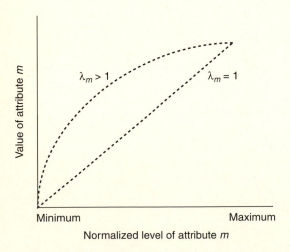

Figure 10.9 Effect of Diminishing Marginal Substitution on the Shape of the Value Function

TABLE 10.2   SCORES FOR ALTERNATIVE RENEWABLE RESOURCES (IDENTICAL ATTRIBUTE WEIGHTS)

Resource	Type	Cost (millions of dollars)	Reliability Index (0–100)	GHG Avoided Emissions (10^3 tons)	Ambient Noise (decibels)	Total Resource Score
(1)	(2)	(3)	(4)	(5)	(6)	(7)
Attribute weight:		25%	25%	25%	25%	
X_1	**Hydro 1**	9	76	24	70	**0.66**
X_2	Wind 1	16	42	92	80	0.42
X_3	**Solar 1**	18	53	95	60	**0.56**
X_4	**Hydro 2**	8	88	0	80	**0.63**
X_5	Biomass 1	17	66	55	100	0.30

Note: Chosen resources appear in **bold**.

each assigned a weight of 5 percent. The revised scores with these new weights are shown in Table 10.3. In this case, solar 1 and wind 1 are the two highest-ranking resources. Seeing that their combined cost equals $34 million, the policymakers can fund development of both resources but no others.

Choosing Weights   A difficult and often misunderstood aspect of multiattribute analysis is how to determine the attribute weights. How are policymakers to know that they have selected the "correct" set of weights for all of the attributes? The reason this is a problem is that multiattribute analysis does not make decisions on its own. Merely presenting attributes and efficiency frontiers does not tell environmental policymakers the "correct" weighting for the different attributes. Thus the

TABLE 10.3   SCORES FOR ALTERNATIVE RENEWABLE RESOURCES WITH GHG WEIGHT EMPHASIZED

Resource	Type	Cost (millions of dollars)	Reliability Index (0–100)	GHG Avoided Emissions (10^3 tons)	Ambient Noise (decibels)	Total Resource Score
(1)	(2)	(3)	(4)	(5)	(6)	(7)
Attribute Weight:		15%	5%	75%	5%	
X_1	Hydro 1	10	76	24	70	0.40
X_2	**Wind 1**	16	42	92	80	**0.78**
X_3	**Solar 1**	18	53	95	60	**0.81**
X_4	Hydro 2	8	88	0	80	0.23
X_5	Biomass 1	17	66	55	100	0.48

Note: Chosen resources appear in **bold**.

approach can be (and sometimes is) criticized for reaching "arbitrary" solutions. This criticism is certainly true in one sense. If all relevant attributes could always be priced directly using willingness-to-pay or willingness-to-accept measures, including equity and rights attributes, there would be no need for policymakers to make difficult decisions. Instead, a computer could spit out a number quickly with the correct choices identified. The real world, unfortunately, is not so simple.

Keeney and Raiffa (1993) address this issue by identifying numerous procedures for determining attribute weights. Some of these procedures are easy; others are difficult. Most of the procedures involve detailed questioning of policymakers to gauge their preferences and trade-offs. Even these procedures, however, can be considered "arbitrary," especially if different decision makers assign different importance to attributes. In such cases, one might imagine assigning a group of individuals to weigh the weights chosen by the different decision makers. Of course, this process could be extended *ad infinitum*, with the result being that no decisions are ever made.

Following our discussion in Chapter 5, however, we assume that all policymakers have as their ultimate goal making "good" decisions and selecting appropriate policy instruments. One approach in addressing the choice of attribute weights, therefore, is to investigate the *sensitivity* of preferred alternatives to different sets of weights. For example, underlying the choice of Hydro 1 over Wind 1 is a shadow price for reduced GHG emissions. Tables 10.2 and 10.3 showed that Solar 1 would be chosen whether GHG emissions were weighed heavily or equally with the other attributes. Therefore, if disagreements over attribute weights focus on the importance of GHG emissions, funding of Solar 1 is unlikely to be an issue. By contrast, selection of Hydro 1 and Hydro 2 *are* sensitive to the weight given to GHG emissions. If the GHG weight is 25 percent, they are selected; if it is 75 percent, they are not.

If the choice of preferred alternatives is found to be sensitive to the choice of attribute weights, policymakers may wish to reassess the available options. They may decide that other attribute weights are more important, or they may determine that other attributes are needed. In choosing a set of renewable resources to fund, for example, some of the different alternatives (e.g., Hydro 1 and Hydro 2) may be functionally equivalent, and it may make little difference from the standpoint of meeting the desired objectives which alternative is selected. More likely, *disagreements about the correct set of weights will probably stem from a failure to identify and agree on overall goals.* Such disagreements will often hinge on the basic moral and ethical values held by policymakers and others, making resolution difficult.

This is one area where shadow prices can be useful. Suppose that one policymaker prefers Wind 1 to Hydro 1, consistent with the weights assumed in Table 10.3. Hydro 1 dominates Wind 1 in terms of reliability and noise. Wind 1 is preferred, therefore, solely because of its lower relative GHG emissions. The cost difference between the projects is $6 million, and the GHG emissions difference is 68,000 tons. This implies a shadow price for reduced GHG emissions of about $88 per ton. Is that price "reasonable"? The answer depends on whether there is information about "real" costs of reducing GHG emissions. Suppose there exists a market for GHG emissions and known GHG-reducing technologies that lead to a market-clearing price of $20 per ton. Then the $88-per-ton shadow price indicates an excessive weight on GHG emissions that should be reduced. By determining that the shadow price associated with a particular choice is inappropriate, policymakers will in essence be adjusting the slope of the tangent line shown in Figure 10.6 to determine a different solution. In that case, the four alternatives can be reevaluated.[14] This approach will not solve all disputes over attribute weights, but it can solve some of them.

Conclusions

Space precludes us from providing a complete review of all multiattribute methods. However, we believe that the technique can be useful in environmental policy applications because many environmental policy decisions involve trade-offs between disparate attributes and objectives. A major drawback of multiattribute techniques is that they can become complex and time-consuming, which may not meet the expectations of some constituent groups who, as we discussed in Chapter 5, want solutions now.

Although we have intentionally avoided any preconceived definitions of "good" outcomes, some interest groups may object to the fact that a multiattribute approach requires that the values used to define policy goals be made explicit. Such clarification of values can make it more difficult for some interest groups to achieve predetermined ends. Even if these are environmental ends, we believe that an explicit consideration of values is to be desired in the long run because, as Oelshlaeger (1991) remarks, "What the members of a democratic society think ultimately makes a difference" (p. ix).

THE REALITIES OF POLITICS AND BUREAUCRACY

The realities of politics and bureaucracy may not always affect the choice of goals for environmental policies but will almost surely affect the weighing of different goals. Environmental and other regulators, entrusted to bring their expertise to bear on complex environmental issues, may also wish to pursue their own more limited agendas. These may reflect genuine concerns over environmental issues; they may also reflect a desire merely to stay in positions of power.

Recall that President Clinton's ill-fated Btu tax, which we discussed in Chapter 2, had three purposes: to raise money so as to reduce the federal deficit, to reduce energy consumption, and to reduce emissions of carbon dioxide produced from the combustion of fossil fuels. It never passed out of Congress, even though almost everyone agreed that the tax would have accomplished the three goals set out. Instead, the disagreements centered on who would bear the burden of the tax.

---

[14]For an application of multiattribute decision analysis to electric utility decisions, see Connors (1992). Lesser and Zerbe (1995) discuss the use of multiattribute analysis in the context of sustainability.

OUT OF SITE?

You probably know the location of several electric-generating stations near where you live. The locations of nuclear power plants, such as Three Mile Island in Pennsylvania or Chernoybl in Ukraine, are probably the best known. But how are decisions to site such facilities made? Ultimately, who is responsible for such siting decisions, and why are those decisions so often controversial?

Energy facility siting can be regulated by both environmental and energy agencies. Environmental agencies may participate in resource choice and siting decisions directly through a formal process, as in siting a power plant or permitting an oil or gas well, or through prohibitions of development at various sites such as parks, critical wildlife habitats, or already polluted areas. Environmental agencies will also affect resource choice and siting indirectly through the regulations they impose on the operation of facilities after they are built. It may be prohibitively expensive or even impossible for some candidate facilities to comply with environmental regulations. Energy regulators may make, or at least approve, the final choice. However, in doing so, they must take the environmental regulations of other agencies as given.

One problem that arises in siting energy facilities is that the goals of these different regulating agencies often diverge. Balancing policy goals between different and often competing regulatory agencies is more difficult than balancing different policy goals that fall under the purview of just one regulator or set of regulations. A fish and wildlife agency that primarily serves the interests of hunters and conservationists may strenuously object to the development of a hydroelectric facility on a popular recreational river. An air pollution agency, by contrast, may favor the hydroelectric facility over higher-polluting coal-fired plants, whose pollution could drift downwind to expose the mostly minority inhabitants of a poor county. An energy-siting agency may prefer the hydroelectric plant to avoid the need to build new and expensive transmission facilities through a national park. The public utility commission may wish to see the coal plant developed because it will mean more affordable electricity for low-income consumers. Balancing all of these environmental and social goals clearly presents difficulties. This is one reason why the development of facilities can be an excruciatingly difficult and costly process.

A particularly glaring siting example in the United States was the construction of the Shoreham nuclear plant by the Long Island Lighting Company (LILCO). Although billions of dollars were spent to construct the plant, it never generated any electricity for commercial purposes, owing to the fervent opposition of many local residents and the governor of New York over the lack of an adequate evacuation plan in case an emergency were to occur at the plant. The squabbling between different interest groups and regulatory agencies was intense. Ultimately, the plant was sold to the state of New York for $1. But because it had generated some electricity in low-level operating tests, the eventual decommissioning of the plant will be far more expensive (because the inside is now radioactive) than if the plant had never been tested or completed. LILCO and its stockholders lost billions of dollars, putting the company on the verge of bankruptcy. No doubt, the ill-fated plant will be on the minds of electricity consumers and taxpayers for years to come.

Every interest group raised numerous objections to its having to bear any burden, whether as a matter of "fairness," lost jobs, or regional disparities such as longer driving distances in western states.

Environmental Regulations and Balancing Policy Goals

As we discussed in Chapter 9, the balancing of policy goals is evident in much environmental legislation and regulation, although not always intentionally so. In that chapter, we discussed a variety of environmental laws, including the Clean Air Act, the Endangered Species Act, and the so-called Superfund Law. For example, we saw that the Clean Air Act incorporates not only aspects of economic efficiency but also human rights to the environment. Even the Endangered Species Act, which purportedly protects species regardless of cost, has an out in the form of a "God squad" that can determine whether the cost of species protection exacts too high a cost on humans.

That environmental legislation balances policy goals should not be surprising. Governments, for good or ill, are often large bureaucracies serving the needs of diverse constituencies. A more important issue is whether environmental legislation and regulation balances different goals consistently. Here the evidence is not compelling.

One of the first difficulties is the often complex web of regulations and regulators. In the United States, environmental and energy regulations are divided among many agencies. Primary responsibility for environmental regulation at the federal level rests with the Environmental Protection Agency. At the state level, it rests with state environmental agencies and with local or regional air and water quality districts. Many other agencies regulate environmental impacts or make decisions with environmental consequences. This often occurs in the granting of permits and licenses, such as the Federal Energy Regulatory Commission's granting hydroelectric licenses, or by local governments. For example, development and use of energy resources that affect local, national, and global environmental quality have often been regulated at the state level by one or more agencies, including utility commissions and specific siting agencies. At the national level, energy development and use have been regulated by the Federal Energy Regulatory Commission and influenced by legislation such as the Clean Air Act, the Fuel Use Act, and the Public Utilities Regulatory Policies Act, to name but three. And still other regulators can affect environmental quality. For example, the U.S. Fish and Wildlife Service is charged with developing a recovery plan for Pacific Northwest salmon species listed under the Endangered Species Act, even though the Northwest Power Planning Council has also been required to develop a recovery plan.

CHAPTER SUMMARY

If you are interested in the ultimate determinations of environmental policies, this chapter is probably one of the most important in this book. We make that assertion not because we believe we have a monopoly on the selection of appropriate policies but because we are convinced that Oelshlaeger's point is well taken. In democratic societies, individuals who hold different values can and should express those values. At some point, to take positive actions, the opinions of these many individuals are aggregated into policy directions. We leave it to you to decide for yourself how effective such aggregations of opinion are. And we remind you that the realities of politics and bureaucracy will also influence environmental policy goals, as will the cost of enforcing different goals. As human beings place greater demands on the environment, policymakers likely will face more difficult choices. To the extent that the reasons behind the choices made can be clarified, society will be better off. So, too, should the environment.

CHAPTER REVIEW

Economic Concepts and Tools

- Multiobjective or multiattribute decision analysis is a method for making the trade-offs between policy goals explicit.
- There are six distinct steps in a multiattribute analysis:
  1. Select and define the policy goals.
  2. Select attributes to measure those goals.
  3. Construct an efficient frontier of options, rejecting options that are dominated (rank lower in all attributes than other options).
  4. Construct a value function.
  5. Calculate the value function for options along the efficient frontier, and choose the option with the highest value.
  6. Use sensitivity tests, if necessary, to address concerns about the importance of the attribute weights selected.
- A good set of attributes will be complete, easily generalized, decomposable into independent subsets, not redundant, and simple, meaning that the smallest possible set of attributes is used.
- The weight given to any given attribute or overall set of attributes will depend on its range of values over all of the policy alternatives under consideration. All other things being equal, larger weights will be associated with greater ranges.

Policy Issues

- Environmental and other policymakers will often have to weigh competing goals for at least two reasons. First, resources are finite; only so much is available with which to improve environmental quality. Second, correction of some environmental problems may exacerbate other problems.
- Some policy goals may be qualitative; they may be satisfied or not. Some policy goals may be quantitative; they may be satisfied in varying degrees and be numerically measurable.
- Political and bureaucratic realities often impede the introduction of "good" environmental policies. Policy goals, however noble, will often be dismissed as politically infeasible.

- Much environmental legislation, implicitly or explicitly, has balanced competing goals. Whether the legislation has done so in an efficient manner is a different issue, although the evidence is not encouraging.
- Disagreements about the correct set of weights to use in a multiattribute analysis will likely stem from a failure to clarify or agree on overall objectives.

DISCUSSION QUESTIONS

1. Ideally, developments whose costs exceed their benefits will not be undertaken. Why, then, do many developments, such as large irrigation projects, go forward when this criterion is not satisfied?
2. The government has determined that only $10 billion is available for restoration of salmon spawning grounds in the Columbia River system and preservation of old-growth forests in the Pacific Northwest. To do both successfully will cost a total of $15 billion. Of 1,000 individuals surveyed, over 70 percent preferred that the government focus on salmon restoration. As a result, the government announces that it will proceed with the spawning ground restoration. Immediately, advocates of old-growth forest protection object, saying that the $10 billion budget constraint is "artificial." How might you answer the old-growth advocates' objection?
3. In a major public policy speech, a representative of an influential environmental rights group states that "improving economic efficiency should never be an important goal because it will lead to a sort of 'Gresham's law' for environmental quality: environmentally 'bad' projects will always drive out environmentally 'good' ones." In the question-and-answer period that follows this speech, how might you respond?
4. What methods would you suggest for determining attribute weights in a multiattribute analysis? Surveys? Referenda? Other? Examine the problems with a multiattribute approach and suggest possible solutions.
5. A nuclear waste dump can either be sited in a sparsely populated county, which is primarily inhabited by poor minorities, or be located near a large tourist destination. In a referendum, 55 percent of the voters in the county said that they would like the dump sited in the county because it would provide them with high-paying jobs. However, a subsequent demographic survey has found that the 45 percent of the voters opposed to the project live in households with over 75 percent of the area's children. Furthermore, the cost of building the waste dump will be higher in the sparsely populated area, owing to a more complex geology. How could you set up a multiattribute analysis for choosing a site? What would your siting decision be?
6. Can you think of some other value functions besides the one in Equation 10.2 that would be useful for a multiattribute analysis?
7. In the motion picture *Star Trek II: The Wrath of Khan*, Mr. Spock sacrifices himself to save the U.S.S. *Enterprise*. As he lays dying, he tells a grieving Captain Kirk, "The good of the many outweighs the good of the few." What does Spock's statement imply, if anything, about attribute weights for the

welfare of the current generation in comparison with the welfare of future generations? Do you think his statement is a reasonable principle for policy development?

REFERENCES

Connors, S. 1992. *Externality Valuation Versus Systemwide Analysis: Identifying Cost and Emissions Reduction Strategies for Electric Service.* Report No. EL92-001WP. Cambridge, Mass.: Energy Laboratory, Massachusetts Institute of Technology.

Keeney, R., and H. Raiffa. 1993. *Decisions with Multiple Objectives.* New York: Cambridge University Press.

Kelman, S. 1981. "Cost-Benefit Analysis: An Ethical Critique." *Regulation* 4(1): 33–40.

Kleindorfer, P., H. Kunruether, and P. Schoemaker. 1993. *Decision Sciences: An Integrative Perspective.* New York: Cambridge University Press.

Lesser, J., and R. Zerbe. 1995. "What Can Economic Analysis Contribute to the Sustainability Debate?" *Contemporary Economic Policy* 13(3): 88–100.

Manheim, M., and F. Hall. 1976. "Abstract Representation of Goals: A Method for Making Decisions in Complex Problems." In *Transportation—A Service: Proceedings of the Sesquicentennial Forum.* New York: New York Academy of Sciences and American Society of Mechanical Engineers.

Oelshlaeger, M. 1991. *The Idea of Wilderness: From Prehistory to the Age of Ecology.* New Haven, Conn.: Yale University Press.

Rawls, J. 1971. *A Theory of Justice.* Cambridge, Mass.: Harvard University Press.

PART III

ENVIRONMENTAL VALUES: MEASUREMENT AND APPLICATION

In Chapter 7, we developed policies to address economic efficiency goals. At the beginning of that chapter, we noted that one critical component—determining whether the environmental "problem" in question was worth correcting—would require that we measure the benefits and the costs of alternative policies. Even policies that are driven primarily by equity or rights considerations, such as preservation of endangered species, cannot be effective if society is unable to determine whether there is an actual environmental problem (is the species truly endangered, or have we just miscounted?) and if so, once a policy is adopted, whether the problem will have been corrected effectively.

Determining whether an environmental problem is worth correcting can depend on the cost of measuring its magnitude. If it takes a $100 million study to show that the benefits of correcting a particular environmental externality are $1 million, society will be worse off. This is one reason why some policymakers and regulators like "proxy" measures of environmental benefits and costs, such as the *costs* of pollution control measures. Without techniques to measure environmental costs and benefits, however, there is little value in discussing, much less implementing, environmental policies. It makes little sense to discuss optimal emissions fees, for example, if society is unable to measure marginal benefit or cost curves. If society cannot determine the distribution of benefits or costs, how can it determine whether policies are fair? If society does not even know what environmental impacts are occurring, how can it be determined whether human rights or the rights of nature are being violated?

Finally, environmental costs and benefits can rarely be measured with certainty. People have different tastes and preferences for the food they eat, the automobiles they drive, and the clothes they wear. They also have different environmental preferences. Like the pollster who takes the nation's political "pulse" and reports a margin of error, the researcher who estimates society's willingness to pay for environmental improvements arrives at just that—an estimate—and will almost certainly trade off precision against cost. Environmental impacts will also be uncertain. No one can say what will be the precise effects of additional carbon dioxide in the atmosphere, nor will all of us be equally sensitive to the effects of different pollutants. Thus policymakers will have to deal with uncertainty.

In Part III, we address all of these issues. You may find some of this material difficult and technical. Yet in terms of the actual development and implementation of environmental policies, this portion of the book is crucial. Without an ability to measure the costs and the benefits of alternative policies or even simply the impacts of alternatives, it will be impossible to know whether any given policy makes sense. Without an ability to deal with the many uncertainties that prevail, policymakers will be unable to address the most critical environmental issues.

In Chapter 11, we examine the techniques used to measure environmental benefits and costs in monetary terms. These techniques vary in their ease of application and cost. Some are applicable only in certain situations because of the types of data they require and their underlying assumptions. Some have been applied widely, and the techniques for applying them are therefore well developed. Others are more experimental and more controversial. We discuss and present examples of direct valuation techniques that include *hedonic pricing models,* which determine values for characteristics of goods and services; *contingent valuation studies,* which are survey instruments; *travel cost models,* which gauge the value of nonmarket goods and services, particularly the value of recreation, by analyzing the characteristics of the individuals who travel to consume these goods and services; and the use of *market costs and prices* to value environmental costs. We also examine nonmonetary valuation techniques, which are sometimes used to form the basis for direct estimates or serve as proxies where direct estimates are not possible. Though some of the applications presented are complex, they illustrate both the power and the difficulty of accurately assessing environmental benefits and costs.

In Chapter 12, we examine how some of these techniques have been applied to a particularly important aspect of environmental costs: the value of life and health. We consider first some philosophical issues associated with valuing life, including whether it is reasonable to estimate and use such values. We argue that in many instances measuring the values people place on life and health is appropriate and that as long as we are clear about what values have been measured, the value of life and health can be important to the development of sound environmental policy. We present the results of several empirical studies that employed the techniques presented in Chapter 11. Last, we discuss some of the equity and rights considerations that environmental policymakers must address when dealing with risks to life and health.

In Chapter 13, we tackle the *intertemporal* nature of the benefits and the costs of many environmental impacts. Pesticides applied to crops today, for example, may lead to an increased incidence of cancers 20 years from now. If global climate change occurs as a result of increased emissions of carbon dioxide, predicted impacts may not occur until hundreds of years into the future. We review the concept of *discounting* and address the choice of appropriate discount rates for environmental policy analysis. We stress the distinction between intertemporal efficiency and equity issues and the different role of discounting in addressing these two types of issues.

In Chapter 14, we discuss the problem of developing environmental policies in the face of uncertainty and risk. To do that, first we define uncertainty and risk. Next we discuss several valuation concepts used in the context of uncertainty, such as option price, and their relationship to willingness-to-pay measures. We ask whether policymakers should approach environmental issues in a risk-averse manner. To answer that question, we discuss the concept of irreversibility and the consequences of environmental irreversibility. We conclude Chapter 14 with a brief review of several decision methodologies useful in evaluating alternative policies when there is uncertainty, including risk-adjusted discount rates, environmental "portfolios," and the multiattribute approach we discussed in Chapter 10.

CHAPTER 11

MEASURING ENVIRONMENTAL COSTS AND BENEFITS

View from the Top: Air Pollution and Changing Vistas at the Grand Canyon

In the Four Corners region of the southwestern United States, where Utah, Colorado, Arizona, and New Mexico meet, several large coal-fired power plants were built. The Four Corners Generating Station began service in 1969. Farther to the west, just south of Lake Powell, the Navajo Station began service in 1974. The air pollution from these plants has contributed to reduced visibility at the Grand Canyon during certain times of the year, although the precise amount of reduction and the primary causes of that reduction are still disputed. At times, for example, pollution from the Los Angeles basin will drift eastward and obscure views.

The owners of the Four Corners power plants have disputed those plants' contribution to visibility reductions. One reason is the requirements for reducing pollutant emissions under the Clean Air Act amendments. Under the act, national parks like the Grand Canyon are classified as Class I airsheds. In these airsheds, the most stringent environmental restrictions apply. Under the act, a set of rules were developed, called the "prevention of significant deterioration" (PSD) requirements, in which aesthetics and atmospheric visibility play a major role in determining air pollution control requirements. Thus if the plants at Four Corners were determined to be the cause of reduced air quality at the Grand Canyon, the emissions controls required for the plants would be more stringent and more expensive. From the standpoint of economic efficiency, it would be nice to know whether the lost economic value from the deterioration in views was greater than the cost of the control measures proposed. To answer such a question, however, requires a way of measuring the value of the view itself.

Unfortunately, one cannot go to the store and buy a view the way one buys a box of cornflakes. Thus the question arose, especially in light of the PSD regulations, as to what a pristine view of the Grand Canyon was worth. Another policy issue that arises is the value to whom? Does a view of a "pristine" Grand Canyon have value only to those who actually visit the park, or does it also hold some value for individuals who may never intend to visit but value knowing that the view is there now and into the future? And do those individuals who have no intent of ever visiting have standing? Should those individuals' values be included in determining required controls at the power plants?

Arriving at answers to these questions involves several critical steps. First, a view must be defined. Generally, when atmospheric visibility is discussed, three definitions are used: (1) visual range (the actual range of visibility for an observer looking at an object), (2) prevailing visibility (which extends the concept of visual range across the horizon—the concept used by air traffic controllers when reporting visibility), and (3) meteorological range (a theoretical concept that is slightly broader than the first two definitions).[1] Although the differences in these definitions may seem slight, the implications can mean significant differences in expenditures for pollution control equipment.

Once the view to be valued has been defined, the next issue to tackle is how to value it. Economists have developed several methods to determine the values of environmental attributes like majestic views, which we discuss and explain in this chapter. None of these methods is perfect. In determining the value of views at the Grand Canyon, most studies have used surveys—essentially, fancy methods of asking individuals what they might pay for a slightly better view or what they might accept in compensation for a slightly poorer view. Other studies have looked at the costs incurred by tourists traveling to the Grand Canyon and used those costs to determine the value of the Grand Canyon recreation "experience," much of which may consist of taking in the view.

The last issue, determining whose values "count" when calculating the overall value of improved views at the Grand Canyon, may be the most difficult of all, representing as it does a philosophical and legal issue for society rather than a strictly economic one. One argument for counting the values of those who do not intend ever to visit the Grand Canyon is that it is a national park preserved for the enjoyment of all citizens. Another argument in favor of counting so-called passive-use values is that all taxpayers pay for upkeep at the park and therefore should be included in overall valuations of views. An argument against counting these nonusers' values is straightforward: if the external damage is the reduction in the view, then since they have no intent of ever "consuming" that view, no external damage will have been caused them. Thus their willingness to pay, if any, to preserve or enhance the view at the Grand Canyon is irrelevant when determining emissions requirements. Ultimately, however, which of these arguments is "best" depends on your point of view.

---

[1]For a detailed description of these definitions, see Horvath and Charlson (1969).

INTRODUCTION

How do we measure environmental benefits and costs? After all, we can't go to the supermarket and buy clean air or protection for endangered species. Nor does the government advertise "blue-light specials" for buying wilderness areas. When environmental policymakers wish to measure nonmarket environmental values, they first have to define those values. As with defining a view across the Grand Canyon, improvements or reductions in environmental quality can be amorphous. Thus unlike well-defined markets for goods and services, where prices are revealed openly, measuring environmental costs and benefits requires more effort. Somehow we must get individuals and markets to reveal environmental values to us. That is the focus of this chapter.

There are two major types of environmental valuation techniques: *monetary* and *nonmonetary* or *physical*. The values that monetary techniques measure can be broken down further into two categories: *use* and *nonuse* (sometimes called *passive-use*) values. As their name implies, direct valuation techniques are those that directly determine the monetary values individuals place on receiving environmental amenities or avoiding environmental costs. For each of the monetary valuation techniques we discuss, we examine their ability to measure use and nonuse values, present empirical examples of past studies using the technique, and review the strengths and weaknesses of each.

Nonmonetary or physical valuation techniques (sometimes called *indirect* valuation techniques) measure physical environmental impacts themselves (e.g., tons of pollution emitted and the effects of such emissions on health), without directly placing a monetary value on those impacts. With these sorts of measurements, *dose-response* models are often applied to identify the effects of pollution on health, vegetation, or materials such as statues and buildings. These physical impacts are then multiplied by values per unit of impact, usually derived from previous applications of direct monetary methods. Nonmonetary methods are most useful when individuals are unaware of the environmental effect in question. For example, if individuals are unaware that acid rain damages buildings, asking them what they would be willing to pay to reduce acid rain damage to buildings would probably not yield useful results.

TYPES OF ENVIRONMENTAL VALUES

Use and nonuse values can be subdivided further, as shown in Table 11.1.[2] As the term implies, use values are values that individuals place on environmental goods and services they actually consume. An individual who enjoys fishing has a direct

---

[2]None of these should be confused with value *systems*. In our context, we refer to environmental values as relating to something that can be measured, albeit imperfectly and perhaps controversially, rather than a particular philosophy or system of beliefs and laws. Of course, the latter often will determine measured values. If we cared not one whiff for whales, for example, it is doubtful that we would place such a high value on their preservation. If our religious beliefs were such that we expected the world to end tomorrow, it is doubtful that we would care about the risk of future global climate change.

TABLE 11.1   ENVIRONMENTAL VALUES

Use Values	Nonuse Values	
	Existence Value	Option Value
"Visited Grand Canyon last summer, but the view was terrible because of the pollution."	"Never intend to visit the Grand Canyon, but glad the views there are majestic."	"May visit the Grand Canyon next summer. Want a guarantee that the view will be great."
	"I want my children and grandchildren to be able to see the Grand Canyon in all its majesty." (bequest motive)	
	"I want my neighbors to be able to enjoy the majesty of the Grand Canyon today." (gift motive)	
	"I feel better knowing that I am helping preserve the Grand Canyon and the plants and animal species that live there." (sympathy motive)	

use value associated with his ability to fish in an unpolluted lake. A hiker has a direct use value for the unspoiled wilderness areas she frequents. A visitor to the Grand Canyon has a direct use value for the majestic views or the rapids in the Colorado River far below. Use values are perhaps the easiest environmental values to measure because we can readily identify them with a specific set of individuals. As we discuss in later sections, we still have to exercise care in measurement. Individuals may have a use value for an environmental amenity even though they do not consume it because the cost of consumption exceeds the value they assign to consumption.

Within the class of nonuse values, we can distinguish between *option* and *existence* values. People may value the existence of an environmental good or service because they *may* use it in the future, even though they do not use it currently. An individual who may be contemplating a trip to the Grand Canyon would assign a value to the Grand Canyon, in the sense that he would wish the scenic beauty to be preserved for his future visit, should it come to pass. This type of value is sometimes called an *option value* (Weisbrod 1964), although it has come to be called the *option price* in the literature today. Because option value and option price are direct consequences of future uncertainty, however, we will postpone our discussion of them until Chapter 14, when we take up the subject of uncertainty and its importance to estimating environmental values.

Of course, individuals who neither fish nor hike may also value the existence of unpolluted lakes, pristine wilderness areas, and animal and plant species. Similarly, even if I have no intention of visiting the Grand Canyon, I may prefer it to exist as is, rather than being turned into a strip mine. In some cases, the total value placed on an environmental amenity by many nonusers may be much larger than the total use value. Thus it is important to address techniques that can measure these nonuse values.

Essentially, an *existence value* is a value placed on an environmental good or service that is unrelated to consumption of that good or service. Even though I may never have seen a live whale and have no intention of ever seeing one, I may value the existence of whales for a variety of reasons.[3] Economists often break down these reasons for caring about the existence of species or places into three broad categories: *bequest motives, gift motives,* and *sympathy motives.* Each motive can be thought of as a form of altruism to the future.

Bequest motives refer to individuals' wishing to provide their descendants with a supply of environmental resources. Their descendants may use the resources, and a bequesting individual values the resources because of that. This potential future use value may be the basis of currently living people's bequest motives, but it is not the same thing.[4] I cannot know whether my great-great-grandchildren living 100 years from now will visit the Grand Canyon. I cannot even be certain that I will have great-great-grandchildren. However, I can still value the opportunity that my future great-great-grandchildren will have to visit the Grand Canyon should they want to.

Gift motives are similar to bequest motives. The difference is that the gift is usually to members of the current generation instead of to members of a future generation. Although I may never climb Denali Peak (Mount McKinley) and look down on the Brooks Range, I may value the fact that others do. Again, my nonuse value is based on someone else's use but is not the same thing as that person's use value. There is no connection necessarily between the value someone places on an experience and the value someone else places on that person's being able to have the experience.

Sympathy motives perhaps reflect existence values most closely. Individuals may value environmental resources because of the respect or "sympathy" they have for the humans, the plants, and the animals that occupy rain forests, wilderness areas, and oceans.[5] Sympathy motives are not based on use values, or at least not on use values associated with consumption of environmental amenities by an outsider. For example, bequest and gift motives for preservation of an underdeveloped area could be based on a desire for current and future tourists from outside to be able to visit and appreciate its beauty. Sympathy motives lead to a desire to preserve the area, even if that means excluding current and future uses. Sympathy

---

[3]Krutilla (1967) refers to individuals who gain pleasure from indirect exposure to environments or species (through television, books, etc.) as having a *vicarious use value.* To define *existence value,* Krutilla uses the example of individuals placing a value on the preservation of wilderness areas, even though they would be terrified by the prospect of actually visiting one.

[4]For a somewhat different view, see Pearce and Turner (1990), chap. 9. See also Randall and Stoll (1983).

[5]Although the literature refers to "sympathy" values, the meaning is not in the narrow sense of "feeling sorry for" plants, animals, and so on.

for plants, animals, and humans can imply that society is willing to grant those species some degree of rights. Thus sympathy values can express a willingness to pay to preserve the rights of nature.

MONETARY VALUATION TECHNIQUES

There are four major categories of direct valuation techniques. These are (1) the use of market prices to value economic costs and benefits arising from changes in environmental quality; (2) the hedonic pricing approach, which decomposes market prices into components encompassing environmental and other characteristics; (3) the contingent valuation approach, which is a nonmarket technique using surveys to ask people to reveal the values they place on environmental amenities; and (4) the travel cost approach, which is a market-based technique that uses travel costs as a surrogate for the price of unpriced recreational amenities. Each of these approaches has its advantages and disadvantages, both from a theoretical standpoint and from the standpoint of empirical applicability.

Using Market Prices

The first, and easiest, valuation technique is to estimate environmental costs and benefits from market prices. Obviously, this method works only for environmental goods that *have* market prices. We cannot measure the value of a lost view simply by traveling to the local shopping mall and inquiring the price of views today because no one explicitly sells views. By contrast, it may be possible to place values on the damage caused by pollution on such goods as crops because we can easily determine their market prices.

A standard result in microeconomics is that if a good sells in competitive markets and there are no externalities or underemployed resources, the market price will equal *both* the marginal buyers' willingness to pay and the opportunity cost of supplying that good. For example, suppose that pollution reduces wheat yields by exactly 1 bushel when the same supply of land, labor, equipment, fertilizer, water, and other inputs is used and that total production of wheat is measured in millions of tons. Thus the loss of 1 bushel of wheat can be considered a very small (marginal) change in supply, and the value of the lost production will just equal the market price of that one bushel of wheat.

Often, however, the situation is more complicated. First, not all resources may be fully employed. There may be unemployed laborers, whose opportunity cost of labor is below prevailing wage rates. Plant and equipment may be idle, rather than being used in production. In such cases, the market price will be greater than the opportunity cost, and using the market price will overestimate pollution damages. Markets themselves may also not be fully competitive. A monopolist producer of wheat would produce less than a competitive industry and charge a price greater than the opportunity cost.[6] Therefore, using the monopolist's market price to value

---

[6]This result is demonstrated in all standard microeconomics textbooks.

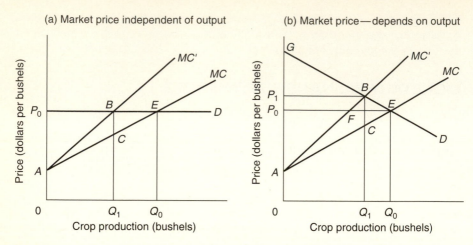

Figure 11.1   Measuring the Welfare Implications of Pollution Using Market Prices

the loss of that bushel of wheat production will overstate monetary damages. Markets may also be distorted for other reasons, such as subsidies, quotas, taxes, or tariffs. If pollution causes farmers to grow less of the crops for which they receive subsidies and for which the value to consumers is less than the cost, reducing subsidized grain production may be a net benefit to society, rather than a cost. Conversely, reducing production of a good whose production is already limited by price controls will cause a loss greater than that shown by the market price.

   If the necessary conditions of competition, full employment, and no externalities are all met, the market price gives an accurate value of a marginal change. If there are significant violations of these conditions, the market price may differ from willingness to pay (*WTP*) or opportunity cost. In that case, the market price may be an appropriate starting point for estimating *WTP* or opportunity cost.[7]

   If an environmental impact causes a nonmarginal change, then use of the market price will no longer be valid. Instead, we must examine changes in consumers' and producers' surplus. To see this, suppose that air pollutants emitted by a coal-fired power plant have been determined to reduce wheat yields up to 100 miles downwind of the plant. Figure 11.1 illustrates how we would measure the environmental damages associated with the plant. There are two cases to consider.[8] In the first, the reduction in crop output is assumed to have no effect on market price. Suppose that local farmers produce less wheat. Because the demand curve they face for wheat is completely elastic, there will be no price increase. This case is shown in Figure 11.1(a). The gross reduction in farm revenue would be $P_0(Q_1 - Q_0)$, equal to area BEQ_0Q_1. With the change in production costs, there is a net loss of producers' surplus equal to area ABE, which is unambiguously less than the loss

[7]See, for example Mishan (1976), chaps. 13 and 14, or Sassone and Schaffer (1978), chap. 5.

[8]We ignore the issue of subsidies in the agricultural market, although the extension is straightforward.

in revenues.[9] Because of the completely elastic nature of demand, however, the local farmers would bear all of the losses, and consumers would bear none.

In Figure 11.1(b), we assume that the nation's farmers face an aggregate demand curve for wheat that is not completely elastic. A reduction in production will be accompanied by an increase in market price. The reduced production reduces consumers' surplus from the area of triangle P_0EG to area P_1BG. Thus consumers suffer a welfare loss equal to area P_0EBP_1. Farmers' revenues are now P_1Q_1, rather than P_0Q_0. The change in revenues, $P_1Q_1 - P_0Q_0$, may be either positive or negative, depending on whether demand is inelastic or elastic. If it is inelastic, the reduction in wheat production will be accompanied by a greater than proportional increase in wheat prices, resulting in an overall increase in farmers' revenues. Producers' surplus initially equals area AEP_0. After the change, it equals area ABP_1. The change equals area P_0FBP_1 less area AFE. This may be either positive or negative, depending on the elasticity of demand and the elasticity of supply. Consumers, however, are unambiguously worse off because of the higher crop prices. The smaller the overall elasticity of demand, the larger the wealth transfer from consumers to producers because of higher market prices.

Two other factors need to be considered when using market prices or consumers' and producers' surplus to measure environmental benefits and costs. One is that gains to one party may be losses to another. In Figure 11.1(b), consumers' surplus is reduced by the area P_0EBP_1. Part of this loss to consumers is transferred to producers, who gain the area P_0FBP_1. The loss to society can be calculated by summing the net gains and losses of all parties: $P_0FBP_1 - P_0EBP_1 - AEF$. In this case, the net loss to society also can be seen directly as area AEB. Thus, counting the gains and the losses to only one side of the market will miss some losses and ignore the fact that others are actually transfers.

The second factor is that an environmental impact may affect a number of markets. For example, as a result of pollution, some wheat farmers may switch to other crops less affected by the pollution. (Indeed, the Coase theorem would suggest this as one outcome.) If so, valuing the environmental damage based on the value of lost wheat production only may overstate total damages. Reductions in consumers' and producers' surplus in the wheat market may be offset in part by increases in the markets for the substitute crop.

In some cases, the use of market prices to estimate changes in environmental values, either by themselves or as a starting point to value environmental benefits and costs, will be appropriate. In these cases, we can use the standard tools of welfare economics, such as consumers' and producers' surplus, to determine values. Because there are many interesting policy cases that do not involve market prices, however, development of sound environmental policies will often require

---

[9]Total variable production costs equal the area under the marginal cost curve. Initially, this was equal to area $0AEQ_0$. With the change, production costs equal the area under the MC' curve, at the new level of production. This is just $0ABQ_1$. The loss in producers' surplus equals triangle ABE, whose area equals $(BE)(P_0A)/2$. The loss in revenues equals the lost production times the fixed market price. This equals $P_0 \times (Q_1 - Q_0) = P_0 \cdot BE$, which by simple geometry is greater than the loss in producers' surplus.

methodologies that can determine environmental costs and benefits in the *absence* of markets. These methods are the subject of the next three sections.

The Hedonic Pricing Approach

Goods that do not have market prices themselves can often affect the prices of market goods. Houses located near airports, for example, tend to sell at lower prices than comparable houses elsewhere, owing to aircraft noise. Similarly, houses located downwind from oil refineries and slaughterhouses probably have lower prices than comparable houses that are not subject to such olfactory challenges. Houses along the Oregon coast that have panoramic views of the Pacific Ocean command higher selling prices than similar houses without such views. Even though there are no "markets" for noise, smell, or ocean views, their effects *on* market prices can often be measured.

In many cases, differences in values can be attributed to differences in the *characteristics* of goods. One ways of measuring the contribution to value of the different characteristics of goods is known as the *hedonic pricing approach* (HPA), initially developed by Ridker (1967). *Hedonic* pertains to pleasure; we place a positive value on such goods as beautiful views presumably because we derive pleasure from them. We also derive pleasure from the absence of negative characteristics, such as noise and smell.

The HPA is based on a straightforward premise: the value of an asset, whether a piece of land, a car, or a house, depends on the stream of benefits that are derived from that asset. These include the benefits of environmental amenities. One of the most common applications of the HPA has been the use of differences in the values of real estate with different environmental amenities to estimate the value of those amenities. Houses may have different views or be located in areas with better schools or lower crime rates. Houses may also differ in their exposure to pollution. By using regression techniques,[10] an HPA model can, in theory, identify what portion of property value differences can be attributed solely to environmental differences and infer individuals' *WTP* for environmental amenities and therefore the overall social value of a given amenity. The HPA can also be used to estimate *WTP* to avoid disamenities.

In the case of environmental externalities, the HPA is often applied to environmental attributes associated with specific commodities.[11] An HPA model may not be applicable to certain environmental externalities, however, if those externalities cannot be *decomposed* or *differentiated* within existing market prices. One example is housing prices and atmospheric carbon dioxide levels. Because carbon dioxide emissions are a global issue, we should not expect housing price differentials to depend on local emissions of carbon dioxide.

---

[10]Appendix B at the end of the book contains a brief overview of regression techniques.

[11]See Brookshire and colleagues (1982) for an example applied to rent values and pollution levels in Los Angeles. Consistent with theory, the authors found that rents were directly correlated with reduced pollution levels and that surveyed *WTP* to avoid pollution was less than the observed rent differentials.

The usefulness of HPA studies depends on the accuracy of identifying key attributes, the quality of the data used to develop the statistical models, and, most important, the ability to identify differential impacts. Identifying relevant attributes will sometimes be difficult. For example, individuals may be willing to accept lower wages in the Pacific Northwest to enjoy the additional environmental amenities, but defining the specific amenities they are enjoying may be difficult. And even if those amenities are identified, determining which of them (Mount Ranier? Puget Sound? the Sawtooth Range?) is the primary driver may not be possible. Nevertheless, to the extent that attributes can be identified correctly and completely and that reasonable statistical work can be performed, the HPA may offer a good sense of the "market value" of environmental amenities (Cummings, Brookshire, and Schulze 1986).

The How-To's of Hedonic Models   To identify differences in property prices because of differences in environmental amenities, data are taken from a sample of similar residential properties over a period of years (time-series analysis), on a larger set of dissimilar properties at a given point in time (cross-sectional analysis), or using a mixture of both types of data (pooled analysis). In actual empirical studies, the cross-sectional approach has been used most often because it is difficult to control for all of the variables that may affect property prices over time.

Often an analyst will choose a log-linear model because such a model allows the effects of different attributes to be separated. The general form of a log-linear hedonic model looks like Equation 11.1:

$$\ln P_H = f(A_1, A_2, \ldots, A_N) = \beta_0 + \beta_1 \ln A_1 + \beta_2 \ln A_2 + \ldots + \beta_N \ln A_N \qquad (11.1)$$

where P_H is the market price of the house and the A_i are the attributes to be valued, $i = 1, N$. If A_1 is the attribute we are interested in—say, amount of view—the goal of the regression analysis is to get an estimate of β_1 that is both accurate and precise. We want an estimate of β_1 that, on average, is as close to the true value as possible, and we want the range of uncertainty of the estimate to be as small as possible. These goals are formalized in the concepts of the *bias* and the *standard error* of an estimator.[12] Ideally, we want an estimate that is unbiased and has the smallest possible standard error. Unfortunately, in practice, it may be impossible to achieve both goals at once.

An estimated coefficient may be biased if the form of the regression equation is incorrect. There are many ways in which misspecification of a regression equation can lead to bias. One is if other important explanatory variables have been left out of the regression. Suppose that we develop an HPA model of housing prices and we are most interested in the relationship between housing price and airport noise. Now, the value of an individual house depends on numerous factors. Some of the more obvious factors include the physical attributes of each house (e.g., total

---

[12]We discuss these terms in Appendix B at the end of the book.

size, number of bathrooms, whether the yard is fenced), attributes that describe the nearby surroundings (e.g., accessibility to public transit, quality of neighborhood schools and other public facilities), and environmental attributes (e.g., auto traffic, noise, air pollution, presence of views).

Next suppose that we develop a model similar to Equation 11.1. However, because of a lack of data, we omit the variable defining the amount of view. Instead of using Equation 11.1, we estimate the model

$$\ln P_H = \beta_0 + \beta_2 \ln A_2 + \dots + \beta_N \ln A_N \tag{11.2}$$

Suppose that coefficient A_N refers to airport noise. By omitting A_1, the coefficient β_N may "pick up" a portion of the true value of β_1, which in Equation 11.2 has been implicitly set to zero.

How much omitting the amount of view as an explanatory variable will bias the estimate of the coefficient on noise level depends on how correlated the omitted variable (number of bathrooms) is with the dependent variable (total property value) and on how correlated the omitted variable is with views. For example, it may be that houses near the airport are older and smaller. Thus they may have a tendency to have only one bathroom, unlike large, expensive houses in the newer suburbs. As a result, the number of bathrooms will be positively correlated with housing prices and inversely correlated with airport noise. A regression based on Equation 11.2 will therefore tend to bias the estimate of noise on property values upward.

Another type of misspecification that can lead to biased coefficient estimates is use of the wrong mathematical function. In Equation 11.1, we discussed a log-linear model. However, if the relationship between property values and view is not log-linear, using that form of model can lead to bias. Bias can also arise if the relationship between views and property values really needs to be modeled as one of a set of several simultaneous equations, but we estimate only the single equation.[13]

The bias from excluding variables that should be in the regression may tempt you to include as many variables as possible on the chance that some might be relevant. Including irrelevant variables does not lead to biased estimates, but it generally does reduce the *precision* of estimated coefficients (increases their standard error). Thus including the homeowner's astrological sign in the regression will not bias the noise coefficient estimate, but it will reduce the precision of that coefficient.

Another factor leading to low precision of estimated coefficients is correlation between different explanatory variables, or *multicollinearity*. For example, both noise and traffic congestion are correlated with distance from the airport; including both in the regression may lead to large standard errors on the coefficients of one or both. This poses a dilemma. Including the traffic coefficient may lead to an imprecise estimate of the effect of noise on property values, but excluding it may lead to a biased estimate. However, in doing an HPA study, there is a way around

---

[13]If you would like to explore the problems caused by an omitted variable in regression analysis more fully, consult one of the econometric textbook references shown at the end of Appendix B.

this dilemma. The dilemma arises because of the fact that noise, traffic congestion, and property values are all correlated in our sample data. If we expand the sample of houses to include areas away from the airport, where traffic congestion depends primarily on factors other than distance from the airport, we can reduce the correlation between noise and congestion and thereby reduce the problem. Unfortunately, it may not always be possible to do this. If we want to estimate the impact of carbon monoxide levels on property values, multicollinearity will be a problem if carbon monoxide levels are correlated with the levels of other pollutants, such as particulates and nitrogen oxides. In this case, we may have to settle for estimating the impact of an index of all pollutants on property values without having precise estimates of the impact of any one pollutant (Pearce and Markandya 1989).

Another critical issue is data measurement. To estimate Equation 11.1, we need to have reasonable estimates of both the price of each house in the sample and the attributes themselves. For the housing price, P_H, the value most often used is the selling price, although one also could use values derived from professional appraisals. Generally, obtaining good data on prices is not a problem. Obtaining good data on the different attributes, however, may be problematic.

To see this, suppose that we are interested in the effects of air pollution levels on home values. Air pollution will vary almost continuously. It may be bad at certain times of the year, perhaps in the winter when more wood stoves are used; it may be bad at certain hours of the day, such as at commuting rush hours. The case may also be that air pollution is a concern only at times of peak concentration, such as in an atmospheric inversion in winter, or it may be a problem at all times. Thus the question arises as to the most appropriate air pollution measure. Unfortunately, there may be no easy way to reduce air pollution to a single index. Other environmental variables can pose similar difficulties. Suppose that we were interested in the quality of a view. Should that view be measured in terms of distance on pristine days, the average distance on all days, the number of days that the view is available, or some other variable? Again, there is no uniquely correct answer. It will depend on the context of the analysis.

If we want to infer individuals' *WTP* for different levels of environmental quality, we must proceed beyond estimation of Equation 11.1. The reason is that equation 11.1 tells us only the *aggregate WTP* for marginal changes in environmental attributes. To see this, consider Figure 11.2. Panel (a) represents the estimated relationship between environmental quality (e.g., the amount of view) and the price of a house. As environmental quality rises, the value of that house rises as well, although at a decreasing rate. This is shown as curve $P(E)$. Panel (b) illustrates the *slope* of $P(E)$ versus the level of environmental quality. In fact, it shows the aggregate demand curve for environmental quality, D_{TOT}. Because the slope of $P(E)$ decreases as environmental quality increases, D_{TOT} slopes downward. Thus at a level of environmental quality equal to E_0, the slope of $P(E)$ equals r_2. At other levels of environmental quality, there will be different slopes, such as $r_1 = \beta_1(P_H/A_1)$, which is just the derivative of Equation 11.1 with respect to A_1. Given a robust set of data, we can identify this aggregate household demand curve for environmental quality.

If the level of views changes very slightly, household WTP will also be measured by r_1. If all households are identical (same number of persons, ages,

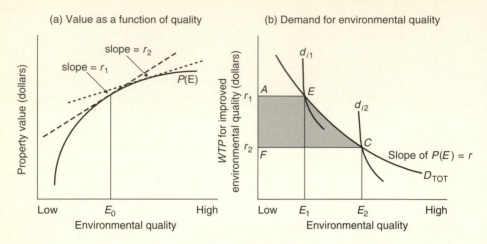

Figure 11.2   Using the Hedonic Method to Estimate *WTP* for Environmental Quality

incomes, etc.), the individual household demand curves d_{ij} will be identical to the aggregate demand curve D_{TOT}. If, as is far more likely to be the case, individual households are different, then a regression equation will have identified only single points (at r_i) on the individual household demand curves. Thus to estimate the individual household demands for views, we will have to run another regression on the r's estimated from Equation 11.1 on individual household characteristics of the form $r = f(\text{view}, \mathbf{z})$, where $\mathbf{z}$ is a vector of household characteristics such as income, race, age, and family size.

To value an improvement in environmental quality, we could use the results from this second estimated equation. Suppose that overall environmental quality increases from E_1 to E_2. The total increase in consumers surplus would equal area *AECF* in panel (b) of Figure 11.2, which would equal the sum of the individual changes in comsumers surplus.[14]

Examples of Empirical Studies   In this section, we consider several studies that used the HPA to value reductions in noise and air pollution. Tables 11.2, 11.3, and 11.4 summarize findings from studies of automobile noise, aircraft noise, and air pollution, respectively. Table 11.2 indicates that a 1 percent increase (decrease) in airport noise would decrease (increase) housing values between 0.5 and 2.0 percent. Table 11.3 indicates that a 1 percent increase (decrease) in traffic noise would decrease (increase) property values between 0.08 and 0.65 percent. In both cases, however, it is possible that these results are biased because of omitted variables. For example, traffic noise is probably strongly correlated with levels of ambient air pollution. Thus it is not clear whether the empirical results truly mea-

---

[14]There are several other more technical empirical issues associated with determinations of total value. These are summarized in Pearce and Markandya (1989) and Cropper and Oates (1992).

TABLE 11.2   PERCENTAGE CHANGE IN HOUSING PRICES CAUSED BY A PERCENTAGE INCREASE IN AIRCRAFT NOISE

Location	Impact of a 1-Unit Change in NEF[a]
New York	−1.60–2.00
San Francisco	−0.50
Washington, D.C.	−1.00
Boston	−0.83
Minneapolis	−0.58

[a]NEF is a measure of aircraft noise related to human hearing and discomfort.

Source: Nelson (1980); Pearce and Markandya (1989, p. 30).

sure only the effects of traffic noise on property values or if they are measuring aggregate effects. Finally, as was illustrated in panel (a) of Figure 11.2, the values estimated will not necessarily be constant over the entire range of noise.

The same sort of issue arises with the results on air pollution shown in Table 11.4. In many cases, it will be difficult, if not impossible, to distinguish between different forms of air pollution and the reasons individuals value reductions in pollution. Trijonis (1984), for example, looked at the effects of improvements in visibility on housing prices in San Francisco. He found that households would, on average, pay an additional $200 per year for a 10 percent improvement in visibility. It is difficult to know, however, whether this value is net of changes in air pollution, if it merely reflects living higher up on one of San Francisco's many hills, or other effects. Furthermore, it is not clear what a "10 percent increase in visibility" means to homeowners. Is it a 10 percent increase in the length of the view or seeing the same distance 10 percent more of the time, perhaps because of local variations in weather patterns in different parts of the city?

Conclusions   The HPA has often been used to value changes in environmental effects on property values. If this method is to be used, particular care must be paid to the type and form of data collected and the estimation methods, to avoid the problems of multicollinearity and uncertainty about how the results of studies may be interpreted.

TABLE 11.3   PERCENTAGE CHANGE IN HOUSING PRICES CAUSED BY A PERCENTAGE INCREASE IN TRAFFIC NOISE

Location	Impact of a 1-Unit Change in L_{eq}[a]
North Virginia	−0.15
Chicago	−0.65
Spokane	−0.08
Towson	−0.54
North King County	−0.30

[a]L_{eq} is the level of equivalent continuous sound, measured in decibels, that has the same sound energy over a given period of time as the measured fluctuations in sound because of traffic noise.

Source: Nelson (1982); Pearce and Markandya (1989, p. 30).

TABLE 11.4   ELASTICITY OF HOUSING PRICE WITH RESPECT TO AIR POLLUTION LEVEL

City	Year of Property Data/Pollution Data	Pollutant	Elasticity of House Value with Respect to Pollution Levels
St. Louis	1960/1963	Sulfates and particulates	−0.06–0.10 −0.12–0.14
Washington, D.C.	1970/1967–1968	Oxidants and particulates	−0.05–0.12 −0.01–0.02
Chicago[a]	1964–1967/1964–1967	Sulfates and particulates	−0.20–0.50
Philadelphia	1960/1969	Sulfates and particulates	−0.10–0.12
Pittsburgh[a]	1970/1969	Sulfates and dust	−0.09–0.15
Los Angeles[a]	1977–1878/1977–1978	Particulates and oxidants	−0.22

[a]Joint effects of both pollutants.

Sources: Freeman (1979); Brookshire et al. (1982); Pearce and Markandya (1989, p. 31).

The Contingent Valuation Method

The premise of the contingent valuation methodology (CVM) is straightforward: if you wish to know the value people place on something (a view, clean air, safety, etc.), just ask them. CVM asks people what they are willing to pay for an environmental benefit or what they are willing to accept to tolerate an environmental cost. This asking may be done through the use of direct questionnaires or surveys or through the use of experiments that determine how individuals respond. The biggest potential advantage of CVM is that it should be applicable to all situations. Whereas a hedonic study might be unable to distinguish between the effects of different pollutants, a CVM could ask individuals about specific pollutants and the desired environmental change (less noise, improved visibility at the Grand Canyon, etc.) directly. CVM also allows researchers to ask people about choices that they may not actually make in real life, such as making direct payments for cleaner air.

CVM is also uniquely suited to address nonuse values. Many CVM studies have attempted to determine nonuse values of environmental amenities through surveys. Still others, as we discuss in Chapter 12, have attempted to elicit values individuals place on reducing their risk of premature death. A few examples of CVM studies include valuing improvements in water quality for recreation use (Carson and Mitchell 1988; Duffield, Neher, and Brown 1992), valuing improvements in visibility at the Grand Canyon (Schulze and Brookshire 1983), and valuing preservation of endangered species (Boyle and Bishop 1987). Other studies have focused on the values of passive users of environmental amenities, such as those associated with the 1989 Exxon *Valdez* oil spill described in the box (Carson et al. 1992).

Next we will review the CVM method itself, using the Exxon *Valdez* study as a guide. Although there have been hundreds of CVM studies performed, the Exxon *Valdez* study is particularly noteworthy because of its high profile and the care that was taken in its design and execution. Following the discussion of the how-to's of

CVM IN THE LAST FRONTIER: THE CASE OF THE EXXON *VALDEZ*

When the Exxon *Valdez* ran aground on March 24, 1989, it spilled millions of gallons of crude oil into the pristine waters of Prince William Sound in southeastern Alaska. It also set off a major debate as to the accuracy and the relevance of CVM in determining the monetary liability of the Exxon Company associated with the spill.

Although the obvious questions of the use values associated with the lost income of fishermen put out of work because of the spill were addressed in the damage claims, other damage and liability questions were raised. What was the damage done to sea otters? Was it relevant to include the existence-value damage to people who had no intent of ever visiting Prince William Sound yet were aware that the area had been sullied by the spilled crude oil? How could biological complexities be represented in a CVM survey?* Last, how should damage to future generations, who might otherwise be able to enjoy the benefits of a pristine Prince William Sound, be incorporated, if at all?

The Comprehensive Environmental Response, Compensation, and Liability Act (CERCLA) of 1980† and the Oil Pollution Act of 1990 allow recovery of passive-use damages for injuries to natural resources resulting from the release of hazardous substances and crude oil. This passive-use liability can affect the precautions firms take to prevent environmental damage (i.e., how much firms insure themselves) and the level of required restoration should environmental damage occur. Because of this legal liability, the use of CVM came under intense scrutiny: lawyers for Exxon and major petroleum-using industries vehemently opposed the validity of CVM as a valuation measure, while environmental advocates insisted as fiercely that the damages estimated by CVM were valid.

There is little doubt that poorly designed CVM studies will produce unreliable estimates of environmental valuation. The arguments over CVM, however, have focused on whether such design flaws are *inherent* to CVM. If so, CVM is a poor estimation tool and hence a poor tool on which to base economic policy and legal liability. But if careful survey design can produce reasonably accurate measurements of environmental resource valuation, CVM is a much more potent and useful tool. The Exxon *Valdez* CVM study was performed at the request of the attorney general of the state of Alaska to help establish damages in a lawsuit the state brought against Exxon.

Rather than address damages associated with lost use values, the CVM study focused on lost passive-use values. For example, one of the key questions in the CVM survey referred to a proposal to require escort ships to help prevent and contain future oil spills by asking the individuals surveyed to imagine that they could travel back in time and, by paying a fee for this program, prevent the Exxon *Valdez* accident from occurring. The results of the study indicated lost passive-use values of around $3 billion.

Desvouges, Smith, and McGivney (1993), as well as Diamond and Hausman (1994), argue that this type of question is not a valid basis for determining legal liability. They argue that respondents will often base their answers on emotional values rather than economic ones. In well-publicized cases such as

(continued)

oil spills, respondents will often feel a sense of outrage that will bias their answers. As both sets of authors point out, such emotional values will cause respondents to assign the same valuation to a minor oil spill that does little damage as a major one that does significant damage. In many cases, these authors have found respondents' *WTP* to prevent damage absurdly high, often higher than their annual incomes. And they argue that respondents often fail to consider substitution effects: individuals may wish to prevent oil spills, but they may also wish to have cleaner air, more national parks, safer streets, and better schools. Economic theory teaches us that individuals must make choices among their unlimited wants that reflect their limited incomes.

Despite these criticisms, Randall (1993) and Hanemann (1994) argue that CVM does provide information useful for establishing legal liability. They state that courts are used to dealing with controversial damage claims and with well-qualified experts arguing conflicting testimony. They argue that there is no need to demonstrate that CVM is an absolutely foolproof methodology, merely that it can provide an adequate basis for evidentiary requirements in civil damage cases. These authors reject arguments that were made by Exxon and the oil industry that CVM is too unreliable to determine passive-use damages and that such damages should therefore be eliminated from consideration in liability cases.

No doubt, the debate over CVM and the determination of passive-use damage values for legal liability will continue. Ironically, even though the Exxon *Valdez* case brought CVM to the forefront of legal and economic scrutiny, no final decisions as to the accuracy of CVM for calculating passive-use values arose from it. In an out-of-court settlement negotiated before the completion of the various CVM studies, Exxon agreed to pay $1.1 billion in damages, on top of the cleanup costs associated with the spill.

*See Carson, Meade, and Smith (1993); Desvouges et al. (1993); and Randall (1993) for an excellent readable debate on the passive-use issue. See also Castle, Berrens, and Adams (1994).

†See Chapter 9 for more discussion of CERCLA, which is better known as the Superfund Law.

CVM, we discuss some of the problems associated with CVM studies that can affect the reliability of the derived *WTP* and willingness-to-accept (*WTA*) values.[15] We conclude with a brief review of several other CVM studies, including a study of the value of instream flows for recreational use and two studies that formed the basis for the case study on visibility at the Grand Canyon that began the chapter.

---

[15]*WTP* and *WTA* are reviewed in Chapter 3.

The How-To's of CVM   A CVM study requires three basic items. First, a CVM study must carefully describe the environmental commodity to be valued. Is the environmental good in question a lost view? Is it lost recreational opportunities because a river has become polluted or because too much water has been diverted for irrigation? Is the study considering the loss of endangered species? Second, a CVM study requires a method by which individuals' payments (hypothetical or perhaps real) are to be made. For example, a study of the value of a recreation-related good might require payment in the form of a user fee or an increase in taxes. A study asking individuals what they would be willing to pay for a better view at the Grand Canyon might ask those individuals if they were willing to pay a larger electric bill. Third, a study must have a method of converting those individual payments to overall *WTP* or *WTA* values. Thus if a study determines that the average *WTP* is $50 per year for improving views at the Grand Canyon, it is still necessary to estimate overall *WTP* by determining the relevant population—is it all U.S. citizens, everyone in North America, or some other population?

CVM studies also require a method with which to convey information to potential respondents and analyze their responses. There are numerous types of survey instruments, each having its own benefits and costs. Phone surveys, for example, have higher response rates than mail surveys. However, they are more expensive to undertake. They also preclude the use of visual material, such as photographs showing different pollution levels. Face-to-face interviews are the most reliable survey method but also the most costly. Mail surveys are generally the cheapest but can have low response rates and provide no opportunities to explain questions that respondents find confusing or to clarify confusing answers.

Study designers must use a large enough sample of the population to guarantee results with the desired degree of precision. Nonresponse bias is always a concern with surveys. If people who do not answer a question or do not cooperate at all differ systematically from those who do, a survey's results will be biased. The survey will not accurately reflect the population as a whole.

To determine maximum *WTP* an individual respondent might simply be asked to name an amount (in an *open-ended* survey) or asked whether or not she would be willing to pay a given amount (a *closed-ended* survey, sometimes called a *referendum* or *take-it-or-leave-it* survey format). Closed-ended surveys do not directly yield individual *WTP* estimates. However, the fraction of respondents willing to pay different amounts can be used to estimate aggregate *WTP*. Closed-ended surveys have several advantages over open-ended ones. First, most people are comfortable with referendum questions because many markets operate on a take-it-or-leave-it basis (Freeman 1993). When you buy cornflakes from the supermarket, the price is not negotiable; you either pay the marked price or forgo the cornflakes. A second advantage of closed-ended surveys is that the decision problem they pose is straightforward. Either you are willing to pay a stated amount for an action or you are not. As a result, closed-ended surveys usually have higher response rates than open-ended ones. That can be an important consideration because of the high cost of surveys, especially in-person ones. Researchers will always want to get the

TABLE 11.5   EXXON *VALDEZ* VALUATION QUESTIONS BY SURVEY VERSION

Survey Version	Question		
	A-15	A-16	A-17
A	$10	$30	$5
B	$30	$60	$10
C	$60	$120	$30
D	$120	$250	$60

Source: Carson et al. (1992), p. 3-59.

largest amount of usable data from the smallest reliable sample of individuals possible.

In the case of the Exxon *Valdez* study, four different versions of close-ended *WTP* questions were asked of respondents to gauge their *WTP*. In essence, researchers asked the respondents to go back in time before the spill occurred. Respondents were asked what they would be willing to pay for a program that would escort all ships through Prince William Sound and that would prevent the spill from ever happening (Carson et al. 1992):[16]

> A-15: *At present*, government officials estimate the program will cost your household a total of $(specified amount here). You would pay this as a special one-time charge in addition to your regular federal taxes. This money would *only* be used for the program to prevent damage from another large oil spill in Prince William Sound. (p. 3-56, emphasis in original)

The "specified amount here" refers to one of four sets of values, shown in Table 11.5, that were used for different surveys. Different respondents were asked question A-15 (and one of the two follow-up questions after it) using these different sets of values to get a better estimate of *WTP*. The reason is that by using different referendum amounts, the researchers could increase the possible range of values using a smaller set of individuals. If the respondent indicated that he or she would be willing to pay the specified dollar amount in question A-15, a follow-up question was asked:

> A-16: What if the final cost estimates showed that the program would cost your household a total of $(amount)? Would you vote for or against the program?

As shown in Table 11.5, this follow-up question had a higher threshold value. For example, version A respondents were asked question A-15 using a value of $10. If they indicated that they were willing to pay that amount, question A-16 asked whether they would be willing to pay a value of $30.

If a respondent was *unwilling* to pay the specified amount in question A-15, a different follow-up question with a lower threshold value was used:

---

[16] This is an example of a lost passive-use value. Another excellent example of this type of survey for a very different type of environmental good can be found in NRDA (1994).

A-17: What if the final cost estimates showed that the program would cost your household a total of $(amount)? Would you vote for or against the program?

Of course, some respondents were not willing to pay the amount specified in question A-15 or A-17. For these respondents, additional follow-up questions were asked to determine the reasons for this unwillingness to pay. It turned out that about a third of those who said they would be unwilling to pay the lower amount in question A-17 did so because they thought the oil companies should pay. About one-fourth said they could not afford to pay the specified amount. Fewer than 10 percent thought protecting Prince William Sound was not worth as much as they were asked, and another 40 percent either were unsure, opposed any new taxes, or thought the government would be unable to operate the program effectively.

From Individual Values to Aggregate Values   Because CVM studies survey individuals, researchers first determine a representative value of individual *WTP* or *WTA*. What CVM studies ultimately seek, however, are aggregate values of an environmental amenity. To go from individual values to total values, however, first requires defining the relevant *population*. Before we tell you the population used for the Exxon *Valdez* study, ask yourself what might be most relevant: all individuals living in the state of Alaska? in the United States? North America? the world? In many cases, identifying the relevant population is not straightforward.

To determine the relevant population, it helps to define the relationship between beneficiaries of an environmental good and those who pay for the good. This is shown in Table 11.6. Category I represents the "ideal" population for a CVM study. Individuals in category I benefit from the environmental good, and payment vehicles that move individuals into this category should be designed, if possible. For example, presumably residents living near an airport would benefit from reduced airplane noise, while residents far away from the airport would not. The latter residents will be in category III or IV. The relevant population will be only those households that are affected. So a potential payment vehicle might be increased property taxes for homeowners living near the airport.

Individuals in category II benefit from the environmental good but will not necessarily pay for it. For example, out-of-town relatives may visit and experience the airport noise. They, too, might be willing to pay to reduce airport noise so as to

TABLE 11.6   RELATIONSHIP BETWEEN BENEFICIARIES OF AND PAYERS FOR AN ENVIRONMENTAL GOOD

		Pays for the Good?	
		Yes	No
Benefits from the Good?	Yes	I	II
	No	III	IV

Source: After Mitchell and Carson (1989).

sleep better while visiting. Thus category II individuals should be moved to category I, if possible. Category III residents could include people living in the neighborhood who are deaf, as well as absentee landlords whose market rents are lower than at comparable residences because of the airport noise. Ideally, they would be moved to category IV.

When the environmental good in question is less clearly defined than airport noise affecting a single neighborhood, determining the relevant population becomes more difficult. The relevant population benefiting from improved visibility at Grand Canyon National Park, for example, would include local Arizonans who frequently visited the park (category I) but could also include individuals who have existence values from merely knowing the view is fantastic. Thus a researcher who determined an aggregate *WTP* value for improved visibility using only the local population would tend to undervalue true *WTP*. Conversely, including the population of a country whose residents had never heard of the Grand Canyon would tend to overvalue improved visibility.

Unfortunately, there are no concrete rules for determining a relevant population. Most populations will include users and nonusers. Although it is always appropriate to include users, researchers need to determine which nonusers have positive existence and option values. That determination requires careful judgment.

In the case of the the Exxon *Valdez* study, the researchers defined the relevant population as *all English-speaking U.S. households.* They did this because the environmental services in Prince William Sound are held in trust for all present and future generations of Americans (Carson et al. 1992). Defining the relevant population soley as Alaskans would have undervalued total *WTP*, and including individuals outside of the United States, for whom the environmental services are not held specifically in trust and for whom there are no direct payment vehicles (e.g. higher U.S. income taxes), would have overvalued total *WTP*.

Having a relevant population, to estimate an overall *WTP* value the researchers used the *median* WTP estimate of the individuals surveyed. The median *WTP* was used instead of the *mean WTP* for two reasons. First, because the mean value was greater than the median value,[17] using the median would determine a lower-bound value that could be reported as "conservative." Second, it turns out that the mean is quite sensitive to the assumptions made about the actual shape of the overall distribution of *WTP* values. Rather than determining a mean subject to much uncertainty, the researchers chose to use the more stable median value.

With a median *WTP* of $31 and the population of households estimated to be about 91 million, the overall valuation was estimated to be $2.8 billion, with a confidence interval between $2.4 and $3.2 billion.

Estimating a Valuation Function†   Frequently, overall *WTP* is estimated using a *valuation function*. A valuation function relates respondents' characteristics to

---

[17] The mean was greater than median because of the skewed nature of the distribution of *WTP* values. No respondents valued preserving environmental quality in Prince William Sound below zero dollars (meaning that they preferred a dirty, oil-slicked sound), but some cited very high values.

†*NOTE:* Sections marked with a dagger refer to material that is more advanced.

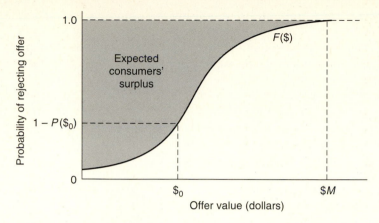

Figure 11.3   Logit Model and Expected Consumers' Surplus

their *WTP* estimates. In the Exxon *Valdez* study, for example, the researchers determined the probability that a given respondent would say yes to the values in questions A-15 through A-17, based on that respondent's education, personal income, education level, race, and other demographic variables.

Once a valuation function like this is estimated, overall *WTP* can be determined using the same population. First, the valuation function is estimated using standard regression techniques. For the Exxon *Valdez* study, the researchers used a *logit* (log-odds) model.[18] A logit model provides a convenient way of estimating an individual's probability of saying "Yes, I would be willing to pay $X" because it allows a linear model to be developed, even though predicted probabilities must always lie between 0 and 1. In the Exxon *Valdez* study, the probability of responding yes to a given amount was found to increase with income, just as we would expect from our discussion of the demand for environmental quality in Chapter 9.

Once the model is estimated, the results are used to estimate total expected consumers' surplus, which will be the same as total *WTP*. This is shown in Figure 11.3. The curve $F(\$)$ is a cumulative density function. As the take-it-or-leave-it offer value is increased, more respondents will be *unwilling* to pay the specified amount. At some offer value $\$M$, no individual will be willing to accept the offer. Thus the probability of rejection will equal 1.0. This value can be thought of as describing the intercept point on a demand curve. As the offer price decreases to $\$_0$, the probability of a respondent's rejecting the offer will equal $P(\$_0)$, and so the probability of accepting the offer will equal $1 - P(\$_0)$. Expected consumers' surplus just equals the area *above* $F(\$)$ and below the probability value 1.0, that is, $1 - F(\$)$, in the same way the integral under a demand curve equals consumers' surplus.[19]

---

[18]The logit model is one form of a class of models known as *dichotomous choice* models. More information about these models can be found in Maddala (1983).

[19]A detailed proof can be found in Freeman (1993).

Reliability of the CVM Approach For a surprisingly simple premise, there is a voluminous literature on the accuracy of CVM, reflecting the ongoing controversy with the method.[20] A large portion of the Exxon *Valdez* study, for example, addresses concerns about biases in the survey, the use of pretests to evaluate potential flaws in the survey, and other design issues. Just as you might expect surveys commissioned by individual political candidates to be biased, there is much concern that CVM surveys will suffer from a variety of biases because of the way the questions are asked.

Because of the difficulties associated with survey instruments, a great deal of the CVM literature has dealt with the accuracy and the reliability of the derived *WTP* and *WTA* estimates (Smith 1993a, 1993b).[21] There is, for example, concern about possible biases in CVM estimates because the survey approach most commonly has dealt only with payments that are *hypothetical* (Arrow et al. 1993). CVM studies may also be vulnerable to strategic behavior by respondents, who may think that they can influence a decision by answering untruthfully. Still other respondents may refuse to play along with hypothetical scenarios. They may respond with what are called *protest bids,* saying, for example, that they would not tolerate even the smallest increase in pollution at a national park no matter what the compensation. Or they may think that the hypothetical scenario makes no sense. Someone who lives next door to the Grand Canyon, for example, may not understand how their cost of enjoying the Grand Canyon could increase.

The potential biases in the results of CVM studies have generally been separated into five separate categories: *strategic, design, information, hypothetical,* and *operational bias.* Whether any of these biases causes problems in applied work is a matter of ongoing controversy.

Strategic bias refers to the problem of getting individuals to reveal their true preferences when, by not telling the truth, they can still obtain benefits. This is similar to the free-rider problem. Suppose that a city is considering the development of a new park that will provide recreation benefits. Individuals are told that the park will be developed if *WTP* on the part of taxpayers is greater than the cost of development. Furthermore, suppose that taxpayers will each be charged their individual *WTP* values. Under these circumstances, there will be an incentive for individuals to understate *WTP,* that is, to enjoy the benefits of the park without paying their true maximum *WTP.* The park has attributes of a public good in that, once developed, it is difficult to exclude anyone from enjoying its benefits. Many other environmental quality issues, such as views at the Grand Canyon, share these public good attributes.[22]

---

[20]Good summaries can be found in Mitchell and Carson (1989) and Cummings, Brookshire, and Schulze (1986). See also "The Price of Imagining Arden" (1994). An excellent and readable case for CVM is made by Hanemann (1994). Pessimistic views of the CVM method can be found in Arrow et al. (1993) and in Diamond and Hausman (1994).

[21]Accuracy of CVM estimates is the main subject of the book by Cummings, Brookshire, and Schulze (1986).

[22]Recall from Chapter 6 the definition of a public good and the aggregation of public good benefits.

Although a CVM survey may offer respondents opportunities for this type of game playing, actually giving an answer based on strategic considerations requires recognizing that a strategic answer is possible and deciding which way and how much to distort the answer. Particularly in face-to-face and phone surveys, respondents may simply not have time to figure out how to misrepresent their preferences. Even on mail surveys, people may tell the truth simply because the potential gains from lying are not worth the effort. Individuals who make protest or strategic responses can sometimes be identified with follow-up questions. It is possible to perform statistical tests on results from the whole sample to determine whether they are affected by strategic bias.

Design bias primarily encompasses two distinct effects. The first is called *starting-point bias.* Starting-point bias refers to situations where the interviewer suggests the initial bid. If the starting point of *WTP* for the new park, for example, is $100 per year, the ultimate *WTP* the respondent decides on may differ from a survey where the initial bid was only $50 per year. The problem arises if respondents are influenced by the starting point, which in itself conveys information to respondents about the potential value of the environmental good. Whether starting-point bias is a significant problem is still inconclusive (Cummings, Brookshire, and Schulze 1986). One of the reasons that the Exxon *Valdez* study and more recent CVM studies use a take-it-or-leave-it format to determine *WTP* is the ability to overcome starting-point bias.

A second component of design bias is called *vehicle bias.* Vehicle bias refers to the choice of payment vehicle. The vehicle for the new national park might be direct, such as with an entrance fee, or indirect in the form of higher overall property taxes. In the case of the Exxon *Valdez* study, the payment vehicle was an increase in the respondent's income tax bill.

Respondents may be sensitive to the type of payment vehicle. They may show a higher *WTP* if the payment were in the form of property taxes, for example, than if there were an entrance fee. This might arise because of a perception of sunk versus variable costs: with higher property taxes, additional visits to the park would have no marginal cost (except the cost of physically getting to the park), whereas with an entrance fee, the marginal cost would be higher. Vehicle bias can also arise from a respondent's attitude toward the payment vehicle itself. Someone who places a high value on parks may nevertheless express a low or zero *WTP* if the payment vehicle is higher taxes and the person believes that taxes are too high or if the vehicle is a fee and the person believes that all parks should be free. Testing for vehicle bias is straightforward but can be expensive. To test for this bias, one would test for statistical differences among different payment vehicles. If a bias existed, a more difficult issue would be deciding on a "neutral" payment vehicle.

Respondents' *WTP* will also be influenced by the information they have. This, not surprisingly, is called *information bias.* The amount and quality of information supplied to respondents will almost certainly affect their *WTP* values, much as information can affect *WTP* for market goods. To take a simple example, suppose that a researcher wishes to ascertain *WTP* to avoid exposure to electromagnetic fields (EMF). If the question is simply, "What would you pay to avoid EMF?" the answer will depend on whether the respondent knows what EMF is. If, however, the question asks, "What will you pay to avoid EMF, which has been shown to cause cancer in children?" the answer may be much higher. Determining whether or not information bias exists is difficult. Usually, it involves eliciting responses from separate groups that are given different amounts of information. If a difference in *WTP* is observed, however, it may not be clear what is the "right" amount of information on which to base estimates of *WTP*. In the Exxon *Valdez* study, individuals were shown a variety of maps of Prince William Sound and pictures of the sound, heavily oiled shorelines before cleanup, and wildlife such as sea otters.

As we stated earlier, most CVM studies involve hypothetical payments. For example, the people questioned in the Exxon *Valdez* study did not actually have to pay more in income taxes. The fact that payments are usually hypothetical can be a source of *hypothetical bias* because in actual markets, purchasers pay for their mistakes.[23] Consider the example of a trip to the Grand Canyon. Suppose that a respondent indicated a *WTP* of $20 for one visit to the Grand Canyon after being shown a picture of its magnificent vistas. If the respondent actually paid $20 and then visited the Grand Canyon, only to discover hordes of tourists jostling one another to see the view, the respondent may feel anger at having paid so high a price.

Finally, *operational bias* may occur if consumers are unfamiliar with the good to be valued. The main issues with operational bias is whether respondents are familiar with the goods they are asked to provide values for and whether their picture of what they are valuing is the same as the researchers'. Operational bias may be a problem with CVM estimates of nonuse values. For example, researchers may ask respondents' *WTP* for continued existence of the harlequin duck, holding all other goods and environmental attributes constant (except for any environmental attributes that must be changed to preserve the duck). Respondents may give the "desired" answer, they may express their *WTP* for preservation of endangered species in general, or they may express their willingness to give to a good cause. Researchers must take great care to ensure that they are getting answers to the "right" questions.

Other Empirical Examples of CVM Studies   Next we examine two additional empirical CVM studies. We focus on two distinct environmental goods: the value of improvements in stream flows and water quality in the Rocky Mountain West and the value of additional visibility in the southwestern United States. For each environmental good, we compare two separate studies and examine the differences in their results.

Valuing Instream Flows for Recreation   Duffield, Neher, and Brown (1992) used a CVM study to determine the recreation values of instream flows in Montana's Big Hole and Bitterroot rivers. Unlike the Exxon *Valdez* study, which focused on nonuse values, this study focused on use values. Duffield and colleagues sought to determine what value recreationists placed on additional river

---

[23]Some researchers have used actual experiments to determine *WTP*. See, for example, Bishop, Heberlein, and Kealy (1983).

flows. Such values are important because there are several existing and potential uses for the water in these rivers. If there is too much irrigation, there will be too little water for recreation. Reserve too much water for recreation, however, and economic losses are incurred because of lost crop production. Thus, allocating river flows between recreational use and consumptive use (such as water for irrigation) to maximize total economic value will depend on the values of both uses. Measuring the economic value of crop production is relatively straightforward, but measuring the economic value of recreation requires a nonmarket approach. Hence the CVM study.

The principal recreation forms for the two rivers are different. The Big Hole River is best known for its trout fishing and attracts anglers from across the United States. The Bitterroot River, while also a good fishery, is used primarily by boaters and shoreline recreationists. Instream flows in these rivers vary significantly by season. They are highest in spring because of melting mountain snowpack. Flows peak in June and reach a minimum usually in August or September.

To develop the database for the model, on-site surveys were conducted along portions of each river that are used heavily for recreation. The survey data were collected in the summer of 1988. The survey used a closed-ended survey format to determine *WTP*. As with the Exxon *Valdez* study, a range of values was developed beforehand, and each survey form contained a dollar value. Respondents were asked a question of the form "Would you have made this trip if your costs were X dollars more?"[24] The respondents' answers were correlated with measured flows to determine a model linking flow levels and *WTP*. The respondents were also asked to supply demographic data about themselves, such as their household income and their age, as well as the distance they had traveled and the number of days in their trip. This was done to develop the overall valuation function linking *WTP* and demographic data, again in a manner similar to the Exxon *Valdez* study.

Specific data relating to recreation conditions were also collected so as better to assess the determinants of value. For example, data were collected on whether a given survey day was cold or windy and whether the respondent felt that the river was "crowded." By using the data collected, the authors were able to develop a model that predicted the probability that a respondent would be willing to pay a given amount in addition to the trip expenses. The estimated model for *WTP* was then combined with a model on use of the rivers.

As expected, the authors found that higher instream flows were correlated with higher *WTP* for a trip. In other words, a given user would pay more for the privilege of recreating with higher flows. The number of users initially increased as flow levels increased but, after some high level of flows, declined. This makes

---

[24]It is important to note that this question is not the same as "How much did you spend on this trip?" Although that is an interesting question, it is different. It could tell us how much recreationists are willing to spend on gasoline, food, fishing tackle, and beer. It does *not* tell us how much they value the recreation site or its attributes. As we discuss in the section on the travel cost method, *WTP* for an unpriced recreation site is the difference between *WTP* for the whole trip and what is paid for all the market goods that go into the trip.

intuitive sense. We would expect that at very low flows, use would be low. Use would also be low during periods of flooding, when instream flows were greatest. Using their model, the authors were able to estimate the value of additional instream flows. They found that at low flow levels, around 100 cubic feet per second (cfs), the marginal value of additional flows was $10.31 per acre-foot of water on the Bitterroot River and $25.45 on the Big Hole River. Marginal values approached zero at flow levels of about 1,900 cfs on the Bitterroot River and at about 2,200 cfs on the Big Hole River. Using these results and estimates of the total number of visitors, the authors estimated that for the entire recreation season (May 1 to September 30), the overall recreation values were $2.4 million on the Bitterroot River and $8.1 million on the Big Hole River.

Valuing Improvements in Visibility   Next we consider two studies that valued a pure public environmental good: improved visibility. The first study, conducted by Rowe, d'Arge, and Brookshire (1980), estimated the value associated with improved visibility in the Four Corners region of the southwestern United States. A later study by Schulze and Brookshire (1983) valued improvements in air quality at the Grand Canyon and several other national parks in the U.S. Southwest.

Rowe and colleagues used photographs to determine respondents' values for preserving visibility. They conducted an in-person survey of 93 individuals living near the area, eliciting from each *WTP* and *WTA* amounts. The hypothetical payment vehicle was the respondents' electric utility bills.

The authors used an open-ended *bidding-game* format to determine *WTP* and *WTA* values. This approach is the oldest CVM method used and is based on the premise of an auction. In the bidding game, respondents are asked to "bid" an amount that they would be willing to pay for an environmental improvement or willing to accept for environmental deterioration. Unfortunately, as the authors confirmed, bidding games are susceptible to starting-point bias. Like an auction, the initial bid tends to imply a value for the good in question (Mitchell and Carson 1989).

Despite the presence of starting-point bias, the authors were able to derive average *WTA* values for decreases in visibility. These values are shown in Table 11.7. The authors also compared the results of their study to a previous visibility

TABLE 11.7   VALUES ASSOCIATED WITH MAINTAINING VISIBILITY IN THE SOUTHWEST

Study	Average Yearly Bid (dollars)
Rowe, d'Arge, and Brookshire (1980)	
Best-to-worst visibility	82.20
Best-to-average visibility	57.00
Randall, Ives, and Eastman (1974)	
Best-to-worst visibility	85.00
Best-to-average visibility	50.00
Schulze and Brookshire (1983)	
Preservation value (average visibility)	79.32–115.68

study, which also used a bidding-game approach, for the Four Corners region (Randall, Ives, and Eastman 1974). These values are also shown in Table 11.7. The results are surprisingly similar, given the different goods valued in the surveys.

The premise of the study by Schulze and Brookshire (1983) was to compare the benefits of visibility with the costs of pollution control measures, much as we discussed at the beginning of the chapter. Their study surveyed over 600 households. Respondents were shown pictures of the Grand Canyon and were asked their *WTP* (also in the form of higher electric bills) to preserve the view shown. The authors used a survey design that asked respondents to check off their maximum *WTP*, without specifying an initial bid amount as with the Rowe study. The authors argued that this approach avoided the starting-point bias found in the Rowe study.

The results of the study indicated that individuals would be willing to pay between $3.72 and $5.14 per month to preserve the view they were shown. *WTP* increased to between $6.61 and $9.64 per month when visibility protection was expanded to include the three national parks in the area (Grand Canyon, Mesa Verde, and Zion). (Annual values are shown in Table 11.7.) By extrapolating to the entire U.S. population, the authors concluded that the total value of visibility preservation was $3.5 billion each year for the Grand Canyon alone and $6.2 billion each year for the three parks combined. The authors also estimated present-value benefits associated with improved visibility, corresponding to the anticipated 30-year lifetimes of the coal-fired power plants that are major contributors to air pollution in the region. These present values ranged between $70 and $130 billion, depending on the discount rate used.[25]

Conclusions   CVM is being used more often to value environmental amenities that are difficult to observe in the marketplace. Whether or not CVM is a reasonable approach, and the extent to which the potential biases in CVM studies are significant, is still debated. The report by Arrow and colleagues (1993) is pessimistic about the CVM approach. Cummings, Brookshire, and Schulze (1986) and Mitchell and Carson (1989) are more positive. Carson and colleagues (1995) tested some of the suggestions raised by Arrow using the data from the Exxon *Valdez* study and found no difference in the results. Knetsch (1990, 1994) has raised numerous critical issues about CVM, most notably the large disparity between *WTP* and *WTA* estimates in experiments. Knetsch has also questioned the conventional wisdom of linking *WTP*- or *WTA*-based values to the assignment of property rights. Instead, he advocates a determination of the "normal" or "prevailing" environmental state as the correct determinant.

The results of CVM studies, like the results of anything else, will probably be challenged by the parties for whom the results portend economic losses. For example, utilities facing billions of dollars' worth of expenditures for additional scrubbers because their coal-fired power plants' pollution is reducing views at the Grand

---

[25]We take up the issue of appropriate discount rates for environmental goods in Chapter 13.

Canyon might be tempted to challenge the results of CVM studies concluding that improved visibility is valued more highly than the cost of the scrubbers. Despite the potential (and real) difficulties with CVM, we believe that it remains a useful tool. We are stronger in our belief that CVM will continue to be used to value environmental amenities. As such, policymakers should understand both the benefits and the potential drawbacks of the approach.

Travel Cost Methods

Here we present a third technique used to estimate the value of environmental amenities, the *travel cost method* (TCM). This method is often used to estimate the value of public recreation sites, which usually have a zero or nominal admission price. The travel cost method is based on three observations. First, the cost of using a recreation site is more than the admission price. It includes the monetary and time costs of traveling to the site and may include other costs. Second, people who live different distances from a recreation site face different costs for using the site. Third, if the value that people place on a site does not vary systematically with distance, travel costs can be used as a proxy for price in deriving a demand curve for the recreation site.

The How-To's of Travel Cost Models   We can begin to develop the theory behind travel cost models by examining the relationship between distance from a recreation site and number of visits for a single individual. Suppose that we want to know the value that individuals place on trips to a pristine beach that lies within Acadia National Park, off the coast of Maine. An individual taking a day trip to this beach will incur several costs. The monetary costs of the trip will include gasoline, food, wear-and-tear, and the admission price to the park. A less obvious type of cost is the *opportunity cost of time*. Time spent at the beach and traveling to and from the beach could have been spent in other ways. It could have been spent in other leisure activities; it could have been spent studying or writing; it could have been spent working. The value of the time used for the trip toward its next best use— that is, the opportunity cost of time—is part of the cost of spending the day at the beach. In many cases, it will be the largest component of total cost.

Both the direct monetary costs of a day at the beach and the opportunity cost of time depend on the distance, and therefore time, to get to the beach. An example of this is shown in Table 11.8, which shows five types of costs associated with a day at the beach for people living three different distances from the beach. Expenditures on gasoline are proportional to distance. In the example, we have assumed that a car gets 25 miles per gallon and gasoline costs $1.30 per gallon. Little or none of the wear on the car is a current expense, but it is a current cost. Driving an additional mile reduces the value of the car because it reduces the remaining life of the car. It may also increase future maintenance expenses or shorten the time until they are incurred. We have assumed that this cost is proportional to distance at 10 cents per mile. The cost of parking at the beach is independent of the distance traveled to get there. We have assumed that parking costs are a constant $5

TABLE 11.8 OPPORTUNITY COSTS OF VISITING THE BEACH AT ACADIA NATIONAL PARK (IN DOLLARS)

Expense Item		Distance from Home to Beach		
		10 Miles	50 Miles	100 Miles
Gasoline		1.04	5.20	10.40
Wear on car		2.00	10.00	20.00
Parking		5.00	5.00	5.00
Time at beach (hours)	8	8	8	
@ $10 per hour		80.00	80.00	80.00
Travel time (hours)	1	$2\frac{2}{3}$	$4\frac{1}{3}$	
@ $10 per hour		10.00	26.67	43.33
TOTAL		98.04	126.87	158.73

per day. We have assumed a value of time of $10 per hour. We have also assumed that in each case, eight hours are spent at the beach. Travel time may or may not be proportional to distance. Suppose that the last 10 miles to the beach are on a narrow road full of other beachgoers and that the average speed for this 10-mile stretch is 20 miles per hour. If the rest of the trip is on interstate highways with an average speed of 60 miles per hour, round-trip travel time is an hour plus two minutes for every mile over 10.

Suppose that a typical individual living 50 miles from the beach would visit it ten times during the summer if the cost were $100 (point A, in Figure 11.4), six times if the cost were $125 (point B), twice if the cost were $150 (point C), and not at all if the cost were $162.50 or higher (point D). These values trace out four

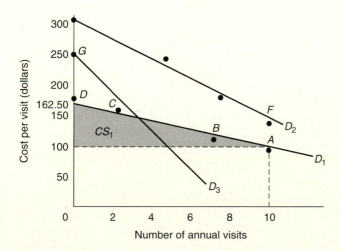

Figure 11.4 Plot of Annual Visits and Costs to the Beach for Three Different Consumers

points on a demand curve, D_1, which is plotted in the figure. Next suppose that we estimated similar demand curves for two other typical individuals living 10 and 100 miles from the beach. These are labeled D_2 and D_3. If the actual cost to visit the beach were greater than $162.50, individual 1 would not visit the beach at all and would derive zero consumers' surplus from *using* the beach. (Individual 1 may still derive a nonuse value from knowing that the beach exists.) If the actual price of a visit were only $100, however, individual 1 would visit the beach ten times per year and derive consumers' surplus from using the beach equal to the area below the demand curve D_1 and above the horizontal line at $100. With the linear demand curve shown, this individual's consumer surplus would be $312.50.[26] By contrast, if the actual cost were $150, individual 1's consumers' surplus would be only $12.50. These estimates of consumers' surplus apply only to individual 1. From a policy perspective, however, we will be more interested in the overall market demand for using the beach and the overall estimate of consumers' surplus.

Ignoring any nonuse values, the value of the recreation site is the sum of the consumers' surplus for *all* relevant users. If users differ only in the distance they travel to the site, this is fairly straightforward. The consumers' surplus for a visitor coming from a given distance is multiplied by the number of visitors who travel that same distance. This is done for all distances, and then these products are summed. For example, if there are 1,000 people facing a $100 cost for using the beach and 10,000 people facing a $150 cost for using the beach, the total use value of the beach is

$$1,000 \times \$312.50 + 10,000 \times \$12.50 = \$312,500 + \$125,000 = \$437,500$$

In this case, most of the value derives from the relatively high consumers' surplus of the relatively few people living close to the beach, but that is not always so. If the population facing a cost of $150 for using the beach were 100,000, most of the value of the beach would derive from the large number of users who each received relatively small consumers' surplus from it.

In reality, we cannot assume that everyone has the same preferences. In Figure 11.4, for example, the consumers' surplus estimates associated with individuals 2 and 3 will be different from that of individual 1 because demand curves D_2 and D_3 are different from D_1. Fortunately, this is not a problem in general.

A typical empirical procedure is to estimate average, or per capita, consumers' surplus as a function of distance and then multiply that value by the populations living at various distances from the recreation site. The fact that different individuals living the same distance from the site have different preferences does not affect the procedure. However, the TCM depends *crucially* on the assumption that the distribution of preferences among the populations at different distances from the site is the same. In other words, the TCM attributes differences in numbers of trips to a site *only* to differences in the cost of visiting the site and not to differences in the preferences of different individuals. This assumption is valid only if

---

[26](10 × $62.50)/2 equals the area of the shaded triangle.

other attributes of populations facing different travel costs either are constant or are controlled for. Differences in observable variables, such as income, can be controlled for by including them in the regression equation estimating the relationship between travel cost and visits. However, systematic differences in unobservable variables, such as preferences, can lead to inaccurate and unreliable results. The best way of overcoming this problem is to include observable variables (such as occupation and whether the person lives in an urban, suburban, or rural area) that are likely to be highly correlated with differences in preferences.

If estimation biases are not overcome, the value of travel cost studies for policy purposes will be limited. For example, suppose that in response to a TCM study that derived an overall value of $20 million for beach visits, federal policymakers decided that it was not worth expanding Acadia National Park to encompass another 1,000 acres of rocky beach because the cost of purchasing the land would be over $50 million. If the study significantly underestimated use value (not to mention nonuse value), a beneficial environmental improvement would not be undertaken.

Estimation Techniques   Like CVM studies, data for TCM studies are always derived from some type of survey. For example, a low-budget but not particularly reliable study can be based on counting license plates at a park gate or in a parking lot. Accurate and reliable results require more extensive surveys. As with any survey, it is important to design and administer the survey to avoid sampling bias and nonresponse bias and to test the data for evidence of such biases. And like all regression analyses, it is important to minimize the possibility of bias from omitting explanatory variables or other types of misspecification. To summarize, the data needed for a good travel cost study are data on travel cost and travel time to the site in question, data characteristics of individuals visiting the site, data on attributes of recreational facilities themselves, and data on substitutes for the site.

Data on travel costs and travel time to a site should include the actual transportation costs to the site, plus the opportunity cost of the round-trip travel time. Data on actual transportation costs is straightforward to obtain and verify. We can easily measure travel distance, gasoline consumption, hotel and meal expenses, and the like. In some cases, it is important to know whether the site was the ultimate destination or a stop along the way on a longer trip. In the latter case, it is necessary to use some judgment in allocating part of the cost of the trip to this site or to exclude such respondents from the analysis.

Obtaining data on the opportunity cost of time may be more problematic. Unfortunately, these data often are the most crucial to a TCM study. Without inclusion of the opportunity cost of time, the demand curves shown in Figure 11.4 will shift downward and be less steep. For example, if we ignored individual 1's opportunity cost in terms of forgone earnings, point A in Figure 11.4 would reflect ten annual visits at a cost of $20 per visit. The higher an individual's opportunity cost of time, the greater the downward shift. All other things being equal, individuals with the highest opportunity costs of time are least likely to visit. Omission of opportunity costs will tend to shift down points like B and F more than points like

G or D. Thus it will be important to have accurate estimates of the opportunity costs of time for different individuals.

In the example in Table 11.8, we assumed that an individual's opportunity cost of time equaled his forgone wage earnings. Unfortunately, in empirical studies, this is not always true. First, wage income received will be less than wages earned because of income taxes. If wages are taxed at 20 percent, for example, an individual whose wage rate is $10 per hour will have an after-tax income of $8 per hour. Second, there may be costs associated with working (e.g., stress) that are not incurred while traveling. Third, individuals may not have been able to work even if they were not traveling or may have been able to work while traveling. (Many people work on airplanes, for example.) In a review of many TCM studies, Cesario (1976) concluded that the value of time while traveling was between 25 and 50 percent of the wage rate. As a result, travel costs to a site would equal transportation costs plus perhaps one-third of the forgone wage income.[27]

Another empirical TCM study issue is the time actually spent at a recreation site. Different individuals spend different amounts of time at a site. For example, even though they may have a higher overall demand for recreation, higher-income individuals may spend less time at a site than lower-income individuals because of the former's higher opportunity cost of time. In addition, individuals who travel farther to a given recreation site may stay longer than individuals who live in close proximity. Ignoring these effects may bias the estimated demand curves for site visits and therefore the estimates of overall consumers' surplus. Unfortunately, it is not clear how important inclusion of site visitation time is to the actual estimation of demand curves. Desvouges, Smith, and McGivney (1983), for example, looked at 23 travel studies and found that the slopes of the demand curves were not affected significantly when time spent at the site was omitted. Nevertheless, such data should probably be incorporated into TCM studies when available.

The relationship between travel time and time spent at a given site can be important in defining the good to be valued. Is the good the number of trips to the site or the days spent at the site? If it is trips, then trips with different lengths of stay will have different values. If it is days actually spent at the site regardless of travel time, then stays of different length will have different travel costs per day.

Another issue concerns the probability that an individual will be sampled. That probability will be proportional to the number of days spent at the site. Individuals who make only a few day trips to a site are less likely to be pestered by nosy economists than individuals who stay for weeks at a time. A study based on the number of trips taken to a site that ignores length of stay or a study based on the number of days spent at a site that ignores the number of trips will produce biased results. This is one reason that any TCM study should account for *both* trips and length of stay. Whether policymakers are interested in the total value of a site or the relationship between value and site or visitor attributes, total value will equal value per

---

[27]This assumption was tested by Desvouges, Smith, and McGivney (1983), who found that there was more support for using an actual wage rate than one-third of the wage rate, although their results were not conclusive.

day at the site times the number of visitor days, which is the average stay times the number of trips. Thus, policymakers will ultimately be interested in the number of visits, the length of stays, and how both vary with site and visitors' attributes.

Data on characteristics of the individuals visiting sites ordinarily include income because the demand for recreation generally increases with income. Other data often included in empirical studies are the age of the individual and the level of education attainment. The significance of these variables usually depends on the specific site involved. The Desvouges, Smith, and McGivney (1983) study found that although the sign of the income coefficient was correct (i.e., *WTP* increased as income increased), the value of the coefficient was often not statistically significant (i.e., different from zero).

Household characteristic data also can be used as proxies for wage rates and therefore opportunity costs of time. Desvouges and colleagues (1983) used data on age, educational attainment, gender, and other demographic details, to develop a *hedonic wage rate equation* that could be used to predict wage rates of site visitors, which could then be used in developing the subsequent demand curve estimates.

A Two-Stage Procedure†   The characteristics of recreational facilities can be incorporated in numerous ways. Data may include such items as water quality, miles of shoreline available, miles of hiking trails, and total land area of the facility. Because many site characteristics are fixed, estimating the effects of changing site characteristics often requires using a *two-stage* procedure (Freeman 1979). In the first stage, the number of visits made is estimated as a function of individual or household characteristics, especially individual or household travel costs to the site. Thus for each site i, we have

$$V_{ki} = \beta_{0i} + \beta_{1i}TC_{ki} + \sum \beta_{mi}CHR_{km} \tag{11.3}$$

where V_{ki} is the number of visits to site i made by respondent k, TC_{ki} is the total travel cost to site i for respondent k, and CHR_{km} is a vector of m characteristics of respondent k (e.g., income, age).

Regressions are run on different sites to obtain values for the coefficients β_{0i}, β_{1i}, β_{2i}, . . . , β_{mi} for each site. In the second stage, the estimated values for β_{ji} are regressed against the different site characteristics to assess the latter's impact on the former. Thus in the second stage, we estimate

$$\beta_j = \sum_{w=1}^{M} \gamma_w CHR_w \tag{11.4}$$

where CHR_w is the vector of M site characteristics, $w = 1, M$.

Freeman's (1979) study, for example, found that only improved water quality at a site was a significant explanatory variable. This does not mean that TCMs of all facilities should ignore other site characteristics. Indeed, the individual nature of many recreation sites warrants a careful examination of site characteristics and their impacts, especially if environmental policies under consideration are aimed at those characteristics. A TCM study of visits to the Grand Canyon, for example, would probably be more concerned with air quality and visibility above the canyon than with water quality in the Colorado River below.

The Problem of Nonvisitors   Throughout this discussion of estimation techniques, one question you might have asked yourself concerns the value to people *not* observed to visit the beach at Acadia. The TCM assumes that nonvisitors place no value on the site. This raises two important issues. First, is it appropriate to assume that nonvisitors value the beach at zero? Second, does *not* accounting for nonvisitors affect the estimated values of visitors? Nonvisitors may have option values if they believe that they may wish to visit the beach in the future or existence values if they do not intend to visit but value knowing that the beach exists.

The importance of option and existence values on the total value of an environmental good or an improvement in environmental quality will depend on the type of good to be valued. For example, a TCM study by Smith and Desvouges (1986) on the value of water quality improvements in five counties in Pennsylvania showed a mean value of about $25 per household to improve water quality from its being merely usable by boats to its being usable by fishermen. Using a CVM approach, however, Carson and Mitchell (1988) determined an average value for the same improvement in water quality to be about $80 per household (in 1983 dollars). Clearly, in situations such as this, nonuse values are important. Thus TCM studies may need to be incorporated with other estimation techniques, as Randall (1994) argues.[28]

It also turns out that omitting nonvisitors can significantly affect regression estimates of models such as that in Equation 11.3. Without going into too much detail, which requires an understanding of *censored regression techniques*,[29] imagine that we have developed a set of costs per visit and visits to Yellowstone Park, as shown in Figure 11.5. Estimation of the demand for visits at the beach ignoring nonvisitors yields the demand curve *D*. Nonvisitors, for whom the cost of visiting is sufficiently high, will be clustered on the *y*-axis. Including these nonvisitors when estimating the demand for visits will yield the new demand curve *D'*. The overall value of beach visits or of improvements to the beach, measured using consumer surplus, will differ for *D* and *D'*.

Example of an Empirical Study   Duffield (1984) represents a "typical" TCM study. Duffield developed a TCM to estimate the recreational value associated with visiting Kootenai Falls, the site of a proposed hydroelectric facility in northwestern Montana. Using data collected in the summer of 1981, he developed regression equations for the value associated with a visit. Following Equation 11.3, the functional form he used was

$$\ln V_i = \beta_0 + \beta_1 D_i + \beta_2 S_i + \beta_3 Y_i \qquad (11.5)$$

---

[28]Randall (1994) goes further in his criticism of TCM. He asserts that TCM "cannot serve as a standalone technique for estimating recreation benefits" (p. 88). See his article for a complete discussion.
[29]For a thorough discussion, see Maddala (1983).

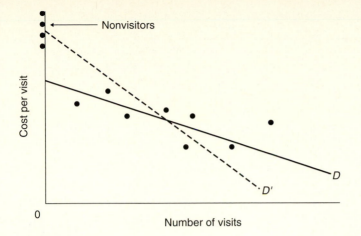

Figure 11.5   Bias in Demand Estimation from Omission of Nonvisitors

where V_i = per capita visits from travel zone i
  D_i = distance to the site from zone i
  Y_i = mean income for zone i
  S_i = the substitute measure (defined as either existence or relative dis-
    tance to substitute)
  β_i = parameters to be estimated

Unlike Equation 11.3, however, Duffield estimated visits per capita as a function of distance traveled rather than travel cost. Thus he needed to convert distance driven into a dollar estimate. He did this by using estimates of the value of time and the unit costs of travel of the respondents. In this way, Duffield was able to derive an estimate of the consumers' surplus associated with visiting Kootenai Falls for subgroups of respondents for whom the falls were their main destination and those for whom the falls were one of many destinations.[30] The total values depended on the exact empirical specification and ranged between $243,000 and $420,000 (in 1981 dollars). These results are shown in Table 11.9.

Duffield (1984) also developed CVM estimates for the value of the falls to compare the two methodologies. These also are shown in Table 11.9. He used several different payment vehicles, including entrance fees and higher electric utility bills, as well as estimated values for willingness to drive (*WTD*). Last, he developed an estimate based on willingness to accept compensation for loss of use of the falls. The *WTD* estimate provides the most direct comparison with the travel cost estimates and is relatively similar. The *WTP* estimates for higher utility bills, as well as the compensation estimate, may include indirect (nonuse) values and so could be

[30]Duffield's derivation of aggregate consumers' surplus, which is somewhat technical, is shown in the appendix to this chapter.

TABLE 11.9   ESTIMATES OF THE ANNUAL RECREATION-RELATED VALUE OF KOOTENAI FALLS

Estimation Method	Travel Cost Estimates of Total Value (1981 dollars)	
	Specification 1	Specification 2
By Demand Subgroup		
Main-destination subgroup	80,200	259,100
Multiple destination subgroup	163,100	160,800
Total	243,300	419,900
By Direct Survey Methods		
Willingness to pay entrance fees	90,600	
Willingness to pay utility bills	1,001,800	
Willingness to drive	536,000	
Willingness to accept compensation	699,500	

Source: Adapted from Duffield (1984).

expected to exceed the direct travel cost and *WTD* estimates. Duffield notes that the discrepancy between the travel cost estimate and the estimate of entrance fee *WTP* may have arisen because of individuals' expectations about actual entrance fees at similar sites.

Conclusions   The results obtained from TCMs have generally been positive. However, there are some disadvantages to the technique. First, it requires a large amount of data to estimate regressions accurately of the form in Equations 11.3 and 11.4. Collecting that much data is both time-consuming and expensive, two drawbacks with which policymakers will not often want to be saddled. Second, the methodology also assumes that travel to a given site is for the sole purpose of visiting that site. There is no way that the methodology can allocate costs between multipurpose trips other than in an arbitrary manner. Despite these limitations, the methodology should be considered when adequate data are available, especially in situation where many users visit a site solely for recreational purposes.

NONMONETARY VALUATION TECHNIQUES

So far, we have discussed methodologies that allow us to place a monetary value directly on environmental costs and benefits. In some cases, however, it may be impossible to do this. For example, individuals may be unaware of the corrosive effects on metals associated with exposure to certain pollutants. If so, asking them to value reductions in exposure levels to these corrosives may be problematic. In such cases, a direct approach will not reveal the "true" value that individuals or societies place on reductions in exposure levels (Pearce and Markandya 1989).

Nonmonetary valuation methods, sometimes called *indirect* valuation methods, generally use measures of *dose* and *response*. Examples include the effects of air pollution on human health, agricultural production, or corrosion of buildings. In principle, such *dose-response* functions can always be measured, although the degree of precision of the measurement may be questioned. In some (but not all) cases, nonmonetary valuation can form the basis for monetary valuation. If we can measure the effects of air pollution on human health and can estimate the values that individuals place on reducing risks to their health, we can value reductions in air pollution directly.[31]

Estimating Dose-Response Functions†

The basic procedure begins with estimation of the dose-response function. Physical damages D are related to the level of the suspected pollutants P_i, as well as any other related variables. Thus, we estimate a regression model of the form

$$D = \beta_0 + \beta_1 P_1 + \beta_2 P_2 + \beta_3 P_3 \tag{11.6}$$

The coefficients β_1, β_2, and β_3 measure the change in damage because of a change in the level of the pollutants.[32] Once the dose-response function is estimated, either damages can be expressed in physical terms or, in some cases, monetary values may be assigned, such as with crop losses.

Empirical Examples

A great deal of empirical dose-response function estimation has been done in the area of human health. For example, Lave and Seskin (1977) estimated the effects of air pollution on mortality rates. They found that statistically significant relationships existed between sulfate and particulate concentrations and mortality. According to their study, a 1 percent reduction in these pollutants would reduce mortality by 0.12 percent. Applying estimates of projected reductions in the levels of these two pollutants, one could calculate the overall expected reduction in mortality. By improving on the data, Lipfert (1984) was able to reexamine the Lave and Seskin analysis. He found that the coefficient on sulfate was reduced to the point where it was no longer statistically significant, meaning that reductions in sulfate concentrations would not reduce mortality.

In addition to studies on pollution levels and mortality, there have also been studies relating pollution levels to *morbidity,* which refers to nonfatal illnesses. One major study was performed by Ostro (1983, 1987). Ostro used data from a 1976 health interview survey of 50,000 households in the United States. These health data were matched with data on pollution levels of sulfur and particulates and other information (income, race, age level, etc.) in the metropolitan areas that the survey covered. Ostro measured morbidity in two separate ways: the number of days absent from work, or "work loss days" (WLD), and number of days affected by ill

---

[31]We discuss the values that individuals place on their lives and their health in Chapter 12.

[32]There may also be cross-effects. In other words, the damage caused by pollutant X may depend on the level of pollutant Y, and so on. If so, these effects will also need to be incorporated into the regression.

health, which he called "restricted activity days" (RAD). Unlike the WLD measure, RAD refers to both workers and nonworkers.

With these data, Ostro estimated dose-response regressions similar to those in Equation 11.6 for different groups of individuals. He developed regression estimates for all individuals, and for a variety of subgroups, including nonsmokers and males. Ostro found no statistically significant relationship between mean sulfur levels and morbidity.

A COMPARISON OF THE METHODOLOGIES

Now that we have discussed the basic methodologies and presented some empirical examples of each, we need to address three major concerns of environmental policymakers. First, policymakers will want to know which of these methodologies, if any, is most appropriate to the specific environmental attributes to be measured. Second, they will want to know which of the methodologies will yield the most accurate measure of the value of those environmental attributes. Third, they will want to employ the most cost-effective methodology. In other words, they will want accurate and reliable results that don't cost too much to obtain.

All of the methodologies presented have some drawbacks. None is capable of determining a uniquely correct answer. However, the fact that all of these techniques will be imperfect in some ways does not mean that all attempts at measurement should be abandoned. Instead, policymakers will have to apply imperfect measures as best they can. (We take up the issue of using imperfect information in Chapter 14.)

Despite many studies that have compared the different methodologies, disagreement remains as to the most appropriate technique in different situations. Clearly, there will be cases where one or more methodologies may be inappropriate. It would be difficult, for example, to use the HPA for a study on the value of visibility at the Grand Canyon. Similarly, TCM studies are appropriate for determining user values of recreational facilities but, by definition, say nothing about nonuser values. CVM studies are most appropriate where well-defined markets do not exist. It would be silly to design a CVM study to determine the value of cornflakes at the store since there is a well-functioning market that reveals the price easily.

Based on the existing literature (Smith 1993a; Cropper and Oates 1992; Cummings, Brookshire, and Schulze 1986), it appears that CVM is a reasonable, though potentially biased, methodology. Much progress has been made in designing CVM studies that can avoid the various biases we have discussed, as is evidenced by the Exxon *Valdez* study. Nevertheless, the debate is far from settled (Portney 1994; Hanemann 1994; Diamond and Hausman 1994; Knetsch 1994; Arrow et al. 1993). CVM studies must be approached with care, as the form of the questioning has been shown to induce biases in responses. CVM does have the benefit of being the only methodology able to elicit nonuse values, which for many environmental goods will be of paramount importance. Comparisons of user values derived using CVM have a mixed record as to consistency with values derived through TCM and HPA. Of course, though consistency among methodologies does not guarantee accuracy, it is comforting to know that the different methodologies can yield similar results.

One potential drawback with CVM studies, which is rarely mentioned but is critical in policy applications, is their cost. Undertaking large surveys can be a time-consuming and expensive process. A quick and inexpensive survey may not yield robust estimates, even if it is designed carefully. Hence, if CVM is to be used, it is imperative that sufficient resources be devoted to ensure reliable results. This same criticism can apply to TCM, which also requires survey data. An advantage of HPA is that much of the data used can be gleaned from market transactions, which will usually be more readily available.

Finally, the use of market prices to estimate damages can be easily misinterpreted. Changes in the value of outputs will be valid measures only for marginal changes in competitive markets. Otherwise, such changes must examine changes in producers' and consumers' surplus, not only in the directly affected market but in indirect markets as well. Hence, this measure should be approached with great care.

CHAPTER SUMMARY

In this chapter, we have presented a variety of empirical techniques to estimate environmental benefits and costs. We identified four major techniques for the direct evaluation of environmental benefits and costs: hedonic price models, contingent valuation studies, travel cost studies, and direct use of market prices and costs. All of these techniques have advantages and disadvantages in terms of ease of use, accuracy, and cost. We also looked at indirect valuation techniques, specifically the use of dose-response relationships, that can be used as the basis for further direct valuations or as stand-alone results.

Whatever methodologies are adopted to measure environmental benefits and costs, there may be significant implementation issues when such estimates are used as the basis for environmental policy decisions. What this implies is that measuring environmental impacts accurately, especially measuring them in monetary terms, must be done with great care and will not come cheap.

CHAPTER REVIEW

Economic Concepts and Tools

- Use values are those associated with actual consumption of an environmental asset.
- Nonuse values, sometimes called passive-use values, arise because people who do not intend ever to consume environmental assets themselves either want those assets to be available for others to use or derive satisfaction from knowing that the assets exist. This latter valuation is called an existence value.
- Direct valuation techniques are those that directly determine values of environmental assets. Three major valuation techniques are generally used: the hedonic pricing method, the travel cost method, and the contingent valuation method.

- The hedonic pricing method is designed to infer values of nonmarket attributes from market prices of goods and services. Using this method, differences in the prices of market goods can be attributed to differences in the levels of nonmarket attributes.

- Use of the hedonic pricing method requires that the individual attributes of a good can be identified. A hedonic pricing study requires a sample of sales of the market good where the observations differ in the amount of nonmarket attributes. Regression techniques are then used to estimate the contribution (positive or negative) of a unit of the nonmarket attribute to the overall value of the market good. This provides a measure of the marginal *WTP* for the unpriced attribute.

- The travel cost method is designed to infer values of nonmarket assets, primarily recreational ones, from the behavior of individuals who use those assets. The travel cost method is used less frequently now than it has been in the past.

- The travel cost method is based on three assumptions. First, the cost of using a recreation site is more than the admission price. It includes the monetary and the time costs of traveling to the site and may include other costs. Second, people who live different distances from a recreation site face different costs for using the site. Third, if the value that people place on a site does not vary systematically with distance, travel costs can be used as a proxy for price in deriving a demand curve for the recreation site. The data for a travel cost study are collected through surveys of potential visitors, asking whether they visit a site, or through surveys of visitors at the site itself. The survey data are used to econometrically estimate a market demand curve, with the number of visits per capita a function of the distance or travel cost. The per capita consumers' surplus at each distance from the site is weighted by the population living that distance from the site to yield an aggregate consumers' surplus for the site. The overall consumers' surplus will depend on the assumed value of travel time, which remains an area of controversy.

- The contingent valuation method estimates the value of nonmarket goods by using surveys that directly ask the value of the good or that ask respondents to make choices designed to reveal the value of the good. Open-ended CVM surveys ask respondents to tell the maximum amount they would pay to acquire a nonmarket good, or avoid a bad. Closed-ended or referendum CVM surveys ask respondents to say yes or no to receiving a good or avoiding a bad and paying a specific amount. This amount is varied across different surveys and individuals to get more robust results.

- A CVM study requires three items. First, a CVM study must carefully describe the environmental commodity to be valued. Second, it requires a method by which payment (usually hypothetical but in some cases real) is to be made. Third, the study must have a method of converting payments to *WTP* or *WTA* values.

- The CVM method remains controversial, for several reasons. First, writing good survey questions is difficult because the CVM estimates derived are subject to numerous biases that can arise because of poor survey design. There is also controversy about the appropriateness of *WTP* or *WTA* measures. Much of this controversy stems from conflict over the identification of the "normal" state.

Economists do not agree whether CVM can provide reliable measures of the value of nonmarket goods. Despite this, CVM estimates continue to be used widely.

Policy Issues

- Measurement of environmental costs and benefits, whether in total or to various parties, will often be a consideration in environmental policy decisions. There will always be concerns about the relevant populations and the uncertainty of statistical estimates.
- All of the methodologies presented have some drawbacks. None is capable of determining a uniquely correct answer. However, the fact that all of these techniques will be in some way imperfect does not mean that all attempts at measurement should be abandoned. Instead, policymakers will have to apply imperfect measures as best they can and decide whether that information will nevertheless help them make better decisions than in the absence of any information.
- The use of market prices to estimate damages can be easily misinterpreted. Changes in the value of outputs will be valid measures only for marginal changes in competitive markets.
- Environmental policymakers will likely have three major concerns about measuring nonmarket environmental values. First, not all techniques can be used to measure all types of values. Policymakers will want to know which methodology, if any, is most appropriate to the specific environmental good to be measured. Second, some techniques can produce biased estimates of environmental values. This is true particularly when researchers must rely on data collected for other purposes or when the environmental good in question is difficult to define or describe precisely. Third, the accuracy of estimates will depend on the sample size of the data collected and the valuation technique used. Because gathering data will almost always be expensive, policymakers will want to employ the methodology that is the most cost-effective while still providing an acceptable level of precision.

DISCUSSION QUESTIONS

1. How would you determine the value of living in an area of the country that was less prone to earthquakes than, say, San Francisco?
2. How can the attributes of environmental "goods" be identified? For example, what are the attributes of the Grand Canyon? How can attributes be differentiated from one another?
3. "The value of fishing for recreational purposes should be no more than the commercial value of the fish." Comment.
4. What do you believe to be a suitable trade-off between the accuracy of a valuation study and its cost? How could such a trade-off be determined?
5. Why do you think the Exxon *Valdez* researchers used only the number of English-speaking households as their population, rather than including all U.S. households?

6. Find examples of each type of monetary valuation methodology in the literature and critique them. How do different researchers cope with the weaknesses of the different techniques?

REFERENCES

Arrow, K., R. Solow, P. Portney, E. Leamer, R. Radner, and H. Schuman. 1993. *Report of the NOAA Panel on Contingent Valuation.* Washington, D.C.: National Oceanic and Atmospheric Administration.

Bishop. R., T. Heberlein, and M. Kealy. 1983. "Hypothetical Bias in Contingent Valuation: Results from a Simulated Market." *Natural Resources Journal* 23(3): 619–633.

Boyle, K., and R. Bishop. 1987. "Valuing Wildlife in Benefit-Cost Analysis: A Case Study Involving Endangered Species." *Water Resources Research* 23: 943–950.

Brookshire, D., M. Thayer, W. Schulze, and R. d'Arge. 1982. "The Valuation of Public Goods: A Comparison of Survey and Hedonic Approaches." *American Economic Review* 72(1): 165–177.

Carson, R., N. Meade, and V. Smith. 1993. "Contingent Valuation and Passive Use Values: Introducing the Issues." *Choices* 8(2): 5–8.

Carson, R., and R. Mitchell. 1988. "The Value of Clean Water: The Public's Willingness to Pay for Boatable, Fishable, and Swimmable Quality Water." Discussion Paper No. 88-13, University of San Diego.

Carson, R., R. Mitchell, W. Hanemann, R. Kopp, S. Presser, and P. Ruud. 1992. *A Contingent Valuation Study of Lost Passive Use Values Resulting from the Exxon* Valdez *Oil Spill.* Report to the attorney general of the state of Alaska. La Jolla, Calif.: Natural Resource Damage Assessment, Inc.

Carson, R., W. Hanemann, R. Kopp, J. Krosnick, R. Mitchell, S. Presser, P. Ruud, and V. Smith. 1995. "Referendum Design and Contingent Valuation: The NOAA Panel's No-Vote Recommendation." Discussion Paper No. 96-05. Washington, D.C.: Resources for the Future.

Castle, E., R. Berrens, and R. Adams. 1994. "Natural Resource Damage Assessment: Speculations About a Missing Perspective." *Land Economics* 70(3): 378–385.

Cesario, F. 1976. "Value of Time and Recreation Benefit Studies." *Land Economics* 52(1): 32–41.

Cropper, M., and W. Oates. 1992. "Environmental Economics: A Survey." *Journal of Economic Literature* 30(3): 675–740.

Cummings, R., D. Brookshire, and W. Schulze (eds.) 1986. *Valuing Environmental Goods: An Assessment of the Contingent Valuation Method.* Lanham, Md.: Rowman & Littlefield.

Daubert, J., and R. Young. 1981. "Recreational Demands for Maintaining Instream Flows: A Contingent Valuation Approach." *American Journal of Agricultural Economics* 63: 666–676.

Desvouges, W., A. Gable, R. Dunford, and S. Hudson. 1993. "Contingent Valuation: The Wrong Tool to Measure Passive Use Values." *Choices* 8(2): 9–11.

Desvouges, W., V. Smith, and M. McGivney. 1983. *A Comparison of Alternative Approaches for Estimating Recreation and Related Benefits of Water Quality Improvements.* Office of Policy Analysis Report No. EPA-230-05-83-001. Washington, D.C.: U.S. Environmental Protection Agency.

Diamond, P., and J. Hausman. 1994. "Contingent Valuation: Is Some Number Better than No Number?" *Journal of Economic Perspectives* 8(4): 45–64.

Duffield, J. 1984. "Travel Cost and Contingent Valuation." In *Advances in Applied Microeconomics*, ed. V. Smith Greenwich, Conn.: JAI Press.

Duffield, J., C. Neher, and T. Brown. 1992. "Recreation Benefits of Instream Flow: Application to Montana's Big Hole and Bitterroot Rivers." *Water Resources Research* 28: 2169–2181.

Freeman, A. 1979. *The Benefits of Environmental Improvement: Theory and Practice.* Baltimore: Johns Hopkins University Press.

———. 1993. *The Measurement of Environmental and Resource Values.* Washington, D.C.: Resources for the Future.

Hanemann, W. 1994. "Valuing the Environment Through Contingent Valuation." *Journal of Economic Perspectives* 8(4): 19–43.

Horvath, H., and R. Charlson. 1969. "The Direct Optical Measurement of Atmospheric Air Pollution." *Journal of the American Industrial Hygiene Association 26:* 500–509.

Knetsch, J. 1990. "Environmental Policy Implications of Disparities Between Willingness to Pay and Compensation Demanded Measures of Values." *Journal of Environmental Economics and Management* 18(2): 227–237.

———. 1994. "Asking the Right Question: The Reference Point and Measures of Welfare Change." Paper presented at the 69th annual meeting of the Western Economic Association, Vancouver, British Columbia.

Krutilla, J. 1967. "Conservation Reconsidered." *American Economic Review* 57: 777–786.

Lave, L., and E. Seskin. 1977. *Air Pollution and Human Health.* Baltimore: Johns Hopkins University Press.

Lipfert, F. 1984. "Air Pollution and Mortality: Specification Searches Using SMSA-Based Data." *Journal of Environmental Economics and Management* 11: 371–382.

Maddala, G, 1983. *Limited Dependent Variables and Qualitative Variables in Econometrics.* New York: Cambridge University Press.

Mishan, E. 1976. *Cost-Benefit Analysis.* New York: Praeger.

Mitchell, R., and R. Carson. 1989. *Using Surveys to Value Public Goods: The Contingent Valuation Method.* Washington, D.C.: Resources for the Future.

Natural Resource Damage Assessment (NRDA). 1994. *Prospective Interim Lost Use Value Due to DDT and PCB Contamination in the Southern California Bight.* Report to the National Oceanic and Atmospheric Administration, San Diego, CA.

Nelson, J. 1980. "Airports and Property Values: A Survey of Recent Evidence." *Journal of Transport Economics and Policy* XIV: 37–52.

————. 1982. "Highway Noise and Property Values: A Survey of Recent Evidence." *Journal of Transport Economics and Policy* XVI: 117–130.

Ostro, B. 1983. "The Effects of Air Pollution on Work Loss and Morbidity." *Journal of Environmental Economics and Management* 10: 371–382.

————. 1987. "Air Pollution and Morbidity Revisited: A Specification Test." *Journal of Environmental Economics and Management* 14: 87–98.

Pearce, D., and A. Markandya. 1989. *Environmental Policy Benefits: Monetary Valuation.* Paris: Organization for Economic Cooperation and Development.

Pearce, D., and R. Turner. 1990. *Economics of Natural Resources and the Environment.* Baltimore: Johns Hopkins University Press.

Portney, P. 1994. "The Contingent Valuation Debate: Why Economists Should Care." *Journal of Economic Perspectives* 8(4): 3–17.

"The Price of Imagining Arden." 1994. *Economist,* December, 1994, p. 80.

Randall, A. 1993. "Passive-Use Values and Contingent Valuation: Valid for Damage Assessment." *Choices* 8(2): 12–15.

————. 1994. "A Difficulty with the Travel Cost Method." *Land Economics* 70(1): 88–96.

Randall, A., B. Ives, and C. Eastman. 1974. "Bidding Games for Valuation of Aesthetic Environmental Improvements." *Journal of Environmental Economics and Management* 1: 132–149.

Randall, A., and J. Stoll. 1983. "Existence Value in a Total Valuation Framework." In *Managing Air Quality and Scenic Resources at National Parks and Wilderness Areas,* ed. R. Rowe and L. Chestnut. Boulder, Colo.: Westview Press.

Ridker, R. 1967. *Economic Costs of Air Pollution.* New York: Praeger.

Rosen, S. 1974. "Hedonic Prices and Implicit Markets: Product Differentiation in Pure Competition." *Journal of Political Economy* 82: 34–55.

Rowe, R., R. d'Arge, and D. Brookshire. 1980. "An Experiment on the Economic Value of Visibility." *Journal of Environmental Economics and Management* 7: 1–19.

Sassone, P., and W. Schaffer. 1978. *Cost-Benefit Analysis: A Handbook.* Orlando, Fla.: Academic Press.

Schulze, W., and D. Brookshire. 1983. "The Economic Benefits of Preserving Visibility on the National Parklands of the Southwest." *Natural Resources Journal* 23(1): 149–173.

Smith, V. 1993a. "Nonmarket Valuation of Environmental Resources." *Land Economics* 69(1): 1–26.

————. 1993b. "Welfare Effects, Omitted Variables, and the Extent of the Market." *Land Economics* 69(2): 121–131.

Smith, V., and W. Desvouges. 1986. *Measuring Water Quality Benefits.* Boston: Kluwer-Nijhoff.

Trijonis, J. 1984. *Air Quality Benefits for Los Angeles and San Francisco Based on Housing Values and Visibility.* Final Report for the California Air Resources Board, Sacramento.

Weisbrod, B. 1964. "Collective Consumption Services of Individual Consumption Goods." *Quarterly Journal of Economics* 77(3): 71–77.

APPENDIX TO CHAPTER 11

Derivation of Consumers' Surplus for the Travel Cost Model

We begin the derivation using the specification in Equation 11.5. Thus

$$\ln V_i = \beta_0 + \beta_1 D_i + \beta_2 S_i + \beta_3 Y_i \tag{11A.1}$$

Exponentiating, we have

$$V_i = \exp(\beta_0 + \beta_1 D_i + \beta_2 S_i + \beta_3 Y_i) \tag{11A.2}$$

Equation 11A.2 traces out a demand curve with annual trips per year as a function of distance. To convert that to a monetary measure, we need to convert distance traveled in miles into dollars. Travel costs for a given distance D_i will equal the direct variable travel costs (gasoline, hotels, etc.) plus the cost of time. Thus

$$T_i = \delta + \frac{\omega}{\nu} \tag{11A.3}$$

where δ = direct variable travel costs, in dollars per mile
ω = average wage rate, in dollars per hour
ν = average velocity of the trip, in miles per hour
T_i = travel cost per mile

To determine the consumers' surplus associated with a trip, we convert Equation 11A.2 into dollars. This is done by multiplying it by T_i. To get the consumers' surplus (CS), we take the area under this new demand curve by integrating with respect to distance. Thus

$$CS = \int_{D_i}^{D_{\max}} V_i(D) \, dD \tag{11A.4}$$

Thus

$$CS_i = \left(\delta + \frac{\omega}{\nu}\right) P_i \frac{e^{\beta_0}}{\beta_1} e^{\beta_2 S_i + \beta_3 Y_i} (e^{\beta_1 D_{\max}} - e^{\beta_1 D_i}) \tag{11A.5}$$

where P_i is the population of zone i. The aggregate consumers' surplus is the sum of the consumers' surplus for each travel zone. Thus

$$CS = \left(\delta + \frac{\omega}{\nu}\right) P_i \frac{e^{\beta_0}}{\beta_1} \sum_i e^{\beta_2 S_i + \beta_3 Y_i} (e^{\beta_1 D_{\max}} - e^{\beta_1 D_i}) \tag{11A.6}$$

where CS = aggregate consumers' surplus. Equation 11A.6 may at first glance appear counterintuitive, as it shows that CS increases as travel costs increase. However, note that the original travel demand function holds the value of time and the variable costs of travel constant. Thus if we observe two individuals who live in the same location and who have different travel costs making the same number of trips, the individual with the higher travel cost must have a greater consumers' surplus associated with the trip.

CHAPTER 12

MEASURING THE VALUE OF LIFE AND HEALTH

Is Life Cheap? The Case of Asbestos Regulation

In the United States, only two environmental statutes—the Federal Insecticide, Fungicide, and Rodenticide Act (FIFRA) and the Toxic Substances Control Act (TSCA)—require that the benefits and the costs of regulations be balanced in setting environmental exposure standards. In 1985, under the rules of the TSCA, the Environmental Protection Agency proposed a ban on the use of asbestos in 39 products, ranging from brake linings in cars to roof coatings to protective clothing.

There is little doubt that some forms of asbestos are human carcinogens. No doubt, you have seen pictures of school classrooms ripped asunder in order to remove asbestos-containing ceiling tiles or insulation. Animal and epidemiological studies have shown that exposure to some forms of asbestos cause cancer of the lung, the stomach, and the abdominal lining, although the latency period (the time between exposure and the actual occurrence of disease) can be many years. Under the TSCA, the EPA appeared justified in developing regulations covering asbestos exposure.

The EPA was able to develop estimates of the number of cancer cases that would be avoided for 31 of the 39 products considered for regulation. (These estimates assumed that the use of asbestos in these products would be banned in 1992 and that substitute products would all be harmless.) The EPA was also able to estimate the cost of the ban by developing estimates of lost consumers' and producers' surplus from the use of substitute products. Given estimates of the costs of the ban and the predicted number of cancer deaths avoided, dollar values per life saved could be calculated. A sampling of these values are shown in Table 12.1. Eventually, the EPA banned 27 of the 39 products examined.

An analysis by Van Houtven and Cropper (1993) showed that benefit and cost considerations alone explained 85 percent of the EPA's decisions regarding which products to ban. However, their analysis also showed that the EPA valued

TABLE 12.1 COSTS AND BENEFITS OF BANNING ASBESTOS

Product	Gross Total Loss (millions of 1989 dollars)	Cancer Cases Avoided	Cost per Cancer Case Avoided (millions of 1989 dollars)
Selected Products Banned			
Drum brake linings	13.87	136.39	0.10
Pipeline wrap	0.55	1.12	0.49
Roofing felt	4.04	0.97	4.16
Clutch facings	10.93	0.54	20.08
A/C shingles	31.66	0.41	77.01
Automatic transmission components	0.20	0.00	500.00
Products Not Banned			
Asbestos packing	0.49	0.01	42.98
High-grade electrical paper	58.79	0.51	115.12
Acetylene cylinders	0.08	0.00	2,666.67
Missile liner	1,001.67	0.32	3,168.84

Source: Van Houtven and Cropper (1993), p. 20.

a "statistical life" at almost $45 million, a figure that is generally considered high when compared to the empirical literature. (We present estimates of the statistical value of life later in this chapter.) Thus the EPA may have banned too many products containing asbestos.

The Van Houtven and Cropper (1993) study also showed that the EPA valued reductions in the higher levels of workplace exposures to asbestos far more highly than it valued reductions in the lower level of exposure to which the general population was exposed. That is, the EPA required tougher standards for individuals exposed in the workplace than for individuals exposed elsewhere. That result is not surprising because additional risks are usually valued more highly the higher the original, or baseline, level of risk. In addition, workers who die from cancer can be more easily linked to asbestos exposure than members of the general populace can. Workers' exposure may also be more "voluntary" than that of other groups, especially schoolchildren, because many workers who are exposed to asbestos are compensated for the higher risks they take in the form of higher wages. Thus the premium placed by the EPA on exposure in the workplace may have been misguided, in effect double-counting the value of the risk to workers.[1]

There are two critical policy issues in the regulation of hazardous pollutants like asbestos: what are the trade-offs between costs and benefits, and what is the critical population on which to base policy decisions? If asbestos exposure were

---

[1]Recall the discussion in Chapter 8 as to whether individuals who bear external costs should be compensated for them.

limited to schoolchildren, society might on the one hand be unwilling simply to evaluate the benefits and the costs of exposure and might instead provide children with a statutory right not to be exposed regardless of the cost. On the other hand, to the extent that asbestos was used to reduce other risks (e.g., fire hazards, brake failure), some balancing would inevitably be called for. If exposure were limited to workers who received additional compensation for the risks they faced, the balancing of regulations might be quite different.

The timing of risks and benefits is also a crucial factor. A worker exposed to asbestos might not develop lung cancer for 30 years. The avoided costs from reduced cancer deaths would need to be discounted and compared with the potential loss of more immediate benefits, such as fire protection.[2] Van Houtven and Cropper (1993) estimated that if exposure to asbestos caused cancer after only 10 years rather than at once, the $45 million figure the EPA calculated for the value of a statistical life would increase to almost $65 million, raising further issues of how future costs and benefits should be discounted.

INTRODUCTION

In Chapter 9, we summarized some of the major U.S. environmental legislation that contains policy goals other than economic efficiency. As that summary made clear, many environmental policies were enacted to protect human health and well-being, including the Clean Air Act, the Clean Water Act, and Superfund, among many others. From an economic efficiency perspective, has all of this legislation been worth the cost? Has the regulatory expense been worth the lives saved?

Some people consider even asking such questions to be reprehensible, much less providing answers to them. How, they may argue, can we "put a price tag" on lives in order to make trade-offs between risks to human life and health on the one hand and lower-priced goods and services on the other? Doesn't the U.S. Congress, as well as other regulatory bodies, have a moral duty to protect U.S. citizens and residents? The question became particularly relevant in 1995 when the Republican-controlled Congress passed legislation requiring that all new federal regulations costing more than $100 million be subjected to cost-benefit tests.

All of us want to be safe. We do not want children eating lead paint or attending school in asbestos-laced classrooms. Yet trade-offs between cost and safety exist because resources are scarce. Application of certain pesticides to agricultural crops may reduce damage done by insects and increase food supplies but may cause cancer in some consumers or farmworkers who work and harvest those crops. Which is more important? Well, when you went to the store last week, did you buy a regular head of lettuce or a more expensive "organically grown" one? Reducing air pollution emissions from power plants may reduce exposure to harmful pollutants, such as sulfur dioxide, but it will also increase the cost of generating electricity. Are you willing to pay more for the electricity you use to heat your

---

[2]Discounting is discussd in Chapter 13.

house so that the air will be cleaner? Can society strike a balance between risk and economic growth, and if so, how?

Environmental policymakers are often called on to answer such questions and make these sorts of trade-offs. Individuals make these same trade-offs every day. In many instances, individuals voluntarily choose to assume certain levels of risk, through the choice of the cars they drive, the foods they eat, and the leisure activities they pursue. Society also determines the level of other risks, as with highway safety programs. Some of these trade-offs will involve not only questions of economic efficiency but also questions of equity and rights. From a policy perspective, an individual choosing to accept a higher level of risk is quite different from a higher level of risk being involuntarily *imposed* on that individual. Observing the sacrifices that people are willing to make to protect their life and health and the risks that people are willing to take to earn rewards and measuring them in monetary terms not only makes sense but is also essential to the development of sound environmental policies.

CAN ECONOMIC CONCEPTS BE APPLIED TO LIFE AND HEALTH?

Many regulations that reduce the risks we face impose their own costs. This immediately raises the question of the "value of life," an explosive subject due to confusion as to just what the expression means. There are numerous philosophical issues associated with valuing life and health, including whether placing a monetary value on life or health ever makes sense (Viscusi 1992).

One of the main reasons that applying economic concepts to life and health is controversial is that it is often misunderstood. If you learn nothing else from this chapter, we want you to remember this one crucial idea: *economists do not place values on others' life and health; they measure the values people place on their own (and others') lives and health.*

People show the values they place on life, health, and risks in exactly the same way they show the values they place on bubble gum, opera, and cheeseburgers: through the choices they make. People constantly make choices about life and health, or at least about the risks they will face. We decide whether to step into the crosswalk or wait two seconds to be certain that an oncoming car will stop. We decide whether to walk home from a party or ride with a friend who has been drinking. We decide whether to buy a large, heavy, expensive, and dull but relatively safe late-model family sedan or a small, fast, and great-looking sports car. We decide whether to become economists or ironworkers. In all of these cases, there is a cost that must be paid to protect life and health or reduce risks. Whether it is a two-second wait at the crosswalk, a half-hour walk home from a party, or lower lifetime earnings, that cost can be converted to monetary terms in exactly the same way that other trade-offs can.

Whether we *can* value life and health is not an issue; we can. What is at issue is whether we *should* measure the values people place on life and health and use those values in developing public policies. At one extreme is the position that not only is it never appropriate to use monetary values for life and health in policy deliberations, but such values should also never be estimated. If we estimate values of life and health, we will be tempted to use them, and allowing people to become accustomed to thinking of life and health in monetary terms will corrupt their ethical judgments. At the other extreme is the position that there is nothing special about life and health and we should routinely use monetary values of life and health in formulating public policy. The latter more closely resembles the legislation passed by Congress to subject all regulations to cost-benefit analysis.

We take a stance midway between these positions. Using monetary values for life and health is appropriate in some circumstances and not in others. Whether it is appropriate depends on the issues and values involved. We believe that we can give some general guidance on the issues and values questions where monetary values for life and health can help provide answers, and we believe that we can do this without excessive judgment of the values people actually hold. We note also that courts routinely require payments for wrongful injury and death, and although it would be incorrect to regard these payments as the same as payments for commodities, they do contain an element of compensation.

The four situations we will outline here cover a range of areas where it is or is not appropriate to use monetary values for life and how the value of life should be used where its use is appropriate.

Inalienable Rights to Life

If, as in the Declaration of Independence, there is a basic, inalienable right to life, the right to harm or kill someone cannot be bought and sold or transferred in any way. That is what inalienable means. A society that holds this value has ruled out any trade-offs between deliberate harm to another human and any other good. In such a society, public decisions determining whether any specific individual will live or die should not be based on whether that person's death will have financial or psychic benefits to others.

This is not a value that has been held by all societies throughout history. In some, but not all, societies with the institution of slavery (e.g., the Roman Empire), a slave owner had the right to kill a slave. The right to kill a specific person could be bought and sold, as long as that person was a slave. In parts of pre-Christian Europe, while the right to kill someone could not be bought and sold, it generally was agreed that payment to the victim's family would completely absolve a murderer. This after-the-fact payment for a human life is the *wergeld* (literally, "man payment") mentioned in *Beowulf* and the *Nibelungenlied*. For a society with the institution of *wergeld*, some of the techniques we will discuss for estimating the value of a particular life might have been useful in determining the payment required for any given murder.

Compensation for Premature Death

Whether the right to life is inalienable or alienable, people hurt and kill each other both accidentally and deliberately. Many contemporary societies require compensation in such cases. Whether such compensation should be based on economic calculations depends on its purpose. If the purpose of the compensation is punishment or to provide an incentive for people to be careful, the value of the victim's life or health is probably not a good basis for determining the level of compensation. The responsible party's degree of responsibility and ability to pay would be better bases for punishment. The elasticity of carelessness with respect to the compensation level would be a better basis for setting compensation as a deterrent.

If the compensation truly is intended to be compensatory, to make up for the loss suffered, the value of life or health may be an appropriate basis. Compensation for accident victims who are unable to return to their jobs is often based on lost earnings. Compensation to the family of someone killed in an accident can also be based on lost earnings, as well as intangible values such as the loss of companionship. Of course, compensation for the loss of a life is not a good substitute for the emotional loss. But is the only form of compensation available.

Individual Trade-Offs Between Risk to Life and Health and Other Goods

People make choices where they voluntarily face trade-offs between risks to life and health and other goods. All other things being equal, people generally require higher wages to perform more dangerous jobs. All other things being equal, people will generally pay more for safer products. How much more people must be paid for more dangerous jobs and how much more people will pay for safer products give direct monetary measures of the value people place on risks to life and health. It is difficult to see how there can be objections to the use of values for life and health in such situations. People contemplating such choices may want to know quantitative measures of the risks they face and the value they are implicitly placing on their life or health by making different choices. However, such choices are generally not matters of public policy.

Imposing Risks on Others: The Value of a Statistical Life

The value people place on risks is often expressed in terms of the *value of a statistical life*. This is the amount that people are willing to pay to avoid a risk (or willing to accept to be exposed to a risk) times the probability of death from that risk. The expression "value of a statistical life" is somewhat misleading. It is a measure of the value we place on *small* changes in the risk to life, not the value of a particular life like that of your grandmother. Determining how Grandmother weighs the risks she faces and calculating a statistical value of life based on that behavior does not imply that she will then agree to forgo her life in exchange for the calculated amount.

The value of a statistical life can be computed by examining small changes to the amount of risk faced by random individuals. Calculating a statistical value of life is straightforward. Suppose that you are willing to accept $10 for a one-in-a-million (1×10^{-6}) chance of a fatal injury. In that case, your statistical value of life would be $10 / (1 \times 10^{-6})$, or $10 million.

To assess the value of a statistical life, researchers have usually already determined the willingness to pay (*WTP*) for a *slightly* lower risk to life or the willingness to accept (*WTA*) for a *slightly* higher risk. Assuming that one has a right to life, the value of accepting a slightly higher risk is the amount one is willing to accept to undertake that risk. Similarly, we can calculate an individual's *WTA* for a slightly higher risk in exchange for a monetary payment. As we discussed in Chapter 11, large discrepancies between these measures have been found in certain empirical studies. Therefore, setting the context for the risk whether an individual has a right not to face a risk (in which case a *WTA* measure is appropriate) or can pay a premium to avoid it (in which case a *WTP* measure is appropriate) is crucial.

The statistical value of life is a *risk premium* and is specific to the degree of risk faced. The reason we deal with small changes in risk is to get consistent values for this risk premium. An individual may accept $10 in exchange for an increased risk of death of one in a million (1×10^{-6}), but that does not mean that the individual will accept $5 million for facing a 50 percent (1 in 2) higher risk of death or will accept a $10 million payment to his heirs in exchange for certain death. We would expect that the risk premium demanded would increase as the degree of risk increased.

METHODS OF CALCULATING THE VALUE OF A STATISTICAL LIFE

The approaches to estimating *WTP* to reduce the risks of death and injury fall into four basic categories:[3] wage rate differentials between alternative occupations with different statistical risks; contingent valuation studies, where respondents are asked to assess their *WTP* to avoid hypothetical risks; consumer market studies that examine observable trade-offs consumers make between risks and benefits in their consumption decisions; and forgone earnings.[4]

Wage Differential Studies

The most common method to develop a value of a statistical life are wage rate studies. This method is based on the observation that certain occupations pay higher wages than others because of the risks involved. The underlying concept is that of risk aversion, in which risk is regarded as a bad. (A person who refuses to pay, say, $50 to win $100 on the flip of a coin—that is, who refuses a fair bet—is said to be "risk-averse.") Ironworkers, who build skyscrapers, face higher risks than clerical workers, who do not. Similarly, coal miners face greater risks to their health than

---

[3]A more rigorous discussion of valuation methodologies can be found in Freeman (1993).

[4]The category of forgone earnings is primarily found in tort awards, which are monetary damages awarded by juries in cases of negligent death, injury, or disease. However, jury awards are fundamentally different from the other categories in that they represent payments to specific individuals affected by known events. Thus jury awards will not necessarily apply to risks facing many individuals simultaneously. See Viscusi (1990) for further discussion.

do economists who write environmental policy textbooks. The additional risk faced in high-risk professions will be internalized at least in part through higher wage payments. The greater the additional risk, the higher the expected risk premium. For example, an ironworker who demands a $100 annual wage differential for facing a 1 in 10,000 annual increase in the risk of death is said to have a value of life equal to $100 times 10,000, or $1 million.

Several questions immediately arise with this methodology. First, can valuations of life at the specified level of risk be generalized to other levels, such as those from exposure to pesticides, air pollutants, or electromagnetic fields? Second, how can valuations of different individuals, with different degrees of aversion to life-threatening risk, be aggregated?

To illustrate these points, consider Figure 12.1. Suppose that there are three different groups of individuals, each with differing degrees of aversion to life-threatening risk. Group 1 is assumed to be the most averse to life-threatening risk. As a result, for a given level of risk, R, this group will demand a wage premium of W_1. Individuals in group 2 are less risk-averse. They will demand a wage premium of only W_2. Individuals in group 3 are the least risk-averse and will demand a premium of only W_3. For each group, the value of life will be calculated as $W_i R$. In addition, for each group, the wage premium required will increase with the degree of risk faced. This is shown by the upward-sloping curves WP_i. So the value of a statistical life will differ among the three groups. Although it would be possible to determine an average overall value based on the number of individuals in each group and their respective wage premiums, there is no guarantee that the resulting value would be efficient for policymaking purposes.

An Empirical Issue: Different Employer Costs of Providing Safety†

Wage rate differential analysis is complicated further because employers have different costs of providing safety, just as they have different costs of production. How

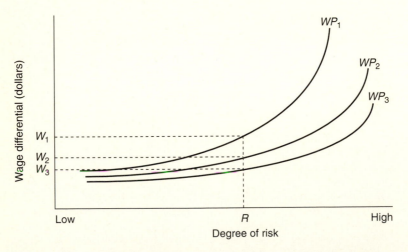

Figure 12.1   Wage Differentials and the Value of a Statistical Life

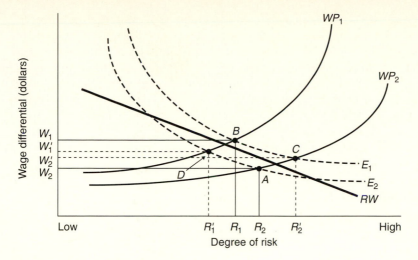

Figure 12.2   Observed Wage Premiums and the Value of Life

much of a wage premium an employer will *actually* pay a worker depends on whether it is cheaper to pay the premium or to increase the level of safety. This is shown in Figure 12.2.

Suppose that there are two types of employers who have different marginal costs of providing greater safety, given by curves E_1 and E_2. These curves slope downward because it is assumed that the cost of the employer to reduce risk *further* (move toward the left) *increases* as the level of risk decreases. For example, it might be simple to install a low-cost fan that removes 99.9 percent of carbon monoxide in an automobile repair shop. If the carbon monoxide were not removed, all of the mechanics would die with certainty (a high risk indeed!). To remove the remaining 0.1 percent, however, might require installation of an expensive filtration system. Thus the marginal cost of reducing that last bit of risk would be high. However, the risk of death associated with the remaining 0.1 percent would be quite small.

As shown in Figure 12.2, for any given level of risk R, employer group 1 will have a higher cost of reducing risk at the margin than will employer group 2 ($E_1 > E_2$). If employer group 2 hires group 1 workers, the degree of risk will be reduced to R_1' (point D). But if this employer group can hire group 2 workers, the degree of risk need only be reduced to R_2 (point A). For employer group 1, if group 1 workers are hired, the degree of risk will be R_1 (point B), while for group 2 workers it will be R_2' (point C).

In the marketplace, all four wage differentials and risk levels may be observed, rather than either of the wage-risk curves WP_1 and WP_2. Given these four observations, a regression on the four observations could look like the solid line RW in Figure 12.2 and have a declining slope. (Depending on where the observations were, the regression line also could have a positive slope.) As drawn in Figure 12.2, the regression would show a *decline* in the risk premium required as the degree of risk *increased,* contrary to common sense. In fact, just this sort of counterintuitive wage-risk behavior has been observed in the marketplace (Olson 1981; Viscusi 1983). What this means is that studies of high-risk occupations can show a lower average value of a statistical life than studies that focus on low-risk occupations. This is an example of a common problem in applied econometrics and can result in flawed policies if not corrected. Observed behavior generally represents points of intersection of supply and demand curves. These points trace out either a supply or a demand curve in special circumstances. Fortunately, if is often possible to estimate both the supply and demand curves using simultaneous equation techniques.[5]

Empirical Estimates   The literature contains many empirical studies relating the trade-off between risk and wage rates, covering a variety of occupations.[6] Not surprisingly, estimates of the value of increased risk differ significantly in these studies, ranging from under $1 million per statistical life to well over $10 million. Reasons for the wide range of estimates, other than the usual potential for statistical error, are related to several assumptions inherent in wage-risk studies. First, all wage-risk studies assume that workers are aware of differing risks across jobs (Fisher, Chestnut, Violette 1989). If that is not the case, workers will tend to overvalue the higher-risk job and accept lower wage payments. This will tend to bias estimated values for risks downward. A second assumption is that workers can move freely between jobs. If this assumption is violated, wage-risk studies may also exhibit a downward bias. The existence and magnitude of these biases, however, remain unclear (Fisher, Chestnut, and Violette 1989).

Wage-risk studies also have other limitations. Most such studies have not examined the risks associated with nonfatal accidents (Fisher, Chestnut, and Violette 1989), even though the majority of workplace accidents are nonfatal. This can lead to a measurement problem if wage premiums are ascribed entirely to fatal risks. To understand this point, suppose that writers of environmental economics textbooks suffer many nonfatal risks (sore fingers, carpal tunnel syndrome, cerebral atrophy, etc.) but few fatal ones. A researcher estimating wage premiums for these writers, based only on data incorporating fatal accidents, would derive too high a value for a statistical life because all of the wage premium would mistakenly be assumed to cover fatal risks.

Using workers' compensation payments may reduce this potential wage differential bias. However, while workers' compensation covers some nonfatal risks, some risks may not be accounted for in these compensation payments. Furthermore, workers' compensation will often be less than the full wage rate. Last, exposure to some risks may not be represented accurately. Certain airborne pollutants,

---

[5]For a discussion of these techniques, see Johnston (1984).
[6]See Fisher, Chestnut, and Violette (1989) and Violette and Chestnut (1983) for more detailed summaries of wage rate studies.

for example, may increase the incidence of respiratory ailments among workers but may not be covered under workers' compensation rules.

Wage-risk studies have generally relied on wages alone, rather than total compensation packages (wages plus health and insurance benefits, retirement contributions, etc.) to estimate risk premiums. If the ratio of wages to total compensation is constant across occupations, there will be a consistent downward bias in the estimated risk premium. Suppose that wages always equal 80 percent of total compensation. If coal miners' wages are on average $1,000 more than economists', their total compensation will exceed that of economists by $1,250. As a result, a calculated value of $10 million per statistical life will actually be $12.5 million per statistical life, and the wage-risk study will be biased downward. Finally, wage-risk studies can evaluate only directly affected individuals' *WTP* to reduce the risk of death. They do not include the values held by other affected individuals, such as family members. Again, this omission will also tend to bias value-of-life estimates downward.

A summary of empirical estimates is presented in Table 12.2.

Dillingham (1985) examined earlier wage-risk studies, including his own, and concluded that much of the variation in the estimates could be explained by differences in the specification of the risk variables. If different definitions of risk are used, such as the probability of a fatal accident in a given year versus the probability of a fatal accident over a career (which will be higher), it is likely that different wage-risk points, such as those in Figure 12.2, will be estimated. Moore and Viscusi (1988) reexamined earlier estimates as well, focusing their efforts on better estimates of risk. Their research led them to higher estimates of the value of life than had generally been found previously, between $5.2 and $6.6 million (in 1986 dollars).

TABLE 12.2 SELECTED VALUE-OF-LIFE ESTIMATES FROM WAGE-RISK STUDIES

Study (Year)	Implicit Value of a Life (millions of 1990 dollars)	Data Source
Thaler and Rosen (1976)	0.8	Survey of Economic Opportunities
Viscusi (1978)	4.1	Survey of Working Conditions, 1969–1970
Brown (1980)	1.5	National Longitudinal Study of Young Men, 1966–1971, 1973
Viscusi (1981)	6.5	Panel Study of Income Dynamics, 1976
Olson (1981)	5.2	Current Population Survey (CPS), 1978
Arnould and Nichols (1983)	0.9	U.S. Census, 1980
Smith and Gilbert (1984)	0.7	CPS (1978)
Dillingham (1985)	2.5–5.3	Census and Workers Compensation Data, 1970
Moore and Viscusi (1989)	7.8	Panel Study of Income Dynamics, 1982
Moore and Viscusi (1990)	16.2	Panel Study of Income Dynamics, 1982
Gegax, Gerking, and Schulze (1991)	1.6	Authors' mail survey

Source: After Viscusi (1993), Table 2, pp. 1926–1927.

Contingent Valuation Studies

As we described in Chapter 11, contingent valuation methodology (CVM) studies measure *WTP* through the use of survey data. In studies estimating the values of reducing risks of death or injury, individuals are asked their *WTP* for alternative levels of safety. Thus the CVM approach can be used to describe situations for which actual market data (such as wage rate differentials) do not exist.

While there have been far fewer contingent valuation studies of risk, the more recent studies have yielded results consistent with wage-risk studies (Fisher, Chestnut, and Violette 1989). One example, a study on motorists' *WTP* to reduce the risk of serious accidents (Jones-Lee, Hammerton, and Philips 1985), indicated *WTP* estimates between $1.9 and $5.2 million (in 1990 dollars). Another study by Gerking and colleagues (1988) derived a value of $2.6 million (in 1984 dollars). These are both within the range shown in Table 12.2.

The major criticism of most CVM studies is that the payments are hypothetical and that individuals are not actually required to pay the amounts indicated to reduce risk (Arrow et al. 1993). However, in the opinion of Fisher, Chestnut, and Violette (1989), the consistent results of CVM studies with the wage-risk studies indicate that the CVM studies did not suffer from any unusual or systematic biases that made them unsuitable.

Consumer Market Studies

Consumer market studies examine the observed trade-offs individuals make between the risks and the benefits of consuming various products and services. Unlike CVM studies, consumer market studies examine observed consumer behavior. Thus they share some of the traits of wage-risk studies and may be compared to the hedonic pricing studies discussed in Chapter 11.

Unfortunately, there have been relatively few such studies. Fisher, Chestnut, and Violette (1989) report results from only four, which estimated statistical values of life between about $300,000 and $1.5 million (in 1990 dollars). Most of the studies cited, such as those related to increases in automobile safety from the use of seat belts (Blomquist 1979, 1981), focused on whether markets respond to differences in safety, rather than the value of a statistical life. However, one could infer values for statistical lives from the results of the studies. For example, if consumers were observed to pay $500 for an air bag that would reduce their risk of death by 1 in 10,000, the inferred statistical value of life would be $5 million.

Using this approach requires careful measurement of the costs of risk reduction. If these costs are underestimated, the estimated value of life will be too high, and vice versa. For example, Blomquist (1981) identified the cost of using seat belts as the time needed to buckle up. For many people, the nuisance of using seat belts may be a much higher cost than the time. A valuation of a statistical life based on seat belt use using only this cost could result in a downward-biased value.

Ippolito and Ippolito (1984) used information about the market for cigarettes to estimate value of a statistical life. They compared changes in available information about the health hazards of cigarette smoking and estimates of changes in life expectancy with changes in individuals' demand for cigarettes. They determined what the demand for cigarettes would have been in 1980 had no health information been available and compared those figures with actual demand. The reduction in demand was then compared to the perceived changes in risk to determine a value of life. The results of their study indicated a value of $460,000 in 1985 dollars, or about $600,000 in 1990 dollars. Of course, to the extent that cigarettes are addictive, individuals may be unable to change their consumption behavior as much as might otherwise be expected. This also would tend to bias the calculations downward.

Studies of Forgone Earnings

The forgone-earnings approach, sometimes known as the *human capital* approach, is quite different from the economists' approach using either willingness to pay to avoid risk or willingness to accept increased risk. However, the human capital approach is used most frequently by courts in determining damages. Its applicability to environmental policy is unclear. However, in cases where individuals or groups are exposed to *involuntary* risks, it may be relevant.

Human capital estimates use the contribution that an individual makes to society to estimate a value of life. In this approach, the value of life is derived from an individual's contribution to the economy. To take an example, suppose that one's annual income was expected to be $20,000 per year for the next 30 years, adjusted for inflation. If this stream of earnings were not discounted, the total value of this lifetime stream would be $600,000. Thus this person's value of life would be $600,000.

This approach has the advantage of being easily measured. However, it does not measure the same thing as the other approaches to valuing life or health.[7] Human capital studies do not measure *WTP* to avoid a risk. They measure the loss in productivity resulting from a specific person's injury or death. Even as a measure of this loss, a human capital study is open to at least five objections. First, it may be biased against women and minorities, who tend to have lower wage rates (Fisher, Chestnut, and Violette 1989). Second, the approach assigns no value to the lives of the very old and the retired.[8] Third, it does not include the value to all individuals from the reduced risk, only the value of the individual life "saved." Fourth, it assigns no value to leisure time. Fifth, and perhaps most crucial, it does not take into account that one's *WTP* or *WTA* may be substantially different from one's income.

---

[7]Some unpublished work indicates that human capital estimates may produce consistent *fractions* of estimates derived using *WTP* and *WTA* approaches.

[8]Calculating the value of life for children can be quite tricky too, as it is impossible to project a child's future income stream from an as-yet-unknown career.

APPLYING THE VALUE OF A STATISTICAL LIFE: ENVIRONMENTAL POLICY CONSIDERATIONS

Individually and collectively, we make decisions that impose risks on others. Sewage discharged into a river may pose health risks for people living downstream. Wastes buried in a landfill may pose risks to future generations if the landfill ever leaks. Knowing the value of a statistical life and health may help us quantify the risks in this type of situation, but the primary considerations are the rights of the parties having risks imposed on them and the distribution of gains and losses. Monetary values for life and health give us no information about the rights in question or the justice of the distribution of gains and losses.

From our discussions so far, we can extract three principles:

1. It may be appropriate to consider the value of a particular individual's life or health when we are considering compensation for a harm that has already occurred, but generally it is not appropriate to consider the value of a particular individual's life or health (other than one's own) when prospectively considering actions that might harm that person.
2. In cases where the value of life or health is an appropriate consideration in forward-looking public policy debates, we are generally dealing with risks to life and health, not certain harm to a specific person.
3. Other considerations, such as equity and individual rights, will likely be important in cases where it is useful and appropriate to consider the value of life and health.

Even though the economist's approach to the valuation of life is consistent with the valuation of other goods and services, there remain important considerations for environmental policymakers who must rely on such values. Willingness to pay for or willingness to accept risk will be different for different individuals and will be affected by wealth. Someone who is rich is obviously able to pay more to reduce a particular risk than someone who is poor. Furthermore, wealthier individuals generally have higher *WTP* and *WTA* values than less wealthy individuals. However, this does not mean that the lives of rich people are inherently more valuable than the lives of the poor, nor does it mean that dumping environmental wastes in a poor neighborhood is preferable to dumping them in a rich neighborhood.

Only on economic efficiency grounds may dumping wastes in poor neighborhoods be preferable and not an example of "environmental racism" such as discussed in Chapter 9. It is on *equity* grounds that arguments against such dumping can be made. Dumping wastes in poor neighborhoods will likely make those neighborhoods even poorer, encouraging (on efficiency grounds) still more dumping. Thus environmental "disamenities" such as waste dumps should be sited voluntarily, as the parties affected will be better off in the process. The importance of separating efficiency and equity issues, as well as clarifying voluntary and involuntary risks in value-of-life considerations, is illustrated in the accompanying box.

In general, environmental policymakers who wish to incorporate the value of a staistical life into policy development must keep five issues in mind: the overall

THE VALUE OF LIFE IN POOR COUNTRIES VERSUS RICH COUNTRIES

In February 1992, *The Economist* printed portions of an internal memorandum written by Lawrence Summers of the World Bank in December 1991 ("Let Them Eat Pollution" 1992). The memorandum discussed the reasonableness of a strategy to encourage dirty industries in less developed countries (LDCs). Summers gave three reasons for this recommendation. First, he argued that the health cost of pollution was based on forgone earnings. Thus countries with the lowest relative wage rates would have the lowest value of life. These countries are the LDCs. Second, he argued that because the first increments of pollution have the lowest marginal cost (recall the discussion in Chapter 6), many of the underpopulated countries in Africa are "vastly *underpolluted*": their air quality is "probably vastly inefficiently low compared to Los Angeles or Mexico City." Third, he argued that the demand for a clean environment, "for aesthetic and health reasons," would have a high income elasticity. (Recall the discussion in Chapter 8 about wealth and the demand for environmental quality.) In other words, individuals don't care about clean air, clean water, and scenic views unless they are rich. He concluded that arguments against the proposal for more pollution in the LDCs (social concerns, intrinsic rights, morality, etc.) could be used against every development proposal made by the World Bank. Of course, Summers assumed that an LDC would accept the dumping voluntarily in exchange for compensation. (This raises the issue of who in the LDC is compensated, a particularly acute problem in some autocratic countries.)

Not surprisingly, the report caused quite a stir both inside and outside the Bank. Yet the economic arguments he made require debate. It is also interesting to note that a subsequent World Bank report issued in 1992, titled *World Development Report, 1992: Development and the Environment,* concluded that development and improved environmental quality go together. Economic development cannot occur without clean water, good sanitation, clean air, and the like, but these cannot be achieved until there is sufficient income to pay for them. Such issues will probably increase in importance over time and will have to be wrestled with by environmental policymakers.

level of risk and the class of risk, the value of life to others, whether or not the risk is voluntary, how risks are distributed, and perceived versus actuarial risks, in cases where the public's perception of risks differs significantly from the actual value.

Level of Risk

Appropriate risk premiums will depend on the level of risk. Is the risk extremely small, or is it large? In addition, what individuals are bearing the risk? Empirical evidence indicates that individuals who voluntarily expose themselves to additional risk will have a lower value of life than individuals who are exposed to involuntary risks. With consumer market studies, exposure to risk and valuation are insepara-ble. For example, cigarette smokers are voluntarily exposing themselves to known health risks, while nonsmokers are avoiding those risks.

For occupational studies, individuals who are least averse to risk will be drawn into the highest-risk occupations because the wage premiums required to induce such individuals to choose those occupations will be lowest. Thus when consider-ing environmental policy, it will be important to know which group of workers is most likely to be exposed.

Value of Life to Others

An individual whose life is at risk will probably also have value to his or her rela-tives. This is most obvious for families and, especially, children, who must rely on a parent's income for support. But there may also be considerations of friends and other, unrelated individuals who might be willing to pay to reduce risks to the indi-vidual. There may also be altruistic individuals who are willing to pay to reduce risks to the populace at large. Obviously, incorporating these values will be difficult for policymakers, but they do remain a consideration.[9]

Voluntary Versus Involuntary Exposure to Risk

One of the most important policy issues is the crucial difference between voluntary and involuntary exposure to increased risk. This difference is the choice of individ-uals to face differing levels of risk. Though individuals may value voluntary expo-sure to risks quite differently, involuntary exposure is probably best assigned a uni-form value among all individuals for purposes of equity (and, possibly, political expediency). This may be a particularly important issue where young children are exposed involuntarily to environmental risks, such as lead paint. Undoubtedly, sig-nificant moral issues will be raised if involuntary exposure to risks by certain groups of individuals is valued differently by other groups.

It is also likely that any uniform value chosen would be higher than values for voluntary exposure to risks because the involuntary category will include highly risk-averse individuals who do not expose themselves to many risks voluntarily. To take an example, individuals who fear heights would likely assign much higher val-ues (be willing to pay more) to avoid mountain-climbing risks than professional mountaineers would.

WTP estimates should also include the value that other individuals receive from affected individuals. In other words, because individuals' lives will affect other individuals, estimating the value of a statistical life may need to include not only the directly affected individual's responses to small changes in risk but also the

---

[9]Needleman (1976), for example, examined willingness to pay on the part of family or friends to save a life in the context of kidney donors.

value that others place on changes to that individual's risk. For example, *WTP* estimates may also need to include existence values for, say, an individual's family (Cropper and Sussman 1988) or even altruists who would be affected in the event of the individual's death.

There has been some empirical work on how to value involuntary as opposed to voluntary exposure to risks. Slovic, Lichtenstein, and Fischhoff (1979) performed a study in which a panel of adults was asked to rank different risks by assigning relative social values to different types of risks. Voluntary risks, such as mountain climbing, were assigned an index value of 1. Deaths from voluntary exposure to more common risks, such as from automobile accidents, were assigned a value of about 1.25. Involuntary risks, such as exposure to pesticides, were assigned values between 1.5 and 2. Using these data, one could argue that *WTP* estimates for voluntary exposure to risks should be increased between 50 and 100 percent in order to develop willingness-to-pay estimates for involuntary exposure to risks, based on how individuals perceive such risks differently.[10]

Distribution of Risk

Dumping hazardous wastes in poor countries is just one example of the importance of environmental policy to the distribution of risks. The value of a statistical life will not always be placed in an efficiency context. Often it will involve questions of equity and rights, especially when exposure to risk is involuntary. In equity contexts, it may still be necessary to weigh monetary values of life to determine an estimate of the distribution of risks. However, equity considerations may not lend themselves (at least not without great controversy) to different values of life for different classes of individuals.

When rights are considered, which will often be the case with involuntary risks, it may be more useful to estimate numbers of lives and not assign value to those lives. Policy questions might then be aimed toward maximizing the *number* of lives saved rather than maximizing the *value* of lives saved.

Perceived Versus Actuarial Risk

One final problem that appears often in the context of environmental policy issues and statistical value-of-life estimates is the perception of risk versus the statistical, or actuarial, risk. Individuals often perceive risks as being smaller or larger than they actually are, sometimes by orders of magnitude. This is an important issue for policymaking because individuals act on the basis of their *perceived* risks. Many individuals who think nothing of driving off in their automobiles without wearing a seat belt will refuse to fly in airplanes because they believe flying to be a high-risk

---

[10]This may explain why people are more afraid of flying than driving, even thought the latter is more risky on a statistical basis. Often people perceive themselves as having no control when flying. Thus they are at the mercy of the pilots, weather, and other external forces. Driving a car, however, they often feel that they can take some action to reduce the severity of an accident and therefore the risks to themselves.

TROUBLE IN HAPPYVILLE

Portney (1992) considers the mythical town of Happyville (pop. 1,000), which has an above-average incidence of cancer. The drinking water there contains a naturally occurring substance that every resident believes is responsible for the high cancer rate. The residents have asked you, the director of environmental protection, to build an expensive water treatment facility costing $8 million. Each resident is willing to pay $10,000 to remove the substance from the drinking water, which will more than cover the cost of the facility. The only complicating factor is that the ten best risk assessors in the world have tested the substance in the water and all have found it *not* to cause cancer. You face a policy dilemma: do you build the facility that the residents want, even though "experts" insist it will do nothing toward solving the problem identified?

activity, even though the actuarial risk of flying is many times lower in comparison. Similarly, individuals may be terrified by stories of the potential harm from certain food additives such as Alar or BGH, even though the estimated risks are negligible, yet continue to smoke cigarettes.

The sort of problem described in the accompanying box arises in real-world policy decisions. In Seattle, for example, residents of a local neighborhood opposed locating a tuberculosis sanitarium there, even though health experts assured them that the risks of contamination were extremely small. Neighborhood residents have also opposed locating facilities to house AIDS patients (Zerbe 1991). The courts have addressed some of these issues. In one 1983 Supreme Court case, *Metropolitan Edison* v. *People Against Nuclear Energy,* the latter group opposed operation of a nuclear power plant because of the *psychological* harm it would cause, seeing that people were frightened of nuclear power. But the Court held that the Nuclear Regulatory Commission, which regulates nuclear plant operations, need not consider psychological harm that derives from fears not substantiated by expert perception.

These issues are relevant for estimating the value of a statistical life because estimates based on the perception of risk may differ significantly from those based on actuarial risks. Where perceived risk exceeds actuarial risk, *WTP* or *WTA* to avoid risk will be too high. Risk-averse individuals will be willing to pay higher risk premiums to avoid uncertainty than would be warranted on the basis of the actual risk. This reduces economic efficiency. Of course, there may also be cases where perceived risks are much lower than actuarial risks. In those cases, individuals may not be willing to pay to reduce actuarial risks when there is economic justification to do so.[11] These disparities can affect economic behavior and will almost surely

---

[11]See, for example, the discussion by Broome (1982) on the use of seat belts (pp. 206–207).

influence the choice of environmental policies, as policymakers do not determine environmental policy in a vacuum.

There are no easy answers to this issue. Some observers argue that actuarial risks cannot be trusted and that perceived risks are consequently important for policymaking. This may be a legitimate concern for some environmental issues, such as nuclear waste disposal, where there is insufficient statistical evidence to develop actuarial risks, or predictions of global climate change, because our predictive abilities and computer models have yet to master the vast complexities of the earth's climate.

There is also no question but that the media may materially affect the perception of risk. Certainly policy development in an atmosphere of hysteria is unlikely to produce effective policies. The way in which the discussion is framed and the process by which a decision is reached can give rise to values that are relevant to the decision. Perhaps the difference between experts' and the public's estimates or risk reflect something important about the nature of risk—that exposure to it is involuntary rather than voluntary, that it involves outcomes that are regarded with particular loathing, and so forth. A process that is inclusive and that allows room for an expression of different points of view is more likely to produce more acceptable policy decisions.

CHAPTER SUMMARY

Estimates of the value of a statistical life will be critical to many environmental policy issues. There are many empirical estimates of such values that together can provide useful policy guidance. The controversy surrounding those estimates, such as the debate over the "morality" of assigning monetary values to life, stems from confusion over the policy goals involved. Considerations of human rights do not lend themselves to monetary estimates of the value of life. Considerations of economic efficiency and equity, by contrast, will almost certainly need to rely on monetary values for the simple reason that money is the most useful comparison vehicle. When dealing with environmental risks, policymakers will have to consider actuarial and perceived risks. Where perceived risks differ substantially from actuarial risks, a policy process that helps spell out *why* those differences exist can lead to better policy decisions.

CHAPTER REVIEW

Economic Concepts and Tools

- Economics does not place values on human life and health. Economics can be used to measure the values that individuals place on their own and others' life and health by estimating the value that individuals place on small changes to the risks they face.
- The value of a statistical life can be estimated in four different ways:
  1. Wage rate differentials between alternative occupations

2. Contingent valuation studies
3. Consumer market studies
4. Human capital and forgone earnings

- The wage differential approach is based on the premise that people choose jobs based on the wages paid, the risks inherent in the jobs, and other factors. All other factors being equal, wage differences between jobs should reflect the value people place on the differences in risk. Market wage differences will reflect differences in risks and in other job characteristics.

- Because individuals differ in their attitudes toward risk, people who are less risk-averse will end up in riskier occupations. As a result, observed market wage differences will understate individuals' marginal willingness to pay to avoid risk. To overcome this problem, wage differential studies should use simultaneous equation regression techniques to account for differences in both risk and preferences.

- Contingent valuation studies ask respondents to assess their *WTP* to avoid hypothetical risks, much as CVM studies determine individuals' *WTP* for environmental goods.

- Consumer market studies estimate *WTP* to avoid risks from observed *WTP* to obtain safer products. They can be performed using techniques similar to those used in wage differential studies.

- The human capital approach uses lost lifetime earnings to measure the value of life and health.

- Wage differential studies, consumer market studies, and CVM can be used to estimate individuals' *WTP* to avoid risks to their own life and health. The human capital approach measures the cost of a risk to society as a whole, not to the individual at risk. CVM can also be used to estimate individual's *WTP* to avoid risks to others' life and health. These are three different types of value, not three different measures of the same value.

Policy Issues

- Whether we can measure the value of risks to life and health in economic terms is not an issue; we can. Whether we should base any particular decision on such economic values may be an issue. If the decision is whether to risk, take, or save a particular life, economic values are probably not relevant. Economic values may be relevant for setting compensation for actual harm when the goal is to compensate the victim. They may be less relevant when the goal is to deter future harmful acts. Economic values may be one relevant factor in deciding whether to accept individual or collective risks. Economic values may also be relevant in deciding whether to impose risks on others, but primary consideration is likely to be given to distributional or procedural justice.

- Willingness to pay or accept risk will be different for different individuals and will be affected by wealth. Someone who is rich can pay more to reduce a particular risk than someone who is poor. Because of this, it is important to keep both equity and efficiency in mind when allocating health risks. This does not mean that the lives of rich people are inherently more valuable than the lives of the poor, but basing decisions solely on total WTP may inadvertently treat them as more valuable.

- Because different economic values of life and health can be measured, it is important to match the right value with the policy question being asked.
- Actuarial risks may differ substantially from perceived risks. In such cases, one benefit that policymakers can provide is educating consumers so that more rational decisions may be made.
- Empirical studies have produced a wide range of estimates of the statistical value of life This does not mean such estimates have no relevance to policy development. In does mean that estimates should be used to provide broad guidance for the desirability of various policies, rather than to make precise trade-offs.

DISCUSSION QUESTIONS

1. Should a statistical-value-of-life approach be used in wrongful-death cases? Why or why not?
2. We are often told that flying is far safer than driving. Yet most people are much more afraid of flying than driving. What explains this anomaly? Should airline safety policies be enacted on the basis of perceived or actual risks?
3. A policy that reduces atmospheric lead concentrations will reduce the incidence of life-threatening diseases to 1 million at-risk children. However, the resources used to institute and enforce the policy will mean forgoing investments that can prolong the lives of 2 million senior citizens. What role, if any, do statistical values of life play in determining whether the policy should be enacted?
4. The Environmental Protection Agency is considering a more stringent regulation to control exposure to benzene in the workplace. The benefits estimates from reduced exposure have been based on a contingent valuation survey of a random sample of U.S. citizens. The cost and benefit schedules are shown in the table.

Exposure (parts per billion)	Total Cost (millions of dollars)	Total Benefits (*WTP*) (millions of dollars)
20	100	300
10	150	400
5	175	430
2	190	450
1	300	460

a. If the figures in the table are accepted, at what level should the EPA set the benzene standard?
b. An analyst hired by the EPA questions the use of the benefits figures on the grounds that the population sampled is more risk-averse than workers

exposed to benzene. If this analyst is correct, would the optimal level of regulation tend to be higher or lower than it is now? Why?

   c. At a citizens' hearing before the EPA, a plant official, John Smith, maintains that benefits should not vary with the risk adversity of the exposed population. Rather, he argues, benefits should be based on estimates of the medical costs avoided at different levels of exposure so that there will be a uniform value of life for lives lost. What are the merits of and problems with Smith's proposal? Should the lost wages of workers made ill by exposure to benzene be included if Smith's approach is used?

5. Return to the Happyville example. As director of environmental protection, would you recommend building the water treatment facility?

REFERENCES

Arnould, R., and L. Nichols. 1983. "Wage-Risk Premiums and Worker's Compensation: A Refinement of Estimates of Compensating Wage Differential." *Journal of Political Economy* 91(2): 332–340.

Arrow, K., R. Solow, P. Portney, E. Leamer, R. Radner, and H. Schuman. 1993. *Report of the NOAA Panel on Contingent Valuation.* Washington, D.C.: National Oceanic and Atmospheric Administration.

Blomquist, G. 1979. "Value of Life Savings: Implications of Consumption Activity." *Journal of Political Economy* 87(3): 540–558.

———. 1981. "The Value of Human Life: An Empirical Perspective." *Economic Inquiry* 29(2): 156–164.

Broome, J. 1982. "Uncertainty in Welfare Economics and the Value of Life." In *The Value of Life and Safety,* ed. M. Jones. Amsterdam: Elsevier North-Holland.

Brown, C. 1980. "Equalizing Differences in the Labor Market." *Quarterly Journal of Economics* 94(1): 113–134.

Cropper, M., and F. Sussman. 1988. "Families and the Economics of Risks to Life." *American Economic Review* 78(1): 255–260.

Dillingham, A. 1985. "The Influence of Risk-Variable Definition on Value-of-Life Estimates." *Economic Inquiry* 24(2): 277–294.

Fisher, A., L. Chestnut, and D. Violette. 1989. "The Value of Reducing Risks to Death: A Note on New Evidence." *Journal of Policy Analysis and Management* 8(1): 88–100.

Freeman, A. 1993. *The Measurement of Environmental and Resource Values.* Washington, D.C.: Resources for the Future.

Gegax, D., S. Gerking, and W. Schulze. 1991. "Perceived Risk and the Marginal Value of Safety." *Review of Economics and Statistics* 73(4): 589–596.

Gerking, S., M. OcHaan, and W. Schulze. 1988. "The Marginal Value of Job Safety: A Contingent Valuation Study." *Journal of Risk and Uncertainty* 1(1): 57–74.

Ippolito, P., and R. Ippolito. 1984. "Measuring the Value of Life Savings from Consumer Reaction to New Information." *Journal of Public Economics* 25: 53–81.

Johnston, J. 1984. *Econometric Methods.* New York: McGraw-Hill.

Jones-Lee, M., M. Hammerton, and P. Philips. 1985. "The Value of Safety: Results of a National Sample Survey." *Economic Journal* 95(1): 49–72.

"Let Them Eat Pollution." 1992. *Economist,* February 8, 1992, p. 66.

Moore, M., and W. Viscusi. 1988. "Doubling the Estimated Value of Life: Results Using New Occupational Fatality Data." *Journal of Policy Analysis and Management* 7: 476–490.

———. 1989. "Promoting Safety Through Workers' Compensation." *Rand Journal of Economics* 20(4): 499–515.

———. 1990. "Environmental Health Risks: New Evidence and Policy Implications." *Journal of Environmental Economics and Management* 18(2): 551–562.

Needleman, L. 1976. "Valuing Other People's Lives." *Manchester School of Economic and Social Studies* 44: 309–342.

Olson, C. 1981. "An Analysis of Wage Differentials Received by Workers on Dangerous Jobs." *Journal of Human Resources* 16(2): 165–181.

Portney, P. (1992). "Trouble in Happyville." *Journal of Policy Analysis and Management* 11(1): 131–132.

Slovic, P., S. Lichtenstein, and B. Fischhoff. 1979. "Images of Disaster: Perception and Acceptance of Risks from Perceived Nuclear Power." In *Energy Risk Management,* ed. G. Goodmand and W. Rose. London: Academic Press.

Smith, V., and C. Gilbert. 1984. "The Implicit Risks to Life: A Comparative Analysis." *Economic Letters* 16: 393–399.

Thaler, R., and S. Rosen. 1976. "The Value of Saving a Life: Evidence from the Labor Market." In *Household Production and Consumption: Studies in Income and Wealth,* Vol. 40, ed. N. Terleckyj. New York: Columbia University Press.

Van Houtven, G., and M. Cropper. 1993. "When Is a Life Too Costly to Save? The Evidence from Environmental Regulations." Discussion Paper No. CRM 93-02. Washington, D.C.: Resources for the Future.

Violette, D., and L. Chestnut. 1983. *Valuing Reductions in Risk: A Review of the Empirical Estimates.* Report prepared for the U.S. Environmental Protection Agency, Washington, D.C.

Viscusi, W. 1978. "Labor Market Valuations of Life and Limb: Empirical Estimates and Policy Implications." *Public Policy* 26(3): 359–386.

———. 1981. "Occupational Safety and Health Regulation: Its Impact and Policy Alternatives." In *Research in Public Policy Analysis and Management,* Vol. 2, ed. J. Crecine. Greenwich, Conn.: JAI Press.

———. 1983. *Risk by Choice: Regulating Health and Safety in the Workplace.* Cambridge: Harvard University Press.

———. 1990. "The Value of Life: Has Voodoo Economics Come to the Courts?" *Journal of Forensic Economics* 3(3): 1–15.

———. 1992. *Fatal Trade-Offs.* New York: Oxford University Press.

———. 1993. "The Value of Risks to Life and Health." *Journal of Economic Literature* 31(4): 1912–1946.

Willig, R. 1976. "Consumer's Surplus Without Apology." *American Economic Review* 66(4): 589–597.

World Bank. 1992. *World Development Report, 1992: Development and the Environment.* New York: Oxford University Press.

Zerbe, R. 1991. "Comment: Does Benefit-Cost Analysis Stand Alone? Rights and Standing." *Journal of Policy Analysis and Management* 10(1): 96–105.

Graphical Interpretation of *WTP* and *WTA* Changes in Risk Levels

WTP and *WTA* estimates for changes in risk levels can be represented by an individual's indifference curve map. This is shown in Figure 12A.1. Although the figure appears complex, its elements are familiar. In this figure, the individual is able to trade off some portion of his income, M, for varying degrees of safety, where the degree of safety, S, is defined as 1 minus the probability of death. If the probability of death is 2 percent, the degree of safety is 98 percent. Suppose that the individual is initially at point A. This point is tangent to the individual's indifference curve U_0 assuming an initial price of safety of P_0. The individual chooses a level of safety equal to S_a. Now suppose that the price of safety decreases from P_0 to P_1 because of some technological improvement, such as automobile air bags. At this new lower price of safety, the individual will choose a higher level of safety S_b and will achieve a higher overall level of utility U_1.

To determine the individual's willingness to pay for the price decrease in safety and hence the decrease in risk, we can determine the amount of income that the individual would be willing to forgo that would leave him as well off after the price decrease as he was prior to it. To get the income effect, we draw a budget line shown by the dotted line tangent to U_0 and parallel to the P_1 budget line that is tangent at B. From the discussion in Chapter 3 on *WTP*, we know that the difference

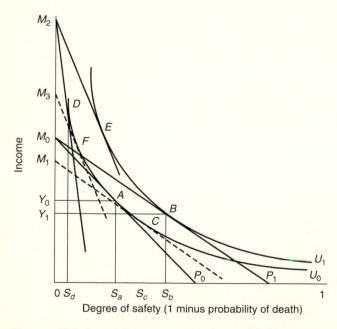

Figure 12A.1 Willingness to Pay for Reduced Risk

in these parallel budget lines measures the value in income from moving from U_0 to U_1 and that this amount of income equals $M_1 - M_0$. (This is the compensating variation, CV.)

As the level of safety *decreases*, the marginal rate of substitution between safety and income will *increase*. Thus the individual will be willing to pay more for additional safety or require more compensation to forgo additional safety. If the individual were initially at point D and faced a price decrease, the compensating variation of moving from point D to point E would equal $M_2 - M_3$, which is larger than $M_1 - M_0$ because the overall level of safety at point D, S_d, is lower than at point A.

WTP essentially assumes that the individual must purchase the decrease in risk. For example, if the individual wished to have better automobile seat belts, he would be required to purchase them. Suppose instead that the individual is guaranteed a right to the better seat belts. We can then ask what the individual would be willing to accept to forgo the price decrease. (This is the equivalent variation, EV.) In other words, what level of compensation would the individual accept in lieu of the better seat belts? This amount will be greater (for a normal good) than the willingness to pay for the price decrease because it is unconstrained by income. In asking the willingness-to-accept question, we are granting the individual a higher indifference curve as the initial or starting point. This is shown in Figure 12A.2. Without the newer seat belts, the individual is initially at point A along indifference curve U_0. However, the individual is now assumed to have a right to the newer seat belts, which will reduce his risk. Thus the individual has the right to move to point B along indifference curve U_1, if he so chooses, at no cost to himself.

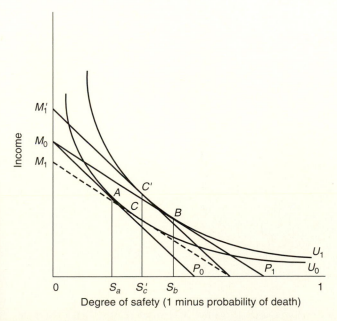

Figure 12A.2   Willingness to Accept Higher Risk

The automobile manufacturer, wishing to avoid the additional expense of the new seat belts, asks what the individual would be willing to accept to forgo the new seat belts. To determine this, we find the amount of income that the individual will accept such that, at the original price of risk P_0 (no new seat belts), he would be as well off as with the new seat belts. The individual will demand a payment sufficient to boost him to from indifference curve U_0 to indifference curve U_1, at the original price P_1. This is the point C'. The amount of income is given by $M_1' - M_0$. With this payment, the individual faces the original, higher price of safety but is still as well off as with the lower price of safety. Note that as drawn, $(M_0' - M_0) > (M_1 - M_0)$.[1] This difference can be quite large when values of life are involved.

---

[1]Recall from Chapter 3 that this is to be expected for normal goods, although the difference theoretically should be small (Willig 1976).

CHAPTER 13

DISCOUNTING ENVIRONMENTAL BENEFITS AND COSTS OVER TIME

From Now Until Forever: International Approaches to Radioactive Waste Disposal

High- and low-level radioactive waste disposal continues to be a contentious issue in the United States.[1] Some of these wastes, such as plutonium, will remain dangerously radioactive for thousands of years; others will become "harmless" in only a few. For the past 50 years, radioactive wastes have been produced not only by civilian nuclear power plants but also at nuclear weapons plants including Hanford, in southeastern Washington State; Rocky Flats, east of Denver, Colorado; and Oak Ridge, in eastern Tennessee. Cleaning up these sites will cost billions of dollars over many years yet will still result in some areas' being off limits to humans for centuries.

Issues surrounding the disposal of radioactive wastes are not confined to the United States. Other countries, especially in Europe, have also been grappling with the issue of safely disposing of radioactive materials.[2] Perhaps most frightening of all, however, are the cleanup and disposal problems in the former Soviet Union. The 1986 accident at the Chernoybl nuclear power plant in Ukraine revealed to the world the poor safety standards of Soviet civilian reactors. The subsequent breakup

---

[1]Recall the discussion of the Nuclear Waste Policy Act in Chapter 9.
[2]Other problem countries include North Korea, Israel, India, and China.

of the Soviet Union showed that radioactive waste disposal was scarcely better. A survey in the May 1991 Bulletin of the Atomic Scientist *discussed how radioactive wastes from Chelyabinsk-40, a Soviet nuclear weapons plant east of the Ural Mountains and north of the Kazakhstan border, were simply pumped into nearby Karachay Lake. Off the northern coast, near the port city of Murmansk, radioactive wastes have been dumped into the Barents and Kara seas for 20 years. It was thus not surprising that in 1989, a Soviet biologist, Alexei Yablokov, claimed that 20 percent of the Soviet population, some 50 million people, lived in what he called "ecological disaster zones."*

Countries such as France, Great Britain, and Sweden are also addressing radioactive waste disposal solutions. According to a 1994 report by the General Accounting Office, like the United States, most of these countries plan to bury nuclear wastes underground. None plans to have ready a facility to do so until the year 2020.[3] In the meantime, continued operation of nuclear power plants, which are the major generators of new nuclear wastes, remains controversial. The wastes generated at these plants continue to be stored on-site, either aboveground or in shallow containment pools. Environmentalists are concerned that money set aside by law now for decommissioning plants (including safe disposal of wastes and site cleanup) will be woefully inadequate for the actual task. Furthermore, they question the legacy that today's generation is leaving future generations.

There are many policy issues associated with radioactive waste disposal. How should the wastes be disposed of? How "clean" should civilian and military sites be made? For how long must "safety" be ensured to protect future generations? If "accidents" do occur in the future, what will be the monetary value of the damages? Should money be set aside today in a "nuclear waste compensation fund" for future generations? If so, how much should be set aside? What is the current generation willing to pay to reduce risks to future generations from continued production of radioactive wastes? Given the potential dangers to future generations, what are the true social costs of continued nuclear power plant operation?

These questions cover the entire spectrum of environmental policy issues that we have discussed in earlier chapters. They also pose immense conflicts and dilemmas for policymakers. A guarantee of absolute safety for a specified time period (if even possible), for example, grants a right to individuals not to be put at risk rather than determining an efficient level of risk. Questions of absolute safety are therefore not questions of economic efficiency. Yet can the current generation really "guarantee" safe (riskless) disposal for thousands of years? Even if such a guarantee were possible, how long should it extend into the future? One year seems too short; one million years seems too long.

At the same time, many environmental groups fervently oppose siting any permanent waste disposal site, even though such a site would probably provide greater safety than the current patchwork of temporary on-site facilities. In the United

---

[3]In the 1970s, Charles Hollister, a biologist at the Woods Hole Oceanographic Institute, proposed disposing of nuclear wastes beneath thick mud that carpets the ocean floor (see "Nuclear Burial at Sea" 1992).

States, tremendous opposition has been raised to developing a high-level waste repository at Yucca Flats, Nevada (which was supposed to open in 1998), and to the opening of the Waste Isolation Pilot Project (WIPP) near Carlsbad, New Mexico. Charges of politically motivated decisions for the choice of Yucca Flats (no doubt having a ring of truth), as well as opposition to transporting wastes to the WIPP, have slowed progress in "solving" the disposal issue. Although this opposition may protect some parties today, it places others at risk. How these trade-offs should be made is rarely discussed.

The risks of nuclear power and waste disposal, because they conceivably extend into the distant future, raise questions of how to compare future costs and benefits with today's costs and benefits. Investments in nuclear power may also preclude investments in other, less environmentally hazardous energy resources, even though the latter appear to be more expensive today. All of this raises the issue of how society should compare future environmental costs and benefits to present ones. That is the subject of this chapter; it is known as discounting. Not surprisingly, the role of discounting and the appropriate discount rate have been fiercely debated. Yet many of those debates arise from misunderstandings about the role of discounting and the priority of different policy goals.

INTRODUCTION

Fortunately, not all comparisons between present and future environmental costs and benefits are so complex. Many involve well-defined timelines that are comprehensible to individuals and do not involve other complex issues simultaneously. However, addressing future environmental costs and benefits from an economic efficiency standpoint can often be intertwined with other policy goals.

For example, suppose that the legislature of the state of Hypochondria has $100 million available to protect the quality of aquifers that supply municipal water. Environmentalists have identified the two biggest threats to the quality of water in this aquifer as a leaking landfill and inadequate sewage treatment facilities. The landfill leak, if left untreated, will eventually release toxic wastes into the aquifer 50 years from now. If left untreated, the cleanup cost is estimated to be $6 billion. The inadequate sewage treatment is currently releasing disease-causing bacteria into the aquifer that are making people ill. Repairing the landfill leak will cost the entire $100 million, as will upgrading the sewage treatment facilities. The legislative committee that decides such matters has turned to its crackerjack staff economist to provide them with recommendations on how the $100 million should be spent.

The economist examines the issues carefully and tells the committee members that they must compare two impacts that will occur at different times. The economist estimates how much is spent each year on treating people for the waterborne bacterial illnesses and develops a forecast of future costs based on projections of population growth in the area over the next 50 years. The economist presents the committee with his results, which are shown in Table 13.1.

One of the legislators asks the economist what "present-value cost" means and what a "discount rate is." The economist explains that the discount rate is used to

TABLE 13.1   PROJECTED FUTURE COSTS OF WATERBORNE ILLNESS IN THE STATE OF
HYPOCHONDRIA

Year	Estimated Cost (millions of dollars)
1996	10
1997	12
. . .	. . .
2045	108
Present-value cost of future waterborne illness	1,212
Present value of future aquifer damage from landfill leak	1,369

Note: Discount rate = 3.0 percent.

"bring back" future costs and benefits to the present, in order to determine the present-value cost. The legislator, a quick study, nods in understanding and suggests to the economist that even though the present-value damages from future aquifer deterioration is larger than the present-value cost of future waterborne illness, he will vote to recommend funding for the sewage treatment plant. The economist explains that economic efficiency would be better served by addressing the future damage from the landfill because the present-value damages are larger. The legislator explains, however, that he will not be seeking reelection 50 years from now and thus prefers to address his constituents' needs today. Then he fires the economist.

If policymakers are going to improve economic efficiency, they need a mechanism to compare benefits and costs that occur at *different times*. The premier tool used by economists to do this is called *discounting*. Of course, policymakers must often address other issues besides improving economic efficiency and will want to know whether discounting is appropriate in these other situations. If they decide that nuclear waste disposal really is an issue of future human rights, is discounting appropriate? Should Congress require that the value of future lives saved be discounted in comparison to saving lives today? Can *any* future environmental costs or benefits be discounted, or will that always be inappropriate? And as our hypothetical legislator from Hypochondria demonstrates, policymakers may have still other, less benevolent motives.

In this chapter, for the benefit of readers unfamiliar with the concepts or needing some review, we first go over the basics of discounting, the determination of the market rate of interest when borrowing and lending can occur, and the determination of the optimal societal discount rate that would be realized in the absence of any imperfections in capital markets. Readers familiar with these concepts can skip to the section, Discounting Environmental Benefits and Costs on p. 351. Next, we delve more deeply into the issue of discounting as it applies to environmental policy decisions. We examine the impacts on the discount rate when capital market imperfections exist and ask what is an appropriate discount rate to use. Then we examine the more controversial issues surrounding whether it is fair to discount future environmental benefits and costs at all. Specifically, we look at the issue of *intergenerational equity*, which may be one of the most important considerations when addressing environmental impacts that may not occur for decades or centuries. We show that arguments against discounting environmental costs and benefits confuse equity and efficiency goals. The chapter concludes by discussing one of the most controversial and misunderstood of environmental policy issues, discounting future human lives.

DISCOUNTING DEFINED

Imagine that you have just won $10 million in a lottery. While dreaming of your newfound riches, you read the fine print on your ticket and discover that you will not receive all of the money today. Instead, you will receive a check for $500,000 each year for the next 20 years. Your heart sinks, because you had hoped for all of the money today. Fortunately, you are in luck, because a rich aunt offers to buy your ticket and asks how much money you would accept today in lieu of the 20 annual payments. Depending on the strength of your desire for more money today, you will almost surely accept an amount less than the full $10 million. This is the basis of discounting. People are generally willing to exchange future gains for a smaller gain today. Future gains sell at a discount today.

We are probably all used to treating money this way without thinking about it. Suppose that I borrow $1,000 from the bank today and have to repay $1,100 in a year. The price of an additional $1,000 now is $1,100 one year from now. If I put $950 in the bank today, I can withdraw $1,000 one year from now. The price of receiving $1,000 in a year is discounted to $950 today. In both cases, a dollar a year from now buys and sells for less than a dollar now. A dollar a year from now is discounted relative to a dollar now. The degree to which future dollars are discounted relative to current dollars is called the *discount rate.*

The value today of a sum to be paid or collected in the future is called its *present value.* Present value is related to the discount rate in a straightforward way. Let V_1 be a sum due one year from now and PV be its present value. The discount rate, r, is the difference between V and PV, divided by PV. Thus

$$r = \frac{V_1 - PV}{PV} \tag{13.1}$$

This can be expressed equivalently as

$$\frac{V_1}{PV} = 1 + r \tag{13.2}$$

and as

$$PV = \frac{V_1}{1 + r} \tag{13.3}$$

These concepts can be easily extended farther into the future. The sum V_1 due one year from now may itself be the value a year from now of a sum V_2 due in two years. Thus

$$V_1 = \frac{V_2}{1 + r}$$

$$PV = \frac{V_1}{1 + r} = \frac{V_2/(1 + r)}{1 + r} = \frac{V_2}{(1 + r)^2} \tag{13.4}$$

The same process can be applied to give the present value of a sum due any number of years in the future by applying Equation 13.3 recursively. Thus for a sum V_t to be paid t years in the future, the present value of V_t is calculated as follows:

$$PV = \frac{V_t}{(1 + r)^t} \tag{13.5}$$

Because the present values of two sums due on different dates are both expressed in *today's* dollars, they can be added or subtracted. In each year t, if an action will cause a stream of benefits, B_t, and costs, C_t, extending a total of T years into the future, their present value is as follows:

$$PV = \frac{B_1 - C_1}{1 + r} + \frac{B_2 - C_2}{(1 + r)^2} + \cdots + \frac{B_T - C_T}{(1 + r)^T} = \sum_{t=1}^{T} \frac{B_t - C_t}{(1 + r)^t} \tag{13.6}$$

Equation 13.6 is one basis for comparing intertemporal streams of benefits and costs and is one foundation of applied benefit-cost analysis.[4]

INTEREST RATES, BEHAVIOR, AND EFFICIENCY

When you take out a loan from a bank, you are charged interest. The interest you pay is the price of the loan. In other words, it is the price the bank charges you for the use of the bank's (really, other depositors') money. Similarly, when you put money in your bank savings account, you are providing the bank with a loan. The interest you receive is the price you are charging the bank for their use of your money. Thus interest rates simply are market prices.[5] Like all market prices, they are determined by the interaction of supply and demand. They are determined by how much people who want to borrow are willing to pay and by how much others must be paid to be willing to lend.

Individual Choices and the Interest Rate

People may want to borrow or lend money for a number of reasons. Some people are simply impatient and wish to increase their consumption now even if it means less consumption in the future. Some prefer postponing current consumption for greater future consumption.

---

[4]The continuous time analogue of Equation 13.6 is $PV = \int_0^T (B_t - C_t)e^{-rt}\, dt$.

[5]This section discusses one overall "interest rate" solely for simplicity. As we will discuss shortly, there are many interest rates, corresponding to financial commitments with different maturities and different risks.

The premium that someone will pay to increase current consumption by $1—that is, to borrow $1 more or lend $1 less—is called that person's *rate of time preference,* or *RTP.* It is the discount rate an individual applies to consumption decisions. Individuals' rates of time preference vary with their consumption preferences. For example, a person with low current income and bright future prospects may have a high *RTP*—that is, may be willing to pay a lot to increase current consumption. But the same person might have a lower *RTP* if current income is high and anticipated future income is low.

The rate of time preference is not a fixed number, even for a single individual. It depends on personal preferences, current income and wealth, and expected future income. This is illustrated in Figure 13.1. At point *A,* for example, the individual's preferred consumption pattern $1,500 this year and $2,000 next year. Point *B* represents $2,500 of consumption today but only $500 next year. The curve $U_{T,T+1}$ is the set of all combinations of consumption this year and consumption next year that this person regards as being just as good as that at point *A.* Because points *A* and *B* both lie on $U_{T,T+1}$, the individual is *indifferent* to the two consumption patterns.

Points above and to the right of $U_{T,T+1}$ are preferred to point *A.* Point *A,* however, is preferred to points below and to the left of $U_{T,T+1}$. The *RTP* is determined by the slope of $U_{T,T+1}$ and equals the *absolute value of the slope minus 1.* At point *A,* for example, the slope of $U_{T,T+1}$ equals -2.0, and the *RTP* equals 1.0. The positive magnitude of the *RTP* means that the individual would prefer to forgo future consumption for additional current consumption at a rate of $2 forgone next year to $1 gained today.

As we did in Chapter 3 for two goods, we can draw a budget line for consumption during the two time periods. The budget line goes through the point

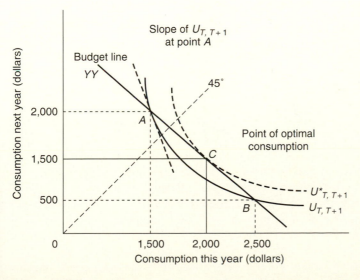

Figure 13.1   Indifference Curves and the Rate of Time Preference

on the graph representing the individual's income in each of the two periods, assumed here to be point A. The slope of the budget line shows the rate at which consumption at one date can be exchanged in the market (through borrowing and lending) for consumption at the other date and equals $-(1 + r)$. Thus if the individual in Figure 13.1 has an income stream of $1,500 today and $2,000 next year and the interest rate is zero, the budget line will go through point A and slope downward to the right at 45 degrees. This is shown as line YY. By borrowing money today, this individual can move from point A to point C, which represents a higher level of satisfaction $U^*_{T, T+1}$. The budget line shows those combinations of current and future consumption that can be reached with lending and borrowing.

The difference between the RTP and the market interest rate is straightforward. The RTP is the premium a person would be *willing to pay* for an extra dollar of consumption today; the market interest rate is the premium a person would be *required to pay* for an extra dollar of consumption today. For example, with an RTP of 5 percent, I would be willing to pay $105 in a year for an extra $100 today. If the market interest rate charged by the bank is 9 percent, then I must pay $109 in a year for an extra $100 today. Because the market interest rate is greater than my RTP, I will choose not to borrow the extra $100.

An individual whose RTP is greater than the market interest rate is willing to give up more in the future for a dollar of current consumption than required by the market. If such an individual is a borrower, he or she will prefer to borrow more at the market interest rate. If a lender, the individual will prefer to lend less. Borrowing more or lending less allows more current consumption but leaves less available to spend on future consumption. The more future consumption is traded for current consumption, the smaller the premium someone will be willing to pay for another dollar of current consumption. In other words, as debt increases (or net wealth decreases), the rate of time preference *falls*. People will reduce future consumption to increase current consumption only to the point where their rate of time preference has fallen to the level of the interest rate. Similarly, an individual whose RTP is *less* than the interest rate is unwilling to give up as much future consumption for additional current consumption as is required by the market. If such an individual is a borrower, he or she will wish to borrow less. If a lender, the individual will wish to lend more. Individuals whose RTP is not equal to the market interest rate will prefer changing their time pattern of consumption because such a change will improve their economic welfare, such as moving from point A in Figure 13.1 to point C.

These types of trade-offs apply to environmental goods just as much as consumer goods bought and sold in markets. An individual can purchase an environmental good such as recreation at a beautiful lake today in exchange for fewer consumption goods in the future. Society can require that owners of coal-fired electric generating plants purchase additional scrubbing equipment today in order to reduce air pollution in the future and thus "buy" greater quantities of pristine views at the Grand Canyon. The state of Hypochondria's legislature can vote to raise taxes today (decreasing residents' current consumption) in order to improve water quality for the next 50 years.

The Market for Loans and the Interest Rate

Different people may respond differently to the same interest rate. This is partly because of differences in preferences but is largely because of differences in income, wealth, expected future income, and age. At any time, young adults are likely to be going into debt to start families and buy houses and other durables. The middle-aged will be paying off their debts, supporting their children, and saving for retirement. The old will be living off their accumulated savings. The old live by trading assets for the labor of the young and middle-aged. The young live beyond their current means by going into debt to the more productive middle-aged. The middle-aged appear to bear a disproportionate burden but do so in exchange for previously having gone into debt to their elders and the promise of being repaid by their juniors.

Figure 13.2 shows how differences in preferences can lead to lending and borrowing. The indifference curves I and I' belong to one individual and J and J' belong to another. Individual I's indifference curves are steeper throughout. Individual I can be characterized as more impatient than person J. Initially, both have consumption now of C_1^0 and consumption next year of C_2^0 (point A). At this point, I's *RTP* is greater than J's. I is willing to borrow to increase current consumption at an interest rate at which J is willing to lend.

Individual I will borrow up to the point where the market interest rate equals his *RTP* at point X_i. Individual J will lend up to the point where the interest rate equals her *RTP* at point X_j. With only one lender and one borrower in the market, they will set the interest rate themselves. They will set it so that the amount I wants to borrow at that rate just equals the amount J wants to lend. Thus $C_1^I - C_1^0 = C_1^0 - C_1^J$ and

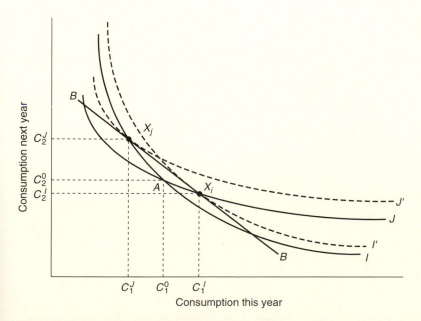

Figure 13.2 Lending and Borrowing Behavior

$C_2^J - C_2^0 = C_2^0 - C_2^I$. Both I and J are better off. This is shown on the graph by the fact that both move to higher indifference curves.

The same principle holds with more individuals and for societies. The loan market reaches equilibrium when everyone, both lenders and borrowers, has the same rate of time preference and no one wants to lend or borrow a different amount. The market interest rate equals this universal *RTP*, which is called the *social rate of time preference* (*SRTP*). The *SRTP* reflects the trade-offs that society as a whole is willing to make between present and future consumption.[6] In the United States, the *SRTP* is often equated with the rate of interest on long-term Treasury securities, which have generally averaged between 2 and 3 percent in real (inflation-adjusted) terms.

Investment and the Interest Rate

It is also possible to trade present goods for future goods directly by *investing* in productive assets, such as new machinery, technologies, or environmental assets. Such investments involve a current expenditure and future net returns. Because tangible assets (e.g., land, homes) and many intangible assets (e.g., stocks and bonds) can be sold at any time, it is possible to treat most investments as if they lasted only one period. An expenditure on an asset today will result in a net return next period and an asset with a possibly different value. If the asset is worn out or used up after one period, its value at the end of the period will be zero. Longer-lived assets will generally have a positive value after one period.

Let P_0 be the price of the asset today; let R_1 be the net revenue from the asset, to be realized at the beginning of the next period; and let P_1 be the price of the asset next period. The one-period rate of return from buying an asset is

$$\frac{R_1 + P_1 - P_0}{P_0} = \frac{R_1 + P_1}{P_0} - 1 \tag{13.7}$$

Different investment opportunities will have different one-period rates of return. Thus individuals will be willing to buy assets offering a rate of return greater than their *RTP* for the same reasons they are willing to lend to another person who offers to pay an interest rate greater than the lender's *RTP*. Businesses and individuals wanting to make investments enter the loan market in the same way as individuals wanting to borrow for current investment. They will invest their own funds up to the point where the one-period rate of return on the marginal investment equals their *RTP*. They will borrow to invest up to the point where the marginal rate of return equals the market interest rate, which will equal lenders' *RTP*. Because efficiency requires that borrowers and lenders have the same *RTP*, it also requires that the *SRTP* equal the one-period rate of return on the marginal investment. Equilibrium in the loan market requires all of these to be equal to the market interest rate.

---

[6]We will discuss shortly the issue of which society is relevant. In other words, there may be more than one relevant *SRTP* that policymakers must consider.

DISCOUNTING ENVIRONMENTAL BENEFITS AND COSTS: THE CASE OF EFFICIENCY

By way of review, Pareto efficiency over time requires that there be no unexploited gains from trading over time. Economic efficiency over time also requires that every investment that will pay a return at least as high as the *SRTP* be undertaken and that no investment yielding a lower return be undertaken. Economic efficiency over time therefore requires that the *SRTP* be equal to the *marginal return on investment*. This is equivalent to the familiar rule that investments should be undertaken if the present value of the returns is at least as great as the present value of costs. Thus for an investment to be undertaken, the present value of benefits should exceed the present value of costs. However, contrary to what your intuition might tell you, economic efficiency over time does not necessarily require the discount rate to be positive. It merely requires that all decisions be based on the same discount rate.[7]

This rule applies to environmental costs and benefits as well. As we have discussed, production of many goods involves environmental costs and benefits at other dates. The construction of a hydroelectric dam may disrupt recreation and fish habitats for several years before the project begins producing electricity. The operation of a chemical plant may leave wastes that will seep into groundwater supplies years or even decades after the plant ceases operation. Many pollution control technologies require substantial up-front investments but result in less pollution over a long time span.

The fact that there are trade-offs over time is independent of whether the trade-offs go through a market or are externalities. Investments in pollution control equipment and in new stamping mills both involve giving up current consumption to make investments that will yield future benefits. Efficiency over time requires that the trade-off between a dollar of current investment and the future benefits from that investment be made on the same basis whether the benefits will come in the form of cleaner air or car fenders. An investment should be made if the present value of its benefits exceeds its costs.

In a first best world (one without any economic distortions such as taxes), we can state two general principles for maximizing welfare where decisions have future benefits and costs:

1. Future environmental benefits and costs should be discounted at the *SRTP*.
2. The action or investment that should be chosen is the one with the highest net present value.

---

[7]This is strictly true only if all investments have the same degree of risk. Efficiency over time requires that all decisions involving the same degree of risk be based on the same discount rate and that the difference between the discount rates applied to decisions with different degrees of risk be just enough to compensate for the difference in risk. This is discussed in Chapter 14.

DAM DISTORTIONS: WATER PROJECT DEVELOPMENT IN THE AMERICAN WEST

Do discount rates really matter? Can using the "wrong" discount rate lead to environmental catastrophe? Yes! The evidence lies in many parts of the western United States, where over the past century, the U.S. Bureau of Reclamation and the U.S. Army Corps of Engineers battled each other for domination of water projects. Between them, these two agencies built hundreds of water projects—hydroelectric dams, irrigation projects, and canals.* Their cost-benefit "analyses" were often little more than shams. The agencies would inflate future project benefits using low discount rates. Sometimes they didn't even bother to discount future benefits whatsoever. In that way, benefits far into the future (dams last quite a long time) could appear to be much larger than costs borne by taxpayers during construction. (In many cases, they also fudged the calculations of the benefits and the costs themselves, but that's another story.)

The discount rates used by the Army Corps of Engineers have varied greatly over time. During the 1950s and 1960s, the official discount rate was as low as 2.5 percent. In the 1980s, it was as high as 10 percent. These discount rates have been determined either by internal policy decisions, by Congress, or by independent federal agencies such as the Water Resources Council (WRC). Between 1968 and 1978, for example, the WRC stated that the discount rate used should reflect the coupon rate on long-term government bonds.† Then, from 1978 until 1982, the WRC recommended the use of the yield to maturity (*YTM*) on long-term government bonds.‡ Today, development of water resource projects is done under the guidelines of the Water Resources Development Act of 1974, which uses the *YTM* on government bonds as the discount rate.

If "correct" discount rates had been used, many projects' direct monetary benefits would not have exceeded their costs. Taking into account some of the environmental damage that accompanied water project development—siltation, salinity and loss of agricultural productivity, loss of wetlands, destruction of wildlife habitats and fisheries—many projects made even less economic sense.

One noteworthy example of a boondoggle is the Garrison Diversion Project in west-central North Dakota. The project was first conceived back in the 1940s as a way of irrigating North Dakota farmlands. The project involves a series of canals, pipelines, and reservoirs designed to carry water from Lake Sakakawea behind Garrison Dam to several hundred thousand acres of farmland in the northern and the eastern parts of the state. Construction of Garrison Dam alone in the 1950s resulted in a loss of 350,000 acres of productive farmland that were flooded behind the reservoir. Not only has the project been an ecological disaster, destroying wetlands and wildlife habitats, but the economics of the project were also never justified. It is estimated that the few farmers who benefit from the diversion project will be paying less than 3 percent of the actual cost of bringing water to their lands.

Of course, some projects were well thought out. Others, like Grand Coulee Dam in Washington State, one of the largest dams in the world, extracted a large environmental price but provided large benefits. Grand

Coulee was a major factor in the United States' defeating Germany and Japan in World War II: the electricity it produced was used to build thousands of planes and ships.

The moral of the story is that discount rates do matter. Adjusting discount rates, or benefits and costs themselves, can extract a significant environmental price. Policymakers with short time horizons (and high personal discount rates) would do well to remember this.

*One of the best indictments of the Bureau and Corps work is Reisner (1993). We discuss water resource development in more detail in Chapter 17.

†A coupon rate is the published rate on a bond. For example, a bond with a $1,000 face value and 10 percent coupon rate would pay $100 interest each year, in addition to paying $1,000 if held to maturity.

‡The yield to maturity on a bond equals the interest that would equate the discounted stream of bond payments with the bond's price today. Suppose that the $1,000 ten-year bond with the 10 percent coupon rate could be purchased for $800 today. The YTM would equal the discount rate, r, such that $800 = \sum_{t=1}^{10} \$100/(1 + r)^t + \$1,000/(1 + r)^{10}$. In this example, the YTM turns out to be about 13.8 percent.

Distortions in Markets

The real world is full of distortions. Capital markets are imperfect. Individuals may have different levels of information and a different willingness to accept risk. And of course, there are always taxes, which are not always assessed at the same rate for different individuals and corporations. Thus in reality, the market does not produce a situation where all individuals have the same RTP and where this $SRTP$ is equated with the rate of return on the marginal investment. The comparison and selection of policies that capture environmental benefits may be influenced by these distortions. Environmental policymakers need to be aware of such distortions and their impacts on the entire economy.[8]

How does all of this relate to environmental benefits? Improving environmental quality is an investment. Policies to reduce air pollution or purchase

---

[8]The impact of income taxes, for example, can be seen as follows. Suppose that a $1 investment in a business will return $1.10 next year. This gives a rate of return of 10 percent. If the business owner pays a marginal income tax rate of 38 percent, the after-tax return is $1.062, or 6.2 percent. The business owner will invest up to the point where the rate of time preference equals the after-tax rate of return, not the pretax rate of return. Thus income taxes create a *wedge* between the marginal rate of return on investment (ROI) and the rate of time preference. In the presence of income taxes, the RTP at the margin will be less than the return on private investment. With a tax rate of τ percent, the after-tax return on investment, ROI_a, will equal $(1 - \tau)ROI_b$, where ROI_b equals the pretax return. In equilibrium, the RTP will be equated with ROI_a. Thus the higher the marginal tax rate, the larger the wedge between the RTP and ROI_b.

wetlands are investments, trading off reduced consumption today for increased consumption (of environmental assets) in the future. In some cases, environmental investments may be pure public investments, as when the government purchases land for a new national park or improves facilities at an existing one. In other cases, however, private actions will be required. For example, a utility's decision to invest in a new scrubber for a coal plant versus purchasing additional sulfur dioxide emissions permits may be affected by the respective tax treatments of these investments. It is possible that, from society's perspective, the most efficient investment would be the purchase of the emissions permits, yet from the utility's perspective, the scrubber will make more sense.[9]

Because of their public-good nature, investments in environmental assets are often financed by the government. Government investments can be financed through taxes or by government borrowing. (They can also be financed by the government's printing money, but that is really a form of borrowing.) In either case, government spending can displace, or *crowd out,* private sector spending. Unless the supply of capital is perfectly elastic, increased government borrowing will increase the interest rate, causing a reduction in private sector borrowing.[10] This is shown in Figure 13.3.

A reduction in private sector borrowing because of government borrowing can be considered an additional cost of government-financed investments and thus may need to be factored into evaluations of the benefits and the costs of purchasing environmental assets. So if the choice is between government-financed investment in environmental improvements and private sector–financed investment, the additional cost of government borrowing should be accounted for.

Determining the magnitude of this additional cost depends on how the displaced private sector spending would have been otherwise used. Some of the displaced private sector spending would have been for consumption, and some would have been for investment. If there were no crowding out, there would be no displacement of private capital. With complete crowding out, all of the costs of the public project would displace private capital. When public investment displaces a dollar's worth of private *consumption,* there is no problem in measuring this cost. It is $1 of current consumption. Because it is current consumption, it is not discounted, and capital market distortions do not affect it.

When public investment completely crowds out a dollar's worth of private *investment,* things are not so simple. The private investment would not have been planned unless it would have earned the pretax marginal rate of return. Hence the present value of the private investment, discounted at the *SRTP,* will be greater than $1.

---

[9]In fact, this is a real issue for many electric utilities and a significant source of uncertainty because there has been confusion as to the tax treatment of emissions permits. Are emissions permits utility "assets"? If the market price of emissions permits increases, is that treated as a "capital gain" and subject to taxation? Are purchases of emissions permits a deductible utility expense?

[10]For readers familiar with macroeconomics, the crowding out we refer to here is the same sort of crowding out displayed in IS-LM analysis.

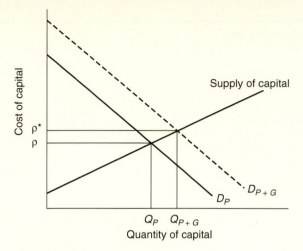

Figure 13.3   Crowding Out of Private Investment Because of Government Borrowing

For example, suppose that the *SRTP* is 6 percent and the pretax private rate of return is 16 percent. Displacing $1 of private investment today means giving up $1.16 a year from now. Discounted at the *SRTP*, the present value of $1.16 is $1.16/1.06 = $1.094 > $1.00. If the private sector investment would not have matured for two years, the loss in two years would be ($1.16)($1.16) = $1.346. Its present value, when discounted at the *SRTP* of 6 percent, is $1.198. The longer-lived the private investment that is displaced, the greater the actual value of each dollar of displaced investment. If this investment's yield were all in the thirtieth year, to give a rate of return of 16 percent, it would have to yield $85.85 after 30 years for each dollar invested. This has a present value of $14.19 at 6 percent.

This value of a dollar of displaced private investment is termed the *shadow price of capital* (*SPC*).[11] It is the value of current and future potential consumption given up by displacing a dollar of private investment. The shadow price of capital is generally thought to be between a factor of 2.5 and 3, based on estimates of the average lives of private investments and the fraction of returns that are reinvested. In other words, by forgoing $1 worth of private investment today, we are forgoing future private consumption with a present value between $2.50 and $3.00.

The fraction of private spending displaced by a public investment that would have been private investment must be weighted by the shadow price of capital to show all the costs of the public investment correctly. Doing so puts all costs on an

---

[11]See Lind (1982, 1990). For a mathematical treatment, see the appendix to this chapter. See also Lesser and Zerbe (1994).

equal footing by measuring them in terms of forgone consumption and allows for comparisons that will maximize economic efficiency.[12]

Compensating for Distortions

With an income tax, the *SRTP* will be less than the marginal rate of return on private investment. With crowding out of private investment, the true cost of government borrowing will be higher than the market interest rate. This raises the question of what will be the appropriate rate to use to discount environmental costs and benefits.

Thinking about the concept of efficiency for a second makes the answer clear. Economic efficiency consists of giving people what they want when they want it. Inefficiency over time consists of people giving up more than they want in one period to get goods in another period. To judge whether we have efficiency over time, we need to know the rate at which people will trade goods at one time for goods at another. It is the *SRTP* that tells us this.

Discounting environmental benefits and costs at the *SRTP* tells us what future benefits and costs are worth today. Using the rate of return on private investment, or some intermediate rate, will undervalue future benefits and costs. Discounting at another rate, such as the rate of return on private investment, can lead to the same environmental costs and benefits being discounted at different rates.

Suppose that two electric utilities each own half of a coal-fired power plant. The first utility, Goodguys Power and Light, is well managed. Goodguys has an after-tax cost of capital equal to 8 percent. The other utility, Fly-by-Night Electric, is poorly managed. It is perceived by the investment community as much riskier than Goodguys. Potential investors will want a higher after-tax rate of return to compensate for the additional risk. (We discuss risk and discount rates in detail in Chapter 14.) Because the utilities have equal shares of the coal plant, the environmental costs in each year will be the same for both. But because Fly-by-Night gets to use a higher after-tax cost of capital as a discount rate than Goodguys does, it will value the future environmental costs resulting from operation of the plant less than Goodguys. Thus Fly-by-Night will see the coal plant as a cheaper resource, even though the actual environmental costs associated with each utility's share of the electric output must be identical. This is certainly a perverse result: future environmental costs are valued *less* because they are produced by a badly managed company.

This example should convince you that the presence of distortions in the capital market does not require adjusting the discount rate. The *SRTP* will still be the appropriate discount rate to use, with or without distortions. This does not mean that distortions in capital markets have no effects whatsoever. They may. *The way to correct these distortions, however, is to adjust the benefit and cost streams themselves.* To see this, suppose that a unit of government is considering investing in a

---

[12]See Bradford (1975), Lind (1982), and Zerbe and Dively (1994) for derivations of the shadow price of capital.

sewage treatment plant. If the plant has benefits of $1 million per year for 50 years, the present value of those benefits is

$$PV_b = \sum_{t=1}^{50} \frac{1,000,000}{(1 + SRTP)^t} \qquad (13.8)$$

The plant will be worth building if the present value of the benefits is greater than the present value of the costs. If there were no distortions in capital markets, this would be straightforward to determine. If there are distortions, the stream of benefits should be reduced to reflect crowding out. For example, the consumption equivalent of the stream of benefits may be only $950,000 each year. If so, Equation 13.8 should be reevaluated using that lower benefits value, again discounting at the *SRTP*.

Are Distortions a Problem for Evaluating Environmental Projects?

According to Lind (1990), international capital markets are probably highly elastic in most cases. Even if there were some crowding out of private investment, a procedure that discounted ordinary benefits and costs by the *SRTP* and then performed a sensitivity test would be all that was required. For projects that did not pass a sensitivity test, further work could be done to determine the benefits and costs of the project more precisely and the degree of crowding out, if any, that might occur as a result of project financing.[13]

Unfortunately, despite overall highly elastic capital markets, some countries have limited access to capital markets, either because of market inefficiencies or political sanctions (e.g., embargo on Iraq, freezing of Iranian assets in international banks). Thus in some cases, capital market distortions may still present a significant *environmental* problem. A country choosing between investing in private sector environmental infrastructure like sewers and water treatment facilities may significantly reduce limited private investment toward economic growth. If that reduces the economic well-being of citizens, it may result in *more* environmental harm than if the infrastructure investment did not occur.[14] Thus capital market distortions should not be dismissed out of hand; rather, they should be assessed carefully.

The Choice of Social Discount Rate

We discussed how, in an ideal world with perfect capital markets, everyone would have the same rate of time preference, which we now know is called the *SRTP*. However, in the real world, there may be groups within society that do not interact

---

[13]Of course, it would also be important to determine why the project was being undertaken. If it was to meet equity or rights concerns, a traditional benefit-cost test would be insufficient. See Zerbe (1991) for further discussion.

[14]We discuss environmental quality and economic well-being in Chapter 19.

through capital markets and therefore have different rates of time preference. The benefits and the costs of pollution or pollution control may accrue to members of groups with different rates of time preference. Therefore, the value assigned to future environmental impacts will depend on *whose RTP* is used. Cummings (1991) discusses this issue in terms of the reserved water rights of Indian tribes. U.S. courts have generally accepted the principle that tribes' reserved water rights must be based on the amount of water that can economically be used to irrigate reservation land. In analyzing the economic feasibility of reservation irrigation, the courts have used discount rates derived from U.S. society as a whole, even though tribes' investment behavior appears to indicate different, and in some cases "negative," discount rates.[15]

The same type of situation could arise in other environmental areas. In Chapter 8 we briefly discussed the "exporting" of pollution across international boundaries. Emissions of sulfur dioxide from coal-fired power plants in the midwestern United States, for example, have been prime contributors to acid rain and forest destruction in eastern Canada. Radioactive fallout from the Chernoybl nuclear power plant in Ukraine spread over many European countries. In both cases, the populations that benefited from the power plants and the populations that bore some of the environmental impacts were separate and may have different rates of time preference.

For example, suppose that Canadians have a lower *RTP* than Americans. In that case, the present value of the costs of acid rain would be greater, as the Canadians would evaluate them, than would be the costs when evaluated using the American rate of time preference. This situation raises both efficiency and equity issues. The fact that two groups have different rates of time preference indicates that there is some imperfection in the capital market: there are investments or lending opportunities in the larger society that the group with the lower *RTP* would be willing to take advantage of. If capital market imperfections could be removed, the two groups' *RTP*s would be brought into equality, and the group with the lower *RTP* would have its wealth increased in the process. However, this would also lower the value of future environmental costs as evaluated by the group that now has the lower *RTP*. This is an issue that policymakers need to be aware of but for which there is no general principle for resolving. Things are somewhat more straightforward when we turn to *strict* equity questions.

DISCOUNTING AND INTERGENERATIONAL EQUITY

As we have seen, discounting plays a vital role in analyzing whether an action increases overall economic welfare. So far, however, we have not looked at how that welfare may be *distributed* over time. The distribution of welfare over time is central to many ongoing environmental policy controversies, such as global warm-

---

[15]Rogers (1994) provides intriguing evidence for changing time preferences as a result of natural selection over many generations.

ing and preservation of endangered species. This section examines the relationship between discounting and intergenerational equity. We look at three questions.

1. Is discounting appropriate in deciding whether intergenerational inequities exist?
2. Will discounting future benefits and costs to measure welfare changes from actions with future impacts necessarily lead to intergenerational inequity?
3. Should the discount rate used to analyze the overall benefits and costs of an environmental policy depend on considerations of intergenerational equity?

It is not hard to think of intergenerational environmental impacts. Most of the local environments inhabited by humans have been changed significantly by human activities. Forests have been cut down, converted to farmland, and sometimes paved over or even reforested. Our actions today can affect our descendants for thousands of years, possibly in drastic ways that we cannot fully comprehend today. Emissions of greenhouse gases may alter the earth's climate permanently; dams we build today will be in place for decades or centuries; nuclear wastes we leave behind may be toxic for centuries or millennia.

Alternative Concepts of Intergenerational Fairness

There is a large literature focusing on the definition of intergenerational fairness that builds on the concepts of fairness we discussed in Chapter 4. Broadly speaking, intergenerational fairness considers two issues: the nature of the current generation's responsibility to future generations and the possibility of a moral commitment to biological and institutional integrity. Instrumental in both of these concerns is the substitutability between "natural" and other forms of capital. As Toman (1994) notes, these definitions have been the focus of debates over the ethical implications of the present-value criterion, which some analysts believe weighs the preferences of the current generation at the expense of future generations.[16] Though these concerns predate more recent debates over "sustainability,"[17] they have been linked to sustainability owing to the 1987 report by the World Commission on Environment and Development, Our Common Future, better known as the Bruntland Commission report, which describes "sustainable development" as "development that meets the needs of the present generation without compromising the ability of future generations to meet their own needs."

How well do these more recent characterizations fit with other definitions of intergenerational fairness? As you may recall from Chapter 4, Rawls (1971) developed principles of justice that he proposed to apply across generations as well as between contemporaries. According to Rawls, there is justice between generations when the worst-off generation is as well off as possible. We are being unjust to

---

[16]These debates are set out in a series of papers by Howarth and Norgaard. References can be found in Toman (1994). Oberhofer (1989) refers to a "cultural" discount rate, which he sees as increasing in the United States, reflecting decreasing concern for the future.

[17]We discuss definitions of sustainability and its measurement in more detail in Chapter 19.

future generations if some of them will be worse off than we are and we could improve the lot of the worst-off generation. Another recent conception of justice holds that a situation is fair if no one envies anyone else in the sense of being willing to trade places.[18] This conception of fairness also makes it possible to say that a situation is fair, or more than fair, to some individuals but not to others. A situation is fair to individual X if there is no one that X wants to trade places with.

This conception of fairness can be extended to intergenerational equity. The present generation is being unfair to future generations if those future generations would be willing to trade places with us. A third conception deals directly with the choice of discount rate. In this conception, an individual is allowed to *choose* the discount rate that will be used to compare the welfare of current and future generations. However, that individual cannot choose the generation into which he or she is placed. Thus someone who chose a high discount rate in the hope of being placed in the present generation may be rudely surprised.

All of these conceptions of intergenerational justice come down to the same idea: we are being unfair to future generations if they will be worse off than we are *because of our actions today* (Barry 1977). Thus one definition of a sustainable future is one in which the current generation's actions do not jeopardize the ability of future generations to be as well off as we are today. If future generations will be at least as well off as we are, we are not being unfair to the future. This can be applied to individual members of future generations as well as to future generations as a whole. A decision made today is unfair to specific members of future generations if it would cause them to be willing to trade places with people alive today. Other ideas of intergenerational justice are possible, but we will use this one for the remainder of the chapter. We encourage readers who have another idea of intergenerational fairness to work through the arguments in the rest of this chapter using it.

It is important to notice that this conception of intergenerational fairness requires comparing the welfare of members of different generations, not comparing any one individual's welfare with what it *could have been*. To see the difference, consider the following example. Suppose that people alive today have a choice of two actions. One will give all individuals alive today an annual income of $12,000 and their grandchildren 50 years from now an annual income of $50,000. The other will give all persons alive today an annual income of $12,500 and their grandchildren an annual income of $40,000. Choosing the second does not violate this conception of fairness to the future, even though it reduces future incomes by $10,000 in exchange for a small increase in income today. This is because either choice leaves our grandchildren much better off than we are. We may want to give up $500 a year so that our grandchildren can have an extra $10,000 per year, but that would be *benevolence* on our part, not the fulfillment of an obligation. Failure to realize this fact would lead to the absurd conclusion that each generation should work like slaves and save like misers while freezing and starving in the dark,

---

[18]See, for example, Varian (1975, 1984) and Baumol (1986).

because any consumption or leisure represents an expenditure of resources that could have been devoted to making future generations better off.

How Practical Are Concepts of Intergenerational Fairness?

Time travel notwithstanding, we cannot ask someone from the future if he or she would care to trade places with us. Nor can we know with certainty whether our actions today will make future generations worse or better off, not only because we cannot predict the future with certainty, but also because there is no unique definition of well-being.

If we accept the definition that we are being unfair to future generations if our actions today will make them worse off than they otherwise would be and that there should be rough equity in how benefits and costs are allocated, how can we compare the welfare of different generations? We do so *imperfectly,* by comparing monetary measures of income or wealth or some wider measure of quality of life. Thus in considering broad questions of environmental policy issues, an "intergenerational fairness" test could ask if future generations will be better off than we are and whether, for a particular project, the benefits will be gained by those who bear the costs.

It is important to understand that this type of comparison does *not* involve discounting the welfare of future generations. For example, I might want to compare the value I place on my situation today with the value my grandchildren will place on their situation 100 years from now. Discounting my grandchildren's welfare would show how much value *I* place today on events 100 years from now but would *not* provide information on how my grandchildren will value those events. Hence if the primary goal of a policy analysis is to evaluate the fairness of a proposed action on future generations, the costs and the benefits of that action should *not* be discounted.

Is a Positive Discount Rate Unfair to the Future?

We have just stated that when equity is the primary policy goal, future benefits and costs should not be discounted. Does this mean that using a positive discount rate for analyzing the economic *efficiency* of environmental projects and policies is necessarily unfair to future generations because less weight is placed on future benefits and costs? The answer is no. Placing more or less weight on future benefits and costs is a matter of attitudes or decision procedures. As we have defined it, fairness to future generations is an issue of distributional justice as defined in Chapter 4. It is a matter of consequences of our actions today. If discounting is unfair to the future, *it must either cause future generations to be worse off than we are or be part of a procedure that causes future generations to be worse off than we are.*

We now examine whether such a connection exists. As we discussed earlier in the chapter, there is no single factor that determines the interest rate. Some people are willing to pay a positive interest rate to borrow. Others are willing to lend only if they receive a positive interest rate. And there are investment opportunities available that are expected to yield a positive rate of return. The factors that determine interest rates also affect overall economic growth in the economy and future wealth. By using a simple economic growth model, we can examine how the various forces that determine interest rates affect the economy over time and therefore the welfare of different generations. Even though the model is simple, it is relevant to environmental policy discussions *because it illustrates the danger of equating specific discount rates to "fair" outcomes.*

There are many models of economic growth in the literature, most of which do not model different generations explicitly. One type of model that does, one that we use here, is called an *overlapping-generations model,* which was developed first by Samuelson (1958). As the name indicates, the distinguishing feature of this type of model is that it models explicitly two or more generations with overlapping lifetimes. (We present the specific mathematical form of the model and derive the equilibrium conditions in the appendix to this chapter.)

In this model, we assume away many features of the real world that do not affect the results, and we make some simplifying assumptions about the features we are interested in. First, we assume that there are three relevant groups in the model at any time. There are two generations of people alive at any time, the young and the old, and there are many identical firms.

We assume that population is constant over time. Each generation lives for two periods. People are born with no wealth, and there is no inheritance. The younger generation consists entirely of working adults. (If you like, you can assume that children lurk in the background but do not participate in the market economy.) The young enter the labor force without any assets except their human capital. They earn income only from their labor. We also assume that this labor supply is inelastic: the young supply the same amount and quality of labor regardless of the wage rate. The young can buy only two things: consumer goods and shares of stock in the many identical companies.[19]

The old are retired and have income. They must live off the shares of stock they accumulated in the previous period when they were young. They receive dividends and then they sell their shares. At the end of the second period, they die. To keep things simple, we assume that there are no inheritances. Assets pass from one generation to the next by the old selling their stock to the young. Thus the people in this model face only one choice in their lives: how to divide their income when they are young between consumption and saving for their retirement. We have assumed away all other individual choices except this intertemporal choice.

All capital goods are owned by the firms, which hire the younger generation to operate them. The firms pay the young wages equal to the value of the marginal product of labor. Each share of stock represents a constant ownership share in one firm. Each firm's physical capital may change over time, but it is fixed within each period, so firms pay dividends proportional to the value of the marginal product of capital. The firms produce both consumer and capital goods. The consumer goods

---

[19]Because we assume that the companies are identical, their stocks are interchangeable. That allows us to assume away any nasty portfolio issues.

are sold, while the capital goods are kept for use in future production. Firms divide their output between consumer and capital goods to maximize their profits. Thus firms must respond to consumers' demands. For example, if the young want more current consumption (and therefore want to save less), the price of consumer goods will rise, and the price of shares will fall. Firms will increase production of consumer goods up to the point where the price of consumer goods equals marginal cost. This will require reducing production of capital goods, and net investment will be smaller. It may even be negative.

Now, we know that one factor that affects interest rates is individuals' preferences between current and future consumption. For the old, this is a moot question. They have no future, and they consume all of their dividend income and the entire proceeds from the sale of their accumulated shares. The young, however, do have a choice between current and future consumption. To make this factor easier to deal with, we assume that everyone has the same preference between current and future consumption. This preference is characterized by one parameter, R, which equals the *RTP* when consumption is the same in the two periods. In Figure 13.4, R is just the absolute value of the slope of the utility curve at point A minus 1. The distribution of production possibilities between now and next year is shown by the line *PPF*. This line represents combinations of production that are feasible given the resources and technology that society possesses.

R can be thought of as a measure of impatience. When $R = 0$, a person facing an interest rate of zero will divide consumption equally between the two periods, as at point A in Figure 13.4. A more impatient person with $R > 0$ will require the reward of a positive interest rate to be willing to consume the same amount in the two periods. For this person, an interest rate of zero will lead to a consumption allocation such as point B ("bird in the hand"). A person with $R < 0$ prefers consumption in the future to consumption today. If the interest rate is zero, this person will choose a consumption allocation such as point C ("rainy-day saver"). We

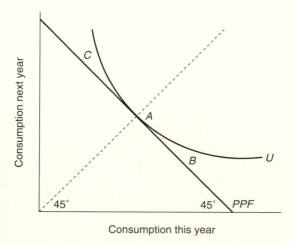

Figure 13.4   Two-Period Consumption Allocation

TABLE 13.2   BASE-CASE SCENARIO

Technology Factor, γ	Capital Productivity Factor, P	Impatience Factor, R	Initial Capital Stock, K_0
0.0	0.5	0.0	5.00

assume that each generation also is selfish in that each cares only about its own consumption. There is no malevolence or altruism toward other generations, just indifference.

A second factor that will determine the interest rate is the production process and the return it can pay on investment. In our model, we assume a simple production function that can be characterized by two parameters, P and γ.[20] P is an index of the relative productivity of capital and labor. If $P = 0.5$, capital and labor are equally productive. If $P > 0.5$, the productivity of capital increases relative to that of labor, and if $P < 0.5$, the productivity of capital falls relative to that of labor. The importance of this relative productivity factor is that it will help determine how much investment there is in new capital goods. The other parameter, γ, is an index of the rate of improvement in technology. The output produced by a given combination of capital and labor increases by 100γ percent each period. If γ is zero, technology is stagnant; if γ is positive, technology is improving over time, and capital and labor are both becoming more productive. In terms of a production isoquant, P tells us the shape of the isoquant, and γ tells us how the isoquant shifts from year to year.

To run the model and determine an equilibrium interest rate, we need to provide a value for the initial capital stock, K_0, and values for P, R, and γ. The initial capital stock can be thought of as an endowment of natural resources, such as minerals, crude oil, forests, and productive land for agriculture. The greater the stock of natural resources, the larger K_0 will be and the better off all generations will be.

With these inputs, the model calculates a series of values for the capital stock, income and consumption for each of the two generations alive in each period, and the interest rate. In doing so, *the model allows us to explore whether there is a connection between a positive interest rate and declining welfare, when welfare is measured by consumption.* Thus the model can test the hypothesis that a positive discount rate is unfair to future generations because it encourages the current generation to consume at the expense of the future.

To test the hypothesis, we begin by constructing a base-case scenario. The base case has an interest rate of zero and constant consumption over time. One of the many combinations of parameters that will give us this result is shown in Table 13.2. If we solve the model using this set of parameters, consumption of both the young and the old will be constant in each period, and the capital stock will remain constant at its initial level of 5 units. The equilibrium interest rate will also be a constant

---

[20]We assume that the same production process produces either consumer or capital goods.

TABLE 13.3   CASES 1 AND 2

	Technology Factor, γ	Capital Productivity Factor, P	Impatience Factor, R	Initial Capital Stock, K_0
Base case	0.0	0.5	0.0	5.00
Case 1	0.0	0.5	0.10	4.65
Case 2	0.0	0.5	−0.10	5.40

0 percent. Thus in the base case, the younger generation in each period is willing to trade current consumption for future consumption on a one-for-one basis, and investment possibilities are such that they will repay any investment exactly with neither gain nor loss.

Any change in these four input parameters will change the model's behavior. The model can show us how changes in any of these parameters affect the equilibrium interest rate and the consumption levels of the two generations. *If we observe that higher equilibrium interest rates coincide with a shift in consumption patterns from the future to the present, we can deduce that higher interest rates lead to unfair outcomes for the future.*

The easiest way to test this hypothesis is to change consumers' degree of impatience, since "selfishness" is often seen as a key driver of "unfairness" to the future. First we increase impatience, and then we decrease it. It turns out that by increasing R, we must change K_0 so that it remains constant over time.[21] We set the initial capital stock where the rate of time preference equals the return on investment and save the effects of capital accumulation for later cases. For our first two cases, we select the four parameters in Table 13.3. The only difference between case 1 and case 2 is that in case 1 the impatience factor is positive and in case 2 it is negative. Using these parameters, we can determine the steady-state levels of consumption, capital stock, and interest rates. Using these inputs in the model, the results for consumption, the capital stock, and the equilibrium interest rate shown in Table 13.4 are derived.

In case 1, the young in each period require a higher rate of return for each level of saving. That is not surprising, as the young now are more impatient. With decreasing marginal productivity of capital, a *higher* rate of return per unit of investment can be paid only with a *smaller* capital stock. Thus the return on investment and the rate of time preference will be equal at a *lower* level of saving. This results in higher consumption for the young but a lower capital stock and lower total consumption. Compared to the base case, with its 0 percent interest rate, all generations are worse off in case 1, with its positive interest rate. In addition, the members of each generation are worse off when they are old than when they are

---

[21]Changing the degree of impatience changes the size of capital stock at which the rate of time preference is equated to the return on investment. If we had not done so, the model would converge to a steady state in only a few generations. If you examine the model equations in the appendix, you can convince yourself of this.

TABLE 13.4   STEADY-STATE CONSUMPTION, CAPITAL STOCK, AND INTEREST RATES: CASES 1 AND 2

	Consumption of Old	Consumption of Young	Capital Stock	Interest Rate (percent)
Case 1	4.88	5.11	4.65	5.00
Case 2	5.13	4.86	5.40	−5.00
Base case	5.00	5.00	5.00	0.00

young. However, all generations in case 1 are equally well off. All generations consume 5.11 units when they are young and 4.88 units when they are old.

In case 2, the results are reversed. The savings of a less impatient population support a larger steady-state capital stock and a negative interest rate. All generations are better off than in the base case, and each generation is better off when old than when young. Again, however, all generations are equally well off.

Just by changing the degree of impatience, we produced *both* positive and negative interest rates. Both were associated with steady states where future generations are as well off as the present one. According to our definition of unfairness, the present generation is not being unfair to the future. In case 1, greater impatience made *all* generations worse off, but it did not lead to a declining standard of living over time.

Next we examine the differences from the base case when we change the relative productivity of capital and labor. In case 3, we make capital relatively more productive than labor by setting $P = 0.6$. In case 4, we make capital relatively less productive than labor by setting $P = 0.4$. The input parameters for these two cases are shown in Table 13.5.

Whether we change the initial capital stock or leave it at 5 units, within a few generations it will converge to the new steady-state value. Once the steady state is reached, the levels of consumption, capital stock, and interest rate will be those shown in Table 13.6. The higher productivity of capital in case 3 results in higher consumption than in the base case and a positive interest rate. This makes economic sense: a larger, more productive capital stock will make all generations better off. Both the young and the old can increase their consumption. Conversely, the lower productivity of capital in case 4 results in lower consumption than in the base case and a negative interest rate.

TABLE 13.5   CASES 3 AND 4

	Technology Factor, γ	Capital Productivity Factor, P	Impatience Factor, R	Initial Capital Stock, K_0
Base case	0.0	0.5	0.0	5.00
Case 3	0.0	0.6	0.0	5.00
Case 4	0.0	0.4	0.0	5.00

TABLE 13.6   STEADY-STATE CONSUMPTION, CAPITAL STOCK, AND INTEREST RATES: CASES 3 AND 4

	Consumption of Old	Consumption of Young	Capital Stock	Interest Rate (percent)
Case 3	6.02	5.02	5.02	20.0
Case 4	3.96	4.95	4.95	−20.0
Base case	5.00	5.00	5.00	0.00

In case 3, the old consume more than the young, yet the interest rate is *positive*. In case 4, the young consume more than the old, yet the interest rate is *negative*. In both cases, however, all generations have the same lifetime consumption, and total consumption is the same in all periods. Based on these four cases, there seems to be no unique relationship between the relative welfare of current and future generations and the interest rate.

So far, we have seen constant levels of consumption coexisting with zero, positive, and negative interest rates. In cases 5 and 6, we demonstrate consumption levels that are not constant over time. In these cases (see Table 13.7), the initial capital stock differs from its steady-state level. All of the parameters except the initial capital stock are set to their values in case 1.

In case 5, our economy starts out much poorer than in the base case. The initial capital stock is only 2 units. In case 6, by contrast, the economy starts out much richer than in the base case, with an initial capital stock of 8. This could be comparable to the wealth of two generations, one with an rich endowment of natural resources and the other with few natural resources.

In case 5, the smaller initial capital stock supports a positive interest rate (less capital, higher marginal productivity of capital), which induces the young to save more than is required to replace the existing capital stock. This net positive saving continues until the capital stock grows to its steady-state level. As the capital stock grows, consumption grows with it to the steady-state level. (With this combination of P and R, consumption of the two generations is always the same.) The interest rate is positive as long as the capital stock is less than its steady-state level. Figure 13.5 shows the time paths of the capital stock, consumption, and the interest rate.

In case 6, the capital stock starts out larger than its steady-state level. This larger capital stock can only pay a negative rate of return on investment. As a result, the

TABLE 13.7   CASES 5 AND 6

	Technology Factor, γ	Capital Productivity Factor, P	Impatience Factor, R	Initial Capital Stock, K_0
Base case	0.0	0.5	0.0	5.00
Case 5	0.0	0.5	0.0	2.0
Case 6	0.0	0.5	0.0	8.0

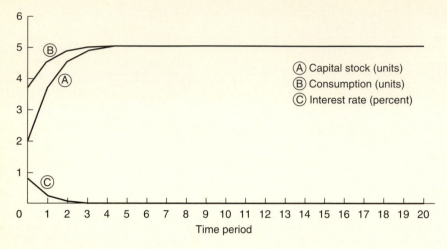

Figure 13.5   Case 5: Time paths of Capital Stock, Consumption and the Interest Rate, Capital Stock less than Steady-State Amount

young are not willing to save enough to maintain the capital stock at its current level. Both consumption and the capital stock decline toward their steady-state level, and the interest rate *rises* until it reaches its steady-state level of 0 percent. Figure 13.6 shows the time paths of the capital stock, consumption, and the interest rate in case 6.

In case 5, the capital accumulation and resulting increase in consumption meet our criterion for fairness to future generations, even though they are accompanied by a positive interest rate. In case 6, however, early generations leave their successors worse off than they are, even though they could have done otherwise. They could have maintained the capital stock at its initial level but chose not to.

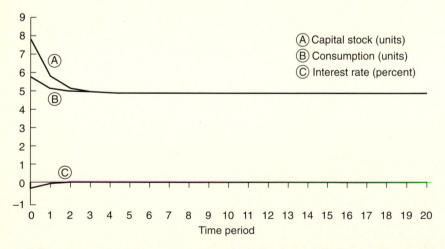

Figure 13.6   Case 6: Time Paths of Capital Stock, Consumption and the Interest Rate, Capital Stock Larger than Steady-State Amount

Thus the actions of early generations are unfair to future generations, but this unfairness is accompanied by a *negative* interest rate.

Many other cases can be constructed with this model and other economic growth models. The computer disk accompanying this book contains a computer spreadsheet of this model and some suggested cases to try.[22] Cases can be constructed by varying two or more parameters at once. It is possible to construct cases where there are positive interest rates and each generation is unfair to its successors. It is also possible to be fair, or more than fair, to the future with negative interest rates.

The lesson to be drawn from this simple model is that *having a positive discount rate does not cause us to be unfair to future generations, nor does it tell us whether we are being unfair.* Each generation passes on an inheritance of capital, resources, and technology to its successors. Environmental assets, including environmental quality and stocks of natural resources, will be part of this inheritance. We are being fair, or more than fair, to our descendants if the inheritance we pass on is enough to sustain a steady or rising standard of living. We are being unfair if it is not.

In general, positive interest rates do not mean that we are living off the future's inheritance. In fact, positive interest rates are associated with capital accumulation and improving technology, two actions that will make the future better off. It is also possible for greater technology growth to substitute for capital assets. Thus even though we deplete stocks of certain resources over time, such as oil and minerals, we can overcome that "loss" through improved technology and utilization of the remaining stocks. That is precisely what has happened over time.[23]

The common misconception that discounting at a positive rate means treating the future unfairly results from confusing *attitudes that motivate behavior* and the *consequences of that behavior.* It is true that people seem less concerned about their grandchildren's consumption than about their own. People appear to be even less concerned about their descendants 50 generations hence. This does not necessarily translate into living off their inheritance. People may accumulate capital that benefits future generations from selfish or shortsighted motives. The increasing wealth and welfare of the past few centuries have been the result of technological change and capital accumulation. It may be true that most people are more concerned with the immediate future than the distant future and more concerned about their own welfare than the welfare of their distant descendants.

The preference for the present over the future is one factor influencing interest rates, but not the only one. A shortsighted 25-year-old may be willing to go deeply into debt to buy a BMW with little thought for the consequences. However, it is possible for a person to borrow only if someone else is willing to lend. As long as the more sober-minded middle-aged are willing to save more than enough

---

[22]Available upon request from the publisher.
[23]As we discuss in Chapter 19, one of the critical arguments about creating a "sustainable" future is whether technology and "synthetic" capital assets really can substitute for stocks of "natural" capital, including biodiversity, forests, and other environmental goods.

of their income to cover their juniors' debt-financed consumption, there will be funds left over for productive investments that will make even greater consumption available in the future. Though the impatience of human nature may push for a positive discount rate, it is the *productivity of investment* that allows it. It is conceivable that a society could reach a point where so much investment had been made in the past that the rate of interest had been driven to zero. However, this is unlikely in a society with ongoing technological change. With improving technology, the real return from a dollar of investment next year will be higher than it is this year, and it will be even higher the year after. So even if the productivity of investment were driven to zero in one year, new technology would raise it above zero the next. The continuing improvements in technology that are largely responsible for increasing income over time are also largely responsible for interest rates generally being positive.

The misconception that discounting is necessarily unfair to the future may also result from confusing individual and social behavior. People living on pensions are living off their capital. A well-managed pension fund would have no assets left when the last pensioner dies. That does not mean that society as a whole is living off its capital. Pensioners live off their capital by selling off assets, not by eating stock certificates. Every asset that a pensioner sells off is bought by someone else. It is most likely to be bought by or on behalf of people in the workforce accumulating assets to fund their pensions. As long as each generation adds to the total, the future will be better off, despite the fact that each generation will sell off most of its assets before it dies.

Will Adjusting Discount Rates Promote Intergenerational Equity?

It is conceivable that certain actions taken by the present generation could treat future generations unfairly. The following is an example of the argument. Consider a toxic-waste "time bomb" that will cause enormous environmental costs sometime far in the future. Suppose that current disposal technology can contain this waste for 5,000 years but that the waste will remain toxic for 10,000 years. Sometime between 5,000 and 10,000 years from now, the waste will escape its sarcophagus. The estimated costs of the environmental damage that would occur are $6,000 quadrillion, about 1,000 times the current U.S. gross domestic product. The present value of that environmental damage, discounted at a 3 percent social rate of time preference (*SRTP*), is far less than one penny. In fact, it is 4.3×10^{-50}. Suppose that not creating the waste time bomb would have cost an additional $1 million today. Discounting the damage from the escaping wastes at the *SRTP* in a decision process that looked only at net present value would lead to their being ignored.

An easy response is to argue that using lower, or possibly zero, discount rates will avoid such time bombs (e.g., Schulze, Brookshire, and Sandler, 1981). Will that approach work here? If we use a 2 percent discount rate, the present-value costs of the time bomb are 2.2×10^{-28}. With a 1 percent discount rate, the costs are 1.2×10^{-6}. The present value reaches $1 million only if we lower the discount rate to 0.45 percent. There are two problems in this example. First, using a lower discount rate cannot tell us whether there is an intergenerational equity problem. We know that there is a problem, because the time bomb will impose huge costs on future generations, even though avoiding those costs requires a relatively minor expenditure today. Using a present-value criterion with a predetermined discount rate does not tell us this. We can adjust the discount rate to give us the "correct" answer to the equity question, but only if we already know the answer that we want. The second problem is that using a discount rate below the *SRTP* would lead to economic inefficiency by justifying investments with lower future returns than the people who pay for the investments are willing to accept in exchange for the current opportunity cost.

Thus the approach of adjusting discounting rates to incorporate intergenerational equity concerns has little merit, and its appeal is based largely on confusion between economic efficiency and intergenerational equity. Using a discount rate below the *SRTP* will lead to economic inefficiency by justifying investments with insufficient returns. An approach based on inefficiently low discount rates tries to prevent inequities by adjusting prices. The result is that *inequity* appears to be *inefficiency.* Some advocates of this approach even argue for using *negative* discount rates to evaluate future environmental benefits and costs. However, this leads to the absurd conclusion that the more distant in time an event, the greater will be its value today. In that case, the rational strategy for every generation would be to impoverish itself so as to protect the consumption possibilities of future generations, although that generation would always be far off. This dramatically illustrates the importance of separating equity and efficiency issues.

Compensating Future Environmental Damage

The time bomb example we discussed at the beginning of this section could be addressed through the use of a "savings account" where current dollars are invested to pay for anticipated future damage. A similar concept is applied to electric utilities with operating nuclear power plants. Those utilities are required to set aside a certain amount of income to pay for decommissioning costs in the future. Such a savings account could be set up to fund the smaller of compensation for future damage or the costs of future actions to avoid damage, such as redisposal of toxic wastes using better technologies in the future. A requirement for such a savings account in essence provides future generations with a form of property rights to future environmental quality. The present generation can take actions that violate future generations' property rights only if we pay for doing so.

This idea would necessarily result in a limited approximation of property rights. Future generations do not yet exist, so we cannot bargain directly with them. They have no way of expressing their *WTA* for damage we might impose on them or of telling us the costs of future technologies for avoiding such damage. Any savings account arrangement would have to be based on the current generation's estimates of future costs. Future generations also have no way of withholding consent from bargains struck on their behalf. Savings account arrangements provide an imperfect way of protecting the interests of future generations, but that may be better than giving future generations no protection.

A KEY ENVIRONMENTAL POLICY APPLICATION: DISCOUNTING HUMAN LIVES

As we have discussed, environmental policy decisions will affect the levels of these risks, not only today but also far into the future. Thus it seems appropriate to address the issue of discounting future costs and benefits associated with policies that affect the statistical risks to humans. Consider again our example of the Hypochondria state legislature and the need to decide whether to spend $100 million on a sewage treatment facility that will reduce waterborne illnesses in the populace or on landfill improvements so as to prevent poisoning of the aquifer 50 years from now. In that example, the staff economist used a discount rate of 3 percent. Why is that number appropriate? Why did the economist not use 0 percent? After all, aren't future lives just as valuable as lives today? Should we value a small increase in risk today exactly the same as the same increase in risk ten years from now, implying a zero discount rate? Do risks to future lives solely involve issues of economic efficiency, or are there equity issues as well? And if there are both, how do we distinguish between them?

In essence, there are two opposing viewpoints on discounting future risks to human life. The first is that risks to human life should be treated in exactly the same way as other environmental risks. This is an argument for using the principles of economic efficiency when addressing issues affecting life and health. Empirical studies (e.g., Moore and Viscusi 1990; Cropper and Sussman 1990; Cropper, Aydede, and Portney 1992) show that individuals *do* discount future health risks at rates that are quite similar to those used in financial markets. As a result, these authors conclude that future health risks should be discounted in the same way as other future costs and benefits.

The second argument, which opposes discounting, is based on considerations of equity. This argument states that risks to the health of future generations should not be discounted by the current generation. Health risks in the future should be weighed equally with those today. Within this debate, there are several policy issues. First, it matters whether the future deaths at issue will affect members of the current generation or whether they will solely affect future generations. Whether or not my exposure to a pesticide today will cause cancer ten years from now is a different issue from whether my burning fossil fuels will lead to global climate change and the environmental ills associated with it 200 years from now. In the former, exposure to the pesticide is directly affecting my own welfare; in the latter, my actions may affect future generations. Second, depending on how society today decides to treat future health risks, it still must decide how to weigh benefits and costs. In other words, if pesticide exposure is to be treated on strict efficiency grounds, what is the appropriate discount rate? What if exposure is an equity issue? Is a zero discount rate appropriate? Should other procedures be used to deal with the issue?

We can make the distinction between intertemporal efficiency and intergenerational equity clearer with a couple of examples. First, suppose that we are asked to evaluate the fairly common situation of a medical treatment that reduces the probability of death from a given disease but has the risk of side effects that may eventually be fatal. In this case, we are comparing the risk of immediate death with the risk of death sometime in the future. Our beliefs about intergenerational equity are irrelevant because we are dealing with only one generation. The fact that people facing this risk have a lower *WTP* to avoid future risks than present risks is certainly relevant for evaluating this medical treatment.

Next, suppose that we are asked to evaluate a different medical treatment, which reduces the probability of death from this disease but poses a risk of fatal birth defects for the grandchildren of patients who are given the treatment. In this case, the fact that the patients may have a higher *WTP* for avoiding present risks than for risks to their grandchildren seems less relevant, if it is relevant at all. This is definitely an equity issue because different people are involved. In fact, entirely different groups receive the benefits of the treatment and bear its risks. The fact that they are different generations is less significant than the fact that they are distinct groups of people.

Treating deaths in different generations equitably does not necessarily mean aggregating benefits and costs using a zero discount rate. It may mean not aggregating or comparing benefits and costs at all. It may mean using the same criteria to allow or prohibit risky actions regardless of when the risks occur. It may mean prohibiting actions with risks that increase over time. It may mean prohibiting actions that impose risks on generations that do not receive any benefits. It may mean taking the same actions to protect members of all generations or the same actions to compensate victims regardless of when they are victimized.

All of these are requirements for intergenerational equity and are in addition to the requirements of economic efficiency. Using a zero discount rate to evaluate projects that have future health risks will lead to economic inefficiency and may not prevent inequity. Using a zero discount rate only for health risks to future generations and using the *SRTP* to discount all other benefits and costs likely will cause less inefficiency but still may not prevent inequities.

To take another example, suppose that the value of a statistical life has been calculated to be $3 million. Suppose also that without accounting for health risks, a particular project has a net present value of $3 billion. Finally, suppose that all of the benefits of the project accrue to the current generation but all of the health risks fall on the next generation. Using a zero discount rate for health risks would allow the project to go ahead as long as it caused fewer than 1,000 deaths in the next generation. Using a positive discount rate would allow even more deaths; the zero discount rate does not *in itself* prevent or even point out the obvious inequity.

Looking at net present value does not tell whether there are intergenerational inequities, and manipulating net present values through the choice of discount rates is not a good way to prevent them. Intergenerational equity issues that involve health risks are clearest when they are left in terms of mortality and morbidity and not monetized at all. The real equity issue in the example in the preceding paragraph is that 1,000 people who do not benefit from the project will die because of it. The fact that the victims will be in another generation seems secondary, at best. In this sense, a zero discount rate for health risks does seem appropriate, but only when analyzing equity. Someone must make a decision of whether $1 billion in benefits is worth 1,000 premature deaths among people who do not receive any benefits. The decision that is made can be used to infer the decision makers' value for a nonbeneficiary's death. Intergenerational equity requires that this implicit value *not* depend on *whose* premature death it is. However, this zero discounting is in the context of an explicit equity analysis that is separate from the consideration of the project's overall benefits and costs.

CHAPTER SUMMARY

Perhaps the most important concept you can take from this chapter is that *how* benefits and costs at different dates should be compared depends on *why* they are being compared. In deciding whether an action increases economic efficiency, future environmental benefits and costs should be discounted because discounting is necessary for economic efficiency. An action increases overall economic welfare if the present value of its benefits exceeds the present value of its costs. In general, environmental benefits and costs should be discounted at the social rate of time preference. All investments should be valued in terms of forgone consumption. With public investments, which most environmental investments are, this may require adjusting costs and benefits by the shadow price of capital before discounting. Other capital market imperfections may require similar types of adjustments.

When it comes to equity and fairness for future generations, discounting neither causes nor is evidence of unfairness to the future. There are no valid equity arguments for using a zero discount rate in evaluating the overall welfare impacts of an action. A zero discount rate no more guarantees fair outcomes than positive discount rates do. Actions that leave the future worse off or are unfair to members of future generations should be avoided because they are unfair (presuming, of course, that society values "fairness"). Discount rates and values for future benefits and costs should not be tampered with to make an equity problem look like an inefficiency. Deciding *whether* an intergenerational inequity exists may require comparing (undiscounted) measures of wealth or income at different dates or comparing benefits with (undiscounted) numbers of premature deaths. However, this equity analysis is separate from the evaluation of the net benefits of an action.

Whether the benefits of an action are greater than the costs is a different question than whether we are being unfair to future generations. Time plays fundamentally different roles in the two questions. In one case, we are asking whether we are willing to make a sacrifice at one time in exchange for a gain at another. The difference in times is essential, and discounting is the appropriate technique for making the comparison. In the other case, we are asking whether an action treats some individual or group fairly. This is a question about how the action affects the welfare of different people; whether the impacts are at the same time or different times is not material. Answering this question requires making undiscounted welfare comparisons.

CHAPTER REVIEW

Economic Concepts and Tools

- The degree to which future dollars are discounted relative to current dollars is called the *discount rate*. Present value (*PV*) is the value today of a benefit or cost that will accrue some time in the future. For a benefit *B* accruing *T* years in the future, $PV = B/(1 + r)^T$, where *r* equals the discount rate.
- The rate of time preference (*RTP*) is the discount rate implicit in an individual's consumption decisions. The *RTP* is not a fixed number but depends on an individual's preferences, current wealth, and future income. For an individual, the marginal rate of substitution between current and future consumption is $1 + RTP$.
- The *RTP* is the premium a person would be *willing to pay* for an extra dollar of consumption today; the market interest rate is the premium a person would be *required to pay* for an extra dollar of consumption today. The interest rate is determined by the production process and the return it can pay on investment.
- When two individuals have different *RTPs*, both can increase their welfare if the person with the higher *RTP* borrows from the person with the lower *RTP*. Gains from trade will have been exhausted and efficiency reached only when everyone has the same *RTP*. When everyone has the same *RTP*, it is natural to speak of a social rate of time preference (*SRTP*). This is the premium that society as a whole requires to postpone a dollar of consumption.
- Because efficiency requires that borrowers and lenders have the same *RTP*, it also requires that *SRTP* equal the one-period rate of return on the marginal investment. Equilibrium in the loan market requires that all of these be equal to the market rate of interest.
- Economic efficiency does *not* require a positive *SRTP*. Instead, the *SRTP* will be determined by the stock and productivity of capital, as well as the rate of technological change.
- Distortions in capital markets, such as taxes, should be adjusted by valuing future benefit and cost streams using the shadow price of capital (*SPC*), not by adjusting the discount rate. The *SPC* is the value of current and future potential consumption given up by displacing a dollar of private investment. The *SRTP* is the appropriate discount rate to use, with or without distortions.

Policy Issues

- Discounting at the *SRTP* is appropriate and necessary for evaluating intertemporal efficiency.

- Discounting is inappropriate for comparing the respective welfare of different generations.
- Several concepts of fairness produce the same basic judgment about intergenerational equity: we are being fair to future generations if we leave them at least as well off as we are; we are being unfair to future generations if we leave them worse off than we are when we could have left them better off.
- A positive discount rate neither causes unfairness to the future nor indicates the presence of such unfairness. In practice, a positive interest rate has been associated with capital accumulation and technological change, which have made future generations better off. The common misconception that discounting at a positive rate means treating the future unfairly is the result of confusing attitudes that motivate behavior with the consequences of that behavior.
- Negative discount rates have no economic rationale in policymaking decisions. Such an approach leads to absurd conclusions because the more distant in time an event, the greater will be its value today.

DISCUSSION QUESTIONS

1. Often lawyers will seek damages for workers who are injured or killed on the job. Most of the time, these damages are based on the potential future income of their clients. Is it fair to discount such an income stream? Why or why not?
2. Indian tribes have sometimes argued that their customs and reverence for future generations result in a negative *SRTP*. Is this a valid statement? Why or why not? If capital markets are perfectly elastic, will there be different *SRTP*s among different societies? Does your answer change if capital markets are not perfectly elastic?
3. Suppose that a $50 million investment in a sewage treatment plant will save the lives of 100,000 people who would otherwise die from cholera next year. If that money is invested in technologies that promise lower carbon dioxide emissions, however, it has been predicted that 200,000 lives will be saved 100 years from now. If a government has only $50 million to spend, what should it do?
4. In Figure 13.4, what happens when *PPF* rotates upward, reflecting increased opportunities for economic growth through investment? What happens to the discount rate if the utility function between current and future consumption is still tangent to the new *PPF* along the 45 degree line?
5. Suppose that society decides that benefit streams associated with projects that may have long-term environmental risks should not be discounted. How does society allocate resources? Should there be some threshold level of probable risk? What constitutes the long term?
6. Using the overlapping-generations model described in the appendix to this chapter, examine the impacts of positive and negative technological change

on the welfare of future generations, interest rates, and fairness. Specifically, use values of $+0.05$ and -0.05 for the technology parameter γ, and use base-case values for the other parameters. Are the situations unfair?

REFERENCES

Barry, B. 1977. "Justice Between Generations." In *Law, Morality and Society*, ed. P. Hacker and J., Raz. Oxford: Clarendon Press.

Baumol, W. 1986. *Superfairness: Applications and Theory*. Cambridge, Mass.: MIT Press.

Bradford, D. 1975. "Constraints on Government Investment Opportunities and the Choice of Discount Rate." *American Economic Review* 65(4): 887–899.

Cline, W. 1992. *The Economics of Global Warming*. Washington, D.C.: Institute for International Economics.

Cropper, M., and F. Sussman. 1990. "Valuing Future Risks to Life." *Journal of Environmental Economics and Management* 19: 160–174.

Cropper, M., S. Aydede, and P. Portney. 1992. *Public Preferences for Life Saving*. Center for Risk Management, Discussion Paper No. CRM 92-01. Washington, D.C.: Resources for the Future.

Cummings, R. 1991. "Legal and Administrative Uses of Economic Paradigms: A Critique." *Natural Resources Journal* 31(4): 463–473.

Dixit, A., and R. Pindyck. 1994. *Investment Under Uncertainty*. Princeton, N.J.: Princeton University Press.

Kolb, J., and J. Scheraga. 1990. "Discounting the Benefits and Costs of Environmental Regulations." *Journal of Policy Analysis and Management* 9(2): 381–390.

Lesser, J., and R. Zerbe. 1994. "Discounting Procedures Rate for Environmental and Other Projects: A Note on Kolb and Scheraga." *Journal of Policy Analysis and Management* 13(1): 140–156.

Lind, R. 1982. "A Primer on the Major Issues Relating to the Discount Rate for Evaluating National Energy Options." In *Discounting for Time and Risk in Energy Policy*, ed. R. Lind. Baltimore: Johns Hopkins University Press.

———. 1990. "Reassessing the Government's Discount Rate Policy in Light of New Theory and Data in a World Economy with Integrated Capital Markets." *Journal of Environmental Economics and Management* 18: S8–S28.

Moore, M., and W. Viscusi. 1990. "Discounting Environmental Health Risks: New Evidence and Policy Implications." *Journal of Environmental Economics and Management* 18: S51–S62.

"Nuclear Burial at Sea." 1992. *Technology Review*, February-March, pp. 22–23.

Oberhofer, T. 1989. "The Changing Cultural Discount Rate." *Review of Social Economy* 13(1): 43–54.

Plater, Z., R. Abrams, and W. Goldfarb. 1992. *Environmental Law and Policy: A Coursebook on Nature, Law, and Society*. St. Paul, Minn.: West.

Rawls, J. 1971. *A Theory of Justice*. Cambridge: Harvard University Press.

Reisner, M. 1993. *Cadillac Desert* (2d ed.) New York: Viking Penguin.

Rogers, A. 1994. "Evolution of Time Preference by Natural Selection." *American Economic Review* 84(3): 460–481.

Samuelson, P. 1958. "An Exact Consumption-Loan Model of Interest with or Without the Social Contrivance of Money." *Journal of Political Economy* 66(6): 467–482.

Schulze, W., D. Brookshire, and T. Sandler. 1981. "The Social Rate of Discount for Nuclear Waste Storage: Economics or Ethics?" *Natural Resources Journal* 21(4): 811–832.

Toman, M. 1994. "Economics and 'Sustainability': Balancing Trade-offs and Imperatives." *Land Economics* 70(4): 399–412.

Varian, H. 1975. "Distributive Justice, Welfare Economics, and the Theory of Fairness." *Philosophy and Public Affairs* 4: 223–247.

———. 1984. "Equity, Envy and Efficiency." *Journal of Economic Theory* 9(1): 63–91.

World Commission on Environment and Development. 1987. *Our Common Future.* New York: Oxford University Press.

Zerbe, R. 1991. "Comment: Does Benefit-Cost Analysis Stand Alone? Rights and Standing." *Journal of Policy Analysis and Management* 10: 96–105.

Zerbe, R., and D. Dively. 1994. *Benefit-Cost Analysis in Theory and Practice.* New York: HarperCollins.

Shadow Prices and the Overlapping-Generations Model

THE SHADOW PRICE OF CAPITAL: SIMPLIFYING THE APPROACH

It turns out that in many cases, the *SPC* approach may be simplified. To see this, it is useful to ask what information is required to implement the *SPC* approach in practice. To evaluate a government-financed environmental project's benefits and costs, first we convert the dollar flows into their private consumption equivalents by accounting for gains or losses of private capital (Lind 1982). In other words, the benefits and the costs of the government project are redefined so as to account for any displacement of or returns to private capital, based on the value of the shadow price of capital.

Let C_t be the cost of a public sector project in year t. Let Θ_c be the fraction of that cost that takes the form of displaced private investment so that $1 - \Theta_c$ is the fraction that directly displaces consumption. Let V be the shadow price of capital, and let C_t^* be the cost in terms of lost consumption. Thus C_t^* is the sum of the value of displaced consumption in year t and the value of displaced investment multiplied by the shadow price of capital:[1]

$$C_t^* = \Theta_c C_t V + (1 - \Theta_c) C_t = C_t \left[\Theta_c V + (1 - \Theta_c) \right] \qquad (13A.1)$$

The benefits from a public investment may take the form of increased consumption or increased private investment. For example, suppose that a government-financed sewage treatment plant improves water quality in a river. The better-quality water can now be used by an industry downstream in its manufacturing

---

[1]There remains disagreement over the actual calculation of the *SPC*. Cline (1992), for example, believes Lind's formulation, itself a correction of Bradford (1975), to be too explosive to be useful for public policy decisions. Cline's formulation is based on the present value of an annuity $A_{r,T}$, where r is the internal rate of return for an annuity of T years. In Cline's formulation,

$$V = \sum_{t=1}^{T} \frac{A_{r,T}}{(1 + i)^t}$$

Cline's reasoning is that the *SPC* should reflect the difference between a unit of consumption now and a smaller amount of consumption annually for T years. Cline's *SPC* is just the ratio of this stream of consumption discounted at the *SRTP*. To take an example, Kolb and Scheraga (1990) use Lind's formulation of the *SPC* to show that given a private cost of capital of 7 percent and an *SRTP* of 3 percent, the *SPC* equals 2.94. Under Cline's formulation, the *SPC* would directly equal 1.215, which is what Kolb and Scheraga derive using the two-stage approach for the present-value cost of a $1 investment. Thus Cline's *SPC* appears to be what Kolb and Scheraga derive using the two-stage procedure. Under his formulation, Cline's *SPC* will be bounded by Bradford's one-year *SPC* = $(1 + r)/(1 + i)$, and r/i for an investment of infinite duration. Cline (1992) argues that Lind's (1982) formulation of the *SPC* is too explosive unless, as Lind (1982) notes, $0.4 \le i/r \le 0.5$, where r is the private cost of capital. Cline argues that this may not be the case in many small countries. However, the observed high degree of elasticity of world capital markets makes Lind's assumption far more plausible.

process without the industry's having to clean the water itself. The industry becomes more profitable and can now afford to expand, or further improve its technology. To account for these sorts of benefits accruing to the private sector, we have to perform the same sort of adjustment as we did for costs. This latter adjustment will reflect the fact that a dollar of private investment resulting from a public project will have returns worth more than a dollar when they are discounted at the *SRTP*.

Let B_t be the benefits from a project occurring in year t, let Θ_b be the fraction of those benefits occurring as private investment, and let B_t^* be the benefits converted to their consumption equivalent. Then

$$B_t^* = \Theta_b B_b V + (1 - \Theta_b)B_t = B_t[\Theta_b V + (1 - \Theta_b)] \tag{13A.2}$$

Thus the net present value (*NPV*) for a given investment I, $NPV(I)$, will be

$$NPV(I) = \sum_{t=1}^{T} \frac{B_t^* - C_t^*}{(1 + i)^t} \tag{13A.3}$$

Equations 13A.1 and 13A.2 convert ordinary benefits and costs into their consumption equivalents at time t, by multiplying Θ_b and Θ_c by the SPC. Equation 13A.3 differs from that used in discounting ordinary (unadjusted) benefits and costs by the *SRTP* only because costs and benefits have been converted into their consumption equivalents.[2] So letting $M = [\Theta_b V + (1 - \Theta_b)]$ and $N = [\Theta_c V + (1 - \Theta_c)]$, Equation 13A.1 can be rewritten as

$$NPV(I) = M \sum_{t=1}^{T} \frac{B_t - (N/M)C_t}{(1 + SRTP)^t} \tag{13A.4}$$

If none of the project benefits take the form of returns to private capital, $\Theta_b = 0$, $M = 1$, and Equation 13A.4 reduces to

$$NPV(I) = \sum_{t=1}^{T} \frac{B_t - NC_t}{(1 + SRTP)^t} \tag{13A.5}$$

Equation 13A.5 shows that any remaining bias introduced by discounting ordinary benefits and costs depend on the displacement of private capital and hence the value of N. The value of N, in turn, will depend on the elasticity of the supply of capital. As the elasticity increases, Θ_c will approach zero, the value of N will approach unity, and the SPC approach will be more closely approximated by discounting ordinary benefits and costs.

---

[2]The usual benefit-cost criterion is to accept a project whose *NPV* is positive or, if projects are mutually exclusive, to choose the one with the largest *NPV*. For investments where uncertainty is present, the criterion may be far more complex. See Dixit and Pindyck (1994) for a thorough treatment.

In the situation in which the percentage of costs displacing private capital are equal to the percentage of benefits that contribute to private capital formation (i.e., $\Theta_b = \Theta_c$), then $M = N$, and Equation 13A.4 can be written as

$$NPV(I) = M \sum_{t=1}^{T} \frac{B_t - C_t}{(1 + SRTP)^t} \tag{13A.6}$$

The *sign* of the *NPV* as calculated in Equation 13A.6 will be the same as the sign when ordinary benefits and costs are discounted by the *SRTP*. Since the usual decision criterion is to accept a project whose *NPV* is positive, it is the sign that is important.[3] Clearly, if the cases represented by Equations 13A.5 and 13A.6 are common, this approach reduces to one that is straightforward. Furthermore, as long as the fraction of project costs coming from private capital is not large and as long as the ratio between this fraction and the fraction of benefits returning to private capital is within a broad range, ordinary benefits and costs may simply be discounted by the *SRTP*. Whether the results of a project comparison are sensitive to the values of M and N should be tested by calculating Equation 13A.6 for each project with M and N taking several values in their likely ranges. If the actual decision is not sensitive to the values of M and N, there is nothing to be gained from the effort required to estimate them (Lesser and Zerbe 1994).

For example, suppose that $\Theta_c = 0.10$, $\Theta_b = 0.05$, and $V = 2.5$. Furthermore, suppose that the ordinary benefits from a policy are estimated to be \$1,000 each year for 20 years. The ordinary cost is \$975, also for 20 years. If we look only at ordinary benefits and costs, the policy makes sense because irrespective of the actual value of the *SRTP*, *NPV* will be positive. If we convert ordinary benefits and costs to their consumption equivalents, however, the policy does not look like such a good idea:

$$B_t^* = \Theta_b B_b V + (1 - \Theta_b)B_t = (0.05)(\$1,000)(2.5) + (0.95)(\$1,000) = \$1,075$$

and

$$C_t^* = \Theta_c C_t V + (1 - \Theta_c)C_t = (0.10)(\$975)(2.5) + (0.9)(\$975) = \$1,121.25$$

In this example, the adjusted costs are greater than the adjusted benefits, and the policy should not be implemented.

THE OVERLAPPING-GENERATIONS MODEL

Here we present the mathematics behind the examples in the text. The specific functions used were chosen for their computational simplicity. The same kind of model could be constructed with other functional forms. All members of each

---

[3] In comparing projects, one chooses the project with the highest *NPV* so that magnitude as well as sign is important.

generation are assumed to be identical so that their aggregate behavior can be represented by the preferences of a representative individual. Each generation's preferences between consumption when it is young and when it is old are represented with a Cobb-Douglas utility function:.

$$U_1 = C_{1,1}^a C_{1,2}^{1-a} \tag{13A.7}$$

where $C_{1,1}$ is consumption by the first generation in the first period and $C_{1,2}$ is consumption by the first generation in the second period. The "impatience" parameter defined in the text, R, equals $[a/(1 - a)] - 1$. Notice that the consumption of other generations does not enter into the utility function. Each generation is unaffected by, and indifferent toward, the welfare of other generations.

The production function is an augmented Cobb-Douglas with Hicks-neutral technical change (i.e., technological change that does not alter the desired ratio of capital to labor). Total output in period t equals

$$Y_t = G_0(1 + \gamma)^t L_t^{1-d} K_t^d = G_0(1 + \gamma)^t L_t^{1/1+P} K_t^{P/1+P} \tag{13A.8}$$

where Y_t = output in period t
L_t = labor in period t
K_t = capital in period t
γ = rate of technological improvement

The relative factor productivity parameter used in the text, P, equals $P = d/(1 - d)$, where $0 < d < 1$. Labor supply is assumed to be completely inelastic. This allows us to choose units for labor so that the quantity supplied always equals one unit of labor. This allows Equation 13A.2 to be rewritten as

$$Y_t = G_0(1 + \gamma)^t K_t^{P/1 + P} \tag{13A.9}$$

To make the results of the base case come out to round numbers, G_0 was set to 8.772052. Output Y_t can be consumed by the young, consumed by the old, or set aside by the young for use as capital in the next period. Thus, $Y_t = C_{t,t} + C_{t-1,t} + K_{t+1}$. The income of the old is the amount of capital (which they saved in the previous period) times the marginal product of capital. Being that there is only one good, its price can be set to 1. Then the marginal products of labor and capital are also values of marginal product. (Recall that $VMP = P \times MP$.) Differentiating Equation 13A.3 with respect to labor and capital, we have

$$MPL_t = \frac{Y_t}{L_t} = \left(\frac{1}{1 + P}\right) G_0(1 + \gamma)^t K_t^{P/1+P} \tag{13A.10}$$

and

$$MPK_t = \frac{Y_t}{K_t} = \left(\frac{P}{1 + P}\right) G_0(1 + \gamma)^t K_t^{-1/1+P} \tag{13A.11}$$

Each generation maximizes the utility of its consumption subject to its income constraint. For the young, income is entirely wage income, while for the old, income consists of the returns earned on the previous period's investments. Because the amount of labor is normalized to one unit, total wage income in period t just equals MPL_t. (Recall, in equilibrium, the wage rate will equal the value of the marginal product of labor.) Because the total income of the young equals MPL_t, the young will save $MPL_t - C_{t,t}$. At the beginning of the next period, this investment is used to produce more output in the economy. The formerly young's (now the old's) savings are returned with the interest earned. The amount of interest earned, of course, is determined by MPK_t.

The Cobb-Douglas utility function is convenient because the share of income spent on each good equals the ratio of the exponent of that good to the sum of the exponents. (This is not a general property of utility functions.) When the goods are consumed in different periods, income must be interpreted as the present value of income in all periods. We have given consumers a particularly convenient budget constraint (convenient for us). Income in the second period equals savings in the first period plus interest earned on those savings. The present value, in the first period, of income in the second is just equal to savings in the first. Thus the present value of lifetime income is just equal to income in the first period, or MPL_t. Because $a/(a + 1 - a) = a$, consumption in the first period is

$$C_{t,t} = aMPL_t = \left(\frac{R + 1}{R + 2}\right) MPL_t = \left(\frac{R + 1}{R + 2}\right)\left(\frac{1}{1 + P}\right) G_0(1 + \gamma)^t K_t^{P/1\,+P}(13A.12)$$

The interest rate, ρ, will just equal the net return on savings. Thus

$$\rho = MPK_{t+1} - 1 = \left(\frac{P}{1 + P}\right) G_0(1 + \gamma)^t K_t^{-1/1+P} - 1 \qquad (13A.13)$$

CHAPTER 14

RISK, UNCERTAINTY, AND ENVIRONMENTAL POLICY

Snake Eyes? The Value of Preserving Biodiversity

What did you eat for lunch today? What did your lunch (when it was still alive) eat for lunch? What did your lunch's lunch eat? The livelihoods of different species, including Homo sapiens, are linked in a complex web that we are only beginning to understand. A break in the chain of these linkages can have adverse effects on the entire ecosystem. The extinction of a species amounts to a reduction in genetic diversity, which may affect overall ecological stability. Some ecologists argue that the more complex the ecosystem, the greater its resilience. Thus the case can be made that the conservation of biological diversity is necessary if ecosystems are to function properly.

Yet thousands of species came and went long before humans existed. The earth survived a mass extinction of species some 60 million years ago caused by a large comet or asteroid striking the earth. Although vast numbers of species were wiped out, many more flourished afterward.

Today, scientists estimate that because of relentless human activities, 20 to 50 percent of all species may become extinct over the next century. Increasing population pressures are accelerating the conversion of undeveloped lands into agricultural and residential habitats, decreasing the available habitats for wildlife. Swanson and Barbier (1992) estimate that in the decade of the 1980s, 2 percent of all the world's forests were cleared. Almost all of the undeveloped and species-rich lands that still exist are in developing countries, including Brazil, Mexico, Colombia, and

Indonesia. Nonetheless, the consequences of decreasing biodiversity will be felt globally.

The complexities and uncertainties surrounding biodiversity argue for policies to maintain it. But how much of our limited resources should be spent to maintain, and perhaps increase, biodiversity? How should it be accomplished? How can biodiversity be traded off, if at all, with human activities that decrease it? And how should resources be allocated between preserving biodiversity and achieving other environmental goals? Diplomats from many nations continue to struggle with these questions. For example, biodiversity was a prominent topic on the agendas of the World Conservation Strategy sessions of the United Nations Conference on Environment and Development in 1980 and 1992 and was part of the agenda at the summit on climate change in Rio de Janeiro in 1993.

Policies that address biodiversity cannot be separated from broader questions of land tenure, rural poverty, and agricultural development, both at the national and the international level. Policies must also confront efficiency and equity questions: how much should be spent, who should spend it, and what should the money be spent on?

Conservation programs are costly. Yet for some countries, so-called ecotourism has become a major source of revenue. Developed countries are in a better position to pay for maintaining biodiversity but do not have property rights to the species-rich lands that are located in developing countries. But developed countries have an incentive to pay, as they are the primary users of fragile ecosystems. For example, in 1992, an American pharmaceutical company, Merck, Sharp, and Dohme, agreed to pay Costa Rica a $1 million "prospector's fee," plus royalties, on any products developed from genetic materials discovered in that country. Many public institutions, such as the World Bank and the United Nations, as well as many private organizations, have programs that funnel aid to developing countries for conservation projects. Developed countries, however, will be even more willing to pay if they are provided with assurances that the money will be used effectively.

Complicating the protection of species and biodiversity is the fact that regardless of the cost of programs to promote it, success is uncertain. Uncertainty arises from the limited information available about the biological and genetic processes of plants and microorganisms and their future values. There is uncertainty as to the genetic strength of species that are preserved. And there is uncertainty as to how biodiversity should be measured. In the case of Pacific Northwest salmon, for example, debate persists over the viability of fish raised in hatcheries as a means of preservation. Some environmentalists refer to such hatchery fish as "stupid" fish because they are too "dumb" to swim downstream, avoid predators, and do other things wild salmon do. But without the hatcheries, there would be far fewer salmon.

There is also uncertainty about the existence of species themselves. Is the plant that harbors the cure for all cancers waiting to be discovered deep in some Amazon jungle? Or has it already been destroyed by human activity? Does it even exist? Clearly, scientists cannot predict the significance of incompletely studied organisms, much less those whose existence is unknown. That a species is not considered valuable today does not mean that it may not prove valuable in the future.

This, unfortunately, leaves policymakers in the difficult position of making decisions with only limited information. How much weight should they put on new genetic discoveries? Should they approach environmental decisions involving biodiversity preservation from a risk-averse perspective, and if so, how risk-averse should they be?

Biodiversity will also be affected by ecosystem stability. From an economic perspective, if more species are better because they increase ecosystem stability, the marginal increase in stability is worth the risk premium paid. In other words, buying an ecosystem "insurance policy" will be worth the cost. But what price should be paid? What is the value of the insurance policy? What is its policy consequence, seeing that species loss is irreversible? Should irreversibility concerns promote environmental preservation through the elimination of development projects that might increase the welfare of humans? What weight should be given to such changes and policies and the consequences on all of the affected parties, human and otherwise? None of these questions is easily answered, nor is any without controversy. Yet perhaps the worst solution is to make no attempt whatsoever to answer them.

INTRODUCTION

Until now, we have paid little attention to the fact that the future is *uncertain*. Yet uncertainty lies at the heart of many environmental policy issues, and developing environmental policies in the face of uncertainty is difficult and controversial. At the individual level, many of us don't know whether we will use an environmental asset in the future. Will you visit the Grand Canyon next year? What about visiting Yosemite National Park ten years from now? How can we account for environmental benefits, in the form of use values, if we don't know who the users will be and when they may be users? At the other end of the spectrum, there remains tremendous uncertainty as to the potential effects of global climate change and the loss of biodiversity. How likely is it that the spotted owl will survive current preservation efforts? What if it doesn't survive? What will the world have lost? How should society develop policies in the face of such uncertainty? How much risk should society be willing to take?

This chapter makes a start at remedying the omission of uncertainty and society's approach to taking risks in environmental policy development. We first look at how people value uncertain future events and how to measure those values and provide several additional foundation concepts needed to develop the tools for policy analysis in the presence of uncertainty. Some of these concepts can be hard slogging but are important to grasp nevertheless in order to understand policy applications. We begin with some basic definitions, examining uncertainty and people's behavior when they face it, in a nontechnical way. Then we introduce a concept that economists have often used to model consumers' approach to taking risks: *expected utility theory.* Students familiar with the subject can skip this discussion if they wish. In the section, The Value of Information, we use expected utility theory to show the value of additional information. Environmental policymakers will always want to know more about complex interactions, such as biodiversity and global warming, but the tougher question is knowing when additional information is worth its price. The section, Option Price, Expected Consumers' Surplus, and Option Value, deals with issues in measuring nonmarket values that are affected by uncertain future events.

We then turn to environmental policy issues and the tools available to evaluate environmental policy alternatives in the presence of uncertainty. In the section, Should Environmental Policymakers Be Risk-Averse?, we begin by asking whether environmental policymakers representing the interests of society should pay to avoid future risks. If so, they must determine how much to pay, especially in the context of potentially irreversible consequences, for these can raise significant efficiency and, perhaps even more important for policy purposes, equity questions. Following that, we examine several decision methodologies that can be useful to policymakers who must make decisions in the presence of uncertainty, including an extension of the multiattribute analysis work from Chapter 10. Finally, in the last section, we review the use of risk assessment in federal government decision making, focusing on how governments can determine the highest-priority risks given limited budgets.

Unfortunately, none of these methodologies can guarantee environmental policymakers a uniquely "correct" policy response because policymakers cannot know whether their actions are correct until after the fact. Instead, the best that can be hoped for is that the methodologies will shed light on crucial aspects of decisions. Ultimately, for society and environmental policymakers, the presence of uncertainty and risk means, "You pays your money, and you takes your choice."

UNCERTAINTY, RISK, AND RISK AVERSION

The only certainty about the future is its uncertainty. We can imagine what it will be like, we may even be able to assign probabilities to future events, but we do not know what will happen. In ordinary language, we use the terms *risk* and *uncertainty* interchangeably to describe this fact. But when economists use *risk* and *uncertainty*, they mean two different things.[1] We may suspect that exposure to a certain pollutant causes cancer, but until epidemiological studies have been done, we do not know the probability that a person who has been exposed will develop the disease. The riskiness inherent in different investments or policies can be estimated as a sort of scientific exercise, but the public's evaluation of those risks may differ materially from that of the expert, and different people may assess the level of risk quite differently. In addition, even if the level of risk is known and agreed on, people may react differently to it.

---

[1]Knight (1933) distinguished between risk and uncertainty on a technical level. He stated that *risk* refers to situations where we know the possible future outcomes of a situation and the probabilities of those outcomes. For example, gambling on the flip of a coin involves risk because the possible outcomes, heads or tails, and their probabilities, .5 each for a fair coin, are known in advance. *Uncertainty,* by contrast, refers to events whose probabilities are not known or decisions where all possible outcomes are not known.

When we discuss risk in this chapter, we will mean how individuals and societies approach decisions that have uncertain outcomes, that is, their *risk preferences*. Economists often refer to individual behavior as *risk-averse, risk-neutral*, or *risk-loving*. Most of the time, people behave as if they are risk-averse. What this means is that they are willing to pay more than the expected value of possible losses to avoid a risk. One everyday example of this is homeowner's insurance. Risk-averse homeowners will be willing to pay, and risk-averse banks will insist on, a monthly premium to protect themselves against catastrophic loss from, say, fire, even though the future payments will exceed the cost of replacing a house and its contents multiplied by the probability that they will be destroyed in a fire. Thus with a 30-year mortgage on a $100,000 house, the insurance company may believe that the probability of the house's burning down over the life of the mortgage is 5 percent. If the value of the contents is also $100,000, the expected loss will be (.05)($200,000) = $10,000. If the cost of the insurance policy is $400 per year, the insurance company will collect $12,000 over the life of the mortgage, $2,000 more than the expected loss. Risk-neutral individuals will not take out insurance policies of this type.[2] Risk-loving individuals are willing to pay to take on risks. Gambling in a casino is risk-loving behavior because the odds are set so that on average, the house will come out slightly ahead and the gamblers will come out slightly behind.[3]

Risk-averse individuals require a higher expected rate of return on risky investments than either risk-neutral or risk-loving individuals. A risk-averse individual, given a choice between a guaranteed 8 percent rate of return on a Treasury bond and a similar *expected* rate for an alternative investment, would always prefer the certainty of the Treasury bond. However, a risk-averse investor might choose the riskier investment if its expected rate of return were higher than 8 percent. Suppose that the investor would be indifferent between the two investments if the risky investment offered a 10 percent expected rate of return. The 2 percent difference in rates can be thought of as the *risk premium* that the investor requires for accepting the risk associated with the latter investment. Speculators in financial markets are generally not risk lovers. They only need to be less risk-averse than the hedgers (or better able to reduce risks by diversifying).

EXPECTED UTILITY THEORY

In Chapter 3, we discussed how a person's choices can be represented by a utility function. It turns out that when the choices involve risk, we can say more about what a person's utility function looks like than when there is no risk involved. Expected utility theory is a useful concept when we deal with uncertainty and risk.[4]

---

[2]For a precise development of risk aversion and its implications, see Hirschleifer (1992). See also Hey (1979) and Freeman (1993).

[3]Risk-neutral and risk-averse people may gamble in casinos because the rest of the experience compensates for their gambling losses.

[4]Expected utility theory does have some significant weaknesses. A good summary of these can be found in Thaler (1991).

Given enough information about the riskless choices a person would make between bundles of goods and services, we can construct a utility function. This utility function will assign a numerical utility index that is the same for all bundles toward which the person is indifferent and is higher for bundles the person prefers. We can construct such an index if this person meets some very minimal conditions for consistency in making choices (von Neumann and Morginstern 1947). Although the technical details are left to the appendix to this chapter, expected utility theory boils down to an ability to construct indices based on the mathematical expectation of uncertain events, thereby ranking those events. That turns out to be important, because we will want to compare economic well-being in different states of the world, before we know which of those states will come to pass. Expected utility theory allows us to do that.

For example, suppose that we are considering a policy that will require spending $100 million to preserve the northern spotted owl. Suppose that if we spend the $100 million on owl preservation, we will not be able to increase the size of Yellowstone National Park. If we spend the money on increasing the size of the park, we know that society will be better off because the danger posed by mining activities just outside the park will be rendered moot. And if we spend the money on preserving the spotted owl, the efforts may still be insufficient to prevent its extinction. Perhaps there is a 50-50 chance that the expenditure will save the owl. The choice that policymakers prefer will depend on their attitude toward risk. By using expected utility theory, we can rank the different options and, based on policymakers' attitudes toward risk, compare the average outcome (in this case, the average utility associated with spending money to save the spotted owl) with the "sure thing" of increasing the size of the park.

Utility is ordinal and not cardinal, so we cannot give any meaning to specific numerical values of a utility function. We can, however, glean information from the *curvature* of a utility function. This is an important result because *the curvature of the utility function tells us the person's attitude toward risk*. A concave utility function indicates risk aversion, a linear utility function indicates risk neutrality, and a convex utility function indicates risk loving. This is shown in Figure 14.1.

Figure 14.1 shows a concave function of utility that depends on wealth. As wealth increases, utility increases, but at a decreasing rate. This is termed *diminishing marginal utility of income*.

In Figure 14.1, an income of $10,000 gives utility of 1,000 units, an income of $10,500 gives utility of 1,035 units, and an income of $11,000 gives utility of 1,070 units.[5] What is the individual's expected utility if his income is uncertain? Figure 14.1 can be used to determine it. Suppose that this person participates in a profit-sharing program. If the company he works for has a good year, there will be a $1,000 bonus on top of his base salary of $10,000. The utility associated with this uncertain income is the expected value of the utilities associated with the possible outcomes. If there is a 50 percent probability of a good year, the expected utility is

---

[5]These utility numbers have a degree of arbitrariness. Remember that only the curvature of the utility function tells us any information. We can change the scale and the intercept on the vertical axis without losing that information.

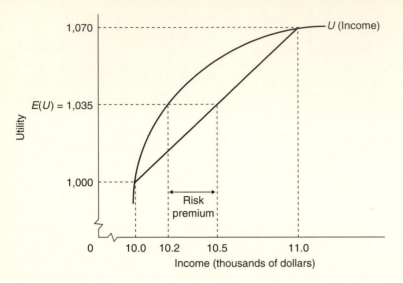

Figure 14.1   A Utility Function for Someone Who Is Risk-Averse

$$[.5]U(\$10,000) + [.5]U(\$11,000) = [.5]1,000 + [.5]1,070 = 1,035$$

This is the midpoint of the line segment connecting the points ($10,000, 1,000) and ($11,000, 1,070).[6] The expected value of income is $10,500, and the expected utility associated with this income is 1,035 units. Notice, however, that if this person were offered a *guaranteed* income of $10,200, her utility also would equal 1,035 units. The $10,200 income figure is called the *certainty equivalent*. The difference between the expected income level and the certainty equivalent can be thought of as a *risk premium,* just like an insurance premium.

A risk lover has a convex utility function such as that shown in Figure 14.2. Here an income of $10,000 gives utility of 1,000 units, an income of $10,500 gives utility of 1,060 units, and an income of $11,000 gives utility of 1,130 units. Note that for this risk-loving person, the marginal utility of income increases. This person's expected utility from the uncertain income from the profit sharing program is

$$[.5]U(\$10,000) + [.5]U(\$11,000) = [.5]1,000 + [.5]1,130 = 1,065$$

For this risk lover, an equivalent utility could be achieved with a guaranteed income of $10,800. Thus for a risk-loving individual, the premium paid for a certainty equivalent will be negative.

---

[6]If the probabilities had been different, the expected utility would be found at a different point on the line segment. If the probability of a good year is α, the expected utility is found the fraction α of the way along the segment from ($10,000, 1,000) to ($11,000, 1,070).

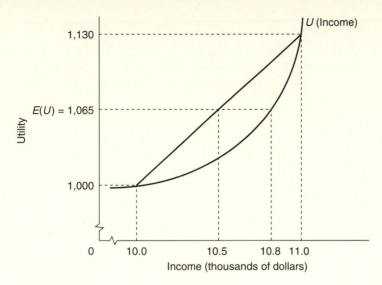

Figure 14.2   An Indirect Utility Function for Someone Who Is Risk-Loving

If the expected outcomes of two events are the same, the risk-averse individual will prefer the less risky one. This is shown in Figure 14.3. In this figure, we assume that the individual's base salary has been increased to $10,200. There is still a 50 percent chance of getting a bonus. However, now the bonus will be only $600. The expected income level is the same as previously, $10,500. The expected utility, however, increases to 1,050 units. Even though the individual's average

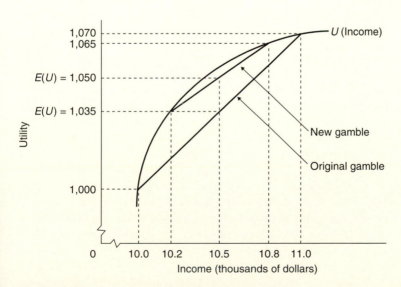

Figure 14.3   Increasing Risk and Preferences

income will be same in both cases, the individual will prefer the less risky salary-plus-profit-sharing plan.

The equivalence between risk aversion and declining marginal utility of income makes intuitive sense. Risk-averse people are unwilling to take a gamble with an expected outcome of $0 because they value $1 of potential gains less than they value $1 of potential losses.[7] Concave indifference curves indicate a preference for consuming a mix of goods over consumption dominated by one or a few goods. Ben Franklin's admonition to practice "moderation in all things and all things in moderation" also turns out to be a prescription for risk aversion.

THE VALUE OF INFORMATION

In George Orwell's bleak novel of the future, *Nineteen Eighty-Four,* one of the sayings in "Newspeak" was "Ignorance is bliss." Yet intuitively, we know that more information will usually be preferred to less. Expected utility theory allows us to examine why this is true and whether it is always true. Information can be a critical component of environmental policy decisions. Separate from any rights-of-nature considerations, a decision on the value of preserving a particular species will be improved with additional knowledge of that species. The external costs associated with air pollution emissions from a specific coal-fired power plant will be known with greater certainty if policymakers have a better knowledge of the prevailing air dispersion patterns nearby and hence better knowledge of the affected populations.

To determine the value of new information, it is useful to use "decision trees," which provide a convenient representation of possible decisions and their consequences in different future states of the world. Consider the following example. Suppose that you face a choice between two actions and that each of these actions has two possible outcomes, depending on the state of the world. The choice could be walking to class tomorrow morning or taking the bus. The two possible states of the world are that it rains and that it does not, and the weather report you heard as you were setting your alarm clock put the probability of rain at one-half. If you walk to class and it does not rain, you will get some exercise and be able to see the campus cherry trees in full bloom, which you particularly enjoy. If you walk and it does rain, your clothes will be ruined. We can represent the possible decisions and outcomes with the matrix shown in Table 14.1. We assign the (No rain, Walk) outcome a utility of 1,000 (the origin of your utility scale is totally arbitrary). If you walk and it rains, you will get soaked. We assign that outcome a utility of 0. If you ride the bus, you will arrive safe, dry, and bored, regardless of the weather. We assign this outcome a utility of 700, which is not arbitrary. Once we have arbitrarily set utility levels for two outcomes, in principle we can determine the utility of any other outcome by confronting you

---

[7]You may wish to look again at the discussion in Chapter 3 on loss aversion and kinked indifference curves to note the similarities.

TABLE 14.1

		Decision	
		Walk	Ride
State of the World	Rain	0	700
	No rain	1,000	700

with options and observing your choices. This situation can be represented by the decision tree shown in Figure 14.4.

The leftmost node represents the choice you must make between walking and riding the bus. The intermediate nodes represent nature's (uncertain) chance event: rain or no rain. The ends of the branches show the outcomes in each case. We can see which choice you should make by calculating the expected utility on each of the decision branches. If you walk, your expected utility will be

$$E[U(\text{walk})] = [.5]1,000 + [.5]0 = 500$$

However, if you take the bus, your expected utility will be

$$E[U(\text{bus})] = [.5]700 + [.5]700 = 700$$

So if you are risk-neutral or risk-averse, you should, and presumably will, take the bus because $E[U(\text{bus})] > E[U(\text{walk})]$.

Now suppose that you have another option. Tonight's weather forecast reported that there is a cold front 100 miles to the west. There is a 90 percent probability of rain if the cold front moves through overnight and a 10 percent probability of rain if the cold front stalls. If you set your alarm for 15 minutes earlier than usual

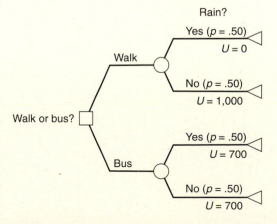

Figure 14.4   Decision Tree of Choices and Utility

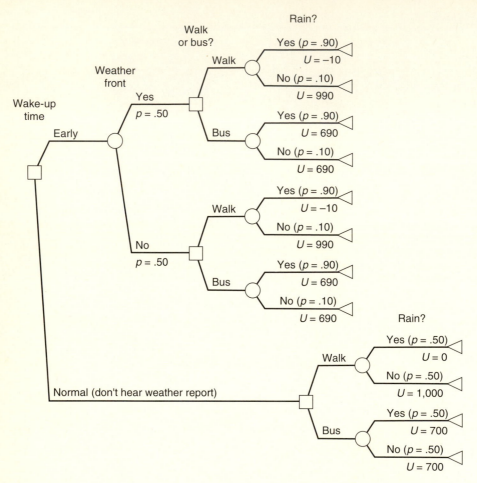

Figure 14.5   Extended Decision Tree with Additional Information

and listen to the weather report in the morning, you will know which of these events has taken place. Of course, getting up earlier has a cost, which we will show by reducing the utility of all outcomes that involve getting up earlier by 10 units. We can illustrate this new situation with the expanded decision tree in Figure 14.5.

Now the leftmost node of the decision tree is the decision on whether or not to get up early. If you do not get up early, the bottom branch from that first node duplicates the decision tree of Figure 14.4. Without watching the weather report, the probability of rain tomorrow is .5. Tomorrow morning, the probability of rain, conditional on the information you will have if you do not get up early, still will be .5.[8] If you decide not to get up early, and if you are risk-neutral or risk-averse, your best decision in the morning will be to ride the bus. We know that that decision provides you with an expected utility of 700. If you do decide to get up early and watch the weather report, you will have additional information about the front. By reading off the rightmost endpoints of the decision tree and the associated probabilities of each outcome, we can determine expected utility and the preferred decision. For example, if the front has passed through and you walk, your expected utility will be

$$E[U(\text{front, walk})] = [.1]990 + [.9](-10) = 90$$

If the front has passed through and you do not walk, your expected utility will be

$$E[U(\text{front, ride})] = [.1]690 + [.9]690 = 690$$

Thus if you decide to get up early and hear that the front has passed through, you should ride the bus. If the front has stalled and you walk, your expected utility will be

$$E[U(\text{no front, walk})] = [.9]990 + [.1](-10) = 890$$

If the front has stalled and you ride the bus, your expected utility will be

$$E[U(\text{no front, ride})] = [.9]690 + [.9]690 = 690$$

Thus if you get up early and hear that the front has not passed through, unless you are extremely risk-averse, you will want to walk to class and enjoy the cherry blossoms.

Tonight, you know what decision you will make in the morning for each of the possible weather reports. However, *you do not have to make that decision tonight.* You just have to decide whether to listen to the weather report. If you do not, your expected utility is the same as if you did not have the option, 700. If you do get up early to catch the weather report, your expected utility is

$E[U(\text{get up early})] = [.5]E[U(\text{front, ride})] + [.5]E[U(\text{no front, walk})] = [.5]690$
$+ [.5]890 = 790$

Your best *option* is almost certainly to get up early and decide whether to walk on the basis of the weather report.[9] In that case, the additional information you will receive from getting up early is worth its cost to you (in terms of forgone sleep). Why? Because it allowed you to make a better final decision, and the expected benefit of that better decision outweighed the expected cost.[10] If you listen to the weather report and it says rain is likely, you will ride the bus and be slightly worse

---

[9]Again, if you are extremely risk-averse, you may still prefer the sure thing of riding the bus.

[10]This is an example of a real option, which is similar to the concept of financial market options. See Dixit and Pindyck (1994).

off than if you had slept later. However, if you hear the weather report say rain is unlikely, you will walk and be much better off than if you had slept later. If you do not listen to the weather report, you will ride the bus, even if you would have been better off walking. In essence, by deciding to get up early, you are buying a type of insurance option. You are forgoing additional sleep in exchange for reducing your risk of deciding to walk when it will rain.

The additional information would not have been worth it to you if it would not have changed your final decision. If your decision would have been to ride the bus even with the new weather report, you would not have been willing to make any sacrifice to hear a later weather report. The additional information would also not have been worthwhile if the cost of obtaining it had been greater than the expected gain from having it. Thus if losing 15 minutes of sleep resulted in your falling asleep during your final exam and flunking class, you might choose instead to face a greater chance of ruined clothes and a passing grade.

OPTION PRICE, EXPECTED CONSUMERS' SURPLUS, AND OPTION VALUE†

In the example in the preceding section, your decision of whether to walk or ride the bus depended on information that would become available in the future. This is a common situation, as few of us can say exactly what we will be doing a week or a month from now because we know that what we do will depend on what happens between now and then.

Suppose that in our example, the question was not whether you should get up early but whether the bus should be run. The revenue the bus generates may barely be enough to justify running it, especially if it has few riders on nice days. However, you and all the other riders may claim that having the bus there every day is worth more than the average of the fares you pay on days you ride and the nothing you pay on days you don't. In fact, you might be willing to pay more for a monthly pass than the daily fare times the average number of days you ride per month, or you might even be willing to pay a small daily fee for the option to ride the bus at the regular fare. Weisbrod (1964) recognized this possibility and gave the name *option value* to the difference between the value someone places on having a good available and the expectation of the possible values the person will receive from consuming the good in the various possible future states of the world. Weisbrod intuitively assumed that option value would be positive. He also did not give it a formal definition. In the decades since Weisbrod's original paper, countless journal articles have tried to pin down this concept. We will not bore you with all of the controversies about option value, but we will touch on it as we present the current thinking on the subject and its importance to environmental policy decisions.

With goods that are bought and sold in a market, it is often possible to set up markets for *options* on those goods. For example, there are well-organized options markets for financial assets and commodities. Some of these options are sold through market exchanges such as the Chicago Board of Trade or the New York Mercantile Exchange. Unfortunately, when there are no well-defined markets for goods, as is the case with many environmental goods, there may be no way to set up an options market.[11] This is why environmental economists have debated the relevance of option value in determining the values of environmental assets.

Weisbrod and others originally believed that option value would always be positive and that it was another type of *nonuse value,* to be added to use values in estimating total willingness to pay (*WTP*) for a good. Option value was thought to be relevant especially for irreversible environmental decisions, such as those involving the extinction of a species or the destruction of a scenic view. Although option value might be difficult to measure, if it were positive, we could be certain that *observable* measures of willingness to pay, primarily expected consumers' surplus, would provide a lower bound on the value of an environmental resource. Unfortunately, it turns out that option value may be positive, negative, or zero, further complicating environmental policy decisions.

The technical details of why option value need not be positive depend on the properties of the *indirect utility* function. Indirect utility functions can be thought of as a mirror image of the "normal" utility functions we discussed in Chapter 3. Instead of being functions of quantities of goods, they are a function solely of income because the demand for different goods will themselves be functions of income. It turns out that option price can be determined from indirect utility levels in different states of the world.[12]

Option Price and Option Value

Now we are ready to define *option price.* Suppose that you are on vacation in Arizona, a short drive away from the Grand Canyon. If the weather is clear tomorrow, you will consider visiting the Grand Canyon. If you go there, you will have to pay an admission fee. However, if it is raining and cloudy tomorrow, you will prefer visiting a museum for free. In fact, in that state of the world, you would prefer visiting the museum even if visiting the park were free. You will probably wait until tomorrow, see whether it is clear or raining, and then pay to go to the park if it is clear. Conceivably, the Park Service could set up a system where you could buy a ticket one day in advance that would allow you to visit the park if you wanted. You would not be willing to pay as much for such an advance ticket today because you might not use it tomorrow. Now suppose that the Park Service sold *only* advance tickets; either you buy it today or you do not have the opportunity to visit the park tomorrow. The maximum amount you would pay for an advance ticket you might not use, rather than be certain of not visiting the park at all, is your *option price.*

---

[11]Despite this limitation, the concept of an option price is somewhat analogous to financial market options, which can influence optimal investment decisions. See Dixit and Pindyck (1994) for a thorough discussion.

[12]The formal derivation of the indirect utility function is presented in the appendix to this chapter.

Option price is defined as the price of the advance ticket that would make you indifferent between buying the ticket and not buying it. Paying your option price will result in identical levels of expected utility, regardless of whether or not you buy the ticket.[13]

Society frequently faces this sort of environmental policy choice. For example, society must decide whether to invest in different environmental assets—preserving natural environments, reducing air pollution, or protecting endangered species—without knowing who will benefit or how much they will benefit. It turns out that the sum of option prices for all potential beneficiaries is the appropriate measure of total *WTP* when society faces such an irreversible decision. The problem for the applied policy analyst is that option price *cannot* be measured directly.

If you buy the ticket to visit the Grand Canyon, you will have reduced your income, whether or not you ultimately go there. That reduction in income will reduce your utility. If you are risk-averse, your indirect utility function will be concave. Thus the more income you start with, the less the reduction in income will reduce your utility. For example, if your income were initially $1,000, a loss of $10 would reduce your utility *less* than if your income were initially $10. That is simply a consequence of the diminishing marginal utility of income.

Suppose that you are not willing to pay more than $20 for the advance ticket. By definition, if you pay this amount, you will be indifferent between buying the ticket and taking your chance that you will not want to visit the park anyway tomorrow. Suppose that if the weather were clear tomorrow, you would be willing to pay $30 to visit the park. (If it is cloudy and rainy tomorrow, you will not want to visit, so your *WTP* will be zero.) If there is a 50 percent probability of rain tomorrow, your expected consumers' surplus will be $15 ([.5]$30 + [.5]$0). The $5 difference between option price and expected consumers' surplus is your *option value*.

If option value were *always* positive, option price would be greater than the expected value of future *WTP*. Will this always be true? No. Option *value* will be zero if, over the relevant range of incomes, we have risk neutrality *and* the difference in utility between visiting the Grand Canyon and visiting the museum is independent of the level of income. In other words, the relationship between option price and expected consumers' surplus depends on the level of income in each state of the world and whether the consumer experiences diminishing marginal utility of income. That is why option price can be positive, zero, or even negative. There may be certain cases where you will prefer to take your chances on an uncertain outcome rather than eliminate that uncertainty by purchasing an option.

Originally, positive option value was thought to be a consequence of risk aversion. In reality, whether option value is positive depends on the relationship between a person's attitudes toward risk *in different states of the world*. The result is that we cannot say that a measure of expected *WTP* of users gives us a lower bound on *WTP* for provision of a good that people may or may not consume.

---

[13]The formal derivation of option price is shown in the appendix to this chapter.

The Use of Option Price in Applied Environmental Policy Work

If we were to ask what is an individual's *WTP* to maintain or enhance biodiversity, the lesson of the preceding section is that the use of expected consumers' surplus will not give the correct answer. Instead, the correct answer will be given by option price. Expected consumers' surplus may be greater or less than option price, so we cannot use expected consumers' surplus as a bound to the correct value.

The determination of option price is difficult but possible. Contingent valuation studies can be used to elicit values that are contingent on the state of the world. Such studies hold the possibility of obtaining option values in some (perhaps limited) circumstances. These questionnaires could ask for a hypothetical commitment to be made prior to project completion, such as the value of preserving a wetland or keeping a river free-flowing.[14] However, because use value already contains expected consumers' surplus, if we add use value and option price together, we will be double-counting. It is option value, rather than option price, that should be added to consumers' surplus.[15]

To see this, consider three groups of consumers and their consumption of an environmental good such as the view at the Grand Canyon. Group A consumers will visit the Grand Canyon regardless of the state of the world (regardless of whether it is sunny or raining). Group B consumers will visit, but only if the weather is sunny. Group C consumers have no intention of ever visiting the Grand Canyon; however, they do value its existence. The analyst measures the consumers' surplus of group A, perhaps through a travel cost study, and finds it to be $10 million. Because this figure does not include the potential consumers' surplus of group B and the existence values of group C, it underestimates the total value of the Grand Canyon view. Suppose that the option price for group B equals $6 million and the existence value for group C is $30 million. Then the total value of the Grand Canyon view equals $46 million.

If the world were this neat, option price would be a positive value added to consumers' surplus.[16] This sort of positive addition to value may be what some analysts have in mind when they treat option value as positive. Unfortunately, as we saw in Chapter 11, environmental values are not usually calculated this way. Ordinarily, we will estimate consumers' surplus for a sample of members from groups who are observed to consume a good, and we will estimate associated probabilities that all individuals in each group will consume the good. From these estimates we can calculate total expected consumers' surplus. To add option price to this set of

---

[14]For examples of past studies that implement this procedure, see Brookshire, Eubanks, and Randall (1983) and Desvousges, Smith, and McGivney (1983).

[15]In the late 1980s, additional controversy arose as to the nature of option price, expected consumers' surplus, and option value, questioning whether the definition of option value as option price less expected consumers' surplus made any sense. A good summary of this controversy can be found in Randall (1991). From an empirical standpoint, however, the arguments appear to have little relevance.

[16]Note that option value here is not necessarily positive. We don't know what it is because we have not calculated expected consumers' surplus for group B.

values would be to double-count because option price and expected consumers' surplus are *alternative WTP* measures.

We might calculate expected consumers' surplus from existing use of a recreational facility, for example, by performing a travel cost study. Expected consumers' surplus would consist of the consumer surplus of not only the members of group A but also those of group B. How many of the group B individuals would use the facility would depend on the state of the world existing during the period during which data were collected. Provided that data collection covered the different states of the world that influenced actual use (e.g., rain or no rain), an *ex post* (after the fact) estimate of use and thereby consumers' surplus would be obtained, reflecting one measure of *WTP*.

Should an additional amount be added for those group B members who did not use the facility? After all, they have some positive option price. The revealed consumers' surplus of group B members who actually used the facilities, however, will exceed their option price. Whether or not the revealed consumers' surplus for group B users in the *aggregate* exceeds their option price cannot be determined. To see this, suppose that group B consists of two individuals, Dick and Dan, each with an option price of $45. If, during the time we collect data, we observe only Dick using the facility, and his consumers' surplus is $100, then the total recorded consumers' surplus for group B will be $100, whereas total option price is $90. If we arbitrarily add a dollar amount to the measured consumers' surplus to represent the option value for group B nonusers (i.e., Dan), we will have inflated the actual value. By covering reasonable variations in all states of the world during the data collection process, we allow all group B members to stand up and be counted. *Ex post* values may or may not be reasonable estimates of *ex ante* (before the fact) consumers' surplus. Again, however, adding option price to these values would double-count total value.

The twin complications that option value may not be measurable and that one will often be measuring *ex post* values has led a number of economists to despair (Bishop 1986). The situation does not seem so pessimistic to us. In practice, risks can often be spread so that the information one can collect on the likely *ex post WTP* is useful in determining an *ex ante* value. Consider the situation in which only group B consumers exist. Then all of the estimates we have of the future value of the park are *ex post* revealed estimates of those who actually use the park, but who were previously unsure that they would be able to use the park. Suppose that, on average over the different states of the world, 40 percent of those with a prior option demand actually show up. It does not seem unreasonable to decide on whether or not to preserve the park by estimating the *ex post WTP* of these people and comparing this with the costs of preservation. Private entrepreneurs bear risk and undertake projects on the basis of expected *ex post* demand. Why not proceed with public projects on the same basis? The risk of preserving the park today may be undertaken by bondholders who are paid *ex post* from the fees collected by demanders. In both cases, we are asking if users will pay for the values received.

The contingent valuation methodology discussed in Chapter 11 is the most amenable to determining *ex ante* use, existence, and total values. The total value of an environmental amenity can always be decomposed into its use value and existence value components. In the presence of uncertainty, all of these valuation concepts will be *ex ante*.

If uncertainty is critical, perhaps because a wrong decision could lead to irreversible damage, then measurement techniques should attempt to incorporate this uncertainty. Market techniques, such as travel cost and hedonic price studies, will be unlikely to incorporate uncertainty because those techniques focus on *ex post* observed or implicit market values. If properly designed, CVM studies can determine *ex ante* values for use and existence values alike. Thus *the applied researcher must first determine how important uncertainty is to the specific environmental amenity or policy to be valued and then select an appropriate valuation technique.*

SHOULD ENVIRONMENTAL POLICYMAKERS BE RISK-AVERSE?

Because we often observe individuals behaving as if they are averse to risk, should society behave the same way when confronted with environmental issues? If so, is there a "correct" amount of risk aversion from society's standpoint? As Smith (1986) discusses, there are no easy answers to these questions, for a number of reasons. First, environmental issues may reflect *actuarial* risks and *perceived* risks that differ significantly.[17] People may be terrified of Alar on their apples yet drive without wearing their seat belts, even though the latter is far riskier than the former. Should society invest resources to reduce perceived risks when the actuarial risks do not justify the investment? Or should society invest resources to reduce actuarial risks when perceived risks are much lower? Second, there are different sorts of environmental risks. Some affect economic efficiency; others may involve equity and rights. Many, like preserving biodiversity, can involve both. That means that policymakers must determine which effects are most important.

Some authors (Hirschleifer 1970; Sandmo 1972) have argued that all public projects be treated the same as private ones. Thus public investments and public goods—and developing many environmental amenities such as national parks are public investments—should earn "rates of return" as high as private investments. This would require that future environmental project benefits and costs be determined and discounted using the *shadow price of capital* (*SPC*) approach presented in Chapter 13. Other authors (Arrow and Lind 1970) have argued that public investments should be required to earn only a risk-free rate of return.

One problem with both of these views comes to mind immediately: how do we measure the "rate of return" on environmental goods, such as clean air or preserving biodiversity? In some cases, we can measure the rate of return the same way as for private goods—if individuals are willing to pay for environmental investments, they can be evaluated like private investments. Of course, this addresses environmental investments only from the point of view of economic efficiency. It makes little sense to talk about rates of return for investments in human rights, equity, and the rights of nature.

Ultimately, whether or not environmental policies should be developed in a risk-averse or risk-neutral manner hinges on three factors: the irreversibility of

---

[17] Recall the Happyville example of Chapter 12.

environmental impacts, the ability to reduce environmental risks through diversification, and equity and fairness concerns.

Irreversibility and Uncertainty

Many development decisions have uncertain environmental benefits and potentially irreversible environmental costs. Grand Coulee Dam, for all of its economic benefits, contributed to the near extinction of some salmon species on the Columbia River. The economics literature has addressed this issue in an attempt to determine whether irreversibility should lead to greater environmental preservation and less resource development (Arrow and Fisher 1974; Krutilla and Fisher 1985; Orian, Brown, and Swiezbinski 1985; Fisher and Hanemann 1986).

Often the focus on irreversible decisions is on the value of information that may be gained by delaying development. In the case of potential environmental costs, there may be a value to an evaluation of strategies that can provide information about uncertainties (Freeman 1986). Uncertainty arises from a lack of information about decisions. For example, one benefit to delaying construction of a dam that might result in the extinction of a salmon species would be the information that could be gathered on the value of preservation or on other options to pursue development without extinction. This does not mean that dam construction should be halted because of potential extinction of the species—although there may be legal requirements that effectively lead to that decision—but that there may be benefits to delaying development until more information can be gathered about the value of preservation or of options to prevent extinction.

In the context of economic efficiency, decisions about irreversible development involve comparisons between the rate of change in the present-value benefits associated with development and the rate of change in the present-value costs associated with reduced environmental quality. (Clearly, the choice of discount rate in such comparisons can make a big difference in the findings.) Essentially, these models state that investment should be halted if the returns from development are decreasing relative to the returns associated with preservation (Krutilla and Fisher 1985). This is the approach Krutilla and Fisher used in their Hell's Canyon study (see box on p. 403). In general, it will make sense to stop development when the optimal size of the development (determined on the basis of return) is decreasing.[18]

Figure 14.6 provides a simple illustration in the case of certainty, where the value of electricity production and whitewater recreation are plotted over time. Initially, the value of whitewater recreation over time (the dashed line) increases more rapidly than the value of electricity production (line EE). After T^* years, however, the increase in the value of whitewater recreation slows, shown by the decrease in the slope of the dashed line, so that the rate of increase in the value of electricity production is larger than that associated with whitewater recreation. Thus in this example, it would make sense to delay development of the dam for T^* years.

---

[18]The math associated with this result is somewhat complicated and involves a technique known as *optimal control theory* (see Kamien and Schwartz 1981; see also Dixit and Pindyck 1994 for a discussion of optimal control techniques and the determination of investment "options").

TAMING A WILD RIVER: THE CASE OF HELL'S CANYON

The Snake River passes through a 200-mile stretch of the border between Oregon and Idaho known as Hell's Canyon. It is one of the most scenic rivers in the United States, described in a letter dated November 8, 1968, by then U.S. Secretary of Agriculture Orville Freeman as "an awesome stream consisting of a series of swift white-water rapids flowing into deep pools in one of the deepest Canyons in the United States. . . . There is no doubt that this stretch of the Snake River represents one of the last of this country's great rivers."

Hell's Canyon was also an attractive site to build hydroelectric dams for the same reasons. Development was considered as far back as the 1940s by the U.S. Army Corps of Engineers, as part of its overall development plan for the Columbia River System. In the late 1950s, the Federal Power Commission (FPC), which was the precursor to the Federal Energy Regulatory Commission (FERC), licensed three sites in the upper reach of Hell's Canyon for development. In 1964, the FPC granted a license to the Pacific Northwest Power Corporation to develop the lower reach of Hell's Canyon. That development would have eliminated forever the whitewater rapids that Secretary Freeman wrote so eloquently about.

The secretary of the interior challenged the FPC decision, and in 1967, the U.S. Supreme Court ruled that the FPC had not considered other benefits of the area that would be lost forever should development occur, including the loss of salmon species. The Court ordered the FPC to reconsider the license application. In 1969, economists John Krutilla and Anthony Fisher undertook to measure the environmental costs associated with development, submitting a "friend of the commission" study. They were able to measure some of these environmental costs, including the potential loss of recreation opportunities, but they noted that other costs, such as the extinction of salmon species, were impossible to measure. Their findings are summarized in Krutilla and Fisher (1985, chaps. 5 and 6.)

Krutilla and Fisher quantified and incorporated into their benefit-cost analysis the environmental opportunity costs associated with hydroelectric development. They estimated measurable preservation benefits and primarily recreation benefits and then determined how large those benefits would have to be in order for the *total* preservation benefits to equal the benefits of development. They found that annual preservation benefits would have to be at least $80,000 in order to equal annual development benefits. However, their study found that the quantifiable benefits alone from preservation were almost $900,000 annually, far exceeding the annual benefits from development. Ultimately, Congress prohibited further development of Hell's Canyon.

In the presence of uncertainty, things can get more complicated. First, future returns may be uncertain. Because the future prices of electricity and substitute forms of energy will not be known, the benefits associated with development of the dam will be uncertain. Similarly, we will not know with certainty the number of future recreationists should the dam not be built. Thus we have to modify Figure 14.6 to incorporate bounds on future benefits and costs, as shown in Figure 14.7.

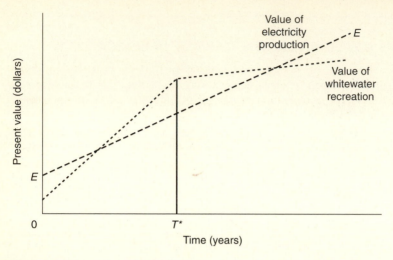

Figure 14.6 Value of Development Versus Preservation

In this example, it is not clear whether development should be delayed and, if so, whether the dam should ever be built. If the value of electricity production follows VE_{low} and the value of whitewater rafting follows VR_{high}, the dam should never be built because the value of rafting will always be greater than the value of electricity. Reverse the situation, however, with a value for electricity production of VE_{high} and value of rafting equal to VR_{low}, and the dam should be built immediately. What may make the most sense is to delay development while more information is gathered that will *reduce* the uncertainty. Thus, delaying development may have an *option value* (Dixit and Pindyck 1994).[19] Although the terms are the

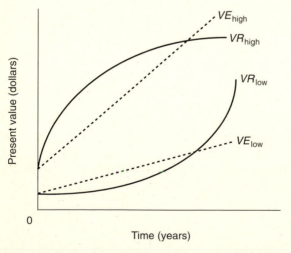

Figure 14.7 Development Versus Preservation When Values Are Uncertain

same, this option value resembles a financial option (e.g., an option to buy or sell a stock) and not the concept we defined earlier in this chapter.

Estimating preservation benefits can be complicated further because of the diversity of the benefits. For example, new information that increases the relative importance of preserving a wilderness area may be brought forth. The genetic value of various species may prove to be valuable in the future. Or it may be that removal of an individual species of plant or animal would contribute to the irreversible breakdown of an entire ecosystem. And preferences may change over time, increasing or decreasing the values that individuals place on environmental preservation. Thus even if we could accurately determine the number of future whitewater recreationists, the value they place on their recreation opportunities could change over time.

Irreversibility and Equity

Whether or not decision makers will benefit from better information that may be revealed in the future, irreversibility clearly involves issues beyond strict economic efficiency goals. As we have stated throughout the book, environmental issues often do not focus solely on economic efficiency. Other considerations are often made by policymakers. When these factors are considered, optimal decisions made for preservation or development may appear to be intertemporally *inefficient*.

Some authors (e.g., Margolis 1959) have argued that policymakers may be better off adopting a risk-averse viewpoint when concerns about equity are paramount, such as the poorest members of society's not bearing disproportionate shares of environmental costs. In general, if environmental benefits and costs are distributed asymmetrically, in that the beneficiaries of policies do not bear the costs, efficiency may no longer be the primary concern. The losers from today's policy responses may also be future generations who have had no say in today's resource choices or individuals who do not reap the benefits of development but bear the costs.

Diversification of Environmental Risk

A crucial and often disputed issue associated with assessments of the environmental costs of development is the ability to *diversify* environmental risks. Diversifying environmental risks can be thought of in the same way as diversifying financial risks, such as an investor buying a mutual fund instead of an individual stock. Indeed, as we will discuss shortly, a fundamental theory of finance may be useful in environmental policy applications. Once a species is gone, we cannot recreate it, popular fiction and movies to the contrary. However, what is less clear is whether we can *substitute* for the loss of the species, thus diversifying away the environmental risk.

---

[19]This is similar to the concept of a financial option. It is unfortunate that the financial literature and the environmental literature use the same term to mean different things.

Substituting for an extinct species may seem an odd concept. After all, a dolphin cannot substitute for a deer, nor can a catfish stand in for a crocodile. That is one reason the ability to diversify away environmental risks remains controversial, as we discuss in more detail in Chapter 19. But this is not the concept of substitution we mean. Instead, arguments in favor of environmental substitution recognize that many species became extinct in the past prior to human existence, yet the environment continued to survive. Thus there may be particular species that are less genetically "important" than others. A rare and isolated subspecies of bird living on a remote tropical island may be less genetically important than a species of plankton that serves as the initial link in the food chain. Then again, that particular species of bird may be immune to cancer. Until we have a definitive way of *measuring* genetic "value," it will never be clear what is the value lost by species extinction and whether that loss can be completely diversified away.[20]

Concerns about environmental risk diversification will not necessarily be limited to questions of species extinction and irreversible impacts. Mere reductions in the level of certain environmental assets may not be fully diversifiable. For example, if humans cannot adapt sufficiently to global climate change, a reduction in the atmosphere's ability to absorb additional greenhouse gases may lead to our species' demise. Even though there would still be remaining absorptive capacity, it would have fallen below a level that can be adequately substituted for and thus not fully diversifiable.

Conclusion: Adopt a Risk-Averse Viewpoint

Given the potential importance of irreversible consequences from development, the likelihood that many environmental costs will have equity and rights impacts, and the uncertainty over whether environmental costs are fully diversifiable, it seems reasonable to advocate that environmental policymakers approach their decisions in a risk-averse manner. While there is no way to "prove" this assertion formally, there is also no way to disprove it. For some environmental issues, it may be that risks *can* be sufficiently diversified away and their impacts limited to those affecting economic efficiency. Converting a large open space in the middle of a city into an urban park with nature trails and recreation facilities will probably not have critical irreversible consequences. In such a case, the arguments of Arrow and Lind (1970) are probably appropriate, and policymakers would do well to evaluate the benefits and the costs of that development using the SPC approach.

But for many environmental issues, especially global issues like climate change, ozone depletion, and species extinction and biodiversity, there may be both irreversible and disproportionate consequences. For these environmental impacts, it may be difficult or impossible to diversify risk. And even if it were pos-

---

[20]Many ecologists and some economists also raise moral arguments to humans' contributing to the loss of species.

sible, there is no guarantee that efficient diversification would guarantee outcomes that were perceived as fair or just.

The recommendation to adopt a risk-averse viewpoint carries with it an important follow-up question: *how* risk-averse should policymakers be? Adopting a risk-averse attitude should not preclude all development, as policymakers will often be required to trade off environmental costs and benefits from different projects. For example, development of a new sewer treatment facility along a lakeshore may damage a wetland but improve overall water quality and therefore human health. But with uncertainty, one must be cognizant that it can "go both ways." An uncertain environmental cost may prove higher *or lower* than expected. In Chapter 9, for example, we discussed the controversy over the development of Tellico Dam, which centered on the endangered status of the snail darter, thought to live only where the dam was to be built. Further research, however, found the species living elsewhere. Thus it was found to be less endangered than previously thought. We also have a tendency to overestimate certain environmental risks. The case of spraying Alar on apples, which we discussed in Chapter 5, is an example. Whether such spraying is economically efficient, *not* spraying based on wildly overblown risks makes little sense from a policy standpoint.

DECISION METHODOLOGIES THAT INCORPORATE RISK AVERSION

Considering that we have recommended that environmental policymakers adopt a risk-averse approach in addressing environmental costs and benefits, we turn now to a discussion of tools that policymakers can use to make decisions. Some of these tools obviate the need to define precisely what level of risk aversion, if any, is "best." Others can illustrate the sensitivity of specific decisions to different levels of risk and point to areas for further study. But no methodology provides an automatic answer. Once we incorporate uncertainty and risk, the "best" decisions will require a dose of sound judgment. Although space prevents a complete discussion of decision analysis techniques, in this section we provide an overview of several alternative methods that can be used.[21]

Risk-Adjusted Discount Rates and the Capital Asset Pricing Model

In Chapter 13, we stated that it is appropriate to discount future environmental benefits and costs (adjusted to their consumption equivalents) for efficiency considerations so that accurate comparisons between resources can be made. We argued that it was most appropriate to use the *social rate of time preference (SRTP)*

---

[21]See, for example, Keeney and Raiffa (1993) or Kleindorfer, Kunruether, and Schoemaker (1993).

as the discount rate. Absent considerations of risk, if there were uncertainty in the benefit and cost streams in year T, then we would discount the value of the future expected benefits and costs in year T using the *SRTP*.[22]

Once we incorporate risk into the decision framework, however, it may no longer be appropriate to discount *all* future cash flows at the *SRTP*. There are two possible alternatives: adjust the benefits and cost streams themselves, or adjust the rate at which the original benefit and cost streams are discounted. In their study of Hell's Canyon, Krutilla and Fisher (1985) in effect did the former by determining a "break-even" level of forgone environmental benefits were development to occur. However, adjusting benefit and cost streams themselves, except in the context of the *SPC* approach, is difficult because there is no inherent method for adjusting them. For example, should the estimated future benefits from hydroelectric development in Hell's Canyon have been lowered, or should the environmental costs have been increased, and if so, by how much?

Suppose that we must decide whether to invest in a solar energy company, a new national park, or more stringent safety regulations.[23] All three projects have the same net present value when discounted by the *SRTP*. For the solar project, we are confident that the higher future energy prices from fossil fuel sources are, the greater the return on the investment will be. Furthermore, because most linked energy-economic models predict that higher energy costs will reduce economic growth, we also know that the benefits from the solar energy investment will be higher when economic growth is lower. In other words, the solar energy company will provide the largest amount of wealth when overall wealth is lower, rather like a rich uncle giving you the most money when you are a poor and starving student. This implies that investment in the solar energy technology will be negatively correlated (have a negative *covariance*) with gross domestic product (GDP).[24] We also assume that the returns from the park project are not correlated with variance in community wealth or income. And we assume that returns from the new safety regulations will be positively correlated with community wealth, since the value of safety is greater the more people are employed, and the number of people employed is directly related to community wealth.

Why should we care that the returns will likely be highest when overall economic growth is lowest? The reason goes back to our discussion earlier in this chapter linking declining marginal utility of income to our definition of risk aversion. For a risk-averse individual, an additional dollar of wealth will be valued less if she is already rich than if she is poor. Similarly, the return on an investment in the solar energy company will act like an insurance policy: the returns will be greatest when they are valued the most because high energy prices will be accompanied by lower GDP and national wealth. If such an investment is thought of as a "public"

---

[22]Lind (1982a) notes that this point appears to be misunderstood by some authors. If project A's benefits in year T were more uncertain than project B's, they would discount project A's benefits at a higher rate.

[23]See Awerbuch (1995) for further discussion.

[24]GDP is the value of all domestically produced final goods and services. It is one (albeit imperfect) measure of national wealth.

investment, the solar energy company will provide the greatest benefit when society values that benefit most.

What does this have to do with "risk-adjusted" discount rates and environmental assets? Well, like any investment over time, we will want to evaluate the present value of the solar company investment with the present value of the alternative investments, in this case assumed to be the purchase of land for a new national park and more stringent environmental safety regulations that are expected to save lives in the future. To do so, however, we must use an appropriate discount rate. When uncertainty is present, one of the most common, controversial, and misunderstood methods is to use risk-adjusted discount rates.

Sometimes discount rates are adjusted for risk arbitrarily, along the lines we discussed in Chapter 13. Advocates of developing the national park, for example, might recommend that its future benefits not be discounted at all. At other times, discount rates are adjusted on the basis of a particular project or policy's own risk, usually (and sometimes erroneously) using the variance of estimated benefits and costs. Opponents of the more stringent safety regulations might argue that the potential range (probability distribution) of lives saved is large and therefore that the benefits should be discounted at a higher rate than "normal." Neither of these procedures is likely to be correct. Fortunately, there is a common model used in financial portfolio theory that under certain conditions can provide appropriate risk-adjusted discount rates: the *capital asset pricing model* (CAPM). In essence, the CAPM provides risk-adjusted discount rates that enable us to compare the present value of uncertain future cash flows to the value of known cash flows.[25]

The CAPM is based on a fundamental proposition about risk: *the risk inherent in a project is not its own risk but its risk relative to everything else* (Sharpe 1964). As shown by Lind (1982a), this risk is reflected by the *correlation* of returns from an investment and the relevant *wealth portfolio.*

Individuals hold a variety of assets. They may own homes, stocks and bonds, money in savings accounts, gold bars under mattresses, and other assets. The collection of these assets can be called an individual's *wealth portfolio.* The value of these individual assets may rise and fall; the price of gold, for example, may increase during periods when the economy does poorly because many people see owning gold as valuable during "hard times" or during periods of extreme inflation. By contrast, if the economy is especially robust, the price of gold may fall. The value of other assets in the portfolio may behave differently. Unlike gold, the value of a home may fall when the economy is doing poorly. The relationships between the value of individual assets and the value of an overall wealth portfolio make it possible to define the riskiness of holding individual assets. Assets like gold may be a form of insurance for maintaining a higher overall level of wealth, paying the most when the level of wealth is lowest. Other assets may not have this insurance characteristic. The relationship between the return on an individual asset and the return on an entire wealth portfolio forms the basis for determining the riskiness

---

[25]Lind (1982a) also notes that theorists with diverse views on the treatment of public projects (Hirschleifer 1965; Sandmo 1972; Arrow and Lind 1970) all implicitly agree on the applicability of risk-adjusted discount rates.

TABLE 14.2   WEALTH AND RETURN FROM SOLAR PROJECT INVESTMENT

State of the World	World "Wealth"	Value of Investment
Large global climate change	Low	High
Small global climate change	High	Low

of individual assets. This relationship provides a method for determining risk-adjusted discount rates in the framework of the CAPM.

There is no intrinsic reason that the value of environmental policies cannot be examined using a portfolio approach. For example, the solar energy investment will reduce the production of greenhouse gases linked to global climate change. If global climate change turns out to be large and costly to society, GDP will be reduced, but society's investment in the solar project will have a larger payoff. This payoff will be more valuable because it will occur when national income is lower because of global climate change.[26] Even if global climate change turns out to be beneficial, the loss from investments in solar energy that reduced greenhouse gas emissions would occur when GDP was highest. Losses would be less "harmful" because total wealth would be higher. These results are summarized in Table 14.2. As we will discuss shortly, it is this *correlation* between wealth and return that will determine the proper discount rate to use.[27]

To develop the concept of risk-adjusted discount rates based on wealth portfolios, we can use the concept of the certainty equivalent (CEQ) that we illustrated previously in Figure 14.1. The present value of the CEQ can be used to derive a risk-adjusted discount rate. For example, suppose that the cost of the solar project is $100 million. The return ten years from now will be $250 million if global climate change is severe or $150 million if it is not. If the probability of each of these states is .5, the expected return will equal $200 million. Suppose that policymakers are indifferent between these uncertain returns and a guaranteed return of $180 million. Then there will be some risk-adjusted interest rate, R, such that discounting the expected cash flow from the solar investment will have the same present value as $180 million discounted at the *SRTP*. Thus for some R,

$$\frac{\$200 \text{ million}}{(1 + R)^{10}} = \frac{\$180 \text{ million}}{(1 + SRTP)^{10}} = \$133.9 \text{ million} \tag{14.1}$$

Solving Equation 14.1 shows that $R = 0.041$, or 4.1 percent. Using this risk-adjusted discount rate, we can discount the uncertain future cash flows from the solar project to equate to the value of the expected cash flow from the solar energy project and the certain cash flow from a risk-free investment.

---

[26]This assumes that society is risk-averse and therefore that there is diminishing marginal utility of income.

[27]For example, Lind (1982b) argues that most energy investments should be discounted at a rate *lower* than the *SRTP* due to their insurance characteristics.

This sort of analysis is fine as long as the investor's wealth portfolio contains only one asset. However, if the investor's wealth portfolio has more than one asset, this approach is inadequate. The relevant risk will not be that the cash flows from the solar project are uncertain but rather how the uncertainty of those cash flows is related to the value of the investor's overall portfolio of assets. This is where the CAPM comes in: it relates the riskiness of an individual asset to the portfolio of assets held.

William Sharpe, the economist credited with developing the CAPM, showed that under certain conditions, the relationship between the expected return on an asset and its risk will be linear. This is shown in Figure 14.8. In this figure, it is assumed that there exists a risk-free asset. (The closest example is U.S. government Treasury bonds.) There also are an infinite combination of assets that have different risk-return relationships, such as points P, Q, R, S, and M. The riskiness of any individual portfolio of assets is assumed to be captured by that portfolio's covariance σ with the market. Investors who prefer higher expected returns but lower risk will never choose portfolios like P, Q, and R because those portfolios will always be dominated by portfolios M and S, which have higher expected returns and less risk. The curve LL is called the *efficient set* of portfolios. All portfolios along LL may be chosen because none is dominated by another. An investor choosing portfolio S, for example, is selecting a lower-risk portfolio than M but also a portfolio with a lower expected return. Portfolio M is special. It is called the *market portfolio*, meaning that it contains combinations of every asset. Of course, in reality this is not possible, but there are close approximations. For example, today investors can purchase stock index funds, which contain shares of the Standard and Poor's list of 500 stocks on the New York Stock Exchange. The market portfolio is the most diversified portfolio that exists because it contains some of everything. Any risk associated with this portfolio is called *systematic* or *nondiversifiable* risk.

Sharpe (1964) showed that investors with preferences given by the indifference curve U_I would be best off by selecting some combination of the risk-free asset and the market portfolio M, and in doing so reach a higher indifference curve

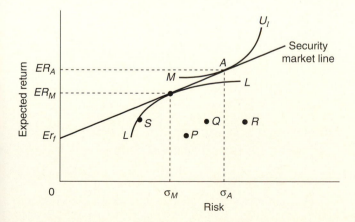

Figure 14.8   The Capital Asset Pricing Model

tangent to the security market line. Sharpe also showed that the relationship between the expected return on any portfolio of assets and its risk would be linear. That linear relationship is the foundation of the CAPM. For any portfolio of assets i, the expected return on i will equal the risk-free rate plus a risk premium. This relationship is shown in Equation 14.2:

$$E(R_i) = R_F + \beta[E(R_M) - R_F] \tag{14.2}$$

where β ("beta") is the ratio of an asset's covariance with the market portfolio to the variance of the return on the market portfolio. A beta of 1.00 means that the riskiness of the asset in question is perfectly correlated with the market portfolio. A beta greater that 1.00 means that the riskiness of the asset is more exaggerated than the market portfolio. A negative beta means that the riskiness of the asset is inversely correlated with the market portfolio. The solar energy company investment, for example, has a negative beta.

Risk-adjusted discount rates can be developed using the CAPM. To do this, we need to know the correlation between returns from the particular investment project under consideration and the overall wealth portfolio. We can derive an expression for the correct risk-adjusted discount rate, which will be based on the *SRTP* and an overall market interest rate that reflected the overall risk in the market. Although we leave the formal derivation to the appendix to this chapter,[28] the risk-adjusted discount rate for a particular project can be shown to equal

$$R_A = R_F + \beta(R_M - R_F) \tag{14.3}$$

where R_A = the risk-adjusted discount rate reflecting portfolio risk
$\quad\quad\ \beta$ = the project's beta
$\quad\quad R_F$ = the risk-free rate of interest
$\quad\quad R_M$ = the market interest rate[29]

For example, suppose that the rate of return on the market portfolio is 9 percent, that the risk-free rate (again assumed equal to the *SRTP*) equals 3 percent, and that we have estimated the beta for the solar energy facility as -0.3. According to Equation 14.3, the risk-adjusted discount rate to use for the solar energy project will equal $0.03 + (-0.3)/(0.09 - 0.03) = 1.2$ percent. In this case, the returns from the solar energy project (including the avoided external environmental costs) would be discounted using a risk-adjusted rate of 1.2 percent.

Equation 14.3 deals with an investment that lasts for just one period. To extend it to the more realistic case of many periods, it is necessary to assume that the estimate of beta remains constant over time. This is equivalent to stating that although

---

[28]See Copeland and Weston (1983) for a more detailed derivation of this model, as well as critiques of it.

[29]The market interest rate will reflect the overall level of risk because it is not possible to diversify away risk from the entire market portfolio. (The market portfolio is by definition as diversified as possible because it contains all possible investments.)

the risk is constant in any period, it accumulates over time so that returns farther into the future are riskier. If this assumption is unreasonable, then the returns in different periods must be broken up into segments where beta is constant.[30]

Determining a Relevant Wealth Portfolio

The CAPM deals primarily with well-established financial markets, such as the stock market. Investors can read published betas for different stocks. Unfortunately, most environmental attributes are not traded in markets. How can we determine a relevant wealth portfolio for investments that either produce or reduce environmental externalities as well as environmental betas? Unfortunately, this question has not been dealt with in much detail in the literature. Furthermore, we doubt that you will be able to look up betas for clean air or beautiful mountain vistas.

Nevertheless, one possible answer may lie with the nature of environmental costs and benefits. Because externalities can affect entire communities or even have global effects, relevant portfolios can be taken as the relevant area's overall wealth. For example, to the extent that global climate change is a problem, the relevant portfolio would seem to be worldwide wealth.[31] For pollutants that have much more localized impacts, such as local effects on groundwater supplies, the wealth of the affected community would better represent the relevant portfolio when measuring returns for a given environmental investment. Development of a new national park would consider the country's overall wealth because, although the park would be located in a specific area, it would provide benefits to all citizens.

How could this be done in practice? Consider again the case of preservation of Hell's Canyon, where the benefits of preservation were primarily recreational and the benefits of development were in the form of power production. In light of evidence that the demand for environmental quality increases with wealth, we could assume that the value of recreational benefits would be highest in high-wealth states of the world. Likewise, benefits would be valued the least in low-wealth states of the world. Thus an argument could be made that the benefits associated with whitewater recreation be discounted at a rate greater than the *SRTP*.

In terms of the future power production benefits, an adjustment to the *SRTP* is not clear. On the one hand, like the solar power company example, we can argue that the benefits of hydroelectric production will be greatest when fossil fuel prices are high and economic wealth is low. This supports the use of a discount rate below the *SRTP*. On the other hand, a low-wealth state of the world likely means a reduced demand for electricity, which will tend to reduce the value of the hydroelectric plant's output. This argues for a discount rate greater than the *SRTP*.

Given the order-of-magnitude difference between estimated power production benefits and estimated recreational benefits, it is unlikely that adjusting the

---

[30]See Lind (1982a) or Zerbe and Dively (1994) for more detail.
[31]Measures of wealth are taken up in Chapter 19.

discount rates used to determine net present values of preservation and development would have changed the ultimate recommendation for preservation. In other cases, however, policymakers would be wise to perform *sensitivity analyses* on the choice of discount rates.[32]

Other Stochastic Methodologies

In certain cases, the use of risk-adjusted discount rates derived from the CAPM may be inappropriate. The CAPM is based on the returns on financial investments being distributed normally (along a bell-shaped curve). The reason is that for a normal distribution, the variance completely describes the risk. If returns are not distributed normally, we cannot use the CAPM to derive risk-adjusted discount rates because risk may not be captured completely in the variance term. Instead, there may be other important properties, such as whether a distribution is skewed in one direction or the other. Environmental costs, however, may not always be distributed normally over all future states of the world. In fact, we would be surprised if they always were. For example, the potential environmental costs associated with global climate change are likely skewed significantly, reflecting a small probability that there may be catastrophic damage.

One alternative would be for decision makers to adopt other rules that incorporate information about the distributions of environmental costs. For example, decision makers could examine the probability that a project's environmental costs exceed some critical threshold level that has been set. This is the basis for the "safe minimum standard" approach discussed in Chapter 9. Or they might examine the probability that a project's costs exceed its benefits. There are also methodologies that can evaluate entire distributions of costs. These methods may be able to eliminate certain projects and thus enable decision makers to focus efforts to value environmental costs further for a smaller set of resources.

Consider Figure 14.9, which shows hypothetical distributions of external environmental costs associated with two alternative hydroelectric resources, A and B. These resources are assumed to be identical except for the estimated environmental damage they will cause. In this example, the mean (expected) external cost for resource A is $21 million, and the mean external cost for resource B is $23 million. However, the probability that resource A will have very high external costs is greater than the probability for B. In such a situation, risk-averse decision makers face a dilemma: the expected cost of the riskier hydroelectric resource is $2 million lower. The decision maker must decide whether the additional risk associated with resource A is worth $2 million in expected savings.

In situations such as this, decision makers could resort to arbitrary decision rules—for example, they could choose the resource with the lowest probability of some arbitrarily set level of environmental costs. This type of decision rule is known as a *mini-max* rule because it minimizes the maximum loss associated with a particular decision. If, as shown in Figure 14.9, this level was set to anything

---

[32] See Zerbe and Dively (1994) for a discussion of sensitivity analysis.

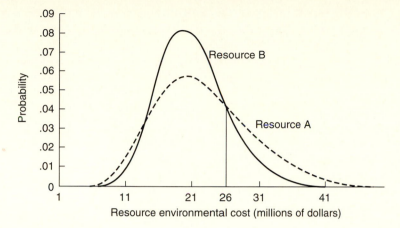

Figure 14.9   The Mini-Max Decision Rule

above $26 million, resource B would be chosen. Otherwise, resource A would be chosen. The biggest limitation with this type of decision rule is selecting the cutoff level. Should it be set to $26 million, $30 million, or some other value? The choice will always be arbitrary and will depend on the policymaker's degree of risk aversion.[33] Krutilla and Fisher's (1985) analysis of the environmental benefits of Hell's Canyon was in fact an example of this type of mini-max decision rule.

Stochastic Dominance   There are also more rigorous analytical methods available to choose between resources. One method, called *stochastic dominance,* has been used extensively in financial analysis and has numerous other applications.[34] In fact, we introduced the concept indirectly in Chapter 10 when we discussed how alternatives that did not lie on the efficient frontier were said to be *dominated* and could therefore be eliminated from consideration.

The advantage of stochastic dominance is that it can rank options for risk-averse decision makers regardless of precisely how risk-averse they may be.[35] The concept is based on expected utility theory. Stochastic dominance can allow us to rank a set of alternatives (investments, etc.) without knowing much about the underlying preferences of decision makers or regulators. If all we know is that decision makers are risk-averse, stochastic dominance may allow us to eliminate certain resources from consideration without having to know that regulator A is only half as risk-averse as regulator B, and the like. Using stochastic dominance, we may be able to determine that resource A and resource B both dominate resource C and hence eliminate C from further consideration. With this technique, the

---

[33]As was mentioned earlier, however, one possible cutoff point would be a level that represents a societal budget constraint.

[34]See, for example, Whitmore and Findlay (1978).

[35]See, for example, Cochran (1986). Stochastic dominance can also be defined relative to an Arrow-Pratt measure of risk aversion.

number of resources to be examined may be narrowed, allowing better decisions to be made about the environmental impacts associated with the remaining resources.

Although multiattribute analysis employs a simple form of stochastic dominance, the concept is itself broader, in some case allowing alternatives along an efficient frontier to be ranked. Formally, stochastic dominance is defined by looking at the *cumulative density functions* (cdfs) of two probability distributions, $F(x)$ and $G(x)$, for the random variable x. We say that "F dominates G in the first degree" if and only if $G(x) > F(x)$ for all values of x. For example, in Figure 14.10(a), the cdf $G(x)$ always lies above and to the left of the cdf $F(x)$ for all possible values of x. Thus G dominates F in the first degree. First-degree stochastic dominance is powerful because it means that a decision maker will prefer G to F whether risk-averse or not.

First-degree dominance is rare, however. In many cases, the benefits from one project will be greater than another project in some states of the world and less than the other project in other states of the world. This is shown in Figure 14.10(b). In such cases, the expected value of alternative G may be greater than the expected value of F, but there may also be more uncertainty associated with G. In cases like this, first-degree stochastic dominance will not hold, but *second-degree stochastic dominance* may. With second-degree dominance, all risk-averse decision makers, regardless of how risk-averse they are, will prefer the hydro plant option. Formally, we say that $F(x)$ dominates $G(x)$ in the second degree if and only if the area under the cumulative density function $G(x)$ is always larger than the area under the cdf $F(x)$ for all possible values of x. Even though the cdfs may cross, the accumulated excess in area will preserve the domination of one alternative over the other, allowing second-degree dominance to be established. With first-degree dominance, the cdf of one alternative is always above the cdf of the other.

Consider the following example. Suppose that we are evaluating the net benefits from preserving a free-flowing river versus the net benefits of development for power production. For simplicity's sake, assume that we have discounted the benefits associated with both alternatives and derived two probability distributions

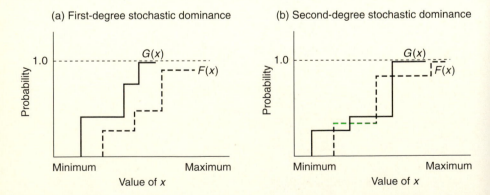

Figure 14.10   First- and Second-Degree Stochastic Dominance

TABLE 14.3 DISTRIBUTION OF NPV BENEFITS: PRESERVATION VERSUS DEVELOPMENT

State of the World	Cumulative Probability	Project 1 Development (millions of dollars)	Project 2 Preservation (millions of dollars)
1	.1	20	50
2	.2	25	50
3	.3	40	50
4	.4	60	70
5	.5	80	70
6	.6	100	70
7	.7	120	110
8	.8	120	120
9	.9	140	150
10	1.0	150	160

of the net present-value benefits over ten discrete future states of the world. We have sorted and ranked the benefits in both cases. These are shown in Table 14.3.

Figure 14.11 graphs the two cumulative density functions for projects 1 and 2. Because the cdfs for the two functions cross, neither dominates the other in the first degree. To determine whether there is second-degree stochastic dominance, we need to determine the area under each of the cdfs. In this example, project 2 will dominate project 1 in the second degree if the area under the cdf of project 1 is always greater than the area under the cdf for project 2 at any given probability level. (Determining these areas is left as an exercise.)

Multiattribute Analysis Under Uncertainty† We conclude our discussion of stochastic methodologies by returning to multiattribute analysis, which we first introduced in Chapter 10. As we stated in that chapter, when there is no uncertainty,

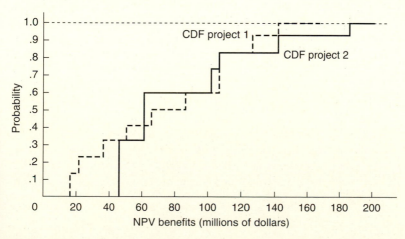

Figure 14.11 Determination of Second-Degree Stochastic Dominance

TABLE 14.4 ATTRIBUTES OF ALTERNATIVE RENEWABLE RESOURCES

Resource	Type	Cost (millions of dollars)	Reliability Index (0–100)	GHG Avoided Emissions (10^3 tons) (Low)	(High)	Ambient Noise (decibels)
(1)	**(2)**	**(3)**	**(4)**	**(5)**	**(6)**	**(7)**
X_1	Hydro 1	9	76	20	30	70
X_2	Wind 1	16	42	35	130	80
X_3	Solar 1	18	53	40	150	60
X_4	Hydro 2	8	88	15	0	80
X_5	Biomass 1	17	66	0	60	100
Minimum value:		8	42	0	0	60
Maximum value:		18	88	40	150	100

multiattribute analysis can show stochastic dominance graphically by examining the relevant attribute space. In many cases, we will be able to eliminate some project or policy alternatives through the use of stochastic dominance. Just as likely, however, there will remain a more limited set of alternative for which we cannot establish dominance. In these cases, multiattribute analysis offers a convenient way to incorporate uncertainty and select a preferred action.

In Chapter 10, we defined a multiattribute value function V as follows:

$$V_m(a_m) = \left(\frac{a_{jm} - a_{jm}^{\min}}{a_{jm}^{\max} - a_{jm}^{\min}} \right)^{1/\lambda_m} \qquad \lambda_m \geq 1 \qquad (14.4)$$

where a_{jm} represents the mth attribute value of the jth alternative and λ_m is a constant that measures the curvature of V.

Recall that the quantity $(a_{jm} - a_{jm}^{\min})/(a_{jm}^{\max} - a_{jm}^{\min})$ will lie between 0 and 1 for all values of the attribute a_m. As we discussed in Chapter 10, raising the entire quantity to the $1/\lambda_m$ power changes the curvature of the function. As λ_m increases, the value function becomes more convex. But as we discussed earlier in this chapter, convexity of a utility function measures risk aversion. Thus it turns out that by increasing λ_m for different attributes, we can represent the policymaker's level of risk aversion for a particular attribute. Then, consistent with expected utility theory, we can determine the expected value of the sum of the individual attribute value functions. (Because the mathematics is somewhat complex, we won't derive it here.)[36]

To examine the influence of risk aversion, we use the example of renewable resource development from Chapter 10. However, in this case we assume that green house gas (GHG) emissions are uncertain. Thus as shown in Table 14.4, *avoided* GHG emissions have a high and low range as shown in columns 5 and 6.

---

[36]Additional detail on the structure of multiattribute utility functions can be found in Keeney and Raiffa (1993). A short discussion is contained in Kleindorfer, Kunreuther, and Schoemaker (1993).

If in column 5, Biomass 1 has the highest overall GHG emissions and thus avoids none, while Solar 1 avoids 40,000 tons of GHGs. In column 6, however, it is Hydro 2 with the highest level of GHG emissions, so it avoids none, while Solar 1 avoids 150,000 tons. Using this range of avoided GHG emissions, we can determine value function scores when there are different attribute weights and different values of λ. A sample of these are shown in Table 14.5.

If you examine Table 14.5, you will notice that the changes in resource rankings are most noticeable for resources in the middle of the pack. Biomass 1, for example, is always dominated by the other resources, and so its ranking does not change. As the weight on GHG emissions increases, Solar 1's rank increases from 3 to 1. As the level of risk aversion is increased (increasing λ), its ranking is not affected for a given GHG weight. The reason is that Solar 1 always avoids the maximum amount of GHGs. Hence uncertainty in GHG emissions does not affect its relative rank.

This points out an important policy implication in general: *sometimes uncertainty and decision maker's attitudes toward risk will not matter much because the preferred strategy (given well-defined policy goals) will be insensitive to the uncertainty.* Thus if preventing species extinction is of paramount importance, uncertainty in the cost of a policy that has no impact on species need not be considered

TABLE 14.5 RESOURCE RANKINGS WITH ALTERNATIVE VALUE FUNCTION CURVATURES (λ AND ATTRIBUTE WEIGHTS)

Resource	GHG Weight				
	0.2	0.3	0.4	0.5	0.6
			$\lambda = 1$		
Hydro 1	1	1	2	2	3
Wind 1	4	4	4	3	2
Solar 1	3	3	1	1	1
Hydro 2	2	2	3	4	4
Biomass 1	5	5	5	5	5
			$\lambda = 2$		
Hydro 1	2	1	2	3	3
Wind 1	4	4	4	2	2
Solar 1	3	3	1	1	1
Hydro 2	1	1	3	4	4
Biomass 1	5	5	5	5	5
			$\lambda = 5$		
Hydro 1	2	3	3	2	4
Wind 1	4	4	4	4	2
Solar 1	3	1	1	1	1
Hydro 2	1	2	2	2	3
Biomass 1	5	5	5	5	5

because cost is not a high-priority goal. What may happen, however, is that uncertainty in cost becomes an important secondary consideration once a reduced set of policy alternatives are determined. If we determine that the GHG weight should be 0.5, for example, and rank Solar 1 and Wind 1 the highest of the five resources, we may want to take a closer look at their costs. But we still will not care about the costs of Biomass 1.

SETTING GOVERNMENT PRIORITIES: COMPARATIVE RISK ASSESSMENT

We have discussed a number of risk-related issues in this chapter. We have advocated policymakers' taking a risk-averse attitude in their approach to environmental risks. We have discussed a variety of methodologies and valuation techniques for environmental assets in the presence of uncertainty. What we haven't discussed is how different environmental risks—whether atmospheric sulfur dioxide emissions, stratospheric ozone depletion, or water pollution—should be dealt with in the face of limited resources to do so. This is especially true for many environmental risks because government action will be required to address them. For example, governments may need to develop markets where none had existed previously, as with air pollution permits. Or governments may need to ban the production and use of chlorofluorocarbons. Or national governments may need to impose specific requirements on municipalities for sewage treatment and water quality.

Even after we have valued environmental risks, using the techniques described earlier in this chapter or other techniques, the ranking process will not be complete because risks can affect a number of policy dimensions. But regardless of the environmental risks to be addressed, there will be only limited resources available to address them. Even market mechanisms, such as emissions taxes, will require monitoring, collection, and enforcement. That takes resources. And when environmental risks cannot be addressed through market mechanisms, as with the storage of high-level nuclear wastes, government must decide on appropriate policies in consideration of many other priorities.

In 1987, the Environmental Protection Agency completed a report that compared the risks addressed by the multitude of the agency's environmental programs. By 1989, then EPA administrator, William Reilly, had made risk-based priority setting the centerpiece of his administration (Davies 1996). *Comparative risk assessment* (CRA) was born. CRA encompasses a broad set of methods to rank multiple risks. It can compare similar risks, such as risks of various cancers associated with exposure to different pesticides. It also can compare dissimilar risks, such as the health risk of lead poisoning versus the risk of death in an automobile accident. And CRAs can compare alternative risk reduction policies, such as whether water should be purified using chlorine or ultraviolet light or whether reducing groundwater contamination should take priority over reducing ground-level ozone.

Performing a CRA requires some form of risk analysis. First, it requires determining the sources of an individual risk (e.g., does Alar really cause cancer?) and the development of dose-response models, such as those we discussed in Chapter 11, to establish the relationship between exposure and harm. Second, it requires determining who (or what) will be exposed. By combining all of this information with other similar studies, CRA can value and rank different risks. Determining and valuing the impacts of air pollution emitted from midwestern coal-fired power plants, for example, requires an estimate of who and what will be exposed, what that exposure will cause (cancer, asthma, acidification of lakes, etc.), and how society will value reducing those adverse impacts.

A CRA will not determine a policy response in itself. For example, a CRA may determine that the overall risk from pesticide exposure is greater than the risk posed by Alar, but will say nothing about how policymakers should address the two risks. CRAs may even address questions of equity and fairness, should these be included in developing risk rankings. But the ultimate development of policy responses will be left to policymakers and regulators, who can use the results of the CRA as an input to make decisions.

CRA and Multiattribute Analysis

CRA is really a form of multiattribute analysis in which risks are compared using a variety of metrics. For example, analyses can be based on monetary measures of risk, e.g., value of statistical life estimates (Chapter 12) or contingent valuation studies of WTP to avoid environmental risks such as oil spills (Chapter 11). Metrics can also incorporate nonmonetary measures, including geographic, socioeconomic, and even philosophical factors. For example, are emissions of atmospheric lead concentrated disproportionately in areas populated by minorities? Are Superfund sites predominately located near poor neighborhoods? Do certain risks have irreversible consequences, such as species extinction?

An analyst performing a CRA study will probably have to account for a multitude of values. As Morgan and colleagues (1996) point out, even if there are no resource constraints, value judgments will still enter risk rankings. For example, they use the example of lost life expectancy as a measure of risk versus premature death. In Chapter 12, we discussed development of monetary values for the statistical value of life. Those values, and the empirical estimates presented, were all based on premature death. In that respect, there would be no difference between increased risks to infants and children (e.g., the Alar scare) and increased risks to the aged. However, values of a statistical life calculated on the basis of lost life *expectancy* would obviously rank the risks to infants and children more highly than for the population as a whole. Though that may seem reasonable in some respects, older individuals might take a dim view that their lives are somehow "less valuable" because they will soon be dying anyway.

Another critical attribute will be public values. This relates to the issue of perceived versus actual risks that we discussed in Chapter 12. Policymakers who rank different risks need to appear credible by incorporating public values (Graham and Hammitt 1996). The problem is trying to figure out what those values are, especially if the public has no clue how to rank different and unfamiliar risks. Furthermore, just as with the residents of the mythical Happyville, when public perceptions differ completely from reality (or at least expert judgment), maintaining a credible risk reduction policy becomes even more difficult. The public may be more inclined to heed the warnings about Alar from an earnest celebrity such as Meryl Streep than to believe the reassurances provided by some "faceless bureaucrat." The best solution will be education. Individuals' perceived risks are more likely to approach reality if they have a better understanding of the basis for those risks.

Morgan and colleagues (1996) describe a six-step process to rank different risks. These steps are as follows:

1. Categorize the risks.
2. Identify the risk attributes.
3. Describe the risks in terms of the attributes.
4. Select a group to do the ranking.
5. Perform the analysis.
6. Summarize the results for use by decision makers and the public.

If you were to review the discussion in Chapter 10 about performing a multiat-tribute analysis, you would notice many similarities. Consider an analysis of the risk of premature death in humans because of environmental degradation. One way of categorizing those risks is by type, such as chemical risks (e.g., lead, mercury, Clean Air Act criteria pollutants), bacteriological risks (e.g., lack of clean water), and radi-ological risks (e.g., high- and low-level nuclear wastes, radon). Once the risks are categorized, the next step is defining the risk attributes. These attributes should fit the criteria we discussed in Chapter 10.[37] For example, one attribute could be number of deaths. Another might be size of the exposed population. Still others could include socioeconomic characteristics of the exposed population. There could also be psychological attributes. For example, exposure to nuclear wastes may inspire more sheer terror among the public (mutation, slow and painful death from radiation sickness, attacks by giant insects, etc.) than exposure to radon gas, even though the latter is statistically more risky because it is so ubiquitous. Once that step is completed, the specific risks must be described to the group that will perform the ranking, and the analysis is then performed. The group should include risk experts and risk managers but should probably also include members of the public so as to enhance credibility. The subsequent analysis will need to include developing attribute weights and specifying some of functional form (such as Equation 14.4) that will be used to perform the analysis.

Equity Versus Efficiency

If you have read this far in the book, you will not be surprised by the heading of this final section on CRA. Good decisions require clarity. Policy exercises that rank dif-ferent risks must be based on an understanding of what goals are sought. We

---

[37]Recall that attributes should be comprehensive, measurable, preferentially independent, nonredun-dant, and simple.

should not be surprised if risks ranked in terms of their economic efficiency impacts differ from those ranked in terms of their equity and fairness impacts. The reduction in economic efficiency arising because children are exposed to lead may be less than the reduction in efficiency caused by agricultural workers exposed to pesticides or workers in factories that make insulation. But which is the most "unfair" risk? What if the agricultural workers are primarily minorities and the factory workers are not? Should risks to minorities be ranked more highly than risks faced by the majority? Should risks faced by the poor be ranked more highly than risks faced by the rich?

Answering such questions requires defining equity and grounding the definition in a moral philosophy, such as those we discussed in Chapter 4. Although credible risk assessment studies may include attributes of equity and fairness, doing so can make the analyses more susceptible to politics. Recall the discussion in Chapter 9 about "environmental racism." What sort of political pressure would be applied to CRA studies that identified what might appear to be racist but was in fact a consequence of economics? Furthermore, how should equity and rights components be merged with observed differences in the demand for environmental quality, differences that are often found to be based on income and education levels? The entire issue can become still more problematic when risks affecting the rights of nature are ranked. Are hydroelectric dams that endanger salmon species more "risky" than the clearcutting of forests that endanger spotted owls? Should saving whales take priority over saving plant species? Because we cannot ask these members of the "public" to rank the risks they face, people must serve as surrogates. Finally, how do we compare risks that cross a multitude of equity concerns, whether between different ethnic groups, generations, or species? Although CRA will not resolve all such issues, by providing data about and consequences of different risks, it may enhance the treatment of equity concerns.

CHAPTER SUMMARY

In this chapter, we have focused on the issue of measuring environmental benefits and costs in the presence of uncertainty and risk. We distinguished risk from uncertainty and defined the concept of risk aversion and expected utility. We then considered risk and uncertainty as reflections of willingness to pay, and we examined the value of additional information. We also saw that there are alternative measures of *WTP*, including expected consumers' surplus and option price. We discussed the concept of option value and showed that contrary to the intuition of many, option values could be either positive or negative. Last, we discussed the use of option price in empirical work and reviewed the benefits of CVM for its ability to determine existence values and option price.

We concluded that there are good reasons for environmental policymakers to be risk-averse, owing to irreversibilities and their equity impacts, as well as limited abilities to diversify certain environmental risks. We then addressed several useful methodologies to evaluate environmental policies in the presence of uncertainty and risk aversion.

Ultimately, even if policymakers do everything "right," they may still make "wrong" decisions. A particular environmental policy may have only a 1-in-1,000,000 chance of failure, yet it may still fail. We will never be able to eliminate environmental risks entirely, nor should we attempt to do so. And it is unlikely that we will ever have complete information about any environmental policy decision. However, as long as society must continue to allocate scarce resources to meet environmental and other goals, it will be better off from having attempted to make consistent and logical decisions.

CHAPTER REVIEW

Economic Concepts and Tools

- Risk and uncertainty are not the same thing, even though the terms are often used interchangeably. Economists often refer to uncertainty when not all of the possible outcomes are known or not all of their probabilities are known. Risk refers to how individuals and societies approach decisions that have uncertain outcomes.
- Economists often classify individual behavior as risk-averse, risk-neutral, or risk-loving. Someone who is risk-averse is willing to pay more than the expected value of a possible loss (or willing to accept less than the expected gain) to avoid a risk. Someone who is risk-loving is willing to pay only some amount less than the expected value of a possible loss (or will accept only more than the expected gain) to avoid a risk. Someone who is risk-neutral is willing to pay the expected value of a possible loss (or accept the expected gain) to avoid a risk.
- An indirect utility function shows the maximum utility obtainable for a given level of income. An individual who is risk-averse will also have a declining marginal utility of income.
- Information is valuable when having more information results in better decisions with higher expected utility.
- Option price equals an individual's *WTP* for the *right* to consume a good, even though the individual may or may not *wish* to consume the good, depending on the state of the world. Option price is an *ex ante* (before the fact) measure of value. The concept of option price in environmental economics is somewhat analogous to financial market options.
- Expected consumers' surplus is an *ex post* (after the fact) measure of value. It is the consumers' surplus associated with each possible future state of the world times the probabilities of those states.
- Option value is the difference between expected consumers' surplus and option price. It may be positive, zero, or negative. Thus an *ex post* measure of expected consumers' surplus is not a lower bound for *ex ante WTP*.
- Economic irreversibility exists when the costs of changing a decision after it is made are prohibitive. In the extreme, an irreversible decision cannot be

changed once it is made. At this time, allowing the extinction of a species is irreversible. Allowing a single, small wetland is not because the cost of restoring it is not prohibitive.

- There are at least three components of any irreversible decision: (1) whether it should be rejected because the costs are greater than the benefits, (2) whether it should be delayed because the net present value of benefits is greater with delay (e.g., because net benefits will increase faster than the rate of interest), and (3) whether it should be delayed because the value of information that can be learned during a delay is greater than the cost of the delay.

- Decision makers' attitudes toward risk can sometimes be incorporated in a decision based on expected net present value by using risk-adjusted discount rates to discount the benefits and the costs of risky projects. A risk-adjusted discount rate is derived by constructing an artificial option called a *certainty equivalent*, which has a certain value equal to the expected future value of the project less the value of the change in riskiness of the portfolio of assets because of the addition of the project. The risk-adjusted discount rate is the rate of return of the certainty equivalent.

- Decision makers with different degrees of risk aversion will have different discount rates.

- A risky project whose benefits are negatively correlated with those of other assets may make the overall portfolio of assets less risky.

- Any risk-averse decision maker will prefer one option over another if the first shows either first- or second-degree stochastic dominance. Option A dominates option B stochastically in the first degree if the cumulative density function (cdf) of B is always above the cdf of option A. Option A dominates option B in the second degree if the area under the cdf of B is always greater than the area under the cdf of A for all possible values of the underlying random variable.

- Multiattribute decision analysis can address uncertainty by adjusting the concavity of value functions as a proxy for risk aversion. Alternatively, specific measures of risk, such as the variance of expected net benefits, can be directly incorporated as attributes to be valued.

- Comparative risk assessment (CRA) is a method to rank alternative risks. It is a form of multiattribute analysis. CRA was developed by the EPA and is increasingly being used by other federal agencies to set priorities for addressing risks in the face of limited governmental resources.

Policy Issues

- The contingent valuation methodology is the most amenable to determining *ex ante* use, existence, and total values. The total value of an environmental amenity can always be decomposed into its component parts, consisting of use values and existence value. In the presence of uncertainty, all of these valuation concepts will be *ex ante*.

- If society can diversify away the risks inherent in public decisions, both for society as a whole and for individuals, an argument can be made that public decision makers should be risk-neutral, even if individual members of the society are risk-averse. These conditions are seldom met for environmental projects. Therefore, public sector decision makers should generally be risk-averse when evaluating these projects. There is little agreement as to how well environmental risks can be diversified away.
- There are limits to the amount of information that policymakers can absorb and use. To be effective, economists must summarize information about the risks of a decision in ways that are meaningful but easy to understand.

DISCUSSION QUESTIONS

1. Explain the difference between financial market "options" and the concept of environmental options. Are there situations where the option price for an environmental project would have a precise analogy in financial markets?
2. How could a society's aversion to future environmental risk be measured?
3. How do you explain an individual who both buys insurance and gambles in Las Vegas?
4. If, for a given environmental amenity, the proper valuation is based on willingness to *accept,* is there a role for the use of option price?
5. Discuss alternative ways in which uncertain environmental impacts that may occur 100 or more years into the future should be addressed.
6. We concluded that there appear to be sufficient reasons for policymakers be risk-averse when confronting environmental impacts. There are many degrees of risk aversion, however. Thus it is natural to ask how risk-averse policymakers should be. Discuss.
7. Suppose that state environmental policymakers are considering the level of an emissions cap for particulates, which can cause a variety of health impacts, in the state's largest city. If the cap is set too stringently, it may prevent any future industrial development. If set too leniently, it may allow too many adverse health impacts. Also, there is significant uncertainty as to the amount of future population growth in the city. What should the policymakers do to establish the emissions cap?
8. A specific policy is designed to reduce emissions of carbon dioxide, which scientists believe may be contributing to global climate change. Given the current state of scientific knowledge, the magnitude and pace of that change, if any, are uncertain. How should the policy be evaluated? At what rate should its future costs and benefits be discounted? Is the risk from global climate change diversifiable? How could such diversification be measured empirically?
9. Using the data in Table 14.3, determine whether project 2 (preservation) dominates project 1 (development) in the second degree.

REFERENCES

Arrow, K. 1972. "Exposition of the Theory of Choice Under Uncertainty." In *Decision and Organization*, ed. C. B. McGuire and R. Radner. Amsterdam: Elsevier.

Arrow, K., and A. Fisher. 1974. "Environmental Preservation, Uncertainty, and Irreversibility." *Quarterly Journal of Economics* 88(2): 313–319.

Arrow, K., and R. Lind. 1970. "Uncertainty and the Evaluation of Public Investment Decisions." *American Economic Review* 60(2): 364–378.

Awerbuch, S. 1995. "Market-Based IRP: It's Easy!" *Electricity Journal* 8(3): 50–67.

Bishop, R. 1986. "Resource Valuation Under Uncertainty." In *Advances in Applied Micro-Economics*, Vol. 4, ed. V. Smith. Greenwich, Conn.: JAI Press.

Brookshire, D., L. Eubanks, and A. Randall. 1983. "Estimating Option Prices and Existence Values for Wildlife Resources." *Land Economics* 59: 1–15.

Cochran, M. 1986. "Stochastic Dominance. The State of the Art in Agricultural Economics." In *Risk Analysis for Agricultural Production Firms: Concepts, Information Requirements, and Policy Issues.* Dept. of Agricultural Economics, Washington State University, Pullman.

Copeland, T., and J. Weston. 1989. *Financial Theory and Corporate Policy*, 3d ed. Reading, Mass.: Addison-Wesley.

Davies, J. (ed). 1996. *Comparing Environmental Risks: Tools for Setting Government Priorities.* Washington, D.C.: Resources for the Future.

Desvouges, W., V. Smith, and M. McGivney. 1983. *A Comparison of Alternative Approaches for Estimating Recreation and Related Benefits of Water Quality Improvements.* U.S. Office of Policy Analysis Report No. EPA-230-05-83-001. Washington, D.C.: Environmental Protection Agency.

Dixit, A., and R. Pindyck. 1994. *Investment Under Uncertainty.* Princeton, N.J.: Princeton University Press.

Fisher. A., and M. Hanemann. 1986. "Option Value and the Extinction of Species." In *Advances in Applied Micro-Economics*, Vol. 4, ed. V. Smith. Greenwich, Conn.: JAI Press.

Freeman, A. 1986. "Uncertainty and Environmental Policy: The Role of Option and Quasi-Option Value." In *Advances in Applied Micro-Economics*, Vol. 4, ed. V. Smith. Greenwich, Conn.: JAI Press.

———. 1993. *The Measurement of Environmental and Resource Values.* Washington, D.C.: Resources for the Future.

Graham, J., and J. Hammitt. 1996. "Refining the CRA Framework." In *Comparing Environmental Risks: Tools for Setting Government Priorities*, ed. J. Davies. Washington, D.C.: Resources for the Future.

Hey, J. 1979. *Uncertainty in Microeconomics.* New York: New York University Press.

Hirschleifer, J. 1970. *Investment, Interest, and Capital.* Upper Saddle River, N.J.: Prentice Hall.

Kamien, M., and N. Schwartz. 1981. *Dynamic Optimization: The Calculus of Variations and Optional Control in Economics and Management.* New York: Elsevier.

Keeney, R., and H. Raiffa. 1993. *Decisions with Multiple Objectives.* New York: Cambridge University Press.

Kleindorfer, P., H. Kunruether, and P. Schoemaker. 1993. *Decision Sciences: An Integrative Perspective*. New York: Cambridge University Press.

Knight, F. 1933. *Risk, Uncertainty, and Profit*. Boston: Houghton Mifflin.

Krutilla, J., and A. Fisher. 1985. *The Economics of Natural Environments: Studies in the Valuation of Commodity and Amenity Resources*, 2d ed. Baltimore: Johns Hopkins University Press.

Lind, R. 1982a. "A Primer on the Major Issues Relating to the Discount Rate for Evaluating National Energy Options." In *Discounting for Time and Risk in Energy Policy*, ed. R. Lind. Baltimore: Johns Hopkins University Press.

———. 1982b. "The Rate of Discount and the Application of Social Benefit-Cost Analysis in the Context of Energy Policy Decisions." In *Discounting for Time and Risk in Energy Policy*, ed. R. Lind. Baltimore: Johns Hopkins University Press.

Margolis, J. 1959. "The Economic Evaluation of Federal Water Resource Development." *American Economic Review* 49(1): 96–111.

Morgan, M., B. Fischoff, L. Lave, and P. Fishbeck. 1996. "A Proposal for Ranking Risk Within Federal Agencies." In *Comparing Environmental Risks: Tools for Setting Government Priorities*, ed. J. Davies. Washington, D.C.: Resources for the Future.

Orian, G., G. Brown, and J. Swierzbinski. 1985. *The Preservation and Valuation of Biological Resources*. Seattle: University of Washington Press.

Pratt, J. 1964. "Risk Aversion in the Small and in the Large." *Econometrica* 32: 122–136.

Randall, A. 1991. "Total and Nonuse Values." In *Measuring the Demand for Environmental Quality*, ed. J. Braden and C. Kolstad. New York: Elsevier.

Sandmo, A. 1972. "Discount Rates for Public Investment Under Uncertainty." *International Economic Review* 13(2): 287–302.

Savage, L. 1954. *The Foundations of Statistics*. New York: Wiley.

Sharpe, W. 1964. "Capital Asset Prices: A Theory of Market Equilibrium Under Conditions of Risk." *Journal of Finance* 19(3): 425–442.

Smith, V. 1986. "A Conceptual Overview of the Foundations of Benefit-Cost Analysis." In *Benefit Assessment: The State of the Art*, ed. J. Bentkover et al. Dordrecht, Netherlands: Reidel.

Swanson, T., and E. Barbier (eds.). 1992. *Economics for the Wilds: Wildlife, Diversity, and Development*. Washington, D.C.: Island Press.

Thaler, R. 1991. *Quasi-Rational Economics*. New York: Russell Sage Foundation.

von Neumann, J., and O. Morgenstern. 1947. *Theory of Games and Economic Behavior*. Princeton, N.J.: Princeton University Press.

Weisbrod, B. 1964. "Collective Consumption Services of Individual Consumption Goods." *Quarterly Journal of Economics* 78: 471–477.

Whitmore, G., and M. Findlay (eds.). 1978. *Stochastic Dominance*. Lexington: D.C. Heath.

Zerbe, R., and D. Dively 1994. *Benefit-Cost Analysis in Theory and Practice*. New York: HarperCollins.

APPENDIX TO CHAPTER 14

The Mathematics of Risk and Utility

EXPECTED UTILITY

Expected utility theory begins with several postulates about individual behavior. The first postulate is *completeness of preferences*. For any two bundles of goods, the person either consistently prefers one over the other or is indifferent between them. When asked whether I prefer A or B, I can answer "I don't care" but not "I don't know." The second postulate is that *preferences and choices are transitive*. If I have transitive preferences and I pick A over B and B over C, I will choose A over C.

We can construct a utility function describing someone's preferences unless they violate one of these two postulates. However, there are an infinite number of utility functions that can describe the same preferences. If we take one utility function describing a person's preferences, any monotonically increasing function of that utility function is also a utility function describing those preferences.[1] In practical terms, this means that the only information in such a utility function is the ranking of various bundles of goods. Neither the slope of the utility function nor its curvature nor its value for any particular bundle of goods conveys any information.

When we are dealing with choices involving risk, if these choices satisfy some additional postulates, we can define a utility function in such a way that its curvature does convey information. This information is the person's attitude toward risk. Recall that the first two postulates are completeness and transitivity, which apply to preferences and choices between actions, even when those actions have uncertain outcomes. If these two postulates are satisfied, we can construct a utility function describing a person's preferences between actions.

The remaining postulates can be stated in several ways. All of them relate *preferences* between actions to the *consequences* of those actions and their probabilities. In a situation of risk, the consequences of any action will be determined by which state of the world occurs in the future; different states of the world have definite probabilities, and those probabilities add up to 1. The state of the world does not have to be a complete description of the universe. It merely has to specify which of a set of mutually exclusive events occurs. It may tell whether a coin came up heads or tails, whether the Dallas Cowboys beat the Detroit Lions on Thanksgiving, or whether a particular individual has a genetic predisposition to develop cancer when exposed to benzene.

---

[1] A monotonically increasing function slopes upward to the right. Formally, F is monotonically increasing if $F(x) > F(y)$ for any $x > y$.

The first additional postulate (the third postulate) is what Savage (1954) called the *"sure-thing principle."* This postulate states that for each possible state of the world, if the consequence of action A in that state is preferred to the consequence of action B, then action A is preferred to action B. For example, consider the following two states of the world: (1) I will develop lung cancer if I smoke, and (2) I will not develop lung cancer if I smoke. Suppose that I do not enjoy smoking and do not want to get lung cancer. If the first state of the world comes to pass, I will have both cancer and a habit I do not enjoy if I smoke and will have neither if I do not. If the second state of the world comes to pass, I will only have a habit I do not enjoy if I smoke, and I will not have it if I do not. If I satisfy the sure-thing principle, since I prefer the consequences of not smoking in both possible states of the world, I will prefer not to smoke. In addition to its obvious rationality requirement, this postulate also requires that preferences between actions depend only on the consequences of those actions and their probabilities.

The second additional postulate (fourth postulate) is *continuity of preferences over probabilities.* This postulate states that if consequence X is preferred to consequence Y, which is preferred to consequence Z, there must be some nonzero probability π such that an action that would give Z with probability π and X with probability $1 - \pi$ is preferred to an action producing Y with certainty.[2] Despite its name, this postulate is really a requirement that all consequences be comparable.

For example, let Y be nothing in particular happening, let X be winning $20 million, and let Z be dying a slow and horrible death. This postulate requires that you would be willing to risk some infinitesimal probability of a slow, horrible death in exchange for an almost certain $20 million. Would 1/1,000 be a small enough probability π? Would 10^{-10}? Or $10^{-10,000}$? Confronting the risk of death in such stark mathematical terms may make people uncomfortable, but as we discussed in Chapter 12, many daily activities involve small but positive risks of serious injury or death.

The third additional postulate (fifth postulate) is the *independence of preferences and beliefs.* A person's preferences between consequences must not depend on the states of the world in which those consequences occur, and the probabilities we assign to possible states of the world must not depend on their consequences. This postulate requires two things. It requires psychological objectivity. It rules out wishful thinking and paranoia. Thus it requires dealing with actuarial risks rather than perceived risks. It also requires an ability to define states of the world in a way that does not involve their consequences for the person in question.

If these three additional postulates are satisfied, a somewhat surprising result follows, which is known as the *expected utility theorem:* If a person's preferences and choices satisfy these five postulates:

1. Completeness of preferences
2. Transitivity of preferences

---

[2] This postulate can be stated in a weaker but less intuitive form; see, for example, Arrow (1972).

3. The sure-thing principle
4. Continuity of preferences over probabilities
5. Independence of preferences and belief

it is possible to define a utility function such that the utility of an action is the mathematical expectation of the utilities of its possible consequences.

Such a utility function is not unique, but all of the utility functions we can define to represent the preferences of someone who satisfies these five postulates are *linear transformations* of one another. Any one can be obtained from another by multiplying by a constant and adding a constant. Although this means that we cannot give any meaning to the numerical value of the utility function or its slope, there is information to be gleaned from its *curvature,* as was shown in Figures 14.2 and 14.3.

THE INDIRECT UTILITY FUNCTION AND THE CALCULATION OF OPTION PRICE

The indirect utility function can be derived as follows. Begin with the familiar utility function showing utility as a function of N goods and services consumed:

$$U = U(x_1, \ldots, x_N) \tag{14A.1}$$

An individual's demand curves for these goods and services can be derived from the utility function and will depend on the prices of the N goods and the individual's income level Y:

$$x_i = x_i^* (p_1, \ldots, p_N, Y) \tag{14A.2}$$

where p_i equals the price of good i and Y equals income. Substituting Equation 14A.2 into Equation 14A.1, we have

$$U = (x_1(p_1, \ldots, p_N, Y), \ldots, x_n(p_1, \ldots, p_N, Y), Y) = V(p_1, \ldots, p_N, Y) \tag{14A.3}$$

The utility function that was determined directly by the levels of consumption of the N goods has been rewritten as a function only of prices and income in Equation 14A.3. $V(p_1, \ldots, p_N, Y)$ is called the *indirect utility function.* The indirect utility function is convenient for use in applied work. It also is useful for working directly with the compensating variation (CV) and equivalent variation (EV) measures of welfare change we introduced in Chapter 3.

Recall that the compensating variation is the amount of money that would need to be taken from (or given to) a consumer to make the person indifferent between staying in the initial position and experiencing some change, such as a fall in the price of some good. The indirect utility function gives a convenient way to show this directly. Let CV be the compensating variation for a price change from p_0 to p_1. Then

$$V(p_0, Y) = V(p_1, Y - CV) \tag{14A.4}$$

This will prove useful in investigating the relationship between option price and another measure of WTP that may be easier to measure, expected consumers' surplus.

Let π be the probability that it will be a bright and sunny day tomorrow, and let OP be the option price. Let $V_C(Y)$ be your indirect utility function if it is bright and sunny tomorrow, and let $V_R(Y)$ be your indirect utility function if it is rainy and you visit the museum. (V_C and V_R are functions of prices, but since we are not changing any prices, it is not necessary to show them explicitly.) Let Y^0 be your current wealth. If you do not purchase the advance ticket, you will visit the museum regardless of the weather, and your utility will be $V_R(Y^0)$. If you pay \$T to purchase the advance ticket, you will visit the Grand Canyon if it is clear, and your utility will be $V_C(Y^0 - T)$. If you purchase the ticket and it rains, your utility will be $V_R(Y^0 - T)$. Your *option price* is defined as the price of the advance ticket that would make you indifferent between buying the ticket and not buying it. Thus your option price will be the price that results in identical levels of expected utility, regardless of whether or not you buy the ticket. Mathematically, this can be written as

$$\pi V_C(Y^0 - OP) + (1 - \pi) V_R(Y^0 - OP) = \pi V_R(Y^0) + (1 - \pi) V_R(Y^0) = V_R(Y^0) \tag{14A.5}$$

Look carefully at Equation 14A.5. If you do not buy a ticket, you cannot go to the Grand Canyon regardless of the weather, and you therefore visit the museum. The utility associated with that visit is shown in the right-hand side of the equation. If you buy the ticket for price OP, there is a probability of π that you will see the Grand Canyon and derive utility $V_C(Y^0 - OP)$ and a probability of $(1 - \pi)$ that you will be rained out and will go to the museum instead, deriving utility of $V_R(Y^0 - OP)$.

A numerical example may clarify things. Suppose that the probability that tomorrow will be bright and sunny equals 0.6. Suppose also that your income Y^0 equals \$100, that $V_C = 2Y^{1/2}$, and that $V_R = Y^{1/2}$. Then, using Equation 14A.5, OP will solve the equation:

$$(0.6)V_C(100 - OP) + (0.4)V_R(100 - OP) = V_R(100)$$

or

$$(0.6)(2)(100 - OP)^{1/2} + (0.4)(100 - OP)^{1/2} = (100)^{1/2} = 10 \tag{14A.6}$$

Solving for OP, it is easy to show that it is about \$61. Therefore, you would be willing to pay \$61 for a ticket guaranteeing your right to see the Grand Canyon tomorrow. What would you be willing to pay for a ticket if you knew tomorrow would be sunny? That figure can be found by using Equation 14A.4. Thus we can solve for

CV as follows: $100^{1/2} = 2(100 - CV)^{1/2}$, so $CV = \$75$. Thus if you *knew* that tomorrow would be sunny, you would be willing to pay $75 to see the Grand Canyon. But because you are risk-averse and *don't know* what tomorrow's weather will be, you are willing to purchase the ticket in advance for only $61.

THE ARROW-PRATT MEASURES OF RISK AVERSION

In general, given an expected utility function $U(W)$, where W refers to wealth, if $U''(W) < 0$, there is aversion to risk; if $U''(W) = 0$, there is risk neutrality; and if $U''(W) > 0$, there is risk-loving behavior. There are several useful measures of the degree of risk aversion. These were developed independently by Pratt (1964) and Arrow and are known as the Arrow-Pratt measures of absolute and relative risk aversion.

Because the utility function $U(W)$ is unique only up to a linear transformation, the "risk preference indicator" embodied in $U''(W)$ could be arbitrarily changed. To get around this problem, Arrow and Pratt divided $U''(W)$ by $-U'(W)$, which represents the negative of the slope of the expected utility function. This measure, denoted $R_A(W)$, is known as the *Arrow-Pratt measure of absolute risk aversion.* Thus

$$R_A(W) = \frac{-U''(W)}{U'(W)} \tag{14A.7}$$

$R_A(W)$ has the following properties: if it is positive, zero, or negative, then the individual displays risk-averse, risk-neutral, or risk-loving preferences, respectively; the larger $R_A(W)$ is, the more risk-averse the individual is; and $R_A(W)$ is invariant to a linear transformation.

An alternative measure similar to $R_A(W)$ that it is unaffected by the choice of units of W is called the *Arrow-Pratt measure of relative risk aversion,* $R_R(W)$. $R_R(W) = WR_A(W) = -WU''(W)/U'(W)$.

For example, let $u(W) = a - be^{-Rw}$. It can be easily shown that $R_A(W) = R$, for all $W > 0$. Similarly, if $U(W) = a - bW^{1-R}$, it can be shown that $R_R(W) = R$, for all $W > 0$. As Hey (1979) points out, these forms of the utility function have proved popular because the expected utilities can be easily computed for any given distribution of W. It can be shown that $EU(W) = a - bM_W(R)$, where $M_W(R)$ is the moment-generating function for the probability distribution of W, evaluated at R.

THE PRICE OF RISK, COVARIANCE, AND BETA

The finance literature has developed a useful expression for the price of risk, which is based on the *SRTP,* the interest rate in the "market," and the variability of returns in the market. This derivation is used in much of the financial literature.

Suppose that we denote the variability in the market portfolio, for example, the stock market, as σ_m^2. Specifically, let σ_m^2 equal the variance in the returns to the market portfolio.[3] This is the market risk. Because the stock market goes up and down, investors would face risk even if they purchased every stock listed. So an investor who wished to borrow money would be charged some market rate of interest that reflected the overall risk of all investments. Presumably, this interest rate, R_m, would be higher than the interest rate charged for risk-free investments that had no variability in their returns. If we call the interest rate for risk-free investments R_f, which in an ideal economy would just equal the *SRTP*, we can represent the market price of risk as the interest rate premium $(R_m - R_f)$ per unit of market risk σ_m^2. Thus the market price of risk can be written

$$\frac{R_m - R_f}{\sigma_m^2} = \frac{R_m - SRTP}{\sigma_m^2} \tag{14A.8}$$

Suppose that our investor wishes to purchase shares in a solar energy company. As we argued before, the value of solar energy will be higher when fossil fuel prices are higher. Furthermore, because we would expect that higher energy prices would reduce economic growth and cause the stock market to be lower than with high growth, the investment in the solar energy company will likely have a negative correlation with returns in the stock market as a whole. The correlation of returns between the solar energy company and the stock market as a whole will reflect the amount of risk associated with the project. The more negative this correlation, the more successful the investor will be in diversifying away risk.

Let the covariance of the returns between the solar energy company and the stock market as a whole be denoted as σ_{se}, where s equals returns to the solar energy company and e equals stock market returns. In the case of the solar energy investment, σ_{se} would be negative. The total price of risk for the solar energy company investment would therefore equal the market price per unit of risk times the amount of risk associated with the project. Thus the total price of risk would be $[(R_m - SRTP)/\sigma_m^2]\sigma_{se}$.

In general, the certainty equivalent of a return one year from now (CEQ) will equal the expected return $E(C_1)$ minus the total cost of risk. Thus we have

$$CEQ = E(C_1) - \frac{R_m - R_f}{\sigma_m^2}\, \sigma_{se} \tag{14A.9}$$

By combining Equations 14A.8 and 14A.9, using some algebra and properties of the covariance, we can derive an expression for the risk-adjusted interest rate, R:

$$R = R_f + \frac{R_m - R_f}{\sigma_m^2}\, \sigma_{se} \tag{14A.10}$$

Equation 14A.10 is the basis for the CAPM, which has been studied and used extensively in the financial literature. If the covariance between the market portfolio

---

[3] The variance is a simple measure of the dispersion of a random variable. For further explanation in the context of investment returns, see Copeland and Weston (1989).

and the project is zero, then the second term in Equation 14A.10 is zero, and the risk-adjusted discount rate will just be the risk-free rate, which we argue is just the *SRTP.* If, as in the case of the solar energy project example, the covariance is negative, then the risk-adjusted discount rate will be less than the *SRTP.*

The term σ_m^2/σ_{se} is the *beta* (β) referred to in the finance literature. Beta is the covariance of a project's rate of return as a percentage of the variance of the market. Thus we can rewrite Equation 14A.10 as

$$R = R_f + \beta(R_m - R_f) \tag{14A.11}$$

which provides a risk-adjusted discount rate.

PART IV

SELECTED
POLICY TOPICS

The first three parts of this book were designed to provide you a solid foundation of key concepts and tools with which to understand environmental economics and evaluate cogent policies. In Part IV, we turn our attention to a variety of topics that are at the forefront of many environmental policy issues.

We begin in Chapters 15 and 16 with a discussion of exhaustible and renewable resources. These two chapters are designed to provide a solid footing in the principles of natural resource use while addressing some of the key policies that have grown up around the management (and mismanagement) of such resources, including the world's fisheries and forests. These chapters contain some of the standard mathematics of natural resource economics, but readers unfamiliar with the math used will still be able to understand the underlying concepts and policy implications.

Chapter 17 focuses on water resources, primarily issues of how water is allocated and used. Water can be both a renewable resource and a depletable one, but that classification can sometimes be influenced by how it is allocated. So first we provide an overview of water allocation in the United States, which has been dominated by federal policies. Next we turn to policy instruments that can allocate water efficiently and equitably. We conclude the chapter with a discussion of measuring the "value" of water, which can be a driver in determining the efficient level of water quality.

Chapter 18 examines energy resources. Energy production and use are the most significant sources of pollution and environmental degradation in the world. We focus on two areas: energy used in transportation, and its effects on the environment; and the electric utility industry, which converts various forms of energy to electricity. We look at alternative policies that have been used to reduce transportation-related pollution and alternatives used to combat stationary source pollution. We also address equity and rights issues, which for stationary sources such as electricity-generating facilities, have become increasingly important.

Chapter 19 tackles the interrelated issues of economic development, environmental quality, and the increasing interest in developing policies that promote a "sustainable" future. We first consider the relationship between population growth and environmental quality. This is an important issue because meeting the economic needs of increasing numbers of people will require more efficient use of our resources. And, as we will discuss, not meeting the needs of people is often one of the primary drivers of environmental degradation. The chapter then turns to sustainability, which remains a poorly defined concept. We present some of the most common, but still competing, definitions. Last, because policies that promote or promise sustainability ultimately will need to be verified, we discuss the empirical techniques that have been proposed to do just that.

Chapters 20 and 21 explore international environmental issues. Chapter 20 examines international environmental problems that are localized: they cross individual borders but are generally confined to specific areas. We begin by presenting some of the basic theory associated with transboundary impacts and the effects of cooperative and noncooperative solutions. Then we turn to a discussion of acid deposition, commonly (and somewhat mistakenly) called "acid rain," and finally to selected issues concerning transboundary water use, allocation, and pollution.

Chapter 21 moves on to global environmental issues. We begin with chlorofluorocarbons (CFCs), which have been implicated in the depletion of atmospheric ozone. Though a serious problem, CFCs represent an environmental policy "success story." Their use is now declining, and although there remain some difficult issues to be dealt with, such as illicit trading in CFCs, their use should continue to decline. We devote the majority of the chapter to the environmental policy issue we began the book with: global climate change. We provide a summary of what it is, why it may be a problem, and what its physical and economic impacts may be. Then we discuss the policy issues associated with global climate change, which encompass all of the key concepts—efficiency, equity, human rights, and rights of nature—that we have addressed throughout this book.

Chapter 22 provides some concluding thoughts. We summarize the challenges that face environmental policymakers, the problem of managing competing and sometimes conflicting environmental goals, and the challenge of measuring impacts and progress toward chosen environmental goals.

CHAPTER 15

EXHAUSTIBLE RESOURCES

Are We Running Out of Oil?

In the 1970s, there was a widespread perception that we had an energy crisis. The Organization of Petroleum Exporting Countries (OPEC) appeared able to increase oil prices at will, the United States government placed restrictions on the use of natural gas to conserve apparently meager and fast-dwindling reserves, and electricity rates skyrocketed as utilities passed on the costs of new power plants that were being built to meet growing demand. We seemed to be entering an era when energy was becoming scarce and more expensive.

    The "energy crisis" era was ushered in by Middle Eastern oil producers' 1973 embargo of the United States and other Western countries. There were numerous policy responses to this embargo, few of which were based on coherent economic analysis. The first was the Emergency Petroleum Allocation Act of 1973, which extended price controls on oil and thus exacerbated shortages. In 1974, Project Independence was launched, with the objective of making the United States independent of any foreign energy supplies, especially crude oil, by 1980. Other legislation followed. In 1977, the U.S. Department of Energy was created. In 1978, the Power Plant and Industrial Fuel Use Act, which restricted the use of natural gas (whose price was still controlled) at industrial facilities, was passed. Also in 1978, Congress enacted the Public Utilities Regulatory Policy Act (PURPA), which was designed to encourage independent development of nontraditional and renewable energy source power generating facilities, including wind, hydro, solar, and biomass.[1] Congress even created industries, such as U.S. Synfuels, which was to develop synthetic petroleum from the vast oil shale deposits in the western United States and Canada. The nation also began the Strategic Petroleum Reserve, which was designed to meet domestic demand for several months in the event of another

---

[1]Energy issues are discussed in more detail in Chapter 18. As this is being written in 1996, Congress is considering repeal of PURPA because of structural changes in the electric industry.

439

embargo. And in 1978, the government began imposing "corporate average fuel efficiency" (CAFE) standards for new cars and light trucks. As a result, by 1993, the efficiency of a new domestic car was 50 percent greater than in 1978.

In the 1990s, the energy crisis seems like a vaguely remembered bad dream. After adjusting for inflation, gasoline is as cheap as it has ever been, natural gas consumption is increasing and prices are falling every year, and the biggest worry facing electric utilities is deregulation and competition, along with getting someone to pay for power plants built in the 1970s that cannot compete in today's market. Why has there been such a dramatic turnaround? Were we wrong to think we were running out of oil, or have we just postponed the day of reckoning?

We were wrong to think we were running out of oil in the 1970s. Most of the events that people interpreted as an energy crisis had other causes. The oil crises of 1974 and 1979 were politically motivated embargoes. Oil producers cut off supplies to the United States and other countries in 1973 in retaliation for American and European support for Israel during the 1973 Arab-Israeli war and in 1979 in response to support for the Shah of Iran. Neither of these events had anything to do with actual scarcity of crude oil, but both were made possible by the fact that a few countries had a large share of international trade in oil. These embargoes showed OPEC the market power it had, and the OPEC members decided to exploit the situation and raise prices. A number of prominent economists publicly predicted that OPEC would collapse because of the incentives for cartel members to cheat on each other and exceed their production quotas. These predictions were right, but for the wrong reasons. OPEC's market power collapsed primarily because it could not prevent entry into the world oil market, not because it could not control its own production. With higher oil prices, oil companies were willing to take the risk of exploring for oil in new territories, and they found it. England, Norway, Mexico, and Venezuela all became significant oil producers.

The apparent shortage of natural gas in the United States was the result of ill-conceived regulation. Interstate sales of natural gas were subject to federal price controls, while intrastate sales were unregulated or subject to state regulation. When OPEC drove up oil prices, the prices of substitutes, including natural gas, rose as well. When the market prices for intrastate gas sales rose above the federally regulated prices for interstate sales, gas producers naturally sold as much as they could inside producing states and as little as they could in other states. The resulting shortages disappeared when federal regulation of natural gas prices was phased out beginning in 1978.

Similarly, increases in electric rates were more the result of regulatory quirks than of increasing scarcity. Until the recent impetus to deregulate the electric utility industry, American electric utility regulation was based primarily on the premise that a regulated monopoly should be allowed to earn a "just" rate of return on its investments but no more. In practice, this came to mean that each year, a utility's rates were set to cover that year's accounting depreciation and the allowed rate of return on the remaining undepreciated value of the utility's assets. The result was utility rates that overstated economic costs when a utility's assets were mostly new and greatly understated economic costs when a utility's assets were mostly old. In the 1970s, many American utilities had aging plants and faced rapidly rising demand due, in part, to rates that understated costs. As they built new plants to replace old ones and meet growing demand, their rates rose.

Even though the energy crisis of the 1970s was not the result of the world's hitting either physical or economic limits on energy production, the earth does have finite stocks of oil, natural gas, and many other materials. Do we face real oil, or aluminum, or even gravel crises in the future as we use up these finite stocks?

INTRODUCTION

In earlier chapters, we have looked at issues relating to environmental quality. We have viewed the environment as a place to live. The environment plays an equally important role as the source of raw materials that make our lives possible. Our food ultimately comes from sunlight and soil. Our clothes, shelter, automobiles, and video games ultimately come from the same sources or from holes in the ground—mines and wells. The next two chapters introduce the economics of nature as a source of raw materials and some of the environmental implications.

This chapter is an introduction to the economics of exhaustible resources or stock resources. These are resources, such as minerals, the use of which consumes part of the resource stock—the same resource cannot be used now and in the future. The next chapter will introduce the economics of renewable resources or flow resources. Those are resources, such as wind or sunlight, that occur as a naturally recurring flow, and use today does not necessarily preclude use of the same resource tomorrow.

Natural resource economics is a considerable field in its own right, and we cannot do more than scratch its surface in two chapters. Therefore, in these two chapters, we will concentrate on how the work of resource economists over the years sheds light on the current debates over the concept of *sustainability*. Although we discuss its specifics in Chapter 19, many advocates of sustainability urge us to limit our use of exhaustible resources and to rely on renewable resources to the greatest extent possible. There are several arguments for this position. One is that we will force our descendants back into another dark age by using up resources that are essential for the maintenance of civilization. Another is that free markets consistently undervalue exhaustible resources and therefore encourage inefficient overuse. A third is that we do not know what the future will be like and therefore do not know what will be valuable in the future. Thus we should not squander limited natural resources on low-value uses today when they may be needed for more valuable but unforeseen uses in the future. A knowledge of natural resource economics will help us evaluate these and other arguments about sustainability.

We begin by looking at the decisions facing a mining or petroleum firm, and how these decisions determine prices and production rates. We will start by determining the conditions to maximize the value of production from a single mine or well. Then we will look at an ongoing firm that in addition to extracting minerals is exploring for new reserves as its old reserves are exhausted. Last, we will look at an industry composed of many such firms. This development follows the traditional textbook exposition of the competitive market, rather than the traditional expositions of the economics of exhaustible resources. For example, one traditional exposition begins, "Suppose that you are stranded on a desert island and all you have is a cake of given finite size. Every day, you can eat any amount of cake you want, but when the cake is gone, you will die. What is the optimal way to allocate your cake over time?"

There are at least three reasons why we do not take this traditional approach. One is that the "cake-eating" model is a special case of a more general theory. The model omits several important features of the real world. As a result, it produces several very striking predictions that are special cases of more general results produced by more general models. Unfortunately, the most striking results of the "cake-eating" model are due to its most unrealistic features, and the model predicts behavior that is not observed in any real-world mineral industries. We present the "cake-eating" model as a special case of the more general model presented in this chapter.

The second reason for taking our approach is that the "cake-eating" model is a model of optimal use of a limited resource. However, our primary concern is with the market *allocation* of exhaustible resources. Once we have seen how resources are allocated, we will ask whether that allocation is efficient. But we prefer to start with market allocation rather than start with efficient allocation, and argue that markets can and will achieve it.

A third reason for taking our approach is that the real world is both more complicated and more interesting than can be presented in the simpler "cake-eating" model. All of the issues we will raise in this chapter have been incorporated into the theory, but the mathematics involved (stochastic optimal control theory) is far beyond what we expect students to be comfortable with. In fact, there are sections of this chapter that we expect to be mathematically challenging for most students. Those sections have been highlighted with a dagger and can be omitted without missing any of the main points of this chapter. However, students who do work through them will be rewarded with a deeper understanding of those points.

A SINGLE MINE OR WELL

Imagine that there is a single, price-taking firm, Antoinette & Robespierre, Inc. (ARI), created solely to exploit a single mineral deposit. The firm will be liquidated when the deposit is exhausted. This allows us to start by making only a few modifications to the familiar model of the competitive firm. It is also not an unusual situation in the real world. Firms are often organized for the purpose of exploiting a single mineral deposit or oil field. Sometimes these firms are independent companies. Often they are joint ventures with several parent companies. Such joint ventures are very common in oil and gas production, where the initial investment required to develop a field is larger than any one firm wants to make. Joint ventures are frequently formed to spread the risks of exploration and are then continued through production when an exploration program has been successful.

The owners of ARI must make investments to buy the mineral deposit and buy and set up the plant and equipment needed to extract, and possibly process, the mineral. The owners plan to recoup their investment while earning a competitive return in every time period on ARI's remaining stock of assets. When the deposit is exhausted, they expect to sell off any remaining assets. This arrangement gives us a convenient unit for analysis. It gives us a process with a definite termination, and it allows us temporarily to put off the market determination of mineral prices by assuming that ARI is a price taker.

The Simplest Case: Constant Price, Fixed Initial Resource of Uniform Grade, Costs Proportional to Depth

Let us begin with a stylized mining operation of the important mineral "sheetcake." Sheetcake is found in a rectangular deposit, with no variations in mineral quality, extending a great distance into the earth. ARI's cost of production in each period depends on the rate of production and the depth that the deposit has already been mined. At any time, the sheetcake mine has conventional U-shaped cost curves for production in the current period: average extraction cost (AEC) is at a minimum at some positive level of production, marginal extraction cost (MEC) equals average extraction cost at the production level that minimizes average extraction cost, marginal extraction cost is less than average extraction cost at lower levels of production, and marginal extraction cost exceeds average extraction costs at higher production levels. As the deposit is worked, mining is carried on at greater depths, and the cost to bring the mineral to the surface increases. This causes the mine's cost curves to shift upward over time. For now, we will assume that this shift is proportional to depth. This is shown in Figure 15.1.

Suppose that for the foreseeable future, the price of sheetcake is known to be P. It is easy to confirm that ARI will eventually close the mine. When mining has

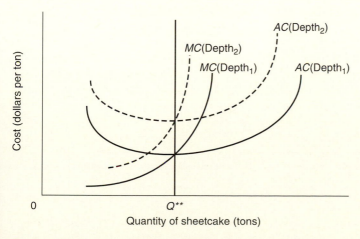

Figure 15.1   Cost of Mining Sheetcake over Time

reached the depth where the minimum average extraction cost equals P, the mine will just break even if the mineral is extracted at the rate that minimizes average extraction cost, Q^{**}. Continuing to operate the mine at greater depths would continue to shift the mine's cost curves upward. Average extraction cost would be greater than price at all positive production levels, and the mine would make a loss in every period. Therefore, ARI's owners will close the mine at this point, regardless of whether there is any mineral remaining.

This demonstrates an important point: *resource exhaustion is an economic concept.* A mineral deposit is economically exhausted when the minimum average cost of production from that deposit exceeds the value of the mineral.

Before the point of economic exhaustion is reached, the value of the firm (the present value of present and future net revenues) is maximized by producing at the point where marginal cost equals price. In this, a mining firm is no different from a manufacturing or service firm. However, except at the point of economic exhaustion, a mining firm's marginal cost includes more than its current marginal extraction cost. Marginal extraction cost includes the costs of all inputs purchased and used up in the current period, the costs of inputs previously purchased and used in this period, and the costs of marginal depreciation on plant and equipment. It leaves out one important economic cost. Every ton of sheetcake ore produced this year raises the costs of producing in future years because future mining will be carried out at slightly deeper levels than if the marginal ton had not been extracted this year. This component of the mine's marginal cost is called *user cost.*[2] User cost is *the present value of all increases in future costs because of an additional increment of output today.*

ARI's value is maximized by producing at the point where the firm's marginal cost, which is the sum of marginal extraction cost and user cost, equals the price at each instant during the life of the mine. This is shown in Figure 15.2.

What is the value of user cost? At exhaustion, user cost is zero. When the deposit is economically exhausted and the mine is closed, there are no future costs that can be affected by current production. Thus at the time of exhaustion, marginal cost equals marginal extraction cost. When the mine has one year of operation left, user cost is the present value of the increase in costs next year that will be caused by marginal production this year. For the stylized mine we are considering here, the extraction cost is the sum of two components: the cost of mining the mineral and the cost of transporting it to the surface. Call these components of extraction cost C_m and C_t. Let us assume that C_m depends only on the rate of production. This is consistent with our assumption of uniform grade. Let us also assume that the cost of transporting the mineral to the surface is proportional to depth. Thus $C_t = ALQ_t$ where L is depth, Q_t is the rate of production in tons, and A is a constant. If there are α tons of ore per foot of depth in the deposit, the increase in C_t because

---

[2]The idea of user cost was first developed in 1936 by John Maynard Keynes in *The General Theory of Employment, Interest, and Money.* Keynes considered user cost a vital part of his theory, though the point has been forgotten by succeeding generations of macroeconomists.

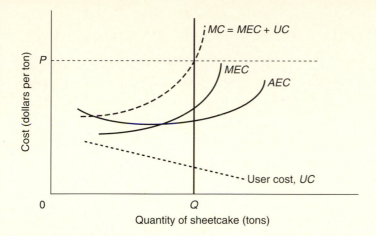

Figure 15.2 Maximizing the Value of the Mining Firm

of a marginal increase in Q_{t-1} is just $dC_t/dQ_{t-1} = AQ_t/\alpha$.[3] Thus at one year before exhaustion (time $T - 1$), user cost, UC_{T-1}, will be calculated as follows:

$$UC_{T-1} = \frac{AQ_T}{\alpha(1 + r)} \tag{15.1}$$

where r is the discount rate. Two years before exhaustion, user cost equals the present value of increases in costs in year $T - 1$ and year T from a marginal increase in production in year $T - 2$. Thus

$$UC_{T-2} = \frac{AQ_{T-1}}{\alpha(1 + r)} + \frac{AQ_T}{\alpha(1 + r)^2} \tag{15.2}$$

Following this same logic, user cost at any time τ years before exhaustion will be calculated as follows:

$$UC_{T-\tau} = \sum_{\tau=t+1}^{T} \frac{AQ_\tau}{\alpha(1 + r)^{T-\tau}} \tag{15.3}$$

With more complex cost functions, the formula for user cost is more complex, but user cost is always *the present value of future cost increases because of an increment in current output*. In general, where $\partial C_t/\partial Q_t$ equals marginal extraction cost at time t,

---

[3] To see this, note that at any time t, $L_t = L_{t-1} + Q_{t-1}/\alpha$. Thus a change in Q_{t-1} results in a change in depth L_t, ΔL, of $\Delta Q_{t-1}/\alpha$. The change in extraction cost will reflect the change in depth. Thus $\Delta C_t = A(\Delta L)Q_t$. But since $\Delta L = \Delta Q_{t-1}/\alpha$, $\Delta C_t = A(\Delta Q_{t-1}/\alpha)Q_t$. So the change in extraction cost because of a marginal change in Q_{t-1} will just equal $\Delta C_t/\Delta Q_{t-1} = AQ_t/\alpha$. As the change in Q_{t-1} goes to zero in the limit, we have the derivative of C_t with respect to Q_{t-1}. Thus we have $dC_t/dQ_{t-1} = AQ_t/\alpha$.

$$UC_t = \sum_{\tau=t+1}^{T} \frac{\partial C_\tau / \partial Q_t}{(1+r)^{T-\tau}} \qquad (15.4)$$

User cost is not constant over the life of a mine. Two opposing factors tend to change it. First, because each year there is one less year in the remaining life of the mine, each year there is one less term in the sum defining user cost. This tends to make user cost decline over time. Conversely, each of the remaining terms is discounted one year less. This tends to increase user cost. Near the end of the life of a mine, the first effect is stronger. It eventually dominates and drives user cost to zero at the time of exhaustion. Earlier in the life of the mine, user cost may either increase or decrease from year to year, depending on the relative impact of production today on extraction costs in different years in the future.

Figure 15.3 shows extraction costs and user costs, and therefore production rates, at three different points during the life of a mine. MEC_t, AEC_t, and MC_t are marginal extraction cost, average extraction cost, and marginal cost, which equals marginal extraction cost plus user cost, at time t. At time T, current profits and the present value of net revenues over the remaining life of the mine are the same. Profit is maximized at the production rate Q_T. At time t', setting marginal cost equal to price gives the production rate $Q_{t'}$. This rate of production at t' maximizes the present value of net revenues over the life of the mine, assuming that the value-maximizing rule will be followed for the rest of the mine's life. The same holds true at time t, where setting marginal cost equal to price gives the production rate Q_t.

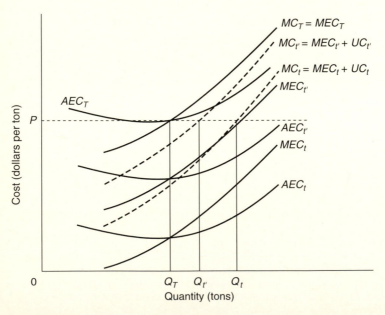

Figure 15.3   User Cost, Production Cost, and Extraction Cost

An Example†   Let's look at a numerical example based on ARI's simple sheet-cake mine.[4] This is a case where total extraction cost is a linear function of depth and a quadratic function of the rate of output:

$$TEC_t = C_0 + AL_tQ_t + \frac{BQ_t^2}{2} \tag{15.5}$$

Differentiating Equation 15.5 with respect to output gives marginal extraction cost; dividing Equation 15.5 by Q_t yields average extraction cost. Thus we have

$$MEC_t = AL_t + BQ_t \tag{15.6}$$

and

$$AEC_t = \frac{C_0}{Q_t} + AL_t + \frac{BQ_t}{2} \tag{15.7}$$

where MEC_t equals marginal extraction cost and AEC_t equals average extraction cost. We know that in the last period of the mine's operation, it will produce the level of output with the minimum average cost (minac). This is where the derivative of AEC_t with respect to Q is zero:

$$\frac{\partial AEC}{\partial Q} = -\frac{C_0}{Q^2} + \frac{B}{2} = 0 \tag{15.8}$$

Solving Equation 15.8 for Q yields the solution:

$$Q_T = Q_{\text{minac}} = \sqrt{\frac{2C_0}{B}} \tag{15.9}$$

We also know that in the last period of operation, T, user cost is zero. This means that price is equal to marginal extraction cost. Thus from Equation 15.6,

$$P_T = AL_T + BQ_{\text{minac}}$$

This can be solved for the final depth:

$$L_T = \frac{P - BQ_{\text{minac}}}{A} \tag{15.10}$$

Now let's put some numbers into these equations. Let $A = 0.01$, $B = 0.01$, and $C_0 = 1,000$. From Equation 15.9, we have $Q_{\text{minac}} = 447.2$. If $P_T = 10$, then from Equation 15.10, we have $L_T = 552.8$.

---

[4]A second, more complex example is contained in the appendix to this chapter.

Recall that user cost in the last period is zero. From Equation 15.1, user cost in the next-to-last period is $UC_{T-1} = AQ_T/\alpha(1 + r)$. Let $r = 0.08$ and $\alpha = 50$. Then $UC_{T-1} = 0.083$. Output in period $T - 1$ should be chosen to equate marginal cost and price. Thus

$$P_{T-1} = AL_{T-1} + BQ_{T-1} + UC_{T-1} \tag{15.11}$$

Depth in period $T - 1$ will just equal the final depth D_T less the extraction that took place in period T. Thus, $L_{T-1} = L_T - Q_T/\alpha$, or $L_T = 552.8 - (447.2/50) = 543.8$ feet. If we repeat this procedure at time $T - 1$, we set marginal cost to price, remembering to include the now nonzero user cost UC_{T-1}. Thus from Equations 15.1 and 15.11, $Q_{T-1} = 447.9$.

We can continue this procedure, moving backward from the last period of operation using an interesting and important property of the formula for user cost. As long as extraction at one date influences extraction cost at later dates *only* through its effect on the remaining mineral stock, then

$$UC_t = \frac{UC_{t+1}}{1 + r} + \frac{\partial C_{t+1}}{\partial Q_t} \tag{15.12}$$

or

$$UC_t = \frac{UC_{t+1} + AQ_{t+1}/\alpha}{1 + r} \tag{15.13}$$

Equation 15.13 can be used to solve for user cost, and therefore sheetcake production, at every date before the last. The actual date of the last period is determined by the number of periods we have to work backward to reach a depth of zero. Figure 15.4 shows the time path of output for the simplest mine, and Figure 15.5 shows the time path of user cost.

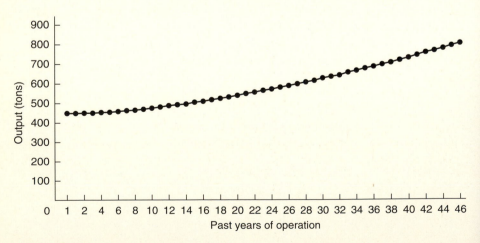

Figure 15.4 Production Rate in Simplest Mine Example

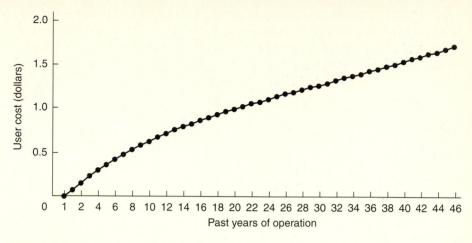

Figure 15.5   User Cost for Simplest Mine Example

The Value of Mineral in the Ground

A mineral deposit is an asset, the same as a piece of machinery. It is valuable to the mine's owners because it contributes to their future net revenues. In fact, the value of a mineral deposit is the contribution of the deposit to the present value of the firm's net revenues. If the present value of the costs of all inputs over the life of a mine, including capital, labor, and management, is subtracted from the present value of the revenue stream the mine will earn, the remainder is the value of the mineral in the ground, V. Thus

$$V = \sum_t \frac{P_t Q_t - C_t}{(1 + r)^t} \qquad (15.14)$$

Any asset should be used up to the point where the return from the last increment of use equals the cost of that last increment of use. A mining firm that produced at the point where *MEC* equals price would be ignoring the cost of using up its stock of ore. It would be ignoring the value of the mineral deposit it was mining. This would be like a manufacturing firm ignoring the depreciation of its plant and equipment.

Manufacturing equipment (or mining equipment, for that matter) wears out over time. The economic aspect of this wearing out is called *depreciation*—the decline in the value of an asset over time. Depreciation as calculated by accountants is an approximation of economic depreciation. Accountants calculate the decrease in the book value of an asset; economic depreciation is the decline in the economic value of the asset. Depreciation of equipment occurs partly because of the passage of time (e.g., rust, technological obsolescence) and partly because of use (e.g., operating costs, wear and tear). Using a machine a little harder—running it faster or using it more hours per day—increases the wear and tear on the machine. This has costs for the firm. In the future, it will have to spend more on maintenance, replace the machine sooner, or settle for reduced productivity. The present value of these future costs is marginal economic depreciation or user cost. The manufacturing firm faces a trade-off over time. Increasing production now has costs in the future, as well as in the present. A value-maximizing firm will operate its machinery at an intensity where the value of marginal product of the increased machine intensity (holding all other inputs fixed) is equal to marginal economic depreciation or user cost.

A mining firm faces the same kind of trade-off. Ore produced today will not be available in the future. Because a mining firm that maximizes its value will produce the cheapest ore first, extracting more ore today increases future extraction costs.[5] A mine should take the same action in the face of this trade-off over time involving its stock of ore as a manufacturing firm makes regarding its machinery (or as the mine makes regarding its machinery). It should set the intensity of use of its stock of ore (the extraction rate) where the current marginal contribution to net revenues, $P - MEC$, equals the present value of the resulting incremental future costs, user cost.

Recall that we defined user cost as the change in the value of a mineral deposit because of an increment of current production. Therefore, user cost is the marginal value of the mineral in the ground. However, the current user cost is the marginal value only of minerals that will be extracted in the current period. Minerals that will be extracted in future periods must be valued using the user costs for those future periods. Their values must also be discounted because they will be realized in the future. The marginal value today of minerals extracted in period t is the present value of user cost in period t. This gives another way to measure the value of a mineral deposit. It is the present value of future production valued at future user costs:

$$V = \Sigma_t \frac{UC_t Q_t}{(1 + r)^t} \tag{15.15}$$

These two measures of value will be equal for a mine that is being operated to maximize the present value of net revenue.

Prices Changing over Time

We defined economic exhaustion of a mine as the point when minimum average extraction cost has risen to the level of the market price. A higher price means that this will occur when cumulative production from the mine is greater. If the price rises over time, exhaustion will occur later and with higher cumulative production than if price were constant. This is shown in Figure 15.6. Conversely, a falling price will lead to earlier economic exhaustion and lower cumulative extraction. It is important to note that we are talking about economic exhaustion, not physical

---

[5]In our example, the mine has to extract the cheapest ore first, but even if it is not a physical necessity, it is economically rational. If $C_2 > C_1$, $[P_1 - C_1 + (P_2 - C_2)/(1 + r)] - [P_1 - C_2 + (P_2 - C_1)/(1 + r)] = C_2 - C_1 + (C_1 - C_2)/(1 + r) > 0$ for all P_1 and P_2, and all $r > 0$.

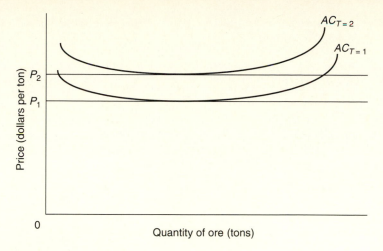

Figure 15.6   Price and Economic Exhaustion

exhaustion of the deposit. Higher future prices will lead to later economic exhaustion, but a smaller stock of ore left in the ground as uneconomic. Lower future prices will lead to earlier economic exhaustion, but more ore left in the ground as uneconomic.

The rule that the value of a mine is maximized by setting the rate of production so that price equals the sum of marginal extraction cost and user cost holds regardless of the price at any date before exhaustion and regardless of the time path of prices. However, in comparing the effect of prices on production at any date, we need to look at prices over the life of the mine because user cost also depends on expected future prices.

To see this, let's consider ARI's sheetcake mine again, where total extraction costs are a linear function of depth. The total cost of mining sheetcake equals the extraction cost plus the cost of transporting sheetcake to the surface. Thus

$$TEC_T(Q_T) = C_1(Q_T) + AD_TQ_T \qquad (15.16)$$

where $C_1(Q)$ equals extraction cost and AD_TQ_T equals transport cost. If economic exhaustion occurs at the end of period T, then setting price equal to marginal cost and remembering that user cost is zero in the last period, we have

$$MEC_T = MC_1(Q_T) + AD_T = P_T \qquad (15.17)$$

One period before exhaustion, present value is maximized by setting

$$MC_1(Q_{T-1}) + AD_{T-1} + \frac{AQ_T}{\alpha(1 + r)} = P_{T-1} \qquad (15.18)$$

where now $UC_{T-1} = AQ_T/\alpha(1 + r)$.[6] Similarly, two periods before exhaustion, present value is maximized by setting

$$MC_1(Q_{T-2}) + AD_{T-2} + \frac{AQ_{T-1}}{\alpha(1 + r)} + \frac{AQ_T}{\alpha(1 + r)^2} = P_{T-2} \qquad (15.19)$$

and so on for earlier periods. The extraction rate at each date depends on the price at that date and user cost at that date. However, in each period except the last, user cost depends on the rate of extraction in following periods. But extraction in future periods depends on the prices in those periods. This leads to a general principle: *user cost depends on expected future prices.* The exact dependence depends on the structure of the extraction cost, but in general, higher expected future prices translate into higher user cost, and lower expected future prices translate into lower user cost. A consequence of this addresses one concern of those advocating sustainability: as the price of a depletable resource increases, the incentive for additional exploration, technological innovation, and recycling all increase as well. For example, that's why predictions in the 1970s that we would run out of natural gas within ten years proved to be wrong. Higher natural gas prices created huge incentives to explore and, in fact, massive reserves have been discovered and developed.

Technological Change in Extraction

Improvements in technology will lower the cost of extracting minerals. This will affect the behavior of the extractive firm in four ways. First, it may affect the current price and expected future prices. We will leave this for a later section and assume that the technological change affects only one firm, whose behavior does not affect the market price. With no change in price, the second effect of improving technology will be an increase in the ultimate cumulative production from the deposit. This will make economic exhaustion occur at a later date. Third, technological change will affect current production by decreasing marginal extraction cost at each level of output. With no change in price, this would result in faster extraction if user cost were fixed. However, the fourth way that technological change affects the mine is by changing user cost.

The change in user cost caused by an improvement in technology can be separated into two parts, as shown in Figure 15.7. The cost curves labeled AEC_1 and MEC_1 are the current extraction cost curves before the change in technology. If the technological improvement produces a parallel downward shift of the cost curves, the new extraction cost curves will look like AEC_2 and MEC_2. With our simplest cost function, with cost depending linearly on depth, the extraction cost curves will rise over time as mining goes deeper until they have returned to AEC_1 and MEC_1. Call the time this occurs time S. At time S, as far as current and future costs are concerned, the situation is exactly the same as it was immediately before the technological change. From S forward, the extraction cost curves and user cost

---

[6]We derived the expression for user cost using the example in the text.

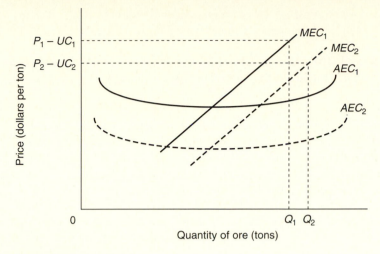

Figure 15.7   User Cost and Technological Change

will follow the same paths they would have initially followed if there had been no technological change. Thus user cost at time S equals user cost immediately before the technological change: $UC_S = UC_0$. We saw that user cost consists of a sum of terms, each of which is the impact of marginal current production on future costs. User cost immediately after the technological change includes all the terms that are in user cost immediately before the change, but these terms are now discounted by S periods. However, it includes the sum of S new terms, showing the impact of marginal current production on extraction cost in the next S periods. Therefore, user cost immediately after the technological change is $U_0' = A + U_0/(1 + r)^S$. Usually, but not always, A will be greater than $U_0' - U_0/(1 + r)^S$, and user cost will increase.

Immediately before the technological change, the value-maximizing production rate, Q_1, equates price P with marginal cost $MEC_1 + UC_1$ or, alternatively, MEC_1 with $P - UC_1$. Immediately after the technological change, the value-maximizing production rate, Q_2, equates MEC_2 with $P - UC_2$. Because the MEC_2 curve is below the MEC_1 curve, Q_2 is greater than Q_1. However, Q_2 is generally less than Q', the output that would result from ignoring the change in user cost.

In mineral industries, as in most sectors of the economy, technological change is an ongoing process. Though any particular change may catch firms in the industry by surprise, they should expect ongoing change and incorporate that change into their price expectations. We will return to this point when we move from the individual firm to the mining industry.

Special Cases

Until now, we have considered extractive firms in general and used a specific, but not very typical, firm as an example. We now consider three important real-world examples: the case of multiple grades of ore, a mine with a processing plant located at the mine to reduce shipping costs, and a typical oil or natural gas well.

Multiple Grades of Ore Minerals differ in their quality between deposits and even within a deposit. This means that the same effort expended on extraction will produce different results.

Imagine our stylized mine laid on its side. However, instead of having cost increase with depth, let the grade of ore decrease uniformly along the length of the deposit. With our vertical mine, we were obliged to begin mining at the surface because we could not reach the deeper ore without first removing the ore above it. In this case, however, we can start anywhere on the deposit. Should our mining firm begin mining with the richest ore? To maximize the value of the mine, it should. The present value of net revenues is maximized by making those expenditures with the greatest return first. To see why, suppose that extracting any given ton of ore costs C and that the richest ton of ore will sell for R_1 and the next richest will sell for R_2, where $R_1 > R_2$. If we extract the richest ton in period 1 and the next richest in period 2, the present value of net revenue will be as follows:

$$PV_1 = (R_1 - C) + \frac{R_2 - C}{1 + r} \tag{15.20}$$

Conversely, if we extract the second-richest ton first in period 1 and the richest ton in period 2, the present value of net revenue will be as follows:

$$PV_2 = (R_2 - C) + \frac{R_1 - C}{1 + r} \tag{15.21}$$

Subtracting Equation 15.21 from Equation 15.20, we have:

$$PV_1 - PV_2 = R_1 + \frac{R_2}{1 + r} - R_2 - \frac{R_1}{1 + r} = (R_1 - R_2)\frac{r}{1 + r} > 0 \tag{15.22}$$

Therefore, the net return per ton of ore extracted will be highest with the richest ore. To maximize the present value of net returns, the highest return should be taken first. The richest ore having the highest return is the same as the cost per ton of concentrated mineral extracted being the lowest for the richest ore. Thus if we view output as concentrated mineral, our simple model can be used for a mine with increasing cost per ton of ore, with decreasing grades of ore, or both.

A Mine with a Fixed Processing Plant Most minerals undergo some processing at the mine. The ore is crushed, cleaned of some impurities, and concentrated. In some cases, it is subjected to chemical reactions. Our stylized mine had an extraction cost function with two terms. The first depended on the rate of extraction, and the second depended on the depth of the mine. Processing adds a third term to the cost function for concentrated ore: $C_1(Q) + C_2(L) + C_3(Q)$, where C_3 is processing cost.

The processing plant is likely to have a U-shaped long-run average cost curve. It will have an optimal size, and this optimal size may not match the optimal extraction rate in any year when only extraction costs are considered. In addition, the plant may be inflexible. Once it is built, it may be too expensive to change its size during the life of the mine. Therefore, once the size of the processing plant has been chosen, the corresponding short-run cost curves will apply for the life of the mine.

As Figure 15.8 shows, the effect is that the sum of marginal cost curves is much steeper than the marginal extraction cost curve. The impact of this is to restrict optimal extraction rates to a narrower range.

Our simplest mine model predicted that output would decline over the life of the mine. Most real mining operations have relatively stable levels of output. This is sometimes taken by "practical" people associated with mineral industries as evidence that the economic theory is wrong or inapplicable. We have just seen, however, that when the relevant features are incorporated into the theory, it does predict the kind of behavior seen in actual mines.

An Oil or Natural Gas Well†   An oil or gas well presents one of the simplest cases of resource extraction. Once the well is drilled and developed and the pumps

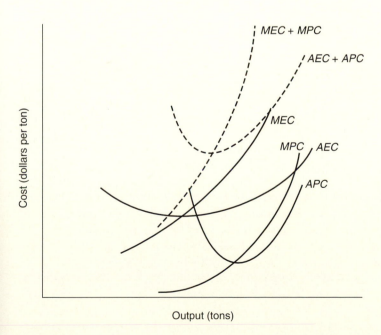

Figure 15.8   Cost Curves for a Mine with Fixed Processing Plant

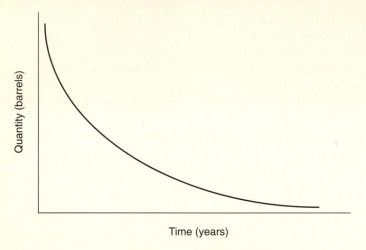

Figure 15.9 Oil Well Production Decline Curve

are installed, the operating cost per unit of time is roughly constant.[7] The suction of the pump creates a pressure differential in the porous rocks of the oil or gas reservoir, and the oil or gas flows through the rock to the well casing and then up the well. At first, the well is drawing oil or gas from the immediate vicinity. Over time, the oil or gas that is produced has to travel farther through the rock to get to the well, and the rate of production slows down. (That's one reason why ownership and extraction rates in oil and gas fields can be complex: one firm's extraction rate will affect others', much as any common-property resource like those we discussed first in Chapter 6.)

Petroleum engineers collectively have experience with hundreds of thousands of wells and are able to predict future production rates for a well from the production early in its life. A graph of production over time, such as Figure 15.9, is called a *decline curve*. The height of the curve at any date is the rate of production expected at that date, and the area under the curve up to that date is the cumulative production up to that date. This gives a particularly simple cost function. The marginal extraction cost function is vertical at any date and shifts to the left over time.

Ignoring any common-property issues, the firm developing the well faces only two choices: it must decide on the size of the pump to install when the well is put into production, and it must decide when to stop pumping and abandon the well. The decision of when to stop pumping is the same as we saw for a mine. The well should be operated as long as price is at least as high as average cost. The choice of the size of the pump determines the rate of extraction and the cost in each period the well is operated. With this simple form, the conditions for maximizing the pre-

---

[7]We will ignore the fact that pumps can be stopped and restarted or in some cases run at less than full capacity. We will also ignore the fact that later in a well's life, water or steam is often injected into a nearby well to help move the oil or gas.

sent value of net revenue are easiest to derive working in continuous time. The present value of net revenue is as follows:

$$PV = Q_0 \int_0^T P_t e^{-(\delta+r)t} \, dt - C(Q_0) \int_0^T e^{-rt} \, dt \qquad (15.23)$$

where extraction cost is denoted by $C(Q_0)$ to show that it depends only on the initial choice of pump size. Now let $Q_t = Q_0 e^{-\delta t}$, where Q_0 equals the initial production and δ equals the rate of decay of production. Then we can rewrite Equation 15.23 as

$$PV = \int_0^T [P_t Q_t - C(Q_0)] e^{-rt} \, dt \qquad (15.24)$$

To determine the maximum present value, we differentiate Equation 15.24 with respect to Q_0:

$$\frac{\partial PV}{\partial Q_0} = \int_0^T P_t e^{-(\delta+r)t} \, dt - \frac{dC}{dQ_0} \int_0^T e^{-rt} \, dt = 0 \qquad (15.25)$$

Equation 15.25 can be rewritten as

$$\frac{dC}{dQ_0} = \int_0^T P_t e^{-\delta t} \, dt \qquad (15.26)$$

Now, $e^{-\delta t}$ is the ratio of Q_t to Q_0. This means that the pump should be sized so that the annual cost due to having a pump that will produce one more unit of oil or gas initially is equated to a weighted average of prices over the life of the well, with the weights being the (Q_t/Q_0)s. When the well is abandoned at time $t = T$, it must be the case that average cost has risen to equal price:

$$P_T = \frac{C(Q_0 e^{-\delta T})}{Q_0 e^{-\delta T}} \qquad (15.27)$$

From Equation 15.27, it can be seen that if future prices are known, the choice of the initial pump size also determines the date that the well will be abandoned.

Summary

The economics of the single mine differs from the economics of the single manufacturing plant or single service establishment in two important ways. First, it is impossible to analyze a mine without explicitly taking time into account. With a manufacturing or service firm, it is possible to hold the firm's stock of assets fixed and do short-run static analysis or take the stock of assets as a choice variable, assume that the firm's assets will be held constant once chosen, and do long-run static analysis. These options are not available with a mine. It is the mine's business to use up its primary asset, its stock of mineral. The primary decision for the mine's owners is how much of that stock to extract today and how much to leave to extract in the future. However, both the analytical techniques and the results are the same for the mine and for the manufacturing firm when we allow the stock of assets to vary over time. Any firm maximizes its present value by equating marginal revenue with marginal cost, where marginal cost includes the user cost of each of the firm's assets. For human-produced assets, user cost is the additional economic depreciation that results from the incremental use of the asset. For minerals, user cost is the present value of future costs that would result from leaving a marginally smaller deposit for the future.

The second difference between a mine and other firms is that the owners of a mine *plan* to shut down in the foreseeable future. Though other types of firms regularly go out of business, there is nothing inherent in their nature that says they must. At least conceptually, all of the assets of a manufacturing or service business can be maintained indefinitely or replaced when they wear out. The main asset of a mine can be replaced only by discovering another deposit and opening another mine. Any individual mine will be shut down eventually. However, the mining firm can stay in business by discovering new deposits. We turn next to the process of exploration and discovery.

EXPLORATION FOR NEW RESERVES

So far, we have looked at a single mine in a competitive industry. One of the features of this type of operation is that it eventually shuts down when average extraction cost is no longer less than price. For an extractive industry to continue to exist over time, new mines must be opened to replace those that are exhausted. The same is true of the individual firm. It can go out of business when its current reserves are exhausted, or it can find new reserves and stay in business. Thus one part of an ongoing extractive industry will necessarily be exploration for new deposits.

There is another reason for exploration: to find lower-cost deposits. Deposits of different quality will have different extraction cost. A firm that finds a deposit with higher quality and lower cost than the deposits its competitors are mining will be able to earn higher than normal profits. In industries where extraction costs for a single deposit rise as the deposit is exhausted, finding new deposits of the same quality will provide a cost advantage over firms working partially exhausted deposits.

The circumstances of exploration differ between industries. In some cases, such as coal in the United States, the location and size of unexploited deposits is well known. In others, such as oil, gas, and many minerals, it is not. Where the location and size of additional deposits is well known, it is usually a by-product of other activities or the result of government action. In industries where there is not a known stock of unexploited deposits, exploration is a costly and risky activity. Firms considering exploring for minerals must decide whether to explore, where to explore, and when to explore.

Exploration of a Single Prospect

Let's start with a simple case for our hypothetical mining firm. We assume that there is a known probability that an area either does or does not contain a deposit of sheetcake of known size and quality. Exploration of this prospect can therefore have one of two well-defined outcomes. Although this is an unrealistic scenario, the *structure* of the decision problem is exactly the same as that faced by any mineral firm in the real world. The only difference is that the real firm faces many more possible outcomes.

In this example, Antoinette & Robespierre, Inc., faces two decisions: *whether* to explore the prospect and, if so, *when* to explore it. The decision of whether to explore comes down to whether the *expected value* of the potential deposit is greater than the cost of exploration, which may include the cost of acquiring the mineral rights.[8] Let π be the probability that there is a deposit, and let V be the value of the possible deposit if it is mined optimally. The expected value of the gamble of exploration is $\pi V + (1 - \pi)0 = \pi V$. If the cost of exploring is C, the prospect is not worth exploring at all if $\pi V < C$.

Of course, exploration can always be *postponed*. If exploration is postponed, so are its costs. This reduces the present value of costs.[9] However, delaying exploration also delays the date at which mining begins. This delays the receipt of net revenues from the mine and reduces their present value. If prices are expected to stay unchanged into the future, delaying exploration reduces the present value of costs and expected net revenues by the same proportion, and there is nothing to be gained from delay.

If prices are expected to rise over time but costs are not, there *is* a gain from delaying exploration.[10] Consider the decision to explore this year or delay for a year. (The same decision can be repeated for next year and the year after and so on so that the decision of when to explore can be broken down into a series of decisions of whether to delay.) The decision to explore hinges on whether the expected net present value of exploring today, $\pi V_1 - C$, is greater than the expected net present value from exploring next year, $(\pi V_2 - C)/(1 + r)$.

Letting $V_2 = \alpha V_1$, our firm should explore this year if $\pi[V_1 - \alpha V_1/(1 + r)] > rC/(1 + r)$. This inequality can be rearranged to give $[(1 - \alpha + r)/(1 + r)]\pi V_1 > [r/(1 + r)]C$. This inequality will be true if two things are true: first, $\pi V_1 > C$—that is, the prospect is worth exploring—and second, $\alpha < 1$—that is, $V_1 > V_2$. Since the deposit is the same, regardless of when the plot is explored, the only thing that can cause V_1 and V_2 to be different is if the price stream that the mine will face if exploration and extraction begin now is different from the price stream that will be faced a year later. V_1 will be greater than V_2 only if prices are higher now than they will be in the future. With constant prices or steadily rising prices,

---

[8] We are assuming that the firm is risk-neutral, even though Antoinette & Robespierre may themselves be risk-averse individuals.

[9] The costs of exploration can also be uncertain, which adds a further complication to the decision.

[10] This is an example of applying the concept of "real" options to exploration decisions. See Dixit and Pindyck (1994) for a discussion of so-called real options.

exploration should be delayed. With steadily falling prices or prices that fall and then rise, it may be more profitable to explore now than to wait. What this means is that exploration of a prospect should be delayed until the prospect of a shortage will drive the price up but not so long that others' exploration and discoveries drive prices back down. The prospect of higher mineral prices may also drive up the price of mineral rights, increasing the cost of exploration.

For any prospect, generally there will be a date when the difference between expected net revenues and exploration cost, including the cost of acquiring the mineral rights, is greatest. This date will depend on the exploring firm's expectations of future prices and on the mineral rights owner's expectations of future prices. Thus we will have to move from analyzing an individual price-taking firm and look at the *market* determination of prices, which we do later in this chapter.

In our example, we assumed that there were only two possible outcomes of exploration. In the real world, of course, there are many possible outcomes of the exploration of any one prospect. There may be different deposit sizes, different grades of mineral, different ore body shapes, and different types and level of impurities. The list of potential differences that can affect extraction costs or mineral value is virtually endless. However, this does not change the basic problem for a firm considering exploring a prospect. It still must compare the expected present value of net revenues from mining the deposit with the cost of exploration and compare the saving from delaying exploration with the reduction in expected return. This calculation can be extremely complicated in the real world. It is likely to be approximated or even guessed at but is conceptually the same as the simple calculation we have examined.

The *Ex Ante* Value of a Prospect

We saw that the value of a known deposit is the maximum present value of net revenues that can be realized from exploiting it. For an unexplored prospect, this amount is uncertain. Because of this uncertainty, the value that a mineral prospect has to any potential owner has two components. One is the expected present value of net revenues that could be earned from the prospect. This is the difference between the expected present value of net revenues from extracting the minerals that may be in the deposit and the present value of exploration cost. The other component of the value of a mineral prospect is a *risk premium*. Most people are risk-averse and, given a choice between two assets, will choose the one with less uncertain returns unless the expected return of the riskier asset is higher.[11] For a mineral prospect, the expected present value of net revenues depends on the information that is known about the prospect and is fixed for any given level of information (although it may be different for people who have different information). The potential return that a buyer can expect therefore depends on the mineral price. The greater the uncertainty about the prospect and the more risk-averse the potential buyer, the lower will be that buyer's maximum offer.

---

[11]You may wish to review the discussion of risk aversion in Chapter 14.

This allows us to make several qualitative statements about markets for mineral rights. The first is that prices in these markets will tend to be slightly lower than the expected present value of net revenues from future mineral production. The second is that investors who buy and hold mineral rights will tend to be less risk-averse than investors who hold less risky assets. A third qualitative statement we can make about these markets is that successful long-term participation in such markets requires continuous investment in specialized knowledge. Estimating the value of a mineral prospect requires information about the prospect itself, about current and future costs of exploiting the types of minerals that might be found in the prospect, and about current and future prices of those minerals. A party consistently acting on less or lower-quality information than others in the market will soon get into trouble. On prospects where poorer information leads to a lower value, someone else will make a higher bid. On prospects where poorer information leads to a higher value, that value will generally be higher than the true value of the prospect given all existing information. The result is that trading in mineral rights tends to be concentrated among parties who already have reasons for having the required specialized information—mineral extraction firms. Within those firms, there often are individuals who specialize in acquiring mineral rights—traditionally called *landsmen* in the petroleum industry.

For someone to be willing to hold mineral rights as an investment, the yield must be comparable to that from other investments with similar risks.[12] The only way that mineral rights in an unexplored prospect can have a positive yield is if they are appreciating in price. To have the same yield as other assets, mineral rights must appreciate at the rate of interest, plus a premium for the degree of risk associated with holding them. Therefore, the value of a prospect at any time should be the expected present value of net revenues less exploration costs, discounted back from the time when the prospect will be explored, less a risk premium. In the example in the last section, the value of the prospect immediately before it is explored is πV. Ignoring any risk premium, the value at any time t before the date of exploration T is just $\pi V e^{-r(T-t)}$.

This smooth appreciation of mineral rights contrasts sharply with the capital gains or losses that occur when a prospect is explored. Immediately after it is explored, the value of the prospect in the example will be either V or 0. If the prospect contains a mineral deposit, the mineral rights owner has a capital gain of $V - \pi V = (1 - \pi)V$. If the prospect does not contain a deposit, the mineral rights owner has a capital loss of $0 - \pi V = -\pi V$. The only case in which exploration will not produce a capital gain or loss is when the value of one of the possible outcomes of exploration equals the expectation of the values of all possible outcomes and that outcome is realized.

The owner of the rights to a prospect can also experience capital gains or losses when other prospects are explored, for two reasons. First, the value of a prospect depends on expectations of future prices. Larger than expected discoveries will lower expected future prices and therefore reduce the value of an unexplored

---

prospect. Smaller than expected discoveries will have the opposite effect. Expectations of future prices will rise, and the value of an unexplored prospect will rise with them. Second, the value of a prospect can be affected by exploration of other prospects, if exploring other prospects produces information that changes the distribution of possible values for the first prospect. For example, if the owners of the rights to oil and gas in part of a geologic formation drill a dry hole, the owners of other prospects in that formation may revise downward their beliefs about the probability that they will find oil or gas. Conversely, if the well hits oil or gas, the owners of the rest of the formation may revise their expectations upward. Exploration of one prospect may affect the value of other prospects in both ways. A discovery in a type of formation that was considered unpromising may increase expectations of the total resource base and increase the value of similar prospects. In our example, exploration of other prospects can cause both V and π to change. If they change from V_0 and π_0 to V_1 and π_1, the capital gain or loss is $\pi_1 V_1 - \pi_0 V_0$.

In this discussion, we have assumed a competitive market for privately owned mineral rights. This is the exception rather than the rule. In most of the world, minerals are owned by governments. Governments have their own goals, and maximizing the present value of net revenues from mineral extraction is seldom one of them. In some cases, governments regard minerals as revenue sources and do seek to maximize revenue, but often in the short run rather than the long run. In other cases, governments see development of a country's mineral resources as a path to economic development. This may lead them to transfer mineral rights to extractive firms at below market prices. Both of these goals can affect sustainability concerns as well.

Ongoing Exploration Programs

Most extractive industries consist of many firms working many deposits. Generally, some of these deposits are nearing exhaustion, and firms in the industry are exploring to replace them or find new deposits with lower costs. Sometimes the same firm explores and mines. In other cases, firms specialize in exploration. Either they sell their discoveries to firms that specialize in production or work on contract for producers. As exploration has come to depend more and more on specialized knowledge and technology, it has increasingly become the domain of the specialized firm or the specialized department or subsidiary of a larger firm.

Finding Cost   People working in mineral industries often speak of the *finding cost* of new reserves. This is just the ratio of the cost of exploration to the quantity of new reserves discovered. It is expressed in dollars per ton or per barrel or per some other physical unit. Any particular exploration project will incur certain costs and as a result find a deposit of a certain size, which may be zero. The deposit's size and characteristics are beyond the firm's control and cannot be known ahead of time. Thus for any particular exploration project, the finding cost for that project cannot be known ahead of time. It can be calculated only after the fact. Before the project starts, its finding cost looks like a random variable. If the firm's expectations are concrete enough to put in the form of a probability distribution, it is possible to define an *ex ante expected finding cost.* It is also possible, and more common, to speak of an *ex post average finding cost,* which is just the sum of exploration costs divided by the sum of new reserves discovered during a period.

When measured in terms of dollars per unit of final mineral recovered, finding cost implicitly takes differences in mineral quality into account in a physical sense. However, it ignores the economic implication of differences in quality, namely, differences in extraction cost. Two discoveries may have the same physical quantity of reserves and have cost the same to discover; they therefore have the same finding cost. However, if one has a higher grade of ore or some other extraction cost advantage, it is more valuable.

Finding cost for an industry as a whole is total exploration cost divided by total new reserves. Since finding cost for each prospect explored is a random variable, so is finding cost for the industry. This allows us to give a more precise statement of the relationship between exploration success in general and the value of unexplored prospects. When discoveries are greater than expected, realized finding cost is lower than its *ex ante* expected value. When realized finding cost is lower than expected, owners of unexplored prospects will experience capital losses. Conversely, when discoveries are less than expected, realized finding cost is higher than expected, and mineral rights owners experience a capital gain.

Determining Which Prospects to Explore First   We saw that exploration of a single prospect should be delayed until just before new reserves are needed. However, we ignored the fact that there are generally many prospects that could be explored at any time. A mineral exploration firm must decide which prospects to explore first, as well as when to explore any given prospect.

Three things enter into this decision: the expected return from exploring each prospect, the degree of risk of each prospect, and the firm's attitude toward risk. Ignoring risk for a moment, the deposit with the higher expected present value of net revenue from mining less exploration cost should be explored first. This is obvious if the expected present value of one of two prospects is negative. Exploration of that prospect should be postponed until sometime in the future when prices have risen or costs have fallen enough to make its expected present value profitable.

It is also true if both prospects have positive expected present values, just as we showed in the previous discussion on multiple grades of ore. Suppose that $EPV_1 > EPV_2$. Also suppose that only one prospect can be explored in each period. If prospect 1 is explored first, the total expected present value is $EPV_1 + EPV_2/(1 + r)$. If prospect 2 is explored first, the total expected present value is $EPV_2 + EPV_1/(1 + r)$. The difference in expected present value between exploring prospect 1 first and exploring prospect 2 first is then

$$EPV_1 + \frac{EPV_2}{1 + r} - EPV_2 - \frac{EPV_1}{1 + r} = (EPV_1 - EPV_2)\frac{r}{1 + r} > 0 \qquad (15.28)$$

This is true regardless of the ratio of cost to return for the two prospects. This rule also can be expressed in terms of finding cost: if there are no differences in quality, the prospect with the lowest expected finding cost should be explored first.

Differences in the riskiness of prospects may modify this. A risk-averse firm would explore the less risky of two otherwise identical prospects first. Two firms with different attitudes toward risk may even disagree about which of two prospects should be explored first. Suppose that in the example in the last paragraph, prospect 1 was the riskier of the two. Each of the two firms will subtract a risk premium from the expected present value of each prospect. For a firm that has very little aversion to risk, this risk premium will be small. Suppose that firm 1 attaches risk premiums P_1^1 and P_2^1 to the two prospects. Firm 1 is not very risk-averse, and $EPV_1 - P_1^1 > EPV_2 - P_2^1$. Suppose that firm 2 is more risk-averse and its risk premiums are P_1^2 and P_2^2, where P_2^2 is slightly greater than P_2^1 and P_1^2 is much greater than P_1^1. Then it is possible that $EPV_1 - P_1^2 > EPV_2 - P_2^2$.

In general, the "best" prospects should be explored first, and will be, where "best" is a combination of expected finding cost, expected grade (or other influences on extraction cost), risk, and transportation cost. In principle, it would be possible to construct a risk-adjusted, grade-adjusted, and location-adjusted measure of finding cost. You should keep in mind that "finding cost" means "finding cost subject to all these adjustments" or "finding cost per ton of mineral deliverable to market."

Trends in Finding Cost and Price   Sometimes concern is expressed that finding costs have increased greatly over time, which again leads to speculation that the world will soon run out of certain resources. When crude oil was first discoverd, one could practically poke a hole in the ground to get a "gusher." Now oil companies explore and extract oil in places that are far less hospitable, such as the North Sea and the Arctic. As the best prospects are exhausted, they have to be replaced. The remaining prospects will have a lower probability of containing large, low-cost deposits. This is the equivalent for a mineral industry of the depletion of its deposit for a single mine, and it has similar consequences for costs. With the prospects remaining to be explored declining in expected value over time, expected finding cost will tend to rise. All other things being equal, this would result in rising mineral prices and declining consumption. With constant exploration cost and constant price, the expected return on exploration would fall. If exploration is less attractive, it will slow, and fewer reserves will be discovered. Coupled with rising extraction cost for existing reserves (assuming constant technology) and constant demand, price would rise.

There is a second factor tending to cause the prices of extractive resources to rise over time. Over time, not only will extraction cost from existing deposits rise, but the cost of discovering new reserves will also tend to rise, and eventually, extraction costs from new reserves that are discovered will rise.

However, even if extraction costs and expected finding costs that both increased with the exhaustion of the best prospects were the only influences on mineral prices, there would be times of falling prices. This is because the actual results of exploration are not known ahead of time. Actual discoveries may be higher or lower than *ex ante* expectations. New deposits may have higher or lower extraction cost than the *ex ante* expectation. A greater than expected rate of discovery, or even a single unexpectedly large discovery with low extraction costs, can lower prices. Conversely, a smaller rate of discovery than expected can cause prices temporarily to rise faster than expected. If exhaustion of deposits and of prospects were the only forces acting on mineral prices, we would expect to see prices behave something like what is shown in Figure 15.10, where the solid line shows the long-run trend and the dashed line shows actual prices varying around this trend.

Just as technological change in extraction can lower the cost of extracting any grade of ore, technological change in exploration can lower the cost of exploring any given prospect. Exploration consists of several stages, and technical improvements can occur at any stage. The final stage generally consists of drilling into a suspected deposit. With oil and gas, there is an overlap between the final stages of exploration and the first stages of production because the same well that is used to determine whether a deposit is actually present will generally be used for production. With solid minerals, this last stage of exploration consists of drilling through a suspected deposit to determine the extent of the deposit and collect samples to determine the type and grade of ore and the level and type of impurities. Improvements in drilling technology can lower the cost of this final phase of exploration.

Technological change can also occur in the preceding phases of exploration and may be more important there. No one throws a dart at a map and then drills a well. The entire exploration process consists of finding out more information about places where minerals might exist. Long before the final direct phase of exploration, other, indirect methods of obtaining information are used. Information may be gathered from aerial or satellite photography, from geologists walking around looking at rocks, from reading variations in the earth's magnetic field, or from observing shock waves that have passed through the earth. Technological change in the preliminary phases of exploration can take the form of improvements in existing techniques or the development of new techniques. Two of the most important areas of technical improvement in the past few decades have been in remote data gathering and in the use of computers to analyze data.

Improvements in exploration technologies can lower finding costs in two ways. All else being equal, technological change will lower the cost of exploring any given prospect that appears promising enough to be worth exploring. However, greater

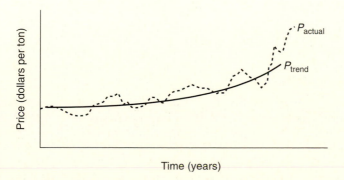

Figure 15.10 Short-Run and Long-Run Trends in Mineral Prices

cost savings generally come from distinguishing good prospects from poor ones at an early stage in the exploration process and stopping the process on the poor ones. This increases the success rate for the overall exploration process and therefore reduces finding cost.

Consider the following example. Suppose that ARI has a list of prospects. Half of the prospects actually have a 75 percent probability of having a deposit of size X and a 25 percent probability of having no deposit. The other half actually have a probability of 25 percent of having a deposit of size X and a 75 percent probability of having no deposit. However, with the information ARI has, it cannot tell them apart. As far as the company can tell, all of them have a 50 percent probability of containing a deposit. On average, half the exploratory wells it drills will be in high-probability prospects, and half will be in low-probability prospects. The success rate will be $(.5)(.75) + (.5)(.25) = .5$. If final exploration of each prospect will cost C, expected finding cost is $C/.5X = \$2C/X$.

Now suppose that a new type of preliminary exploration work, with a cost of D per prospect, where D is much less than C, can distinguish between the two types of prospects. If the preliminary work is done on all prospects, only those with a high probability of having a deposit will be explored. On average, this will be half of the prospects on which preliminary work is done. Each prospect where exploration is completed will incur costs of $C + \$D$, and each prospect where exploration is stopped after the preliminary work will incur costs of D. Thus on average, for each prospect where exploration is completed, $C + 2\$D$ in costs will have been incurred. However, 75 percent of these prospects will have deposits. The average discovery per prospect explored will be $.75X$. The average finding cost therefore will be $\$(C + 2D)/.75X = \$1.33(C + 2D)/X$. This is less than the finding cost without preliminary work, $\$2C/X$, if $D < C/4$.[13]

Summary

Extractive firms and extractive industries must explore for new deposits to replace depleted reserves. Extractive firms may also explore in the hope of finding deposits with lower extraction cost than current reserves have. Exploration is a risky investment activity because its results are uncertain. Holding mineral rights as an asset is also risky. There is a high probability that mineral rights holders will experience capital gains or losses. There is near certainty that holders of the rights to unexplored prospects will experience capital gains or losses when their prospects are explored.

We have seen that there are two factors tending to increase mineral prices over time, exhaustion of the lowest-cost minerals and exploration of the most likely prospects, and two factors tending to decrease price over time, technical change in extraction and technical change in exploration. Over any time span, the general trend of prices may be upward, downward, or flat. In addition, there will be short-

---

[13]In fact, this is a simple example of a real option. By investing in preliminary exploration work, we can increase the probability of future success.

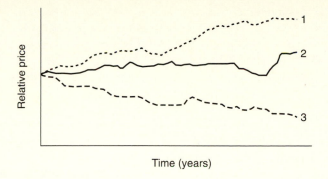

Figure 15.11   Trends in Mineral Prices with Technical Change

term deviations from whatever the long-term trend is because of discoveries' being larger or smaller than expected. Thus mineral prices may follow a time path like any of the three shown in Figure 15.11.

In the short run, exploration costs, and therefore finding costs, are influenced by another factor: modern mineral exploration is capital-intensive, and most of that capital is specialized—it has few alternative uses. Many phases of exploration also require specialized skills. The equipment used in exploration generally has long construction times, and the skills take years to acquire. So in the short run, the capital goods and labor required for exploration both have very inelastic supply. Over periods of a few years, changes in the demand for their services will lead to relatively large changes in their prices. A rise in mineral prices will lead to increased demand for exploration and therefore higher exploration costs. A fall in mineral prices will have the opposite effect.

What will happen to mineral prices in the long run? To answer that question, we need to look at an extractive industry as a whole and at its place in the overall economy.

THE EXTRACTIVE INDUSTRY

At any time, there are equilibrium conditions that apply for each of the participants in a competitive mineral industry. Mineral rights owners are willing to hold mineral rights only if they expect them to appreciate at the rate of interest. Minerals will be extracted from known deposits at a rate where marginal cost, including user cost, equals the price of the mineral. Mineral firms will explore prospects where the expected present value of revenue from exploiting a deposit that may be found is at least as great as the sum of the market value of the prospect and exploration cost. These will be the most promising prospects. All other prospects will be left to explore in the future. These conditions all describe the *supply* side of the industry.

The *demand* side of a mineral industry is indistinguishable from the demand side of any other industry. If the mineral is bought for final consumption, the buyers' demand is determined by exactly the same factors—income, prices, and tastes—that determine the demand for any other consumer good. If the mineral is bought as an input for production, the buyers' demand is determine in exactly the same way as any other derived demand for an input. For the buyers, the fact that they are buying an exhaustible resource is irrelevant, unless the buyer has some emotional or philosophical reaction to that fact.

The Industry in the Long Run

These equilibrium conditions, combined with the physical characteristics of the resource stock, determine the behavior of the industry over the very long run. Over the long run, the *supply side* of a mineral industry differs from that of a manufacturing industry in two important ways. First, exploration and production proceed from the most promising prospects and the best-known deposits to less promising prospects and poorer deposits. In the absence of any other forces, this will tend to drive prices up over time. Second, even if we assume an infinite future, the ultimate cumulative production from a mineral industry can never exceed the initial mineral stock. If extraction cost for some deposits exceeds the highest price anyone will ever be willing to pay for the mineral, ultimate cumulative extraction will be less than the initial mineral stock.

For ultimate cumulative extraction to be finite, production must go to zero, at least asymptotically. This statement may seem obvious, but it contains a potential that may not be obvious: *a finite resource stock can be made to last forever without extraction ever dropping to zero.* This can happen if the rate of use declines toward zero at least as fast as the stock does. For example, if half the remaining stock is used each year, both the remaining stock and the rate of use will be halved each year.[14] Each year, the remaining stock will get closer to zero, but at every finite date, there will still be some left.

In either case, demand must go to zero, in either finite time or infinite time. There are several forces that can make this happen. Most of the literature on exhaustible resources focuses on one: rising price. In the absence of countervailing forces, the price of an exhaustible resource will eventually rise as exhaustion nears. When exhaustion occurs, the price will have risen to the point where demand is completely choked off so that the price reaches the maximum amount anyone will pay for the resource at the instant that no more is available.

In actual experience, prolonged rises in mineral prices are rare, and real prices of most minerals show level or declining long-term trends.[15] There are two possible explanations for this fact. One is that we are still far from exhausting the stocks of most minerals, and the rising prices that will accompany imminent exhaustion are still in the future. The other is that other forces are at work that are generally assumed away in theoretical treatments of mineral economics. We have already discussed one force that is definitely applicable to most mineral industries: technological change in extraction and exploration. This can and does lead to steady or

---

[14]The same principle applies for any fraction between zero and one.
[15]See Barnett and Morse (1963) and Adelman (1991).

falling mineral prices, but ultimately price must rise as exhaustion nears, even with continuing technological change. New technologies can lower the cost of exploring any given mineral prospect and can lower the cost of extracting minerals from any given deposit once it has been found, but they cannot overcome the ultimate scarcity of a limited resource. Once all deposits have been found, finding cost becomes infinite. Once all deposits have been exhausted, extraction cost becomes infinite.

Another force that can lead to steady or falling prices is the development of substitutes, be it recycling previously extracted and processed deposits (e.g., aluminum cans, copper) or different materials (e.g., ceramics instead of steel, carbon fiber instead of aluminum). New substitutes or increases in the supply of existing substitutes will reduce the demand for a resource. This has happened many times in history. Flint was once one of the most important exhaustible resources. Together with other stones that could be flaked to form sharp edges, it was central to human technology for thousands of years. The development of metallurgy made flint tools obsolete, and the demand for flint dropped to essentially zero. Plastics and ceramics are currently cutting into the demand for several metals. Recycled materials can be substituted for newly mined minerals.

Another force that can reduce the demand for a resource is technological change in resource-using industries. This can take many forms. Improvements in combustion efficiency and thermal efficiency of boilers can reduce the demand for mineral fuels. Changes in production processes and in products themselves can lead to equivalent products being supplied that use fewer natural resources. Finally, improvements in mineral processing can lead to less ore needing to be extracted to produce the same quantity of mineral.

Thus the decline in production that must ultimately be the fate of any extractive industry can result from rising prices or from declining demand due to the development of substitutes or other technological changes. In that case, price may, but need not, rise as exhaustion approaches.

Modeling a Competitive Extractive Industry†

Generally, we construct a model of a competitive industry by aggregating the demand functions of all buyers to give an industry demand function and aggregating the supply functions of all sellers to give an industry supply function. We can follow that route with an extractive industry, but the result is far too complicated for our purposes here. That is because the supply functions of individual firms do not aggregate in the relatively clean way they do for manufacturing or commercial firms. As in any industry, each firm's supply function is defined by the upward-sloping part of its marginal cost curve, where the firm's supply price equals its marginal cost. Equilibrium for the industry means that price equals marginal cost and marginal cost is equalized across firms.

The complexity for an extractive industry comes when we decompose marginal cost into marginal extraction cost and user cost. Whereas any two firms will have the same marginal cost, they will have the same marginal extraction cost (and the same user cost) only by accident. In general, user cost (and therefore marginal

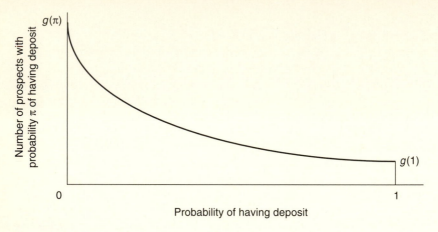

Figure 15.12   Density Function of Prospects

extraction cost) will differ across firms. This would be true even if all firms were identical except for being different ages—we saw that user cost changes over the life of a mine and goes to zero at the end of the mine's life. We can construct an aggregate supply curve for an extractive industry, but we cannot construct aggregate marginal extraction cost and user cost curves. And because user cost depends on expected future prices, we cannot use the industry supply curve to look at different time paths of prices.

To get around this complexity, we use a model that abstracts from all firm-level detail. We assume perfect competition, where all individual entities are infinitesimally small relative to the market, and we will assume that exploration of a single prospect and extraction of all the mineral in an individual deposit are instantaneous—they occur in infinitesimal time spans. With individual deposits having infinitesimal lives, the concept of user cost does not arise at the firm level. We get around our inability to aggregate user cost by assuming it away. Most of the literature on the theory of exhaustible resource economics takes a slightly different approach of ignoring the aggregation problem and constructing industry-level cost functions. Either way, the result is a model that provides information about the behavior of the industry as a whole that we could not get if we insisted on keeping all the firm-level detail.

Model Assumptions   Each prospect either does or does not contain a mineral deposit. All deposits are of uniform size and grade.[16] Prospects do differ in their probability of having a deposit. Call this probability π, where $0 \leq \pi \leq 1$. For each π, the total supply of prospects with that probability of having a deposit is $g(\pi)$. Thus $g(\pi)$ is the density function of π, as shown in Figure 15.12. However, the integral of $g(\pi)$ is not one, as with a probability density function. It is the total stock of unexplored prospects.

---

[16]Differences in grade and deposit size can also be built into the model.

The cost of exploring any prospect is fixed at each date. Call it b_t. There are no cost differences due to location, geology, or any other factors. Exploration cost may decline over time due to improvements in technology; we can express this as $\dot{b} \leq 0$, where $\dot{b}$ represents the change in exploring costs over time.

Once a prospect is found to contain a deposit, extraction of that deposit is instantaneous. This assumption allows us to aggregate extraction cost across firms and get a meaningful aggregate function. Without this assumption, we can aggregate extraction cost, but the resulting aggregate function has no simple relationship to any aggregate behavior.

All deposits contain one unit of mineral. Let c_t be the total cost for mining one deposit, including a normal return on capital. Extraction cost is uniform across all deposits at any time. There are no differences in grade and no transport cost differences. Over time, technological change may reduce extraction cost: $\dot{c} \leq 0$.

Demand at time t depends on the mineral's own price, P_t, and on the prices of substitutes and complements, which we will represent with one aggregate "other" price, P_t^0. Demand also depends on a host of other factors, including technology in industries that use the mineral, tastes, and population size. We will represent all these factors by another aggregate variable, Z_t. This gives the industry demand function

$$Q^D = Q^D (P_t, P_t^0, Z_t) \tag{15.29}$$

Mineral rights are initially owned by individuals. Firms specializing in exploration buy mineral rights, paying a price ρ_t for each prospect. These exploration firms turn around and sell the deposits they find to firms specializing in extraction. The price of deposits is δ_t.

We also make the very strong and unrealistic assumption of perfect foresight. Everyone knows everything about the present and future except whether individual prospects contain deposits. This means that there is no uncertainty about the aggregate results of mineral exploration. If X_t prospects are explored, $\pi_t X_t$ deposits will be discovered. The only uncertainty is which prospects they will be discovered on. We also assume either that exploration firms are large enough relative to individual prospects that they face no uncertainty or that they are risk-neutral and thus maximize expected net revenue.

Equilibrium for Exploration Firms There are three groups of actors on the supply side of this model. Exploration firms and extractive firms maximize profits while mineral rights owners maximize the present value of their income from selling mineral rights. We need to examine equilibrium conditions for each of these three groups.

Prospects with the highest probability of containing a deposit will be explored first. Thus at any instant t, the prospects being explored will be uniform, and we can denote the fraction of prospects found to contain deposits at t by π_t. As the better prospects are explored, π_t will decline over time. Exploration is instantaneous, and exploration firms sell deposits as they discover them. Individual exploration firms will try to maximize profits, but firms will enter the market up to the point where there are no economic profits. Exploration firms will recover all their costs (at least on average), including a normal return on capital. Thus revenue from selling deposits to extraction firms must just equal aggregate exploration costs plus payments for mineral rights:

$$P_t Q_t = b_t X_t + \rho_t X_t \tag{15.30}$$

where $Q_t = \pi_t X_t$.

Equilibrium for Extraction Firms   With instantaneous extraction and identical deposits, there is no reason to build up a stock of unexploited reserves. Deposits are mined as they are explored. Individual extraction firms try to maximize profits, but free entry guarantees that there are no economic profits. Revenue from selling extracted mineral must just equal aggregate extraction costs, including a normal return on capital, plus payments for deposits:

$$P_t Q_t = b_t Q_t + \delta_t Q_t \tag{15.31}$$

The zero economic profit conditions for exploration firms and extraction firms can be combined to give the market supply function:

$$P_t Q_t = c_t Q_t + b_t X_t + \rho_t X_t = c_t Q_t + (b_t + \rho_t)\frac{Q_t}{\pi_t} \tag{15.32}$$

or

$$P_t = c_t + \frac{b_t + \rho_t}{\pi_t} \tag{15.33}$$

The market is in equilibrium when this supply function and the demand function are simultaneously satisfied:

$$Q_t = Q^D\!\left(c_t + \frac{b_t + \rho_t}{\pi_t}\ P_t^0, Z_t\right) \tag{15.34}$$

Equilibrium for Mineral Rights Owners   The owners of mineral rights hold them as assets until the time they sell them for exploration. Two conditions are necessary for equilibrium in the market for mineral rights. First, the owners of prospects that will be explored in the future must earn a competitive return from holding them. Otherwise no one would be willing to hold mineral rights. Second, the price that exploration firms pay for mineral rights must equal the cost to society from reducing the stock of the mineral. If this condition is not satisfied, there are gains to be captured, either by mineral rights owners or exploration firms, from speeding up or slowing down the pace of exploration.

The first equilibrium condition takes a fairly simple form. Since the only way that mineral rights owners can earn a return from holding them is for their price to rise, equilibrium in the mineral rights market requires mineral rights prices to rise at the rate of interest. Rights to prospects with different probabilities of containing a deposit will sell for different prices, but all will be appreciating at the rate of interest. Let $\rho_t(\pi)$ be the price of mineral rights with probability of success π, and let π_t be π for prospects being explored at time t. Then $\dot{\rho}_t(\pi) = r\rho_t(\pi)$ for $\pi_t < \pi$.

The second condition is the industry-level equivalent of accounting for user cost at the level of the single firm. The cost of exploring, and possibly mining, an additional prospect today is the present value of future cost increases that will result from having marginally lower-quality prospects available at every date in the future. The price of prospects being explored at t must be

$$\rho_t \pi_t = -\int_t^T (P_s - c_s)\dot{\pi}_s e^{-r(s-t)}\, ds \tag{15.35}$$

where T is the date when all prospects are exhausted.[17] $P_s - c_s$ is the net value of marginal mineral production at time s, and $-\dot{\pi}_s$ is the loss of production at time s from having a marginally smaller stock of prospects. (Remember that $\dot{\pi} < 0$.)

Differentiating Equation 15.35 with respect to time yields further insight into the dynamics of the mineral rights market:

$$\dot{\rho} = r\rho - (P - c)(-\dot{\pi}) \tag{15.36}$$

The two terms in Equation 15.36 reflect the two factors acting on the price of mineral rights. The price of each vintage of mineral rights must appreciate at the rate of interest, or people will not hold them. However, over time, lower-quality prospects with lower values are explored, and the second term is the marginal price differential between vintages of mineral rights.

This is shown graphically in Figure 15.12. The curves $\rho(\pi_0)$ through $\rho(\pi_3)$ show the prices of four different vintages of mineral rights rising at the rate of interest. The curve ρ_t shows the movement of the price exploration firms pay for prospects as they explore them. It always rises at less than the rate of interest and may fall.

Time Paths of Mineral Price and Consumption   At every instant of time, the price of the mineral and the quantity produced are determined by the equilibrium of supply and demand. We can determine the price and quantity by simultaneously solving the supply and demand functions:

$$P_t = c_t + \frac{b_t}{\pi_t} + \frac{\rho_t}{\pi_t} \tag{15.37}$$

---

[17]T may be infinite. See the discussion of time paths of prices in this section.

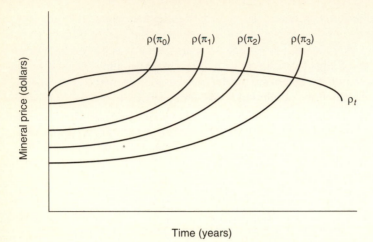

Figure 15.13 Time Paths of Mineral Rights Prices

$$Q_t = Q^D (P_t, P_t^0, Z_t) \tag{15.38}$$

Since these two equations must be satisfied at every moment, any changes in the variables appearing in these equations must occur in ways that maintain their relationships. This means that differentiating these two equations with respect to time will give us two simultaneous equations in the rates of change of the variables in the supply and demand functions:

$$\dot{P} = \dot{c} + \frac{b}{\pi} - \frac{b\dot{\pi}}{\pi^2} + \frac{\dot{\rho}}{\pi} - \frac{\rho\dot{\pi}}{\pi^2} \tag{15.39}$$

$$\dot{Q} = \frac{\partial Q^D}{\partial P} \dot{P} + \frac{\partial Q^D}{\partial P^0} \dot{P}^0 + \frac{\partial Q^D}{\partial Z} \dot{Z} \tag{15.40}$$

The definition of the stock of prospects, $g(\pi)$, implies that $\dot{\pi} = - X/g(\pi)$. Substituting $- X/g(\pi)$ for $\dot{\pi}$ and $\rho - (P - c)X/g(\pi)$ for $\dot{\rho}$ (Equation 15.40), in the differentiated demand function gives

$$\dot{P} = \dot{c} + \frac{b}{\pi} + \frac{bX}{\pi^2 g(\pi)} + \frac{r\rho}{\pi} - \frac{(P-c)X}{\pi g(\pi)} + \frac{\rho X}{\pi^2 g(\pi)}$$

$$= \dot{c} + \frac{b}{\pi} + \frac{r\rho}{\pi} - \left(P - c - \frac{b}{\pi} - \frac{\rho}{\pi}\right) \frac{X}{\pi g(\pi)} \tag{15.41}$$

But $P - c - \dfrac{b}{\pi} - \dfrac{\rho}{\pi} = 0$, from Equation 15.37, so Equation 15.41 reduces to

$$\dot{P} = \dot{c} + \frac{\dot{b}}{\pi} + \frac{r\rho}{\pi}$$

$$(?) \ (-) \ (-) \ (+) \qquad\qquad (15.42)$$

where the sign of each term is shown in the parentheses. The three terms on the right-hand side are not all the same, so the sign of $\dot{P}$ can be $+$ or $-$, or $\dot{P}$ can be zero. Technological change in extraction and exploration ($\dot{c} < 0$ and $\dot{b} < 0$) work to lower P over time. The fact that mineral rights owners have a positive rate of time preference and demand a positive return for holding them ($r > 0$ and $\rho > 0$) tends to increase P over time.

Whether consumption rises or falls also depends on three factors: whether price is rising or falling ($\dot{P}$), whether prices of substitutes are rising or falling ($\dot{P}^0$), and whether demand is rising or falling because of other factors such as technological change in resource using industries ($\dot{Z}$).

There are three possibilities for the ultimate fate of our model industry. The industry may exhaust the physical stock of mineral in finite time, it may reach economic exhaustion in finite time, or exhaustion may be approached asymptotically with the stock lasting forever.

Economic exhaustion will occur in finite time if the sum of exploration and finding cost exceeds the maximum price buyers are willing to pay for the mineral. In our model, this is $Q^D(\overline{P}) = 0$ for some $\overline{P} < c + b/\pi_{min}$ where π_{min} is the lowest probability of finding mineral on any prospect. As Figure 15.11 is drawn, this is certainly possible because the minimum value of π is zero. If there is no technological change in exploration, finding cost will eventually become infinite. Physical exhaustion can occur in finite time only if the sum of exploration and finding cost never exceeds the maximum price buyers are willing to pay for the mineral. In our model, this is $Q^D(c + b/\pi_{min}) > 0$. As Figure 15.12 is drawn, this is impossible. Physical exhaustion is possible only if $g(\pi)$ stops short of the vertical axis. This is possible for minerals that are found in discrete units in well-defined circumstances and are not found at all elsewhere. It is not possible for minerals, such as most metals, that are found virtually everywhere in some concentration, however small. We may eventually find all of the world's diamonds, but if we stop mining iron, it will be because of economic exhaustion, not physical exhaustion.[18]

In our model industry, the remaining stock will asymptotically approach, but never reach, zero if π/X is always at least as great as some positive constant. This will be true if X approaches zero at least as fast as π does, that is,

$$\frac{\dot{\pi}}{\pi} \geq \frac{\dot{X}}{X} \qquad\qquad (15.43)$$

---

[18]If our model had differences in deposit sizes and qualities, economic exhaustion could occur because of extraction cost increasing as extraction moves to lower-quality deposits over time.

(Remember that both sides of this inequality are negative.) Equation 15.43 can be converted to an equation in $\dot{X}$ by using the fact that $Q = \pi X$ and therefore $\dot{Q} = \pi \dot{X} + X \dot{\pi}$:

$$\dot{X} = -\frac{\dot{\pi}X}{\pi} + \frac{\partial Q^D}{\partial P}\frac{\dot{P}}{\pi} + \frac{\partial Q^D}{\partial P^0}\frac{\dot{P}^0}{\pi} + \frac{\partial Q^D}{\partial Z}\frac{\dot{Z}}{\pi} \tag{15.44}$$

Substituting this for $\dot{X}$ and multiplying both sides by πX gives

$$2\dot{\pi}X \geq \frac{\partial Q^D}{\partial P}\dot{P} + \frac{\partial Q^D}{\partial P^0}\dot{P}^0 + \frac{\partial Q^D}{\partial Z}\dot{Z} \tag{15.45}$$

Extraction will decline faster than the remaining stock only if consumption is choked off at the correct rate by prices rising fast enough or demand falling fast enough. Thus an infinite life for a finite resource stock requires a special balance between technological change, the declining resource stock, the shape of the demand curve at low quantities, and shifts in demand due to development of substitutes, changing consumer tastes, or technological change in resource-using industries.

A Special Case Very little of the literature on exhaustible resources has explicitly incorporated technological change. It has focused on the economic consequences of having a finite, exhaustible stock. If there is no technological change, our mineral industry model is considerably simpler, and its behavior is simpler. If we go back to Equation 15.42 and set $\dot{c} = 0$ and $\dot{b} = 0$, we get

$$\dot{P} = \frac{r\rho}{\pi} \tag{15.46}$$

Thus the mineral price always rises. This rise is driven by mineral rights owners' demand to earn a competitive rate of return and the fact that the best prospects are explored first so that finding cost rises over time. The ultimate fate of the industry is also simpler. There are two possibilities. Either the stock of prospects is physically exhausted in finite time, or the price rises to the maximum demand price (perhaps asymptotically) before all prospects are explored and some prospects are ignored as uneconomic.

If we simplify the model further by assuming that all prospects have the same π, our model is driven entirely by two factors—the finite stock of prospects and mineral rights owners' demand to earn a competitive return. In this simplest model, there is only one final outcome: physical exhaustion of the resource. Until that time, the behavior of the model is governed by Equation 15.46 with $\pi = 1$:

$$\frac{\dot{P}}{\rho} = r \tag{15.47}$$

The mineral rights price, which is the difference between the mineral price and the sum of extraction and finding cost, rises at the rate of interest. This is often called *Hotelling's rule* because it was first derived by Hotelling (1931). However, it is a rule that applies only in a very special case, as Hotelling's original article and many others show. We should not be surprised that actual prices of many exhaustible resources, such as crude oil, do not follow this path.

Does the Market Promote Efficient Resource Use?

Occasionally, noneconomists claim that a market economy leads to inefficient use (which always means excessive use) of exhaustible resources because it does not take the costs of resource exhaustion into account. Does this claim have any merit? We have looked at the costs of resource exhaustion and at the decisions made by all the parties in an extractive industry. Have we seen any costs of exhaustion that are not being properly accounted for?

For both society and individuals, the problem posed by resource exhaustion is when to use the limited resource stock. The marginal cost of resource use is the sum of the direct costs of production and the opportunity cost of using an increment of the resource today rather than leaving it for the future. Mining firms see this cost in two places. For mineral deposits they own, they see this opportunity cost in the form of their user cost. A profit-maximizing mining firm has the same incentives to decide between current and future extraction as society as a whole. The decision that maximizes profits for the firm is also the efficient decision. For other known deposits and for unexplored prospects, the opportunity cost of the resource is reflected in the price of the mineral rights. Again, the owners of mineral rights face the same incentives as society as a whole. For each prospect, there is a present-value-maximizing date for exploring it and bringing it into production if minerals are found. Exploring and beginning production either earlier or later gives a lower present value.

At this point, skeptics about markets are likely to bring up the noted impatience of the human species, much as we discussed in Chapter 13. They may claim that people want a return now, that they won't wait for the optimal time. That may be true, but if so, it is an indictment of humans, not of markets as a means of coordinating human activities. As with any other assets, the owners of mineral rights can sell them at any time. In equilibrium, mineral rights will appreciate at the rate of interest, so it is not necessary to hold them "to maturity" to earn a return and recoup the initial investment. With regard to mineral rights, the market performs two allocation functions simultaneously. It allocates the stock of resources over time, and it guarantees that the best prospects are exploited first. It offers attractive bids only on those prospects that should be explored today while offering the promise of higher bids in the future for less attractive prospects.

In a competitive resource market, the prices of mineral rights will reflect the opportunity cost of resource exhaustion, and this will cause all participants in the market to take that opportunity cost into account. The result will be efficiency. Of course, real-world markets for exhaustible resources may be imperfect for all the same reasons that other markets are imperfect. There may be market power on the supply side, the demand side, or both. There may be uninternalized external costs or benefits. There will likely be taxes and government regulations. An additional source of market imperfection is the fact that in much of the world, stocks of many exhaustible resources are owned by governments. However, none of these potential sources of inefficiency is unique to an exhaustible-resource industry. The only one that relates specifically to the opportunity cost of resource exhaustion is government ownership. Governments have complex sets of motives and goals. Maximizing the present value of returns from natural resources is seldom a dominant government goal.

EXHAUSTIBLE RESOURCES AND THE ECONOMY: POSSIBLE LONG-RUN FUTURES

Exhaustible resources play an import part in our economy. Coal, oil, natural gas, and uranium supply much of our energy. Our homes, offices, and factories are full of iron, copper, and aluminum. Even the roads and sidewalks under our feet are made using sand, gravel, limestone, and asphalt, which are mined from the ground and exist in finite amounts. How will our economy be affected as we use up naturally occurring stocks of minerals? Will resource exhaustion bring the end of civilization as we know it, or will it hardly be noticed? What, if anything, can we do to prepare for the possible consequences? Should we, as advocates of sustainability argue, switch to using renewable resources? Can we? The answers to these questions depend on how any particular exhaustible resource fits into the overall economy. We can examine four possibilities.

Alternative 1: Exhaustible Resources Are Inessential

It may be that we can get by very well without any particular exhaustible resource or combination of exhaustible resources. There are substitutes for virtually everything, and we can expect improving technology to continue to develop more substitutes for goods that seem essential to us now. We use a lot of iron, but there are few things we do with iron that we could not do with something else if we ran out of iron. We can also recycle most materials. If we ran out of iron ore, we would still have huge stocks of iron in the form of automobiles, machinery, and I-beams. We could continue to make new goods out of iron by recycling old ones.

If exhaustible resources turn out to be inessential, we would still face all the intergenerational equity questions we examined in Chapter 13 because even inessential resources could play a crucial role in intergenerational equity. We use the natural resources we do because they allow us to supply the goods and services consumers want at lower cost than other ways of supplying them. If we use up an inessential resource, our descendants will be able to consume the same goods and services we do, but their costs may be higher. In particular, they may need a larger capital stock to support the same level of consumption. They may also need a different mix of capital goods.

If exhaustible resources turn out to be inessential, our fairness to future generations hinges on whether we leave them enough capital to make up for the fact that we used up some natural resources. But in this case, natural resources play a role no different than that of any other assets.

Alternative 2: Exhaustible Resources Are Essential and Irreplaceable

It is difficult to think of any particular exhaustible resource that might be essential for human life. Our ancestors fumbled along for millennia without most of the goods and services that we think of as essential. Yet it is quite conceivable that one or more exhaustible resources might be essential to civilization as we know it. For example, we may never develop acceptable substitutes for fossil fuels that can be supplied at costs and in quantities comparable to our current use of such fuels.

If some minimum annual consumption of an exhaustible resource is essential for civilization, we are out of luck. Civilization will eventually come to an end when we have used all of the essential resource. Conserving the resource or relying on other renewable resources can delay the end but not prevent it. In this case, we have an irreconcilable conflict between generations. No matter how stingy we are with our own resource use, every gram we use speeds the return of the dark ages.

Alternative 3: Exhaustible Resources Are Essential but Have Good Substitutes

Suppose that civilization is impossible without some use of an exhaustible resource but that as long as some positive amount of the resource is available, a standard of living comparable to ours can be maintained if the capital stock is large enough. For example, suppose that we absolutely cannot maintain civilization as we know it without an annual infusion of freshly mined copper. We can recycle copper, and we can use substitutes, but we absolutely need some small amount of new copper every year to replace copper that is lost and unrecyclable. The fact that we can make a finite natural resource stock last forever by making consumption go to zero asymptotically at least as fast as the stock does becomes key in this case. If we can accumulate capital fast enough to make up for our continually declining resource use, we can also maintain our standard of living forever. Whether we can do this depends on how easy it is to substitute capital for the resource. If substitution is easy, it is possible. If substitution is difficult, we (or our descendants) are doomed.[19]

Is capital a good enough substitute for exhaustible resources that we can maintain our standard of living with ever smaller amounts of resources? Dasgupta and Heal (1980) argue that production functions estimated for industrial countries in the twentieth century allow more than enough substitution between resources and

---

[19]Exactly what is required for easy substitution depends on the characteristics of the social production function. See Solow (1974), Stiglitz (1974a, 1974b), or Dasgupta and Heal (1980, chap. 7).

capital. However, they warn that it is not the degree of substitutability we have now that is really relevant but rather the ease of substitution that will exist in the distant future when resource stocks are nearly exhausted.

Alternative 4: Exhaustible Resources Are Essential, but Technological Change Reduces Resource Requirements over Time

Suppose that we have technological change occurring in resource-using industries. Further suppose that thanks to this change, every year, the same output as last year can be produced using some fraction $\alpha < 1$ of the resource used last year and the same or smaller inputs of capital and labor. If R_{t-1} units of the resource were required last year, $R_t = \alpha R_{t-1}$ are required this year to produce the same output. We have seen that a finite stock of a resource can be made to last forever if a constant fraction of that stock is consumed every year. Let the stock be X and call the fraction consumed each year β, so $R_t = \beta X_t$. Substituting αR_{t-1} for R_t and $X_{t-1} - R_{t-1}$ for X_t and solving for α gives $\alpha = 1 - \beta$. For example, if the same output can be produced in year t with, 99 percent of the resource input used in year $t - 1$, the resource stock can be made to last forever if no more than 1 percent of the stock is used each year.

Conclusion

Which of these four alternatives is most applicable? The answer probably depends on your point of view. History provides numerous examples where one resource has been substituted for another. Whether this occurred owing to scarcity or technological change is not clear. There appear to be examples of both. However, past experience may not be repeated in the future. Perhaps there are resources we use today that will turn out to be irreplaceable. Advocates of far greater reliance on renewable resources complain that faith in future technological change are misplaced; we cannot and should not "eat our seed corn" in the belief that technology will rescue us later. They have a point. Pollyannaish faith in the future is probably as misplaced as a fatalistic presumption that "the end is nigh."

We cannot tell you what the "correct" balance point is. That is a matter of your faith and philosophy. We *can* suggest that applying sound economic principles will help matters greatly. Policies that promote efficient resource extraction will be far more useful than policies that prevent economic efficiency. Those policies will in turn create incentives for new technologies, discoveries, and innovation. If the situation really is as described in Alternative 2, where there are resources that are both essential and irreplaceable, we are all doomed no matter what we do. So it will do us no harm to promote as much efficiency as possible and thereby end civilization with a bang and not a whimper.

CHAPTER SUMMARY

To their owners, minerals in the ground are assets, much like any others. A mining firm, and a mineral industry, can be analyzed using the standard tools of microeconomic theory once the costs of using up a resource stock have been properly defined. The cost of extracting an additional increment is called user cost and is the present value of resulting increases in future extraction costs. The value of an individual mine is maximized when price (or marginal revenue) is equated to the sum of marginal extraction cost and user cost. An individual mine will be exploited until its average extraction cost has risen to equal price. At this point, economic exhaustion of the deposit occurs. Most mineral industries have ongoing programs for exploring new prospects. The time path of a mineral price is determined by the need to pay mineral rights owners a competitive return for holding a scarce asset, by technological change in extraction and exploration, by the stocks of resources of different qualities, by the shapes of the demand and cost curves, and by technological change in resource-using industries.

Whether a mining industry is economically efficient depends on the same factors that determine whether any industry is economically efficient, such as whether it is competitive and whether it has external costs or benefits. Markets do not systematically undervalue exhaustible resources. Even if a mineral industry is efficient, the act of using up finite resources, or just the best-quality resources, raises issues of intergenerational equity. These issues have been addressed in Chapter 13 and will be addressed again in Chapter 19. Whether exhaustion of resource stocks will make it impossible for future generations to maintain their standard of living depends on whether capital can be substituted easily for resources and whether there will be continuous technological change in resource-using industries.

CHAPTER REVIEW

Economic Concepts and Tools

- *User cost* is the reduction in the value of an asset that results from using that asset rather than leaving it unused.
- The marginal cost of mineral production is the sum of marginal extraction cost and marginal user cost, that is, the sum of capital and labor costs and the reduction in the value of the deposit from marginal extraction.
- The value of a mine (present value of net revenues) is maximized by setting output to the sum of marginal extraction cost and marginal user cost to equate price (or marginal revenue) in every period.
- The user cost of mineral extraction is the present value of all future cost increases resulting from marginal current extraction.
- *Economic exhaustion* of a mineral deposit occurs when average extraction cost has risen to equal the price.

Policy Issues

- Market allocation of exhaustible resource stocks will lead to the costs of resource exhaustion being taken into account. Mineral industries may fail to achieve efficiency for all the same reasons that other industries fail to achieve efficiency, but there are no special market failures relating to the intertemporal decisions of a mineral industry.

- Exhaustible resources are assets just as much as human-produced capital goods. Fairness between generations hinges on the stock of assets one generation hands on to the next. Stocks of exhaustible resources need to be included in the calculation.
- Many stocks of exhaustible resources are owned by governments rather than individuals or businesses. Governments generally have other goals in addition to or instead of maximizing the present value of net revenues from mineral exploitation.

DISCUSSION QUESTIONS

1. Unreclaimed mines often impose external costs on their neighbors. Because of this, many jurisdictions require mine owners to reclaim abandoned mines. Does a mining company have incentives to reclaim a mine on its own? How does a requirement that mined land be reclaimed affect the mining firm's problem? Under what conditions will reclamation requirements affect the mine's production decisions?

2. When Iraq invaded Kuwait in August 1990, the price of a barrel of oil immediately rose on world markets by about 50 percent. Explain the dynamics of the market in this situation. What role does the concept of user cost play in your explanation?

3. In the 1970s, there were numerous predictions that natural gas supplies would be exhausted within a decade. Yet decades later, the amount of reserves has increased. Why were these predictions wrong? What did they leave out?

4. "Because the earth is finite, all resources will be exhausted eventually." Comment on this statement.

5. Some individuals have suggested that we develop mining operations on the moon or capture asteroids. In doing so, we would increase our resource stocks immeasurably. When should we begin, if ever?

REFERENCES

Adelman, M. 1991. "U.S. Oil/Gas Production Cost: Recent Changes." *Energy Economics* 13(2): 235–237.

Barnett, H., and C. Morse. 1963. *Scarcity and Growth.* Baltimore: Johns Hopkins University Press.

Dasgupta, P., and G. Heal. 1980. *Economic Theory and Exhaustible Resources.* London: Cambridge University Press.

Dixit, A., and R. Pindyck. 1994. *Investment Under Uncertainty.* Cambridge, Mass.: MIT Press.

Hotelling, H. 1931. "The Economics of Exhaustible Resources." *Journal of Political Economy* 39(1): 137–175.

Keynes, J. 1936. *The General Theory of Employment, Interest, and Money.* Old Tappan, N.J.: Macmillan.

Solow, R. 1974. "Intergenerational Equity and Exhaustible Resources." *Review of Economic Studies Symposium on the Economics of Exhaustible Resources:* 29–45.

Stiglitz, J. 1974a. "Growth with Exhaustible Natural Resources: The Competitive Economy." *Review of Economic Studies Symposium on the Economics of Exhaustible Resources:* 139–52.

———. 1974b. "Growth with Exhaustible Natural Resources: Efficient and Optimal Paths." *Review of Economic Studies Symposium on the Economics of Exhaustible Resources:* 123–37.

APPENDIX TO CHAPTER 15

User Cost with Quadratic Extraction Cost

In this example, extraction costs increase far faster than the increase in depth.

$$TEC_t = C_0 + (A_1D_t + A_2D^2)Q_t + \frac{BQ_t^2}{2} \tag{15A.1}$$

(Compare this with the extraction cost in the previous example: $TEC_t = C_0 + AD_tQ_t + BQ_t^2/2$.)

Marginal and average extraction cost will be as follows:

$$MEC_t = A_1D_t + A_2D_t^2 + BQ_t \tag{15A.2}$$

$$AEC_t = \frac{C_0}{Q_t} + A_1D_t + A_2D_t^2 + \frac{BQ_t}{2} \tag{15A.3}$$

Again, we start by looking at the date of economic exhaustion. Q_T and D_T can be found in the same way as the previous example. Q_T is unchanged. D_T is found by setting $MEC_T = P$. Thus $P = A_1D_T + A_2D_T^2 + BQ_T$. This quadratic equation in D_T has a positive root:

$$D_T = \frac{-A_1 + \sqrt{A_1^2 - 4A_2(BQ_T - P)}}{2A_2} \tag{15A.4}$$

Leaving all the parameters at their previous values and letting $A_1 = 0.00001$ and $A_2 = 0.00001$, then $D_T = 743.0$. Once again, user cost is zero in period T. In each previous period, user cost will be as follows:

$$UC_t = \frac{UC_{t+1} + (A_1Q_{t+1} + 2A_2D_{t+1}Q_{t+1})/\alpha}{1 + r} \tag{15A.5}$$

Following the procedure we used in the text, we can solve Equation 15A.5 backward from period T to give user cost and output in each preceding period.

Figure 15A.1 shows the time path of user cost for this mine. Compare the time path of user cost with the example shown in Figure 15.5. Note that in the current example, user cost first increases before decreasing to its final value of zero.

---

[1]With a discount rate of 8 percent, the present value of a 39-year string of $X payments is $11.95X, and a 40-year string of $X payments has a present value of $11.99X.

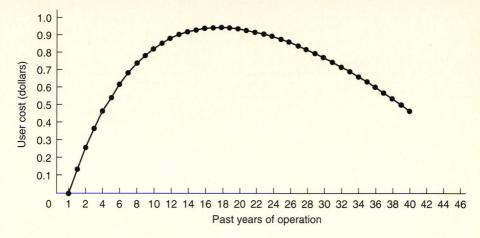

Figure 15A.1   User Cost with Quadratic Extraction Costs Because of Depth

This shows the importance of the two factors affecting user cost over time. Early in the mine's life, the remaining life is so long that shortening that remaining life by one year has little effect on the present value of costs.[1] However, with cost being a quadratic function of depth, the near-future costs of extracting an additional ton of ore rise rapidly as depth increases over time. Later in the mine's life, the shortening of the remaining life over time dominates, and user cost falls for the last 18 years.[2]

---

[2]With a discount rate of 8 percent, the present value of five-year string of $X payments is $4.12X, whereas a four-year string of $X payments has a present value of $3.42X.

CHAPTER 16

RENEWABLE
RESOURCES

Knock on Wood: Clearcutting on Vancouver Island, British Columbia

When they hear the term rain forest, *most people picture the lush tropical forests of the Amazon in Brazil or the island forests in the East Indies. Rarely do people from other areas associate* rain forest *with northwestern North America. Yet British Columbia and Alaska are home to the largest tracts of untouched temperate rain forest in the world.*

On the western coast of Vancouver Island, the land surrounding Clayoquot Sound contains over 600,000 acres of untouched stands of fir, cedar, and spruce trees. Logging and the forest products industries have always been a mainstay of the British Columbia economy and have dominated its politics as well. In April 1993, then premier Michael Harcourt announced a plan that would protect one-third of Clayoquot, allow limited logging on an additional 17 percent, and extensive but "managed" harvesting on the remaining half. In this way, it was hoped, the region would be seen as a model of peaceful coexistence between timber and environmental interests. That has not happened.

Past logging in the province has often been environmentally disastrous. British Columbia's relatively lax regulations, which are weaker than those in the United States, have reportedly gone unenforced. Large clearcut areas have caused mudslides on treeless slopes, and rain-swept mud has destroyed salmon spawning grounds in nearby streams. Although some areas have been replanted, many have not, and well-publicized pictures of denuded hillsides and dead streams have not helped the government, which owns 95 percent of forested lands.

After attempts at negotiating a compromise between timber and environmental interests failed, the provincial government unilaterally imposed a "settlement" in the spring of 1994. That settlement kept the protected one-third of Clayoquot, slightly reduced the amount that could be logged extensively, and imposed more rigid multipurpose restrictions on the remainder, where logging would be allowed,

486

but only if it could still meet requirements for preserving recreation, wildlife, and scenic values. The plan would also almost double stumpage (cutting) fees paid to the government.

Not surprisingly, the government was excoriated by everyone. Environmentalists complained that the compromise plan would still destroy far too much old-growth forest and called for international consumer boycotts of British Columbia forest products worth some U.S. $7.5 billion annually. Timber interests protested that the plan would wipe out thousands of jobs. No doubt, Clayoquot will ultimately be logged; how much and how soon are still to be decided.

How can a forest be "managed"? Or is a "managed forest" an oxymoron? How can the legitimate needs for wood and wood products be met while also providing diverse environmental, recreational, and even social benefits that forests supply? These are difficult questions, in part because there are questions as to the "benefits" that Clayoquot provides and who has the rights to those benefits.

Any given tree can be replanted. Left alone for several hundred or more years, it can become "old growth" just as well as a tree growing in a forest that has never been disturbed. Unfortunately, humans in technologically based societies have generally not shown a preference for such long-term horizons. Furthermore, rather than cutting a single tree hither and yon, we have tended to cut whole swaths, leaving forests no more than a collection of stumps. This is less costly than selecting individual trees for harvest and has contributed to the low relative cost of wood and paper products, which have provided many benefits to many individuals.

Increasingly, there is a demand for "multiple-use" management of forests. This type of management recognizes that forests provide a multitude of goods and services, including goods and services when left undisturbed. A critical issue, therefore, is how to allocate forests to meet the demands for these multiple uses and how best to manage forests to provide the largest net value. That cannot be done until it is also determined what all of the uses are and who owns the rights to those uses.

In the case of Clayoquot, several arguments have been made. Some are persuasive; others are less so. Perhaps the least persuasive arguments have been those urging logging for the sake of jobs. Even though loggers, with good reason, consider jobs an important "use," society should not. Forests no more exist to create jobs for loggers than schools exist to create jobs for school bus drivers. But never cutting any trees would fail to use a valuable resource that is renewable. And bitter court battles would seem to benefit no one.

The fight over Clayoquot, like those over the world's other old-growth forests, will continue as long as benefits and rights are unclear. Multiple-use forestry may mean specialization of different forests; some will be best suited to provide timber, while others will be best suited to provide recreation, biodiversity, and carbon sinks. The British Columbia government's solution left all parties with less than they sought but perhaps more than they might otherwise have.

INTRODUCTION

Unlike minerals and crude oil, many resources can regenerate themselves, if given the chance. Unfortunately, a legacy of barren rivers where once fish battled for space and scarred and eroding mountains where once forests grew thick are but two ugly reminders that such chances are not always forthcoming. Depletion of such *renewable* resources is a major environmental policy issue: spending to restore endangered Columbia River salmon has run into the hundreds of millions of dollars each year, and concern over destruction of the rain forest has encompassed everything from the loss of potentially valuable species to destruction of native people's habitat to changes in the earth's climate. Are renewable resources being depleted out of ignorance or just simple greed? Should all renewable resources be owned by society, rather than left in private hands? What sorts of policies can restore renewable resources and maintain them?

In this chapter, we explore these policy issues. We begin with trees and examine the factors that determine typical "optimal" planting and harvesting cycles. We incorporate the fact that trees have value not only as timber for someone's house or paper for textbooks but also left alone standing in forests. Unlike other renewable resources, such as ocean fisheries, trees often are privately owned. We examine how ownership differences can affect harvesting rates and explore the consequences of forests that can supply a multitude of environmental benefits. Because harvesting decisions can depend critically on discount rates, we also return to the controversial policy issue of the appropriate discount rate, a major concern with some authors who wish to develop environmentally "sustainable" harvesting.[1]

Next, we turn to fisheries resources, which we briefly introduced in Chapter 6. Unlike forests, almost all major fisheries are open-access, or at least common-property, resources. And unlike forests, there is far more uncertainty associated with stock levels, for keeping track of what moves about under the ocean is far more difficult than surveying what remains standing on land. Nevertheless, there are numerous policies that can be used to manage such common-property resources efficiently.

DETERMINING OPTIMAL HARVESTING RATES

Unlike stocks of depletable resources, such as oil and copper, stocks of renewable resources such as trees can be increased over time. However, there will be some finite level beyond which any given stocks of renewable resources cannot increase. The forest biomass on an acre of land will be limited by the amount of light and nutrients available for new trees. At high levels of biomass, disease, decay, and accidents start to catch up to the rate of new growth. Similarly, fisheries stocks will

---

[1]We take up sustainability in Chapter 19.

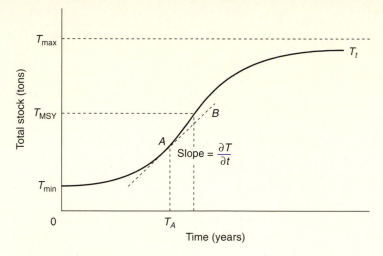

Figure 16.1 Logistic Growth Curve for a Biomass Stock

be limited by available food and the impacts of predators. The greater the number of fish, the more predation will occur.

To examine optimal harvesting rates for a self-renewing biological resource, we begin with a typical *growth curve,* as shown in Figure 16.1. At low levels of biomass, the stock will increase at an increasing rate over time. When biomass is low, as with a stand of young trees or a thinned-out population of trees or fish, the growth rate is low because either there are too few individuals to capture all the resources available for growth (e.g., light, nutrients), there is a low reproductive rate, or both. At some point, however, the rate of increase will begin falling until eventually a maximum level of the stock will be reached.[2] This maximum stock value sometimes is called the *carrying capacity* (Pearce and Turner 1990).

The growth curve T_t has a logistic shape. At any point on the curve, the growth rate is the slope of a line tangent to the curve. Thus at time T_A, the growth rate corresponds to $\partial T / \partial t$ at point A. The maximum biomass, T_{max}, will be determined by the carrying capacity of the environment. The minimum stock, T_{min}, corresponds to a minimum self-sustaining population. If harvesting occurs below this point, the population will be too small to reproduce successfully.

If we call the rate of growth in biomass $F(T)$ and plot it against the total biomass stock, we can determine the *maximum sustainable yield* (*MSY*). *MSY* represents the maximum harvest per unit of time that is possible while keeping the total biomass constant. Thus, at *MSY*, the net annual growth is being harvested each year. This is shown in Figure 16.2, where the stock level T_{MSY} corresponds to the maximum sustainable yield at point B. This also corresponds to point B in Figure 16.1, where the slope of the growth curve is steepest.

---

[2]In some cases, as with trees, it may also make sense to refer to the volume of the resource, rather than simply the number.

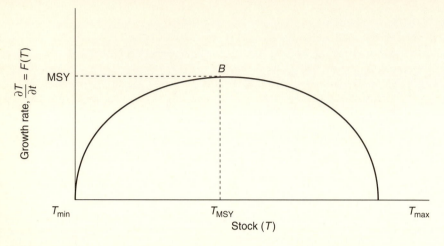

Figure 16.2 Growth Curve and Maximum Sustainable Yield

Optimal Harvest Rates I: Optimal Stock in the Long Run

It is tempting to conclude that *MSY* is the optimal level of harvest and that stocks should be maintained at the level that will support *MSY*. After all, if a renewable resource is harvested at that rate, it will not diminish over time. As it turns out, however, *MSY* generally will *not* be the optimal harvest rate.

There is one hypothetical case where *MSY* is optimal. Suppose that we can pick any stock level between T_{min} and T_{max}, but then we have to maintain that stock forever. Any harvest level below *MSY* is suboptimal in this case because we can harvest more. No harvest level above *MSY* is feasible because it cannot be sustained.

Of course, in real life, we cannot choose the initial stock level, and we can allow the stock to change over time. We can allow a renewable resource stock to grow by harvesting less than the natural increase. We can reduce the stock over time by harvesting more than the natural increase. Just as with an exhaustible resource, we face an *intertemporal choice*. Consuming more leaves a lower stock for the future; consuming less leaves a larger stock. The only difference is that the stock replaces itself and can grow over time.

If the stock we have inherited is less than the optimal stock, there should be an incentive to allow the stock to grow. If the stock is more than optimal, there should be an incentive to reduce the stock. If the stock happens to be optimal, there should be no incentive to change it. Put another way, the incentives to use and preserve the resource stock should be in balance when the stock is optimal. We can look at this balance of incentives by looking at the costs and returns from harvesting the resource stock.

Define the harvest rate as *H*, with the optimal harvest rate given by *H**. Harvesting is not free. The cost of harvesting a resource often depends on both the amount harvested and the stock of the resource. It is easier to cut a given volume of timber from a forest if the trees are larger and there are more of them. Similarly, it is easier to catch a given weight of fish if there are more fish (so that less time has to be spent looking for them) and if the fish are larger. Because of this, the cost function for harvesting biological resources is often broken into two parts. One is a relationship between harvest and *effort*. The other is the cost of a unit of effort.

We will assume that effort, E, is a function of the amount harvested, H, and the stock, T. Thus we can write the total effort expended for harvesting as $E(H,T)$. We assume that effort has a constant unit cost, ω. The total cost of harvesting will be given by $\omega E(H,T)$.

The net revenue from harvesting the resource is π, which can be written as

$$\pi(H) = P/H - \omega E(H,T) \tag{16.1}$$

where P equals the price per unit harvested. The present value of net revenue from harvesting H forever, while maintaining the stock T, is

$$\frac{\pi}{r} = \frac{PH}{r} - \frac{\omega E(H,T)}{r} \tag{16.2}^3$$

Reducing the current harvest will have a cost in terms of forgone current net revenues. It will also have a benefit in terms of a larger stock, which will allow greater future harvests and reduce the effort needed for any future harvest level. The cost of a marginal increase in future stocks is the sacrifice of current harvest needed to achieve it. This is determined by the inverse of the marginal rate of natural increase, $1/F'(T)$. Thus the cost of a marginal increase in future stocks is as follows:

$$\frac{\partial\pi/\partial H}{F'(T)} = \frac{P - \omega(\partial E/\partial H)}{F'(T)} \tag{16.3}$$

The value of a marginal increase in future stock is just the present value of the change in net revenue that would be made possible by a larger stock:

$$\frac{\partial(\pi/r)}{\partial T} = -\frac{\omega}{r}\frac{\partial E}{\partial T} \tag{16.4}$$

The optimal stock is the one where the cost and the value of a marginal increase in the stock are just equal:

$$-\frac{\omega}{r}\frac{\partial E}{\partial T} = \frac{P - \omega(\partial E/\partial H)}{F'(T)} \tag{16.5}$$

---

[3]Equation 16.2 can be derived by noting that the present value of an infinite payment stream is just the nominal payment stream divided by the discount rate.

This can be rearranged to give

$$F'\left(\frac{-\omega\,\partial E/\partial T}{P-\omega\,\partial E/\partial H}\right)=r \qquad (16.6)$$

This is a striking but intuitively appealing result when you think about it. The slope of the growth curve, which can be thought of as the physical rate of return on an investment in the resource stock, must be proportional to the rate of interest. The numerator of the term in parentheses is the value of the reduction in effort made possible by a marginal increase in the stock. The denominator is price less marginal harvesting cost. Thus this term accounts for the fact that the per-unit value of the physical stock changes with the stock. A larger stock means lower harvesting costs, all else being equal, but the larger sustained harvest made possible by a larger stock means higher marginal harvesting cost, all else being equal.

If the interest rate is positive, the optimal long-run stock must be less than the stock that will support the maximum sustainable yield. *MSY* occurs where the slope of the growth function is zero. The slope of the growth function is positive for lower stocks. At stock levels above the optimal stock, including the *MSY* stock, the rate of return on the resource stock is lower than the rate of return on other assets. Therefore, it is economically rational to shift part of society's stock of assets out of a low-yielding biological asset and into other higher-yielding assets. This can be done by harvesting more than the natural increase each period until the optimal stock is reached. If the actual stock inherited from the past is less than the optimal stock, the rate of return on the biological asset is greater than the rate of return offered by society's other assets, and it makes sense to invest in the resource stock by harvesting less than the natural increase for several periods until the stock has risen to the optimal level.

At first glance, there may seem to be a conflict between economic efficiency and intergenerational equity here. On the face of it, starting with a resource stock that would sustain MSY indefinitely and intentionally reducing it appears to be unfair to future generations because it reduces the yield that will be available to them. This would be true only if society had no other assets. In fact, there need not be any conflict between efficiency and equity because the two impose different, though interacting, requirements. Intergenerational equity is concerned with the amount of assets we pass on to future generations. In this case, economic efficiency is concerned with the mix of assets. Economic efficiency demands that if trees or fish give a rate of return lower than other assets, we should shift part of the wealth we have in trees or fish into other assets until we have equalized the rate of return on all of them. Intergenerational equity demands that if we reduce the stocks of trees or fish because their rates of return are too low, we reinvest the proceeds in other, higher-yielding assets rather than consume them.

Optimal Harvest Rates II: A Commercial Forest

Commercial timber is more often managed like a crop than like a wild forest. Trees are planted, harvested, and replanted in rotations. Seedlings are planted, left to grow, and harvested. Then the cycle can begin over again. We wish to determine what will be the optimal planting and harvesting cycle and how that solution will differ from a case where the forest will be harvested only once.

In the case of private ownership, the owner of the forest will want to maximize the present discounted value of profits. We know intuitively that as the trees grow, the value of the harvest will increase.[4] *The owner will wish to harvest when the rate of increase in the value of the trees is just equal to his opportunity cost of capital.* Suppose that the best alternative for the owner would be investing the money he receives from selling his trees and putting it into a bank account earning 5 percent interest. If the value of his stand of trees is increasing 10 percent per year, he will not harvest. However, he will harvest when the value of the trees is growing at 5 percent. This is a fundamental result that can explain much of the environmental controversy over cutting down forests.

The optimal harvesting decision will also depend on whether the owner intends to replant. If the forest is to be replanted, it will be harvested sooner than if it is not to be replanted. Initially, this seems counterintuitive. After all, whether or not the forest is to be replanted, won't the owner harvest when the increase in the value of the trees to be cut equals the opportunity cost? The answer is yes, but the opportunity costs in the two cases differ.

The difference arises from the cost of delaying replanting. If the owner does not intend to replant, the cost of delay is zero. If the owner intends to replant, however, there is an additional opportunity cost associated with delaying replanting. By not harvesting, the owner delays the time when he will be able to replant and then harvest the next cycle. (You can think of this additional opportunity cost as the present discounted value of net benefits from the next cycle.)

A further complication occurs when we consider that forests may have a standing value. That is, if we assume that the forest provides other benefits of value, such as biodiversity or recreational benefits, the optimal harvesting decision changes. Of course, given sufficiently high nontimber benefits, the optimal course of action may be never to harvest (Hartman 1976; Strang 1982; Bowes and Krutilla 1985). These nontimber benefits can include recreational benefits afforded hikers and campers, the species diversity provided by old-growth forests, and scenic values. A further difficulty can arise because these nontimber benefits have significant public good aspects that a private owner may not account for. For environmental policymakers, the difficulty becomes one of measuring these nontimber benefits and, if they are external benefits, internalizing them to the harvesting decision.[5] We will discuss these policy implications later in the chapter.

The Mathematical Solution†   To make the mathematics tractable, assume that we begin with a stand of seedlings that has just been planted. When harvest time comes, all of the trees will be harvested. Then the planting-harvesting cycle

---

[4]We assume that the price of the harvested lumber remains constant over time.
[5]This will be especially difficult when addressing external benefits that have both intergenerational equity and efficiency aspects, such as biodiversity.

will begin once again. Thus the cost of replanting for the next cycle occurs at the same time that revenue is received from this cycle. Let the cost to harvest and replant be C. Let P equal the known price of the timber harvested. The amount of timber that will be harvested is a function of timber growth over time, which we denote as $A(t)$, where t refers to time. The revenues from selling timber of any age t therefore will equal $PA(t)$. We assume that the tree's growth rate declines with age so that A is concave downward. The landowner seeks to maximize the present discounted value of profits from timber sales. Thus the problem can be stated as

$$\pi = \max_{T} \sum_{i=1}^{\infty} [PA(t) - C]e^{-i\rho T} \tag{16.8}$$

What Equation 16.8 says is that we repeat the plant-harvest cycle an infinite number of times, each time waiting T years before harvesting. The factor $e^{-i\rho T}$ is just the discount rate ρ applied continuously over T years.[6] Writing out the infinite series in Equation 16.8 and simplifying, we have

$$\pi = \max_{T} \frac{PA(t) - C}{e^{\rho T} - 1} \tag{16.9}$$

To determine the maximum value for Equation 16.9, we differentiate with respect to T and set the result equal to zero:

$$\frac{\partial \pi}{\partial T} = \frac{PA'(t)}{e^{\rho T} - 1} - \rho e^{\rho T} \frac{PA(t) - C}{(e^{\rho T} - 1)^2} = 0 \tag{16.10}$$

Simplifying Equation 16.10, it must be the case that

$$PA'(T^*) = \frac{\rho(e^{\rho T^*} - 1)[PA(T^*) - C]}{e^{\rho T^*} - 1} \tag{16.11}$$

or

$$\frac{PA'(T^*)}{PA(T^*) - C} = \frac{\rho}{1 - e^{-\rho T^*}} \tag{16.12}[7]$$

Again, Equations 16.11 and 16.12 state that the optimal time T^* to harvest will be when the rate of change in the value of the stand of trees equals the interest that could be received on the value of the harvest plus the capitalized value of an infi-

---

[6] The relationship between a continuous discount rate and a discrete rate can be seen by setting $(1/1 + r)^t = e^{-\rho T}$. Taking logarithms of both sides and solving for ρ, we have $\rho = \log_e(1 + r)$. As long as r is below 10 percent, ρ will be quite close to it.

[7] This is known as the Faustmann solution, after the forester who originally developed this model in 1849.

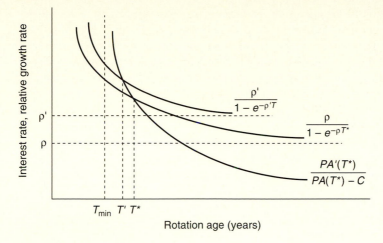

Figure 16.3   Optimal Harvest Timing

nite stream of deferred harvest receipts less deferred planting costs. This is shown graphically in Figure 16.3.

The curve labeled $\rho/(1 - e^{-\rho T^*})$ slopes downward. As T^* approaches infinity, this curve approaches a limiting value equal to ρ. The left side of Equation 16.12 is the relative growth rate in revenues at the time of harvest. As the discount rate increases, the forgone revenues from the interest on the value of the stand that could be received increases, lowering the optimal rotation age. Graphically, the curve labeled $\rho/(1 - e^{-\rho T^*})$ will shift upward to $\rho'/(1 - e^{-\rho' T})$, lowering the optimal rotation age to T'.

Within each cycle, the trees will be left to grow only as long as they are appreciating fast enough to justify delaying the revenue that will be received from harvesting them and from all succeeding harvests. With a higher discount rate, this will occur when the stand is younger. As the cost of harvesting and replanting, C, increases or the price, P, decreases, the curve $PA'(T^*)/[PA(T^*) - C]$ will shift upward. This will tend to lengthen the rotations. A lower P or higher C will reduce the present value of net revenues to be earned after the completion of the first cycle. This makes it worthwhile to delay the time when the higher future returns will be realized in exchange for the higher return in the first cycle that will result from delaying the harvest.

A Few Difficulties Associated with Reality   Although the mathematics and intuition associated with the standard solution just presented may be straightforward, reality provides far more difficult issues. Our model simplifies things. First, future prices will be uncertain; the demand and supply for timber will have unknown elements, including policies that may significantly affect timber supplies. For example, in late 1994, much public forestland in the United States Pacific Northwest was set aside as habitat for spotted owls under the Endangered Species

Act. This has reduced the availability of timber from that region and increased the price of wood products. Whereas a higher *constant* price for timber will tend to shorten the rotation, an *uncertain* future price that tends to increase may either shorten or lengthen rotation, depending on the *expected* rate of increase as well as the "riskiness" of future price streams. The owner of a timber stand may believe that future environmental policies will reduce the supply of timber even more, thus increasing the owner's potential profits if he waits to harvest. Or those same environmental policies may mean that that owner will be unable to harvest his timber, which would tend to encourage him to "cut and run."

Harvesting and replanting costs may also change over time. Technological innovation will tend to reduce harvesting and replanting costs, which will tend to decrease the rotation cycle. Curiously, however, if the cost of replanting and harvest is zero, the rotation age will be independent of timber price and equal to T_{min}, as shown in Figure 16.3. This makes sense if you think about it a moment. If it costs nothing to harvest or replant, the owner will want to harvest when the relative growth rate of the trees just equals the interest rate, regardless of the price of timber.

Multiple-Use Forests†

Until now, we have assumed that forests serve one purpose only: to provide timber. In reality, forests provide a variety of benefits, including recreation, carbon storage, and improved biodiversity. The problem with many of these benefits, like most public goods, is that there is no clear price for them.[8] How should these other uses be accounted for, and how do they affect the optimal rotation schedule? Indeed, given these other uses, should the forest ever be harvested? This is an increasingly important policy question, especially as tracts of old-growth forests (forests that have never been harvested) are gazed on longingly by persons seeking the highest-quality wood.

To address these issues, we begin with Equation 16.9 and add a term reflecting the discounted value of these other amenity benefits. The owner's problem will be to select the rotation age that maximizes profits:

$$\pi = \max_{T} \left\{ \frac{PA(t) - C}{e^{\rho T} - 1} + \int_0^T [B(t)e^{-\rho t}]\, dt \right\} \qquad (16.13)$$

where $B(t)$ equals the value of amenity benefits at any time t.[9] The integral in Equation 16.13 reflects the continuous stream of those amenity benefits. As with

---

[8]It may be possible to develop new market mechanisms to convey information about the value of those benefits. For example, owners of a forest might wish to sell recreation benefits through some sort of admission fee. In that case, there would be a measurable price.

[9]Equation 16.13 really begins with Equation 16.8, the summation of discounted other-use benefits. We have simplified by applying the same reduction technique of the infinite series as we did to derive Equation 16.9.

Equation 16.9, to determine the preferred rotational age T, we differentiate Equation 16.13 with respect to T. A sufficient amount of tedious mathematics leads to a solution analogous to Equation 16.12:

$$(1 - \alpha)\left[\frac{B(\tilde{T})}{\int_0^{\tilde{T}} [B(t)e^{-\rho t}] \, dt}\right] + \alpha\left[\frac{PA'(\tilde{T})}{PA(\tilde{T}) - C}\right] = \frac{\rho}{1 - e^{-\rho\tilde{T}}} \qquad (16.14)^{[10]}$$

The first term in Equation 16.14 captures the amenity benefits associated with the stand, and the second term in brackets is the same as that in Equation 16.12. If the amenity benefits increase with the age of the stand, $\tilde{T}$ will be greater than T^*. That this is so can be shown by noting that if $B(t)$ increases in t—that is, $B'(t) > 0$—then $\int_0^{\tilde{T}} [B(T)e^{-\rho t}] \, dt > \int_0^{\tilde{T}} [B(t)e^{-\rho t}] \, dt$ because $B(\tilde{T}) > B(t)$ for all $t < \tilde{T}$. However,

$$\int_0^{\tilde{T}} [B(\tilde{T})e^{-\rho t}] \, dt = B(\tilde{T}) \int_0^{\tilde{T}} e^{-\rho t} \, dt = B(\tilde{T}) \frac{1 - e^{-\rho\tilde{T}}}{\rho} > \int_0^{\tilde{T}} [B(T)e^{-\rho t}] \, dt$$

Thus

$$\frac{B(\tilde{T})}{\int_0^{\tilde{T}} [B(t)e^{-\rho t}] \, dt} > \frac{\rho}{1 - e^{-\rho\tilde{T}}} \qquad (16.15)$$

Therefore, from Equation 16.14, it must be the case that $\tilde{T} > T^*$. Similarly, it can be shown that if amenity values decrease with age, as could be the case if the primary amenity were wildlife habitat, the optimal rotation age will be smaller than T^*. If the amenity value grows sufficiently fast with age, $\tilde{T}$ may be infinite. In other words, it may never make economic sense to harvest the stand. Of course, this assumes that the landowner can capture the nonamenity benefits. Unfortunately, that is unlikely, as amenity benefits will include pure public goods such as carbon storage and biodiversity, and exclusion costs may be high for other benefits.

Multiple Use, Rotation Age, and an Existing Stand   The foregoing analyses assumed that the stand of timber was planted at time zero. What happens when there is a mature stand at time zero, such as old-growth forest? How does this affect the rotational age? Strang (1982) addressed this issue by modifying Hartman's (1976) analysis. Strang showed that it would be possible for the optimum rotation age to be infinite if there were a mature stand at time zero, even though a finite rotation age would be optimal if the land were initially bare.

Because the mathematics is similar to the preceding case (although a little more tedious), we won't repeat the derivation. We know intuitively, however, that Equation 16.13 will change with the addition of $B(0)$, the initial amenity value. $B(0)$ will also increase over time, although perhaps at a decreasing rate. Thus the

---

[10]For a derivation, see Hartman (1976).

owner must decide if the returns $B(t)$ are large enough that they will always exceed the returns from cutting the stand and then replanting in the future. If $B(0)$ is sufficiently large, it will make sense never to cut the stand.

Of course, it is unlikely that a forest owner would plant a stand of commercial timber and, when it is mature, decide to leave it standing for the amenity values rather than harvest it. Unless the owner can sell these amenity benefits, he will realize no revenues from the public good benefits he provides. The policy trick is to develop methods that allow forest owners to exploit these public benefits, as with some sort of admission fee for recreationists or perhaps some form of tax break for providing biodiversity.

Multiple Use and Specialization   So far, we have confined our discussion to one stand of trees. We showed that under certain conditions, the presence of other amenity benefits could change the decision to harvest and, in some cases, even preclude harvest all together. The presumption has been that any given stand would provide multiple benefits. This was recognized officially in passage of the Multiple-Use Sustained Yield Act of 1960. That act mandated that the U.S. Forest Service adopt a multiple-use philosophy. Unfortunately, the act did not provide guidance for the implementation of such a policy. This situation was remedied slightly in 1964, when the Wilderness Act was passed. That act designated tracts of national forests as wilderness and imposed stringent rules restricting their use, including the prohibition of timber harvesting. For the most part, however, the U.S. Forest Service has pursued policies promoting multiple uses down to the individual-stand level.

Vincent and Binkley (1993), however, show that specialization can make more sense for individual stands. So even if an entire forest may provide multiple benefits, individual stands may be designated as providing timber only, recreation only, biodiversity only, and so on. They also show that specialization can be appropriate even when individual stands in a forest are identical. Vincent and Binkley's results have potentially important policy implications, as they contradict established forestry practices and some suggested new practices that protect biodiversity (Franklin 1989; Behan 1990).

To see why specialization can make sense, consider the following. Suppose that a stand produces only two goods, timber (T) and a nontimber amenity (A). There is a production possibilities frontier (*PPF*) associated with this stand, as shown in Figure 16.4. Given the shape of this frontier, the optimal quantities of timber and the nontimber amenity are T^* and A^*, respectively. These quantities are determined by the relative prices of T and A.

Next, assume that there are two identical stands, each capable of producing only T and A. However, the owner of the two stands can allocate a fixed amount of management effort between the two, where management effort is positively related to production of both timber and the nontimber amenity. For example, increased effort could improve recreational opportunities in a stand, with development of nature trails. Or more effort could be put into harvesting additional timber. As management effort is allocated between the stands, different quantities of T and A may be produced in each. This is shown in Figure 16.5.

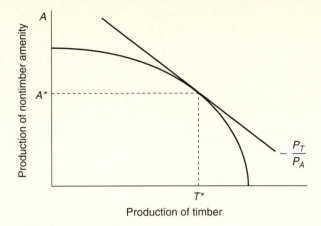

Figure 16.4   Production Possibilities Frontier for Timber and
Nontimber Amenity.

Source: Adapted from Vincent and Binkley (1993), p. 373.

In Figure 16.5, the initial (and identical) frontiers are given by PPF^*. Given
the relative prices P_T and P_A for timber and nontimber amenities, respectively,
point X^* along PPF^* represents the production mix with the highest value. At this
point, the specialization ratio of timber to nontimber amenity production in each
stand is given by T^*/A^*, with corresponding value ratio $P_T T^*/P_A A^*$. Implicit in this
level of production is an identical amount of effort, E^*, devoted to each stand.
Total production of nontimber amenities equals $2A^*$, and total production of timber equals $2T^*$.

Suppose, however, that the level of effort is differentiated between two stands.
Assume that the level of effort is reduced in stand 1 to E_1 and increased in stand 2 to

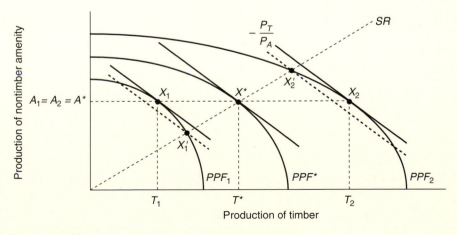

Figure 16.5   Specialization Among Multiple Stands

Source: Adapted from Vincent and Binkley (1993), p. 374.

E_2. This will result in the *PPF* for stand 1 shifting inward to PPF_1 and shifting outward for stand 2 to PPF_2. If the specialization ratio remains constant, production will be along the ray *SR*, at points X_1' and X_2', respectively. This is not the optimal level of production, since at the relative price P_T/P_A, points X_1' and X_2' are not tangent to their respective *PPF*. The tangency points occur at points X_1 and X_2. As a result, stand 1 tends to produce relatively more nontimber amenities, and stand 2 produces relatively more timber. Total production of nontimber amenities remains constant at $2A*$, but as drawn, total timber production increases.[11] Thus, even though the forest produces multiple goods, production in each stand tends to become specialized.[12]

FISHERIES MANAGEMENT

We began this chapter by looking at the renewable resource problem in fairly general terms. We were interested in the economic implications of having a self-renewing asset—one that yields a physical return if left to itself. With forestry, we have been looking at the decisions a value-maximizing manager would make when dealing with a known stock with a well-understood growth function. With fisheries, we have a different set of concerns. We still want to know how to manage fisheries optimally, but property rights to most fish stocks are poorly defined, and we should not expect them to be managed optimally. In addition, wild fish stocks are notoriously uncertain. Stocks at any time can only be estimated, not known, and many fish populations experience wide fluctuations. In many cases, the causes of these fluctuations are not well understood and are therefore difficult to predict. Thus here we will be more concerned with these issues and with ways to make fisheries more economically efficient.[13]

The origin of modern fisheries economics is the seminal article by Gordon (1954).[14] Gordon developed a static (time-independent) model of a fishery. His fishery model is best thought of as showing a long-run equilibrium between fishing effort and fish stocks. It is shown in Figure 16.6, where revenues are a function of the number of fish caught and costs are a function of fishing effort. Total cost is a linear function of effort shown by the line $TC = \omega E$. Total revenue is price times the catch, which depends on effort and the stock. However, in the long run, the stock of fish depends on the fishing effort aimed at it. More effort leads to a smaller stock in the long run. This gives the long-run relationship between effort and harvest, and therefore revenue, shown by the curve *TR*. At low levels of effort, stocks are large, and a marginal increase in effort results in a larger fraction of the

---

[11]This result is a consequence of the shape of the *PPF* curves in Figure 16.5. In actuality, it illustrates the concept of comparative advantage. See Vincent (1993) and Vincent and Binkley (1993) for a more detailed exposition.

[12]Using similar models, many questions about harvest rates, maximum yields, and optimal specialization can be addressed. See Bowes and Krutilla (1985) for further derivations and discussions.

[13]Parts of this discussion are adapted from Munro and Scott (1985).

[14]See also Crutchfield (1956) and the bibliography in Miles, Pealy, and Stokes (1986).

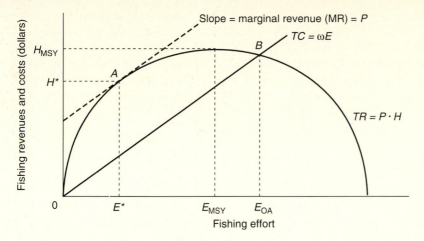

Figure 16.6   Profit-Maximizing Level of Fishing Effort and Profit Dissipation

stock being caught with only a small reduction in the equilibrium stock. At high levels of effort, the opposite occurs. A marginal increase in effort produces a significant relative reduction in the equilibrium stock and a smaller catch. Effort beyond some point will drive the stock to extinction.

The profit-maximizing level of fishing effort is given by E^*, which gives the equilibrium harvest H^*. This level of effort reflects the tangency of marginal revenue and marginal cost curves. A privately owned fishery able to restrict access would produce at this level. If the fishery is subject to open access, additional fishing effort will be expended until all profits are exhausted. That is, additional effort will be expended as long as the average cost of that effort is less than the average revenue to be gained. This occurs at the point labeled B.

Policy Responses

Munro and Scott (1985) distinguish between two types of common-property problems. The first, which they call a Class I common-property problem, is the result of complete nonregulation of a fishery: unlimited numbers of fishermen are allowed to compete for an unconstrained number of fish. The policy responses that have tried to address Class I problems and the resulting fisheries depletion fall into several categories. In general, these policies have tried either to increase harvesting (i.e., increase ω), to restrict access, or do both. If harvesting costs are increased, the TC line in Figure 16.6 will rotate upward. Total fishing effort will be reduced, as will total fisheries harvest. One way to increase costs is to restrict the available technologies that can be used for harvesting. For example, banning huge drift nets increases the cost of catching fish. In the limit, one could insist that all fish be caught individually with rod and reel or with spears, although it is doubtful that such rules could be enforced on the high seas. Nor is it clear that the benefits from reducing the overall harvest would be greater than the costs of significantly reducing supplies of an important world protein source. Restricting access is another time-tested policy response, although it, too, can be difficult to enforce. For example, to address overfishing off the U.S.-Canadian coast, both countries established 200 mile "exclusive economic zones."

The second type of common-property problem identified by Munro and Scott (1985) is called a Class II problem. In Class II situations, fisheries effort is not regulated, but the total catch is limited.[15] In these situations, profits will be dissipated because too many fishermen will seek a fixed number of fish. One obvious policy solution is to combine harvest limits with mechanisms that increase harvest costs.

Multispecies Fisheries

Unlike the models we have discussed so far, most fisheries are home to a number of species. The Georges Bank, for example, which lies east of Cape Cod, is one of the most productive fisheries in the entire world partly because of the variety of species that can be caught there (Pontecorvo 1986). How can such multispecies fisheries be managed effectively? How can models determine optimal harvesting rates, for example, in the presence of extremely complex, and perhaps unknown, biological relationships among the species? Some species, such as sardines and anchovies, may compete for limited food supplies. Some species, such as cod in the Georges Bank preying on capelin, may prey on other species and then be preyed on themselves, as cod are by seals. Prey may even be a predator at different life stages: capelin, for example, are believed to prey on cod eggs (Munro and Scott 1985).

Clark (1988) developed a simple dynamic model, assuming that there existed one species each of predator and prey. Because even this simplified model involves mathematics beyond the scope of this text, we merely frame the model structure and discuss its results. Suppose that the two species are to be harvested. The problem is to determine the optimal rates of harvest. If the prey is harvested too fast, the stock of the predator will decrease because the latter's food supply will have been reduced. Does this mean that the optimal policy will be to drive the predator species to extinction so that the stock of the prey will increase? Not necessarily, not only because the predator species may be more valuable than the prey, but also because of biological uncertainties in the predator-prey relationship. And as we have discussed in other chapters, there may be strong moral components to species preservation, regardless of a species' "economic" value.

In any case, maximization of the net present value of profits will depend on the relative prices of the two species, the stocks over time, and the relative costs of harvest. All of these may be interdependent. For example, the per-unit cost of harvesting North Atlantic cod may increase if there are fewer capelin. A reduced supply of cod will tend to increase the price of cod, which will encourage expending greater effort in harvesting it. But if capelin are feeding on cod eggs, increased har-

---

[15]This includes setting total allowable catches as well as "escapement targets," which are targets with respect to the number of fish allowed to escape the fishermen and be free to spawn. For a discussion of the former, see Scott (1986) and Stokes (1986). Another approach is to restrict the number of fishermen, as well as the total catch. All of these methods establish differing types of property rights.

vesting of cod will reduce the supply of the next generation of cod, and so forth. As Clark (1988, pp. 319–323) shows, determining the "optimal" harvest rates for many of these problems, even simple ones such as in his model, can be difficult or impossible. In essence, the problem can be thought of as managing a "portfolio" of resources, much as one manages a portfolio of stocks and bonds. The value of stocks and bonds can be correlated, as can the value of different species. Ideally, the fisheries portfolio "manager" will want to hold a set of "assets" so that the marginal rate of return on each asset is identical. To do this, Clark advocated development of "practical" approaches to multispecies fisheries management, rather than complex and unworkable but "perfect" approaches.

POLICY ISSUES

The models of forests and fisheries we have examined have two uses for policymakers. They point out areas where policymakers may want to take action or to refrain from interfering with existing behavior. Models can also guide policymakers in setting particular policies, such as license fees or harvest quotas, if the policymakers have information on the model's parameter values. Often policymakers must make decisions with limited information. Real forests and real fisheries are complex. Both are part of dynamic ecosystems that continually change and respond to outside forces. Tree growth, for example, will be affected by changes in yearly weather patterns.

Fisheries can pose even more complex problems for the simple reason that it is difficult to observe them directly. Policies must be developed in the presence of significant uncertainty. Furthermore, enforcing policies that manage fisheries can be far more costly than enforcing forest management policies. Monitoring the behavior of fishing boats on the high seas is extremely difficult, owing to the sheer magnitude of the task. Finally, the goals of forest and fisheries management may extend beyond profit maximization. Each can provide significant nonmarket benefits, such as recreation and biodiversity. Thus policies designed to ensure profit maximization may be inconsistent with capture of nonmarket benefits.

Dealing with Uncertainty

Regulatory policies designed to enhance the productivity and value of fisheries must confront problems of uncertainty. In addition to the usual problems of uncertainty over future prices, fisheries management must address uncertainty of the resources themselves. Managing trees, which are easily seen and tend not to move, is one thing; managing salmon, whose precise number and whereabouts are rarely known, is far more difficult.

What does this mean for effective fisheries management policies? First, the likelihood of unintended "surprises" is more likely (Munro and Scott 1985). The collapse of the Grand Banks cod fishery in the early 1990s, for example, could not be predicted precisely, even though the evidence of overfishing was clear. Second, the optimal form of fisheries management will be far harder to predict.

A steady-state fishery, where the harvest remains constant, for example, may not be optimal or even possible.

Walters and Hilborn (1978) classify uncertainty into three categories, from least difficult to address to most difficult:

1. Random effects whose future occurrence can be determined from past experience
2. Parameter uncertainty that can be reduced by additional research and information gathering
3. Ignorance about the appropriate variables to consider and appropriate model forms

In the easiest cases, we can derive a model of optimal harvesting analogous to the optimal timber-harvesting problem. The result is a rule stating that the effort invested in harvest should equate the *expected* return with the appropriate interest rate.[16] This is analogous to the solution we derived in Equation 16.12. As it turns out, the optimal harvest will not necessarily be the same every year, which is what the deterministic model showed in the section, Determining Optimal Harvest Results. Instead, the optimal harvest will depend on the environmental shocks the fishery is experiencing.

Reality, not surprisingly, introduces further complications. Even if a model showed that a specific number of fish, F^*, should be harvested in a given year, determining whether F^* fish were in fact harvested would be prohibitively expensive for any real fishery. Also, there are different types of solutions. One could attempt to stabilize the population of the fishery with a variable harvest; one could also attempt to stabilize the harvest at some lower level; or one could even stabilize the amount of effort (e.g., number of fishing boats, days of harvesting) devoted to the harvest. Each of these solutions represents a different risk-return trade-off, much as our discussion of the capital asset pricing model (CAPM) in Chapter 14 showed a relationship between risk and return of financial assets. And like the CAPM, there is no unique answer, but rather an infinite number of (risk, return) trade-offs along an efficient frontier. How risk-averse, if at all, fisheries harvest decisions should be in the presence of uncertainty is an unanswerable question. Again, it boils down to the development of policy priorities and then trade-offs of those priorities, perhaps using the multiattribute techniques discussed in Chapters 10 and 14.

The Appropriate Discount Rate

All of the models developed in previous sections. maximized the net present value of profits using an assumed discount rate. This raises the question of what discount rate should be used. Individual fishermen may have different discount rates, none of which may be the same as the social rate of time preference (*SRTP*).[17] Higher

---

[16]See Spulber (1986) for the mathematical derivation, which relies on a technique called dynamic programming.

[17]The concept of the *SRTP* is developed in Chapter 13.

discount rates will tend to decrease rotational ages for forests and encourage greater harvesting of fisheries. But policymakers cannot tell foresters or fishermen to use lower discount rates, at least not without eliciting goggle-eyed stares.

For society, *economically efficient* harvesting decisions will require the use of the *SRTP*. Inclusion of multiple policy goals, such as preservation of endangered species, will require alteration of standard efficient harvesting decisions. Determining *how* this can be done will be complicated. One approach would be to examine the sensitivity of optimal harvest decisions to changes in the discount rate. Policymakers could then impose harvest taxes or quotas on fishermen or loggers consistent with the harvest solutions based on the *SRTP*. Safe minimum standards (SMS) could also be developed, as was discussed in Chapter 9.[18]

Promoting "sustainable" harvesting decisions, though an admirable goal, is probably meaningless from a policy perspective until sustainable solutions are operatively defined. Then, what will be most important is to separate efficiency from equity goals, as we discussed in Chapter 13. Even so, there remains great debate over what constitutes "efficiency" in the context of sustainability and thus what the correct discount rate should be.[19]

Our point here is not to provide the "correct" discount rate, although one based on the social rate of time preference is appropriate when considerations of economic efficiency are paramount. Instead, we raise the issue as "truth in advertising": whenever you see models of optimal harvesting decisions that offhandedly refer to the discount rate ρ, ask yourself what that rate ought to be and how, if public and private actors behave as if they are using different discount rates, policies can alter harvesting decisions to mimic economic efficiency solutions more closely.

Renewable Resource Regulation

We have discussed some of the problems associated with management of renewable resources. What approaches have actually been used? What has worked, and what has not? Regulation of fisheries and forests poses different problems because of the different ownership structures. In North America, for example, most forestland is publicly owned by the government. And unfortunately, some of the worst management abuses have occurred on this land, owing to politics and different government agencies' goals.[20]

Regulation of Fisheries   As we have discussed, the vast majority of fisheries are common-property and open-access resources, with almost no private ownership, although private aquaculture (fish farming) is a rapidly growing industry worldwide. How have fisheries been regulated so as to avoid, or at least limit, common-property problems? Traditionally, there have been several approaches,

---

[18]See Howe (1979) for a more extended discussion of the treatment of risk and uncertainty, as well as discounting.

[19]See, for example, Howarth and Norgaard (1993).

[20]An excellent and comprehensive review of U.S. federal lands policy, including national forests, is Clawson (1983).

including control of harvesting capacity, imposed increases in harvesting costs, and establishment of property rights in certain areas, such as coastal zones. More recently, transferable catch quotas have been established for some species.

We have already discussed the control of harvest capacity and increased harvest costs in a general way. Some of the specific regulations might surprise you. Consider salmon in the U.S. Pacific Northwest, especially the Columbia River Basin. The stocks of these salmon had been greatly reduced from the many millions that plied the waters in the 1800s.[21] Even before passage of the Endangered Species Act, the U.S. government attempted to address the problem of declining runs. The government did this by increasing the cost of harvest. It banned the use of traps and barricades in rivers. Then, when these measures proved insufficient because fishermen switched to other methods, such as trolling, the government began to limit fishing and closing certain areas during each year (Crutchfield and Pontecorvo 1969). None of these methods worked. Technological improvements allowed fishermen to catch more salmon. (The government had also tried banning new technologies, including different types of netting that could not be seen by salmon during the day.)[22] Restrictions of the length of the fishing season increased the intensity of fishing effort during the allowed harvest periods. (In some years, for example, the Alaska halibut season lasts just 24 hours. The intensity of effort during that time period is unimaginable.) Most of these regulations were enacted at the request of fishermen, especially those who were well established. Though this result may seem surprising at first, it is consistent with efforts by many groups to restrict entry into their industry or increase the cost of entry.

In 1982, the United Nations Conference on the International Law of the Sea allowed countries to establish coast management zones, now called exclusive economic zones, that extended 200 miles from their shores. The effect was to restrict access to coastal fisheries to coastal states. The new rules had a significant impact, because over 90 percent of total harvests were caught within these zones. The goal was to improve fisheries management by addressing common-property problems, improving management of transboundary fish stocks such as Pacific Coast salmon, and working out agreements between coastal and noncoastal countries.

How well have these approaches worked? The evidence is not encouraging. Canada and the United States continue to squabble over salmon harvests in the Pacific, and several species of Columbia River salmon have been placed on the U.S. endangered species list. Worse, restrictions on harvest technologies and times have provided incentives for fishermen to circumvent those restrictions.

The problem with these regulatory approaches has been their attempts to restrict behavior, of both salmon and fishermen, without instead providing the relevant economic signals (at least for the fishermen). The 200-mile limit, for example, fails to consider that during the time that they live in the Pacific Ocean, salmon

---

[21]Case studies of Columbia River salmon and implications of the Endangered Species Act are presented in Chapters 8 and 9.

[22]In the Alaska fishery, the government banned the use of boats with engines until the 1950s.

whose spawning grounds lie in Canada or the United States do not always restrict themselves to their respective countries' coastal territory. Nor have these regulatory policies approached the issue in a comprehensive manner. Restrictions on harvest do little to help salmon who are either unable to reach their spawning grounds or find those grounds unsuitable because of low water or poor water quality. At the same time, policies designed to increase the survival rates of juvenile salmon (called smolts) who swim downstream do little to address rapacious takings of those lucky enough to get to the ocean.[23]

Regulation of Forests   In the United States, forest regulation began with the Forest Reserve Act of 1891, which authorized the first permanent system of forest reserves. At that time, there was no allowance made for private harvesting of publicly owned lands. That situation was changed in 1897, when the U.S. Congress provided the funds for the system of forest reserves and authorized private harvesting. In 1905, responsibility for managing these new forest reserves was given to the U.S. Deptartment of Agriculture (USDA). Six years later, Congress passed the Weeks Act, which allowed the newly created Forest Service to acquire additional lands. It did so vigorously.

The head of the USDA, Gifford Pinchot, believed that Forest Service lands should be used. Unlike John Muir, one of his contemporaries and a famous conservationist who wanted Forest Service lands withdrawn from use, Pinchot believed that the Forest Service's goal should be maximizing timber yields on a sustainable basis. Pinchot held little concern for other potential uses for Forest Service lands.

The Forest Service promoted maximum cutting of its landholdings in part to reduce timber price fluctuations. To do so, however, it provided private timber harvesters with taxpayer-financed assistance, including the development of roads that allowed harvesting to take place. Postel and Ryan (1991), for example, cite an estimate of over 300,000 miles of roads—roughly eight times the length of the U.S. interstate highway system. The Forest Service also sold the timber to private harvesters at below-market prices, ostensibly to promote the "public benefits" of harvesting, such as recreation. Of course, in cases where large tracts of forest are clearcut, it is difficult to imagine what public benefits are created.

The Forest Service began to focus more on multiple-use regulation after World War II, specifically with the aforementioned Multiple-Use Sustained Yield Act of 1960 and the Wilderness Act of 1964. In addition, in 1974, Congress passed the Forest and Rangeland Renewable Resources Planning Act. That act required, among other things, that a program for the national forests be developed every five years (Clawson 1983).

Despite all of these policies, the ferocity of the controversies that have developed, such as over cutting of old-growth forests in the Pacific Northwest (Booth

---

[23]In March 1995, the U.S. government proposed buying up scallop fishers' boats to reduce overharvesting off the coastal waters of New England.

1994), indicate that the Forest Service has not managed its resources efficiently or addressed multiple-use management in a consistent manner. At the very least, it should eliminate subsidies to private harvesters, which cannot be justified as a means of increasing economic efficiency. This, of course, is easier said than done in a highly politicized environment.

Multiple-use policies also need to be reconsidered. First, multiple-use benefits, such as recreation, should be estimated accurately. Second, a more comprehensive management approach that determines forest resource priorities, including preservation of biodiversity, should be determined. Third, additional research on forest dynamics should be undertaken. Fourth, less invasive harvesting techniques, such as selective logging and easements along rivers to reduce siltation, should be carefully explored. Although these may increase the private costs of timber harvesting, the benefits (such as restoration of salmon runs) may be far higher. Finally, multiattribute planning methods could be used to define preferred policies more clearly.

Guidelines for "Responsible" Renewable Resource Policies

Howe (1979) developed a set of six principles for "responsible" natural resources policy. They encompassed both exhaustible and renewable resources, but two are particularly useful for developing renewable resources policies.

1. *The avoidance of irreversibilities in all renewable resource systems.* Howe advocates using a safe minimum standard (SMS) approach, which he says must be defined specifically for each renewable resource system. A SMS for a unique natural system, Yellowstone Park, for example, might be defined as a minimum contiguous area needed to permit natural perpetuation of the system.

2. *A clear determination of the role of free markets and prices.* When Howe wrote his principles in 1979, he said that "current practice consists of a bad mixture of attempts at public control and partial reliance on private markets" (p. 336). Almost two decades later, current practice remains glaringly similar. Market prices should be allowed to define actual conditions of scarcity. Subsidies that encourage destructive practices should be eliminated. Regulation should provide market signals wherever possible to encourage efficient behavior. The legacy of failed fisheries regulations that attempted to suppress technological innovation and artificially raise harvest costs should not be forgotten. Better to allow harvest to be done as efficiently as possible, but ensure that the total harvest is limited, in the same way that tradable pollution permits ensure a ceiling on overall pollution levels, but allow those levels to be achieved at the lowest possible cost.

CHAPTER SUMMARY

In this chapter, we have provided an introduction to renewable resources use and policies. Our presentation has been limited, as many books have been written on the subject. Renewable resources, unlike depletable ones, can regenerate themselves. Properly managed, these resources can provide the desired level of services indefinitely. That cannot occur, however, until society first agrees on what services renewable resources ought to provide and balances competing services (e.g., harvesting for food versus preservation of endangered species).

The mathematics of renewable resource management is complex, but the underlying concepts are not. Efficient management of any renewable resource should be undertaken so that the marginal cost of the last unit used—where use can mean either harvest or preservation—equals the marginal cost of use. Remarkably, all of the math really boils down to that concept.

Achieving goals based on equity, human rights, and the rights of nature will be more problematic. Again, however, what is most needed is a better definition of what those goals are and their priority relative to everything else. A permanent ban on all timber harvesting or all fishing so as to save species and promote biodiversity is unrealistic in light of human needs. But the alternative need not be a treeless, fishless, and lifeless planet. There does exist a middle ground—one that may even be shaded.

CHAPTER REVIEW

Economic Concepts and Tools

- Maximum sustainable yield (*MSY*) is the maximum harvest per unit of time that can be sustained while keeping the total resource stock constant. At *MSY*, all growth is being harvested. In general, however, optimal harvest rates will be below *MSY*.
- For a privately held resource, at the profit-maximizing level of harvest, the change in effort relative to harvest will just equal the ratio of the market price to the cost of the additional effort. At this point, marginal harvesting costs will just equal marginal harvest revenues. The owner will wish to harvest when the rate of increase in the value of the trees is just equal to his opportunity cost of capital.
- Pure open-access solutions will occur where *total* harvesting costs equal *total* harvest revenues.
- Optimal timber-harvesting decisions will also depend on whether the owner intends to replant. If the forest is to be replanted, it will be harvested sooner than if it is not to be replanted because the opportunity cost of delay, which equals forgone revenues from the next rotational harvest, is higher. If the owner does not intend to replant, the cost of delay is zero.
- Given sufficiently high nontimber benefits, the optimal course of action may be never to harvest.
- Although an entire forest may provide multiple benefits, specialization can make economic sense for individual stands of timber.
- At an infinite rate of interest, the profit-maximizing harvest solution for a fishery will be the common-property solution, and a zero rate of interest will be the same solution as the static one-period solution.

- Maximization of the net present value of profits for a multispecies fishery will depend on the relative prices of the species, the stocks over time, and the relative costs of harvest. All of these may be interdependent. The fisheries portfolio manager will want to hold a set of "assets" so that the marginal rate of return on each asset is identical.
- Uncertainty about renewable resource stocks can be classified in three categories:
  1. Random effects whose future occurrence can be determined from past experience
  2. Parameter uncertainty that can be reduced by additional research and information gathering
  3. Ignorance about the appropriate variables to consider and appropriate model forms

Policy Issues

- Promoting "sustainable" harvesting decisions, though an admirable goal, is probably meaningless from a policy perspective until sustainable solutions are defined.
- For society, efficient harvesting decisions will require the use of the *SRTP*. Inclusion of multiple policy goals, such as preservation of endangered species, will require alteration of standard efficient harvesting decisions.
- Many regulatory approaches have failed because they attempted to restrict behavior instead of providing relevant economic signals. Subsidies that encourage destructive practices should be eliminated. Regulation should provide market signals wherever possible to encourage efficient behavior.
- A more comprehensive management approach that determines renewable resource priorities, including preservation of biodiversity, should be determined.
- Multiattribute planning methods can be used to define preferred renewable resource policies.

DISCUSSION QUESTIONS

1. What would be the implications of privatizing all Forest Service lands? If this policy were pursued, how would it be made operational?
2. Would fisheries management be improved with a 300-mile exclusive economic zone? What about a 400-mile zone? What are the problems associated with setting such exclusive zones?
3. What would be the implications of a futures market for commercial fisheries? Would it tend to improve management or exacerbate existing common-property and open-access problems?
4. Would it be preferable to limit fishing in a depleted area for 100 years or to place an outright ban on fishing in the area for 50 years? What would you want know before choosing between these two options?

5. Evaluate the following statement: "Sustainable forest management requires the use of a zero discount rate. Otherwise, there won't be any renewable resources left for future generations."
6. When is a resource renewable, and when is it depletable?

REFERENCES

Behan, R. 1990. "Multi-Resource Forest Management: A Paradigmatic Challenge to Professional Forestry." *Journal of Forestry* 88(1): 12–18.

Booth, D. 1994. *Valuing Nature: The Decline and Preservation of Old-Growth Forests.* London: Rowman and Littlefield.

Bowes, M., and J. Krutilla. 1985. "Multiple Use Management of Public Forestlands." In *Handbook of Natural Resources and Energy Economics,* Vol. 2, ed. A. Kneese and J. Sweeney. New York: Elsevier.

Clark, C. 1988. *Mathematical Bionomics: The Optimal Management of Renewable Resources,* 2d ed. New York: Wiley.

Clawson, M. 1983. *The Federal Lands Revisited.* Washington, D.C.: Resources for the Future.

Crutchfield, J. 1956. "Common Property Resources and Factor Allocation." *Canadian Journal of Economics and Political Science* 22(3): 292–300.

Crutchfield, J., and G. Pontecorvo. 1969. *The Pacific Salmon Fisheries: A Study of Irrational Conservation.* Baltimore: Johns Hopkins University Press.

Franklin, J. 1989. "Towards a New Forestry." *American Forestry* 95(1): 37–44.

Gordon, H. 1954. "The Economic Theory of a Common Property Resource: The Fishery." *Journal of Political Economy* 62(2): 124–142.

Hartman, R. 1976. "The Harvesting Decision When a Standing Forest Has Value." *Economic Inquiry* 14(1): 52–58.

Howarth, R., and R. Norgaard. 1993. "Intergenerational Changes and the Social Discount Rate." *Environmental and Resource Economics* 3(4): 337–358.

Howe, C. 1979. *Natural Resource Economics.* New York: Wiley.

Miles, E., R. Pealy, and R. Stokes (eds.). 1986. *Natural Resource Economics and Policy Applications: Essays in Honor of James A. Crutchfield.* Seattle: University of Washington Press.

Munro, G., and A. Scott. 1985. "The Economics of Fisheries Management." In *Handbook of Natural Resources and Energy Economics,* Vol. 2, ed. A. Kneese and J. Sweeney. New York: Elsevier.

Pearce, D., and R. Turner. 1990. *Economics of Natural Resources and the Environment.* Baltimore: Johns Hopkins University Press.

Pontecorvo, G. 1986. "Supply, Demand, and Common Property: The Historical Dynamics of the Fisheries of Georges Bank—Some Preliminary Observations." In *Natural Resource Economics and Policy Applications: Essays in Honor of James A. Crutchfield,* ed E. Miles, R. Pealy, and R. Stokes. Seattle: University of Washington Press.

Postel, S., and J. Ryan. 1991. "Reforming Forestry." In *State of the World, 1991,* ed. L. Brown et al. Washington, D.C.: Worldwatch Institute.

Scott, A. 1986. "Catch Quotas and Shares in the Fishstock as Property Rights." In *Natural Resource Economics and Policy Applications: Essays in Honor of James A. Crutchfield,* ed. E. Miles, R. Pealy, and R. Stokes. Seattle: University of Washington Press.

Spulber, D. 1986. "Fisheries and Uncertainty." In *Progress in Natural Resource Economics,* ed. A. Scott. Oxford: Oxford University Press.

Stokes, R. 1986. "Improving the Relevance of Fisheries Economics Through Political Analysis: Some Suggested Approaches." In *Natural Resource Economics and Policy Applications: Essays in Honor of James A. Crutchfield,* ed E. Miles, R. Pealy, and R. Stokes. Seattle: University of Washington Press.

Strang, W. 1982. "On the Optimal Forest Harvesting Decision." *Economic Inquiry* 20(4): 576–583.

Vincent, J. 1993. "Managing Tropical Forests." *Land Economics* 69(3): 313–318.

Vincent, J., and C. Binkley. 1993. "Efficient Multiple-Use Forestry May Require Land Use Specialization." *Land Economics* 69(4): 370–376.

Walters, C., and R. Hilborn. 1978. "Ecological Optimization and Adaptive Management." *Annual Review of Ecological Systems* 9: 157–188.

CHAPTER 17

WATER
RESOURCES

Dammed with Faint Praise: The Narmada Valley Project in India

Slated as one of the world's largest hydroelectric and irrigation projects, the Narmada Valley Project is part of a long-term plan by the government of India to harness the vast energy of India's 1,300-kilometer-long Narmada River, which flows westward from central India into the Arabian Sea. The project envisions the construction of around 3,200 dams, some 33 of which would be classified as "large" projects generating significant amounts of electricity and providing needed water for irrigation. The project was conceived to address India's ongoing problems of drought, poverty, and starvation, as well as to meet India's energy needs in the pursuit of industrial and economic development. The centerpiece of the project, and largest of the proposed dams, is the Sardar Sarovar Dam, which, if completed, will have an electricity-generating capacity of over 1,200 megawatts (MW) and the potential to irrigate 2 million hectares of land. Construction of the Sardar Sarovar, which was begun in 1987, is estimated to cost around U.S. $1.5 billion. By 1992, the World Bank had already provided around $450 million of the total cost, as well as significant technical assistance.

Despite its great economic potential, the Narmada project has been controversial since it was first authorized in 1979. If completed, the project will flood over 130 hectares (325,000 acres) of land, one-third of which is rich forestland that is home to thousands of small tribal communities. The project has drawn sharp criticism from environmentalists, human rights activists, villagers whose lands will be submerged if the project is completed, and even some economists. In 1991, in response to severe criticisms of the project, the Japanese government withdrew its support for the Sardar Sarovar. A year later, the World Bank released an independent report that concluded that there were significant flaws with the project and recommended reassessment on environmental, social, and economic grounds.

The Narmada Valley Project raises fundamental policy issues: economic efficiency and unbiased benefit-cost analysis, concerns over equity, and changing cultural and "sustainability" priorities. From an economic efficiency standpoint, the Indian government deems the entire project viable if the benefits of the dams, including additional water, agricultural production, and production of "clean" energy (relative to coal or nuclear-generated electricity) exceed by a ratio of 1.5 to 1 the costs of the dams, including environmental damages, full monetary compensation to displaced villagers, and construction costs. Using such a benefit-cost ratio as a criterion for development, however, is flawed from an economic standpoint, for several reasons. First, there are many environmental and health consequences of the project that have yet to be quantified or are intrinsically difficult to measure. These include costs associated with siltation behind the dams, salination, waterlogging of irrigated lands, the release of toxic minerals, a potential increase in the incidence of waterborne diseases, and loss of biodiversity from inundation of forests.

Second, India's past experience with development and construction of large dams and the accompanying benefit-cost studies used to justify development have shown a consistent pattern of miscalculation on the part of government and development agencies, as well as the inability to obtain certain crucial data. In general, the estimated project costs have always been well below actual costs, and delivered benefits have rarely been more than 60 to 70 percent of estimated benefits. Critics of dam development claim that the source of these discrepancies is endemic to a political system that encourages both corruption and collusion among large developers, the various Indian states, and wealthy landowners, all of whom manipulate projects so as disproportionately to benefit themselves. Merely using an arbitrary benefit-cost ratio as justification for development will not eliminate such problems.

From this conflict has also arisen a cultural clash between wealthy landowners and poor villagers. While embracing Western-style development, some Indians now question its viability as a model for their country. The experience of many Indians with large development programs has been one of broken promises of relief for the poor. As a result, some communities are turning to small, locally controlled irrigation and energy schemes as the best way to maintain their communities and grow. Such schemes are not without cost, however, as they are often more expensive and more difficult to finance than larger ones.

For all its problems, development has helped the lot of India's poor as new infrastructure has raised productivity and incomes. Unfortunately, India's problems are complex and extend well beyond simple economics: it is a society divided by region, religion, and caste. Development of the Narmada Valley Project, or any other project, will not solve these issues.

INTRODUCTION

Throughout this book, we have related principles of environmental economics and policy to natural resources. Few resources are as important as water. Adequate supplies of usable water for drinking, agricultural production, and sanitation have enabled civilizations to flourish. The lack of usable water, by contrast, has created immeasurable hardship and suffering in drought-afflicted nations and regions lacking even the most basic sanitation.

In the United States, we are fortunate to be water-rich. We have used our vast water resources to increase our agricultural production, to generate electricity, to transport the goods we produce, to treat the wastes generated by our industries and individuals, and even to provide recreation benefits to millions. Throughout most of our history, we have taken our water supplies for granted. When those supplies dwindled, as in the Great Depression, we have suffered. That devastating drought in the 1930s scarred the Midwest and caused great social upheaval, perhaps best described in John Steinbeck's novel *The Grapes of Wrath.*

Today the world is experiencing more often the pain of apparently inadequate water supplies because of growing populations and increasing industrial demand. Not only do we seem to not have enough water, but there are increasing concerns about the quality of the water resources we do have. As we will explain, water *quantity* and water *quality* are related. Physical scarcity of water supplies, however, does not account for all water quantity and quality problems. Rather, it is *economic scarcity* that is a prime contributor; we have enough water, but we have not applied the policy tools with which to allocate that water efficiently.

In this chapter, we first discuss how allocation mechanisms for scarce water resources were developed historically in the United States. We define different types of water "rights" and explore the federal institutions that enabled more of our water resources to be put to beneficial use but at the same time failed to develop any mechanisms to ensure the *most* beneficial use and *least* environmental degradation. We then turn to a discussion of water allocation policy. Much of that policy has been based not on efficiency goals but on equity goals. We will explore the policy conflicts that have arisen because of misunderstanding of these goals and discuss several alternative policy measures. We also discuss emerging private markets for water resources, which have placed greater emphasis on efficiency goals, and the increasing importance of water quality issues. These policies can address the competing uses for water, such as irrigation and recreation, as well as the disparate distributions of water resources among different geographical regions. Yet they may also lead to real and perceived inequities, such as those associated with the Narmada Valley Project.

WATER ALLOCATION ISSUES

Humans use water in many ways. Some are nonconsumptive—water is used where it is found without reducing the amount available for other uses. Nonconsumptive uses include navigation, hydropower production, recreation, and fish and wildlife habitat. Consumptive uses divert water from its natural course and put it to use somewhere else. Examples of consumptive uses are irrigation, water used to make steam in industrial processes, and household uses for drinking and washing. Except when water is used in chemical reactions, these "consumptive" uses really do not consume water either. Instead, they use water and return it to the environment in a different place and sometimes in a different form. Water diverted for irrigation evaporates, is taken up by plants and transpired, percolates into the groundwater, or flows back into streams or rivers. Water diverted for municipal use evaporates or returns to a stream as sewer discharge.

Many human water uses modify the *hydrologic cycle,* whereby water evaporates from the oceans and other water bodies, returns to earth as precipitation, and flows back toward the oceans until it evaporates again. This gives water three economically interesting properties. First, water—actually the entire hydrologic cycle—is a renewable resource. Most human water use is really exploitation and modification of part of the flow in that cycle. Second, because water flows form a cycle, water uses in one part of the cycle often will affect other water uses. This is not just because many water uses are rivalrous consumption activities. Although it is certainly true that if I drink a glass of water, you cannot drink it, it also true that water used returns to the cycle and becomes available for others, though perhaps in a different place than it would have been available naturally. One person's wastewater, for example, may become someone else's water resource. Third, natural water flows are often highly variable. Precipitation and streamflows can vary dramatically from year to year and even from season to season.

Because of these properties of the hydrologic cycle, economically efficient water allocation institutions need to have five attributes:

1. Water should be allocated to the highest-valued combination of uses. Because of the interconnected nature of water uses, this may not be the same as allocating water to the highest-valued use at each point. For example, diverting all the water from a reach of a river for an irrigation project may be the highest-valued single use of that water but may have a lower value than leaving the water in the reach for navigation and hydropower production and diverting it for irrigation farther downstream.
2. Institutions should be flexible enough to reallocate water when demands change or new demands arise.
3. Institutions should be flexible enough to accommodate the natural variability in water supply. When water is in short supply, the uses that contribute the least to the total value of water use should be cut off first.
4. Water allocation institutions should provide water users with certainty of tenure. People contemplating investments in long-lived projects should know that the water rights they have today will not be reallocated to someone else in the future.
5. Water allocation institutions should minimize uncompensated and involuntary impacts on third parties from changes in water uses. This is important for both efficiency and equity goals and is one of the reasons that large projects like the Narmada Valley project are often controversial.

Water allocation institutions with *all* of these attributes are in very short supply, although they are becoming more prevalent. Many economists see water resources as an area where the Coase theorem should apply: if we can just define water rights correctly, water markets would have these five attributes. Defining water rights correctly seems to be the rub. Existing systems of property in water all have shortcomings, some of them severe. Economists have made many proposals to reform water allocation institutions, usually by making them more market-oriented. We will discuss several of these. None of these proposals has been perfect, but some of them offer the possibility of improving on the status quo. However, many noneconomists object to water markets. Sometimes this opposition stems from a general distrust of markets, but more often it is because specific water market proposals fail to take every interest into account.

Water Allocation Institutions in the United States

In the United States, water law is primarily state law. The U.S. Constitution gives the federal government jurisdiction over navigation and interstate commerce in water. Though these powers have been interpreted fairly broadly, the federal government has left most matters dealing with water to the states. State water laws have some important consistencies and some important differences.[1] One consistency is that water rights are use rights, not ownership rights. Most state constitutions declare that water is owned by the state or the public and held in trust by the state. State constitutions and water laws then set out the rights that individuals have to use water. One important difference divides the country roughly at the Mississippi River. States east of the Mississippi generally follow the *riparian* system of water rights, and western states follow the *prior appropriation* system.

Riparian Water Law   *Riparian* means "on, of, or pertaining to the riverbank or lakeshore." Riparian rights are the rights granted to the owners of land on riverbanks or lakeshores in English common law. The riparian system of water law was developed in medieval England—a slow-changing society in a wet climate. It initially worked fairly well under similar conditions when it was transplanted to eastern North America. The common law was the basis for law in the original 13 states and was carried to new states as they were added to the country. Riparian rights are rights to use the body of water and to divert water for limited use on riparian land, provided that such use does not conflict with the rights of other riparian landowners.[2] Initially, this was interpreted to mean that each landowner had the right to the natural flow past his or her land and to "natural" uses requiring diversion. These "natural" uses were limited to household use, such as a garden or limited livestock watering. These restrictions also allowed water to be diverted to run a mill, as long as the water returned to the stream, but not for irrigation.

Most states have modified the original riparian law concepts in several ways. The restriction of diversions to "natural" uses has generally been relaxed to "reasonable" uses, with the precise definition of "reasonable" often left to the courts. Reasonable has usually come to mean not having a perceptible impact on other riparian landowners. Some states have allowed the severing of riparian rights from land ownership. This allows a riparian landowner to sell the right to divert water to a nonriparian landowner, where the amount that can be diverted is what is "reasonable" for the original riparian landowner.

---

[1]For an introduction to water law, see Goldfarb (1989) or Getches (1984).
[2]Riparian land is generally defined as parcels of land that include a riverbank or lakeshore. Property beginning 1 foot from the high-water mark would not be riparian.

The riparian system of water law is primarily concerned with equity, protecting riparian landowners' rights from adverse effects of others' actions. Riparian water law does little to allocate water to the highest-valued set of uses. It allocates water to traditional uses and can block its reallocation to higher-valued uses away from riparian land. It provides limited flexibility to allocate water to new uses and does little to guarantee that reallocations increase the total value of water use. A new use must be "reasonable" and not "unreasonably" impair existing uses, but once allowed, it has the same legal footing as existing uses. Whether a new use will be allowed is up to the state courts. This is allocation by lawsuit, not allocation through a market. Some state laws deal with supply variability by specifying an order of priority for water uses.

Riparian water law provides strong, but not absolute, tenure. Although existing uses are protected, the quantity of water available for a particular use may be decreased when a new use is found to be reasonable. Riparian water law also provides strong, but not absolute, protection against third-party impacts of reallocations, but it does so by severely limiting reallocations. Because of its inflexibility, it does little to encourage putting water to the highest-valued set of uses. The western states rejected this system of water law, and most eastern states have found it necessary to supplement the riparian system with features borrowed from western water law.

Prior Appropriation Water Law   The prior appropriation system of water law was developed in the western United States in the 1800s, while the western states were still territories. The system had the same impetus as much of the early settlement of western North America: gold fever. The discovery of precious metals (and more mundane ores) drew miners to California, Montana, Colorado, and other areas in the West, where legal institutions were fluid (and formal legal institutions were often distant). Nineteenth-century mining techniques required a lot of water. In the arid West, water was scarce and often was not found where miners wanted it. The miners applied the same legal principle to water that they applied to gold: the first one to claim it owned it. Farmers, who came west to feed the miners, and cattle and sheep ranchers applied the same principle to water for irrigation, and today irrigation is the largest consumptive water use in the western states.

The legal principle of prior appropriation is very simple: any unclaimed water can be diverted for beneficial use, and when there is not enough water to satisfy all uses, older claims (senior water rights) have priority over newer claims (junior water rights). Initially, the act of diversion created a water right. Today, the western states have all formalized their systems for recording water rights and issuing new ones.

The prior appropriation system allocated water fairly efficiently when it was first applied. The best lands for irrigation were settled first, so the first claims for irrigation, which had the highest priority, put water to its highest-valued use. However, prior appropriation law completely ignores one class of water use: instream uses that do not require diversion. Most western states have begun to modify their water laws to recognize instream uses as beneficial uses.

Whether the prior appropriation system has the flexibility to reallocate water as demands change varies from state to state. Some states have requirements that water rights transfers have no adverse impacts on other water right holders. This can be very limiting. In some parts of the West, all of the natural flow in many streams is diverted for irrigation in the late summer, and all of the water actually in the stream is return flow from upstream irrigation. A requirement of no adverse impacts essentially gives downstream water users rights to upstream users' return flows. Downstream users can block any transfer that would reduce, move, or change the timing of return flow. Some states are less restrictive and allow transfers equal to the amount of consumptive use (diversion minus return flow).

The prior appropriation system has limited, or even perverse, incentives for water conservation. In some states, an irrigator who saves water through more efficient irrigation practices is considered to have abandoned the right to the water saved, since it is no longer being put to the use for which it was claimed. The irrigator can make a new claim for this water, to use for additional irrigation, but that claim will be junior to all existing water rights. In addition, increasing irrigation efficiency can reduce return flows, so downstream users may be able to block the new claim.

The prior appropriation system has a strict rule for dealing with variability of supply. When there is not enough water for all users, the ones with the latest claims are cut off first. A century or more after water rights were first claimed, it is unlikely that the relative values of water uses correspond perfectly with their priority dates. A junior water right holder with a high-value use can pay an upstream senior water right holder to leave some water in the stream, but in some states that can be interpreted as abandonment of the senior right. In any case, any intervening user with a less junior water right can legally divert the water before it reaches the party who paid for it.

The prior appropriation system provides very strong certainty of tenure. New water users always have junior water rights and cannot interfere with existing uses. The degree of protection against third-party impacts depends on the state. In some states, the protection is almost absolute. In other states, where transfers of the amount of consumptive use are allowed, there may be third-party impacts from changes in the timing or location of return flows. The prior appropriation system does not provide incentives for affected third parties to become parties to the transaction. It encourages them to litigate to block a change that may have net benefits but harms them rather than negotiate for a share of those net benefits.

Early Federal Involvement in Water Allocation and Ownership

Initially, water allocation in the western United States was primarily a laissez-faire system, with no federal government involvement. Despite this, the federal government had already been involved with water resources, primarily in the development of inland canals and waterways for the transport of goods in the eastern United States. Because water was plentiful, there was far less controversy over allocating water supplies in that region. In the West, however, a desire for rapid economic expansion and concern over efficient water resource development lead to federal involvement and changes in ownership structures. Unfortunately, the development and allocation system that had been initially envisioned (Powell 1879/1962; Stegner 1982) did not occur.

The first major federal action related to water use, specifically irrigation development, was the Desert Lands Act of 1877. This act granted title to 640 acres of land (reduced to 320 acres in an 1890 amendment) at 25 cents per acre, provided that a homesteader diverted water to and reclaimed the land within three years.[3] With that homesteading, however, the water right changed. It became a *usufructory right,* which meant that homesteaders were accorded the right to *use* the water but not to own it. Ownership of the water remained with the state.

Prior to passage of this act, the explorer John Wesley Powell had spent a great deal of time surveying the West, particularly the regions surrounding the Colorado River Basin. These explorations and surveys, which began in 1867, provided the basis for Powell's beliefs on development of land in those arid regions. Powell's background allowed him to compute river flows and determine what percentage of lands might be irrigated (Wahl 1989).[4] Powell determined that (surface) water resources were sufficient to irrigate only a small percentage of the arid western lands. Powell believed that the scarce water resources should be used only for the best areas: land that was both fertile and near streams, where water could be diverted most easily.

Powell also believed that some form of government involvement was necessary to ensure that individual settlers did not reduce the overall potential benefits from irrigation through their actions. Last, Powell feared monopoly control of water resources. Thus Powell implicitly recognized the common-property nature of water resources, as well as economies of scale associated with development of storage reservoirs.

Powell requested that the government provide funds for a comprehensive survey of irrigable land in the West so as to identify land that would best be reserved for reservoir development. In this way, Powell believed, private speculators would be unable to monopolize this land. Unfortunately, settlers began to occupy land surrounding this reserved land, rather than land closest to rivers. As a result, in Powell's view, the pattern of development became worse with federal action than without it.[5] Nevertheless, calls for federal involvement grew. Near the end of the nineteenth century, some state congressional representatives were calling for additional federal assistance with irrigation development (Wahl 1989). Other western representatives opposed grants of land to the states for irrigation development, which had been encouraged under the Carey Act of 1894, in favor of direct federal involvement (Wahl 1989). Not surprisingly, it was claimed that federal developments would be "self-supporting" (Davison 1979, p. 199). By

---

[3] There was also a $1 filing fee per tract.

[4] Powell also defined the "arid West" as lands that received less than 20 inches of rain per year. This corresponds approximately to lands west of the hundredth meridian, which passes through western Kansas around Dodge City. (This also was the inspiration for the title of Stegner's 1982 book about Powell.)

[5] In fact, there was a great deal of private water storage development in the 1870s. Many of these developments failed to deliver the water they had promised to settlers (Robinson 1979; Wahl 1989).

1900, both Republicans and Democrats were favoring federal assistance for irrigation development. This led to the first, and perhaps the most profound, piece of federal legislation ever passed in regards to water resource development, the Reclamation Act of 1902.[6]

The Reclamation Act of 1902   The Reclamation Act was born out of the vision of President Theodore Roosevelt, himself an admirer of John Wesley Powell. Roosevelt was an ardent conservationist, although more in the utilitarian sense, rather than what we might today call a preservationist sense (Reisner 1993). Roosevelt believed that the waters flowing in the great rivers of the West should be used rather than "wasted."

The Reclamation Act created the Reclamation Fund, which had as its source of funds sales of federal lands. The proceeds from these sales were to be used for developing irrigation projects in western states that would deliver water to public land that was homesteaded, as well as existing private land. The fund was to operate as a revolving fund, meaning that settlers who homesteaded would be required to pay back the cost of the irrigation investments after ten years, *without any interest* (Wahl 1989). Unfortunately, despite Roosevelt's admiration for Powell, the provisions of the act did not account for the differences in land quality. Thus homesteaders were given up to 160 acres of land (320 for a husband and wife) regardless of where the land was located (Reisner 1993).

Water rights provided under the Reclamation Act were based primarily on the principle of *beneficial use.* This required the holder of the water right to put that water to some use or lose the right entirely. Unfortunately, nothing in the act defined beneficial use (Wahl 1989). Because many states had previously determined whether water had been put to beneficial use, the federal legislation did not limit states' rights to determine such use. The beneficial use principle provided little incentive to use water efficiently, as reductions in use would be accompanied by an equal reduction in a user's appropriation. Other restrictions on water use and allocation were based on *preferential use* restrictions. Preferential use restrictions determined priorities of use among different categories, such as irrigated agriculture or energy production. Within those categories, water then could be allocated in a variety of ways.[7]

The amount of land provided with irrigation water by Reclamation Act projects grew rapidly in the ensuing decades, owing to the development of many large, multipurpose dams such as Grand Coulee Dam in Washington and Glen Canyon

---

[6]For an exhaustive and fascinating, though not impartial, history of reclamation project development in the West, see Reisner (1993).

[7]Transfers of water were discouraged by both federal and state policies. Wahl (1989) suggests that at least at the federal level, the Reclamation Act did not specifically prohibit transfers, although administrative policy seemed to do so. At the state level, restrictions were sometimes more specific. Gisser and Johnson (1981), for example, discuss the case of transfers in the Middle Rio Grande Conservation District, which the District argued were in violation of state law.

Dam in Arizona. The Bureau of Reclamation also developed large irrigation projects, including the Columbia Basin Project in eastern Washington and the Garrison Project in North Dakota. By the end of the 1970s, there were almost 44 million acres of irrigated land in 17 western states. Of that total, almost 10 million acres were irrigated by the Bureau of Reclamation (Wahl 1989).[8]

Irrigation Subsidies Under the Reclamation Act   Despite the promise of self-sufficiency for federal projects, in reality the programs subsidized irrigators heavily.[9] These irrigation subsidies took two forms: interest-free repayment and the basing of repayment on the Bureau's estimate of irrigators' "ability to pay" (Wahl 1989).

Eckstein (1961) calculated that interest-free repayment of federal debt to construct irrigation projects would repay only small a fraction of the true cost of the loan, primarily because the repayment period was so long (this even before we consider the additional effects arising from discounting and crowding out of private investment that we discussed in Chapter 13). Typically, irrigation projects were financed over 40 or 50 years. Eckstein calculated that at a prevailing interest rate of 4 percent, the required repayment would account for only about 21 percent of the true cost of the development. If the interest rate were 7 percent, the amount recovered fell to less than 7 percent.

Over time, the magnitude of the irrigation subsidies provided under the Reclamation Act grew.[10] Even though the Reclamation Fund was intended to be self-sufficient, with funds repaid after ten years used to construct new projects, it rapidly became clear that the fund would not achieve this goal. As the prevailing interest rate at which the federal government borrowed money rose, so did the degree of the subsidies provided to irrigators. In 1902, for example, the maximum repayment period was ten years. Assuming equal payments of the principal (but without paying any of the interest) and a prevailing federal borrowing rate of 2.7 percent, the simple irrigation interest subsidy equaled 14 percent (Wahl 1989). The subsidy is calculated by comparing the present value of the repayment stream with the initial present value, using the prevailing federal borrowing rate as the dis-

---

[8]A point of clarification concerns the relationship between the Bureau of Reclamation and the U.S. Army Corps of Engineers (COE). The COE is the federal government's construction arm. The Corps built many of the Bureau's irrigation project dams, as well as other construction projects such as aqueducts. Because a dam can serve multiple purposes, including irrigation, flood control, navigation, and power generation, some dams are operated by the Bureau, while others are operated by the COE. Grand Coulee Dam, for example, which lies on the main stem of the Columbia River, is operated by the Bureau. Other dams on the Columbia River, however, such as Bonneville Dam, are operated by the COE. There is a history of rivalry between these two government agencies, a lively description of which is provided by Reisner (1993).

[9]For example, one publication of the Bureau of Reclamation states: "It has long been the philosophy of the Nation that all reclamation project costs for the purpose of irrigation, power, and municipal and industrial water supply should be repaid in full" (U.S. Department of the Interior, Bureau of Reclamation 1972).

[10]For a detailed accounting of the growth in irrigation subsidies, see Rucker and Fishback (1983).

count rate. Thus letting S equal the percentage subsidy and i equal the discount rate, it is straightforward to show that for a loan of T years, the subsidy will equal

$$S = 1 - \frac{1}{T} \sum_{t=1}^{T} \frac{1}{(1 + i)^T} \qquad (17.1)[11]$$

Over time, congressional legislation allowed the Bureau to provide longer repayment periods for its loans. By 1926, the repayment period was 40 years, and the subsidy had increased to just over 50 percent. In 1939, Congress sweetened the subsidy pot even more. The Reclamation Project Act of 1939 allowed a payment-free development period of up to ten years. Thus by 1960, when the prevailing federal borrowing rate was 4 percent, a 40-year, interest-free loan provided an effective subsidy of 84 percent. And in the early 1980s, when the federal borrowing rate was at its highest level ever, almost 14 percent, the effective subsidy was 95 percent.

What had started in 1902 as a small program to provide federal assistance for development of the West grew into a program that provided huge subsidies to irrigators, who then grew subsidized crops. Although one reason for this was much higher inflation rates than in the early years of the program, sympathy for the hardships endured by settlers and a failure of the Bureau to prevent development of projects where soil conditions were poor also contributed to subsidies (Wahl 1989). Perhaps the most pervasive reason, however, was the Bureau's determinations of irrigators' "ability to pay."

Willingness to Pay, Ability to Pay, and Irrigation Project Subsidies   As part of his analysis of reclamation projects, Wahl (1989) estimated WTP for irrigation water and compared it to the Bureau's estimates of irrigators' "ability to pay." The results are striking.

The Bureau defines ability to pay as a percentage of net farm income. The Bureau determines a typical farm budget for those expected on different irrigation projects. Thus the Bureau estimates net farm income by taking expected crop revenues less costs such as seed, equipment, and land (exclusive of water costs).[12] (Total crop revenues are determined by the types of crop grown, those crops' need for water, and how arid is the region.) The Bureau then takes a percentage of this figure, which is usually around 75 percent, and uses the resulting amount to determine average water rates.

Wahl determined the accuracy of this method by comparing the Bureau's estimates of ability to pay (ATP) with estimated WTP for 17 different federal projects. To do this, he examined the prices paid for federal land with and without water

---

[11]Note that this calculation reflects only a simple subsidy. If we accounted for the shadow price of capital (see Chapter 13), the magnitude of the subsidy could be even larger.
[12]Of course, in many cases, the government provides crop subsidies to farmers, raising net farm income, although further distorting economic efficiency.

supplies. In principle, irrigators purchasing irrigated land would pay the full market value of that land and hence the full market value of water. A selection of the results of Wahl's study are reproduced in Table 17.1.[13]

Wahl's results indicated a tremendous discrepancy between the Bureau's *ATP* estimates and irrigators' *WTP*. The ratios range between 1.5 and 51.0 times the actual repayment to the federal government. Wahl noted that *WTP* at the time of project development may have been far lower, owing to uncertainty as to a project's viability and the existence of markets for crops produced. He also noted that for many of the older projects, lands have been resold. Thus current owners will already have paid the market value for water. One further important determinant of *WTP* is the existence of price subsidies for the crops grown.[14] Presumably, farmers guaranteed a subsidized price for their crops would be willing to pay more for irrigation than in the absence of such subsidies because the subsidies would reduce their financial risks in otherwise bad years.

Other Irrigation Project "Benefits"   There is ample evidence that many water development projects in the West were uneconomic. Despite this, many were still developed. Why? There appear to be several reasons. First, in addition to the false claims that most project costs would be repaid (owing to the Bureau's failure to account for the opportunity cost of borrowed funds), the Bureau has long cited other "benefits" from irrigation project development. The benefits claimed take the form of increased federal, state, and local tax revenues and secondary economic impacts. The major problem with such claims is that they are inappropriate in benefit-cost analyses of irrigation (and other) projects. There are two primary reasons for this: many analyses failed to distinguish benefits from transfer payments, and they failed to account for the benefits from project alternatives.[15]

The Bureau's claims of tax and economic development benefits did not address the issue of benefits that might arise elsewhere in the economy from alternative project developments. If the same dollars spent on a particular Bureau project were spent elsewhere, perhaps for a factory, various economic benefits would occur. As we discussed in Chapter 13, to the extent that spending on federal projects displaces private investment, the impacts of these alternative private developments will be even higher.[16] Thus rather than characterizing such effects as *benefits*, they should more properly be described as *impacts*.

---

[13]Torell, Libbin, and Miller (1990) developed an empirical model to determine the market value of water in the Ogallala Aquifer, which spans much of the plains states. Their model, which is discussed in more detail later in this chapter, compares favorably with the values reported by Wahl for the Farwell, Nebraska, project.

[14]This impact is not specifically cited by Wahl, although he does acknowledge other market failures.

[15]Unfortunately, inflated and inaccurate claims for benefits are not confined to federal projects. One particularly misleading claim, which we discussed in Chapter 6, is to label job creation as a *positive externality,* associated with project development. Although it is conceivable that the creation of jobs could be an external benefit to society, it is far more likely to be fully accounted for within the marketplace.

[16]Again, this arises from the shadow price of capital, as described in Chapter 13.

TABLE 17.1 DETERMINATION OF IRRIGATION SUBSIDIES FOR SELECTED FEDERAL WATER PROJECTS.

Irrigation District	In-Service Year	"Ability to Pay"[a] (dollars per acre)	Willingness to Pay[b] (dollars per acre)	Ratio (WTP ÷ ATP)
Glenn-Colusa, California	1938	10	510	51.0
Moon Lake, Utah	1936	44	444	10.1
Elephant Butte, New Mexico	1914	208	1,173	5.9
Truckee-Carson, Nevada	1904	176	1,576	8.5
Lower Yellowstone No. 1, Montana	1905	191	741	3.9
Grand Valley, Colorado	1911	285	1,585	5.6
Imperial Valley, California	1933	54	154	2.9
East Columbia Basin, Washington	1933	55	705	12.8
Malta, Montana	1906	69	344	5.0
Oroville-Tonaskat, Washington	1964	92	142	1.5
Farwell, Nebraska	1958	110	210	1.9

Note: All data expressed in 1978 dollars.

[a]Present value of past and future construction cost repayments using prevailing government borrowing rate.

[b]Difference in land value with and without water supply, plus *ATP.*

Source: Wahl (1989).

525

The second major reason for development of projects that appeared uneconomic may have been the choice of perspective used. This technique, which the Bureau was adept at, restricted the determination of benefits and costs to the geographical areas that would receive project benefits in the form of irrigation water, hydroelectric power, or flood control. Costs borne by those outside the study areas, including the majority of taxpayers, were not included.

Howe (1986) provides a useful case study for a particular Bureau project, the Colorado–Big Thompson (C-BT) project in northeastern Colorado. The C-BT project diverts water from the western slopes of the Rocky Mountains along the Continental Divide to provide water for over 700,000 acres of irrigated land, as well as water for eastern slope cities (Wahl 1989). Howe calculated that, from a *national* perspective, the overall net benefits of the C-BT projects were either −$341.4 million or −$177 million, depending on the number of years looked at in the calculations. Thus the project's costs, paid for primarily by federal taxpayers, were much more than it returned in benefits, most of which were received by irrigators and residents of eastern slope Colorado cities. Howe calculated that regional net benefits of the C-BT were quite large, either $767 million or $1.177 billion, again depending on the number of years looked at. With such large local benefits, the project was approved, thanks in part to political pressure to do so.[17]

Environmental Impacts of Irrigation Project Development   Along with the fact that many Bureau of Reclamation projects could not be justified on the basis of their real economic benefits, the projects also engendered numerous environmental costs that were never accounted for. These environmental costs include increasing salinization of irrigated lands, loss of agriculturally productive river bottomland, loss of fisheries habitat and stocks, and loss of recreation opportunities because of inundation (although other recreation opportunities were created in some cases). Finally, the effectiveness of numerous projects has been reduced steadily, owing to continued silting behind many dams. Thus many of these projects increased usable water quantities, but at the expense of water quality.

Salinization occurs for several reasons. First, water that accumulates in storage reservoirs often passes through soils that are saline or alkaline to begin with. The water leaches some of the salts out of the soil, carrying them into the reservoirs. In addition, water in reservoirs tends to evaporate, especially in the hot, dry climate of the West. This also increases the salinity of the water. This more saline water is then applied to farmlands. A good deal of that water may find its way back into the

---

[17]The C-BT project includes marketable water rights (Wahl 1989), an innovation that has probably improved the economic efficiency of the project. Interestingly, Reisner (1993), one of the Bureau's most vociferous critics, called the C-BT one of the Bureau's "most successful projects. . . . The power produced by the steep drop down the Front Range was enough to justify the expense of the tunnel, and the additional water . . . was welcomed by everyone from canoeists to whooping cranes to irrigators in Colorado and Nebraska" (p. 302).

same or other irrigation reservoirs. These return flows pick up increasing amounts of salt.

When soil drainage is poor and irrigation water does not drain quickly enough from the soil, salt concentrations build up around the root systems of plants. Eventually, salt concentrations build up to levels so high that plants cannot grow in the soil. This is not a new problem, having vexed the Sumerians some 5,000 years ago. Increasing soil salinity continues to be a major problem in most areas of the world that rely on irrigation. Measuring the environmental damage caused by salinization would require estimating the present value of lost crop production over time, assuming that the requirements for using market prices as a measure of damages (discussed in Chapter 11) were met.

The development of many Bureau projects also devastated numerous fisheries. These fisheries provided not only important sources of food but also recreational benefits. Perhaps the largest fisheries impact has occurred in the Columbia River Basin, which we discussed in Chapters 8 and 9. Historically, millions of salmon migrated up the waters of the Columbia River and its tributaries to spawn. Prior to construction of the storage dams in the Columbia River Basin, estimates of the number of salmon that migrated were around 15 to 20 million (Northwest Power Planning Council 1991). In all, 13 dams were built on the main stem of the Columbia River, as well as numerous other dams on the Columbia's tributaries. Some of those dams were quite low, and salmon have been able to negotiate fish ladders around them. But dams such as Grand Coulee, which is the height of a 50-story building, are impenetrable. As a result, the salmon were unable to migrate to their spawning grounds, and numerous runs perished.[18]

As we discussed in Chapter 8, salmon runs today have declined so much along many of the tributaries that there has been an ongoing battle to list numerous runs as endangered species under the Endangered Species Act. The efforts to restore salmon runs have already cost hundreds of millions of dollars, in the form of special fish ladders, protective screens to keep smolts (young salmon migrating downstream) from being sucked into hydroelectric generators, barges used to transport smolts downstream, and higher electric power costs. Efforts to restore these runs continue to be bruising, as the Endangered Species Act does not recognize cost as an excuse for extinction. And because much of the cost of the restoration is now being borne by electric power consumers in the Pacific Northwest, other environmental impacts may occur as utilities and their customers seek alternative forms of electric power, such as from fossil fuel plants, that also impose costs on the environment. These general equilibrium impacts, which we first discussed in Chapter 2 and took up again in Chapter 7, are difficult to trace but can limit the effectiveness of individual environmental policies.

Recreational opportunities have also been damaged by the development of large storage projects. Not only did dams destroy valuable spawning habitat and

---

[18] This does not mean that the dams were useless. Built in the late 1930s, these dams provided needed electricity for the production of aluminum, which was used to manufacture airplanes that helped win World War II.

salmon runs, but they also eliminated recreational benefits associated with white-water rafting and the use of wilderness areas. Those benefits are not insignificant.[19] Of course, dams have created some recreation opportunities, allowing for different sorts of fishing, boating, and swimming. Thus determining the relative effects on overall recreational values is a complex empirical issue.

Another social consequence of project development has been the impacts on Indian tribes (Reisner 1993). The construction of dams along the Columbia River that destroyed the salmon runs also deprived the native tribes of their source of food and livelihood, as well as an important cultural and religious symbol. The Garrison Project in North Dakota is another example. The Mandan, Hidatsa, and Arikara tribes had been granted reservation lands along the Missouri River. The land near the river was fertile and excellent for grazing cattle. In fact, the Bureau of Reclamation considered the land far too productive to inundate. Apparently, however, the U.S. Army Corps of Engineers, which was the main builder of Garrison Dam, thought otherwise. The construction of Garrison inundated most of the tribes' lands and with it their source of income. The tribes requested compensation in the form of hydroelectric power to run irrigation pumps on the arid lands to which they were relocated so that they could raise crops, grazing and watering rights for their cattle along the margins of the reservoir that would be created behind the dam, and a small bridge across a narrow portion of the reservoir that would split their reservation in two. All of these requests were denied.

Such cultural issues are not limited to hydroelectric development in the United States. The Narmada Valley Project involves numerous cultural issues. Another example concerns hydroelectric development by Hydro-Quebéc, the state-owned electric utility of the province of Quebéc. Hydro-Quebéc has developed several very large hydroelectric facilities, including James Bay and Grand Baleen. Although these facilities are not used to provide irrigation benefits (there is plenty of water in the eastern United States and Canada), their construction flooded the traditional homelands of Quebec's Cree Indians. Critics of the projects, most vociferous in the northeastern United States, where most of the electricity generated is sold, have argued that the projects were environmental and cultural disasters whose electric output was not even needed.

The actual environmental costs associated with irrigation project development, in terms of reduced economic efficiency and violations of human rights and the rights of nature, will always be disputed. One of the problems has been that the parties bearing the environmental costs have not always been the same as those enjoying the benefits of irrigation projects. Another difficulty is the length of time over which environmental costs have accrued. In many cases, little attention was paid to the associated environmental costs. Future generations have been paying the environmental price.

---

[19]You might want to reread the summary in Chapter 11 of Duffield's estimation of the value of recreational flows in the Big Hole and Bitteroot rivers in Montana. For those two rivers alone, the value of recreational flows was over $10 million.

None of this is to suggest that irrigation projects are bad per se. Irrigation projects have allowed countries to feed their populations far more effectively and provided the basis for stronger economies and the resources with which to undertake critical environmental improvements, such as water treatment facilities. And like the C-BT, some projects have been well thought out. What should be avoided, therefore, is not irrigation projects but poor water allocation policies. Such policies only encourage wasteful use of water and promote environmental degradation. That is why developing improved water allocation policies is the subject of the next section.

WATER ALLOCATION REFORM PROPOSALS

Here we look at some proposals for market-based reforms of existing institutions. Up to this point, we have only looked at surface water. However, many countries have vast quantities of water in underground aquifers, called *groundwater supplies*. In the United States, for example, one of the largest such aquifers is the Ogallala, which lies beneath most of the High Plains states. Groundwater allocation must be addressed with different policies than surface water because of different *replenishment rates*. In general, surface water supplies are replenished far more quickly than groundwater supplies. Thus surface water can be thought of as a renewable resource, but efficient allocation of groundwater must be considered over time like other depletable resources.[20]

As we discussed in earlier chapters, the efficient allocation of any good, whether water or whales, will require that its marginal values be equated across different users. If this is not the case, then there remain opportunities for beneficial reallocations. These reallocations will increase the overall benefits, which will be approximated by the sum of consumers' surplus for the good in question. Figure 17.1 illustrates this in the case of two competing classes of users of water.

In Figure 17.1, the initial supply curve of water is denoted by S. We assume that the marginal cost of producing water remains constant up to the point of finite supply. This is given by the location of the vertical supply curve. Each class of users has a demand curve for water, given by MB_1 and MB_2. In this two-user-class case, the total market demand curve for water equals the horizontal sum of the individual class demand curves and is shown as the dashed line.[21]

If the supply of water is S, the total quantity of water demanded will be given by Q_T (point W). The efficient allocation of water will be achieved when the marginal benefit of the last gallon of water demanded is the same for both users. Reading off the individual demand curves, the efficient supply of water to each will be Q_1 and Q_2 gallons, respectively.

---

[20] Recall the discussion of depletable resources in Chapter 15.

[21] Recall our discussion of the demand for a public good in Chapter 6. In that case, the individual demand curves were summed vertically. We can also think of the individual demand curves as value-of-marginal-product curves. This might be appropriate in the case of farmers, for whom water is an input to the production of crops.

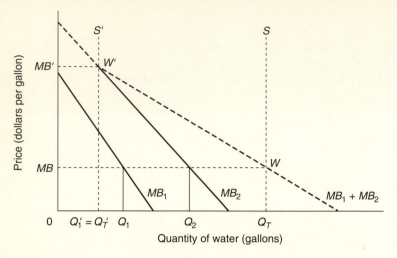

Figure 17.1   Efficient Allocation of Water Supplies

One of the problems with surface water supplies is that they can vary from year to year, primarily because of changes in climate. If water supplies are restricted severely enough, it is possible for the allocation of the existing supply to be limited to one individual. In Figure 17.1, suppose that water supplies are given by S' gallons. S' intersects the market demand curve for water at W'. At W', the marginal benefit of water equals MB'. This is greater than group 1's marginal benefit for even 1 gallon. Thus the entire supply of water will be efficiently allocated to group 2.

Unfortunately, allocation of water based on economic efficiency has been rare. In dry years, for example, water users in group 1 would object to all water being allocated to group 2 users, even though the latter group valued that water more highly. In part, just these sorts of objections have occurred because water has been viewed as an entitlement rather than a tradable resource. Fortunately, proposals have been developed that would increase the economic efficiency of surface water and groundwater allocation. These policies are discussed next.

Surface Water Policies

Traditionally, existing U.S. water law (like water law in many other countries) has done little to encourage transferring water between users to equate marginal values. In particular, the prior appropriation system in many states allows third parties to block a transfer that would affect them, regardless of how small the impact is.

Gisser and Johnson (1981) argue that defining water rights in terms of the amount of *consumptive use* will increase economic efficiency by allowing beneficial transfers. Consumptive use refers to the amount of water that is actually used. To illustrate, suppose that a farmer diverts water from a stream. Some of the water will be used by the farmer's crops, some will evaporate, and some will soak into the ground. Much of the water that escapes into the ground will find its way back into the stream. This water is called *return flow*. So if the farmer diverts 1,000 acre-feet of water, and 400 returns to the stream, the farmer's consumptive use will have been 600 acre-feet.[22]

To understand the crucial nature of return flows, suppose that the full stream-flow prior to any diversion is 1,200 acre-feet per unit of time and suppose that, following Gisser and Johnson (1981), there are three farmers along the stream, A, B, and C. Farmer A diverts 1,000 acre-feet and returns 400. Farmer B diverts 600 acre-feet and returns 300. Farmer C diverts 300 acre-feet and returns 150. The sum of diverted water equals 1,900 acre-feet, 700 acre-feet more than the total initial streamflow. This is illustrated in Figure 17.2.

Now suppose that a nearby city offers to buy farmer A's 1,000 acre-feet for a price of $1.50 per acre-foot. If the value of water for irrigation is $1.00 per acre-foot consumed, farmer A will sell his water for $1,500 and forgo $600 in agricultural production, for a net gain of $900. Unfortunately, the diversion of water to the city means that the 400 acre-feet of return flow that farmers B and C had relied on is no longer present. Instead, farmer B will see only 200 acre-feet of water. He will consume 100 acre-feet and return 100 acre-feet and suffer a loss of $200. Farmer C will have only the 100 acre-feet available. He will consume 50 and will suffer a loss of $100. In addition, flow downstream of farmer C will be only 50 acre-feet, reducing water available for irrigators farther downstream by 100 acre-feet. They will suffer a loss of $100. This gives a net economic gain from the transaction is $500, but farmer A receives all the benefits while farmers B, C, and others downstream pay all the costs.

If property rights are defined in terms of consumptive use, farmer A will be able to sell only 600 acre-feet. This will ensure that 600 acre-feet remain for farmer B. Farmer B has a consumptive right of 300 acre-feet, leaving 300 acre-feet for farmer C, who has a consumptive right of 150 acre-feet. Farmer A makes a gain of $300, and the downstream irrigators are unaffected. If the city wants 1,000 acre-feet, it has to buy water from all three farmers. They will share the gain of $1,500 and will share the cost of $1,000 from reduced crop production.

This solution may work in a climate with a year-round growing season and steady streamflows, but it can break down under other conditions, such as a shorter growing season and seasonal streamflow fluctuations. This is because it takes time for return flows to return to the stream. Many return flows percolate slowly through shallow aquifers that eventually discharge into springs. This can take months. The result is that defining upstream users' rights in terms of consumptive use does not unambiguously define the rights of downstream users.

This can be shown by another example. Suppose that we have the same farmers and the same city but a different climate. The growing season consists of the spring, where natural streamflows are high and evaporation is low, and the summer, where natural streamflows are low and evaporation is high. In addition, return flows from irrigation in the spring return to the stream in the summer, and return

---

[22]An acre-foot of water is the amount of water that would cover 1 acre of land with 1 foot of water, or around 350,000 gallons.

Water Diversion to Farmers   Total Streamflow (acre-feet)

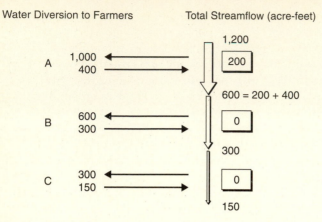

Figure 17.2   Water Diversion and Return Flows

flows from summer irrigation reach the stream in the fall, after the growing season is over. In the spring, flows at farmer A's headgate equal 2,400 acre-feet. Farmer A diverts 1,000 acre-feet, and 400 acre-feet of that is used by his crops or evaporates in the irrigation ditch. This leaves 600 acre-feet to return to the stream during the summer. Flows below farmer A's land in the spring are therefore 1,400 acre-feet. Farmers B and C can divert their 900 acre-feet, and there are 500 acre-feet for downstream users. In the spring, farmers B and C each consume one-third of the water they divert, and the other 600 acre-feet return to the stream in the summer.

In the summer, there are 1,200 acre-feet available at farmer A's headgate. He diverts 1,000, leaving 200 acre-feet in the stream. However, they are augmented by his 600 acre-feet of return flows from spring irrigation so that there are 800 acre-feet available to farmer B. He diverts 600 acre-feet, but return flows from his spring irrigation are 400, so 600 acre-feet are available to farmer C. He diverts 300 acre-feet, but 200 return to the stream from his spring irrigation, so there are 500 acre-feet for downstream users.

In this case, if farmer A sells his consumptive use to the city, downstream users are affected. In the spring, the city can divert only farmer A's consumptive use of 400, so 600 additional acre-feet are left in the stream. However, in the spring, there is already more water than downstream users demand, so these additional flows have no value. They may even have costs if they contribute to flooding. In the summer, the city diverts farmer A's 600 acre-feet, leaving 600 acre-feet in the stream. Since there are no return flows from spring irrigation, farmer B diverts the whole flow. However, the return flows of 400 from farmer B's spring irrigation allow farmer C to continue to divert 300 acre-feet. This leaves 100 acre-feet in the stream. When the 200 acre-feet of return flows from farmer C's spring irrigation are added to this, downstream users have only 300 acre-feet available. They have lost 200 acre-feet in the summer, when their water demands already exceeded the available supply.

In this situation, defining water rights in terms of consumptive use does not protect downstream users. This is because upstream irrigation in the spring actually stores water for use downstream in the summer, when less is available and demand is higher. Defining water rights in terms of consumptive use guarantees downstream users a given amount of water, and in this case, more water actually flows downstream after the transfer. However, it does not guarantee *when* that water will be available. In this case, the transfer harms downstream users by shifting streamflows from summer, when they have a high value, to spring, when the value of additional flows is zero or negative.

The "no third-party impacts" rule used in many prior appropriation states would block this transfer and protect the downstream users. However, the transfer may be beneficial to society as a whole—the benefits from shifting farmer A's irrigation water to a higher-valued use may be greater than the costs to downstream users. Then again, they may not. Which rule comes closer to efficiency depends on circumstances. Both rules are likely to fall short in some cases because they try to deal with third-party impacts through a single rule, rather than by encouraging third parties to become participants in transactions that affect them.

An ideal water rights system in a Coasian world with zero transactions costs would define a complete set of water rights in existing uses, including instream uses, and would require agreement by all affected parties for any change. With zero transactions costs, the losers from any change could bargain for compensation from the gainers as the price of their consenting to the change. Only those changes with net benefits would take place, and all changes with net benefits would be made. The result would be efficient water use. In the real world, with positive transactions costs and an inherited system of water law, the best we can hope for is incremental improvements. Allowing transfers based on consumptive use (or any incremental reform) should not be rejected because it is imperfect any more than it should be embraced universally because it appears to work in some circumstances. Any reform of water allocation institutions needs to be evaluated in the context in which it will be used, and different contexts may call for different solutions.

Market-Based Surface Water Policies for Federal Water Projects   For federal water projects, Wahl (1989) outlined numerous policy changes that could enhance water rights transfers and improve economic efficiency. These changes include removal of limitations on profits from water resale because of provisions of the Warren Act of 1911; removal of limitations on transfers of water outside individual project areas; and removal of acreage restrictions (the 160-acre limit). In addition, the extent of irrigation subsidies discussed previously could be substantially lessened. This would make it less likely that development of uneconomic projects would occur and would encourage transfers of water to higher-valued uses.

Consider a policy that would allow farmers receiving Bureau of Reclamation water at a subsidized price to resell it in an open market. A farmer can sell all or part of his irrigation entitlement. In theory, this should encourage the transfer of water from lower-valued uses to higher-valued ones. However, a potential problem with this approach is noted by Kanazawa (1994). He suggests that the efficiency gains of the market-pricing policy will be reduced if the transfer right is based on historical use rather than the specific entitlement. The reason is straightforward: a farmer who can buy water at a below-market price and then sell it will wish to sell as much as possible. If the farmer's allocation of federal water is based on historical use, the farmer may have an incentive to "waste" water in order to increase his historical use.

Another policy option would be to eliminate the subsidy but maintain the restrictions on reselling water. In this case, the reduction in water use will depend on whether the farmer was initially using his full entitlement or not. If the farmer would prefer using more water at the subsidized price than allowed by his entitlement, the standard efficiency impacts would be observed; prices would increase, and the farmer's usage would decline. Conversely, a farmer who was using less water than allowed might not reduce water usage at all. The reason is that the price would have to rise sufficiently so that the marginal value of the last acre-foot of water use was less than the price (Kanazawa 1994). This is illustrated in Figure 17.3. In this figure, D_W is the farmer's demand curve for water. Assume that the farmer's initial entitlement of water equals W_{E1}. The farmer is entitled to more water than he wishes to purchase, even at the subsidized price, which will equal the farmer's marginal value of water.

Suppose that the price subsidy is now reduced so that the price paid by the farmer increases to P_{new}. At this new price, the marginal cost of water will exceed the farmer's marginal value, and the farmer will reduce water consumption. This is the scenario envisioned by proponents of federal water market reform.

Suppose, however, that the farmer's entitlement is less than his demand—say, W_{E2} acre-feet. Now the farmer's marginal value of water equals P_{E2}. If the subsidized price is increased to P_{min}, the farmer's consumption will remain unchanged because the new price is still below the farmer's marginal value of water.

If restrictions on reselling are eliminated and prices are allowed to increase to their market levels (i.e., the true efficient market proposal), the overall change in existing water consumption will again depend on whether the farmer's entitlement is binding. The observed impact will be less if the existing entitlement is binding.

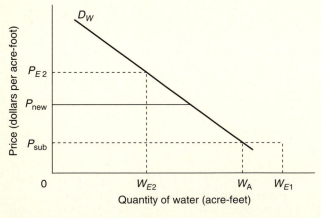

Figure 17.3 Impacts of Increasing Subsidized Water Prices

Source: Adapted from Kanazawa (1994), p. 118.

Another critical market policy issue is the cost of setting up trading mechanisms themselves. The transition to full water markets is not costless. It requires setting up new conveyance mechanism so that water can be physically transferred to different users. It requires more extensive measuring and metering of water use, especially if previous water entitlements were nonbinding, and it requires increasing monitoring and protection of water flows (Zilberman, Macdougall, and Shah 1994). If the efficiency gains from a new market-based system are less than the adjustment costs associated with implementing that system, there will be an overall loss of economic efficiency. Thus if a change is made, it probably should be as widespread as possible to spread the fixed transition costs over the greatest number of users. In their study of water allocation in California, Zilberman and colleagues argue that allocation systems that involve all agricultural users will be less costly than policies restricting trades among farmers using water from California's Central Valley Project. The authors further argue that widespread water allocation mechanisms will have an environmental benefit in California; reducing agricultural water use will free up additional water that can be used to improve water quality in the San Francisco Bay Area.

Water Banks   Water "banks" can be thought of in the same way as their more familiar money-handling cousins. Essentially, a water bank is an arrangement that allows farmers to rent their water to other users. The state of Idaho, for example, formally authorized water rentals in 1980 for water in Bureau of Reclamation reservoirs on the Upper Snake River, although informal rental arrangements had existed since the 1930s (Wahl 1989). The bank leases storage space in Bureau facilities, which allows users to access the water in that storage. However, the bank does not allow unfettered transfers of water. Water rentals are determined by user priority. Top priority is assigned to existing canal companies that own storage space in the Bureau reservoirs. Next priority goes to existing agricultural users who had traditionally used rentals. Then come new agricultural users and, last, other users, especially power companies seeking additional water to generate hydroelectricity.

Another example of a water bank occurred in California, during that state's severe drought in 1976–1977. Under the California program, the Bureau was required to help willing sellers transfer water to willing buyers. However, the program was to be run so that sellers received "no undue profits" (Wahl 1989). Furthermore, the rules of the Bureau program specified priorities among the different buyers. Top priority went to preserving orchards and perennials, next for support crops for cattle (e.g., alfalfa, corn), and last irrigation for all other crops. The bank paid anywhere from $15.00 to $84.50 per acre-foot of water and resold the water at an average price of about $61 per acre-foot.

One of the most innovative banking designs is for Colorado–Big Thompson Project water. The water from the C-BT is distributed by the Northern Colorado Water Conservancy District (NCWCD). Each year, the NCWCD allocates the amount of available C-BT water proportionally among all of the of 310,000 "shares" of water. All shares can be bought, sold, or leased. Thus the NCWCD can be thought of as a "stock market" for water. The price of shares each year varies, depending on total C-BT supplies and the demand for water. Unlike the Idaho and California examples, however, exchanges of NCWCD shares are not fixed in terms of priority groups.

Groundwater Policies

Groundwater allocation policies are complicated by the common-property nature of groundwater resources. As we first discussed in Chapter 6, with no restrictions, common-property resource users will tend to overuse the resource. In the case of an aquifer, such as the Ogallala, theory suggests and empirical evidence confirmed that too much water would be pumped out and too much water would be used by earlier users. Furthermore, because of the nature of aquifer geology, users near the fringes of the aquifer would be the first to experience the adverse impacts of overpumping and reductions in aquifer levels, as the edges would tend to become dry first.

Despite the complications introduced by the common-property nature of groundwater resources, several methods have been proposed to privatize groundwater rights (Anderson, Burt, and Fractor 1981; Smith 1977) or levy "pump taxes" on groundwater (Frederick 1982). Smith's idea is to issue property deeds for a given amount of water to water users in the groundwater basin. Each water user would be granted a right to some amount of flow, as well as a portion of the entire stock. Property rights would be allocated in proportion to the water pumped by the individual users for some base year. (Smith chose 1975 in his example of Tucson Basin, where total use was 224,600 acre-feet.)

Suppose that there are N individual users in the base year, and let the use of the ith individual equal x_i. User i's proportion of total use, p_i, would therefore be $x_i/224,600$. Each individual's right to annual flows would be based on the long-run average recharge rate of the groundwater basin. In the case of the Tucson Basin, average recharge has been estimated at 74,600 acre-feet. Thus the property right or annual flow assigned to each individual would equal $74,600p_i$ acre-feet every year in perpetuity, and the first deed would be renewable. The second deed of groundwater property right would be in the form of a share of the basin's overall stock of water. In 1975, for example, the stock of the Tucson Basin was estimated to be around 30 million acre-feet. Each individual's share would be based on the same proportion p_i. Thus each individual would have a right to pump a total of $30p_i$ million acre-feet at any time in the future. This would be a nonrenewable right. Because the deeds would be fully transferable, water would tend to be allocated to its highest-valued use. Users who consumed less than their annual portion of water would be able to sell the entire component of the second deed. However, users who used more than the renewable portion would be able to sell only the remaining portion of the nonrenewable deed.

There are several potential problems with this approach. First, assignment of the initial allocation is arbitrary. Without careful design, under this scheme, previously "wasteful" users would nevertheless be assigned larger shares of groundwater. Anderson and colleagues (1981) suggest a way of getting around this problem by assigning deeds in proportion to the amount of land overlaying the aquifer. A second potential complication of this allocation scheme is the residual pumping externalities that would remain for edge users of the aquifer. To see this, suppose that some individuals near the center of an aquifer wish to draw down the nonrenewable portions of their water. In such a case, users near the edge of the aquifer could find themselves without water or with rapidly accelerating pumping costs. To solve this issue, Anderson and colleagues (1981) suggest a modification of the property rights to ensure an equilibrium stock of groundwater below which stocks cannot fall.[23]

A "pump tax" on groundwater withdrawals is yet another market-enhancing allocation mechanism (Frederick 1982). The purpose of a pump tax is to reduce the common-property externality associated with excess pumping of an aquifer. The pump tax obliges pumpers to incorporate the scarcity value of groundwater in their water use decisions. A pump tax could be combined with privatization of groundwater rights. For example, one possibility to mitigate the problem for edge users of an aquifer would be to levy differential pump taxes, depending on a user's location above the aquifer. Edge users, who have the least common-property impact, would be charged lower pump taxes than interior users. Obviously, the most difficult issue with establishing a pump tax is setting the tax at the right level. Too low a tax, and the common-property problem will not be abated. Too high a tax, and too little water will be used, reducing economic efficiency.[24]

Despite the implementation difficulties associated with any of these proposals, they represent a clear improvement over existing groundwater allocation policies. For example, the Ogallala aquifer—which underlies parts of Colorado, Kansas, Nebraska, New Mexico, Oklahoma, South Dakota, Texas, and Wyoming—is the largest aquifer in the United States. Over the years, it has been depleted; irrigators have pumped water from it with little regard for future use or for the impacts their pumping could have on others. Implementation of policies that incorporated the methods suggested by Anderson and colleagues or Smith, perhaps in conjunction with the pump tax proposed by Frederick, could increase the efficiency with which water from the Ogallala and other aquifers is used.

Interactions Between Groundwater and Surface Water Policies

Because groundwater and surface water are potential substitutes, allocation and market-enhancing policies addressed to each can affect the other. As a result, policies designed to "fix" one problem, such as inefficient use of Bureau of Reclamation surface water, can be affected by other policies.

---

[23]This raises numerous measurement issues. Measuring groundwater stocks is not precise, much as estimating petroleum reserves in different fields is difficult. See Anderson, Burt, and Fractor (1981) for further details.

[24]This last issue recalls the discussion on Weitzmann's analysis of price versus quantity regulations in Chapter 7.

Kanazawa (1994), for example, examines the relationship between pump taxes and Bureau entitlement ceilings, on the assumption that groundwater is available in addition to Bureau water. Suppose that a farmer's surface water entitlement is binding and that the farmer supplements this allocation with groundwater. Next suppose that a pump tax is imposed to reduce the likelihood of excessive groundwater depletion. The pump tax increases the relative price of groundwater. Because the farmer's surface water entitlement is binding, however, the farmer will not substitute surface water for groundwater, and we will observe a reduction in groundwater use. If the surface water constraint is not binding, however, the farmer will substitute additional Bureau water for groundwater. For policymakers, the key question is whether levying the pump tax in the case of a nonbinding Bureau entitlement would increase or decrease economic efficiency. Unfortunately, determining the efficient depletion rate for groundwater is complicated. Policymakers would have to determine the relevant inefficiencies associated with excessive groundwater pumping and subsidized surface water prices, as well as consider potential environmental costs and benefits. Although the issue is too complex to resolve here, the key point remains: policymakers should carefully consider *all* of the potential impacts of water marketing proposals before implementing them.

WATER PRICING POLICIES

Agriculture is not the only area where water is used inefficiently. This should be obvious to anyone who has seen urban and suburban residents watering the sidewalk next to an already soaked lawn or flushing the toilet to dispose of a tissue. As with federal irrigation projects, the cause of such inefficiency is pricing that does not reflect marginal cost. Few water utilities use marginal cost pricing, because they are either regulated monopolies or branches of local government.

In general, most water utilities have priced at average cost, recovering sufficient revenues to cover their total costs but not reflecting marginal costs. This sort of pricing is similar to that practiced by other regulated utilities. Policies such as increasing block prices, which charges marginal cost for marginal water use while covering average cost on average, and allowing people a minimal level of use at a minimal charge are rare. In some cities, including New York City, individual water demand is often not even metered or water is delivered on a flat-fee basis that does not vary with the amount consumed. In these cases, there is little or no incentive to conserve.

Some cities, such as Tucson, Arizona, have attempted to improve the efficiency of their water pricing policies (Martin et al. 1984). Under these policies, rates for the initial blocks of water can be set low, so as to maintain affordability for an amount of water that is needed for basic survival, and then price subsequent blocks can be priced much higher. Individuals who wish the luxury of, say, large, luxurious lawns in Tucson will pay more for marginal blocks of water.[25]

---

[25]This is essentially the reverse of so-called Ramsey pricing, which calls for the highest prices to be paid by consumers with the least elastic price elasticities of demand.

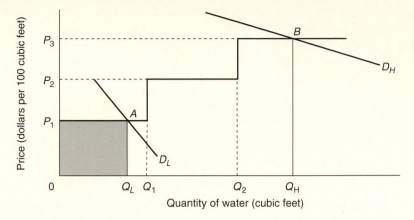

Figure 17.4 Increasing Block Structure for Water Pricing

Increasing block structures are shown in Figure 17.4. Assume that there are two levels of water demand. Demand level D_L represents a low level of water demand. Consumers with this level of demand pay a price of P_1 per 100 cubic feet for a total cost of P_1Q_1. This is shown as the shaded area. Consumers with higher levels of demand D_H, however, pay increasingly higher prices. They pay P_1 for the first Q_1 units, P_2 for the next $Q_2 - Q_1$ units, and P_3 for the last $Q_H - Q_2$ units.

Pricing and the Development of Complete Water Markets

We already have discussed some of the issues associated with developing water markets in relation to existing federal water allocations based on systems of water rights. Of course, not all water is controlled by the federal government. Water resources have been developed by states and municipalities for agriculture, industrial, and residential use. Thus despite the caveats noted by Kanazawa (1994) and Zilberman and colleagues (1994), establishment of fully transferable water markets is an attractive mechanism for improving economic efficiency.

Water markets can be developed like other markets. Instead of basing allocations of water on preexisting water rights, water will flow to its most valued use. Thus a city seeking new water supplies might purchase water from irrigators rather than invest in new infrastructure to increase water supplies (wells, dams, etc.). Like the development of tradable pollution emissions permits that we discussed in Chapter 7, tradable water seems an ideal solution to existing water supply and use policy issues. And there are some examples of institutions like water banks designed to facilitate water transfers among different users. So why has it been so difficult to develop water markets, both in this country and elsewhere?

Wahl (1989) suggests that the difficulty in developing water markets and policies that encourage efficient allocation of water supplies in the United States dates back to the beginnings of federal reclamation policy. In the early part of the twentieth century, federal reclamation policy was designed to allow reclaimed land to compete with other, presumably more productive land. Once water subsidies were granted to different groups, those subsidies became the equivalent of a system of property rights to below-market-price water. Not surprisingly, beneficiaries of such subsidies were loath to forgo them. Consequently, attempts to reform reclamation policies were largely unsuccessful.

It is because these attempts have been unsuccessful that so much policy work has centered around developing efficient water markets like those described earlier. In that way, at least water supplies could be exchanged freely. Although the development of such markets does not directly address equity issues associated with the initial allocation of water subsidies, it would allow water supplies to be allocated to their most beneficial uses.

EMPIRICAL ISSUES: MEASURING THE VALUE OF WATER

Even though it appears that many water allocation decisions will continue to be made by courts, legislatures, or executive-branch agencies, water markets are gaining increased acceptance, both in the United States and in other countries. In many cases, however, water will be purchased by different government entities on behalf of classes of users. For example, the city of Los Angeles may wish to buy water for residents of the city from irrigators in California's Central Valley. If the city wishes to encourage the most efficient use of the water it buys, it will want to determine residents' demand curve for water. In that way, it will be able to establish an efficient price for the water it sells.

In drought situations, where existing supplies of water are restricted, policymakers may need to make specific allocation decisions. Should water be diverted from irrigators to residential users by raising the price to the former? Perhaps, instead, water should be diverted from residential users to irrigators. Or perhaps certain local industries need a lot of water for their production processes. In that case, how should a municipality adjust prices between residential and industrial users? In all of these cases, having information on the different demand curves for water would help make efficient allocation and pricing decisions. In this section, therefore, we examine empirical estimates of the demand for water, specifically for residential and irrigation users.

Before water can be allocated and priced efficiently, the different uses for a given supply of water must be determined, including environmental uses such as recreation or additional river flows for "flushing" fish. Sometimes, however, the alternative uses are difficult to define until the water supplies themselves are defined. For example, construction of Grand Coulee Dam made possible an entire agricultural industry in Washington State. But how would we know what the value of the irrigation water supplied would be before the dam's construction? And in the case of groundwater, which owing to its common-property characteristics may be depleted too quickly, how would we determine water values so as to levy the correct pump tax?

To compare marginal values of water between different classes of users, first we need a common measure that removes the costs of obtaining water. For example, if we observe that the price of water for residential users in Phoenix, Arizona, is $500 per acre-foot while the price to farmers in California is $50 per acre-foot, we *cannot* conclude that water is ten times more valuable to residential consumers in Phoenix than to irrigators in California. The reason is that we must also account for the cost of obtaining the water. In that way, we can determine marginal values of water at the source, whether that is from a river or an aquifer. This is illustrated in Figure 17.5.

In the figure, the prices paid per acre-foot of water by residential users and agricultural users are P_R and P_A, respectively. For residential users, total *WTP* is given by area $ABQ_RQ'_R$, while residential consumers actually pay only the amount given by $CBQ_RQ'_R$. The total *WTP* for agricultural users is given by $A'B'Q_AQ'_A$, while they actually pay $C'B'Q_AQ'_A$. If we assume that the price paid by each exactly reflects the total cost of supplying that water, then the value of water from its source, net of supply costs, will equal the consumers' surplus for each. These are ABC and $A'B'C'$, respectively. Because $ABC < A'B'C'$, consumers' surplus for residential customers is less than that for agricultural customers. Thus even though agricultural consumers may be willing to pay a larger incremental amount for their water than residential customers, the total value to residential customers of that water is still much higher. It is these total values, along with environmental uses of water (recreation benefits from free-flowing rivers, existence values for pristine lakes, etc.) that should be used to compare water allocations.

Residential Value of Water

Gibbons (1986) provides a review of numerous studies that estimated the value of water for residential users. For residential customers, water demand is often seasonal, increasing in summer as residents use water for outdoor activities such as gardening and recreation. Thus the total value of water to residential users can be

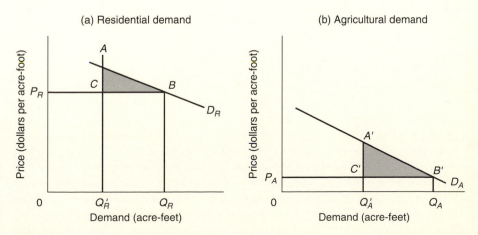

Figure 17.5   Total and Marginal Values for Water

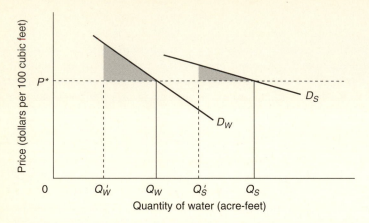

Figure 17.6 Identifying Marginal Values of Water at Different Times of the Year

determined by examining the consumers' surplus associated with different seasonal levels of water consumption. This is illustrated in Figure 17.6.

In the figure, the demand for water in summer is both greater and more elastic than the demand in winter at price P^*. Using data from several studies that had estimated demand curves for water and the accompanying price elasticities of demand, Gibbons (1986) estimated the consumers' surplus associated with different reductions in consumption. In winter, for example, a reduction in consumption from Q_W to Q'_W would be associated with a loss in consumers' surplus equal to the shaded area beneath D_W. A similar reduction in consumption during the summer would entail a loss in consumers' surplus equal to the shaded area below D_S. Because the elasticity of demand in summer is greater than the elasticity of demand in winter, the consumers' surplus loss in winter will be greater than the consumers' surplus in summer (Young et al. 1972). Dividing the consumers' surplus estimates by the change in consumption (either $Q_W - Q'_W$ or $Q_S - Q'_S$), the marginal value of water can be approximated. Gibbons's results are shown in Table 17.2.

Gibbons (1986) notes three important caveats associated with this type of analysis. First, the calculations assume that the elasticity of demand along each of the curves is constant within the interval of the change in quantity of water. Because the demand for water is less elastic as the quantity drops, her methodology will tend to underestimate the marginal value associated with larger quantity reductions. Second, she notes that the share of water in residential household budgets is quite small. Thus prices relative to household income levels are small. This may account for the low elasticity values calculated. The most important caveat, however, is a function of how municipal water utilities obtain their water supplies. In Figure 17.3, it is assumed that the price P^* paid by consumers equals the water utility's average cost for providing water (water pipes, mains, billing services, etc.) but that the raw water receive by the utility is free. If, however, cities purchase

TABLE 17.2 MARGINAL VALUES OF RESIDENTIAL WATER DEMAND

Location (Year)	Season	Price of Water (dollars per 100 cubic feet)	Price Elasticity of Demand	Average Monthly Consumption (hundreds of cubic feet per household)	Marginal Water Value of a 10 Percent Reduction (dollars per acre-foot)
Tucson, Arizona (1979)	Winter	0.72	−0.17	9.44	82
	Summer	0.83	−0.70	16.43	28
Raleigh, North Carolina (1973)	Winter	1.27	−0.305	7.82	105
	Summer	1.17	−1.380	8.81	21
Toronto, Ontario (1967)	Winter	0.79	−0.75	5.30	25
	Summer	0.79	−1.07	6.55	17

Source: Adapted from Gibbons (1986).

water rights in a competitive water market, the marginal value of water would be better reflected by the trading price of water.[26]

Irrigation Value of Water

Irrigation is the single largest use of water in many states, especially in the arid western states, where as much as 90 percent of total water consumption is for agriculture purposes. Thus determining the empirical value of water used for irrigation has been a critical policy task.

Gibbons (1986) presents two alternative valuation methods that have been used: crop water production functions and farm crop budget analysis. Torrell and colleagues (1990) used a different approach. They determined the value of water in the Ogallala aquifer by examining the difference in values for irrigated and dryland farm sales, thus capturing all of the factors that may contribute to the value of water.

Crop water production function analysis simply means that a production function for particular crops is estimated. Various combinations of seed, fertilizer, water, labor, and capital equipment can be used to produce a particular crop. A standard result presented in any microeconomics textbook shows that the choice of combination of these inputs will depend on their relative prices and the values of the marginal product of each. Specifically, the inputs will be combined in such a way that the values of their marginal products are precisely equal to their marginal cost. To determine the marginal value of water using this method, controlled experiments are usually carried out. In these experiments, all other crop inputs are held constant. Additional water is applied to a particular crop to determine the change in overall production. That change, times the price of the crop, will equal the marginal value of the additional water applied.

One of the problems with crop production function analysis is that in many areas, no experiments have been performed. Thus the actual physical productivity of water is unknown. Farm crop budget analysis tries to circumvent this problem by developing representative farm budgets that determine the maximum revenue share of water. In other words, the total revenue of producing a given amount of crop is estimated, usually by agricultural extension agents. From this total revenue, called a *revenue budget,* the cost of all of the nonwater inputs are subtracted. The residual will equal the maximum amount a farmer could pay for water and still cover production costs. Thus the residual amount represents the total on-farm value of water. If the cost of obtaining water is subtracted from this amount, the net value of providing irrigation water can be compared to other values of obtaining water, as was illustrated in Figure 17.3.

A third approach, which has the advantage of being able to determine water values for dryland farming, is to examine price differentials between irrigated and dryland farm sales. Suppose that two adjoining farms are sold at the same time.

---

[26]This is the situation for Colorado towns on the eastern slopes of the Rocky Mountains. See Wahl (1989) for a discussion.

Each has produced the same crop, wheat. The first farm has access to irrigation water and sells for $1,000 per acre. The second farm raises wheat using dryland techniques. This farm sells for $500 per acre. In this approach, it is hypothesized that the $500-per-acre difference in sales prices is attributable to the net earnings potential of water. Dividing this value by the average water thickness at the farm, one can compute the value of water on a per-acre-foot basis (Torell et al. 1990).

Gibbons (1986) summarizes crop production function and farm budget estimates of the value of water. Using experimental data collected by the U.S. Department of Agriculture on crop production functions in six western states, she derives values of water on a per-acre-foot basis. The values depend on crop prices, which are 1980 average national crop prices. The results of the crop production analysis are summarized in Table 17.3. The estimates derived in the production function studies summarized by Gibbons all depend on the efficiency with which irrigation water is used and the price of the crop. As efficiency improves and crop prices rise, so does the value of water applied.

Gibbons cites numerous farm budget studies that determined the net value of water. The values vary greatly. In one case, imputed water values for grain sorghum in three counties in Arizona were found to be negative, although values for other crops in those counties were above zero. These results are reproduced in Table 17.4.

Torell and colleagues (1990) developed estimates for the market value of water using the price differentials between dry and irrigated land in the Ogallala aquifer. Using data supplied by the Farm Credit Service, the authors analyzed prices for almost 7,000 farm sales. The authors took care to ensure that all of the sales represented farms producing crops, eliminating livestock ranches. For their estimation procedure, they determined water characteristics of the farms sold. Specifically, they looked at the depth to the aquifer, the saturated thickness of the aquifer, and the saturation coefficient. The latter two components provide a good proxy for the amount of water contained in the aquifer below a farm, and the depth of the aquifer provides a proxy for the cost of pumping water out of the aquifer.

TABLE 17.3 WATER VALUES REFLECTING CROP PRODUCTION METHOD (DOLLARS PER ACRE-FOOT)

Crop	Value					
	Idaho	Washington	California	Arizona	New Mexico	Texas
Grain sorghum				< 15		113
Wheat		59		22		35
Alfalfa				25	25	
Cotton			71–129	56	61	
Corn					52	57
Sugarbeets		144				
Potatoes	698	282				

Source: Adapted from Gibbons (1986).

TABLE 17.4   WATER VALUES COMPUTED USING THE FARM BUDGET METHOD FOR
FOUR ARIZONA COUNTIES (IN DOLLARS)

Crop	Values			
	Maricopa County	Pinal County	Pima County	Cochise County
Grain sorghum	−7	−1	−6	11
Barley	−6	12	5	8
Wheat	11	25	15	24
Alfalfa	11		25	17
Pima cotton			17	33
Upland cotton	38	55	50	16
Safflower	38	39		
Sugarbeets	49	44		67

Source: Adapted from Gibbons (1986) and from Willitt, Hathorn, and Robertson (1975).

Combining the water quantity variables with estimates of net economic
returns for the farms and several other variables allowed the authors to separate
out other effects on the value of farm sales. The authors estimated two separate
farm price equations, one each for dryland farms and irrigated farms, by state for
the years 1979–1986. A sampling of the results is reproduced in Table 17.5. The
results of their model indicate that water values declined significantly between
1983 and 1986. The magnitude of the decline was different for the different states,
ranging from 30 percent declines in New Mexico to 60 percent declines in
Nebraska. Water values were highest in New Mexico, primarily because of the
risks involved in dryland farming due to New Mexico's being the most arid of the
states and therefore dryland farmers having the fewest options available to them.
To the extent that depletion of the aquifer results in conversions of farms from
irrigated to dryland techniques, the authors' model indicates a significant loss of
market value. This may affect legal claims of environmental damages because of
excessive water depletion out of the aquifer.

The "Piecemeal" Problem

Water is an input to many production processes. Even household consumption of
water can be thought of in this light, with household water an input to production
processes for "outputs" such as clean laundry, showers, and waste disposal. As we
discussed, the marginal value of water will be determined by its value of marginal
product (*VMP*). However, the *VMP* may be affected by other economic distortions.
This is particularly important in determinations of water values for irrigation purposes. A farmer's purchasing subsidized electricity and subsidized water and par-
ticipating in government programs that create artificial price supports for the crops
he grows will affect his marginal value of water. This can further complicate determinations of "efficient" allocations of water, because the *VMP* of water may be significantly distorted. This is sometimes referred to as the "piecemeal" problem and

TABLE 17.5   AVERAGE VALUES OF WATER IN STORAGE, BY STATE

Values	New Mexico	Oklahoma	Northern Colorado	Southern Colorado	Kansas	Nebraska	Average
			State				
Dollars per acre							
1979	579	431	1,004	567	467	429	580
1980	610	325	878	437	432	542	537
1981	639	271	749	312	386	633	498
1982	648	224	668	178	365	695	473
1983	657	226	615	193	349	688	455
1984	603	177	571	156	308	610	406
1985	530	168	569	154	266	476	361
1986	442	173	622	200	253	285	329
Dollars per acre-foot							
1979	7.66	2.54	7.62	5.94	3.07	2.29	4.85
1980	8.24	1.93	6.69	4.58	2.87	2.88	4.53
1981	8.89	1.63	5.73	3.28	2.61	3.38	4.25
1982	9.20	1.36	5.14	2.52	2.49	3.71	4.07
1983	9.49	1.39	4.73	2.06	2.40	3.65	3.95
1984	8.84	1.16	4.41	1.68	2.12	3.17	3.57
1985	7.87	1.05	4.41	1.66	1.85	2.51	3.22
1986	6.64	1.09	4.85	2.17	1.77	1.49	3.00

Source: Adapted from Torell, Libbin, and Miller (1990).

is shown in Figure 17.7, where *VMP* refers to the "true" value of marginal product of water in the absence of economic distortions. The quantity of water used will equal Q gallons. Suppose that the only distortion in the market is that farmers receive a subsidized price for their crops. As a result, the *VMP* for water will shift upward, reflecting the increased value of each additional unit of water. As a result, the quantity of water consumed increases to Q' gallons. Marginal values of water will be higher for given reductions in water supplies.

In addition, as was discussed earlier in the chapter, irrigation can result in negative externalities on land productivity, such as increased salinity, as well as increases in sedimentation in rivers, silting in navigation channels, and increased use of agricultural chemicals. To the extent that none of these impacts are incorporated into empirical estimates of the value of water, those estimates will be distorted. Even in the presence of fully transferable water rights allocation systems, efficient transfers will be distorted to the extent that other economic distortions are present. Policies that are designed to improve economic efficiency will in all likelihood have to be based on second-best considerations, similar to those discussed in Chapter 7.

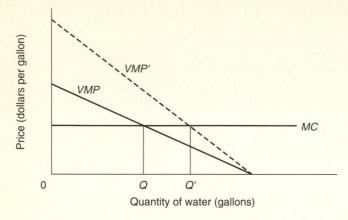

Figure 17.7   Distortions in Water Use Because of Subsidized Crop Prices

CHAPTER SUMMARY

In this chapter, we have briefly addressed issues associated with the allocation and value of water, as well as policies designed to improve allocative efficiency. Although federal involvement in water resource development undoubtedly brought significant economic development benefits to many western states and achieved other social objectives, the price for this involvement has been high. Historically, subsidized water developments have discouraged efficient use of scarce water resources, as have policies that limited property rights to water resources.

Efficient and equitable allocations of water require knowledge of the value of water. We have presented several empirical techniques used to estimate the value of water, but all suffer from the presence of the numerous economic distortions associated with water use. These distortions are particularly significant in agricultural uses of water. Environmental valuations of water, such as those we discussed in Chapter 11, may be particularly important to determine when evaluating water supply policies, such as damming rivers for irrigation projects. Environmental values will also be important when evaluating equity and social concerns, such as those associated with many older Bureau of Reclamation projects, as well as newer foreign ones like the Narmada Valley Project.

Efficient allocations of both surface and groundwater supplies depend on clear determinations of property rights for water. Numerous authors have recommended property rights systems that allow unfettered trading of water supplies, particularly for surface water. Even in the case of groundwater supplies, which are best viewed as depletable resources, property rights systems have been devised that can improve economic efficiency, at least in a second-best context. Last, even though allocation of water is frequently surrounded by discussions of equity, clear systems of property rights may be able to ensure equitable distributions of water supplies in the most efficient manner.

CHAPTER REVIEW

Economic Concepts and Tools

- Under the prior appropriations doctrine, water could be transferred on the basis of willingness to pay, which was naturally based on use value.
- Consumptive use refers to an amount of water that is actually used. Return flow is the amount of water drawn off that returns in the form of runoff.
- The market value of water can be determined by estimating demand functions for water for different classes of users. To compare marginal values of water by class of user, it is first necessary to find a common measure that removes the costs of obtaining water.
- Price differentials between irrigated and dryland farm sales can be used to impute the value of water for irrigation purposes. Care must be taken, however, to account for "piecemeal" effects from other subsidized inputs and outputs.
- A system of private property rights that allows transfers of surface water up to the amount of consumptive use can achieve economic efficiency. Economic efficiency will also require correct pricing of water resources.
- Groundwater supplies have characteristics of common-property resources.

Policy Issues

- Many federal water projects have engendered environmental costs. These include increasing salinization of irrigated lands, which reduces soil productivity; loss of agriculturally productive river bottomland; loss of fisheries habitat and stocks; and loss of recreation opportunities because of inundation (although other recreation opportunities were created in some cases). The effectiveness of numerous projects has also been reduced owing to continued silting behind many dams.
- Water allocation issues have been divisive. In part, this has occurred because of a lack of clarity over primary policy goals. Goals that stress economic efficiency were historically assigned less importance than goals stressing equity. As water demand has increased relative to available supplies, however, efficiency goals have increased in importance.
- Federal water projects were often justified on faulty economic grounds. In some cases, benefits and costs of projects were not discounted. In others, benefits and costs were calculated from different perspectives. As a result, projects that returned local benefits but had much higher national costs were often developed.
- Surface water policies stressing efficient allocation should begin with clear definitions of property rights.
- Groundwater allocation policies are complicated by the common-property nature of groundwater resources. There have been several proposed methods to privatize groundwater rights in which water users would be granted a

right to some amount of flow, as well as a portion of the entire stock. Property rights would be allocated in proportion to the water pumped by the individual users for some base year. In such systems, it will be important to modify property rights to ensure an equilibrium stock of groundwater, below which stocks cannot fall.

- Rarely have water resources been priced correctly by water utilities, owing to their status as regulated monopolies. Further complications can arise if other inputs are priced incorrectly, or if outputs are subsidized. Unfortunately, both often occur in agricultural settings. Policies such as increasing block prices, which reflect higher marginal costs to water users as their consumption increases, are rare.

DISCUSSION QUESTIONS

1. "Governments need only intervene to protect the quality of public water supplies. Private water supplies will be protected without government intervention." Is this a reasonable statement? Will the existence of private property rights to water supplies ensure sufficient water quality?
2. If the costs of many irrigation projects exceeded their benefits, why were so many approved?
3. How can an "optimal" level of water quality be determined? Do all rivers, streams, and lakes need to be equally clean?
4. How will changes in water quality affect the allocation of water supplies?
5. Would policy instruments designed to improve air quality be applicable to improve water quality? Could water pollution be taxed? How would marketable permits for water pollutants work? What about "command and control" water pollution policies, such as those under the Clean Water Act?
6. What is the best way of dealing with the social concerns raised by projects like the Narmada Valley Project? How should equity and efficiency issues be balanced?

REFERENCES

Anderson, T., O. Burt, and D. Fractor. 1981. "Privatizing Groundwater Basins: A Model and Applications." In *Water Rights: Scarce Resource Allocation, Bureaucracy, and the Environment,* ed. T. Anderson. Cambridge: Ballinger.

Davison, S. 1979. *The Leadership of the Reclamation Movement, 1775–1902.* Salem, N.H.: Arno Press.

Eckstein, O. 1961. *Water Resource Development: The Economics of Project Evaluation.* Cambridge, Mass.: Harvard University Press.

Frederick, K. 1982. *Water for Western Agriculture.* Washington, D.C.: Resources for the Future.

Getches, D. 1984. *Water Law in a Nutshell.* St. Paul, Minn.: West.

Gibbons, D. 1986. *The Economic Value of Water.* Washington, D.C.: Resources for the Future.

Gisser, M., and R. Johnson. 1981. "Institutional Restrictions on the Transfer of Water Rights and the Survival of an Agency." In *Water Rights: Scarce Resource Allocation, Bureaucracy, and the Environment,* ed. T. Anderson. Cambridge: Ballinger.

Goldfarb, W. 1989. *Water Law.* Chelsea, Mich.: Lewis.

Howe, C. 1986. "Project Benefits and Costs from National and Regional Viewpoints: Methodological Issues and Case Study of the Colorado–Big Thompson Project." *Natural Resources Journal* 27: 5–20.

Kanazawa, M. 1994. "Water Subsidies, Water Transfers, and Economic Efficiency." *Contemporary Economic Policy* 12(2): 112–122.

Martin, W., H. Ingraim, N. Laney, and A. Griffin. 1984. *Saving Water in a Desert City.* Washington, D.C.: Resources for the Future

Northwest Power Planning Council. 1991. *Northwest Conservation and Electric Power Plan.* Portland, Ore.

Powell, J. 1962. *Report on the Lands of the Arid Region of the United States: With a More Detailed Account of the Lands of Utah.* Cambridge, Mass.: Harvard University Press. (Originally published 1879)

Reisner, M. 1993. *Cadillac Desert,* 2d ed. New York: Viking Penguin.

Robinson, M. 1979. *Water for the West: The Bureau of Reclamation, 1902–1977.* Chicago: Public Works Historical Society.

Rucker, R., and P. Fishback. 1983. "The Federal Reclamation Program: An Analysis of Rent-Seeking Behavior." In *Water Rights: Scarce Resource Allocation, Bureaucracy, and the Environment,* ed. T. Anderson. Cambridge: Ballinger.

Smith, V. 1977. "Water Deeds: A Proposed Solution to the Water Valuation Problem." *Arizona Review* 26: 7–10.

Stegner, W. 1982. *Beyond the Hundredth Meridian: John Wesley Powell and the Second Opening of the West.* Lincoln: University of Nebraska Press.

Torell, L., J. Libbin, and M. Miller. 1990. "The Market Value of Water in the Ogallala Aquifer." *Land Economics* 66(2): 163–175.

U.S. Department of the Interior, Bureau of Reclamation. 1972. *Repayment of Reclamation Projects.* Washington, D.C.: Government Printing Office.

Wahl, R. 1989. *Markets for Federal Water: Subsidies, Property Rights, and the U.S. Bureau of Reclamation.* Washington, D.C.: Resources for the Future.

Willitt, G., S. Hathorn, and C. Robertson. 1975. *The Economic Value of Water Used to Irrigate Field Crops in Central and Southern Arizona, 1975.* Tucson: University of Arizona, Department of Agricultural Economics.

Young, R., S. Gray, R. Held, and R. Mack. 1972. *Economic Value of Water: Concepts and Empirical Estimates.* Technical Report to the National Water Commission, NTIS Publication No. PB210356, Springfield, Va.

Zilberman, D., N. Macdougall, and F. Shah. 1994. "Changes in Water Allocation Mechanisms for California Agriculture." *Contemporary Economic Policy* 12(1): 122–133.

CHAPTER 18

ENERGY
RESOURCES

Bait and Switch? Pollution and
Energy Conservation Policies

In the mid-1970s, the demand for electricity was increasing rapidly. Supplies of natural gas were tight, and the price of natural gas was going up fast. Various pundits were predicting critical natural gas shortages, saying that existing reserves would last only a decade or two. The U.S. government responded by passing the Fuel Use Act of 1978, which strictly limited the ability of electric utilities to build generating plants that used natural gas. Utility planners believed that the economies of scale historically observed for electricity generation facilities would continue. As a result, many utilities committed themselves to building or purchasing shares of large nuclear and coal-fired power plants. These generating plants were to be completed by the early 1980s, in time to meet the increased demand forecast for the next several decades. At the time utilities made these commitments, economic growth was forecast to continue.

Things changed by 1981, however. The U.S. economy was in the midst of a severe recession, which was reducing the demand for electricity. As its electric rates rapidly increased to pay for the new plants that were scheduled to be completed in a few years, many of these same utilities found that consumers were responding to the price increases by reducing their electricity consumption. Some consumers were switching to wood stoves; others were purchasing various devices designed to reduce energy consumption; and still others, especially the poorest consumers, were huddling in colder houses.

Natural gas markets were also changing. The government had begun to deregulate natural gas prices, which was leading to increased exploration. Supplies of natural gas began to increase. Canadian reserves of natural gas also increased rapidly, as suppliers benefited from newly deregulated prices in their markets to the south. As a result, natural gas prices, spurred by the increase in supplies and reduced demand because of the recession, plummeted. As natural gas prices continued to be deregulated and the U.S. economy strengthened, demand for natural gas soared. Yet prices remained low, owing to more rapidly increasing supplies.

By the late 1980s, in an attempt to prevent further planning "disasters," public utility commissions (PUCs) increasingly began ordering the electric utilities they regulated to develop "integrated least-cost plans." These plans were designed to compare the costs of increasing electric supplies with energy conservation programs, such as building retrofits and stricter building codes, as well as with use of other fuels, such as oil, natural gas, and wood. Utilities complied with these orders, even though they were saddled with huge amounts of excess generating capacity.

Also at this time, environmental concerns were increasing. Many PUCs were becoming alarmed by the prospects of global climate change, and much attention was being given to the harmful pollutants emitted by fossil fuel power plants. In response, PUCs began requiring utilities to incorporate externality "adders" in the least-cost planning efforts, to further encourage increased energy efficiency measures and fuel switching. (These adders were incorporated only into new resource acquisition decisions, not the price of electricity.)[1] Some PUCs even ordered electric utilities to pay all of the costs associated with fuel switching and energy efficiency. Many residential consumers could call their electric utility, have their energy use "audited," and receive various energy efficiency measures free of charge.

By the early 1990s, a lot of these utilities were fed up. They objected to PUC requirements to pay for fuel switching and energy efficiency measures, especially when the excess capacity allowed the utilities to supply additional electricity at a lower cost. Some utilities began to fight back. They argued along several fronts: first, that consumers who wish to take advantage of energy efficiency measures ought to pay for those measures, and second, that there were potentially severe environmental consequences from burning greater amounts of natural gas, wood, and oil in their service territories.

The policy issues associated with this case are numerous. First, there is the issue of economic efficiency. How do the environmental impacts within and beyond individual utility service territories compare? There is no doubt that coal-fired power plants pollute, and nuclear waste disposal and storage issues have yet to be solved. How should all of the different environmental impacts be measured? How will those impacts change over time? With mandated fuel switching, will more pollution be generated locally from unregulated sources, especially from consumers who switch from electricity to wood as a fuel? And if so, how do the environmental impacts of that higher local pollution compare to the reductions in environmental impacts from less electricity generation and consumption?

There were also significant equity impacts. Some consumers were unable to take advantage of fuel switching and energy efficiency programs offered. Yet these same consumers were forced to pay for those programs as utility rates were increased to pay for them. As a result, some consumers may have found themselves exposed to additional amounts of air pollution while also paying more for their

---

[1]This is discussed in the appendix to Chapter 7. See also Dodds and Lesser (1994).

electricity. PUC policies also entailed some risk. Suppose, in the future, that prices for these alternate fuels increase significantly. In that case, despite not having their original space and water heating equipment, consumers may be able to easily and quickly switch back to electricity. Utilities could then find themselves having to purchase additional supplies of electricity, some of which may be relatively "dirty."

Ultimately, state PUCs face many difficulties when they address environmental policy. Even though the motives of PUCs were well meaning, they have no control over fully deregulated markets for oil and wood. Were the PUCs correct in trying to establish these environmental policies, many of which will vanish as the electric utility industry is itself deregulated? Why didn't PUCs look to more market-enhancing policies, such as emissions trading and taxes? Finally, what was the role of the federal government, as many forms of pollution the PUCs were concerned about were national and global in nature?

INTRODUCTION

Energy is ubiquitous. We used energy to write this textbook. No doubt, you are using energy in order to read it. Our lives require energy—to cook our food, to heat our homes and offices, and to spirit us to adventures in unspoiled wilderness. Producing and using energy requires still more energy: mile-long trains travel hundreds of miles to deliver coal to plants that produce electricity; natural gas is burned to pressurize pipelines; trucks are used to deliver fuel oil and propane to households.

The production and use of energy has inescapable environmental impacts. As a result, numerous policy issues will arise: What level of emissions should be allowed from an existing coal-fired power plant? What types of new power plants should be built to meet increasing electricity demands? Where can a new natural gas pipeline or electricity transmission line be located? Should exploratory drilling for oil be allowed in "sensitive" environments, such as marine estuaries and remote Arctic tundra? When are policies that increase the technical efficiency with which energy is consumed preferred alternatives to merely meeting increased demands for energy?

Energy policy choices can also affect energy-using technologies. Should fuel efficiency standards for automobiles be raised to reduce gasoline consumption and the resulting pollution? Should electric vehicles, which are often erroneously labeled "zero-pollution" vehicles, be encouraged? Should the use of solar power be encouraged? Should consumers be required to use electricity for some uses, such as lights, but restricted to natural gas or wood for other uses, such as space heating? How can environmental policies accommodate consumers' energy use and lifestyle choices?

The importance of energy policy was made apparent less because of environmental concerns and more because of concerns over the stability of supplies. In 1973, the world was rudely shocked; the supply of oil, the world's major source of energy, appeared to be in the control of "a bunch of desert sheiks" (Carr 1994).

The OPEC oil embargo caused many nations to rethink their energy policies (or lack of policies). More than 20 years later, although the disruptive power of OPEC has waned, energy remains a critical issue. Unlike 1973, however, environmental concerns have become at least as important as concerns about supply adequacy.

To delve completely into the environmental complexities surrounding energy would require several books. In this chapter, we must be content to summarize some major energy policy issues that are linked inexorably to environmental ones. Some of these issues involve concerns over economic efficiency, while others involve controversies over equity, human rights, and the rights of nature. To do this, we have chosen two distinct sectors. We begin with an examination of environmental issues in the largest energy-consuming sector, transportation. America's love affair with the automobile has led to choked highways, fouled air, and polluted water. Yet oddly enough, most of the world's developing countries are racing to experience that love firsthand.

We turn then from the highly mobile world of the automobile to the electricity generating industry. Along with growing demands for automobiles and increased mobility, the demand for electricity is increasing steadily in the developing world, often leading to generating resource development with little regard for the environment. In the United States, however, the electricity-generating industry has been the target of much environmental legislation, most of it well-meaning and, according to the tools of environmental policy we have considered in this book, wrongheaded. With that industry currently in the throes of restructuring efforts that will deregulate many functions, much as in other industries such as airlines, natural gas, and telecommunications, the environmental impacts of the industry will be far less affected by utility regulators.

ENERGY, TRANSPORTATION, AND THE ENVIRONMENT

The transportation sector presents unique challenges for environmental policy. First, there are millions of pollution sources: automobiles, trucks, airplanes, and other vehicles. There are also numerous environmental policy goals involved. Not only will society want to reduce the pollution from these sources cost-effectively, but it will want to do so in a way that is fair. Significant environmental impacts not only arise from the transportation sources themselves but also from the infrastructure surrounding their use. For example, oil tankers bring large quantities of crude oil to refineries. Accidents involving tankers, such as the Exxon *Valdez* and the Amoco *Cadiz*, can have long-term effects on local marine life. Automobiles require roads to travel on. Construction of roads can affect the environment by increasing ambient levels of air pollution, noise, and runoff of polluted water, as well as disturbing wetlands. Furthermore, servicing automobiles and trucks can lead to hazardous waste disposal problems and pollution of groundwater supplies.

Policies That Address Economic Efficiency

In Chapter 7, we showed how emissions taxes could address the three major types of externalities. Emissions taxes for mobile sources like automobiles, however, raise significant technical issues. Ideally, we would monitor emissions from all automobiles and levy emissions taxes that varied by pollutant and location. Thus a driver in New York City would likely be assessed a higher emissions tax on nitrogen oxides than a driver in the middle of North Dakota, owing to the greater population exposed.

Unfortunately, a cheap and reliable technology to monitor emissions continuously from mobile sources like automobiles and to levy emissions taxes that vary by location does not now exist. Thus addressing the economic inefficiency arising from the environmental externalities of automobile pollution will, for the time being, have to rely on taxes on inputs (e.g., gasoline and oil) and outputs (e.g., vehicle miles traveled) or impose command-and-control standards that directly limit emissions.[2]

To get an idea of the difficulties of optimal pollution control, consider the following model of vehicle emissions. Suppose, for the sake of simplicity, that there is only one pollutant, p. Total emissions of p, Q_{TP}, will equal the product of the number of vehicles times the average emissions per mile times the average number of miles traveled per vehicle. Thus

$$Q_{TP} = N \cdot \overline{E} \cdot \overline{M} \tag{18.1}$$

where N = number of vehicles
$\overline{E}$ = average emissions per vehicle per mile
$\overline{M}$ = average number of miles traveled per vehicle

We can break down Equation 18.1 further by accounting for the different *vintages* of vehicles, as individual model years of vehicles will have different pollution characteristics and be driven at different intensities. Thus we can rewrite Equation 18.1 as

$$Q_{TP} = \sum_{v=1}^{K} N_v \cdot \overline{E}_v \cdot \overline{M}_v \tag{18.2}$$

where v refers to one of the K vintages of vehicles assumed to be in operation.[3] We now need to add one further complication to confound policymakers. The number of vehicles of any given vintage, as well as the number of miles traveled, will depend on the relative prices of the different vintages, the cost per mile traveled

---

[2]Tradable emissions permits would probably not be a viable solution for the same reasons that an emissions tax would not work.
[3]We assume that there are no vehicles of age $K + 1$ years or older still in operation.

for each vintage, and the types of policy instruments imposed. Thus we can rewrite Equation 18.2 as

$$Q_{TP} = \sum_{v=1}^{K} N_v(p_1^n, \ldots, p_k^n, G_N) \cdot \overline{E}_v(G_E) \cdot \overline{M}_v(p_1^m, \ldots, p_K^m, G_M) \quad (18.3)$$

where $p_1^n, \ldots, p_K^n$ = the relative prices of the K vintages
$p_1^m, \ldots, p_k^m$ = the relative prices of driving per mile
G_N = government policies relating to the number of vehicles
G_E = government policies relating to average emissions per vintage
G_M = government policies relating to the relative prices of driving per mile

Equation 18.3 looks rather formidable, and in a way, it is, which illustrates the difficulty in determining the most efficient solutions to the problem of vehicle pollution. To understand the complexities, suppose that the government decides to mandate maximum allowable emissions standards for new vehicles. This sort of policy would be reflected by G_E and, in fact, is how vehicle emissions are regulated under the U.S. Clean Air Act. Imposition of emissions standards on new vehicles is assumed to raise the cost of new vehicles relative to older ones.[4] This will induce consumers to hold on to their old vehicles rather than trade them in for newer ones. (In fact, the average age of vehicles has increased since the 1970 Clean Air Act was passed.) As a result, emissions may tend to be reduced less than what policymakers might otherwise have expected.

Now, suppose that the government decides to increase the tax on gasoline so as to encourage reduced driving and presumably pollution. This sort of policy would be reflected in Equation 18.3 through G_M. By increasing the price of gasoline, the cost of driving per mile will increase, and consumers will reduce their driving; the amount of the reduction will depend on both the short- and long-run price elasticity of gasoline.[5] In the short run, the stock of vehicles is assumed to be constant. Thus reductions in the quantity of gasoline demanded will be strictly a function of the price increase. In the long run, however, the stock of vehicles will also change. Consumers will tend to substitute into higher-mileage vehicles. This seems ideal. Unfortunately, the relationship between vehicle mileage per gallon and emissions is generally not linear, with the exception of carbon dioxide.[6] So, government policymakers may again find that emissions will be reduced less than they had anticipated. Furthermore, as gasoline consumption per mile declines, the

---

[4] In general, automobile manufacturers responded to the requirements mandated under the Clean Air Act through the use of relatively expensive technological fixes, such as catalytic converters.

[5] An exhaustive survey of gasoline price elasticity estimates can be found in Dahl (1991).

[6] According to EPA emissions test results, some vehicles with higher mileage per gallon have higher emissions of criteria pollutants (e.g., carbon monoxide, oxides of nitrogen) than vehicles with lower mileage per gallon.

relative marginal cost of driving additional miles will decline.[7] Emissions per mile may decline, but total mileage driven may increase relatively more. This is sometimes called the "rebound effect" (Greene 1992) and has been observed empirically: average annual miles traveled per vehicle (for all vehicle vintages) was 13,186 miles in 1993, up from 10,924 in 1983. Miles traveled by new vehicles are even higher, averaging over 15,000 in 1994 (Davis 1996).

Finally, suppose that the government begins a buyback program for "clunkers—old, highly polluting vehicles. This sort of policy would be reflected by G_N. If the buyback price were sufficiently high, consumers would be induced to turn in their older vehicles for newer models. However, to the extent that these older vehicles were driven less than anticipated, emissions reductions would not be as large as expected.[8] In other words, consumers would be trading in old vehicles that were driven relatively fewer miles for new vehicles that they would drive relatively more.

Empirical Studies of Several Alternative Policies

The potential for conflicting regulatory goals has been tested empirically. Recall from Chapter 7 that a variety of policy tools are available to reduce externalities, including taxes on emissions or the production of goods and command-and-control regulations that directly mandate specific technologies and maximum permissible emissions levels. Though to date there have been no policies enacted to tax the emissions of automobiles, taxes on gasoline and emissions regulations have been used.

Gruenspecht (1982) considered the link between emissions regulations and the composition of the vehicle stock. His analysis showed that more stringent emissions standards prolonged the lives of older, high-emissions vehicles, thus damping the benefits of the standards. Gruenspecht began with a simple scrapping model. In such a model, a decision to scrap occurs when the market value of a vehicle less its scrap value is less than the cost of repairing the vehicle to return it to an operating condition. This is important when considering a buyback program for clunkers. For example, if the market price of a vehicle is $500 and the cash price offered in the buyback program is $50, a "rational" consumer would repair the vehicle as

---

[7]From a consumer's perspective, the cost of driving per mile will also depend on the opportunity cost of time. As a result, changes in government speed limit policies can affect gasoline demand and air pollution emissions. For example, Lesser and Weber (1989) estimated the effect on gasoline demand in Washington when the national speed limit on interstate highways was raised from 55 to 65 miles per hour.

[8]Another approach that has been recommended is differential registration fees. Under such a policy, the registration fee for new vehicles depends on some index of pollution. Purchasers of relatively clean vehicles pay smaller registration fees or may even receive a registration rebate, while purchasers of relatively dirty vehicles pay larger registration fees.

long as the repairs cost less than $450. All else being constant, the greater the market price the less likely a vehicle would be scrapped.[9]

What does this have to do with emissions regulations? Plenty. Increasingly stringent new car emissions standards have raised the price of new cars, which are substitutes for old cars; increase the price or the operating cost of new cars, including costs related to environmental regulations, and there will be increasing substitution to older cars. For example, Crandall and colleagues (1986) estimated that the *full costs* (the actual equipment cost plus the present value of lifetime fuel penalty, maintenance, and unleaded gas premium) of more stringent emissions controls were about $1,600 by 1984. Gruenspecht (1981) found, using the results of an earlier regression model, that relaxing emissions standards or substituting a bounty program on 15-year-old cars for stringent emissions regulations would actually lower overall emissions of certain air pollutants in the short run (a period of one to five years).

Khazzoom (1991) examined the effects of higher gasoline taxes on vehicle emissions. He found evidence that the long-run demand for travel was quite inelastic and therefore that gasoline taxes would have to be increased significantly to reduce vehicle emissions, either through consumers' driving fewer miles or substituting newer, more fuel-efficient vehicles for their existing ones.[10] Khazzoom stated that the EPA's choice of policy instrument—setting standards based on emissions per mile traveled—has resulted in less effective regulation. Instead, he developed a model showing that emissions standards based on emissions per gallon of fuel burned could achieve the same reductions in overall emissions with a far smaller increase in the price of gasoline.

He suggested three potential policy options for tying emission standards to the fuel burned. First, the EPA could set standards in terms of grams per gallon and hold those standards constant. As mileage efficiency increased, grams per mile would have to fall because grams per gallon equals grams per mile times miles per gallon. Second, Khazzoom proposed keeping the grams-per-mile standards but

---

[9]Mathematically, this can be described as follows: Let d_i equal the scrappage rate for a given vintage of automobile i, where $0 < d_i < 1$. Repair costs can be written as $P_R R$, where P_R is the repair price and R is the quantity of repairs. Now, given any vintage of vehicles i, there is an associated probability distribution that any given vehicle will need repairs. Let the probability distribution that a vehicle belonging to a given vintage will need to be repaired at any time be $f_i(R)$. Thus a vehicle of given age will need anywhere from no repairs ($R = 0$) to some "critical" amount of repair, above which a car is scrapped. So if $P_i - SV_i < P_R R$, the car is sold to a clunker program, where SV_i is the price offered by the program and P_i is the market price. (Thus SV reflects the salvage value of the vehicle.) Dividing through by P_R, we can determine the "critical" repair value R. Then the likelihood of scrappage will just equal 1 minus the probability that the amount of repairs needed is less than this critical value. Thus $d_i = 1 - \int_0 (P_i - SV_i)/P_R f_i(R) \, dR$. Note that as the market price increases, the value of the integral increases and the value of d_i falls. That means that the scrapping rate falls with increasing market price, an unsurprising result.

[10]Again, note that vehicles that are more fuel-efficient do not always pollute less than their less efficient counterparts. With the exception of carbon dioxide emissions, emissions depend on a variety of engine characteristics.

indexing them to fuel economy. Last, he suggested a more restrictive grams-per-mile standard for small or fuel-efficient cars. Because this would tend to shift demand to larger cars with less stringent standards, Khazzoom recommended that this policy be coupled with higher fuel efficiency standards.

Benefits and Costs of Clean Air Act Regulations   In the mid-1970s, Schwing and colleagues (1980) performed a cost-benefit analysis of the 1970 Clean Air Act emissions standards. They attempted to determine the economically optimal levels of automobile emissions, including nitrogen oxides, carbon monoxide, and hydrocarbons. The authors developed estimates of both market and nonmarket benefits over a 30-year time horizon and developed a least-cost-of-control curve.

The largest component of economic benefits found was reduced health care expenditures, through reductions in both mortality and morbidity, as well as forgone earnings. In other words, the authors estimated the reductions in lost earnings because of sickness and premature death that were assumed to accompany higher levels of air pollution. These estimates were monetized using estimates of the statistical value of life, such as those we reported in Chapter 12.

The authors estimated the benefits from reductions in damage to buildings, vegetation and soils, and property values, using estimates derived from previous studies, then partitioned those benefits between automobile and nonautomobile sources over the time frame of their study.[11] Adding these benefits to the previously calculated health benefits from reduced emissions, the authors determined a range of annual benefits between $650 million and $7.5 billion in 1968 dollars.

The authors next estimated marginal control cost curves for each of the three categories of pollutants and used these estimates to determine the optimal level of emissions control. Their analysis indicated that the "optimal" level of emissions reductions from an "uncontrolled" base (i.e., 1960 emissions levels) ranged from 43 to 82 percent for hydrocarbons, 24 to 33 percent for carbon monoxide, and 21 to 67 percent for oxides of nitrogen. The resulting 30-year net present value of benefits at these optimal control levels ranged between $2.4 billion and $62.1 billion in 1968 dollars.

Finally, the authors compared the predicted benefits at optimal control levels with those from the more stringent guideline in the 1970 Clean Air Act. Their results showed 30-year net present value benefits of between −$56 billion and $37 billion in 1968 dollars, leading them to conclude that the economically optimal levels of emissions control were below those mandated by the Clean Air Act.[12]

In a much later study, Krupnick and Portney (1991) examined the benefits and costs of reducing urban air pollution. Their study focused primarily on ground-

---

[11]See Chapter 11 for a discussion of the various methods used to estimate such damages.
[12]It should be noted that the authors completed their research prior to enactment of the 1977 Clean Air Act amendments, which further strengthened emissions standards. The authors also conducted their research while employed by General Motors Corporation.

CASH FOR CLUNKERS: A REAL-LIFE EXPERIMENT

In 1992, an accelerated vehicle retirement (AVR) program was tried out in Delaware. The idea was to purchase cars built before 1980 and remove them from use. USGen, a small, independent electricity-generating company, developed the program so that it could reduce air pollution from these old vehicles and then purchase pollution offsets to run one of its coal-fired power plants.

USGen initially estimated that it would have to purchase 125 clunkers to obtain sufficient offsets. It began by trying to enlist some of the over 1,000 cars that had received waivers from Delaware's vehicle inspection and maintenance (I&M) program. Such waivers allow vehicles to be driven after they have been repaired to reduce tailpipe emissions but still fail to pass the emissions test. USGen offered to pay $500 to the owner of any car turned in. Because the company was able to purchase only 60 of these cars, it next contacted 3,000 owners of pre-1980 cars directly, recruiting the remaining 65 cars.

In conjunction with Resources for the Future (RFF), an environmental and natural resource policy think-tank, half of the 125 cars purchased were tested for emissions. The results indicated that the average car emitted about 60 percent more hydrocarbons than a nonwaivered vehicle. RFF then surveyed both owners who had accepted USGen's offer and owners who had refused it to determine just how the cars that were scrapped differed from the overall fleet of pre-1980 cars. RFF asked owners how often they drove their cars, how far they drove, what maintenance was required to keep their cars operating, and how much longer they planned to keep their cars. RFF also asked owners who had refused the USGen offer to name the price, called a *reservation price,* at which they would have been willing to sell.

The RFF study showed that the scrapped cars were driven just as much as cars that were not sold and scrapped. Nor were the replacement cars purchased by owners who had accepted USGen's offer driven more than the cars that had been scrapped. RFF was able to determine that the average cost of hydrocarbons removed was about $4,000 per ton for the waivered cars and about $5,000 per ton for pre-1980 cars overall. Thus the researchers concluded that programs should be targeted at waivered cars rather than clunkers in general. RFF also derived an emissions supply function that estimated the total number of hydrocarbons reduced as a function of the buyback price. The buyback price also helped determine the predicted time a purchased car would be otherwise driven; the higher the price, the longer the expected lifetime of the clunker.

RFF concluded that small-scale programs could be cost-effective if they targeted the most polluting cars. But it noted that such programs would have to be greatly expanded to produce significant emissions reductions. That would tend to increase prices of used cars, reducing program cost effectiveness over time. Nevertheless, buyback programs in conjunction with I&M programs could be better coordinated to achieve less costly emissions reductions.

Source: Alberini et al. (1994).

level ozone resulting from emissions of volatile organic compounds (VOCs) and particulates.[13] Using estimates of the costs of controlling VOCs and particulates developed by the U.S. Office of Technology Assessment (OTA 1989), the authors estimated that the annual cost of achieving a 35 percent reduction in nationwide VOCs (using all available control technologies) would be between $8.8 billion and $12 billion by the year 2004. Reducing the volatility of gasoline would account for the largest percentage reduction of VOCs (14 percent) and would be the most cost-effective measure, reducing VOCs at a cost of between $120 and $740 per ton. At the other end of the control cost spectrum, the costs of using methanol to fuel vehicles would cost between $8,700 and $51,000 per ton of VOCs removed.

The authors used epidemiological data to determine the health benefits from a 35 percent reduction in VOC emissions in the year 2004 for a predicted 129 million people living in 94 metropolitan areas. Krupnick and Portney (1991) then used existing values of willingness to pay for reduced illness to estimate annual benefits from the same 35 percent reduction of VOCs of between $250 million and $800 million per year. Thus they determined that the costs of reducing ground-level ozone were far less than the benefits.

Automobile Fuel Efficiency Standards   Several authors have studied the cost effectiveness of U.S. automobile fuel efficiency standards, known as the "corporate average fuel economy" (CAFE) standards. These studies have examined the impacts of the CAFE standards on global climate change owing to emissions of carbon dioxide (Krupnick, Walls, and Collins 1993), the relative cost effectiveness of future fuel economy improvements (Di Figlio, Duleep, and Greene 1990), and the relative importance of CAFE standards versus higher gasoline prices on new car fuel consumption (Greene 1990). All of these studies have implications for environmental policymakers regarding the efficiency of achieving alternative environmental goals, as well as other, nonenvironmental goals such as reducing dependence on foreign oil and improving vehicle safety.

In 1974, the average fuel efficiency of new U.S. passenger cars reached its lowest point: 14 miles per gallon (mpg). Unfortunately for U.S. consumers and industry, in that same year, OPEC tripled world oil prices and embargoed oil bound for the United States (Greene 1990). The effects—supply shortages, long waits at gas pumps—are still part of this country's folklore. In 1975, the U.S. Congress responded by passing the Energy Policy and Conservation Act, which imposed fuel efficiency standards for passenger cars and light-duty trucks. The act mandated that passenger cars achieve an average of 18 mpg by 1978 and 27.5 mpg by 1985. Compliance was to be measured by computing a corporate average fuel economy (CAFE), based on the number and make of new vehicles sold. Failure to

---

[13]Unlike atmospheric ozone, which protects life from the sun's harmful radiation, ground-level ozone leads to the formation of smog and health problems. Ground-level ozone does not migrate upward to become atmospheric ozone.

comply would result in fines of $5 per vehicle per 0.1 mpg shortfall (Greene 1990). The intent of the CAFE standards was to spur technological change without altering the size distribution of vehicles sold (large, midsize, small). By 1988, despite relaxation of the standards during the Reagan administration, average new car efficiency had doubled to about 28 mpg.

Because gasoline prices had increased at the same time as the standards did, there was much debate over the relative effectiveness of each. Crandall and colleagues (1986) argued that the standards had little effect. Others (von Hippel 1987) argued that consumer response to price changes was limited. Greene (1990) examined the issue from the standpoint of automobile manufacturers required to meet the standards. He separated manufacturers into two categories: constrained and unconstrained. Constrained manufacturers were those whose initial vehicle mix did not meet the standards. Unconstrained manufacturers, primarily Japanese automakers, generally had a more limited product mix that did meet the standards. Greene developed a "penalty" function, reasoning that manufacturers would seek to minimize the combination of monetary penalties imposed by the legislation and the monetary penalties of not producing the most profitable mix of vehicles. His analysis indicated that the CAFE standards were roughly twice as important in determining vehicle fuel efficiency as price changes. He found that the long-run elasticity of fuel efficiency with respect to fuel prices was quite small—about 0.2, meaning that a 10 percent increase in gasoline price would increase mpg figures by about 2 percent.

Gasoline prices have since declined. Inflation-adjusted gasoline prices are currently almost as low as they were prior to the 1973 OPEC embargo. Automobile manufacturers are selling more larger, less fuel-efficient vehicles. And light trucks, which have much lower mileage efficiency standards, have become far more popular. As a result, the overall fuel efficiency of vehicles purchased has fallen from its high of about 28 mpg in 1988 to about 25 mpg (Davis 1996).

Greene's (1990) results raise several environmental policy questions. First, given the relative importance of CAFE standards over price changes in affecting changes in average vehicle mpg, how cost-effective would further increases in CAFE standards be, and relative to what environmental effects? Second, how do further increases in CAFE standards compare relative to other policy initiatives, such as technological forcing of alternative-fueled vehicles and so-called zero-pollution electric vehicles?

The first policy question was addressed by Di Figlio, Duleep, and Greene (1990). Although the policy focus of their research was U.S. dependence on foreign oil, their results have environmental policy implications, especially in the form of reduced emissions of carbon dioxide that may lead to global warming. They estimated the increase in fuel efficiency that could be achieved cost-effectively by the year 2000, using known 1990 technology.

The authors used as a basis for cost effectiveness the estimated change in gasoline prices between 1990 and 2000, assuming that gasoline would cost $1.32 per gallon in 2000. Cost effectiveness would be further influenced by vehicle lifetimes, thus affecting the number of vehicles of a given vintage. (Recall N_v in Equation 18.2.) They found that CAFE standards of over 34.3 mpg could be justified

TABLE 18.1   NET COST EFFECTIVENESS OF REDUCED EMISSIONS (IN DOLLARS PER TON)[a]

Scenario	CAFE Standards	Methanol	Compressed Natural Gas	Reformulated Gasoline
Optimistic	37	172	20	∞[b]
Most likely	106	274	49	∞[b]

[a]GHG equivalents, including VOC reductions.

[b]Infinite because both emissions and costs are higher with reformulated gasoline.

Source: Krupnick, Walls, and Collins (1993).

on the basis of their expected gasoline cost savings without reducing vehicle performance. The maximum technologically feasible increase was found to be 39.4 mpg. However, the authors found that this efficiency level could not be justified on the basis of expected fuel savings alone.

Though Di Figlio and colleagues mentioned other possible benefits, including reduced environmental degradation, they did not include these benefits in their analysis. Krupnick, Walls, and Collins (1993), however, approached the relative cost effectiveness of CAFE standards from just this approach, although they limited their research to emissions of so-called greenhouse gases (GHGs), including carbon dioxide, methane, nitrous oxide, and carbon monoxide;[14] and formation of urban smog from ground-level ozone formed from VOCs.

To compute the cost effectiveness of further CAFE increases, the authors used optimistic and most likely estimates of the upfront cost per vehicle of increasing CAFE standards from 30 to 37.6 mpg, as well as optimistic and most likely estimates of operational costs for alternative-fueled vehicles. These estimates were combined with estimates of reduced gasoline consumption over an assumed 10-year life span per vehicle (including estimated rebound effects from lower marginal driving cost per mile) to derive cost estimates of reduced emissions of GHGs and VOCs. The authors performed the same calculations for alternative-fueled vehicles fueled by compressed natural gas (CNG), methanol, and reformulated gasoline. Table 18.1 presents their results. As the table shows, conversion to CNG-fueled vehicles is the most cost-effective of the strategies in either scenario. The authors point out, however, that there is a great deal of uncertainty associated with their cost estimates, as well as not accounting for related benefits and costs, such as

---

[14]One way of assessing GHG equivalents can be determined by comparing the *radiative forcing* of the different GHGs, which simply means the relative warming potential of one molecule of CO_2 compared with the warming potential of one molecule of methane, nitrous oxide, carbon monoxide, and so on. However, this method assumes linearity of damage from additional GHG emissions.

reduced well-being because of reduced mobility but increased safety because of reduced vehicle congestion.[15]

Future Policy Directions

Despite great improvements in reducing air pollution emissions from individual motor vehicles, large increases in the total number of vehicles and miles driven per vehicle continue to make overall vehicle emissions an increasing source of air pollution, especially emissions of VOCs that produce ozone. Thus a natural policy question is, Where do we go from here?—especially in light of the still more stringent requirements contained in the 1990 Clean Air Act (CAA) amendments. (Of course, we could also ask whether the requirements themselves made economic sense, but that would transform the issues from a cost-effectiveness perspective to a benefit-cost one.)

Harrington, Walls, and McConnell (1994) discuss policy options to meet the emissions standards set by the CAA amendments cost-effectively. They note that even though new-car VOC emissions are 95 percent lower than what they were in the late 1960s, *average* vehicle VOC emissions have not fallen nearly as much. There are several reasons for this. First, emissions controls tend to break down as cars age and are often expensive to repair. Many catalytic converters lose their effectiveness over time and should be replaced. Given their high cost, however, most consumers do not bother to do so. A second reason relates to Equation 18.2, which showed that total emissions were a function of the stock of vehicles of a given vintage. The mean age of the U.S. vehicle fleet has increased, from 5.1 years in 1969 to 8.4 years in 1990 (Davis 1994; 1996). Perhaps because of the high cost of new vehicles, individuals are delaying purchases. As a result, there are more older cars, which tend to pollute more. So even though emissions from new cars are very low, average emissions for the entire vehicle stock have declined less than expected.

The Clean Air Act regulations have focused only on emissions rates per mile and have ignored vehicle miles traveled (VMT). Though emissions rates have decreased, VMT has almost doubled since 1970. Third, until the 1990 CAA amendments, there was no recognition of the role of emissions from fuel evaporation. And fourth, no account has been taken of increasing congestion on roadways, which increases both tailpipe and evaporative emissions.

---

[15]The authors also compare their cost effectiveness estimates with those of several GHG reduction policies that have been proposed, including carbon taxes. They find that under their most likely scenario, increases in CAFE standards are favorable only if policies calling for GHG emissions reductions of almost 90 percent are put into place. Greene and Duleep (1993) develop a partial benefit-cost analysis of future fuel economy improvements, including such things as carbon emissions reductions and energy security "benefits." Their analysis shows that further improvements in fuel economy to about 36 mpg for passenger cars and 27 mpg for light trucks makes economic sense. However, their results are the product of numerous assumptions that are subject to significant uncertainty.

Harrington, Walls, and McConnell (1994) estimated the cost effectiveness of alternative approaches to reducing motor vehicle emissions of VOCs. They compared command-and-control, market-substituting regulations, such as tailpipe standards and inspection and maintenance (I&M) programs, against market-enhancing economic incentives, including accelerated vehicle retirement (AVR) programs, higher gasoline taxes, and emissions-based registration fees. Table 18.2 gives their estimates of the cost effectiveness of these alternative policies. In general, the EPA considers any approach that reduces VOC emissions at a cost below $5,000 per ton to be cost-effective. It considers options that reduce VOCs at a cost below $10,000 per ton reasonable. Harrington and colleagues' research indicates that several of the command-and-control programs, especially those involving methanol and electric vehicles, are not cost-effective. Market-enhancing approaches, such as higher gasoline taxes and especially emissions-based vehicle registration fees, appear far more promising.

As these authors note, these approaches are still imperfect, for several reasons. First, the true cost effectiveness of a given option depends on what has preceded it. A policy of increasing CAFE standards would depend on the existing level of standards; it is less costly to increase fuel efficiency from 10 to 20 mpg than to increase it from 30 to 40 mpg. Second, policies that target reductions in VOCs may not be cost-effective for other pollutants or may exacerbate other policy issues. For example, reducing emissions of carbon monoxide may in some cases increase emissions of oxides of nitrogen. Yet depending on the location, it may be more important in terms of health benefits to reduce one pollutant than another. Third, there will always be a degree of uncertainty in the development of policies. Even though

TABLE 18.2   COST EFFECTIVENESS ESTIMATES OF ALTERNATIVE APPROACHES TO REDUCING MOTOR VEHICLE EMISSIONS

Policy Approach	Cost (dollars per ton of VOCs reduced)
Command-and-control regulations	
Inspection and maintenance programs	
EPA-enhanced	4,500–6,000
Remote-sensing	2,600–6,000
Hybrid	4,000–6,000
Alternative-fueled vehicles	
Compressed natural gas	12,000–22,000
Methanol	30,000–60,000
Electric	29,000–108,000
Economic incentives	
Accelerated vehicle retirement programs	4,000–6,000
Gasoline tax increases	4,500
Emissions-based registration fees	1,650

Source: Harrington, Walls, and McConnell (1994).

an I&M program may effectively target a high-polluting vehicle, for example, the repairs will not always be successful and may sometimes make things worse.

Other Market-Enhancing Regulations

In addition to the three market-enhancing methods of reducing automobile-related air pollution discussed by Harrington, Walls, and McConnell (1994), there are other methods that, with advances in monitoring technology, are becoming increasingly feasible. One possibility, which was first suggested by Mills and White (1978), would tax vehicles on the amount of pollution they generated each year. Properly done, directly taxing vehicle exhaust emissions would be more efficient than levying higher gasoline taxes or charging different registration fees for vehicles with different emissions profiles.

Mills and White envisioned a system that would measure the emissions from a vehicle through a diagnostic test and then multiply this figure by annual miles traveled to determine overall emissions. These emissions would be taxed at a uniform federal level, plus any additional local taxes that were imposed. So drivers in a heavily polluted city like Los Angeles might pay higher taxes for the privilege of driving than drivers in Buffalo, North Dakota, would. In all cases, however, drivers would have an incentive to purchase cleaner vehicles and drive fewer miles.

One of the problems with this approach is accurate measurement of emissions. Under many inspection programs, drivers tune their cars to pass the annual inspection and then ignore emissions the rest of the year. (Another obvious problem is the ability to tamper with vehicle odometers, but that is a much easier problem to remedy.) In the two decades since Mills and White published their article, however, there have been great strides in the technology available to determine emissions. One system under development uses a laser beam to determine emissions of vehicles driving along a road. Coupled with existing technology that can record vehicle use, such as whether a particular vehicle is driving downtown at a particular hour, it would be possible to assess actual emissions on a real-time basis.[16]

The most difficult part of such an emissions tax system would be determining the correct level of the tax. The local nature of many air pollutants, as well as the seasonal nature of some like ozone, would ideally require emissions taxes that varied by location and time of the year. Even so, determining a "correct" value would depend on assigning initial quasi-property rights to clean air. If residents had a right to clean air, then it would be appropriate to base emissions taxes on their willingness to accept (WTA) reduced air quality. If the default level of air quality was that existing prior to imposition of the emissions tax, it would be appropriate to base the taxes on WTP. In either case, empirical studies of the value of cleaner air would have to be undertaken, probably using a combination of hedonic price and contingent valuation methods we discussed in Chapter 11.

---

[16]The vehicle use measurement technology is used in Singapore.

Summary

Although we have presented a minimal sampling of studies, all of them point to the difficulties of designing efficient pollution reduction strategies, especially for mobile sources such as motor vehicles. Determinations of control costs, especially changes in control costs because of changes in future technologies, are difficult and fraught with uncertainty; predicting future benefits in terms of reduced mortality and morbidity is still more so. As Krupnick and Portney (1991) point out eloquently, resources are scarce. Thus not only do alternative vehicle emissions strategies need to be compared among themselves, so too must they be compared with other policies, such as better prenatal care and smoking cessation programs.

As these and other empirical studies have shown, there are numerous dimensions to controlling mobile sources of air pollution. Increasing the cost of gasoline with higher taxes may lead consumers to shift to higher-mileage vehicles, but that will not correspond necessarily to reduced emissions because high-mileage cars do not always pollute less. Stringent control standards may cost far more than the benefits they return and may slow the replacement of older, higher-polluting vehicles. And to the extent that the purchase of a high-fuel-efficiency vehicle is a sunk cost, the marginal cost of additional driving will be lowered, thus encouraging more driving and more pollution.

Still more complex policy issues arise when economic efficiency is addressed in an economywide context, such as presented using the input-output framework of Chapter 2. Gasoline, for example, is used as an intermediate input for the production of numerous goods and services, especially to the extent that such goods are transported using gasoline-intensive methods like trucks (Poterba 1991). Suppose that policymakers increase gasoline taxes in order to reduce gasoline consumption and pollution. What will happen? First, higher gasoline taxes will raise production costs of these goods; it will cost more to deliver them to markets. This will cause ripple effects throughout the economy. Businesses and industries may switch from gasoline-intensive transportation to less intensive modes. Of course, those less intensive approaches may have their own associated environmental impacts. Finally, the overall economywide impacts would depend on how the tax revenues collected were used (Jaeger 1995). Gasoline taxes that are "recycled" (used to reduce other taxes) in the economy will have a different economic impact from taxes that are not recycled.

Given these caveats, what is the environmental policymaker to do? Harrington, Walls, and McConnell (1994) identify three characteristics of "good" motor vehicle emissions policies. First, target them as precisely as possible. If reducing overall air pollutant emissions is the policy goal, it will be better to design policies that reduce those emissions directly than to develop policies that affect emissions per mile. Second, incentives must be consistent. It makes little sense to encourage motorists to purchase cleaner vehicles but drive them far more miles. Third, policies should be designed using actual data rather than engineering estimates.

To these three characteristics, we can add a fourth: once a policy goal (say, reduce automobile air pollution emissions) is identified, policymakers should expand their search for the most efficient agent to achieve the goal. Thus even though air pollution from vehicles may be increasing, it may be more cost-effective to reduce air pollution from factories, or vice versa. This forces policy-makers to examine proposed policies from a first-best perspective instead of a second-best one.

EQUITY AND RIGHTS CONSIDERATIONS

So far we have focused on policies designed to increase economic efficiency, while paying scant attention to the equity and rights impacts of alternative policies. Yet these considerations have often been the focus of mobile-source pollution policies, owing to the revered status of the automobile (and mobility) in our society. The same policies we have already discussed—taxes on gasoline, emissions-based registration fees, command-and-control emissions limits, and I&M and AVR programs—all have equity and rights effects. How much weight these effects should be given relative to the policies' effects on economic efficiency is debatable. What is clear, however, is that equity and rights effects have played a major role in shaping current automobile emissions policy.

To clarify the role of equity and rights considerations, several issues must be considered. First is the *regressivity* of policy alternatives. Do some policies affect the poor relatively more than the well-off? Increases in gasoline taxes, for example, have often been accused of being regressive. Higher CAFE standards will increase the cost of new vehicles and increase the demand for used vehicles. As a consequence, the poor will be less able to afford adequate transportation and will likely substitute lower-mileage vehicles, increasing their overall transportation costs.

A second issue concerns transportation alternatives. It is fine to increase the cost of commuting, as long as affordable substitutes, such as public transit, are available. Often, however, the poor will lack access to such substitutes. For example, an argument against raising gasoline taxes or mileage standards as a means of reducing air pollution is the lack of acceptable substitutes available to the working poor. To the extent that low-income workers need to arrive or leave work at hours when there is no bus service available, they may have few available alternatives. Often, to find affordable housing, the poor live far away from where their jobs are located. Higher travel costs may force them to spend hours traveling by bus because of poorly coordinated bus schedules and routes. Ultimately, the burdens imposed on the working poor may force them onto unemployment, where they become more of a burden on society. Clearly, these are important and difficult policy issues to address.

Other environmental policies related to mobile source emissions may have far-reaching effects beyond the transportation sector. To the extent that higher CAFE standards reduce transport costs for individuals who can afford new vehicles, they may decide to live in more remote areas, which may affect environmental quality. An example concerns forest firefighting techniques in the West. As more people live near national forests and wilderness areas, firefighting techniques will be altered so as to minimize losses to life and property. Ultimately, however, such policies may increase the likelihood of future losses of forest and species habitat by preventing natural burning that removes forest detritus. Thus higher CAFE standards may unwittingly contribute to declines in animal species populations, including endangered species.

Although the availability of transportation alternatives and impacts of mobile-source emissions policies beyond the transportation sector are important, discussing them in detail is beyond the scope of this book. Instead, next we focus on the regressivity of gasoline taxes.

Equity and the Regressivity of Gasoline Taxes

Gasoline taxes have always been thought to be regressive, falling most heavily on the poorest households. This conclusion has been reinforced by income data. For example, consumer expenditure data for 1984 compiled by the U.S. Bureau of Labor Statistics (BLS) showed that the lowest household income quintile spent 15 percent of its pretax income on gasoline, while the highest household income quintile spent just 2.8 percent. Furthermore, research by Sammartino (1987) showed that only about half of all households with incomes less than $5,000 in 1985 purchased gasoline at all, while over 99 percent of households with incomes above $20,000 did. More recent data compiled by the U.S. Department of Energy (USDOE 1993) indicate that only half of all households with incomes below $5,000 owned one or more vehicles in 1991, while over 98 percent of households with annual incomes above $50,000 owned at least one vehicle. (See Table 18.3.) As a result, some of these lowest-income households must spend significantly more than 15 percent of their income on gasoline (Poterba 1989).

Equity arguments are bolstered further by examining data on the fuel efficiency of vehicles purchased by low- and high-income households. As Table 18.3 shows, vehicle efficiency increases generally with household income level. As a result, lower-income households are affected proportionally more per vehicle mile traveled by higher gasoline taxes than higher income households are, further contributing to the regressivity of such taxes.

Poterba (1989, 1991), however, points out several problems with determining regressivity on the basis of income level. Instead, he recommends assessing regres-

TABLE 18.3 VEHICLE OWNERSHIP AND AVERAGE FUEL EFFICIENCY PER VEHICLE BY INCOME CLASS

1990 Pretax Income Level	Percent of Households Owning at Least One Vehicle	Average Fuel Efficiency per Vehicle (miles per gallon)
Less than $5,000	50.0	18.4
$5,000–$9,999	68.3	17.7
$10,000–$19,999	83.8	18.4
$20,000–$34,999	94.4	18.5
$35,000–$49,999	94.6	20.3
$50,000 and over	98.3	20.2

Source: Davis (1994), tab. 4.15. Data from USDOE (1993).

TABLE 18.4   AVERAGE ANNUAL HOUSEHOLD EXPENDITURES ON GASOLINE

Pretax Income Level	Average Expenditures[a]	Gasoline Expenditures as a Percentage of Total Expenditures
Less than $5,000	$13,300	3.7
$5,000–$9,999	$12,250	3.5
$10,000–$14,999	$17,391	3.5
$15,000–$19,999	$21,360	3.9
$20,000–$29,999	$26,071	3.7
$30,000–$39,999	$31,381	3.5
$40,000–$49,999	$39,983	3.3
$50,000–$69,999	$46,735	3.1
$70,000 and over	$69,207	2.3

[a]Average expenditures can exceed income for numerous reasons, such as indebtedness or student status. Public assistance income is included in reported income levels.

Source: Adapted from Davis (1994), tab. 4.2.

sivity in light of *total current expenditures.* The 1984 BLS data, for example, show that the lowest household income quintile devoted 6 percent of expenditures to gasoline, while the second through fourth quintiles spent larger amounts. Data for 1990, reflecting the collapse of oil prices, showed an almost even expenditure pattern by income class, as shown in Table 18.4. Furthermore, expenditure levels are related to age categories. Households at both ends of the age spectrum tend to have higher expenditures than income. This is not surprising. Young households may have heavy expenditures to care for children, finance education, and so forth. By contrast, the elderly and the retired may live off accumulated savings and investments to finance their expenditures.

Based on an expenditure approach, Poterba (1991) argues that gasoline taxes are far less regressive than conventional, income-based analyses suggest. Lower-income households devote a smaller share of their budgets to gasoline than higher-income households. Yet debate over the regressivity of higher gasoline taxes persists and will likely continue to do so in the future.

Policies That Force Technology: The Case of "Zero-Pollution" Electric Vehicles

Electric vehicles have often been touted as a "zero-pollution solution." Of course, this is nonsense. The electricity needed to charge the batteries used in electric vehicles must be generated somewhere, usually in large central plants that burn coal. To represent an efficient environmental policy, purchase and use of an electric vehicle, plus the additional environmental damage arising from the electricity generated to charge them, must be less costly than internal combustion models. To analyze this requires a complex environmental accounting model.

TABLE 18.5   SELECTED ADVANCED BATTERY TECHNOLOGY GOALS OF THE USABC

	Current Sealed Lead-Acid	Mid-Term Goals (1995–1998)	Long-Term Goals (Post-1998)
Power density (watts per liter)		250	600
Energy density (watt-hours per liter)	92	135	400
Specific energy (watt-hours per kilogram)	33	80	200
Lifetime (years)	6	5	10
Recharge cycles	400	600	1,000
Ultimate price (dollars per kilowatt-hour)		< 150	<100
Operating environment		−30°–65°C	−40°–85°C

Source: Adapted from Davis (1994).

At this time, electric vehicles are more costly to purchase and less convenient to operate than standard vehicles. This is primarily because of the lack of significant progress in battery technology, which has progressed little since the development of lead-acid batteries almost a century ago. Although several new types of batteries are undergoing development and tests, their costs are prohibitive when compared to lead-acid batteries.[17] Because the amount of energy stored by lead-acid batteries per kilogram of battery weight is much less than the energy stored per kilogram of gasoline, current electric vehicles have much less range. In addition, lead-acid batteries have a limited recharging cycle ability, effectively shortening their life to around three years.

Despite the current limitations of electric vehicles, the state of California mandated that 10 percent of all vehicles sold in that state by the year 2003 must be electric vehicles. Several states on the East Coast, including New York and Massachusetts, are considering similar legislation to force advances in battery technology. The results of such legislation may not necessarily be less pollution, although it may lead to a redistribution of pollution from higher-polluted areas like cities to lower-polluted rural areas.

In 1991, the United States Advanced Battery Consortium (USABC), consisting of the "Big Three" U.S. auto manufacturers (General Motors, Ford, and Chrysler), the Electric Power Research Institute, the electric utility industry, and the U.S. Department of Energy, was established. The USABC set specific mid-term and long-term battery technology goals, which are shown in Table 18.5. The long-term goals shown in the last column were set to be competitive with internal combustion engines.

Current commercial battery technology has yet to meet the mid-term goals, let alone the long-term ones. Yet California has remained relatively firm in its commitment to these vehicles. If the goals of the USABC are not met by the time the

---

[17]Some alternative technologies include nickel-metal hydride, sodium-sulfur, and lithium-polymer. In addition, several firms are researching flywheel systems that would capture energy dissipated by braking to extend battery life and range.

California requirements take affect, along with other states that may impose similar requirements, it is not clear what will happen. Presumably, most consumers will be loath to purchase more costly vehicles that promise less performance.

Determining the Environmental Benefits of Electric Vehicles

Whether or not the USABC's goals are met, environmental policymakers will want to determine the overall environmental benefits (if any) from greater use of electric vehicles. To do this, they need to determine the environmental impacts of electric vehicles and compare them with the environmental impacts of the gasoline-powered vehicles they replace.

This is not an easy task. Here's why. To determine the overall environmental impacts from electric vehicles, first we have to determine the consumers who will buy or lease them. Will those consumers tend to live in the Pacific Northwest, where electricity is relatively cheap and mostly generated by hydroelectric plants, or in the Midwest, where electricity is generated mostly from coal? All other things being equal, economic theory would predict that the demand for electric vehicles would be higher in regions with lower electric prices.

Of course, all other things are not equal. First, electric vehicles tend to work better in warmer climates. Batteries last longer, and power does not have to be diverted to defrosting the windows or heating the interior. Thus electric vehicles will work better in California than in Maine. The net environmental impacts of electric vehicles will differ in these two states if the sources of electric generation are different, as indeed they are. California consumers get most of their electricity from nuclear power and fossil fuel plants; Maine customers get relatively more of their electricity from hydroelectric plants.

Second, electric vehicles are expensive, even relative to new gasoline-powered cars. Even if they cost the same to purchase, existing battery technology requires the batteries to be replaced every few years. That costs thousands of dollars. Because electric vehicles are expensive, they will probably be purchased by wealthier consumers. But those consumers are the most likely group to have newer, less polluting gasoline-powered cars. Consequently, electric vehicles, wherever they are operated, will tend to be replacing or supplementing the relatively cleanest gasoline-powered vehicles. And to the extent that purchasers are "green" consumers anyway, they will tend to be less reliant on automobiles.

Third, the pollution avoided by electric vehicles (if any) will be valued differently, depending on the location. Except for global pollutants such as carbon dioxide, most pollutants affect local areas. Avoided emissions in Buffalo, New York, will have a higher value to society than avoided emissions in Buffalo, North Dakota. To maximize the environmental benefit of electric vehicles, therefore, policymakers might want to encourage consumers in crowded cities to buy them.

None of this should be taken to imply that electric vehicles are a bad idea. It may be that emissions from electricity-generating plants can be controlled more efficiently than mobile-source emissions can. However, as we explore in the next section, environmental policies that have addressed stationary-source pollution from electricity-generating plants have rarely had economic efficiency as their primary goal. To the extent that electric vehicles are mandated by states in greater numbers, the overall economic cost to society may therefore increase.

STATIONARY-SOURCE POLLUTION: ENVIRONMENTAL POLICY AND ELECTRIC UTILITIES

Having finished our brief discussion of electric vehicles that would be powered by batteries charged with the output from electricity-generating plants, we turn our attention from mobile sources of pollution to stationary sources. Electric-generating plants, especially older coal-fired plants, are a major source of many air pollutants, including sulfur dioxide, oxides of nitrogen, carbon dioxide, particulates, VOCs, and heavy metals. Because they are stationary, however, these generating plants have been easier to regulate than mobile sources of pollution. Because some of this regulation has appeared not to be cost-effective, however, it has contributed to higher electricity prices, which will reduce the attractiveness of electric vehicles.

Economic Efficiency and Command-and-Control Regulation of Utility Sources

The 1990 Clean Air Act amendments set maximum emissions levels for certain pollutants from electricity-generating facilities. In addition, the amendments set maximum allowable sulfur dioxide emissions nationwide. Unlike other pollutants regulated under the Clean Air Act, however, sulfur dioxide emissions credits are tradable between facilities so as to achieve the statutory reductions in the most efficient way possible. (Trading of oxides of nitrogen is expected to go into effect by the end of the 1990s.) Thus emissions control policies are slowly becoming more market-based.

Stationary-Source Regulation Under the Clean Air Act   Under the Clean Air Act and its amendments, the EPA has responsibility for defining ambient air quality standards. There are two types of standards. The *primary standard* is designed to protect human health and is set so as to protect the most sensitive individuals. By statute, the Clean Air Act requires that primary standards be achieved without regard to their cost. Thus primary ambient air standards are based on an absolute human right to a healthy environment. The *secondary standard* is designed to protect other aspects of human welfare for pollutants having effects beyond those on human health, such as aesthetics (e.g., visibility), vegetation, and objects such as houses and monuments (Tietenberg 1995).

The EPA defines the standards, but it is up to individual states to enforce them. Each state is required to develop a state implementation plan (SIP) acceptable to the EPA. Within each state, the SIP further defines alternative control regions, each with its own timetable for meeting the ambient air quality standards set by the EPA. Failure to comply can result in the EPA's imposing sanctions on states. These sanctions can result in the withholding of federal dollars for such projects as highways or even air pollution control programs. Under the SIP, each state determines the best available control technology (BACT) or lowest achievable emissions rate (LAER), which is defined as the lowest emissions rate possible included in any state's SIP, whether or not any pollution source in the state is achieving that rate.

SIP regions were further defined as attainment and nonattainment regions. In essence, attainment regions were those that met the original compliance deadlines in the 1970 Clean Air Act. Those that did not were designated as nonattainment regions in the 1977 CAA amendments and were subject to particularly stringent controls. Lest areas in attainment rest on their laurels, the EPA also defined a "prevention of significant deterioration" (PSD) policy. Under this policy, new pollution sources would have to meet emissions standards sufficient to prevent any significant deterioration of air quality within the designated region. PSD regulations specified allowable increases in pollutant concentrations beyond defined baselines. PSD regions were defined in terms of three airsheds: Class I, which included national parks and wilderness areas, where increases would be the most restricted; Class II, where all other non–Class I regions were placed and where larger pollutant concentration increases were allowed; and Class III, which would allow still higher concentrations.

Because the definitions of BACT and LAER, which are defined at the state level, could change, the Clean Air Act also defined "new source performance standards" (NSPS). The NSPS were designed to serve as a uniform national floor for pollutant emissions and to regulate all new stationary sources.

Environmental Regulation of Electric Utility Generating Units   What do the Clean Air Act regulations have to do with electricity-generating units? Quite a lot. Most electricity-generating units, especially older units, are significant sources of all of the air pollutants regulated. To the extent that these regulations inhibit the operation of these plants, the costs of electricity increase. And since, as we argued in Chapter 8, command-and-control (CAC) regulations would at best achieve only one of the three efficiency goals, these regulations lead to an overall loss of economic well-being.[18] For example, uniform emissions limits per unit of output or time (e.g., grams of nitrogen oxides per kilowatt-hour, grams of carbon monoxide per hour) will fail to correct all three forms of inefficiency. (Recall that these were producing an efficient level of output, using an efficient mix of inputs, and distributing production among different plants correctly.) In general, this type of regulation can hope to achieve the "right" input mix, but there is little, if any, evidence that the Clean Air Act regulations have achieved even this.

One reason for the lack of efficiency of the input mix is the technology-forcing aspects of many CAC regulations. Under BACT and LAER, companies have an incentive *not* to develop more stringent emissions control technologies, for devel-

---

[18]We do not mean to suggest that the Clean Air Act is inappropriate, only that it is inefficient.

opment will lead to redefinition of the standards. Suppose that a generating plant's current emissions control technology permitted emissions of 0.1 grams of carbon monoxide per kilowatt-hour and cost 0.1 cent per kilowatt-hour's worth of lost electric output. The utility comes across a new technology that would reduce emissions by a factor of 10, down to 0.01 gram per kilowatt-hour. However, the cost would increase by a factor of 10, to 1.0 cent per kilowatt-hour. If the utility were to adopt the new technology, it would become the new BACT standard. For example, new scrubber technology might reduce additional sulfur dioxide at a cost of $2,000 per ton removed. Under the emissions trading program for sulfur dioxide that was established by the 1990 CAA amendments, however, the market price (in 1995) was down to about $150 per ton. Forcing a technological solution where there is a much less costly market alternative makes little economic sense. Fortunately, the EPA appears to be moving toward these sorts of market-enhancing regulations, rather than additional CAC regulations.

Another reason for the inefficiency of CAC regulations is their uniformity. To the extent that pollution damage costs differ by area—emissions will be more harmful in Buffalo, New York, than in Buffalo, North Dakota, because of the greater population exposed—uniform regulations fail to distribute pollution efficiently. Furthermore, the standards themselves are set on the basis of "acceptable" health thresholds. Unfortunately, determining an acceptable threshold is difficult. Even though the Clean Air Act requires the threshold to be set such that there is a margin of safety introduced, there may be no level below which adverse affects do not occur. Yet to establish a standard of no emissions whatsoever would be either technically impossible or prohibitively costly.

Equity and Rights Issues

As we discussed in Chapter 9, past regulation of most stationary-source pollutants was not driven primarily by economic efficiency. Instead, the courts have interpreted much of the Clean Air Act legislation as providing various "rights" to an absence of health risks associated with air pollution. One example, which we also discussed in Chapter 9, was President Clinton's executive order of February 1994 to combat "environmental racism." That order required all federal agencies to determine whether their actions would have *disproportionate* environmental impacts on minority or low-income groups. Not surprisingly, attempting to determine a "disproportionate" environmental impact raises the question, disproportionate compared to what? One of the issues is how environmental equity is measured: via proximity or via risk? It also raises questions as to the root causes of environmental impacts borne by particular groups. Are adverse impacts a result of conscious efforts to burden minorities and the poor? Or does the fault lie with environmental policies themselves or with dynamic economic processes?

In addition, *WTP* for improvements in environmental quality will likely differ among different income groups. There is no "correct" value, however. Just as workers choose occupations with different risks and compensation, individuals may weigh decisions about levels of environmental quality and other goods and services

COMMAND-AND-CONTROL ENVIRONMENTAL COSTING FOR NEW ELECTRIC UTILITY GENERATING PLANTS: GOOD INTENTIONS, BAD ECONOMICS

As we discussed at the beginning of this chapter and in Chapter 7, in the late 1980s, many state public utility commissions (PUCs) developed an interest in environmental costing of electric utility plants. The idea was to incorporate the *residual* environmental costs into utilities' resource choice decisions, even though the plants' emissions were already regulated under the Clean Air Act. Most PUCs adopted a "revealed preference" approach. That is, they assumed that the control costs associated with particular regulations were the same as the value of marginal damage. Thus if the current BACT removes half of the 1 percent of remaining oxides of nitrogen (NO_x) produced by a generating plant at a cost of \$5,000 per ton, PUCs assumed the marginal social cost of NO_x to be \$5,000 per ton. In fact, a mandated control cost being the same as marginal damages would occur only by accident. The higher the marginal control cost needed to extract those last few tons of pollutants, the lower the marginal value of the reduced damages.

In the appendix to Chapter 7, we showed that because PUCs operate in a second-best environment (PUCs, unlike the EPA, do not set environmental regulations), the best PUCs could hope to achieve would be to set prices at a *constrained marginal cost,* the constraint being the stringency of existing environmental regulations. We showed further that the correct variable on which to base new resource choice decisions was total social costs, rather than marginal social costs (Dodds and Lesser 1994).

Despite our findings, and those of other economists, many PUCs continue to embrace the idea of environmental costing using CAC cost proxies. (If the electric utility industry is deregulated, PUCs will have far less control over utility generating decisions.) In 1989, the Massachusetts Department of Public Utilities (MDPU), for example, imposed environmental cost "adders" based on the *highest* existing marginal control cost measures. The MDPU also imposed an adder on emissions of carbon dioxide, based on estimates of the cost of planting trees that store carbon dioxide. In 1992, the MDPU again addressed the issue of environmental adders, but decided to maintain the original values. These values are shown in Table 18.6.

TABLE 18.6   MASSACHUSETTS DEPARTMENT OF PUBLIC UTILITIES ENVIRONMENTAL COST ADDERS

Pollutant	Value (1992 dollars per ton)
Sulfur dioxide	1,700
Carbon monoxide	960
Volatile organic compounds	5,900
Particulates	4,400
Oxides of nitrogen	7,200
Methane	240
Carbon dioxide	24

Source: MDPU (1992).

(continued)

Alas, the twists of fate did not bode well for this policy, for several reasons. First, in late 1994, the Massachusetts Supreme Court ruled that the MDPU had exceeded its authority in levying adders. Second, by late 1995, the MDPU itself turned its focus from externality adders to restructuring and deregulation of the entire electric industry. As a result, the MDPU changed its views. Although the agency still wants environmental quality improved, it recognizes that PUCs are not the right entity for setting environmental policy.

differently. Someone who is poor may prefer to live in an area that has more environmental risk for the very reason that housing is more affordable. To the extent that these are conscious choices and not the result of discriminatory *limitations* on choice, it is difficult to discern overt environmental inequity and injustice.

To investigate this issue further, Been (1994) examined the siting of incinerators, landfills, and what have come generally to be called "locally undesirable land uses" (LULUs). Advocates of environmental justice have cited studies showing that communities hosting LULUs have, on average, higher proportions of racial minorities and the poor than other communities. These advocates argue that environmental risks should be distributed equitably among differences races and income classes. Following up on previous studies by the U.S. General Accounting Office (GAO) on siting hazardous waste landfills, Been examined whether LULUs were sited in areas that were *already* inhabited by minorities and the poor, which might indicate discrimination, or whether areas surrounding LULUs *became* disproportionately poor and minority after the LULUs had been sited.

Been examined the demographic characteristics over time in the four areas studied by the GAO, beginning in the year each LULU was sited through 1990. She found that all four areas were predominantly black at the time they were selected as hazardous waste landfills. Her findings were evidence that the landfills did have disproportionate impacts on African Americans. But, as she goes on to discuss, a LULU that has disproportionate impacts on a minority group is not necessarily evidence of discrimination.

The siting of a LULU can affect the characteristics of a neighborhood in several ways. First, an undesirable land use may encourage those who can afford to move from the neighborhood to do so. Second, as higher-income residents move away, property values in the neighborhood will tend to fall, increasing the affordability of housing in the neighborhood and encouraging more lower-income households to locate there. Discrimination in sale and rental housing markets can also force the poor and minorities to locate or remain in the neighborhood. Thus, given the dynamics of housing markets, Been concludes that it would be surprising if LULUs did *not* impose "undue" burdens on the poor and minorities. Nevertheless, Been concludes that no easy generalizations can be made about the causes of the inequity in siting distribution of LULUs because different studies have yielded different findings.

Glickman (1994) examined the issue of measuring environmental equity in general. Most advocates of environmental justice have based their determinations of inequity on proximity-based measurements: how close people are to environmental hazards. As he points out, however, such measurements are inferior to ones that actually measure the risks involved.

Suppose that two neighborhoods surround a toxic waste dump, as shown in Figure 18.1. Neighborhood 1 is located 2 miles upwind of the toxic waste site. Neighborhood 2 is located 10 miles downwind of the site. On a proximity basis, neighborhood 1 would be classified as more "inequitable." However, because the prevailing winds are toward neighborhood 2, on a risk basis it will be more "inequitable" than neighborhood 1. Glickman's (1994) research has shown that with respect to Allegheny County, Pennsylvania, the environmentally riskiest neighborhoods are not necessarily those populated by minorities.

None of this is to suggest that there is no discrimination whatsoever in the siting of LULUs or in housing markets that may lead to minorities and the poor facing higher environmental risks. However, poorly conceived solutions to combat such discrimination that do not recognize the complexities of housing market dynamics are unlikely to achieve their goals.

The increasing difficulty in siting new LULUs, which encompass far more than environmental risks, is the result of greater emphasis on "not in my backyard" (NIMBY) and "build absolutely nothing anywhere near anybody" (BANANA) desires. For example, everyone recognizes the urgent need to develop a permanent nuclear waste storage facility. To do otherwise will mean continued storage of these wastes throughout the country either at nuclear power plants or in other short-term storage facilities. Yet few people wish to have such a facility near them, and fewer still wish to have nuclear wastes transported through their cities and towns. Despite their frustrating nature, however, NIMBY policies can make economic sense. For example, homeowners, wishing to avoid decreases in the value of their property, may view the location of a LULU as a transfer of wealth. Thus one solution to NIMBY concerns may be some form of compensation mechanisms.[19]

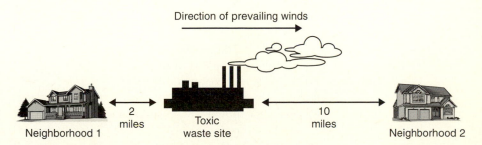

Direction of prevailing winds

2 miles   Toxic waste site   10 miles

Neighborhood 1   Neighborhood 2

Figure 18.1   Locational versus Risk-Based Equity

[19]Such mechanisms would have to be designed carefully, however, to ensure that only those adversely affected received compensation.

BANANA-type sentiments are far more difficult to deal with and may be the most discriminatory of all policies. BANANA sentiments fail to address the needs for economic development. In 1993, for example, the city of Boulder, Colorado, with the intent of preventing continued rapid growth, passed a resolution banning construction of any new housing. In doing so, the city assured existing property owners of increased wealth by fixing the supply of housing and transferred the problems associated with growth to other communities. Such a policy can also prevent low-income individuals from locating in the city and may lead to an exodus of existing low-income individuals who are unable to afford higher rents and property taxes resulting from the constraint on the housing supply.

BANANA environmental policies that prevent the development of, say, new electricity-generating units or mass transit units also fix commodity supplies. They may exacerbate environmental impacts by increasing the value of older, more polluting generating plants or encourage individuals to commute alone in their vehicles.

Deregulation of the Electric Industry and Environmental Quality

With the passage of the Energy Policy Act of 1992 (EPAct), Congress set in motion the beginnings of deregulating the electric utility industry, which has historically been tightly regulated. Ultimately, the EPAct and subsequent state-level policy actions will likely lead to competitive markets for electricity at the *retail* level, much as occurred when long-distance telephone service was fully deregulated in the 1980s.

Though space precludes us from discussing all of the potential ramifications of deregulation and retail competition,[20] one issue it has raised is the effect on future environmental quality and policy. Specifically, will deregulation lead to a situation where cheap but dirty electricity is preferred over clean but more expensive electricity? Some opponents of deregulation of retail electric markets have vehemently answered yes (e.g., Cohen 1994). Proponents have taken a different position. The actual answer, not surprisingly, depends on expectations of the form of future environmental regulations.

If future developers of electricity-generating units believe that environmental regulators will impose stricter regulations in the future, the costs of building cheap and dirty plants today may be much more expensive than building cleaner plants. If buyers wish to sign long-term supply contracts at fixed prices, suppliers will have to estimate the probability that future environmental regulations will be significantly more stringent than today. A supplier will wish to maximize the expected net present value of profit, $E(\pi)$. Thus the supplier will seek to maximize

$$E(\pi) = \int_G \left\{ \sum_{t=1}^{T} [(\tilde{P}_{e,t}\tilde{g})\tilde{Q}_{e,t}(\tilde{g}) - C_{e,t}(\tilde{g})]/(1 + r)^t \right\} f(g)\, dg \qquad (18.4)$$

where $\tilde{g}$ refers to the uncertain future government environmental policy

---

[20]For a general discussion, see Brennan et al. (1996).

$\tilde{P}_{e,t}$ = the uncertain future price of electricity in time period t

$\tilde{Q}_{e,t}$ = the uncertain future quantity of electricity sold in time period t

$\tilde{C}_{e,t}$ = the uncertain future cost of supplying electricity

r = the supplier's discount rate

$f(g)$ = the probability distribution of expected future government environmental policies

As Equation 18.4 makes evident, the simplistic arguments of both proponents and opponents are insufficient. The decision of whether or not to build a cleaner electric plant depends on expectations of that plant's direct costs compared to the market value of electricity with that plant's environmental characteristics. It also depends on the level of deregulation. For example, electricutility rates are now set by PUCs. In a fully deregulated world, electricity prices would be set by markets. Furthermore, the choice of future environmental regulations $f(g)$ will depend on the actions taken by environmental regulators.

For environmental and other policymakers, the best approach will be to develop clear signals for future environmental regulations. A system of emissions taxes or broader markets for tradable emissions permits, for example, will send clear signals to energy resource developers as to the most efficient level of environmental quality for their generating facilities. It may be that the most harmful aspect of deregulation at the retail level is not that suppliers will ignore future environmental impacts but that they will make their decisions in the presence of a great deal of uncertainty.

CHAPTER SUMMARY

In this chapter, we have briefly addressed environmental issues associated with the use of energy. We focused our discussion on two major sources of environmental impacts associated with energy use: mobile and stationary sources. Mobil sources are primarily automobiles and trucks. Their use, which is ubiquitous in this country, is a contributor to major environmental degradation. Yet because of that ubiquitous nature, reducing the impacts from mobile sources in an efficient manner is complex and may have significant impacts on equity considerations.

We focused our discussion of stationary sources of pollution on the electric utility industry, which is one of the largest contributors to pollution. The history of environmental regulation of stationary sources is one of command-and-control regulations. These regulations, such as those embodied in the Clean Air Act and its amendments, have been directed primarily at protecting human health by reducing emissions rates. Unfortunately, many of these regulations have not focused on the true arbiters of health: pollutant concentrations and exposure levels. Fortunately, there is increasing reliance on market-enhancing mechanisms to address stationary-source pollutants.

Improving the economic efficiency of existing regulations that affect energy resource development and use, even in a second-best context, will in the future have to account better for cross-sectoral impacts. Little benefit, and quite possibly significant harm, will come from misguided attempts at regulation that do not examine the impacts on substitute markets.

Environmental equity may also be affected by energy resource and use policies, although perceptions of environmental discrimination against minorities and the poor may be more a reaction to market dynamics than overt discrimination. Equity also needs to be evaluated on a more appropriate basis, that of environmental risks, rather than the more common proximity measures now used. Finally, valuations of environmental quality improvements will likely differ among different income groups. The poor may be more interested in the certain benefits from gainful local employment and less interested in the potential environmental harm they may face. This is observed in occupational decisions, where many workers are compensated for the riskiness of their jobs. There is no reason to believe that it will not be true as well, at least to some extent, for choices where to live.

CHAPTER REVIEW

Economic Concepts and Tools

- The degree of regressivity of gasoline taxes is affected by the definition of income. Lifetime earnings definitions indicate less regressivity than annual earnings comparisons.
- Electric utility regulators must take existing environmental regulations as given. As a result, utility regulators seeking to impose further environmental regulations must operate in a second-best mode.

Policy Issues

- Control of mobile-source emissions such as those from motor vehicles, presents significant challenges to policymakers. Many existing regulations affect the relative demand for new and used vehicles, which can in turn reduce the effectiveness of specific policies. Currently, emissions taxes are impractical, owing to their measurement costs.
- Policies that control emissions may also have significant equity impacts because since lower-income consumers are likely to own older, more polluting vehicles. The regressivity of certain taxes, such as gasoline taxes, however, will depend on whether incomes are defined on the basis of short-term or lifetime earnings.
- "Zero-pollution" vehicles do not exist.
- In the electric utility industry, regulators have pursued a variety of environmental policies. Most of these policies espouse noble ends but have failed to consider second-best issues. Fundamental conflicts between equity and efficiency have arisen.
- Fuel switching, the substitution of central station electricity generation for direct fuel combustion at the site of use, requires difficult efficiency comparisons in that local environmental damage may be difficult to measure. When confronting further deregulation of the electric utility industry, environmental policymakers will have carefully to consider the nature and scope of regulations. Market-enhancing mechanisms, such as emissions taxes and tradable permits, are likely to be far more effective than command-and-control methods.

DISCUSSION QUESTIONS

1. How could a system of pollution-based vehicle registration fees for all vehicles be designed? What would be its ramifications on economic efficiency? On equity? How would such a system account for the impacts of different pollutants?
2. Suppose that a system of emissions taxes for vehicles is too costly for implementation. How could you determine the next-best alternative?
3. What would be the impact of higher CAFE standards on the development of cost-effective electric vehicles? What about higher speed limits? How would you set up an analysis?
4. How should environmental and utility regulators work together to ensure the most efficient regulation of energy sources and use?
5. If the actions of utility regulators affect substitution rates between regulated electricity markets and deregulated fuel markets, should the fuel markets be regulated? Would that make determinations of the "correct" usage levels of all fuels easier? Would it lead to more efficient outcomes? If your answer is no, does that mean that deregulation of electricity markets will lead to a more efficient solution? Why or why not?

REFERENCES

Alberini, A., D. Edlestein, W. Harrington, and V. McConnell. 1994. *Emissions Reduction Credits from Old Cars: The Economics of the Delaware Retirement Program.* Discussion Paper No. 94-27. Washington, D.C.: Resources for the Future.

Been, V. 1994. "Locally Undesirable Land Uses in Minority Neighborhoods: Disproportionate Siting or Market Dynamics?" *Yale Law Journal* 103(2): 1383–1420.

Brennan, T., K. Palmer, R. Kopp, A. Krupnick, V. Stagliano, and D. Burtraw. 1996. *A Shock to the System.* Washington, D.C.: Resources for the Future.

Carr, E. 1994. "Survey on Energy." *Economist,* June 18, 1994.

Cohen, A. 1994. "The Political Economy of Retail Wheeling, or How to Not Refight the Last War." *Electricity Journal* 7(4): 49–61.

Crandall, R., H. Gruenspecht, T. Keeler, and L. Lave. 1986. *Regulating the Automobile.* Washington, D.C.: Brookings Institution.

Dahl, C. 1991. "A Survey of Econometric Gasoline Demand Elasticities." *International Journal of Energy Systems* 11(2): 53–76.

Davis, S. 1994. *Transportation Data Book 14.* Oak Ridge, Tenn.: Oak Ridge National Laboratories.

———. 1996. *Transportation Data Book 16.* Oak Ridge, Tenn.: Oak Ridge National Laboratories.

Di Figlio, C., K. Duleep, and D. Greene. 1990. "Cost-Effectiveness of Future Fuel Economy Improvements." *Energy Journal* 11(1): 65–86.

Dodds, D., and J. Lesser. 1994. "Can Utility Commissions Improve on Environmental Regulations?" *Land Economics* 70(1): 37–56.

Glickman, T. 1994. "Measuring Environmental Equity with Geographical Information Systems." *Resources* 116: 2–6.

Greene, D. 1990. "CAFE or Price? An Analysis of the Federal Fuel Economy Regulations and Gasoline Price on New Car MPG." *Energy Journal* 11(3): 37–57.

———. 1992. "Vehicle Use and Fuel Economy: How Big Is the Rebound Effect?" *Energy Journal* 13(1): 117–143.

Greene, D., and K. Duleep. 1993. "Costs and Benefits of Automotive Fuel Economy Improvement: A Partial Analysis." *Transportation Research* 27A(3): 217–235.

Gruenspecht, H. 1981. "Differentiated Social Regulation in Theory and Practice." Ph.D. dissertation, Yale University.

———. 1982. "Differentiated Regulation: The Case of Automobile Emissions Standards." *American Economic Review* 72(2):328–331.

Harrington, W., M. Walls, and V. McConnell. 1994. *Shifting Gears: New Directions for Cars and Clean Air.* Discussion Paper No. 94–26. Washington, D.C.: Resources for the Future.

Jaeger, W. 1995. *Optimal Environmental Taxation.* Discussion Paper No. 95–10. Seattle: Institute for Economic Research, University of Washington.

Khazzoom, J. 1991. "The Impact of a Gasoline Tax on Auto Exhaust Emissions." *Journal of Policy Analysis and Management* 10(3): 434–454.

Krupnick, A., and P. Portney. 1991. "Controlling Urban Air Pollution: A Benefit-Cost Assessment." *Science* 252: 522–528.

Krupnick, A., M. Walls, and C. Collins. 1993. "Global Warming and Urban Smog: Cost-Effectiveness of CAFE Standards and Alternative Fuels." *Energy Journal* 14(4): 75–97.

Lesser, J., and J. Weber. 1989. "The Impact of the 65 mph Speed Limit on Gasoline Demand in Washington State." *Energy Systems and Policy* 13(3): 193–203.

Massachusetts Department of Public Utilities (MDPU). 1992. *Investigation by the Department of Public Utilities on Its Own Motion as to the Environmental Externality Values to Be Used in Resource Cost-Effectiveness Tests by Electric Companies Subject to the Department's Jurisdiction.* Boston: MDPU.

Mills, E., and L. White. 1978. "Government Policies Towards the Automobile Emissions Control." In *Approaches to Air Pollution Control,* ed. A. Frielander. Cambridge, Mass.: MIT Press.

Office of Technology Assessment (OTA). 1989. *Catching Our Breath: Next Steps for Reducing Urban Ozone.* Washington, D.C.: OTA.

Poterba, J. 1989. "Lifetime Incidence and Distributional Burden of Excise Taxes." *American Economic Review, Papers and Proceedings* 79: 325–330.

———. 1991. "Is the Gasoline Tax Regressive?" In *Tax Policy and the Economy,* Vol. 5. Cambridge, Mass.: MIT Press.

Sammartino, F. 1987. "The Distributional Effects of an Increase in Selected Federal Excise Taxes." Working Paper, Congressional Budget Office, Washington, D.C.

Schwing, R., B. Southworth, C. von Buseck, and C. Jackson. 1980. "Benefit-Cost Analysis of Automotive Emissions Reductions." *Journal of Environmental Economics and Management* 7(1): 44–64.

Tietenberg, T. 1995. *Environmental and Natural Resource Economics,* 4th ed. New York: HarperCollins.

U.S. Department of Energy (USDOE). 1993. *Household Vehicles Survey, 1991.* Washington, D.C.: Energy Information Administration.

von Hippel, F. 1987. "Automobile Fuel Economy." *Energy* 12(10/11): 1063–1071.

CHAPTER 19

ECONOMIC GROWTH, THE ENVIRONMENT, AND SUSTAINABILITY

Economic and Environmental Tragedy

Rightly or wrongly, the mention of Africa conjures up strikingly different images: vast savannas, jungles, and deserts on the one hand; human poverty, deprivation, and misery on the other. Some countries in Africa rank among the world's poorest. And while population growth rates in most areas of the world are declining, birthrates in many African countries remain extremely high. Due to poor farming practices and cruel weather cycles, agricultural productivity cannot keep up. Deforestation to secure more land, much of it only marginally productive for farming and grazing, sets off a vicious cycle. Compounding these problems, desertification and the widespread deterioration of agricultural soils in dryland areas, often from erosion, have decreased harvest yields for many important food crops. And some of the poorest countries have fallen victim to cruel despots, who have exploited these countries as personal fiefdoms and treasuries.

Feeding rapidly increasing populations is but one challenge. There also have been accusations that some African countries, desperate for cash, are allowing themselves to become the dumping ground for the rest of the world's wastes, exposing their populations to severe environmental hazards. Some in Africa have fought this, as when, in 1989, the Organization for African Unity attempted to ban imports of hazardous wastes from developed countries. Some groups in developed countries argue that exporting wastes elsewhere is not only not moral but also not

*sustainable. Others argue that in a market economy, accepting wastes from devel-
oped countries is perfectly rational.*

*Unfortunately, although serving as a dumping ground for the world's wastes may
be a high-profile environmental problem, it is only one of many, and probably one of
lesser importance. Perhaps the most fundamental environmental problem is the lack of
clean drinking water and sanitation facilities, which continues to contribute to a high
incidence of disease and death among millions of people. Because many of the countries lack the financial resources to construct such facilities, much aid has been
received from the developed world to build them. Overshadowing the small degree of
success achieved is the fact that much of that aid has fallen into the hands of despots
and crooks. Environmental improvements that could contribute to economic growth
and human well-being in many countries have been stymied by crass political forces.*

*It thus would seem that many Africans are caught in an endless cycle of pover-
ty and environmental degradation, a cycle that many observers would call* unsustainable. *And the problem is not only limited to African nations. Many developing
nations in Asia and Latin America suffer similar problems, to varying degrees.
Nations with large forests of tropical hardwoods, such as Myanmar (Burma) and
Indonesia, are cutting those forests at an astonishing rate, destroying a valuable
economic and environmental resource. Other countries' development plans may
lead to significant environmental degradation. When completed (if ever), China's
Three Gorges Dam on the Yangtze River will be the largest hydroelectric dam in
the world, dwarfing Grand Coulee Dam on the Columbia River, and will require
the resettlement of millions of people. Critics contend that none of these actions are
supportable if the world is to develop a* sustainable *economy.*

*Yet it seems clear that improving the local environment requires economic and
financial strength that many countries lack. But increasing financial and economic
strength can occur only if resources can be devoted to something besides providing
for the most basic services and needs that individuals in developed countries take
for granted.*

*Most analysts would agree that avoiding or jumping off this environment-
development merry-go-round is crucial. How to do so, however, has been the subject of vigorous debate and disagreement, much of which lies at the core of the sustainability question. Some people argue for more aid from the developed world, in
the form of technology transfers or outright cash. Unfortunately, the track record
for this sort of approach is poor. The lack of basic infrastructure, such as water and
electricity, often makes transferred technologies worthless. A modern electric arc
furnace for producing steel is of little value if there is no electricity; a coal-fired
power plant to generate electricity is of little use if there is no railroad to transport
the necessary coal; railroad tracks are of little use if there is no money to purchase
rail cars. Too often, technology transfers have failed to be mindful of the availability of the needed supporting technology (see, e.g., Schmidheiny 1992).*

*Some proponents of sustainable growth policies argue vociferously for greater
population control measures, reasoning that the burdens placed on a limited supply of natural resources can be reduced only by swiftly reducing population size.
This, too, is controversial, not only for religious and moral reasons but also because
of the economic rationality of large families: the need for more labor to work*

increasingly marginal agricultural lands and the high mortality rate of that labor. Yet as is observed in the developed world, as economic well-being increases, population growth slows, seemingly of its own accord.

Which types of approaches can break the cycle and create a sustainable future—market incentives or command-and-control policies—depends on one's point of view. Because so many poor countries have so few financial resources, policies designed to improve environmental quality should be as cost-effective as possible. Given the large and predatory nature of some of these countries' bureaucracies, it is not surprising that command and control has been the more common approach. Unfortunately, as past chapters have discussed, such approaches have often been the least efficient, squandering limited resources and yielding few benefits. Little regard has been given to the type of environmental problem to be tackled and the resources necessary to impose corrective environmental policies. Yet policies that focused only on increasing economic growth—building roads, hydroelectric dams, and other "big" projects—have also failed. In some cases, they have ignored the support needed to ensure success; in others, the projects themselves caused significant environmental damage.

Though at times it seems that human and environmental horrors may never end, there has been progress. Technology transfer is becoming more appropriate. Environmental quality issues are now addressed carefully prior to funding development projects. More attention is given to providing basic economic infrastructure, in the form of water supplies and water treatment facilities or new institutional policies that better establish property rights and eliminate incentives for the overexploitation of resources. Despite ample reason for skepticism, hope may still be the most important resource of all.

INTRODUCTION

One of the most strident areas of environmental policy debate continues to be the relationship between economic growth and environmental quality. This debate, whether focused on the decline of fisheries or the destruction of tropical rain forests, is often placed in the context of *either* economic growth *or* environmental preservation. Indeed, past evidence indicates that much economic growth has come at the expense of the environment, as there is seemingly no end to the list of environmental horror stories being told throughout the world.[1]

In this chapter, we take a broader look at the relationship between economic growth and environmental quality. We suggest that rather than there existing necessarily an either-or trade-off between economic growth and environmental quality, the relationship is complementary. In the long run, we cannot sustain economic growth and the betterment of human lives without preserving and enhancing

---

[1]The two classic pieces stating opposite positions on the issues are Daly (1971) and Georgescu-Roegen (1971). Daly argues that growth is incompatible with environmental quality, while Georgescu-Roegen contends that such a Malthusian assumption is wrong.

environmental quality. For many areas of the world that are beset by poverty, creating a "sustainable" future is possible.

We begin by framing the issues that have left over 1 billion people living in poverty and the conditions that have fueled the debate over economic development and environmental improvement.[2] Next we address the concepts of *sustainability* and *sustainable development.* These two concepts have become widely invoked and much debated in considerations of environmental and natural resource policies for both developing and developed nations. After discussing the alternative definitions of sustainability and sustainable development, we address how researchers have derived measures of economic growth that incorporate sustainability criteria and the difficulties with these measures. Last, we address the role of economic analysis in the sustainability debate.

Ultimately, meeting the basic needs of billions of individuals, not to mention raising their living standards to Western levels, will require vast resources. Unlike some theorists, however, we do not believe that this is a recipe for global environmental calamity. In fact, as we will argue in the final section of the chapter, properly managed economic growth itself will provide the key to a better environment. Consequently, developing countries should care about environmental quality as much as developed countries, although the former's environmental *priorities* will almost surely differ from the latter's.

ECONOMIC GROWTH, POPULATION, AND ENVIRONMENTAL QUALITY

Perhaps the biggest driver of concerns about growth and environmental quality has been the explosion in the human population. As Figure 19.1 shows, world population has more than doubled since 1950, from about 2.5 billion to around 5.7 billion in 1995. Growth peaked at over 2.1 percent per year between 1965 and 1970. Today that growth rate has declined to about 1.7 percent per year. Despite that decline, however, world population is increasing by almost 100 million each year, primarily in developing countries.

Projections of future population growth vary. By 2000, the World Bank estimates that population will have increased to around 6.5 billion. Farther into the future, population growth will depend on fertility, which has historically declined as economic well-being has improved. The World Bank estimates that by 2100, world population could be as high as 20 billion, if fertility rates remain at their current levels (World Bank 1992).

Eventually, the world's population will stabilize. At what level depends on future growth rates. If world population follows a *logistic growth model,* as it seems to be doing, the decline in observed growth rates indicates eventual stabilization. A logistic growth model resembles an S-shaped curve. Population growth increases

---

[2]A far more complete discussion of development and the environment can be found in World Bank (1992). See also Dasgupta (1995) for an excellent discussion of the linkages between population growth and well-being.

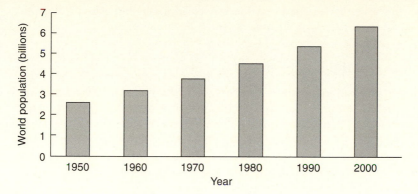

Figure 19.1   World Population Growth, 1950–2000

Source: United Nations.

slowly at first, accelerates to a maximum growth rate, and then gradually levels off to a steady-state population. This is shown in Figure 19.2. For thousands of years, the world's population of human beings increased very slowly. In the last few hundred years, improved technology and better living conditions allowed populations to expand rapidly. In more developed countries, the need for many children (primarily to help with agricultural production and to compensate for high infant mortality) has diminished greatly. That is why population growth in these countries has slowed so significantly. Many less developed countries' economies, however, still are primarily agrarian. As a result, their population growth has slowed little, if at all.

Depending on exactly where on the curve world population is today, growth will stabilize at some overall population level. This is shown as P_{max} in Figure 19.2. That ultimate level may be 20 billion, or it may be significantly less. What is clear, however, is that whatever the world's ultimate population, the demand for

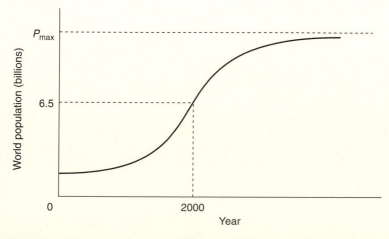

Figure 19.2   Logistic Growth Rate of World Population

resources, including environmental resources like clean air and water, will continue to grow, increasing the need to allocate those resources efficiently.

Population and the Environment

As the world's population increases, the demand for economic goods and services (e.g., food, shelter, clothing, transportation) increases as well. If historical practices are any guide, this increased demand also increases the pressures on natural resources and environmental quality. Bigger populations place greater demands on land resources for agricultural production, on water resources as new supplies of drinkable water are sought, and on timber resources for fuelwood. Bigger populations also increase the need for new sources of employment and increase pressures on urban areas as people migrate in search of work. At the same time, bigger populations mean more wastes that are produced, increasing the strain on the world's carrying capacity.

One region where the pressures of increasing population have been felt most is sub-Saharan Africa (Cleaver and Schreiber 1991). Population growth in this region continues to accelerate. As long as land was abundant, there was little pressure on the environment. But after 1950, improvements in health care allowed populations to expand rapidly. This led to cultivation of lands that were only marginally productive and more rapid deforestation as new supplies of fuelwood were sought. Deforestation and the use of marginally productive lands in turn caused agricultural productivity to fall and further intensified the pressure to use the more productive lands, to the point where they became depleted.[3] The result has been overgrazing, deforestation, depletion of water supplies, and economic stagnation. Unfortunately, where capital is scarce and technology limited, labor becomes the input of choice. Fertility rates in this region have remained high as to provide the needed labor to work marginally productive land. This has reinforced a vicious cycle of environmental degradation and misery.

Compounding these problems has been the trend toward greater urbanization. In 1990, the majority of the world's population lived in rural areas. By 2030, however, urban populations are expected to be twice as large as rural populations (World Bank 1992). This rapid urbanization will continue to increase greatly the environmental stress on cities to provide basic services such as clean water and sanitation. It will also place increasing stress on cities to deal with greater pollution from industrial sources and transportation.

Poverty and the Environment

One of the key goals of economic growth is to improve conditions for the large fraction of individuals living in abject poverty.[4] Unfortunately, the number of indi-

---

[3]One problem is that land has not been allowed to lie fallow so as to recover nutrients.

[4]The World Bank defines the poverty line as $420 in annual income per capita at 1990 prices. See Ravallion, Datt, and Chen (1992) for more information.

viduals expected to be living in poverty by the year 2000 still will be over 1 billion. Though this number represents a declining share of total forecast population, its sheer magnitude raises significant moral issues. The distribution of these individuals will also be uneven, as shown in Figure 19.3. Between 1990 and 2000, all regions save sub-Saharan Africa are expected to see a decline in the percentage of individuals living in poverty. The percentage in the latter, unfortunately, are expected to *increase* to about half of the population.

The poor are the most likely to suffer from environmental degradation, as well as to contribute to it. Because they lack access to the most productive agricultural lands, poor farmers cultivate marginal areas. Many of these marginal lands are prone to erosion, are semiarid where soil nutrients are limited, or are cleared areas in tropical forests. In all three locations, agricultural yields usually decline rapidly, forcing farmers to seek still more marginal lands. Poor families are forced to live in the least desirable areas and often in incredible squalor. In many cases, they survive without access to clean water or sanitation facilities. They may be located in areas prone to flooding, such as in Bangladesh, or in close proximity to heavily polluted industrial sites, as in Mexico City.

Breaking this cycle of environmental degradation and poverty requires the provision of sufficient resources so that the poor can focus on something besides day-to-day subsistence. If investments are made in clean water and sanitation facilities, for example, the health of the poor can be improved. That will increase productivity, income, and future prospects. Many environmental projects are also labor-intensive. Thus they can provide badly needed employment opportunities even as they improve environmental quality. And as the poor become better-off, they will have fewer children. This will reduce future population and environmental pressures.

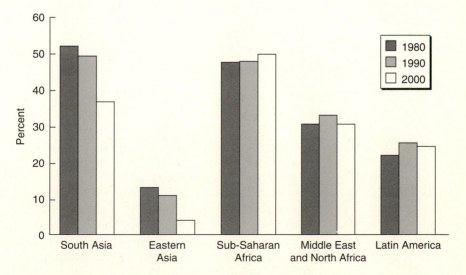

Figure 19.3   Percent of Population Living in Poverty

Source: World Bank (1992), p. 30.

SUSTAINABILITY AND SUSTAINABLE DEVELOPMENT

Fine as it is to argue that breaking the cycle of poverty can reduce environmental degradation, the world has many examples of economic growth that has come at the expense of the environment: strip-mined lands and clearcut forests that resemble moonscapes, depleted stocks of fisheries, rivers and streams choked by industrial wastes, and clouds of pollution that may be irrevocably changing the earth's climate. This is not a pretty picture, and it leads some people to argue that we must fundamentally change our societies and lives toward a nonconsumptive orientation. In other words, we must live with less and seek only economic development that is sustainable if we are to pass on an environmentally sound world to future generations.

So what is "sustainable development?" That simple question has inspired bitter debate and the spilling of much ink. How can we use depletable resources, like oil, if using it today will mean less for future generations? What level of consumption is "sustainable"? Should we allow individuals to make consumption decisions freely, or should these decisions be regulated? Should individuals have the right to procreate at will, or do population pressures require societal actions, perhaps draconian ones, to reduce the global populace?

None of these questions is easy to answer, nor are they questions that most of us want to answer, encompassing as they do economic, ethical, and moral issues. All of these questions, however, can be viewed in the context of actions that the current generation may take that may or may not be fair to "the future." Defining which future and what is in that future is notoriously difficult. Nevertheless, the questions boil down to efficiency, equity, and rights, much like the other environmental issues we have discussed previously. If we are to improve living standards for the world's population, how can we ensure that those improvements do not come at the expense of future generations? At the same time, we must ask, what are reasonable "sacrifices" for the current generation to make? And who in the current generation ought to make those sacrifices?

Even if we come up with an acceptable definition of sustainability, which will be difficult enough, we must then develop operational *measures* to determine whether various economic and environmental actions are sustainable. Thus as with all policies, we need a measuring system, some yardstick by which we can decide whether the goals of sustainable development are being reached and whether standards of living have been improved. Some of these measures may have nothing do with money: declines in infant mortality and increases in education levels, for example, are certainly good indicators of an improving quality of life. Other measures are strictly monetary: increases in gross national product (GNP), equal to the value of all final goods and services consumed, or gross domestic product (GDP), equal to the value of all domestically produced final goods and services consumed.

In addition to these measures, we must then incorporate measures of environmental quality. For example, the amount of pollution emitted into the air, the diversity of species, and the degree of deforestation are all environmental measures that are sometimes incorporated into notions of sustainability. Finally, we must be able to weigh these different measures together, much as we discussed in the context of multiattribute decision analysis in Chapters 10 and 14. Mix with a strong dose of uncertainty and the need to weigh the different attributes of sustainability, and you get an idea of why the problem is so vexing.

As yet, sustainability has no unique operational definition. Thus we cannot state unequivocally that emitting 100,000 tons of a pollutant into the atmosphere would result in an "unsustainable" future, but reducing emissions to 90,000 tons would be sustainable. This complicates the job of policymakers who, if they wish to invoke "sustainable" policies, have little to guide them other than their own beliefs as to an appropriate definition of sustainability. Unfortunately, defining sustainability simply as "I know it when I see it" hardly seems a solid basis on which to develop sound policies.

Yet the concept can nevertheless be useful if it encourages innovative methods of measuring economic and environmental well-being, and therefore policies that can promote such well-being. As we shall see, much work has been done on just this sort of innovation.

Defining Sustainability

Let's begin by discussing the alternative definitions of sustainability. The literature on sustainability is immense and growing.[5] Unfortunately, the term *sustainable* has become a ubiquitous adjective, attached to everything from energy policy to competition. Though this may popularize the term, it provides little guidance for policymakers. And despite the temptation to take the Humpty Dumpty approach to vocabulary,[6] environmental policies that are "sustainable" cannot be defined, nor can progress be measured, until there is agreement on the concept itself.

In its simplest form, *sustainable development* is development that does not occur at the expense of the future, whatever that means. In 1987, the World Commission on Environment and Development (WCED), better known as the Bruntland Commission, defined sustainable development as the current generation's meeting its needs "without compromising the ability of future generations to meet their own needs." This ties in neatly with the concepts of intergenerational equity and fairness that we discussed earlier, especially in Chapters 4 and 13.

One common approach, often seen in textbooks, is defining sustainability in terms of the total welfare of current generations versus future generations. If the welfare of future generations is lower than that of the current generation, the current generation is not pursuing sustainability. The problem with such a definition is that from a policy standpoint, it is meaningless because we cannot measure the welfare of future generations. It is impossible to know whether specific actions today hamper sustainable outcomes or enhance them. For example, is it better to

---

[5]A good summary of the literature is provided by Pezzy (1992).
[6]"When I use a word," Humpty Dumpty said, in rather a scornful tone, "it means just what I choose it to mean—neither more nor less" (Lewis Carroll, *Alice's Adventures in Wonderland*).

spend more money today improving water quality and educational opportunities for the poor in Africa or more on reducing emissions of greenhouse gases? Some proponents of sustainable growth even equate sustainability with no net use of exhaustible resources. From our discussions in Chapters 13 and 15, however, you should understand the fallacy of that viewpoint.

It is because of the lack of clear definitions that much of the debate over sustainability has arisen. Toman (1994) provides an excellent summary of the alternate definitions of sustainability and the problems in rectifying those definitions. For example, the 1992 *World Development Report* (World Bank 1992) defined sustainability in the context of efficient resource management and use. In essence, such a definition states that development will be sustainable as long as property rights are defined and resources are priced efficiently (i.e., where marginal social cost equals marginal social value). This definition is consistent with the economic theory of exhaustible and renewable resources that we discussed in Chapters 15 and 16.

The sustainability literature also has much in common with the "conservationist" writings on the early twentieth century. As Brown (1991) notes, conservationists argued long ago for the "wise use" of natural resources and for the reuse of irreplaceable resources. Gray (1913), for example, wrote an important article in which he argued that the central issue of the conservation movement was the "conflict between the present and the future." Although these authors did not specifically use the term *sustainability* or *sustainable development,* their aims were similar.

Still other authors disagree with "economic" approaches to sustainability. Daly (1990) argues that sustainability can be achieved only if we sharply reduce our use of all resources. Still others argue for policies that combine both environmental and ethical integrity on a worldwide scale, suggesting that sustainability involves responsibilities to the human species as a whole and all of the ecological systems that surround it (Lovelock 1988).

In general, the sustainability literature raises two issues: the nature of the current generation's responsibility to future generations, which we have referred to in earlier chapters as *intergenerational fairness* (some theorists suggest that sustainability advocates also value intragenerational fairness), and the possibility of a *moral commitment* to biological and institutional integrity (Lesser and Zerbe 1995). The first issue relates back to our discussion of intergenerational fairness in Chapter 13, where we discussed the ethical implications of the present-value criterion. There we defined intergenerational fairness in the context of the current generation's actions. We stated that the current generation was being fair to future generations as long as the future generation would not be worse off because of actions taken by the current generation. Thus there was nothing wrong with the current generation increasing its consumption as long as future generations still would be equally well or better off.

There are different definitions of intergenerational fairness. The most controversial definition, which Toman (1994) refers to as the "organicist" position, raises many difficult ethical issues. The organicist position focuses not on the rights of future *individuals* but rather on obligations to the whole of humanity. The reason for this is the difficulty of assigning rights and standing to future "potential" individuals, whose existence depends on the actions of individuals today.[7] The organi-cist position suggests that some important social values cannot be determined through any individual resource valuation, no matter how sophisticated the tech-nique (Toman 1994). And although the organicist position avoids the problems inherent in assigning rights and standing to future individuals, its focus on society as a whole rather than individuals fails to consider the values inherent in many of our important political and social institutions, all of which are derived from the supremacy of individual rights. Unbridled organicism places the rights of the state over those of the individual, a situation that has proved throughout history to be itself a source of much human misery. Thus balancing the rights of individuals ver-sus the need for larger social priorities appears to be a critical part of any definition of sustainability.

The second issue is far broader. It encompasses not only the welfare of future generations of human beings but also the welfare of the entire ecosystem. In this view, we humans must balance our welfare against the welfare of other species. For some individuals, this balance has already been tipped, and they believe that the only way to restore the balance is for humankind to become extinct as soon as possible.[8]

Instrumental to both of these concerns is the substitutability between "natur-al" capital (e.g., natural resources and the environment) and "man-made" capital (e.g., technological improvements, equipment, skills, and social institutions), which can be summarized as follows. Can humans continue to compensate for decreasing supplies of natural resources and environmental goods using improve-ments in technology and better social institutions? For example, could the extinc-tion of the spotted owl be "substituted" by better water treatment facilities that reduce outbreaks of cholera? Can the use of market-enhancing environmental policies substitute for fewer open spaces and more crowded national parks? Given uncertainty about the future, when is increased use of natural resources justified? Are such trade-offs reasonable in some cases? Are they ever reasonable or moral?

The view of many economists, including your authors, is that ultimately all resources are fungible sources of well-being. For example, our simple overlapping generations model from Chapter 13 showed that economic growth can occur with different initial amounts of capital, depending on the availability of other resources and the rate of technological change. Even irreversible events do not preclude sus-tainable growth: as long as there remains sufficient substitutability between the remaining stock of natural capital and man-made capital, growth and improvement in overall well-being can still take place. Therefore, this view of substitutability holds that even major environmental changes, such as global climate change, are not *intrinsically* unacceptable.

---

[7]For example, suppose that you and your spouse have decided to remain childless. Are you being unfair to the children you could potentially bear by not bearing them? Are your consumption decisions today unfair to your "potential" children? And if not, can your actions today be unfair to someone else's future children?

[8] This issue was raised in Discussion Question 6 in Chapter 1.

Many ecologists—and some economists—hold a much different view. They argue that substitutability is inherently limited and morally indefensible. These individuals argue that there must be an absolute moral commitment to biological and institutional integrity. According to this view, physical laws limit the degree to which man-made capital can be substituted for natural resources, including environmental quality. In particular, believers of this view hold that substitutability is limited because of absolute minimums in the amount of scarce energy required for such transformation. Furthermore, because there are limits to the amounts of waste that can be successfully processed by the environment, and all economic activity produces some form of waste, there are absolute limits to economic activity.[9] Thus healthy ecosystems have no practical substitutes, and irreversible changes to ecosystems cannot be compensated for (Pearce and Warford 1994).

To illustrate the importance of this latter concept, Toman (1994) uses the example of assigning responsibility for controlling greenhouse gases to reduce the risk of future environmental damage from global warming. If we believe that investments in technology and other forms of man-made capital will provide only a limited ability to adapt to climate change, then the atmosphere's ability to absorb greenhouse gases such as carbon dioxide is a depletable resource with limited substitutability. If so, then we can assign obligations for controlling future emissions based on past emissions, and the vast majority of the responsibility for control will fall to the industrialized countries. If, however, investments made by industrialized countries have provided significant economic benefits that compensate for depleting the atmosphere's ability to absorb greenhouse gas emissions, then the industrialized nations' responsibility is unclear.

Finally, capital substitutability depends on the extent of environmental impacts (Toman 1994). Local environmental degradation, while potentially serious, is more likely than global degradation to be compensable through migration, economic diversification, and trade. By contrast, restrictions on trade (e.g., tariffs or quotas on imported goods, subsidized domestic industries) may severely restrict the economic opportunities available to developing countries and thereby lessen the likelihood of their developing "sustainable" economies. (We return to this topic later in the chapter.)

All of the alternative concepts of sustainability presented here have some merit. Unfortunately, they contain some elements that are mutually exclusive and impossible to define absolutely. One cannot focus on setting prices "correctly," while at the same promoting concepts that some environmental and social goods simply cannot be valued. One cannot argue that natural capital and man-made capital are substitutable and also argue that they are not. One cannot argue that using some resources is "more moral" than using other resources. These complexities, which lie at the heart of sustainability, make the design and the measurement of policies to promote sustainability difficult. Nevertheless, despite the lack of a unique definition, some economists are attempting to do just that.

---

[9] This is sometimes referred to as *entropy*. See Daly (1992) for a discussion of this view.

MEASURING SUSTAINABLE DEVELOPMENT

Though we cannot settle the definition arguments over sustainability here, we recognize that for it to be a useful concept in a policy context, it must be measurable in some form. There is general agreement that "traditional" monetary measures of economic growth, such as the rate of growth in gross domestic product (GDP), may overstate growth and overall well-being by failing to account for the environmental damage that such growth may have caused. This is important from an equity standpoint because future generations may inherit a depleted environment and be forced to a lower standard of living because of the actions of the present generation. To overcome this accounting problem, new measures of economic growth have been developed that can incorporate environmental quality and thus determine whether that growth is sustainable or whether we are pursuing a path that amounts to "eating our seed corn."

Traditionally, economic growth and social welfare have been measured in terms of GNP and, more recently, GDP.[10] These measures reflect the value of the output in an economy. The implicit assumption made with such measures is that they correlate positively with economic well-being. Unfortunately, neither GNP nor GDP includes the environmental costs associated with that output. Thus they may measure short-term economic growth that is achieved at the expense of long-term growth. To use a simple analogy, suppose that we experience a rapid increase in crime. As a result, the demand for burglar alarms, locks, and weapons increases. All of these items will register as increases in GNP or GDP. We conclude that the sudden increase means that economic well-being has improved. Surely, however, we would not then advocate a policy of releasing all jailed criminals so as to further boost economic growth.

Similar flaws can appear when addressing environmental degradation and economic growth. While these measures account for depreciation of some forms of capital, such as machinery, they do not account for depreciation of environmental quality and depletion of nonrenewable resources. In addition, these measures ignore the services provided by natural resources. GNP does not include the value of using the atmosphere as a dumping ground for pollution, nor does it include the value of forests in preventing soil erosion and enhancing fisheries. Because these services are ignored, policymakers will base their decisions on misleading information. In an economy that is relatively undiversified and heavily dependent on natural resources, that can prove devastating.

There are three general approaches to incorporating natural resources and environmental quality into economic accounting.[11] These are measuring the expenditures on environmental degradation and subtracting those from national income, incorporating depletion of natural resources (i.e., depreciating their values) and incorporating that depreciated value into measures of national income,

---

[10]Both of these measures are based on the United Nations System of National Accounts (SNA).

[11]For a detailed description and analysis, see Lutz (1993).

and physically accounting for environmental assets so as better to link environmental management and economic activity. We shall illustrate each of these three approaches by examining their use in different countries.

Measuring Economic Responses: Pollution Abatement Investments

The simplest approach to accounting for environmental degradation is to change the classification of expenditures for environmental improvements, such as pollution control equipment on fossil-fuel-powered plants, from final goods to intermediate goods. Because both GNP and GDP measure the value of final goods and services, this reclassification will tend to reduce measured economic growth.

Data collected by the U.S. Bureau of the Census indicate that in 1989, expenditures by industry for pollution control equipment totaled over $15 billion. Table 19.1 shows the breakdown of these expenditures by major manufacturing sector. The industries that devoted the most expenditure to pollution control were petroleum refining, chemicals, and primary metal smelting. Even for these industries, however, pollution control expenditures were only about 1.5 percent of the total value of their output, compared to an overall average of just 0.5 percent for the entire manufacturing sector. Nevertheless, these expenditures could represent a significant fraction of GNP growth in a given year. If, for example, overall GNP growth totaled $100 billion (roughly 2 percent of total GNP), 15 percent of that growth would have been for environmental mitigation.

Another closely related approach is to subtract out "defensive" expenditures whose only purpose is to combat environmental degradation (Peskin and Lutz 1990). For example, individuals might purchase air and water purifiers to combat

TABLE 19.1   POLLUTION CONTROL EXPENDITURES BY INDUSTRY, 1989

Industry	Pollution Control Expenditure (millions of dollars)	Expenditure as a Percentage of Total Output
Food and beverages	1,056	0.3
Textiles	136	0.3
Pulp and paper	1,449	1.1
Chemicals	3,509	1.3
Petroleum refining	2,170	1.5
Rubber	403	0.4
Stone, clay, and glass	593	0.9
Primary metals	1,931	1.3
Fabricated metals	896	0.6
Machinery	572	0.2
Electrical equipment	729	0.4
Transport equipment	1,000	0.3
Total manufacturing	15,626	0.5

Source: U.S. Bureau of the Census.

reductions in air and water quality. Rather than *adding* these expenditures to GNP, such expenditures should be subtracted.

There are several problems with these sorts of approaches to environmental accounting. First, almost any expenditure can be labeled "defensive" (Juster 1973). Umbrella purchases defend against rain, pharmaceutical expenditures defend against sickness, and purchases of this environmental economics textbook defends against ignorance and your authors' poverty. Yet these three examples would all be reasonably included as additions to GNP. Indeed, taken far enough, one could envision a system of income accounts in which GNP is always zero.

Perhaps the most significant problem, however, is that *expenditures* to reduce environmental damages may have little relation to the *value* of those damages. As we discussed in Chapters 8 and 9, environmental legislation in the United States has often been aimed at fostering equity rather than improving economic efficiency. And even if economic efficiency were the sole goal of legislation, there is nothing to suggest that legislators will have set standards correctly. Still, some accounting of pollution abatement defensive expenditures is probably a worthwhile endeavor, as both will affect the workings of the economy.

Measuring the Cost of Resource Depletion

Resource depletion costs can be accounted for in several ways. The primary methods that have been applied are a "depreciation" methodology, in which environmental and natural resources are depreciated in much the same way as businesses depreciate machinery and equipment, and a "user cost" methodology that directly calculates resource levels required to maintain a sustainable income flow.

The Depreciation Approach   Depreciation is a well-recognized business concept. By taking account of depreciation, we recognize that consumption cannot be maintained forever without new investments in the capital stock because machines break down and buildings eventually need repairs. When income accounts for countries are developed, they incorporate depreciation on capital assets, such as machinery, buildings, and other manufactured assets. The same sort of reasoning is applied to natural resource assets. Losses of natural resource assets may result is reductions in future production. Thus they should be depreciated like any other capital asset. With the depreciation approach to resource depletion, a nation's natural resource assets are also depreciated, depending on their rate of use, and the lost value is incorporated into national income accounts.

This accounting structure does *not* imply that natural resources ought not to be used. Rather, it allows countries to recognize explicitly that by using their natural resource stocks, they are exchanging one type of assets for another (Repetto 1992). This is easily recognizable if assets are privately held. For example, suppose that you own a stand of timber and cut it down in order to build houses. In addition to timber, you purchase nails, shingles, and drywall, as well as labor to build the houses. Once completed, your balance sheet will look like the one in

TABLE 19.2 BALANCE SHEET FOR HOME CONSTRUCTION (IN THOUSANDS OF DOLLARS)

Item	Credits	Debits
Timber	—	100
Nails, drywall, etc.	—	25
Labor	—	25
New houses	200	—
Profit (new wealth)	—	50
Total	200	200

Table 19.2. In this example, you took your $100,000 asset in the form of timber, combined it with other inputs, and created $200,000 worth of new housing. This action netted you a $50,000 profit, which equals the amount of new wealth created. The national income accounting of this project would be quite different, however. The cutting of the timber would be counted as an increase in national income. Thus the national income accounts would show an increase on $100,000 for timber plus a $200,000 increase for the new houses.[12] Where is the loss of the timber resource accounted for.

Let us take as an example the case of Costa Rica. In Costa Rica, a failure to account for resource depletion has had real environmental and economic implications. Costa Rica has lost a great deal of its natural resources, despite significant actions to restore its ecology. The country has lost over 30 percent of its forests since 1970, primarily to create additional land for grazing. Like most tropical forestland, however, the soil quality is poor and subject to a high degree of erosion. The amount of soil washed away is significant: an estimated 2.2 billion tons between 1970 and 1989, an amount sufficient to bury the capital city of San Jose to a depth of 12 meters (Repetto 1992).

At the same time, the country has overfished its coastal fishery resource, and water pollution has harmed coral reefs important both for fish and as a destination for tourists. Because the country is heavily dependent on timber, fishing, and tourism, the loss of these assets has caused significant economic losses. In 1989 alone, $400 million of timber was destroyed, 36 percent more than the country's foreign debt payments (Repetto 1992). Soil erosion significantly reduced crop and livestock yields. And by 1988, fish harvests and fishing effort combined to eliminate all profits. The loss of these assets was not accounted for in Costa Rica's national income accounts, which continue to show rapid growth.

In the early 1980s, Costa Rica was also experiencing other economic problems, and servicing the country's foreign debt had become difficult. The International Monetary Fund (IMF) helped the country stabilize its monetary base. As Repetto (1992) notes, however, the IMF did not speak about the stabilizing Costa

---

[12] The purchases of nails, drywall, and labor might also count as additions to national income.

Rica's natural resource base, even though the loss of those resources had been the major contributor to the country's inability to meet its debt service payments.

To account more accurately for the losses of the country's assets, the World Resources Institute (WRI) and the Costa Rica Tropical Sciences Center developed natural resource accounts for the country's soils, forests, and fisheries (Repetto et al. 1989; Repetto 1992). The researchers first estimated land use changes because of deforestation. They concluded that over the preceding 20-year period, 28 percent of the country's forests had been lost. The value of this lost timber was derived from stumpage values (the value of standing timber) and data on the species, age, and distance from sawmills of lost trees. They found that real (adjusted for inflation) stumpage prices increased between 400 and 1,000 percent during this time period, with the increases highest for hardwoods.

The researchers next valued depreciation losses because of soil erosion, based on the cost of replacing the lost plant nutrients from topsoil and resulting loss of farm productivity. They found that soil depreciation charges accounted for 13 percent of the value added for livestock production, 17 percent for annual crops, and between 8 and 9 percent for all agricultural production (Repetto 1992). They also developed depreciation values for the country's ocean fishery. They found that the fishery had been virtually wiped out. Depreciation was 100 percent, meaning that the asset value of the fishery was zero.

Adding up the depreciated values between 1970 and 1989, the researchers found that total losses exceeded $5.2 billion in 1990 prices.[13] Costa Rica's 1990 GDP was $5.7 billion (World Bank 1992). Thus the value of the lost resource assets during the 20-year period was almost as large as the country's annual GDP. This estimate of lost resource value, large as it is, does not account for the entire value of lost resources. Forests provide more than timber value; they contribute added value from tourism, nontimber commodities, wildlife habitat, and biodiversity. Soil erosion not only reduces crop yields but also affects soil structure, which also reduces soil fertility. Finally, only losses of principal fish species in one area were valued. The results of this study indicate that depreciating resource assets can represent a significant fraction of a nation's economic output. Countries that fail to account for and reduce this depreciation, especially developing countries, may find their long-term economic prospects bleak.

The depreciation approach is not without its faults, however.[14] First, as El-Serafy (1989) notes, countries with natural resource assets are generally observed to be better off than those without them and can thus enjoy a higher and more sustainable standard of living. The depreciation methodology, however, can result, in extreme cases, in net income streams of zero, which would indicate that a country's standard of living is quite low.

An example of the problem with the depreciation approach can be seen in a country such as Saudi Arabia, which derives almost all of its income from petroleum

---

[13]The figure quoted in Repetto and colleagues (1989) and Repetto (1992) is $4.1 billion in 1984 prices. This figure has been converted to 1990 dollars using the GNP implicit price deflator.
[14]For a detailed criticism, see El-Serafy (1989).

extraction. Ignoring related activities, using the depreciation approach, the value of the petroleum extracted would be subtracted from Saudi Arabia's GDP, leaving a net product of zero. This conclusion, however, conflicts with the observation that having mineral and natural resource wealth can provide significant benefits: Saudi Arabia is a wealthy country.

The other weakness with the depreciation approach is that depreciation is fundamentally an accounting concept rather than an economic one. It is based on tax laws, accounting conventions, and expectations about the future (Hicks 1981). Valuing depreciated natural resource assets may be quite subjective.

The User Cost Approach   To get around objections to the depreciation approach, El-Serafy (1989) proposed a "user cost" methodology for measuring the cost of resource depletion. Although we discussed the concept in Chapter 15, we illustrate it again here using a simple example. Suppose that you pay $1,000 for a machine. Each year, the machine will produce $100 worth of product. If you spend $50 per year on maintenance, the machine will last forever. If this maintenance expenditure is forgone, however, the machine will operate for 10 years and then turn to dust. If we ask, what is the income generated by the machine? two answers come to mind: $100 per year for 10 years or $50 per year forever.

The $100 income stream is not sustainable. By ignoring maintenance, the value of the machine declines each year until at the end of the tenth year its value is zero. Properly maintained, the machine retains its value of $1,000. Thus in this example, if we let the machine turn to dust, the user cost is $1,000. *User cost in this approach is the loss in value of a capital good from optimal use* (Hartwick and Hageman 1991).[15]

For natural resource assets, the idea is to convert a finite stream of net revenues for the sale of an exhaustible resource into a *permanent income stream* by investing part of the revenues over the lifetime of the resource. This investment is called the "user cost allowance" (Bartelmus, Lutz, and Schweinfest 1992). Only the remaining revenues can then be considered "true income" (El-Serafy 1989). Once we know the finite revenue stream, a permanent income stream can be calculated if we also know the discount rate and the lifetime of the resource. If net revenues from the resource are $R each year for N years, define "true income" $X such that a user cost allowance, $R − $X, is accumulated for N years. At the end of N years, the accumulated user cost allowance will generate a permanent income stream of $X.

As an example, suppose that chopping down a hardwood forest will yield revenues of $1 million each year for 20 years, when all of the forest is assumed to be cut down. The discount rate is the social rate of time preference (*SRTP*), which is assumed to equal 3 percent. The permanent income stream $X that can be generated can be calculated as follows:

$$\$X = \$R\left[1 - \frac{1}{(1+r)^{N+1}}\right] \tag{19.1}$$

---

[15]Hartwick and Hageman (1991) provide exhaustive calculations on user cost.

With $\$R = \$1$ million, $N = 20$ years, and $r = 3$ percent, the true income stream $\$X = \$462,450$. Thus the user cost in each year will equal almost $\$540,000$, over half of the income stream generated by harvesting the forest. The lower the discount rate, the higher the user cost and the lower the true income from the asset.

The user cost adjustment can change over time. New discoveries of resources reduce user costs because the amount of income that must be retained to generate permanent income declines. And the market prices of resources can change, as with the rapid increase in hardwood prices that exacerbated the previously described losses to Costa Rica.

Comprehensive Environmental Accounting   The third approach to incorporating the value of natural resource assets in national income accounts is more comprehensive and more difficult. This approach features an accounting of physical resources and natural resource depletion as well as the placement of monetary values on all physical entries (Peskin and Lutz 1990). Think of this approach as follows. The natural environment performs many functions (providing resources for extraction, species diversity, scenic beauty, etc.). There is competition for these functions by the different economic agents that use the resources.[16] Households want clean water for drinking, while industry wants water for waste disposal; recreationists want free-flowing water for fishing, while households want electricity provided by hydroelectric dams. Because of this competition, there may be a "loss of function" from the perspective of certain economic agents, much as an individual whose favorite whitewater rapids are dammed will suffer an economic loss. This loss can be valued as the amount required to restore functions to their "sustainable" levels (Hueting 1980).[17] The cost of restoring functions to those previous levels, plus the cost of other environmental expenditures, is then subtracted from GDP.

A variant of this approach (Peskin 1989) treats the services of environmental and natural resource capital as if all of these services were marketed. The value of those services is entered into the system of accounts as inputs if used by producing sectors of the economy and as outputs if consumed by final demand sectors such as households. Environmental costs, such as pollution from burning coal, are included as negative benefits on the output side. All of the environmental services and damages are treated as if they are traded in private markets and valued according to willingness to pay (WTP). For example, if coal burned to generate electricity produces sulfur dioxide emissions, the environmental damage from those emissions is determined using WTP estimates, which can be derived using techniques discussed in Chapter 11.

---

[16]It can, of course, also be argued that noneconomic agents consisting of animal and plant species are competing for these resources. Unfortunately, they cannot tell us the values they assign. That task must be left to us.

[17]Peskin (1989) refers to this as the "Dutch framework."

The biggest difference between the so-called Dutch approach (Hueting 1980) and Peskin's (1989) approach is in the valuation of environmental services and damages. The Dutch approach determines values for environmental damages *using a cost-of-control proxy*. Thus if scrubbers on the aforementioned coal-fired electric power plant remove sulfur dioxide at a cost of $1,000 per ton, this value is used as a proxy for the damage caused. We discussed the problems with this approach to valuing environmental damages in Chapter 11.

Finally, there remains the policy question of whether comprehensive environmental accounting, if it can be successfully performed, will change the behavior of a country's individuals and better protect the environment and the country's resources. As the following example shows, developing comprehensive environmental accounts for a country is a difficult and time-consuming exercise. If it improves a country's environmental and natural resource policies, so much the better. If it does not, however, it may ultimately be a frustrating exercise.

As an example, let us look at comprehensive environmental accounting in Papua New Guinea. Bartelmus, Lutz, and Schweinfest (1992) performed preliminary work using this approach as a case study for Papua New Guinea, a Pacific Rim nation of 3.5 million inhabitants. The country has few urban areas and little industrialization. Over half of the country's export revenues originated from several copper, silver, and gold mines. GNP per capita is quite low, only about $770 in 1992 dollars. Although the country has abundant natural resources, including good soils, ample rainfall, mineral resources, fisheries, and forests, there are obstructions to balanced development. Because the terrain is so rugged, transportation is difficult, and the transportation infrastructure is limited. There also are disputes over land and resource ownership, low literacy rates, and high unemployment and crime.

To develop integrated accounts, the authors first adjusted the economic accounts to incorporate environmental protection expenditures, accounted for asset balances (e.g., minerals), examined and estimated values for depletion of renewable and nonrenewable natural resources, and developed estimates for the cost of environmental degradation.

The authors next developed two different values for natural resource depletion, using the user cost and depreciation approaches we described. Knowledge of average proven reserves and extraction rates, for example, enabled the authors to calculate the economic life of major mines in the country. Then they used a discount rate of 10 percent and assumed that "normal" rates of return were between 8.8 and 11.4 percent, using data from the International Monetary Fund (IMF 1990). The results of these calculations indicated user costs between 2.6 and 9.5 percent of mining sector value added during the six-year period 1985–1990, corresponding to a reduction of between 0.3 and 1.4 percent of GNP.

The authors then derived depletion values using the depreciation approach favored by Repetto (1992). Traditionally, depreciation is handled in income accounts in two ways. First, there can be depreciation of stocks of goods that are eventually consumed. Second, there can be depreciation of capital assets like machines because of wear and tear. Changes in the quantity or quality of natural resources can exhibit characteristics of both. Soil degradation and erosion, for example, can be thought of as depreciation of a *capital asset*. Depletion of petroleum reserves, by contrast, can best be thought of as a reduction in *stocks* of materials. Forest *stocks* can be depleted as harvesting increases above a sustainable level but can increase as harvests fall below that level. But standing forests can support species diversity, so loss of forested lands can also constitute loss of a capital asset.

Because depletion and degradation of natural resources affect future income, estimates of future income loss are discounted back to the present. Under conditions of perfect competition, it can be shown that the market price of resources, less the costs of factors of production (including a return on capital), called the "net price," reflects this discounted future income stream. This was the approach used by Repetto (1992) for Costa Rica.

Using the net price methodology, the authors derived an overall "environmental depletion cost." They found that after adjusting for resource depletion, the mining sector had an adjusted value added between 50 and 90 percent of original value added, leading to a calculated reduction in GDP of between 1 and 9 percent. In all cases, however, the environmental depletion cost was larger than the values derived using the user cost methodology.

The authors then moved on to valuation of environmental degradation in the country for the agricultural, forestry, and mining sectors. For agriculture, the main losses stem from conversion of forests to cultivated lands, resulting not only in economic losses but also in ecological and spiritual ones. Estimates of losses because of conversion vary between 1.2 and 18 percent of total agricultural value added, because of significant differences in estimates in the rates of forest conversions. As the authors point out, these discrepancies show the need for better measurement of physical resource stocks, as well as better monetary measures of environmental losses. Losses for forest resources themselves are estimated to be between 6.4 and 39.3 percent of total sector value added. In the mining industry, the major cause of environmental degradation is mine tailings. These tailings, which are primarily heavy metals, destroy aquatic life. Cost estimates from these tailings vary between 15 and 44 percent of mining sector value added.

Overall, the results of the study indicated that the environmentally adjusted net domestic product for the country in the years 1986–1990 was between 1.2 and 11.0 percent below the traditionally measured net domestic product. Though the authors stressed the tentative nature of their work owing to the many gaps in available data and requirements for numerous assumptions, they also stressed the feasibility of this sort of integration between environmental and national income accounts. Last, they recommended the gathering of more comprehensive data on natural resources, nationwide monitoring of pollution discharges, monitoring of changes in biodiversity, and development of environmental protection expenditure statistics.

Summary   Although we have presented only the barest introduction to environmental accounting, it should be clear that some sort of environmental accounting is required if "sustainable" development is to be achieved. All of the methodologies presented are based on the notion that natural resources and environmental quality are tangible assets, as much so as machinery or buildings. The accounting procedures discussed differ greatly in their degree of comprehensiveness and difficulty in a   cation.

Accounting for environmental mitigation expenditures is the most straightforward approach. Unfortunately, it provides the least information about environmental and natural resource degradation, owing to the multiple objectives of many environmental laws and the fact that the costs of controlling pollution are likely to be a poor proxy for *WTP* to avoid damage. Measuring the cost of resource depletion, through either a depreciation or a user cost approach, provides a more comprehensive accounting but is still incomplete. The most comprehensive approach, which incorporates environmental mitigation expenditures, determination of resource depletion costs, and accounts for physical resource stocks, can provide a thorough summary for determinations of the sustainability of an economy. Unfortunately, this approach, which is still is in its infancy, requires intensive and expensive data collection. The poor countries most in need of such an accounting may be least able to afford it.

Should comprehensive environmental accounts be developed for countries? Will such accounts be used as the basis for better environmental and natural resource policies? Or is *The Economist* correct when it argues that "it may be better to lobby for policies that actually make people pay the costs of environmental damage than for statistics which show what the world might look like if people did" ("The Price of Everything" 1993)? At present, it appears that comprehensive environmental accounting will not play a major role in policy development. Unless a way is found to develop these accounts more easily, their marginal benefits are unlikely to exceed their marginal costs. Better to develop simpler, incomplete measures that can promote improved policies in a reasonable time frame.

ENVIRONMENTAL QUALITY AND ECONOMIC WELL-BEING

It is common to think of developed nations as having the worst environmental pollution. After all, developed nations have far more vehicles, produce more solid wastes, and are generally perceived to have profligate and wasteful lifestyles. A good example of this thinking is Durning (1991), who writes that "overconsumption by the world's fortunate is an environmental problem unmatched in severity by anything except perhaps population growth." He goes on to say that the developed countries continue to "exhaust or unalterably disfigure forests, soils, water, air, and climate," not to mention destroy "time-honored values that . . . have often been sacrificed in the rush to riches" (p. 153).[18]

---

[18]To be fair, Durning (1991) also notes that "the opposite of overconsumption—poverty—is no solution" and is "infinitely worse for people and bad for the natural world too" (p. 154).

The problem with Durning's direct linking of production and pollution is that it fails to distinguish between producing *less* and producing *differently.* Undoubtedly, we can all point to examples of what we may consider "wasteful" or "conspicuous" consumption. All economic activity involves transforming natural resources; not all economic activity causes environmental degradation. Thus, the relationship between development and environmental quality is complex.

This empirical evidence indicates three distinct patterns between environmental quality and wealth (El-Ashry 1993). Many of these patterns are evidenced in African countries, which range from the desperately poor (Sudan, Rwanda) to the well-off (South Africa). First, some environmental quality indicators increase as per capita income rises. The percentage of a country's population exposed to unsafe water and inadequate sanitation, for example, falls rapidly with higher incomes. Economic growth provides the resources by which investments providing additional public services can be made, further improving productivity and health. The environmental quality indicators in this first group are caused by poverty.

The second group consists of environmental quality indicators that initially worsen but then improve as incomes rise. Most forms of air pollution fall into this category. Unlike the first category, however, improvement is less automatic. Countries must introduce specific policies that address these environmental issues to ensure that resources are devoted to these issues (El-Ashry 1993).

The third group of environmental indicators continue to worsen as incomes increase. This is especially true of solid wastes, carbon dioxide emissions, and emissions of nitrogen oxides. The relationship between pollution exposure and per capita income is shown in Figure 19.4, which is based on the research of Shafik and Bandyopadhyay at the World Bank.

The view that economic activity is a direct cause of environmental damage assumes that it is the size of an economy that leads to environmental degradation. Indeed, this is the basic premise of Durning (1991) discussed earlier. If we recognize that many other factors can contribute to environmental degradation, however, we will be in a much better situation in which to develop environmental policies that can promote economic growth *and* preserve environmental quality.

There are at least four factors that determine environmental quality. First, environmental quality is affected by the structure of an economy (and vice versa). An economy that is primarily agrarian, for example, will face a different set of environmental issues than one that is heavily industrialized. Second, the efficiency with which inputs are used in the economy affects environmental quality. In countries where energy was heavily subsidized, as in the countries of formerly communist eastern Europe, there was little incentive to use energy efficiently. As a result, pollution from the combustion of fossil fuels increased to alarming levels. A third factor is the ability to substitute inputs for one another, especially as some resources become more scarce. The slash-and-burn activities that have greatly reduced tropical rain forests have in part resulted from an inability of the poorest citizens of those countries to purchase the inputs necessary to put existing cultivated acreage to better use. Even though high-quality land has become increasingly scarce in those countries, no alternatives have historically been available. Fourth, newer, "cleaner" technologies and environmental management practices can reduce the

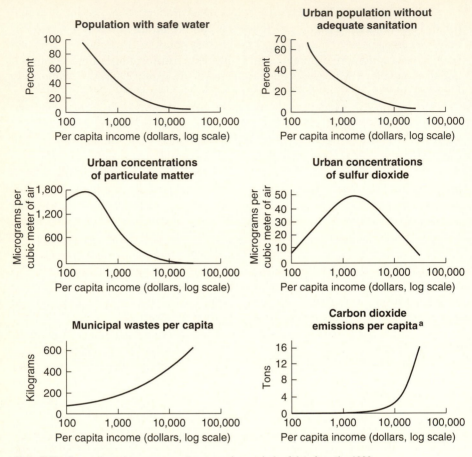

Figure 19.4   Environmental Indicators at Different Country Income Levels

environmental damage associated with every bushel of wheat produced or ton of steel smelted.

Policies that improve economic and environmental well-being in individual countries need to recognize these four factors. Environmental policies that may be appropriate for the United States, for example, may not work well in many African nations. The latters' economies are far more agrarian and labor-intensive. Thus policies focused on new pollution control technologies in the United States may not address important environmental issues in Africa, such as access to clean water. Whatever an economy's structure, efficiency, and ability to substitute man-made capital for natural capital, however, there are several overall policy goals that will have universal application. These are the subject of the next section.

Instituting Sustainable Economic and Environmental Policies

Even assuming that we can overcome the definitional and empirical issues associated with sustainable development, we must still inquire as to what sort of economic and environmental policies will be best suited for achieving sustainability goals. A two-pronged approach may provide the answer. First, environmental policies should stress the positive links between economic growth and environmental quality. Second, policies should ensure that the value of environmental quality is accounted for properly in economic decisions (World Bank 1992).

Policies That Link Economic Growth and Environmental Quality

Environmental degradation is exacerbated by poverty, uncertainty, and ignorance (World Bank 1992). Addressing these three elements is the first step required for effective environmental policies. Accomplishing this will require policies that make sense, even in the absence of environmental benefits. Improving sanitation and water supplies, investing in soil conservation, and improving the health and education levels of the populace, especially women, will be key priorities (World Bank 1992). Providing greater access to health care resources and family planning will help ease the environmental pressures wrought by a rapidly expanding population. A better-educated populace will also more easily adopt more complex environmental management tools. Individuals who are healthy and better fed will be more productive workers and make for a more competitive economy.

Promoting macroeconomic stability (e.g., low inflation rates, a stable and exchangeable currency, and a climate conducive to investment) can also provide a foundation for environmental improvement. Countries that have access to international capital markets and encourage new investment in a stable climate will improve the well-being of their citizens. The economic future of Bosnia, ripped asunder by a civil war that destroyed its economy and reduced its citizens to a barter economy, is far less encouraging than the future of Poland, whose young free-market economy is more stable.

Integration into the global economy can provide greater economic and social benefits. Policies that promote free trade, for example, can improve productivity, introduce newer technologies, and increase economic efficiency by promoting comparative advantage.[19] The drive for many former communist countries in eastern Europe to become members of the European Union is one example. Membership can reduce transactions costs by eliminating tariffs and provide far larger markets for goods and services.

---

[19]The standard economic notion of comparative advantage is disputed by Daly (1993). He argues that in a world of capital mobility, comparative advantage may become absolute advantage, further impoverishing many nations.

Open trade policies are not without controversy, however, for they can increase environmental pressures.[20] Nevertheless, if history provides any guidance, it is probably better to maintain open trade policies in conjunction with environmental protection policies than to restrict trade and its accompanying economic benefits. The North American Free Trade Agreement is a case in point (see accompanying box).[21]

Policy Decisions That Account for Environmental Quality   At first blush, scarcity may seem one of the causes of environmental degradation, rather than a solution. We have already discussed the scarcity of productive agricultural lands, the effects of deforestation, and the lack of clean water in many poor countries. Nevertheless, scarcity can be an important tool in ensuring that resources are used efficiently and to reduce environmental degradation. By allowing scarcity to be fully incorporated into economic decisions, environmental improvements can often be achieved.

In some developing countries—and some developed countries—many resources are subsidized. These subsidies distort markets and reduce incentives to achieve greater economic efficiency. They encourage consumers to be more profligate and increase environmental damage. Charges for water used to irrigate crops is often a fraction of its true economic cost. In Asia, for example, irrigation charges are often less than 20 percent of the true supply cost (El-Ashry 1993). China heavily subsidizes electric power, much of which is generated using low-grade coal that produces vast amounts of sulfur and carbon dioxide. Coal is heavily subsidized in Russia and the Czech Republic. Nitrogen fertilizer is subsidized in Mexico and Sri Lanka. Electric power is subsidized in Brazil so as to develop a domestic aluminum-smelting industry, thus encouraging development of hydroelectric dams.

Resource subsidies are also a problem closer to home. In California, rice is grown in the Sacramento Valley, which has an almost desertlike climate. Growers pay only a small fraction of the price that residential consumers pay and account for 80 percent of total water consumption in the state. Use of public lands is also heavily subsidized in this country. Grazing fees for sheep and cattle are minuscule. Timber royalties in federal forests are low. Under the Mining Law of 1872, firms that wish to mine federal lands need pay only $5 per acre, even though the lands may be worth thousands. Crop subsidies encourage farmers to till marginally productive land; the government now provides subsidies to encourage farmers to let those lands lay fallow.[22]

---

[20]For a lucid summary, see the articles by Bhagwati (1993) and Daly (1993). The General Agreement on Tariffs and Trade (GATT), which was ratified by the U.S. Congress in late 1994, has provoked much argument over reductions in environmental quality.

[21]There is a rapidly growing literature covering reflecting the debate over trade and the environment. Some useful references are Folke et al. (1994), Grossman and Krueger (1993), Bhagwati (1993), and Low (1992).

[22]In 1996, President Clinton signed the Freedom to Farm Act, which will lower crop subsidies and encourage more rational planting decisions. However, the act will expire in 2002 if not renewed by Congress.

THE NORTH AMERICAN FREE TRADE AGREEMENT AND ENVIRONMENTAL QUALITY

One of the fears associated with ratification of the North American Free Trade Agreement (NAFTA), a trade agreement signed in 1992 between the United States, Canada, and Mexico (and ratified by the U.S. Congress in 1994), is that it could lead eventually to reduced environmental quality in northern Mexico and the southwestern United States. NAFTA eliminates tariffs on goods produced by the signatory nations by 2005 and removes most barriers to cross-border investment and to the movement of goods and services. (The agreement also contains provisions for the inclusion of additional member nations. As of this writing, it appears that Chile will be the next country to join.)

Prior to ratification, critics raised three major environmental concerns about NAFTA. First, they noted that environmental degradation is a significant problem in Mexico, and concerns over sustainable development in that country are widespread. Second, they argued that U.S. firms would relocate to Mexico, where labor is cheaper and enforcement of environmental laws has traditionally been lax, in order to reduce their production costs. This fear of "environmental dumping" was frequently raised in congressional debates over NAFTA. Third, the critics feared that NAFTA could undermine environmental laws in the United States as greater economic growth in Mexico created more air and water pollution along the U.S.-Mexican border, increased imports of pesticide-laden agricultural products from Mexico, and ultimately led to an undermining of U.S. environmental laws as U.S. fears about economic growth and jobs took precedence over state and federal environmental standards.*

In an exhaustive examination of the issues, economists Gary Hufbauer and Jeffrey Scott (1992) of the Institute for International Economics looked at the environmental questions surrounding NAFTA. First, they examined recent environmental efforts within Mexico. They noted that Mexico had recently developed a "solid legal framework for protecting the environment" to combat the severe degradation that has occurred; that the country has addressed global environmental issues, such as being the first country to ratify the Montreal Protocol; and that much of Mexico's 1988 General Law for Ecological Equilibrium was modeled on U.S. environmental legislation. The authors also noted that this law has been weakly enforced but that then-President Salinas had made stricter enforcement a priority.

There has already been a great deal of cooperation between the two countries toward combating environmental problems in the border region. The International Boundary Commission, formed in 1889 and later renamed the International Boundary and Water Commission (IBWC), has devoted a great deal of effort to combating water pollution in the region. One of the most contentious issues for the IBWC, for example, has been the salinity of the Colorado River at the U.S.-Mexican border. The La Paz agreement of 1983 committed the U.S. EPA and Mexico's environmental agency, SEDUE, to work together in the areas of air and water pollution, hazardous wastes, and accidental spills.

In the future, parties to NAFTA could also accept new environmental obligations in stages. One such scenario is for each country to strictly enforce its existing environmental standards for three years and subsequently notify the other parties of standards it wanted raised. Only if such harmonization could not be achieved within a reasonable period of time would imports from the offending country be subject to special duties.

(continued)

In the four years after NAFTA was ratified, the overall economic benefits and costs appeared to be smaller than originally predicted. Neither the environmental calamity nor the economic boom predicted have occurred. Rather, it seems that internal events in these countries have had much larger economic impacts on trade. Canada continues to be divided over the separatist leanings of many Quebec residents. Partly as a result, individuals in British Columbia and Alberta, Canada's westernmost provinces, which are endowed with significant natural resources, are also agitating for greater sovereignty. And Mexico's economy has suffered as a result of political upheavals.

These internal impacts have tended to reduce attention given to NAFTA's environmental impacts. Again, however, the dire consequences predicted do not appear to have materialized. Whether NAFTA will eventually lead to significant improvements or reductions in environmental quality in its signatory nations remains to be seen. The evidence to this point is that the impacts will be marginally positive.

*The debate over ratification of the General Agreement on Tariffs and Trade (GATT) by the U.S. Congress in late 1994 raised similar questions over possible reductions in environmental quality (not to mention the usual political concerns over possible harm to narrow economic groups in legislators' states).

Eliminating subsidies is, of course, not easy, as the beneficiaries have strong incentives to maintain them. In many developing countries, subsidies are also used to justify national goals such as food self-sufficiency or rapid industrialization. Such goals will remain elusive in the long run as long as subsidies continue. Yet there have been some success stories. In Indonesia, subsidies on pesticides were eliminated by late 1988. This has reduced pesticide use, promoted development of an integrated pest management system, and saved the government over $120 million each year (World Bank 1992). Brazil eliminated subsidies for ranching, saving over $300 million per year and reducing deforestation pressures in the Amazon rain forest.

Elimination of subsidies must be accompanied by clarification of property rights. Recall our discussion of common-property resources from Chapters 6 and 16. If no one owns a resource, there will be no incentive to conserve that resource, and no individual will bear the full environmental cost of using it. Overexploitation of the resource will often result, as has been observed for many of the world's major fisheries. By assigning property rights to individuals or even groups of individuals, governments can provide incentives for resource conservation. Private owners, who will make self-interested decisions about resource use, will often produce more desirable environmental outcomes. In Nepal, for example, forests were managed for centuries at the local community level. In the 1950s, however, state ownership was instituted. The result was severe deforestation (World Bank 1992).

This does not mean that conversion of all resources to private ownership will magically provide a panacea for environmental degradation. Private owners will make decisions in their self-interest, but those interests may not encompass overall social interests. A private owner of timber will want to maximize yields and profit. Biodiversity, not being a private good, may not enter the owner's decision framework. For these resources, the solution will not be a return to public owner-ship but rather better control of private ownership so that private incentives will match public ones.

Are There Limits to Growth?

Sustainability concerns are often linked to discussions of "how much is enough." Advocates of sustainable economic policies (e.g., Daly 1993; Daly and Cobb 1989) point out that the distribution of wealth throughout the world is highly skewed. They suggest that were all people to be brought up to Western standards of living, the resource drain on the planet, as well as the ability of the earth to absorb all of the resulting pollutants, would be so great as to be unsustainable. They further point out, rightly in our view, that many economists ignore the issue or assume that growth has no limits whatsoever.

Unfortunately, asking how much is enough requires an answer, and debate over the answer will probably never be resolved. How many square feet of living space should people have? Should they be allowed to consume meat or be allowed to possess an automobile or a television set? Should they be allowed to travel? Uncomfortable as we may be individually when we see examples of "conspicuous consumption," the best solution is to price consumption correctly, for the world-wide evidence is that prescriptive limits do not work.

Many who advocate reducing growth or redistributing wealth resort to the same sort of facile arguments made by those who promise limitless growth. It is often pointed out, for example, that the United States, with 5 percent of the world's population, consumes perhaps 30 percent of the world's resources. The implica-tion is that to be equitable, a nation's consumption should precisely mirror its pop-ulation. Such simplistic thinking ignores the real benefits that may result from such imbalances. Extending these arguments, we might as well advocate that oranges be grown in Alaska, rather than Florida, so as to be "fair."

THE ROLE OF ECONOMIC ANALYSIS

There is little doubt that growth cannot continue at the expense of the environ-ment. There are also legitimate concerns that current practices and consumption levels are not sustainable and that new economic policies may affect environmen-tal quality without addressing the broader sustainability issues. And though we do not pretend here to have the answers to all of the issues that have been raised, sev-eral fundamentals strike us as worth repeating. First, ignoring the potential for human ingenuity to address some of these issues will likely lead to the adoption of policies that create too much misery for all concerned. Regarding fundamental economic principles, such as benefits from trade, as incompatible with environ-mental improvement and equity risks a return to policies that do indeed limit growth but may also reduce, rather than improve, environmental quality. Second, if we are to strive for greater social and economic equity, and there is no reason we should not, then we ought to do so aboveboard. Few would argue for unfettered economic growth without any regard to human dignity; we do not condone slavery. Stifling innovation and creativity, however, by invoking policies under the guise of fairness will fail to deliver as promised. Better to develop policies that provide the means to make a bigger (environmentally friendly) pie than to slice a smaller pie into equal slivers.

Economic analysis can and should play an important role in policies that seek sustainability and sustainable development, however defined. Criticisms of economic analysis as relegating future generations to unsustainable futures confuse the proper role of economics in normative analysis, which is not to create or define values but to express them in a way that delineates the consequences of actions. Lesser and Zerbe (1995) define three rules governing the use of benefit-cost analysis, which can also be applied to economic analysis in general: (1) Economic analysis is not a tool to develop values, as it is not suited to the task; (2) the role of economic analysis is to provide information relevant to a decision, not to provide the decision; and (3) values used in economic analysis are best determined by preferences, although rights can also shape values.

Defining sustainability and policies that achieve it cannot be accomplished solely through the use of economic analysis. But achieving those goals cannot be accomplished without some use of the tools of economic analysis. To see this, consider the following example from Lesser and Zerbe (1995). Suppose that heeding the desires and sustainability of the U.S. populace, Congress passes an Endangered Species Act whose sole purpose is to prevent species extinction and therefore maintain biodiversity. In addition, recognizing the cultural definitions of sustainability preferred by the populace, Congress also passes a "Native People's Act" that requires the return of traditional lands to native tribes so as to renew historic cultural values at risk from "modern" society. Both of these congressional actions are applauded as examples of "sustainable" policies.

Now suppose that the land repatriated to a particular tribe contains a large tract of old-growth forest that is the only known home of two endangered species of owls and the only location where a particular species of giant redwoods grows. When the tribe members return to their ancestral lands, they discover that lumber buyers are willing to pay a high price for redwood. If the tribe members sell the timber, which is their absolute right under the Native People's Act, they will improve their standard of living. Of course, the logging will cause the two species of birds to go extinct, not to mention the redwood species itself. After much deliberation, tribal elders vote to permit the logging. Congress is horrified.

A lawsuit is filed to stop the logging, and a benefit-cost analysis is commissioned in connection with the lawsuit. That analysis should consider the values of everyone affected. Citizens who have no well-defined property rights to the land may nevertheless have existence values associated with the redwoods and the bird species. Because these citizens would experience a psychological loss were the logging permitted, their values should be based on a *WTA* measure. The courts may grant standing for these citizens. Were the suit brought before the passage of the Endangered Species Act, the court might not have granted standing. The point is that the benefit-cost analysis should give the same results in either case, unless passage of the Endangered Species Act itself changed the appropriate psychological measures from *WTP* to *WTA* ones.

In this case, the role of economic analysis is not to determine whether the legislation passed met the criteria for sustainability. Instead, economic analysis can, given the assignment of property rights, determine the relevant economic values for tribal members and other citizens. Suppose that the analysis determines that the value of the old-growth forest to citizens in general, even though they do not have well-defined property rights, is $500 million. One policy solution would be to offer to buy the land back from the tribe for that sum, using tax dollars. Another possibility would be for Congress to purchase the standing timber at a price above the current stumpage value. Without economic analysis to determine such values, neither policy option could be considered.

Now suppose that environmentalists have identified three alternate policies to promote sustainability. The first would restore salmon runs and habitat in the Pacific Northwest by restricting salmon fishing for ten years and investing heavily in habitat restoration projects. The second policy, which is a reaction to the decision by the tribal elders to log their lands, would preserve old-growth forests in the Pacific Northwest by eliminating all future logging activities in public and private forests. The third would increase the safety of nuclear wastes stored at the Hanford Nuclear Reservation in southeastern Washington, reducing the likelihood of a catastrophic release of radiation after 1,000 years. The estimated benefits and costs of each of these policies are shown in Table 19.3.

Applying the Kaldor-Hicks criteria introduced in Chapter 4, restoring salmon runs and preserving the old-growth forests are economically efficient policies. But suppose that the government has only $100 million to spend. In that case, only the salmon restoration would be undertaken, since it has the largest net present-value benefits.

Of course, at this point, the analysis may be criticized along several fronts: the numbers are all wrong; society has a moral obligation to future generations regardless of the cost; or the $100 million constraint is "artificial" because the government "really" has more money available. These objections, however valid, have little to do with the role of economic analysis. Instead, they all focus on the relative importance of competing goals, something we discussed in Chapter 10.

TABLE 19.3   BENEFITS AND COSTS OF ALTERNATIVE SUSTAINABILITY POLICIES (IN MILLIONS OF DOLLARS)

	Present-Value Benefits	Present-Value Costs	Net Benefits
Restore salmon runs	180	100	80
Preserve old-growth forest	110	100	10
Improve nuclear waste storage safety	200	8,500	(8,300)

Source: Adapted from Lesser and Zerbe (1995).

The critical issue raised in this example is one of *resource scarcity*. Society does not have the resources to do everything that everyone wants. Economic analysis cannot determine which definition of sustainability is most appropriate. Nor can it determine the most equitable solutions. But the tools of economic analysis can delineate the trade-offs we face and provide a much clearer understanding of the *consequences* of our values and choices. If nothing else about sustainability and sustainable development makes sense to you, you will do well to remember that fundamental concept.

CHAPTER SUMMARY

In this chapter, we have examined the linkages between economic growth and environmental quality and addressed those concepts in the context of calls for sustainable development. Development and the environment are positively linked; sound policies that promote development will also promote environmental quality. Maintaining sustainable economies that can provide benefits to current and future generations will require more direct accounting for natural resources and environmental quality than is now practiced. Although the techniques for accomplishing this are still under development, they show promise. Economic policies that stress positive links to the environment should be enacted, along with policies that accurately incorporate environmental values in economic decisions. The best way of doing this, however, may not be through environmental accounting but rather with direct policies that correctly price environmental services. If we are to deal with issues surrounding limits to growth, we should do so in a positive way that does not remove the human spirit of innovation. Finally, we discussed the role of economic analysis. Although that role is not to define environmental values such as sustainability, economic analysis will clarify the consequences of different choices.

CHAPTER REVIEW

Economic Concepts and Tools

- There is no unique definition of sustainability. Some definitions focus on sending correct resource pricing signals. Other definitions incorporate specific intergenerational equity criteria. Still others reject economic growth and individual choice in favor of social structures that emphasize group welfare.
- Environmental accounting methods are designed to supplement traditional measures of economic well-being, such as GDP per capita, with estimates of natural resource stocks and depletion rates. These methodologies can provide a more complete picture of overall economic growth and well-being.
- In certain cases, economic growth and environmental quality can be viewed as substitutes along a production possibilities frontier. In other cases, they can be viewed as complementary inputs.

- Observed willingness to pay for environmental quality improvements may be higher in rich countries than in poor countries. Relative valuations of different environmental quality improvements will also differ significantly.

Policy Issues

- In the long run, economic growth and environmental quality are not either-or propositions. Neither can be achieved without the other. A lack of potential for economic growth will likely lead to an expanding population, increased natural resource degradation, and bleaker future prospects. Environmental degradation is exacerbated by poverty, uncertainty, and ignorance.
- Wealthier countries will likely have solved many basic environmental issues, such as clean water and sanitation; they are thus likely to focus on broader issues, such as global warming and biodiversity.
- Scarcity can be an important tool in ensuring that resources are used efficiently and to reduce environmental degradation. Environmental improvements can often be achieved by allowing scarcity to be fully incorporated into economic decisions.
- Integration of a developing country into the global economy may be able to provide greater economic and social benefits. Policies that promote free trade, for example, can improve productivity, introduce newer technologies, and increase economic efficiency by promoting comparative advantage. Open trade policies are not without controversy, however, since they can increase environmental pressures in the short run.

DISCUSSION QUESTIONS

1. The organicist definition of sustainability places more value on societies than on individuals. How can individual rights be weighed against societal rights? What determines an environmentally "sustainable" balance?
2. Is affluence a contributor to environmental problems or part of the solution to them?
3. Consider the following approach to population control, first developed by the economist Kenneth Boulding (1964). Each individual would be given a certificate granting the inalienable right to produce one (and only one) child. Couples could pool their certificates and have two children. Over time, this scheme would result in population stabilization, as births would necessarily equal deaths. Certificates could be bought and sold without restriction. Thus families placing a high premium on children could purchase certificates from those who had no particular fondness for parenting. How well does this approach fit into the definitions of sustainability discussed in the chapter? What are the advantages and disadvantages of this approach? What are its ethical implications?
4. "Use of nonrenewable resources today precludes their use by future generations. Therefore, the only sustainable policy is for any generation to use only

renewable resources." Is this a valid definition for sustainability? What are its implications for the substitutability of man-made and natural capital? What are its implications for social discount rates?

5. All of us can probably recall instances when we have decried what we thought were "excesses" in consumption, whether poodles dressed in mink coats, gargantuan houses, or mind-boggling feasts. Those examples provide stark contrast to the images of deprivation we are often shown. Yet it would seem that market economies are aspired to by most individuals and that such economies do a better job than socialist economies. Is there a solution to this dilemma? Is there even a problem to solve?

REFERENCES

Ahmad, Y., S. El-Serafy, and E. Lutz (eds.). 1989. *Environmental Accounting for Sustainable Development.* Washington, D.C.: World Bank.

Bartelmus, P., E. Lutz, and S. Schweinfest. 1992. *Integrated Environmental and Economic Accounting: A Case Study for Papua New Guinea.* Working Paper No. 54. Washington, D.C.: World Bank.

Bhagwati, J. 1993. "The Case for Free Trade." *Scientific American* 269(5): 42–49.

Boulding, K. 1964. *The Meaning of the Twentieth Century.* New York: Harper-Collins.

Brown, G. 1991. *Can the Sustainable Development Criterion Adequately Rank Alternative Equilibria?* Seattle: Department of Economics, University of Washington.

Daly, H. 1971. "Toward a Steady State Economy." In *The Patient Earth,* ed. J. Hart and R. Socolow. Austin, Texas: Holt, Rinehart and Winston.

———. 1990. "Toward Some Operational Principles of Sustainable Development." *Ecological Economics* 6(1): 7–34.

———. 1992. "Is the Entropy Law Relevant to the Economics of Resource Scarcity? Yes, of Course It Is!" *Journal of Environmental Economics and Management* 23(1): 91–95.

———. 1993. "The Perils of Free Trade." *Scientific American* 269(5): 50–57.

Daly, H., and J. Cobb. 1989. *For the Common Good.* Boston: Beacon Press.

Dasgupta, P. 1995. "The Population Problem: Theory and Evidence." *Journal of Economic Literature* 33(4): 1879–1902.

Durning, A. 1991. "Asking How Much Is Enough?" in *State of the World 1991.* New York: W.W. Norton.

El-Ashry, M. 1993. "Balancing Environmental Development with Environmental Protection in Developing and Lesser Developed Countries." *Air and Waste* 43: 18–24.

El-Serafy, S. 1989. "Environmental and Resource Accounting: An Overview." In *Environmental Accounting for Sustainable Development,* ed. Y. Ahmad, S. El-Serafy, and E. Lutz. Washington, D.C.: World Bank.

Folke, C., et al. (eds.). 1994. "International Trade and the Environment." *Ecological Economics* 9 (Special issue).

Georgescu-Roegen, N. 1971. *The Entropy Law and the Economic Process.* Cambridge, Mass.: Harvard University Press.

Gray, L. 1913. "Economic Possibilities of Conservation." *Quarterly Journal of Economics* 27(4): 499–510.

Grossman, G., and A. Krueger. 1993. "Environmental Impacts of a North American Free Trade Agreement." In *The Mexico–U.S. Free Trade Agreement,* ed. P. Garber. Cambridge, Mass.: MIT Press.

Hartwick, J., and A. Hageman. 1991. *Economic Depreciation of Mineral Stocks and the Contribution of El-Serafy.* Working Paper No. 27. Washington, D.C.: World Bank.

Hicks, J. 1981. *Wealth and Welfare: Collected Essays on Economic Theory.* Oxford: Oxford University Press.

Hueting, R. 1980. *New Scarcity and Economic Growth: More Welfare Through Less Production?* Amsterdam: Elsevier.

Hufbauer, G., and J. Scott. 1992. *North American Free Trade: Issues and Recommendations.* Washington, D.C. Institute for International Economics.

International Monetary Fund (IMF). 1990. *International Financial Statistics,* Vol. 42. Washington, D.C.: IMF.

Juster, F. 1973. "A Framework for the Measurement of Economic and Social Performance." In *The Measurement of Economic and Social Performance: Vol. 38. Studies in Income and Wealth,* ed. M. Moss. New York: Columbia University Press.

Lesser, J., and R. Zerbe. 1995. "What Can Economic Analysis Contribute to the Sustainability Debate?" *Contemporary Economic Policy* 13(3): 88–100.

Lovelock, J. 1988. *The Ages of Gaia.* New York: Norton.

Low, P. (ed.). 1992. *International Trade and the Environment.* Washington, D.C.: World Bank.

Lutz, E. (ed.). 1993. *Toward Improved Accounting for the Environment.* Washington, D.C.: World Bank.

Pearce, D., and J. Warford. 1994. *World Without End: Economics, Environment, and Sustainable Development.* New York: Oxford University Press.

Peskin, H. 1989. "A Proposed Environmental Accounting Framework." In *Environmental Accounting for Sustainable Development,* ed. Y. Ahmad, S. El-Serafy, and E. Lutz. Washington, D.C.: World Bank.

Peskin, H., and E. Lutz. 1990. *A Survey of Resource and Environmental Accounting in Industrialized Countries.* Working Paper No. 37. Washington, D.C.: World Bank.

Pezzy, J. 1992. "Sustainability: An Interdisciplinary Guide." *Environmental Values* 1(4): 321–362.

"The Price of Everything, the Value of Nothing." July 31, 1993. *Economist,* p. 63.

Ravallion, M., G. Datt, and S. Chen. 1992. "New Estimates of Aggregate Poverty Measures for the Developing World, 1985–89." Washington, D.C.: The World Bank.

Repetto, R. 1992. "Accounting for Environmental Assets." *Scientific American* 266 (3): 94–100.

Repetto, R. et al. 1989. *Wasting Assets: Natural Resources in the National Income Accounts.* Washington, D.C.: World Resources Institute.

Schmidheiny, S. 1992. *Changing Course: A Global Business Perspective on Development and the Environment.* Cambridge, Mass.: MIT Press.

Toman, M. 1994. "Economics and 'Sustainability': Balancing Trade-offs and Imperatives." *Land Economics* 70(4): 399–412.

World Bank. 1992. *World Development Report 1992: Development and the Environment.* New York: Oxford University Press.

CHAPTER 20

INTERNATIONAL ENVIRONMENTAL AND RESOURCE ISSUES I: LOCAL EFFECTS

Victory over Victoria? Migrating Sewage in the Strait of Juan de Fuca

In the Pacific Northwest region of North America, the United States and Canada share as a common border the Strait of Juan de Fuca, which links the Pacific Ocean to Puget Sound in Washington State. Though the two countries are peaceful neighbors, one important economic function provided by the waterway—sewage disposal—has become a source of conflict.

Every day, Victoria, the largest and southernmost city on Canada's Vancouver Island, releases 20 million gallons of untreated sewage into the strait. Without treatment, smaller solid particles and some toxic heavy metals in the sewage are released into the ocean. Sewage treatment facilities filter these particles out into a separate waste product called sludge.

In contrast to Victoria, Washington's major cities release only treated sewage into the strait, as required by the U.S. Clean Water Act. One of those cities is Port Angeles, which lies directly across the strait from Victoria. Washingtonians suspect that pollution is washing up on their shores as a result of Victoria's sewage disposal. They are also concerned about deteriorating fisheries habitats in the strait, which is a major industry in the region. To protest Victoria's policy, Washington business and consumer groups called for a boycott of tourism and travel to Victoria, which is that city's largest industry.

Victorians insist that damage from sewage disposal is nonexistent and that treatment will not be necessary until the population has become significantly larger. They also argue that the United States has no business complaining about sewage until it cleans up its own environmental actions toward Canada, most prominently those causing acid rain damage to forests in Canada's eastern provinces and pollution in the Great Lakes. However, many businesses in Victoria, fearful of significant economic losses, urged the city to upgrade its sewage treatment facilities. But in a 1992 vote, citizens of Victoria overwhelmingly rejected a proposal to do so because of the higher taxes that would result.

The conflict over sewage disposal invokes several policy issues, including cross-border market failures in pollution control, incongruous environmental laws between nations, scientific accuracy, and determinations of environmental risk priorities.

Cross-border spillovers present particularly troublesome policy dilemmas, in that the adversely affected parties have no centralized authority to whom they can appeal for legislation, compensation, or enforcement. This makes it difficult to internalize the social and economic costs of pollution borne by third parties without entering into bilateral or multilateral agreements. Unfortunately, in many cases there will be little, if any, incentive to enter into such agreements.

Cross-border spillovers also highlight the fact that countries have different environmental laws and institutions. This can make sense for domestic environmental issues because different societies will place different values on reducing environmental costs and different emphases on specific environmental problems. In the case of cross-border spillovers, however, these differences can reduce the effectiveness of an individual country's environmental laws or place the "cleaner" country at a competitive disadvantage with respect to nonenvironmental goods. The U.S. Clean Water Act, for example, prescribes stricter requirements for sewage treatment than Canada does, as well as timetables to phase out ocean sludge dumping altogether. Sewage treatment imposes costs on U.S. businesses and consumers that can provide cost advantages to "dirtier" countries.

The sewage controversy also raises difficult questions as to the adequacy of scientific assessments and trade-offs in the regulation of environmental risks. Opponents of Victoria's sewage dumping practices have no evidence that raw sewage is damaging the ocean environment and the region's fisheries. Scientists also disagree on whether the ocean is capable of processing the waste naturally without harm and, if so, to what extent. Yet the sewage may indeed have irreversible impacts on habitats in the strait and the local ecosystem, permanently damaging the fisheries industry.

Finally, the conflict raises questions over determination of environmental risk priorities. Sewage treatment programs produce sludge, which must then be disposed of. Where should it go? If sludge is dumped on land, for example, will the concentration of toxic metals create water quality problems? How dangerous is the sludge relative to other known environmental hazards that also need mitigation, such as other hazardous wastes, air pollution, and forest depletion? Again, there are no easy answers.

INTRODUCTION

Despite lacking the necessary passports and visas, pollution often fails to respect national boundaries; pollution generated in one country can lead to environmental and economic damage in others. Economists call these situations *transboundary externalities*. There are numerous examples of such externalities, several of which we will discuss in this chapter. The Rhine River in Europe supplies drinking water to numerous countries and provides recreational benefits while at the same time acting as a waste receptacle. Because of agricultural runoff and dams upstream, the Colorado River is both depleted and extremely saline when it reaches the Mexico border. Sulfur and nitrogen dioxide emissions from coal-fired electricity-generating plants in the midwestern United States fall into eastern Canada as acid rain. Of course, the arrow of blame is not always pointed in one direction. Often countries that emit transboundary pollutants are also recipients of such pollution.[1]

Other policy issues can arise because of excessive use of common resources shared by countries. Water is the most frequent resource that suffers from this problem. In many cases, upstream countries will excessively deplete water supplies available to downstream users. Not only is this economically inefficient, but it has also been the cause of much conflict between countries. In many cases, cooperative development of transboundary resources can improve welfare for *all* of the affected countries.

In this chapter and the next, we explore several transboundary environmental and resource issues and examine the policies that have been used to address them. We begin with a brief discussion of the theory of transboundary externalities and their effects on economic welfare and equity. Then we devote the remainder of the chapter to a smorgasbord of examples of localized transboundary externalities, including acid rain, and various water resource allocation and quality issues. These issues, many of which have proved difficult or impossible to solve in any reasonable manner, show that complex environmental issues can be made more so when different countries are involved, all of whom have different laws, policies, and environmental priorities.

Perhaps most vexing is that these policy difficulties surround *local* international environmental issues, whose impacts are limited to several countries only. More difficult still are policies to address global environmental issues, which we take up in the next chapter. We will find that whereas some of the principles discussed in this chapter may apply to global environmental issues, policy solutions are even more difficult to achieve, although it may be much more important to do so.

---

[1]Global pollutants will be discussed in Chapter 21.

INTERNATIONAL ENVIRONMENTAL ISSUES: THEORY

Many environmental issues will have effects that extend beyond any one country's borders. This is most evident in problems such as atmospheric depletion of ozone and global warming. However, other forms of pollution can have international ramifications: air pollutants can cross borders, and the discharge of wastes into rivers can affect water quality downstream. Even pollutants that do not cross international borders can have international impacts, as countries debating whether to invest in improvements in environmental quality will often be concerned about the effects on their businesses' international competitiveness and hence the impacts on domestic employment and economic growth. That was one of the reasons for the controversy surrounding ratification of the North American Free Trade Act (NAFTA), which we discussed in Chapter 19.

Where pollution does cross international boundaries, other issues arise. First, in cases where the "victim" is apparent, there is the question of whether that victim can do anything to reduce the adverse impacts to itself. There is also the possibility for cooperative action. This is most likely to occur when the impacts of transboundary pollution depend on which way the wind blows or where countries share borders along environmental resources such as lakes or oceans. Clearly, cases where cooperative action occur are most likely to achieve efficient and equitable reductions in pollution impacts, using the same sorts of policy instruments (effluent taxes, tradable permits) that can be used for domestic policy. It is, however, noncooperative cases that raise unique issues.

International Impacts of Domestic Pollution

Consider the case where the world consists of two countries, A and B. Each country produces a mix of goods. The production of one of these goods, Q, causes air pollution. However, suppose that there exist production methods that can significantly reduce the amount of pollution that is produced. In a purely domestic case, application of an emissions tax or a tradable permit would lead to the optimal production process and a Pareto-optimal solution. Suppose that country B already has imposed such a policy. In country A, however, there is opposition to imposing such measures because of concerns over international competitiveness and loss of jobs.

The initial situation is shown in Figure 20.1. The first two panels, labeled "Country A" and "Country B," are standard trade figures. Initially, the relevant supply and demand curves for country A are S_A and D_A, with S_B and D_B the corresponding curves for country B. In the initial situation, where country A decides not to impose any pollution control policy, it produces quantity z of good Q, of which only x is consumed domestically and $z - x$ is exported to country B. This corresponds to a total quantity demanded of good Q equal to Q_0 in panel (c) of Figure 20.1, corresponding to the intersection of the overall market supply and demand curves S and D, respectively. If we assume that there are no complications, such as tariffs and transportation costs, the initial price of good Q will equal P_0. At this initial price, country B will import all of its demand for good Q, equal to g, where $g = z - x$.

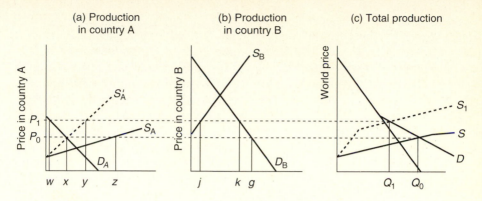

Figure 20.1   Effects of Implementing Pollution Control Measures.

Now suppose that country A imposes some form of pollution control policy. In this case, its new supply curve shifts upward to S_A'. The new world supply curve for good Q will be S_1. The world price increases to P_1, and total world quantity demanded falls to Q_1. Country A's production falls to y, while its domestic consumption falls to w. Country B now produces quantity j while importing quantity $k - j$. Although by *not* imposing the pollution control measures, the world price of good Q will, in general, be lower than if country A does impose the measures, the effect on total pollution is unclear; it depends on the amount of pollution per unit of output in the two countries. If pollution per unit of output in country B is sufficiently higher than in country A, the expansion of production by country B can contribute more additional pollution than the amount of pollution reduced by country A.

One of the main reasons that could be cited by country A for *not* imposing a pollution control policy is that doing so would cause domestic employment to decline. This result, however, need not be the case (Baumol and Oates 1988). The overall effect on employment depends on the production processes with and without the pollution control policy, as well as the elasticity of demand for good Q. Specifically, if the demand for Q is price-inelastic, the imposition of the pollution control measures will increase overall consumer expenditures on Q. This may increase employment in the industry.[2]

Country A's choice of whether to produce good Q without pollution will also have longer-run implications for the distribution of pollution among countries. The reason for this is comparative advantage. Suppose that each country produces two goods. In addition to good Q, each country produces another good, R, which is assumed not to generate any pollution. If country A uses the lower-cost polluting method of production for good Q, then additional production of good R will mean

---

[2]If country A faces a perfectly elastic export demand—in other words, if country A's demand is small compared to world demand—then overall domestic expenditures on good Q would decline. Unless the new production process was more labor-intensive, employment in country A would then be more likely to fall with the pollution control policies. Formal proofs of the employment proposition can be found in Baumol and Oates (1988).

giving up more production of Q. Suppose that the initial price P_0 of good Q is $10 and the international price of good R is $20. Production of an additional unit of R entails forgoing two units of Q. Next suppose that with the pollution control policy, the price of Q rises to $P_1 = \$20$. In this case, production of one unit of R implies forgoing only one unit of Q. If country B is always assumed to use the expensive production process, country A will have a comparative advantage in the production of Q if it does not adopt the pollution control technology. Thus in the long run, country A will tend to specialize in more environmentally damaging industries.

This conclusion has significant implications for international environmental policy. It means that some countries, most likely less developed ones seeking to increase their economic growth, will willingly do the world's "dirty work" (Baumol and Oates 1988). These countries may accept other countries' exports of rubbish and specialize in dirty industries. This problem also lies at the heart of some debates over the "rights" of richer countries to export their pollution to poorer countries.[3] None of this analysis suggests the "correct" solution. A poor country may legitimately seek dirty industries as a way of increasing its supply of capital so as to be able to make investments in education and infrastructure. And rich countries, even without pollution control policies, may have such a comparative advantage in the production of "clean" goods (and services) that "dirtier" industries naturally gravitate toward poorer countries.[4]

Distortions from Noncooperative Solutions

Suppose that in addition to goods Q and R, each country produces another good X. Some of the pollution from the production of good X in country A drifts over the border into country B. Each country must decide whether to implement pollution control policies and, if so, whether those policies should reduce pollution from good Q, good X, or both. For the sake of simplicity, let's suppose that each country will listen to its economists and adopt the most efficient policies relative to the costs and benefits of abatement.

The effect of pollution from the production of good X drifting from country A to country B is to reduce the *perceived* marginal damage function in country A; country A is simply imposing an external cost on country B, much as an individual dumping his garbage in the neighbor's yard is imposing an external cost on that neighbor. Thus from the standpoint of country A (or the garbage-dumping neighbor), the optimal pollution control policy will be determined by equating the marginal cost of control with the marginal benefit of abating just the residual pollution. This is shown in Figure 20.2. Assume that MD_A is the "true" marginal damage function that reflects the total damage of pollution from the production of good X.

---

[3]See, for example, the discussion in Chapter 12 on the value of life in poor countries versus rich countries.

[4]A more detailed exposition of the international impacts of domestic pollution can be found in Baumol and Oates (1988). See also Siebert (1992) for a more mathematical formulation.

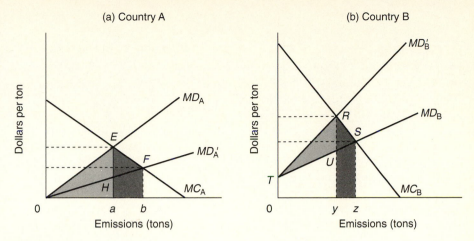

Figure 20.2   Noncooperative Solution to Transboundary Pollution

If country A incorporates this damage into its policy solution, it will reduce emissions to a. If it does not, emissions will be reduced only to the amount b.

Just as the neighbor starts noticing he is producing lots of garbage, from country B's perspective, there is suddenly lots of pollution associated with production of good X. Country B will perceive a higher than usual marginal damage curve. If country A does not account for the impacts of its emissions on country B, B will face the marginal damage curve labeled MD_B' rather than the marginal damage curve MD_B. It is also important to note that the truly efficient solution still results in some transboundary pollution. Even if country A recognizes the true cost of pollution from good X, X still will be produced and some of the resulting pollution still will drift over to country B. Without such cooperation, however, the efficient policy for country B will be to reduce its own emissions further to y from z and incur additional costs represented by the shaded area $RSzy$ in doing so. The overall change in damage to country B will be area TUR − area $USzy$. This may or may not be positive.

So even though country B takes steps to reduce its pollution further, it may see higher overall damage from pollution because of the transboundary contribution from country A. As a result of this noncooperative behavior, total pollution emissions may increase, and overall economic welfare may be reduced.

Second-Best Policies to Address Noncooperation   From a policy standpoint, if country A refuses to cooperate with country B, the issue then becomes one of deciding the best policy action available to country B. This is a second-best issue, much as we discussed in Chapter 7 with regard to electric utility regulators and pollution. Assuming that we rule out such actions as country B declaring war on country A, one possible response is for country B to impose a tariff on the importation of good X from country A.

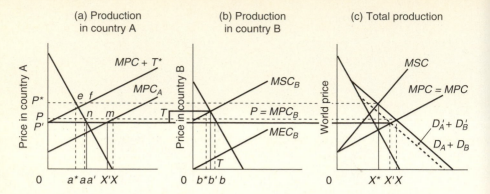

Figure 20.3   Imposition of a Tariff on a Polluting Good.

A tariff can be thought of as the international trade equivalent of an output tax. As we know from Chapter 7, an output tax can force consumers to pay the true social cost of the good produced. However, the tax will not necessarily lead to the correct mix of inputs in the production of a good, for the direct environmental costs faced by the offending producers will still be zero. Nor will a system of tariffs and taxes lead to an internationally optimal allocation of resources, for several reasons (Baumol and Oates 1988). First, a tariff does not directly increase the price of the good in the *exporting* country; in fact, the price of the good in the exporting country either will stay the same or be *lower* than the price without any tariff. Second, tariffs imposed by importing countries will reflect only the damage caused in those countries.[5] Thus consumers in the importing countries will also pay a price for the good that is lower than the good's "true" social cost unless all of the environmental damage accrues in the importing country. Nevertheless, in certain cases, a system of tariffs can achieve a second-best optimum.

To be effective, a country affected by transboundary pollution resulting from the production of a good must import that good. Furthermore, the "victimized" country must import sufficient quantities of the good in question to be able to influence the market price and hence production of the good.

Consider the example shown in Figure 20.3.[6] In this example, country A is assumed to be the sole exporter of good X to country B, which we now assume does not produce any of good X itself. The production cost of good X is given by MPC. Total social cost, including transboundary external costs, equals MSC. Initially, in the absence of the tariff or other distortions, the market price will equal P, based on the intersection of the aggregate demand curve $D_A + D_B$ and MPC. The quantities of X demanded in each country will equal a and b, respectively. Because country B is assumed not to produce X, the quantity b will just equal country A's exports, equal to $X - a$, or line segment $\overline{nm}$.

[5] Of course, this presupposes that the damage can be effectively measured.
[6] See Baumol and Oates (1988) for a more general, trade-theoretical approach.

Now country B imposes a tariff. The size of the tariff will depend on the marginal damage experienced by country B. Thus the marginal social cost for country B will equal the import price of the good ($P = MPC_B$) plus the marginal external cost, MEC_B. This marginal social cost is shown as MSC_B. The magnitude of the tariff imposed, T, will equal the MEC_b at the new equilibrium level of consumption. The imposition of the tariff will reduce the aggregate demand curve for good X to $D_A + D_B'$ and a new *lower* equilibrium price of P'. At this new equilibrium, exports from country A will again equal imports to country B. Consumption in country B will fall to b' because consumers in country B will pay P' plus the tariff T.

How does this solution compare to the first-best optimum? The level of consumption will be at least as large as the optimal level of consumption b^*, and the price will be lower than the optimal price P^*. In country A, the domestic price will *fall* and domestic consumption will increase. Ultimately, however, too much of good X will still be produced and consumed because individuals in country A are not paying the full social cost of X. Nevertheless, from the perspective of country B, imposition of the tariff will result in a second-best solution in that it equates the marginal social cost of importing good X with the marginal value of that good.

Policy Implications   In principle, imposing a tariff can achieve a second-best solution. A better solution, however, would be to design transnational pollution policies in much the same way as domestic pollution policy. An international emissions tax on a pollutant, which equaled the sum of all of the marginal damage imposed on different countries, could achieve a Pareto-optimal solution. Unfortunately, no world body has enforcement powers for such a tax system. And few polluting countries are willing to impose emissions taxes on themselves solely to reduce environmental damage caused outside their borders.

Another possible solution is the use of international marketable permits (Baumol and Oates 1988). In theory, these permits would work just like the domestic variety we discussed in Chapter 7. Countries would be assigned an initial level of permits and would be free to exchange them as they saw fit. In this way, an efficient allocation of permits would be achieved across countries. Again, however, there is the problem of determining the initial quantity and allocation of permits. Although there have been successful negotiations between countries, such negotiations rapidly increase in complexity as the number of parties involved increases. That is one reason why few such agreements are in place.

One problem with a permit approach is that it may turn the "polluter pays" principle on its head, despite Coase's (1960) belief that pollution problems are reciprocal.[7] In this case, it may be the victim who pays. There also are other major problems, such as strategic behavior between two countries (Baumol and Oates 1988). Country A, for example, may have an incentive to issue "excess" permits to its industries so as to lower the cost of compliance. Such behavior will reduce the effectiveness of any joint agreements. Nevertheless, the issuance of international

---

[7]See d'Arge and Kneese (1980) for a discussion of principles that can assign responsibility for transnational pollution.

marketable permits may be a solution worth further examination and a way of arriving at cooperative solutions to the problem of transboundary pollution and resource allocation issues.

TRANSBOUNDARY AIR POLLUTION: ACID RAIN

In some cases, the same pollutants that affect local environments can also be transported hundreds or thousands of miles to become transboundary ones. In this section, we examine several issues associated with transboundary air pollution by discussing the most common pollutant of this type, popularly known as *acid rain.*

Acid rain gets its name from the chemical reaction that takes place between sulfur dioxide (SO_2), nitrogen dioxide (NO_2), and water in clouds. The reaction leads to the creation of sulfuric and nitric acid, which then falls as acidified rain. The term is something of a misnomer because the damage caused by these pollutants, called *acidification,* occurs in two forms, *wet deposition* and *dry deposition.* With dry deposition, SO_2 and NO_2 particles fall to earth, where they subsequently react with water and create sulfuric and nitric acid. In some parts of the world, such as the southwestern U.S., dry deposition is a more serious problem than wet deposition. Nevertheless, the common belief persists that the sole source of damage is wet deposition. Even though there are natural sources of acid deposition, such as volcanic eruptions, the major sources are now *anthropogenic,* or human-caused, such as industry and fossil-fueled electricity-generating plants.

Sources of Acid Deposition

The sources of acid rain differ among countries. In the United States, the main sources are electricity-generating plants that burn high-sulfur coal and oil. These plants are concentrated in the midwestern and eastern United States. In Canada, the major sources are ore smelters, primarily because Canada relies on hydroelectric power for a much higher percentage of its electricity. Similarly, in Europe, the major sources are electricity-generating stations that burn relatively dirty coal. The problem is particularly acute in eastern Europe, where both power stations and heavy industry have installed few, if any, pollution control measures. And because of the relatively small size of many European countries, transboundary acid rain is particularly acute.

Environmental Damage Associated with Acid Deposition

The effects of acid rain are varied. One of the major impacts occurs in lakes and streams. Ironically, acidified lakes often look wonderfully clear and blue. As these become more acidified, fish species decline because few sport fish can tolerate water that is more than mildly acidic. Losses of sport fishing populations reduces recreation values in many areas. The water's clarity is the result of a lack of plant and animal life in the water. In Europe, acid deposition has significantly reduced some fish populations, causing severe economic losses in countries such as Norway, where salmon fishing and farming account for significant portions of the economy.

Acid deposition also damages trees and reduces growth in forests. Pine forests in the eastern United States and Canada have suffered damage. So have many European forests. Acid deposition may also affect the growth of crops, such as wheat and soybeans, although the degree of this damage is less certain (NAPAP 1989).

Acid deposition also can reduce visibility. Fine sulfate particles, which can be formed when sulfuric acid reacts chemically in the atmosphere, have been found to reduce visibility by 50 to 60 percent of "normal" levels (NAPAP 1989). And acid deposition can accelerate corrosion and deterioration of metals and stone, such as galvanized steel and marble. In Rome, for example, deterioration of many ancient buildings and statues has become severe owing to emissions from automobiles.

Empirical Estimates of Damage Costs from Acid Deposition

Empirical estimates of the costs associated with acid deposition worldwide are speculative. To arrive at a comprehensive estimate of overall damages, one would be required to add up the damage arising from crop losses, loss of recreational benefits, damage to buildings, damage to forests, and so on, worldwide. Since even categorizing damage in any comprehensive way is difficult, as is separating the effects of acid deposition from other pollutants, it is doubtful that any reliable damage estimate can be developed.

Numerous authors have estimated damage for different aspects of acid deposition. Mullen and Menz (1985), for example, used the travel cost method (discussed in Chapter 11) to estimate the recreation damage caused by acidification of popular lakes in the Adirondack region of New York State. They concluded that annual losses to recreational anglers who were residents of New York were at least $1 million annually in 1976. This estimated damage occurred because of acid deposition in just one small area of the country and arose from loss of recreational benefits only. One can imagine that the overall damage cost, encompassing all categories of damage for all states, could be quite high.

Calculations of national damage from acid deposition have been performed for several countries. Pearce and Markandya (1989) summarize several of these estimates for West Germany and the Netherlands. The German estimates ranged between 1 and 3 billion 1986 deutsche marks per year (roughly, $600 million to $2 billion), reflecting agricultural and forestry damage, respectively. The latter estimate also incorporates the cost of protecting German forests from acid deposition. Pearce and Markandya also report that a 1986 study by the Netherlands Ministry of Housing and Environment estimated annual damage to cultivated crops and heather regions at between 500 and 700 million Dutch guilders ($250 to $500 million). Another 150 to 500 million guilders ($75 to $250 million) in annual damage was estimated to occur because of reductions in that country's forest harvest.

Policies to Address Transboundary Acid Deposition

Because of the bilateral nature of acid deposition, policies that address acid deposition will often require cooperation between countries.[8] And despite the difficulties in doing so, there have been various international responses to controlling acid rain. In Europe, for example, the Convention on Long Range Transboundary Air Pollution was ratified in 1983. In that same year, Norway proposed that countries sign up to become members of a "30 percent club," where membership would commit those countries to 30 percent reductions in SO_2 emissions from their 1980 levels by 1993 (Pearce and Turner 1990). Though several countries that were the largest sources of SO_2, including the United States, Great Britain, and the eastern bloc countries, rejected the proposal, others agreed, and in 1984 the club was formed. However, there was no mention of the precise policies that would best achieve these reductions. And from a standpoint of economic efficiency, such uniform reductions would be unlikely to achieve such reductions at the lowest cost.

The difficulty of negotiating international agreements almost certainly increases with the number of countries involved. Acid deposition in Europe suffers from this problem. The sheer number of transboundary impacts is quite large. To reduce damage effectively, a large number of contingencies must be dealt with. Examples such as the "30 percent club" point to the difficulties of effectively negotiating reductions. Transboundary issues between the United States, Canada, and Mexico, while still complex, at least have the advantage of smaller numbers of contingencies. As a result, more progress has been made in addressing transboundary air pollution issues in those countries.

The United States and Mexico   In 1983, the United States and Mexico signed the La Paz agreement.[9] This agreement, which covers both air and water quality issues, was developed in response to several severe environmental problems that were occurring in the border areas of the two countries. Addressing these issues on a case-by-case basis would have been tedious. The La Paz agreement was designed to provide a broader framework in which different environmental issues affecting the border regions could be addressed.[10]

Subsequent to the signing of the La Paz agreement, five annexes that addressed specific transboundary issues were agreed to. Two of these focused on air pollution. The first dealt with pollution created by three large copper smelters along the U.S.-Mexican border: a plant owned by Phelps Dodge and located in Arizona; and the Nacozari and Cananea plants in the Mexican state of Sonora.

---

[8]Because significant portions of SO_2 and NO_2 emitted lead to acid deposition within the emitting country, there will often be unilateral policy steps that may be taken to reduce emissions.

[9]This agreement is formally known as the Agreement Between the United States and the United Mexican States on Cooperation for the Protection and Improvement of the Environment in the Border Area and was ratified on August 14, 1983.

[10]The agreement defined the border regions as encompassing the areas within 100 kilometers (about 60 miles) of the two countries' joint border.

(The second annex addressed a growing urban air pollution problem in the El Paso–Ciudad Juarez region.) These smelters, in addition to other pollutants, were a major source of acid deposition. As a result of the annex, the Phelps-Dodge plant was closed, the Nacozari plant was retrofitted to operate a separate facility that would convert previously emitted sulfur dioxide into marketable sulfuric acid, and production at the Cananea plant was fixed at its then current operating capacity (Szekely 1993).

The United States and Canada   For many years, acid deposition in Canada arising from U.S. sources was a major source of strain between the two countries (Scott 1986; Le Marquand 1993). The Canadian government believes that more than 50 percent of the acid deposition in Canada comes from U.S. sources. The 1990 U.S. Clean Air Act amendments, which call for a 10 million–ton reduction in U.S. emissions of sulfur dioxide and a permanent cap at 14.6 million tons by the year 2000, provided a significant boost to cooperation between the two countries (Le Marquand 1993).

The 1990 Clean Air Act amendments led to the signing of an agreement between the two countries in 1991. The Agreement on Air Quality formalizes each country's commitment to reducing acid deposition (Le Marquand 1993). It provides a mechanism for resolving international disputes and a framework for addressing other international air pollution problems, such as air toxics, ground-level ozone, and smog.

EMISSIONS FROM MEXICO TO THE UNITED STATES: THE CARBON II PROJECT

In the northeastern Mexico state of Coahuila, near the city of Piedras Negras, some 20 miles south of the Texas border, a large coal-fired generating plant has been under construction since 1986. This plant, named Carbon II, and its earlier twin, Carbon I, which has been operating since the mid-1980s, has been the subject of vigorous debate and recriminations.

The Carbon II plant represents a major privatization of the electricity-generating industry in Mexico. The plant was to have been jointly owned by the Mexican government's electric utility, known as CFE, and Mission Energy Corporation, a subsidiary of Southern California Edison. Carbon II consists of four individual generating units, each with a capacity of 350 megawatts. The first two units are complete; units 3 and 4 were about half complete by the end of 1993. The units are to burn low-sulfur coal. However, because the units will not be "scrubbed," emissions of SO_2 and particulates will exceed the "new source performance standards" set by the U.S. EPA. However, the plans do meet Mexican air quality standards, which are somewhat lower than those in the United States. The cost of adding scrubbers to the plants would be between $200 and $300 million on top of the $1.6 billion construction cost.

If the Carbon II plant's emissions of SO_2 and particulates remained entirely

(continued)

within Mexico, there would be no controversy (although the plants would still be a source of carbon dioxide, a major greenhouse gas). It is the extent of transboundary pollution that is the source of the controversy. Opponents of the plant argue that the transboundary pollution will enter into Texas and generally degrade air quality in the Southwest. Proponents of the plant argue that it will improve Mexico's air quality by allowing CFE to reduce its heavy dependence on electricity generation using plants that burn high-sulfur oil and produce five times the SO_2 emissions per kilowatt-hour of electricity predicted for the Carbon II plant.

A reasonable question is why the plant was built so near the Mexican-U.S. border. After all, had the plant been built in the middle of Mexico, none of these concerns would have been raised. It turns out that the location is near the only reserve of the proper coal. Locating a generating plant near its fuel source is cheaper than transporting fuel for hundreds of miles.

The issues raised by the construction of the plant involve classic efficiency and equity issues. The plant may reduce overall emissions significantly and provide benefits to individuals in Mexico but may raise emissions in areas of the United States where individuals receive no benefits. Even Solomon might be perplexed as to the right choice of action.

Source: Maize (1993).

SELECTED ISSUES IN TRANSBOUNDARY WATER ALLOCATION, USE, AND QUALITY

Transboundary water allocation and quality issues have also been important. The common-property attributes of both surface and groundwater supplies have resulted in numerous conflicts between nations over the years. Water availability and quality continue to be contentious issues, particularly in regions such as the Middle East where water is scarce. On the positive side, agreements between countries have increased both the usability of existing water supplies and the quality of shared water resources. In North America, for example, the United States and Canada developed joint agreements for the development and use of the Columbia River system and to improve water quality in the Great Lakes.[11] The United States and Mexico have had a more contentious history with shared water resources, focused most notably on disputes over the Colorado River. Even in such politically unstable areas such as the Middle East, agreements between Israel and its Arab neighbors are slowly improving water allocation. Yet as we discussed in the beginning case about sewage treatment, many issues are difficult to solve. And sometimes, as we shall see, cooperative agreements create their own complications.

---

[11]In the case of the Columbia River system, however, the international cooperation that led to beneficial development of the river has exacerbated problems with endangered species of salmon.

The Columbia River Treaty

At the turn of the twentieth century, there were no dams on the Columbia River in either Canada or the United States. The river and its tributaries often flooded, sometimes with devastating results. After the United States began to harness the Columbia for hydroelectric power, the benefits of joint cooperation became more apparent to the two countries.[12] Controlling the river's Canadian headwaters by means of a system of dams in Canada, they reasoned, could reduce the potential for flood damage in the United States and help harness the mighty river's hydroelectric potential. So in 1944, the two governments began to assess the potential for cooperative development of the Columbia River system (see Figure 20.4).

The task of investigating the potential for joint development was given to the International Joint Commission (IJC), which had been formed in 1909 as part of the Boundary Waters Treaty signed by the two countries to help resolve water resource disputes. The IJC was asked by both countries to develop a set of principles that would determine the benefits from joint development and guide the division of those benefits. In 1959, the IJC recommended the development of four major storage projects. Three of these were to be built in British Columbia, where the majority of the water originated. The fourth project was to be built on the Kootenai River, near Libby, Montana. The four projects would permit better control of water flows in the Columbia River system and reduce the likelihood of severe flood damage downstream in the United States (Lesser 1990). And construction of the Canadian storage projects would enable more electricity to be generated at downstream U.S. facilities.

The Columbia River Treaty was signed in 1961, although difficulties with calculation of the downstream flood control and power benefits delayed its ratification until 1964. Eventually, it was determined that the United States would pay Canada a lump sum for flood control benefits equal to one-half of the expected avoided flood damage over the treaty's 60-year life. It was also determined that the power benefits were to be calculated about six years in advance.[13] The additional power generation at U.S. facilities made possible by the Canadian storage facilities was to be shared equally.

Because the transmission lines to return power to Canada did not exist and because the Canadian government did not have the money to finance the three storage dams, Canada sold its half of the power benefits back to the United States for a period of 30 years from the date of completion of each Canadian storage project. That sale expires over a five-year period beginning in 1998, with the Canadian share of the benefits reverting completely to Canada by 2003. In the absence of a future resale of these benefits, which as of this writing is still under negotiation, the United States will be required to deliver electric power to British Columbia beginning in 1998.

Environmental Complications   There can be little doubt that the Columbia River Treaty led to more productive use of the Columbia River system.

---

[12]Development of dams on the Columbia River is discussed in Chapter 8 and 9.
[13]The first of the three Canadian storage projects was completed in 1968. The last was completed in 1973. A discussion of how the power benefits are calculated can be found in Krutilla (1967) and Lesser (1990).

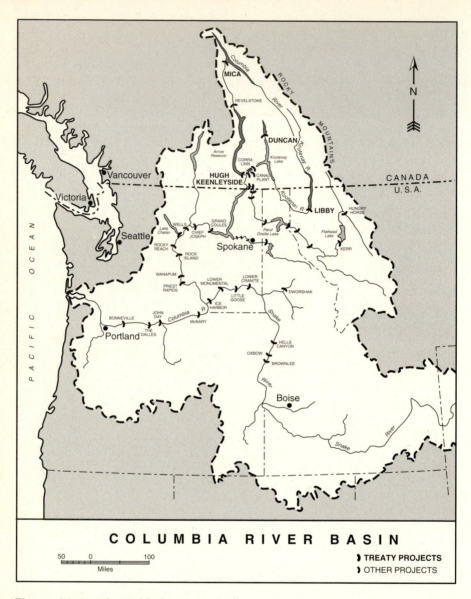

Figure 20.4 The Columbia River System

Source: Bonneville Power Administration

Unfortunately, the treaty has also been "swamped" by unilateral legislation in the United States that was passed to address the problems of declining fisheries stocks in the Columbia River system and, more recently, the strict mandates of the U.S. Endangered Species Act.[14]

---

[14]The Endangered Species Act is discussed in Chapter 9.

In 1980, the Pacific Northwest Electric Conservation and Electric Power Planning Act, usually referred to as the Northwest Power Act, was passed. In addition to developing specific guidelines on how the Pacific Northwest's future electricity requirements were to be met, the act also required that a Columbia Basin Fish and Wildlife Plan be developed.[15] One aspect of this plan was the development of "water budgets." These water budgets were to be used to assist juvenile salmon in their migration to the Pacific Ocean by releasing additional water in the spring. Unfortunately, water that is released in the spring cannot be stored for power generation later in the year, when it is more valuable, owing to peak demands in California in the summer and in the Pacific Northwest in the winter.

The Columbia River Treaty, however, never recognized the fisheries issue, as water for fisheries habitat was never considered a "beneficial use" under the provisions of the treaty. Thus the shared-power benefits are based on a power system that can produce the most power possible without regard to the environmental problems such power production may cause. Yet the Bonneville Power Administration is required to adhere to the rules in the Fish and Wildlife Plan. More recently, several species of salmon and steelhead have been declared endangered species.[16] The Endangered Species Act requires that mitigating actions be invoked without regard to cost. As a result of these listings, more water has been reserved for fish and less for power.

Resolution of these issues remains elusive. Clearly, the potential for conflict exists when one country's environmental legislation requires the cooperative efforts of another country. This is the situation faced by the U.S. parties benefiting from electricity generated in the Columbia River system today. They are constrained not only by U.S. environmental laws but also by an international agreement.

Like many difficult issues, the problems created by the collision of the Columbia River Treaty with subsequent U.S. environmental laws is really an equity issue. Simply put, the key question is: Who will pay the price for the environmental restoration? The issue is complicated further because the proposed pricing mechanisms may exacerbate potential inequities between the parties benefiting from the power made possible by the treaty and those paying the bill.

All of the electricity generated at federal facilities on the Columbia River system is marketed by the Bonneville Power Administration (BPA). Under the Northwest Power Act, the BPA is obligated "to protect, mitigate, and enhance" fish and wildlife. This requirement is the basis for the water budget. In the current situation, the BPA must include the cost of mitigation efforts into the price of the electricity it sells. As it continues to do so, however, the cost effectiveness of substitutes increases; customers, especially the largest industrial users, have a wide range of alternative sources of energy, including on-site generation and use of substitute fuels such as natural gas. To the extent that this form of substitution continues to

---

[15]See Swainson (1986) for further information in the context of the Columbia River Treaty. The plan itself was published by the Northwest Power Planning Council, an entity created by the Northwest Power Act in 1980. See Northwest Power Planning Council (1990).

[16]Steelhead are oceangoing trout.

occur, the costs of mitigation will be borne by remaining users, such as residential customers, with fewer cost-effective alternatives.

The Great Lakes

The Great Lakes are the world's largest freshwater system, covering 84,000 square miles and draining an additional land area of over 200,000 square miles in the Great Lakes Basin, which straddles the United States and Canada. Industrial and residential development along the Great Lakes has proceeded for almost 200 years. Many of both countries' heavy industries, including automobile manufacturing and ore smelting, has been centered in the basin. The area also is home to about 20 percent of the U.S. population and 50 percent of Canada's (Homer 1985).[17]

The primary focus of the Boundary Waters Treaty of 1909 was the Great Lakes. Rather than an upstream-downstream issue, as with the Columbia River Treaty, the Great Lakes represent a common-property resource (Sadler 1986).[18] The primary concerns about the Great Lakes have been lake levels and water quality. Pollution, for example, will be reduced most effectively through joint actions. The Boundary Waters Treaty states that water flowing either way across the boundary would not be so polluted as to damage human health or property in the downstream country. It also states that both countries are responsible for preventing pollution in the Great Lakes, as might be expected for a common-property resource.

Recognizing the importance of the Great Lakes to both countries, in 1972 Canada and the United States signed the Great Lakes Water Quality Agreement, which was later modified in 1978. The 1972 agreement began with a 1964 "reference" (similar to a petition) to the IJC, owing to heightened public and scientific concern about water quality in the lakes. The reference posed three questions (Homer 1985):

1. Were the boundary waters of Lakes Erie and Ontario being polluted on either side to an extent that would violate the Boundary Waters Treaty, in that the pollution was harming human health and property?
2. If so, what were the sources of that pollution?
3. What actions would correct the problem in the most economic manner?

Research on these issues continued for some five years. A final report, which answered the three questions that had been posed, was delivered to the IJC in 1969. The study found that increasing levels of phosphorus was contributing to reductions in dissolved oxygen levels (called *eutrophication*), and reducing fish populations in the lower lakes. The study found that Lakes Erie and Ontario were in advanced stages of eutrophication.

---

[17]See also Dworsky (1985) for a detailed history of the Great Lakes.
[18]Sadler uses the expression "common pool resource"; the meaning is the same, however.

The major source of phosphorus was found to be municipal wastewater, including treated wastewater. The study could not determine that concentrations of phosphorus were the result of actions from specific sources on either side of the boundary; however, it did conclude that the majority of the discharges originated on the U.S. side. The study also determined that contaminants from one country would certainly degrade water quality in the other. The study concluded by saying that urgent measures were needed to improve water quality in the two lakes (Homer 1985).

Policy Actions   With the rise of greater environmental awareness in the late 1960s and early 1970s, the specter of a "dead" Lake Erie proved a powerful force for policy action. The IJC's final report, issued in 1970, identified phosphorus as the major cause but also stated that phosphorous pollution was controllable. Canada's response was to enact the Canada Water Act, which immediately limited the phosphate content of detergents to 20 percent and required a further reduction to 5 percent by 1973. The reduction in detergent phosphate content was identified by the IJC as the most cost-effective approach to reduce phosphorus levels in the lakes (Homer 1985). At first, the United States appeared to be taking similar action. However, in June 1970, the government reversed itself, warning that the substitutes for phosphates in detergent might harm human health.[19] The phosphate debate was never resolved. Instead, many states unilaterally enacted phosphate limitations on their own, and the U.S. government instituted a construction program of new wastewater treatment facilities, even though that was far less cost-effective than removing phosphate from detergent.[20]

Negotiations on the original Great Lakes Water Quality Agreement stalled on a particularly important subject: determining rights to the assimilative capacity (the amount of pollutants that could be absorbed without harming water quality) of the Great Lakes. The Canadians interpreted the Boundary Waters Treaty of 1909 as meaning that Canada and the United States each had a right to half of the assimilative capacity of the Great Lakes. Because U. S. discharges into the lakes were so much higher than Canada's, this interpretation would have forced the United States to bear almost the entire brunt of the cost of reducing pollution discharges, even though more cost-effective reductions could occur on the Canadian side. The United States, citing a different article of the treaty, argued that both countries were equally obligated to clean up the Great Lakes. Eventually, Canada gave up its position, allowing the agreement to proceed.

---

[19]Homer (1985) discusses several possible reasons for the U.S. action, including environmentalists' claims that the Nixon administration had financial ties to Procter & Gamble Corporation, a major manufacturer of household detergents.

[20]In a 1984 report, the IJC stated that the United States and Canada had spent over $7.6 billion on wastewater treatment facilities in the Great Lakes Basin in order to reduce phosphorus concentrations in wastewater to 1.0 milligram per liter.

Under the terms of the 1972 agreement, the IJC was required to report to both countries on progress toward meeting the goals set out in the agreement. In 1975, the IJC noted that progress toward meeting the goals was slow, uneven, and disappointing (Homer 1985). By 1977, it was apparent that the goals set out in 1972 would not be met and a revision of the original objectives was required. This revision was the basis for the second Great Lakes Water Quality Agreement, signed in 1978.

The 1978 agreement reflected better knowledge of ecosystem management. The United States and Canada agreed to implement programs that would control phosphorous inputs, eliminate toxic waste discharges, and minimize hazardous wastes in the Great Lakes (Homer 1985). The commitments in the 1978 agreement are more detailed than those in the original agreement. By the end of 1985, the two countries appeared much closer to approaching the Great Lakes as an integrated ecosystem and articulating policies to implement programs to do so (Dworsky 1986).

The Colorado River

The Colorado River was developed extensively for irrigation and hydroelectric development (Reisner 1993). After it has been tapped for U.S. uses, what little remains of the river flows into northern Mexico. The quantity and quality of the river at the border have been the subjects of bitter disputes between the United States and Mexico for many years.

Millions of residential users and crops grown on over 1 million irrigated acres in the southwestern United States and northwestern Mexico are dependent, to varying degrees, on the Colorado River. As the amount of dissolved mineral salts, called *salinity*, of the river increases, these users are adversely affected. Salinity is usually measured either in milligrams per liter (mg/l) or parts per million (ppm). Concentrations above 500 mg/l harm crops and cause excessive wear on municipal water systems (Gardner and Young 1988). Salinity is a natural development with irrigation. Some of the water that is used for irrigation of plants evaporates, leaving the previously dissolved mineral salts in the soil. To preserve production levels, irrigators have to leach the accumulated salts from the soil, usually through excess irrigation. This requires greater quantities of water, which, as population and irrigation acreage expand, increases the scarcity of existing water supplies.

Salinity emerged as a critical policy issue between the United States and Mexico in the 1960s, but the problems can be traced back much further. The 1944 Water Treaty between the two countries guaranteed Mexico 1.5 million acre-feet (maf) of water from the Colorado River annually (Furnish and Ladman 1975). This amount of water had been promised as far back as 1928, when the Colorado River Compact, an agreement among seven states in the Colorado River Basin— Arizona, California, Colorado, Nevada, New Mexico, Utah, and Wyoming—was signed.[21] The amount of water was quite large by past standards and encouraged expansion of irrigated agriculture (primarily cotton) in the Mexicali Valley. By 1955, the Mexicali Valley had become the leading cotton-producing region in the country. Wheat production also increased in the region, providing needed food supplies. The area's economy grew to serve the needs of the growing agricultural industry.

The 1944 Water Treaty guaranteed Mexico 1.5 maf of water each year, but it contained no specification of the *quality* of the water delivered. Unfortunately, at about the same time that the Mexicali Valley became a major agricultural production area, problems with drainage in subsoil were causing problems upstream for the Welton-Mohawk irrigation project (named for two small desert towns in the area) in Arizona (Furnish and Ladman 1975). Groundwater sources were quite saline and close to the root levels of plants. As a result, irrigation water could not drain. The solution adopted was to drill hundreds of wells in order to pump out this saline groundwater in order to allow the irrigation water to drain properly.

Although pumping the saline groundwater solved the problem at Welton-Mohawk, that water had to be dumped somewhere. The receptacle of choice was the Colorado River. Salinity levels rose dramatically in the Mexicali Valley, reaching 2,700 ppm by 1961, three times the baseline level of around 800 ppm.[22] Not only was the Welton-Mohawk pumping reducing the quality of the water delivered to Mexico, but that pumped water became part of the 1.5 maf quota of Mexico's water. The problem of both quality and quantity then was exacerbated by the filling of Lake Powell, the reservoir behind Glenn Canyon Dam in Arizona. This led to additional economic damages on both sides of the border.[23]

The effects of the increasing salinity levels in Mexico were compounded by other policy changes. In 1965, the United States changed its agricultural policy, which had supported the price of cotton at artificially high levels. As cotton prices declined, production fell while costs per acre increased (Furnish and Ladman 1975). And economic losses in Mexico were made even worse by an infestation of the pink bollworm, which devastated crops in the entire Mexicali Valley.

Policy Actions   Mexico responded with several policy measures. First, it initiated a program to diversify agricultural production, stressing crops that had higher salt tolerance than cotton. Second, Mexico began to rely more on wells for irrigation water, rather than Colorado River water. Third, in 1968 the government initiated a $100 million project to rehabilitate the irrigation systems in the valley in order to increase the efficiency with which the existing groundwater and river supplies could be used.

---

[21]Reisner (1993) provides a lively history of the Colorado River Compact.

[22]Apparently, there was some dispute over how salinity levels were measured. See Furnish and Ladman (1975) and the references cited therein.

[23]See Tamargo and Young (1975) and U.S. Bureau of Reclamation (1980) for specific economic damage estimates.

By 1972, the Colorado River was the subject of much discussion. Both countries pledged to reach a permanent solution to the salinity problem.[24] In 1973, the two countries signed the Colorado River Salinity Agreement.[25] It called for water to be delivered to the Mexican border with a salinity level no higher than 115 ppm (plus or minus 30 ppm) above the level measured upstream at Imperial Dam in 1976 (Reisner 1993). The salinity level measured at the dam turned out to be 879 ppm. In 1974, the U.S. Congress passed the Salinity Control Act, which provided for abatement of both natural and agricultural sources, and authorized construction of four upper-basin (U.S.) salinity control units. This led to the construction of a large desalination plant at Yuma, Arizona, at a cost of over $300 million to treat the wastewater drained from Welton-Mohawk. The cost of treating water at the plant was estimated to be around $300 per acre-foot.

The cost effectiveness of different salinity control strategies has been investigated.[26] In addition to desalination, the standard techniques to reduce external diseconomies that we have discussed in earlier chapters can be examined. These include taxes on water, subsidies for water conservation, taxes on salt discharges, and land and water rights purchases. There is little disagreement that the most expensive policy choice was the desalination plant.[27]

Gardner and Young (1988) evaluated different agricultural strategies to reduce irrigation-induced salinity in the upper Colorado River Basin, which would reduce salinity downstream. The authors first investigated technological control strategies: specific irrigation methods that raise the efficiency with which water is used. They also examined land retirement as a control measure and looked into the costs for different crops. The results of their analysis indicated that these control measures could reduce salt discharges at costs between $0.90 and $55.00 per ton (in 1982 dollars). For several crops, land retirement could reduce salt discharges at a *negative* cost. Pastureland, for example, could be retired and salt discharged at a net cost of −$11.20 per ton. In other words, because of the subsidies for water and the value of pasture, reducing pastureland would increase economic welfare while reducing salt discharges. From an economic efficiency standpoint, therefore, this would be a win-win situation.

Gardner and Young then examined different economic policy instruments, including taxes on effluents, subsidies for irrigation control methods, and tradable permits for salt. As we discussed in Chapter 11, the most efficient solution to the salt problem would be an "emissions" tax on salt discharges. The problem with this policy instrument, however, is that much of the salt is contained in nonpoint irri-

---

[24]Reisner (1993) glibly speculates that the United States' desire to reach agreement with Mexico on the salinity issue might have had something to do with the prospect of large quantities of crude oil discovered there.

[25]This agreement is formally known as Minute 242, titled "Permanent and Definitive Solution to the International Problem of the Salinity of the Colorado River."

[26]See Gardner and Young (1988) and Martin (1975).

[27]As Reisner (1993) states, "What Congress has chosen to do, in effect, is to purify water at a cost of $300 an acre-foot so that upriver irrigators can continue to grow surplus crops with federally subsidized water that costs them $3.50 an acre-foot" (p. 464). Though Reisner's language is not neutral, he illustrates the "piecemeal" problem well.

gation return flows, exacerbating the problem of measuring the original sources of the salt discharges. Nevertheless, Gardner and Young developed a hypothetical model of taxing salt discharges, which showed that salt could be reduced at a cost of between $0.40 and $6.88 per ton.

The authors' model also indicated that irrigation improvement subsidies would reduce salt discharges at a cost of between $0.40 and $12.33 per ton. However, as we discussed in Chapter 7, subsidies for pollution control will only indirectly reduce pollutant discharges and may even lead to increases in overall discharges. A third method investigated was taxing water. This is the input equivalent to a tax on output. A tax on irrigation water would raise the price of water as an input to agricultural production. Because water, like other inputs, would be applied only to the point where the value of the marginal product of the last acre-foot of water equals the price, the tax would reduce water consumption and indirectly reduce salt discharges. The results of a water tax indicated that it would reduce salt discharges at a cost of between $1.58 and $7.16, depending on the original price of water.[28]

The authors concluded that economic efficiency goals have not been paramount in salinity management. This sentiment is strongly echoed by Reisner (1993). In general, upstream irrigators have been able to impose the majority of the costs of desalinization programs on taxpayers in general, rather than set up a more equitable "polluter pays" system. They argue that explicit sharing of desalinization costs by both upstream and downstream users would be a more efficient and equitable solution.

The Middle East

Not surprisingly, the most commonly discussed natural resource in the Middle East is crude oil. But crude oil has been a significant part of the Middle East for less than a century, whereas water, and the lack of it, has been a focus of the Middle East for thousands of years. The region's rapidly increasing population, industrialization, and growing wealth have increased the demand for water significantly in the past few decades, with water demand now exceeding total water availability. The problem is especially acute in Israel and Jordan. Table 20.1 provides a comparison of water availability in the Middle East and North Africa with that in other regions of the world. As the table shows, the Middle East has the lowest amount of renewable water supplies of any region. And water withdrawals in the region represent a far higher percentage of the total supply than in any other region. Per capita water supplies are only around 1,000 cubic meters each year and declining. As much as 80 to 90 percent of this water goes for agricultural purposes, owing to the reliance on irrigation in the predominantly dry climate.

The water problems in the region are exacerbated by a combination of rapidly increasing population, drought, and war. The area seems to face a drought

---

[28]The lower the original price of water, the lower the cost per ton of salt reduced because a given level of water tax will represent a higher percentage increase in the price of water.

TABLE 20.1   WATER AVAILABILITY IN SELECTED REGIONS

Region	Total Annual Internal Water Resources (billions of cubic meters)	Total Annual Water Withdrawals (billions of cubic meters)	Annual Withdrawals as a Percentage of Total Resources	1990 Per Capita Internal Water Resources (cubic meters)	1990 Per Capita Annual Withdrawals (cubic meters)
China and India	14,272	840	18	2,345	520
Members of the OECD	8,365	889	11	10,781	1,230
Middle East and North Africa	276	202	73	1,071	782
East Asia and the Pacific	7,915	631	8	5,009	453
Europe	574	110	19	2,865	589
Latin America and the Caribbean	10,579	173	2	24,390	460
World	40,586	3,017	7	7,744	676

Source: World Bank (1992).

about every four years, and the population is doubling every 25 years. As more people move into cities, their standard of living rises and with it their consumption of water. Farming will be the most affected. Years of conflict, including the Iran-Iraq war, have decimated the infrastructure that controls water quality and allocation.

Given the region's historic animosities, transboundary allocation of these water resources continues to be a source of great concern among the parties. Although it is unlikely that the next war in the Middle East will be over water, rapidly increasing demand and diminishing supplies are creating new tensions ("As Thick as Blood" 1995).

The tensions involve both surface and groundwater supplies. The major sources of surface water in the region are the Tigris and Euphrates rivers, originating in the mountains of Turkey. For centuries, these rivers were relatively undisturbed. However, Turkey has embarked on a major development program, named the Anatolia Project, which when completed will have placed 22 dams on these two rivers. Turkey's aim is to provide irrigation water for farmers as well as hydroelectricity.

The largest of these dams is the Atatürk, completed in 1989. Because the Euphrates flows directly into Syria and then, further downstream, Iraq, this project has caused considerable friction within those two downstream countries. Once the entire project is completed, it is estimated that the downstream flow reaching Syria and Iraq could be reduced by as much as 60 percent (Vesilind 1993). The water that flows into the Euphrates downstream of Atatürk Dam is itself captured in dams. In Syria, for example, power output from a large hydroelectric facility at Tabqa has been diminished. This latter dam has also created concerns farther

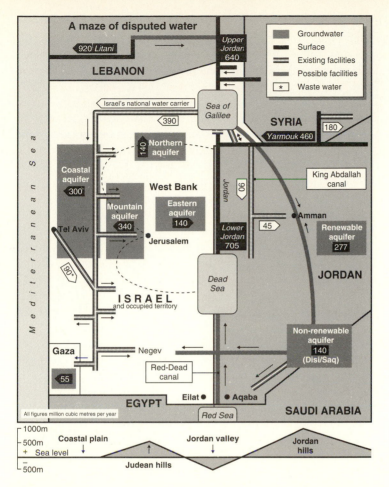

Figure 20.5   A Maze of Disputed Water

Source: "As Thick as Blood," *The Economist,* December 23, 1995–January 5, 1996. p. 53.

downstream in Iraq. The tensions raised by upstream river development nearly led to war between Syria and Iraq in 1975, when the Tabqa reservoir was being filled.

Groundwater supplies are also shared—and disputed, as shown in Figure 20.5. For example, there are three major aquifers in the West Bank, between Israel and Jordan: the Northern, Eastern, and Mountain aquifers. The Mountain and Northern aquifers protrude slightly into Israel, which takes 80 to 90 percent of these aquifers' water. Although countries "downstream" of aquifers have the right to share water with "upstream" countries, Israel's large withdrawals act like a sponge, drying out supplies to the Jordanians.

On the other side of Israel, in the Gaza Strip, the situation is even worse. Individuals living in Gaza get most of their water out of the small aquifer underneath their land. Unfortunately, water is being pumped out of that aquifer twice as fast as it is replenished. As a result, seawater has flowed in, contaminating the aquifer. The water is so saline that using it for irrigation kills citrus trees. Because the Israelis do not share their water with the Gazans, they have no interest in protecting the aquifer, and so the Gazans continue to deplete and destroy it ("As Thick as Blood" 1995).

Israel and Jordan both face limited and shared supplies of fresh water. Jordan relies on water from two main sources: the Jordan River and one of its tributaries, the Yarmuk River. The potential volatility of water issues was recognized in the 1950s when President Eisenhower sent an envoy to attempt to devise a plan for sharing the meager water supplies between Israel, Jordan, Syria, and Lebanon. Though they agreed in principle, the four countries could not agree on allocation rules, and independent development proceeded.

Israel first completed a pipeline project, called the National Water Carrier, which channeled water from the Sea of Galilee to the Negev desert. This enabled Israel to expand irrigated agricultural production greatly but significantly reduced flows in the Southern Jordan River. Then, in the 1976 war, Israel captured almost the entire Jordan River Basin. In that same year, Israel also destroyed the site of a joint Jordanian-Syrian dam on the Yarmuk River. Development of new projects has been stymied by an inability to obtain loan funds. In the meantime, small diversions completed in Syria have further reduced water availability in Jordan.

Because these countries have the least water in a water-poor region and because the populations of both are increasing rapidly, both nations face more severe allocation issues in the future. Israel, for example, has pioneered drip irrigation systems that over the past 20 years have doubled agricultural output with the same amount of water. Israel has also developed systems to recycle urban wastewater for agricultural use. International cooperation between these countries remains limited, even though both might benefit. One possibility is the construction of a desalinization plant, jointly funded by Israel and Jordan. This idea has languished, however, partly because of its cost and partly because of the historic enmity between the countries.

Central Europe

Until the political upheaval in the late 1980s, there was little discussion of environmental quality degradation in the communist countries of eastern Europe.[29] Now, with the veil of secrecy parted, the intense level of water and air quality degradation has become widely realized. Most of the region's rivers and lakes contain levels of pollutants far above international standards, posing both health threats to individuals who rely on those rivers and lakes for drinking water supplies and an economic threat to downstream fisheries, such as those in the Baltic and Black seas.

At the same time that the threat posed by this pollution has become better known, the resources to combat it have declined. The transformation to market-based

---

[29]This section draws on the work of Paulsen and Somlyody (1993).

economies is proceeding slowly and painfully. There have been declines in industrial and agricultural output, accompanied by declines in living standards. The financial resources to install state-of-the-art water treatment facilities simply do not exist. One solution would be to delay any action until the economies are rebuilt. As the region's economies improve, more money should become available for investment in water treatment facilities. Furthermore, delay will result in more of the region's uncompetitive industries failing, obviating the need to address pollutant discharges from those industries.

The problem with this sort of strategy is that, while some of the industrial sources of pollution may disappear, there will still be an increasing demand for sewage treatment facilities as more households and businesses are connected to the existing treatment infrastructure. And consumers in these countries, with a newfound ability to speak their minds, may demand that action be taken sooner rather than later.

One alternative to delaying investments in new water treatment facilities would be to implement policies that required sewage treatment discharges to be reduced to European Union (EU) standards. The problem with this approach is, again, financial. The costs of such policies would likely be more than the new governments would be willing to pay, given the per capita costs of doing so. These costs are shown in Table 20.2, along with some comparison values for the United States. As the table shows, the per capita cost of meeting EU standards is quite high. In Bulgaria, for example, the cost is almost five times the per capita GDP! Furthermore, industrial production in these countries plummeted between 1990 and 1992, further reducing the countries' wealth.

Paulsen (1993) suggests an alternate strategy: focus on the most cost-effective investments to improve water quality. To do this, he suggests examining the behavior of pollutants in river basins. He notes that first, pollutants move downstream and thus water quality will be higher upstream. Second, "conventional" water pollutants, such as nitrogen and phosphorus (common in the runoff from agricultural

TABLE 20.2   COSTS TO IMPROVE WATER QUALITY IN CENTRAL AND EASTERN EUROPE

Country	1992 Population (millions)	1992 GDP (billions of dollars)	1992 Per Capita GDP (dollars)	1992 Per Capita Cost to Meet EU Standards (dollars)	Percentage Change in Industrial Production, 1990–1992
Bulgaria	8.47	6.9	815	3,755	−54
Former Czechoslovakia	15.66	36.1	2,305	4,927	−40
Hungary	10.30	35.5	3,446	2,116	−32
Poland	38.30	72.6	1,895	1,230	−32
Romania	23.20	14.2	610	1,422	−54
United States	260.0	5,600.0	21,500	—	+5

Sources: Paulsen and Somlyody (1993); *Statistical Abstract of the United States* (1993).

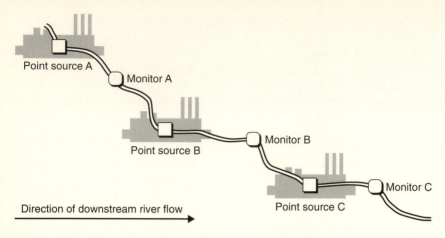

Figure 20.6 Policies to Reduce Point Source Pollution

fertilizers), either decay naturally or settle out of the water column and enter into riverbottom sediments.

The basic idea of the suggested strategy is to control the point sources that have the largest measurable impacts and are the cheapest to control. For example, suppose that there are three water quality monitors along a river and three point sources of pollution directly upstream of each monitor, as shown in Figure 20.6. Suppose further that water quality is worst at monitoring station A. It will make more sense, all else being equal, to reduce discharges from point source A than reducing downstream point sources. If, conversely the worst water quality was measured farthest downstream at monitoring station C, reductions from all of the upstream point sources will improve water quality, but improvement at point source C will likely result in the greatest improvement in water quality because many pollutants discharged farther upstream will have decayed or settled to the bottom by the time they reach monitoring station C.

Case Study of the Nitra River Basin   Paulsen and Solmyody (1993) studied this approach for the Nitra River Basin, which is located in a heavily industrialized area of the Slovak Republic. Their study focused on measurements of the concentrations of dissolved oxygen, which are often used as a broad measure of water quality. The lower the levels of dissolved oxygen, the less likely that aquatic life such as fish will survive and the less healthy the aquatic ecosystem. They considered four alternative policies. The first alternative was a do-nothing policy. This would maintain dissolved oxygen levels in the Nitra River Basin of 0.7 mg/l. The second alternative would be to install the best available control technology (BACT). This would raise dissolved oxygen concentrations almost tenfold, to about

TABLE 20.3   COMPARISON OF COSTS OF INCREASING DISSOLVED OXYGEN LEVELS IN THE NITRA RIVER BASIN

Policy	Minimum Concentration of Dissolved Oxygen (milligrams per liter)	Annual Cost (millions of U.S. dollars)	Percentage of Cost of BACT policy
Do nothing	0.7	0.0	—
BACT	6.9	14.4	100
Least cost I	4.0	2.8	19
Least cost II	6.0	6.6	46

Source: Paulsen and Solmyody (1993).

7 mg/l. A third policy would be to install sufficient control measures to raise the levels to at least 4 mg/l, the minimum necessary for fish and many other types of aquatic life. The last alternative would be to install measures that would raise dissolved oxygen levels to at least 6 mg/l. Paulsen and Solmyody estimated the costs of implementing these policies, as shown in Table 20.3.

Both of the least-cost policies would substantially improve dissolved oxygen levels over the base do-nothing case. Least-cost policy II, for example, would achieve dissolved oxygen levels 80 percent as high as those with the BACT measures, but at less than 50 percent of the cost. Similarly, least-cost policy II would achieve dissolved oxygen levels slightly over half those with BACT, but at less than 20 percent of the cost. Though it is not clear which of the least-cost policies would be preferable, both would improve water quality significantly at a much lower cost than the BACT policy. Despite the prevalence of adoption of BACT policies in the West, however, Paulsen (1993) believes that the severe resource constraints in the Eastern Bloc countries will make such cost-effective policies quite attractive. Of course, because more European countries are adopting U.S. water quality standards, the BACT policies may ultimately be selected.

CHAPTER SUMMARY

In this chapter, we have begun examining transboundary pollution and resource allocation issues by focusing on localized impacts. We began with a presentation of the theory of transnational pollution and examined several policy options that could be considered. Next we considered several case studies of pollution and resource allocation involving the United States and its neighbors Canada and Mexico, Europe, and the Middle East. All of the examples point to the importance and difficulty of achieving cooperative solutions. This seems especially true in the Middle East, where resource allocation issues have proved to be yet another destabilizing factor in that volatile region. In the next chapter, we take up transboundary pollution that is global in nature, examining the problems of ozone depletion and global warming.

CHAPTER REVIEW

Economic Concepts and Tools

- The root causes of transboundary pollution are no different from the cause of pollution within a single country.
- In noncooperative situations, a tariff can be thought of as the international trade equivalent of a tax on output, although a system of tariffs and taxes will not lead to a internationally optimal allocation of resources. Reaching an optimal solution requires cooperation between countries, as well as optimal regulation within each.
- Tariffs do not directly affect the price of the good in the exporting country; the price of the good will be lower than if the optimal tax were directly placed on producers.
- Because tariffs imposed by importing countries reflect only the damage caused in those countries, consumers in the importing countries will pay a price for the good that is lower than the true social cost.

Policy Issues

- International environmental issues introduce additional complexities, as environmental regulations often differ between countries. Noncooperative situations will require second-best solutions.
- To be effective, a country affected by transboundary pollution resulting from the production of a good must import that good. And the "victim" country must import sufficient quantities of the good in question to be able to influence the market price and hence production of the good.
- An international emissions tax on a pollutant, which equaled the sum of all of the marginal damage imposed on different countries, could achieve a Pareto-optimal solution. Unfortunately, no world body has enforcement powers for such a tax system. And it is unlikely that a polluter would willingly impose an emissions tax on itself for damage caused outside of its borders.
- A system of international tradable permits could turn the "polluter pays" principle on its head, since countries who were the victims of transboundary pollution would be required to purchase emissions permits from sources within the polluting country.

DISCUSSION QUESTIONS

1. Can you think of situations where it would be economically efficient for transboundary pollution to exist? Situations where transboundary pollution should be encouraged? Explain.
2. What are the equity implications of international tradable permits?

3. If polluters are unlikely to tax themselves in order to reduce transboundary pollution, what solutions are available to countries on the receiving end of the pollution? Which solutions are likely to be most effective?
4. "The way around transboundary pollution is to redefine international boundaries." Comment.
5. Are solutions to transboundary water pollution problems likely to be easier to solve than transboundary air pollution problems? Why or why not?

REFERENCES

"As Thick as Blood." 1995. *The Economist,* December 23, 1995, pp. 53–55.

Baumol, W., and W. Oates. 1988. *The Theory of Environmental Policy,* 2d ed. New York: Cambridge University Press.

Coase, R. 1960. "The Problem of Social Cost." *Journal of Law and Economics* 1(1): 1–44.

d'Arge, R., and A. Kneese. 1980. "State Liability for International Environmental Degradation." *Natural Resources Journal* (4)20: 430–445.

Dworsky, L. 1986. "The Great Lakes, 1955–1985." *Natural Resources Journal* 26: 291–336.

Frerichs, S., and W. Easter. 1990. "Regulation of Interbasin Transfers and Consumptive Uses from the Great Lakes." *Natural Resources Journal* 30(3): 561–579.

Furnish, D., and J. Ladman. 1975. "The Colorado River Salinity Agreement of 1973 and the Mexicali Valley." *Natural Resources Journal* 15(1): 83–107.

Gardner, R., and R. Young. 1988 "Assessing Strategies for Control of Irrigation-Induced Salinity in the Upper Colorado River Basin." *American Journal of Agricultural Economics* 70(1): 37–49.

Homer, P. 1985. "Lessons from the Great Lakes Water Quality Agreements." In *Acid Rain and Friendly Neighbors,* ed. J. Schmandt and H. Roderick. Durham, N.C.: Duke University Press.

Krutilla, J. 1967. *The Columbia River Treaty: The Economics of an International River Basin Development.* Baltimore: Johns Hopkins University Press.

Le Marquand, D. 1993. "The International Joint Commission and Changing Canada–United States Boundary Relations." *Natural Resources Journal* 33(1): 59–91.

Lesser, J. 1990. "Resale of the Columbia River Treaty Downstream Power Benefits: One Road from Here to There." *Natural Resources Journal* 30(3): 609–628.

Maize, K. 1993. "An Ill Name Blows No Good." *Electricity Journal* 6(8):11–14.

Martin, W. 1975. "Economic Magnitudes and Economic Alternatives in Lower Basin Use of Colorado River Water." *Natural Resources Journal* 15(1): 229–239.

Mullen, J., and F. Menz. 1985. "The Effect of Acidification Damages on the Economic Value of the Adirondack Fishery to New York Anglers." *American Journal of Agricultural Economics* 67(1): 112–119.

National Acid Precipitation Assessment Program (NAPAP). 1989. *1989 Annual Report to the President and Congress.* Washington, D.C.: NAPAP.

Northwest Power Planning Council. 1990. *Columbia Basin Fish and Wildlife Plan.* Portland, Oreg.: Northwest Power Planning Council.

Paulsen, C. 1993. *Policies for Water Quality Management in Central and Eastern Europe.* Discussion Paper No. 20. Washington, D.C.: Resources for the Future.

Paulsen, C., and L. Somlyody. 1993. *Cost-Effective Water Quality Management Strategies in Central and Eastern Europe.* Discussion Paper No. 21. Washington, D.C.: Resources for the Future.

Pearce, D., and A. Markandya. 1989. *Environmental Policy Benefits: Monetary Valuation.* Paris: Organization for Economic Cooperation and Development.

Pearce, D., and R. Turner. 1990. *Economics of Natural Resources and the Environment.* Baltimore: Johns Hopkins University Press.

Reisner, M. 1993. *Cadillac Desert,* rev. ed. New York: Viking Penguin.

Sadler, B. 1986. "The Management of Canada–U.S. Boundary Waters: Retrospect and Prospect." *Natural Resources Journal* 26(3): 359–376.

Scott, A. 1986. "The Canadian-American Problem of Acid Rain." *Natural Resources Journal* 26(3): 337–358.

Siebert, H. 1992. *Economics of the Environment: Theory and Policy.* New York: Springer-Verlag.

Swainson, N. 1986. "The Columbia River Treaty: Where Do We Go from Here?" *Natural Resources Journal* 26: 243–259.

Szekely, A. 1993. "Emerging Boundary Environmental Challenges and Institutional Issues: Mexico and the United States." *Natural Resources Journal* 33(1): 33–46.

Tamargo, F., and R. Young. 1975. "International External Diseconomies: The Colorado River Salinity Problem in Mexico." *Natural Resources Journal* 15(1): 77–89.

U.S. Bureau of Reclamation. 1980. *Colorado River Salinity: Economic Impacts on Agriculture, Municipal, and Industrial Users.* Denver: Colorado River Quality Office.

Vesilind, P. 1993. "Water: The Middle East's Critical Resource." *National Geographic,* May 1993, pp. 38–70.

CHAPTER 21

INTERNATIONAL ENVIRONMENTAL AND RESOURCE ISSUES II: GLOBAL EFFECTS

INTRODUCTION

In Chapter 20, we considered policies and examples of transboundary pollution whose effects are localized, such as upstream pollution affecting downstream users. In this chapter, we consider transboundary pollution that has global impacts, pollutants that affect what can be called the *global commons*. Specifically, we consider two major and controversial environmental issues: the depletion of the earth's ozone layer because of emissions of chlorofluorocarbons and the risk of global climate change because of increased carbon dioxide emissions.

We will begin with a discussion of ozone depletion. The cause and the effects have been fairly well established, primarily through the observance of "holes" in the ozone layer, and policies are in place to address this issue, although it is too soon to tell when these policies will have a measurable impact.

The second issue, global climate change, is far more controversial, and we devote the majority of the chapter to it. Rather than reaching conclusions as to the benefits and costs of specific global climate change policies, we approach the issue as an extended case study from the vantage point of policymakers who are attempting to make decisions with incomplete information. This approach serves two purposes. First, it demonstrates how policymakers must act in the real world. They will never have complete information yet will be called on to make decisions, some with potentially far-reaching consequences. Second, taking this approach will (we hope) reduce future readers' possible puzzlement at the "misinformation" contained in this chapter in light of newer information that will emerge about global climate change. We write this chapter from the vantage point of 1996, and neither theorists nor practicing scientists can incorporate information from discoveries not yet made. No doubt, research will continue to improve our understanding of the earth's climate mechanisms, which will reduce the uncertainty associated with the timing and the magnitude of global climate change in the coming years. Unfortunately, policymakers cannot always wait for more information; they must make decisions in the presence of uncertainty. In some cases, policymakers will conclude that it is better to wait for more information; in others, they will decide that despite the uncertainty, action is warranted.

CHLOROFLUOROCARBONS AND OZONE DEPLETION

Ozone depletion can be a confusing topic because at ground level, ozone is a pollutant that is linked to respiratory irritation and agricultural damage. In the stratosphere, which is the layer of the earth's atmosphere that extends between 6 and 30 miles above the surface of the earth, small amounts of ozone absorb much of the harmful ultraviolet radiation from the sun. By absorbing ultraviolet radiation, stratospheric ozone protects plants and animals. In addition, ozone plays a role in regulating the temperature of the earth by absorbing infrared radiation from the sun.

Certain gases can react chemically with ozone and break it down. One class of these chemicals, called chlorofluorocarbons (CFCs), has been implicated in the breakdown of the ozone layer in two ways. First, CFCs help punch "holes" in the ozone layer, and second, CFCs contribute to an overall reduction, or thinning, of the ozone layer. With both effects, more of the sun's ultraviolet radiation reaches the earth's surface. In humans, the major effect of higher levels of ultraviolet radiation is a higher incidence of skin cancer. In addition, higher levels of ultraviolet radiation reduce plant growth rates and may cause cancers in some animals.

CFCs are a stable class of compounds that have been in widespread use for more than half a century. One major use has been as propellants for such things as aerosol cans. CFCs can be easily substituted in these uses and now generally are. In addition, CFCs have been widely used for refrigeration, in foam packaging for cushioning and insulation, as industrial solvents to clean metals such as that used in the manufacture of computer equipment, and in air conditioning for automobiles and commercial buildings.

The hazards of CFCs were recognized some years ago. In 1978, the EPA banned the production and use of CFCs for aerosol propellants that fall under the Toxic Substances Control Act. This ban was relatively easy to achieve, as there were many good substitutes for CFCs that could be used as aerosol propellants. Because other, primarily industrial, uses had fewer available substitutes, however, the EPA undertook a study of alternative policy tools that could be used to restrict CFC production and use (see Palmer et al. 1980). The results of this study indicat-

---

ANOTHER TYPE OF INCENTIVE: REFRIGERATORS AND GOLDEN CARROTS

Refrigerators have become far more energy-efficient in the past decade. Since the passage of the first national energy efficiency standards in 1983, the average refrigerator's use of electricity has been cut in half. One reason has been the use of better types of insulation. Unfortunately, that insulation has always relied on CFCs. To address this dilemma, the EPA instituted a "golden carrot" contest. A $30 million prize was to be awarded to the manufacturer of a refrigerator using 20 percent less energy than the amount allowed under the 1993 standards *and* not using any CFCs.

The contest represented a change from the usual regulatory burden by offering a positive incentive for efficiency rather than punishment for failing to meet certain standards. The contest was eagerly embraced by the industry and funded in part by U.S. electric utilities. In late 1993, the EPA named Whirlpool Corporation the winner of the contest, and the refrigerators became commercially available in 1995.

---

ed that a system of tradable permits would be the most cost-effective method to reduce total CFC production. The EPA adopted such a system in 1988.

International action was also taken to reduce CFC production and use. Responding to the increasing evidence of ozone depletion and the formation of ozone "holes" over Antarctica, 24 nations signed the Montreal Protocol in 1988. Under the protocol, signing nations agreed to reduce overall production of CFCs by 50 percent from 1986 levels within 12 years. Soon after the accord was signed, however, additional scientific evidence indicated that the deterioration of the ozone layer was progressing faster than anticipated. As a result, 59 nations signed a new, more restrictive agreement in 1990. This agreement calls for the complete elimination of CFCs and related *halons*, or HCFCs, by the end of the century. It also added two additional ozone-destroying chemicals, carbon tetrachloride (a solvent used for dry cleaning) and methyl chloroform (a solvent used for degreasing in industrial processes), which are scheduled for elimination in 2000 and 2005, respectively. The agreement also provides for a fund of $240 million to help developing countries convert to less harmful CFC substitutes. This fund will help sustain economic growth in developing countries by subsidizing the switch to the more expensive substitutes.

Responding to the requirements of the original agreement, in 1988 the U.S. EPA issued regulations establishing a tradable permit system of production allowances, based on 1986 levels of production. Each major producer and consumer of CFCs was allocated 100 percent of its 1986 baseline, with the allowances declining over time down to zero, as agreed to under the Montreal Protocol. The allowances are tradable between producers and consumers, encouraging more efficient use of existing CFC stocks, much as tradable emissions permits for air pollutants like sulfur dioxide have reduced the cost of meeting overall air quality goals. In addition, because the demand for CFCs was quite inelastic owing to the lack of substitutes, the EPA imposed an excise tax on producers and users of CFCs. This purpose of the tax was to reduce "windfall" profits from the sale of increasingly restricted supplies of CFCs, as well as to further encourage the switch to non-CFC substitutes.

GLOBAL CLIMATE CHANGE

Many researchers are convinced that rapidly increasing levels of emissions of certain gases are causing the earth's climate to change more rapidly than ever before. This, it is believed, may lead to significant changes in the ecosystem, with detrimental effects on plant and animal life. As a result, there have been calls for nations to reduce their emissions of so called greenhouse gases and better preserve greenhouse gas "sinks," such as forests. We first summarize the debate over global climate change, briefly reviewing the basic physics in general and the role of carbon dioxide in particular. We note that the problem of greatest possible concern is not climate change in itself, for the earth's climate has changed throughout its history, but rather the *rate* of climate change. Of course, we are not climatologists and are qualified neither to assess the scientific accuracy of the available climate change models nor to validate those models' conclusions. But we can provide a survey of the debates over the findings that have appeared in the literature to date, no doubt many of which will change as new evidence comes to light. We also summarize the effects—both positive and negative—that have been predicted should global warming occur.

Despite the collective uncertainty about predicted impacts, it is possible to discuss policy issues associated with global warming and to develop rational policy responses. In fact, the very uncertainty surrounding global climate change provides an excellent opportunity for a discussion of policy alternatives. We believe that the issue is best examined in the context of intergenerational equity, rather than strictly within the confines of economic efficiency. In our view, the heart of the global warming policy debate centers on potential transfers of wealth between the present and the future, owing to the potential welfare impacts of alternative policies on the current generation. Before cogent policies can be adopted, society must determine whether increased emissions of greenhouse gases, and the climatic changes they may bring, are "unfair" to future generations.

If future generations are made worse off because of higher emissions of greenhouse gases or if there is significant *risk* that they will be worse off, it makes sense to investigate policies designed to reduce future unfairness. Because of the risks involved, policymakers may believe, on the one hand, that there are sufficient equity reasons to impose some form of carbon tax, as well as to develop other nonenergy policies so as to reduce future risks. On the other hand, policymakers must grapple with the benefits from delaying implementation of policies designed to reduce greenhouse gas emissions in the form of greater scientific certainty or lower-cost technological solutions. In other words, policy actions taken today may

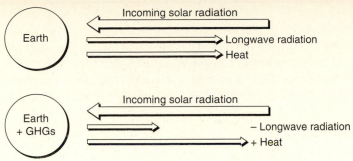

Figure 21.1   Diagrammatic Representation of Radiative Balance

lead to irreversible actions in their own right, much as irreversible impacts on the climate may occur if no action is taken (Dixit and Pindyck 1994).

The Greenhouse Effect: What Is It?

Despite the sense of calamity often associated with the "greenhouse effect" and emissions of carbon dioxide and other gases, the existence of life on earth depends on precisely that effect.[1] The earth's climate is driven by a multitude of factors; perhaps the most basic is the amount of energy the earth receives from the sun. About 30 percent of that energy is immediately reflected back into space by the atmosphere and by the earth itself. The remainder is absorbed by the atmosphere, landmasses, the oceans, and biomass such as trees.

In the long run, the energy absorbed from the incoming solar radiation must be balanced by the radiation reemitted by the earth and its atmosphere. The amount reemitted depends on temperature. The temperature of the earth adjusts until the outgoing radiation, called *longwave radiation,* at the top of the atmosphere balances the incoming solar radiation (Houghton, Jenkins, and Ephraums 1990). This is referred to as *radiative balance.*

Longwave radiation is absorbed by certain trace gases in the atmosphere, called greenhouse gases (GHGs), which reduce the amount of outgoing, or *reflected,* radiation. As the concentration of any one of those gases is increased, more of the longwave radiation is absorbed. To maintain the radiative balance, the increase in absorbed radiation must be compensated by increased emissions elsewhere in the spectrum.[2] These emissions are increased by higher temperatures. Thus increases in GHGs are accompanied by increases in temperatures to maintain the radiative balance, as shown in Figure 21.1.

---

[1]Books and articles on global warming and the greenhouse effect are numerous. Good summaries can be found in OTA (1991), Houghton et al. (1996), and references cited therein. See also Solow (1991).
[2]An analogy is a bucket with a hole in it that is being continuously filled with water. If the flow of water into the bucket is increased, the size of the hole must be made larger to prevent the bucket from overflowing. In this analogy, the bucket is "filled" with incoming solar radiation and is drained by the "hole" created by the reflected longwave radiation.

Another way to look at this is to consider the effects of higher GHG concentrations on surface temperatures. As GHG concentrations increase, more radiation is reflected downward to the earth's surface, resulting in warmer surface temperatures. As those temperatures increase, more energy is transferred to the atmosphere, causing it to heat up and further increase radiation to the surface until the radiative balance is restored. This process of increased atmospheric *opacity* is called the greenhouse effect because the effect is similar to what occurs in a greenhouse. Were it not for this effect, surface temperatures on our planet would be far colder, perhaps by 30 to 35 degrees Celsius (54 to 63 degrees Fahrenheit), making life as we know it impossible.

There are several GHGs, including water vapor (H_2O), carbon dioxide (CO_2), nitrous oxide (N_2O), methane (CH_4), and chlorofluorocarbons (CFC-11, CFC-12). Water vapor, which makes up about 1 percent of the atmosphere, is the most important greenhouse gas in terms of its absorption of solar energy. With the exception of H_2O, however, all or part of the other GHGs are produced wholly or partly by human activities. These GHGs are sometimes referred to as *anthropogenic* GHGs. Unlike the other anthropogenic GHGs, concentrations of CFC-11 and CFC-12 are entirely the result of human activities.[3]

The most important anthropogenic GHG is CO_2, with an atmospheric concentration of 0.04 percent. The amount of CO_2 in the atmosphere changes each year, in part because of human activities but primarily because of natural exchanges with the oceans, plants, and soil.

The earth's climate has also changed throughout its history, varying between periods much warmer than today and ice ages when global temperatures have been colder. This underlying trend of climate change still exists. Variations in atmospheric, surface, and water temperatures occur because of complex interactions (e.g., El Niño) that are not yet fully understood.[4] Despite these variations, however, over time a balance has been maintained between incoming and reemitted solar energy.

The basic physics associated with GHGs are not disputed. Scientists agree that GHGs trap incoming solar radiation. What is still not clearly understood are the precise *linkages* between changes in atmospheric concentrations of GHGs and overall temperature changes. There are also gaps in our understanding of all of the sources and the sinks of GHGs. Estimates of CO_2 emissions, for example, appear to exceed intake of CO_2 by the atmosphere and the oceans. However, because there must be a net balance to maintain equilibrium of the solar radiation budget, there must be additional sinks that are not fully understood at this time.

Rates of Change of Greenhouse Gas Concentrations

As we mentioned, human activity has added an additional variable into the complex equation affecting climate. Combustion of large quantities of fossil fuels, deforestation, and other human activities have contributed to increased concen-

[3]See the discussion of CFCs and the Montreal Protocol earlier in this chapter.
[4]Recent evidence suggests that the earth has gone through many periods of rapid climate change and that climatic stability is the exception rather than the norm.

trations of GHGs over time, most noticeably in the past century. Ambient atmospheric concentrations of CO_2, for example, have increased from around 280 parts per million (ppm) in the year 1800 to about 350 ppm in 1990 (IPPC 1990). The rate of increase appears to have accelerated in the second half of the twentieth century, bringing CO_2 to levels that have never been experienced previously.[5]

At issue are the linkages between concentrations of greenhouse gases and average temperatures. The concern is that if atmospheric concentrations of CO_2 and other GHGs continue to increase because of human activities, the climate system will be pushed beyond its "normal" rate of change, with possibly disastrous consequences. However, the impacts from these increased concentrations have been disputed vigorously.

To examine the effects of changes in GHG concentrations, it is important to distinguish between instantaneous changes in concentrations and the effects those increased concentrations will have over time. The ability of any GHG to affect the radiative properties of the atmosphere depends on its own radiative properties (how strongly and at what wavelengths it absorbs longwave radiation) and its lifetime in the atmosphere. All other things being equal, a onetime emission of a GHG will contribute more to warming the longer its lifetime in the atmosphere. Thus a GHG that is a better reflector of longwave radiation may contribute less to future overall temperature increases than a poorer reflector if it breaks down in the atmosphere more quickly.

To account for both reflective ability, called *radiative forcing,* and lifetime, Lashof and Ahuja (1990) developed a measure that has since been widely adopted. Called the *global warming potential* (GWP), it is defined as the radiative effect over a fixed time period, relative to that of CO_2, for a unit of mass of a greenhouse gas. CO_2 is the least effective greenhouse gas in terms of its radiative capabilities, and CFCs are the most effective. However, atmospheric concentrations of CO_2 are so much larger than the other anthropogenic GHGs that it has the largest greenhouse effect.[6]

Estimated Magnitudes of Global Temperature Change

Estimating changes in the radiative properties of the atmosphere because of changes in concentrations of GHGs is relatively straightforward (Solow 1991). The difficulty lies in translating these radiative changes into temperature changes in the atmosphere and on the earth's surface. Several types of models are used to predict global temperature and climate change. These are essentially sets of mathematical equations that describe the underlying physical processes that affect climate. Specifically, these models estimate climate responses because of changes in incoming solar radiation, movements of large masses of air, evaporation and condensation of water vapor, and many other factors. All of these variables interact. That is

---

[5]Historic atmospheric carbon dioxide levels have been estimated using ice core samples. See Houghton et al. (1996).

[6]Calculated GWPs can be found in Solow (1991) or Houghton et al. (1996).

why modeling climate change, even if only one of the many variables changes, can be quite complex.

The most detailed climate change models are called *general circulation models* (GCMs). These models partition the earth's atmosphere into sections or "cells." These cells are several hundred miles across and several miles deep and are stacked like blocks until they extend 20 miles into the atmosphere. For each cell, all of the mathematical equations predicting the climate are solved for each time period. As a result, predictions of variables such as temperature and wind speed are developed by solving the models many times over.

The limitations of these models are readily apparent. Because their resolution is only several hundred miles, predicted impacts may ignore climatic variations that occur on a smaller scale, which could in turn affect the overall predictions of climate change derived from the models. Thus GCMs may mask important climatic relationships that occur on a smaller scale than is modeled.

Another issue is the empirical relationships themselves. GCMs rely on empirical relationships that have been previously observed. For example, the formation of clouds because of changes in atmospheric temperature and humidity may be modeled on the basis of observed correlations between cloud formation and other climate variables. Thus modelers rely on empirical data collected in the past to develop theoretical models that predict impacts in the future. The problem with such empirically based relationships is that they may hold true only for the current conditions that are observed. If the relationships do not hold under other conditions, predictions of climate change based on them will be erroneous.[7] Unfortunately, despite great advances in computing ability, GCMs are still limited in their resolution and scope.

Using GCMs, predicted temperature changes from a doubling of preindustrial levels of CO_2 have been developed. Estimates obtained from many of these models indicate that the equilibrium warming that would occur is between a modest 1.5 and a scorching 21.5 degrees Celsius (Houghton, Jenkins, and Ephraums 1990). The uncertainty exists for several reasons. First, there is uncertainty about *feedback* effects. These are processes that occur in response to initial warming and act either to dampen or to amplify further warming. The lowest estimate (1.5 degrees) reflects only direct impacts, with little or no amplification from feedback (OTA 1991). The upper end (21.5 degrees) includes feedback effects that are estimated to triple the initial heat-trapping impact.

If temperatures warm, for example, melting snow and ice will tend to reduce the amount of reflected solar radiation, further exacerbating warming because more heat is absorbed. Current models indicate that snow and ice melting would increase warming by only 10 to 20 percent. However, the models do indicate that the feedback would be far stronger in higher latitudes, especially in winter (Ramanathan 1988). So feedback effects may not be uniformly additive. In addi-

---

[7]The problem occurs because the models may be used to predict changes outside the range of the sample data. Climatic relationships that are observed to hold and used as the basis of modeling may not hold if the climate differs from observed conditions in any way.

tion, there is some speculation that cloud formation will be increased by green-house warming, which may result in smaller overall temperature increases and lower overall feedback effects (Ramanathan 1988).

Time Lags Between Changes in Concentrations and Temperatures

The models that have been used to estimate impacts from a doubling of CO_2 concentrations have generally assumed *instantaneous* doubling. This is unrealistic; CO_2 concentrations have increased gradually over time. Furthermore, there is likely to be a time lag between emissions of GHGs and changes in temperatures. There are several reasons for this lag. First, the earth's oceans have an enormous capacity to store heat. The more heat the oceans absorb, the longer warming in the atmosphere is delayed. Second, there is a natural variability in the earth's climate that may mask any changes specifically from greenhouse gas emissions.

The time lag between emissions and temperature changes may be the reason for some of the current controversy over the accuracy of temperature change forecasts, both of predicted future changes and those that have occurred in the past century. Recent estimates suggest that mean global temperatures have increased between 0.5–1.1 °C over the last 100 years (Houghton et al. 1996). The predicted changes because of increasing emissions do not correlate perfectly with predicted temperature changes. In 1988, much interest about global warming was generated publicly by that summer's extreme heat and drought. Perhaps as a consequence, James Hansen (1988), then the director of NASA's Goddard Institute for Space Studies, testified before the U.S. Senate that of the 0.5 degree Celsius warming estimated to have occurred since 1880, most occurred before 1940. He also stated that average temperatures then fell until the mid-1970s and had increased since.

Reversing Climate Change

If it is determined that CO_2 and other GHGs *are* contributing to a significant increase in the rate of climate change, and *if* that change is found to be undesirable, then heat absorption must be slowed, CO_2 emissions must be reduced, or both. In both cases, positive actions would have to be taken. These might involve reducing usage of fossil fuels through efficiency improvements, development of better greenhouse gas controls so as to reduce atmospheric discharges, or "geo-engineering" to reduce the amount of incoming solar radiation that is absorbed. We discuss alternative policies later in this chapter.

Other Explanations for Global Warming

The key issue in such temperature debates is not whether the exact magnitude of the temperature change has been 0.5 degree or 1.0 degree but rather whether GCMs have the ability to predict temperature changes accurately on the basis of changes in greenhouse gas concentrations and to differentiate those predicted changes from the natural variability in climate. Indeed, estimates of natural variability in temperatures developed using ice core samples from Greenland show natural variations on the order of 2 degrees Celsius. It is therefore possible to attribute changes since the late 1800s to natural climatic phenomena. So even though there is little doubt that warming has occurred during the past century, there is still debate over the cause of the increase.

One recent explanation advanced for the temperature changes since the late 1800s is the change in solar luminosity (Kerr 1991; Friis-Christensen and Lassen 1991). According to this argument, there is a striking correlation between changes in solar luminosity—brought about by changes in the sun's magnetic activity—and changes in average global temperatures. This theory suggests that the sun controls climate changes on earth. Records of carbon-14 levels in tree rings (the isotope is a good indicator of solar magnetic activity) also correlate with climatic changes over the past 10,000 years, according to this theory. Finally, the "little ice age" that occurred during the 1700s is cited as evidence that temperature and solar activity are highly correlated.[8]

In one sense, arguments over changes in solar luminosity causing changes in temperatures seem silly. The sun is undoubtedly the final arbiter of the earth's climate. If solar luminosity changed by a large enough amount, the earth's temperature stabilization mechanisms would be overwhelmed, and the planet would become inhospitable to many forms of life. However, no theory is currently able to explain how the known variability in solar luminosity could produce temperature changes as large as those that have been observed in the past century (Cline 1992).

Despite the claims of this theory, an important empirical question remains: are the more recently observed environmental changes caused primarily by human activities or by the natural variability in solar luminosity? If human activities are overwhelming the natural variability in climate that has been caused in the past by changes in solar luminosity, then it makes sense to estimate the magnitude of those human-induced changes and determine whether they will act as positive or negative feedback to further climate change. So even if this theory is correct, there may still be sound reasons to develop policies addressing global climate change.

Potential Physical Impacts of Global Climate Change

A great many studies have attempted to assess the likely physical, economic, and social impacts of climate change.[9] Physical impacts, in addition to higher average temperatures, may include increases in sea levels, resulting in low-level flooding, loss of wetlands, and greater contamination of freshwater supplies; increased intensity of storms; variations in local climates, including localized increases and decreases in rainfall; and changes in biodiversity, because of habitat loss and inability to

---

[8]More recent research by Thomson (1995) casts doubt on the ability of the solar cycle hypothesis to explain the majority of observed temperature changes.

[9]For example, Adams and colleagues (1990) have predicted agricultural impacts in the United States. See also Watson, Zinyowera, and Moss (1996) for overall summaries of impacts, and references therein.

CLOUDED CRYSTAL BALLS

Although publication of the second IPCC assessment of climate change (Houghton et al. 1996) seems to have solidified the argument that global climate change is indeed occurring, the global warming debate still rages on, and not only for purely scientific reasons ("Stormy Weather Ahead" 1996).

In March 1996, a group of 24 scientists published a book called "The Global Warming Debate" (Emsley 1996) which argues that the IPCC's conclusions are less than a scientific certainty. Specifically, they argue that the evidence of global temperature increases presented in the IPCC report is unconvincing and skewed because of faulty data. These scientists suggest that the terrestial data of global temperature increases is skewed because the data have been collected primarily on land in richer countries. Instead, these scientists argue that satellite data, which have been available since around 1980, show no warming trend. Furthermore, this group argues, land-based temperature measurements in developed countries may be measuring the heat produced by industrial economies themselves, rather than underlying changes in the climate. The IPCC scientists respond that they have corrected for this and argue that the satellite temperature data collected has been unduly influenced by recent large volcanic eruptions in Mexico and the Philipines, which have spewed millions of tons of dust and sulfates that have cooled the atmosphere.

Still other scientists in the group of 24 criticize the IPCC results for less charitable reasons. They suggest that the IPCC has a vested interest in elevating fears of global climate change because doing so will maintain a strong flow of research dollars from governments. Not ones to shirk from mudslinging, some of the IPCC scientists counter that the authors of "The Global Warming Debate" have been funded by large, fossil-fuel lobbies.

Whether the criticism of the group or the response of the IPCC scientists are correct, the sniping reinforces the question of uncertainty and the development of a legitimate policy response. Unfortunately, it also reinforces the axiom that no issue is above debate at the lowest possible level.

adjust to rapid change. There could also be changes in river flows because of changing rain and snow patterns, which could affect water supplies and fish and wildlife habitats. Adverse health impacts also would be possible, especially if local drinking water supplies were contaminated.

The physical impacts that may arise from global climate change have generally been estimated by using the output data from GCMs. Not surprisingly, estimates of physical impacts, like those of temperature changes, vary considerably in their severity. These differences matter because one of the major issues is the ability of plants and animals to adapt to rapidly changing climate conditions. Because the primary concern is not climate change itself but rather the rate of climate change, it may be impossible for many species to survive in their current locations or migrate to new habitats. There is also concern about the timing of these effects: would ecosystems be significantly affected in 20 years, 50 years, or more? Cline

(1992) notes that many of the GCM studies arbitrarily double concentrations of CO_2, rather than focusing on impacts in the very long run, on the order of 250 to 300 years.

Data from historic climatological records indicate that many species were able to adapt to past climate change. Oak trees, for example, spread northward from the southeastern United States as glaciers receded after the last ice age, about 18,000 years ago. During that ice age, temperatures were about 5 degrees Celsius cooler than they are today. That temperature difference is roughly equal to the upper bound of currently forecast changes in mean global temperature from a doubling of CO_2 levels. The difference, however, is that the temperature increase took place over thousands of years, rather than during the 100 or so years predicted by some of the GCMs.

A number of potential effects of climate change have been predicted for the United States, including major impacts on forest migration, health, and composition; accelerated reductions in species biodiversity; increasing extinction of species; changes in marine and freshwater fisheries; loss of coastal wetlands because of rising sea levels; and changes in water quality and availability.

Potential Economic Impacts of Global Climate Change

The largest economic impacts that could result from these physical effects are the loss of agricultural lands, which could reduce supplies of agricultural products, increase food costs, and exacerbate famines;[10] the cost of additional investments for flood control systems to protect millions of individuals living in coastal and low-lying areas because of rising sea levels; and the cost to develop new water supplies, especially if rainfall patterns change significantly.

Much of the ongoing debate over climate change has arisen because of the ultimate economic impacts that may be imposed on countries that may be either unprepared or unwilling to address those impacts. If climate change meant only that we would use one less blanket in winter and drink an extra glass or two of lemonade in summer, there would undoubtedly be less uproar over the ultimate impacts. It is precisely the potentially catastrophic economic effects, however, and the costs of reducing those effects, that have focused so much attention on predictions of the physical impacts.[11]

Sea Level Rise   One physical impact often cited is the possibility of rising sea levels and the need either to increase construction of dikes and sea walls to prevent coastal flooding or to relocate coastal inhabitants to areas that will not be affected.

---

[10]Some authors, notably Kimball and colleagues (1993), argue that higher concentrations of carbon dioxide will enhance plant growth, thus increasing food supplies dramatically. These conclusions, however, may hold only if other factors, such as moisture levels, do not limit growth.

[11]This is not meant as a slight to the many moral and ethical issues that have been raised. Nevertheless, there are significant questions about the costs and benefits of reducing greenhouse gas emissions. Because many of these estimates are so large, however, policy discussions have often focused first on economic issues.

Estimates of sea level rise have generally ranged between 10 and 100 centimeters (approximately 4 to 40 inches) over the next century. The magnitude of losses is, not surprisingly, strongly correlated with estimates of the amount of sea level rise itself. Some models have estimated costs between \$30 and \$300 billion for shore protection in the United States, depending on whether sea levels rise 50 or 200 centimeters. Although several hundreds of billions of dollars over many years is a lot of money, it would be a manageably small fraction of the nation's GDP.

Of course, if sea levels rose, there would be worldwide consequences. For poorer countries, the costs of sea wall development might be prohibitive unless some sort of international aid program were established. If global climate change also led to greater storm intensity, more severe storm surges, and the like, the costs of sea wall development would be even higher. Low-lying countries, such as the Maldives, and countries with large coastal populations, such as Bangladesh, could suffer major adverse impacts because of higher sea levels and would be unlikely to have the resources to mitigate those impacts.

The only alternative to constructing sea walls and taking other shore protection measures would be to undertake the large-scale relocation of affected populations. There appear to be no estimates in the literature of the costs of such relocations of potentially affected populations that could be compared to estimates for sea wall construction. Nor would sea wall construction completely mitigate impacts associated with rising sea levels, as presumably it would be difficult to relocate affected plant and animal species. Furthermore, some estimates have shown greater losses of wetlands when densely populated areas are protected with sea walls. Lastly, estimates of the costs of population relocation, especially those that might have to occur on a large scale, must also be tempered by the many questions of equity that would invariably be raised.

Agricultural Impacts   Though there is little doubt that agriculture is sensitive to climate, the impacts of global climate change on agricultural production are still disputed. These disputes center around the potentially conflicting impacts on crop yields because of global warming, as well as other impacts (such as water availability) that may affect production. To the extent that global warming requires greater irrigation of crops, for example, there may be increased competition for scarce water supplies. If these water supplies are themselves affected, due perhaps to changes in rainfall patterns or in snowpacks, crop yields may be adversely affected (Adams et al. 1990; Watson, Zinyawera, and Moss 1996). There is also evidence, however, that increased CO_2 concentrations can enhance the growth rates of crops through CO_2 fertilization (Kimball et al. 1993), although the extent of this effect, if any, is uncertain. Global climate change could thus have a positive overall impact on agricultural production. To the extent that CO_2 leads to the loss of forests, the forest products industry may experience losses. But if CO_2 fertilization dominates forest loss or migration, forest yields could increase, providing overall economic benefits.

The distribution of benefits and costs is also likely to be an issue. Based on the results of GCM modeling, certain areas of the world do appear to become more agriculturally productive as global temperatures increase (Watson, Zinyowera, and Moss 1996). Many areas of the United States, however, are shown to become less productive. Thus the overall value of U.S. agricultural output could rise or fall (Adams et al. 1990). However, given inelastic demand for many agricultural products, increases in the value of output are consistent with *decreases* in total agricultural output.

Health and Biological Impacts   There could also be significant nonmarket impacts associated with global climate change. These include impacts on human health, loss of biodiversity and extinction of species, and loss of recreation opportunities. These nonmarket impacts are probably associated with the greatest degree of uncertainty. That may mean that they are the most important impacts to focus on or prevent, but it may also mean that they could be relatively small and unimportant.

For example, rising sea levels could contaminate freshwater supplies in many low-lying poor countries such as Bangladesh, or changes in rainfall patterns could exacerbate drought conditions in some African nations. In both cases, the results could be reduced water quality and greater incidence of waterborne diseases like cholera. Not only would there have to be investments in new water supplies, but there would also have to be additional investments in emergency health care.

Assessment of such impacts would have to go beyond monetary impacts to include equity, human rights, and the rights of nature.[12] For example, if sea level rise leads to inundation of the Maldives, relocating that country's population would entail significant cost. (A broader question is whether the rest of the world has the right to impose that type of cost on any sovereign nation.)

Other Affected Markets   Global temperature changes are also likely to have several types of energy impacts. First, the demand for energy, especially energy used for space heating and cooling, will be affected. (There will also be some effect on energy used for refrigeration and water heating.) Overall, heating demand will fall and cooling demand will increase. Estimates of overall energy demand impacts also vary significantly, from many billions of dollars down to about $1 billion annually (Nordhaus 1991a).

Energy impacts would not be limited solely to changes in demand. To the extent that hydroelectric generation is affected by changes in water availability, the costs of supplying electricity may increase. Lettenmaier and Sheer (1991), for example, used GCMs to develop estimates of changes in runoff patterns in the Sacramento–San Joaquin river basins. Their study showed that water runoff patterns would be significantly affected, resulting in smaller water deliveries because of limited water storage capabilities. Reduced water deliveries would also have a

---

[12]See, for example, Bruce, Lee, and Haites (1996).

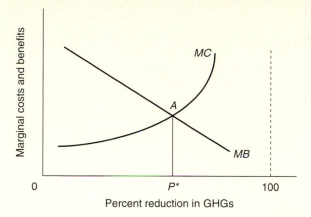

Figure 21.2   Hypothetical Marginal Cost and Benefits Schedules for GHG Abatement

secondary impact on the availability of water for irrigation purposes, thus affecting agricultural production.[13]

Estimates of Overall Economic Costs   Several attempts have been made by economists to determine the overall costs that could accrue to society because of global climate change. Most studies have used these estimates as the basis for determining reasonable strategies to address global climate change, much in the manner of a benefit-cost analysis of pollution reduction strategies (Bruce, Lee, and Haites 1996). In essence, the question that has been asked in these studies is whether the costs of GHG abatement, in terms of reduced levels of GDP, are less than the benefits from that abatement, in terms of avoided damages. In this framework, optimal control of greenhouse gas emissions can be deduced based on marginal cost (MC) and marginal benefit (MB) schedules, as shown in Figure 21.2.

In this framework, the optimal percentage reduction in GHG emissions would occur at point A, reflecting a P^* percent reduction. Beyond this level of reduction, the costs of further reductions exceed the benefits and should not be undertaken. Of course, it is well recognized that the MC and MB schedules are not known with anything approaching certainty.

Benefits of Greenhouse Gas Abatement   The benefits of greenhouse gas abatement would come in the form of avoided costs from excessive warming. If global climate change leads to reductions in agricultural productivity, decreased forestry, increased energy use, loss of wetlands because of sea level rise, construction

---

[13]One alternative would be to increase the amount of available reservoir storage. This would also entail its own costs. Lettenmaier and Sheer (1991) did not perform any sort of benefit-cost analysis on this alternative, however.

TABLE 21.1   ESTIMATES OF ANNUAL DAMAGE TO THE U.S. ECONOMY
RESULTING FROM A DOUBLING OF CO_2 EMISSIONS
(IN BILLIONS OF 1990 DOLLARS)

Sector	Damage[a]
Agriculture	17.5
Forest loss	3.3
Species loss	21.0+
Sea level rise	7.0
Increased energy demand	9.9
Water supplies	7.0
Human life	5.8
Air pollution	3.5+
Hurricanes	0.8
Migration	0.5
Other	**1.8+**
TOTAL	**61.6+**

[a]A + implies that the estimated damage is likely to be higher but of uncertain magnitude.
Source: Cline (1992).

of seawalls, and greater hurricane damage, the portion of those costs that could be avoided through policy actions that reduced GHG emissions would be a measure of policy benefits.

Most of the empirical models that have estimated "optimal" carbon taxes have done so by comparing the benefits of a carbon tax with the costs. The effects of a carbon tax on overall economic activity are estimated, and the feedback from the change in economic activity is then incorporated into estimates of the reduction in carbon emissions.[14]

Cline (1992) notes that Nordhaus's (1991b) study was the only one to place a value on the overall potential damage from global climate change. Nordhaus (1991b) concludes that even if the predictions about global climate change are true, the economic impacts could be relatively small. In a later study, however, he incorporates the effects of uncertainty, including the possibility of catastrophic damage (Nordhaus 1994).

Based on studies done for specific sectors, Cline (1992) provides an estimate of annual damage in the United States because of a doubling of CO_2 emissions. These are summarized in Table 21.1. Some of these studies used the methods we discussed in Chapters 11, 12, and 13 to determine damage estimates. Some estimates, such as agricultural losses, are based on changes in market prices and quantities; others, such as damage to human life, are based on contingent valuation studies. In still other studies (Nordhaus 1994), damage estimates were assumed to be some fraction of world GDP.

---

[14]Nordhaus (1994) contains a detailed explanation of his DICE (Dynamic Integrated Model of Climate and the Economy), which he uses to determine optimal carbon taxes.

In Table 21.1, the annual total economic loss is reported as $61.6 billion plus some unknown cost for additional value from species loss, losses from higher pollution levels, and loss of human amenity values.[15] Cline (1992) also concludes that over the very long term (250 years), damage due to global climate change could easily amount to as much as 6 percent of U.S. GDP.[16]

Costs of Greenhouse Gas Abatement   As Cline (1992) notes, research on the costs of GHG abatement (i.e., the marginal cost curve in Figure 21.2) has progressed much further than research on the marginal benefits. Numerous studies have attempted to identify the *costs* of abatement. These studies fall generally into two categories: *top-down* models and *bottom-up* models.

Top-down models usually begin with an overall model of the economy. In these models, goods and services in the economy are produced using inputs of land, labor, capital, and energy. Reductions in CO_2 emissions require some reduction in energy use or, more correctly, the availability of energy for use in production processes. If there are fixed amounts of the other inputs, economic theory predicts that reductions in energy availability will lead to reductions in production. The reduction in output can then be equated with the economic cost of increased CO_2 emissions. Nordhaus (1994) is an example of a top-down model.[17]

A reduction in CO_2 emissions can be accomplished by substituting less carbon-intensive fuels for more carbon-intensive ones; substituting labor and capital for energy; substituting less energy-intensive products for energy-intensive ones; and reducing deforestation.[18] These substitutions are assumed to impose costs on the economy not only because of the decline in total production from the use of less energy but also because of changing values for goods and services. Instead of purchasing desired product A, consumers will purchase more of product B, which is less energy-intensive. The overall loss of value is typically measured by reductions in GNP or GDP, although, as we discussed in Chapter 19, these can be poor measures of overall societal welfare.[19] The OPEC oil embargo showed that the substitution effect can be quite significant. As Jorgenson and Wilcoxen (1991) note, carbon emissions were no higher in 1987 than in 1972, despite an increase in GNP of 46 percent. Most of the top-down models ultimately derive carbon tax levels required to achieve the given reduction in emissions, based on the degree of substitutability in the models.

---

[15]Cline (1992) also develops some costs for warming over several hundred years, where he assumes that warming of 10 degrees Celsius would occur. His estimate of the associated annual costs is over $300 billion (in 1990 dollars).

[16]There are other studies as well. Several are summarized in Nordhaus (1991a).

[17]Nonmarket costs (species loss, loss of wetlands, etc.) can then be estimated as a function of the change in GDP, as was done by Nordhaus (1994).

[18]A reduction in CO_2 emissions could also be accomplished by reducing overall population, even if emissions per capita remained constant.

[19]As Cline (1992) notes, the Hicksian equivalent variation (see Chapter 3 for a definition) would provide a better welfare measure because it represents the increase in income that would be required to leave consumer no worse off than before the change occurred.

Unlike top-down models, bottom-up models examine reductions in CO_2 emissions by examining engineering changes. These models look at such items as changing from incandescent to fluorescent light bulbs, improved transportation efficiency, use of electric arc furnaces instead of blast furnaces for smelting purposes, and other engineering changes. Because bottom-up models by their nature do not examine the overall impacts of global climate change policies on the economy, we will focus our discussion on a review of major top-down model results.

Top-Down Estimates   Major top-down studies have been conducted by Manne and Richels (1992), Jorgenson and Wilcoxen (1991), Nordhaus (1994), Edmonds and Barnes (1991), Whalley and Wigle (1990), and the OECD (Burniaux et al. 1991). All of the studies that attempt to estimate GHG abatement strategy posit some model of economic growth and overall economic activity, then compare the "potential" level of growth in the absence of any abatement policies with the level of economic activity when policies are in place. This is shown in Figure 21.3.

In the absence of any abatement policies, *GDP* is predicted to grow along the path labeled *GDP.* If abatement policies are introduced, however, *GDP* is predicted to grow more slowly along path *GDP'.* The difference in any year T, $GDP(T) - GDP_a(T)$, equals the net reduction.

Manne and Richels (1992) investigate the costs of limiting CO_2 emissions in the United States at their 1990 levels through the year 2000, then gradually reducing emissions to 80 percent of the 1990 levels by 2020 and maintaining those levels thereafter. Their model combines a production function approach with process analysis of major industries. To achieve the levels of carbon emissions reduction, their model requires a carbon tax that gradually increases to $250 per ton of carbon, roughly equivalent to $30 per barrel of oil.

The Manne and Richels (1992) analysis indicates that the present value of costs imposed on the U.S. economy because of carbon emission restrictions could

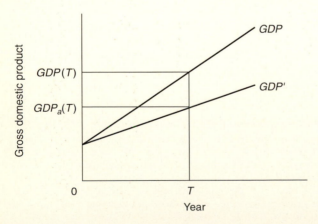

Figure 21.3   Time Path of *GDP* with and without GHG Abatement Policies

be between $0.8 and $3.6 trillion (in 1990 dollars), depending on the strategy used to reduce emissions. These losses translate into reductions in *GDP* of about 3 percent annually in the United States by the year 2030 and remain at about that level through the year 2100. *GDP* losses are higher in other areas of the world, with the highest occurring in China, a 10 percent annual *GDP* loss by the year 2100. The reason for the larger losses in China is that country's heavy reliance on coal for the foreseeable future and the difficulty of substituting other energy sources for coal.

Cline (1992) notes that the Manne and Richels model is limited because of the lack of modeling of trade, in both energy resources and products. Thus each country or region in their model maximizes production using internal resources. With the inclusion of trade possibilities, the costs of meeting the targeted emissions reductions would be expected to decrease, perhaps significantly.

Using his DICE model, Nordhaus (1994) estimates a sequence of optimal carbon taxes under uncertainty. He first examines cases in which there is perfect information, which he calls "learn, then act" (p. 176). In this version of the model, the optimal control rate of carbon emissions rises from about 9 percent in 1995 to just over 12 percent in 2045. The optimal carbon tax rises from $5.24 per ton in 1995 to $13.40 per ton in 2045 (expressed in 1989 dollars). Nordhaus then examines a more realistic case, which he terms "act, then learn." This case reflects the need to undertake policies (including a policy of doing nothing) before knowing the state of the world. In this case, society might enact a high carbon tax only to discover that the global climate change was a far less serious problem than originally thought, or conversely, society might do little only to discover that the impacts were catastrophic. Not surprisingly, the results indicate that more forceful actions are called for in the early years, when the likelihood of not knowing the true implications of global climate change are highest. Nordhaus's results indicate that the optimal carbon tax rises to about $12 per ton in 1995 and to around $26 per ton in 2020. Optimal control rates are also higher, almost 13 percent in 1995, but these rates rise little over the model period.

Jorgensen and Wilcoxen (1991) also investigate the costs of imposing alternate carbon taxes on the U.S. economy in order to achieve specific emissions targets. They investigate three targets: maintaining emissions at projected 2000 levels, maintaining them at 1990 levels, and maintaining them at 80 percent of 1990 levels. The researchers report that the overall impact on GNP would range from a 0.3 percent decline in the least stringent case (year 2000 emission levels) to a 1.6 percent decline in GNP at the most stringent restriction. Although the authors do not explicitly estimate the benefits that would accrue from these emissions reductions, they do urge that benefits be carefully considered before developing policies.

Whalley and Wigle (1990) developed a model to investigate the costs of reducing CO_2 emissions by 50 percent between 1990 and 2030. They hypothesized three different types of carbon tax: a tax on consumers, a tax on producers, and an internationally levied tax whose proceeds were redistributed in proportion to populations.

Their model shows that the carbon tax required to achieve the 50 percent emissions reduction would be about $440 per ton of carbon. The resulting economic losses would amount to about 21.2 percent, in terms of discounted worldwide GNP. This loss figure is quite high, which Cline (1992) attributes to the apparent lack of fossil fuel substitution allowed by their model.

The Organization for Economic Cooperation and Development (OECD) developed a model analyzing the period from 1990 to 2020 (Burniaux et al. 1991). In this model, the authors hypothesize a 20 percent reduction in emissions in the OECD countries and the former Soviet Union by 2010, with emissions remaining frozen at that level through 2020. Emissions in developing countries are permitted to increase somewhat, such that overall carbon emissions are frozen at their 1990 levels through 2020.

By 2020, the carbon tax required to achieve this overall freeze averages $215 per ton worldwide. This average masks wide variations, however. The model predicts a carbon tax of over $300 for OECD countries, but much smaller taxes in countries such as China and the former Soviet Union, primarily because of differences in fuel prices between the different regions modeled. The model predicts a reduction of global *GDP* of about 1.8 percent. Factoring in losses in producers' and consumers' surplus, the model estimates an overall average loss of 2.2 percent of household real income.

Edmonds and Barnes (1991) use an energy-carbon accounting framework instead of directly linking energy and the economy. This accounting is done at 25-year intervals between 1975 and 2100. The model divides the world into nine different regions and nine types of energy. Then it adjusts prices to achieve supply and demand equilibrium between all of the fuels within each region. The authors simulated the effects of imposing carbon taxes on the different energy markets and regions and found that a tax of $170 per ton of carbon was a "break point." Above that level of tax, emissions reductions were relatively small because above that tax level, coal is no longer used. (Thus the marginal cost of abatement curve rises steeply.) The authors also found that by increasing the tax to $250 per ton of carbon, world carbon emissions would be stabilized by the year 2050. The resulting loss in world *GDP* is estimated to be only about 0.9 percent in 2050.

Table 21.2 summarizes the levels of carbon emissions reduction from baseline emission levels, carbon tax requirement to achieve the reduction, and associated economic costs for the years 1990–2100.

Assessment of Economic Studies   The studies we have discussed (and others) show that mitigating global climate change would entail real costs. Imposition of different levels of carbon taxes, for example, would cause real losses in energy industries, which would translate into a reduction in *GDP*. It is not sufficient, however, to examine only the potential costs of GHG abatement. This is equivalent to identifying the *MC* schedule in Figure 21.2.

The studies we have discussed all base their estimates of *GDP* loss on the status quo. In other words, if actions to abate GHG emissions are taken, these studies estimate the loss of *GDP* that would occur relative to no emissions reduction. As Cairncross (1992) points out, however, many of these studies "do not allow for the possibility of nasty surprises . . . nor do they include the incidental environmental benefits that might flow from reducing the output of CO_2 from burning fossil fuels" (p. 18). Such benefits may be significant.

TABLE 21.2   ALTERNATIVE COST ESTIMATES FOR REDUCTIONS IN CARBON
EMISSIONS

Study	Year		
	1990	2025	2050
Manne and Richels (USA)			
Reduction in emissions (percent)	0	52	63
Associated carbon tax (dollars per ton)	0	375	250
GDP loss (percent)	0	3.2	3.3
Nordhaus (World)			
Reduction in emissions (percent)	0	18	41
Associated carbon tax (dollars per ton)	0	33	113
GDP loss (percent)	0	N.A.	N.A.
Jorgenson and Wilcoxen (USA)			
Reduction in emissions (percent)	0	31	36
Associated carbon tax (dollars per ton)	0	43	42
GDP loss (percent)	0	1.1	1.1
Whalley and Wigle (World)			
Reduction in emissions (percent)	0	50[a]	N.A.
Associated carbon tax (dollars per ton)	0	445[a]	N.A.
GDP loss (percent)	0	21.4[a]	N.A.
Burniaux et al./OECD (World)			
Reduction in emissions (percent)	0	−43[b]	N.A.
Associated carbon tax (dollars per ton)	0	215[b]	N.A.
GDP loss (percent)	0	2.2[b,c]	N.A.
Edmonds and Barnes (World)			
Reduction in emissions (percent)	0	−31	−56
Associated carbon tax (dollars per ton)	0	100	280
GDP loss (percent)	0	0.2	0.9

Note: N.A. = not available.
[a]1990–2030; estimate centered in 2010.
[b]In year 2020.
[c]Loss in household real income.
Source: Adapted from Cline (1992).

Estimates of *GDP* losses are of little use without considerations of the losses (if any) that would accrue in the absence of mitigation. These losses reflect, in part, the "nasty surprises" that might result from global climate change. Thus to be more useful, studies showing *GDP* losses should also clarify the losses that might arise from doing nothing. In that way, more theoretically consistent evaluations of policies, at least in the benefit-cost framework underlying these studies, can be developed.

Nordhaus's work (1991a, 1991b, 1994) goes further than most of the other models. He incorporates uncertainty explicitly and proposes an emissions reduction strategy based on identification of the *MB* schedule and therefore the benefits from GHG abatement. As a result, Nordhaus determines an "efficient" level of abatement, taking into account, to the extent possible, reductions in GDP that could occur were no abatement strategies adopted.

A final issue concerns tax revenues. We discussed how to use the revenues collected from an emissions charge in Chapter 7. We showed that the revenues collected would exceed the damage. Thus the issue of what to do with the money collected is nontrivial. As Nordhaus (1994) and others (Jaeger 1995) point out, one argument in favor of high carbon taxes is that the revenues collected can be used to reduce other taxes. Nordhaus terms this "revenue recycling." The idea is to use the revenues collected from a "good" carbon tax to reduce the deadweight loss "wedge" caused by "bad" taxes on consumption, labor, and capital. In essence, one can think of the general equilibrium issues raised by revenue recycling as a variant of the nonconvexity and second-best approaches we explained in Chapter 7.

Assuming revenue recycling in his DICE model, Nordhaus (1994) finds the results significant. In the first decade, the optimal tax rises from $5.24 per ton to $59 per ton. Thus concern about global climate change and a desire for a more efficient tax system justify a much larger carbon tax than could be justified on the basis of the climate change externality alone. As Nordhaus concludes, the "tail of revenue recycling would seem to wag the dog of climate-change policy" (p. 121).

Using a general equilibrium model for an economy, Jaeger (1995) examines the issue of revenue recycling in general. He finds, like Nordhaus, that imposing taxes directly on environmental waste services and then recycling the revenues to reduce the deadweight losses of other taxes is indeed beneficial. Unlike Nordhaus, however, Jaeger finds that the optimal tax in such a situation can be *either* higher or lower than the standard emissions charge solution we derived in Chapter 7.

Summary   There is little doubt that mitigation of GHG emissions may entail certain economic costs, but there also appears to be reason to believe that *not* mitigating GHG emissions may impose far more significant costs. Given the present state of scientific knowledge, the distribution of costs is significantly skewed, with a small probability of catastrophic economic and social costs. There may, however, also be a small probability of net economic and social benefits, although there appears to be less evidence that such benefits, if they come to pass, would be of the same order of magnitude.

The potential impacts from continued global climate change extend beyond economics. Estimates of reductions in world GDP are of interest, but they cannot completely capture the breadth of potential social costs, such as widespread dislocation and migration. Thus in addition to economic efficiency, there appears to be reason to examine equity and rights issues that may be associated with global climate change.

POLICY ISSUES ASSOCIATED WITH GLOBAL CLIMATE CHANGE

The material we have presented is but a small fraction of the information currently available to policymakers. Clearly, any reasonable policymaker might be confused as to what an appropriate course of action would be, in light of the significant uncertainties that remain. In addition, policymakers have to determine what their overall policy goals are: should global climate change to be addressed as an issue of economic efficiency or one of equity?

If global climate change is viewed as primarily an issue of economic efficiency, it may be easy to justify "do nothing" policies, even if costs and benefits are discounted at the social rate of time preference. If predicted impacts do not occur for decades, the discounted value of future costs will be small. The benefits of waiting a comparatively short period of time for new information may very well exceed the discounted costs associated with delay. In addition, there will be benefits to delaying implementation of policies, such as taxes, that will have real economic costs for the current generation.

Although economic efficiency issues must be incorporated into any policy decisions, including decisions to take no action, consideration of equity issues is also critical. As such, rational policies must be based on determinations of several criteria. First, the current generation has to determine whether increased emissions of GHGs are "unfair" to future generations. Some may look askance at such a notion, comparing it to the fox deciding whether eating the chickens is unfair. But future generations aren't around today to be heard and necessarily must rely on our judgment.

Second, equity questions will not be confined solely to concerns of the present versus those of the future. Other equity issues between members of the current generation will also have to be addressed. Is it fair for major producers of GHGs to cause flooding in low-lying countries that produce few GHGs? Do the low-lying countries bear any of the responsibility themselves, perhaps because of policies that encourage development in low-lying areas and rapid expansion of populations?

Neither of these questions can be resolved easily, especially in the presence of uncertainty. Defining unfairness requires some sort of measure of unfairness.[20] While Rawls's (1971) definition, which focuses on whether future generations would change places with us if they could, may be a useful overall guide, it still requires one or more measures on which such a decision might be based. Further difficulties may arise if policies designed to increase fairness to the future are unfair to those in the present who already bear disproportionate costs: this is one aspect of the irreversibility issue. Thus measures of welfare distribution between different segments of each generation might need to be developed.

Despite the existing uncertainties, a reasonable argument can be made that global climate change has the *potential* for extreme unfairness to the future if there are catastrophic impacts. Assuming that such a determination of unfairness can be made, policies to reduce that unfairness must be developed. It is here that rational economic policies will be crucial. Policies that improve equity will improve it more if they are also efficient. It makes no sense to spend $20 for a goal that could just as easily be accomplished by spending $10. In the case of global climate change, however, efficient policies will be clouded by uncertainty. Without knowing with certainty the magnitude and the impacts of global climate change, many different policies could be justified on efficiency grounds. Therefore, a reasonable approach to uncertainty has to be agreed on. Once that is done, efficient policies can be designed and put into place. One of the most common policies discussed has been

---

[20]See Chapter 4 for a discussion of the different types of fairness.

the imposition of some form of carbon tax. Determining an optimal level for such a tax, even in the absence of political issues, is likely to be difficult.

Are Carbon Dioxide Emissions Unfair to Future Generations?

If present climate models are correct and the predicted physical, economic, and social impacts do occur, the current generation may have failed to meet its obligations to the future. This conclusion depends on the answers to two questions: First, are we leaving future generations worse off as a whole than we are? Second, are we doing *avoidable* harm to specific members of future generations?

For example, rising sea levels could impose severe harm on some members of future generations. Residents of low-lying countries, such as the Maldives and Bangladesh, could face inundation of large portions of their countries. This would result in massive dislocation and forced migration to other areas or countries. If global climate change leads to accelerated extinction of species, we may be denying future generations important benefits from those species; if global climate change leads to much lower yields for rice crops, future generations may not have enough food.

There may also be *intragenerational* equity impacts in the future. Differences in the distribution of income between members of any given generation may be exacerbated. If the most impoverished are the most affected by lack of food because of lower crop yields and forced migration to other areas, there will be greater inequity.

If future generations are expected to be twice as rich as we are, but increased CO_2 emissions will make them only slightly less rich, we are not being unfair to the future.[21] Similarly, if future generations will not be as well off as we are in any case, unless CO_2 emissions make them still worse off, we are also not being unfair to the future.[22]

Policymakers cannot determine whether the welfare of future generations will be more or less than that of the current generation without first having some acceptable measure with which to gauge such changes. Ideally, policymakers would need a straightforward measure that is an accurate proxy for well-being. Such proxies are difficult to come by, however, especially when a key component of such measures may be nonmarket levels of environmental quality.

Will the Current Generation Leave Future Generations Worse Off?

Determining whether or not the current generation will leave future generations better or worse off is an extremely complex question. The welfare of future generations, *from the standpoint of the present generation*, will depend not only on their overall level of welfare but also on the uncertainty of future welfare. In Figure 21.4,

---

[21]Sen (1982) suggests that even if future generations are better off, we may still be unfair to the future by reducing their welfare below its potential.

[22]We are abstracting from the possibility that other actions by the present generation are contributing to lower future welfare.

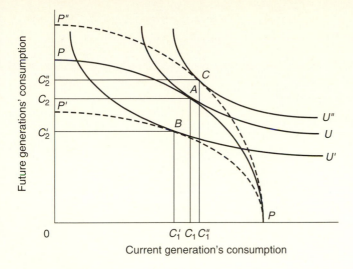

Figure 21.4   Alternative Production Possibilities Between Present and Future Generations

for example, the trade-off between the current generation's consumption C_1 and future generations' consumption C_2 is illustrated. The expected production possibilities frontier is initially given by PP. As a result, optimal intergenerational welfare occurs where the social welfare function is just tangent to PP.[23] This is shown as point A. At A, consumption by the present and future generations equals C_1 and C_2, respectively, and achieves an overall level of social welfare U. This point would assume some base level of global climate change, with its assumed economic impacts.

Because of the uncertainty about the effects of future global climate change, the realized production possibilities curve might be PP', where future production is more limited than expected, or PP'', where future production is greater than expected. If production in the future were more limited, because of greater severity of global climate change, consumption would shift to C_1' and C_2', respectively, where $C_2' < C_2$.

Through their policy choices, decision makers today can influence the shape of the production possibilities frontier, the choice of social welfare function, and the overall level of welfare. This is shown in Figure 21.5. It may be that greater production is possible now with a concomitant reduction in future production. This corresponds to production frontier $P''P''$ and might correspond to a policy decision to pursue a "business as usual" approach to global climate change, without adopting any policies that would reduce future carbon emissions. Consumption by the present generation would increase to C_1'', and consumption by future generations would fall to C_2''. This corresponds to point C.

---

[23] Thus, in Figure 21.4, given the social welfare function, the highest level of welfare that can be attained, given the limits to production, is U.

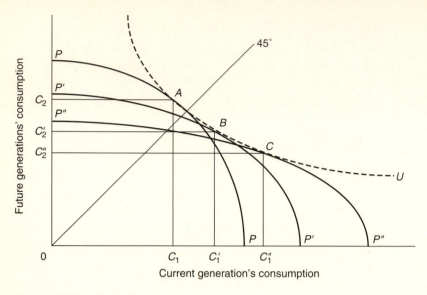

Figure 21.5   Policy Decisions and Intergenerational Welfare

A limited policy of carbon emissions abatement could alter the production possibilities frontier to $P'P'$. In this case, the current generation's consumption would fall to C_1', and future generations' consumption would increase to C_2' (point B). Finally, a stringent program to reduce carbon emissions would result in production frontier PP, where the current generation's consumption fell to C_1 and future generations' consumption increased to C_2 (point A).[24]

In the context of Figure 21.5, movements along the social welfare curve U from points A to B to C reduce future welfare in exchange for increased current welfare. Points below the 45 degree line in the figure represent solutions where future welfare is less than current welfare, while points above the line represent solutions where future welfare is greater than current welfare. Thus solutions B and C may be labeled "unfair" to future generations, and A may be labeled "unfair" to present generations.

Of course, we cannot simply observe the alternative production possibilities frontiers in Figure 21.5, nor can we, in fact, observe any individual frontier. Policies that trade current for future welfare will necessarily involve heroic assumptions and uncertainties.

---

[24]Note that the implied social discount rate is greatest at point A, where the slope of the tangency is steepest, even though current consumption relative to future consumption is lowest. Thus at point A, current consumption is most favorable to future consumption (e.g., discounting future consumption most) despite policies to reduce current consumption in favor of future consumption. See Just, Hueth, and Schmitz (1982) for further discussion.

Will Global Climate Change Impose Costs on Parties Who Receive No Benefits?

Besides policymakers' overall concern about the welfare of current versus future generations, there is also concern about the distribution of that welfare. Specifically, will a *subset* of future generations bear disproportionate costs due to global climate change without receiving any benefits?

As of 1994, there was some evidence that this could be the case. The IPCC (1992) estimated that a 1-meter rise in sea level would result in the loss of about 3 percent of the world's land area. The IPCC study also broke this estimate down by major countries. A 1-meter rise would inundate 12 to 15 percent of Egypt's arable land and 17 percent of the nation of Bangladesh. Given the continued rapid growth of those two countries' populations, the impact from a rise in sea level would disproportionately harm individuals there relative to countries such as the United States.

This IPCC report also estimated the relative annual cost to erect shore protection structures for various affected countries. The effect on overall annual GNP ranged from 0.5 percent for Madagascar to over 34 percent for the low-lying Maldives. Of the 50 countries most affected, all but New Zealand are developing countries. Thus not only are some countries affected much more than others, but the impacts are predicted to be greatest in countries whose inhabitants are relatively less wealthy.

Last, agricultural impacts could also affect developing countries proportionally more than the developed countries. Even though the climatic impacts might be more severe in the more developed countries, the proportion of agriculture relative to total GNP is far higher in developing countries. Furthermore, with limited resources, developing countries may be less able to diversify their economies and improve overall levels of productivity.

Policy Approaches

Questions about policy approaches must begin with who should develop and implement such approaches. Once that is answered, the questions to be answered include the primary goals of the policies ultimately developed and the best policy instruments to achieve those goals.

Who Should Develop and Implement a Policy Response?   Because the risks from global climate change are international, policy responses should ideally be developed at that level. Unitary actions by nations will ultimately fail, owing to the *free-rider* problem. If the United States were to unilaterally impose a carbon tax, for example, the overall effect on reducing carbon emissions would be small, and other countries might gain a competitive advantage. Those countries would enjoy the benefits of reduced carbon emissions without having had to pay a price for those benefits.

This does not mean that individual nations should not develop and implement policy responses. Individual nations will have to consider policies that can best reduce their most prominent sources of greenhouse gases and promote carbon sinks. Thus the United States might want to focus on transportation policies while Brazil focuses on policies to reduce deforestation. Such policies should be developed jointly between environmental and energy regulators.

Policy Responses That Reduce Unfairness   If the current generation is being unfair to the future, it should implement policies to reduce that unfairness. In such a case, the key issue will be the level of investment to apply toward reductions in carbon emissions and the most cost-effective policies with which to achieve those reductions. In an equity framework, the level of investment will no longer be determined by equating the marginal benefits and marginal costs of carbon abatement. Investments that are cost-effective from the current generation's standpoint represent a lower bound for total investments, for those investments should be pursued regardless. Further investments may not directly benefit the current generation but will provide "insurance" for future generations.

Determining the "correct" level of investment for equity purposes is probably impossible. Perhaps the only direct way would be through a contingent valuation study. Policymakers might be able to estimate the current generation's willingness to pay to reduce unfairness to future generations by reducing the risk that future carbon emissions may impose. A contingent valuation study (see Chapter 11) could be used to assess willingness to pay. Respondents could be asked how much they were willing to pay, probably in the form of a carbon tax to reduce carbon emissions and thereby risks to future generations (Poterba 1991).

Unfortunately, there would be at least three difficulties with such a CVM model. First, respondents' *WTP* may be much lower when asked as individuals than when asked as members of society. If individual respondents are unwilling to pay any positive amount to reduce future risks, policymakers must decide whether society as a whole still has a moral obligation to the future, even if its citizens, as individuals, do not think they do. Second, there is the difficulty of asking the right question. The responses to a question about *WTP* to avoid future greenhouse warming may be quite different from the responses to a question focusing on future *GDP*. Last, it can be argued that a CVM model like this would suffer from asking the wrong generation the wrong question. In other words, if equity were of paramount concern, the "correct" CVM basis would be future generations' willingness to accept damage.

Choosing the Right Policy Instrument   Whatever the level of greenhouse policy investment chosen, society will want to achieve the maximum return on that investment. Hence it will be necessary to examine alternative measures for carbon emissions abatement to determine the maximum reduction in emissions achievable for a given cost. In the case of carbon, currently there are no cost-effective control technologies, although there are technologies that can "scrub" carbon that results from burning fossil fuels. (These techniques, however, create a massive disposal problem for the solid residue.) Lower emissions can only come from choosing lower-emission technologies (switching from coal to natural gas, wind, geothermal, solar, etc.) and the choice of final goods and services to be produced. Thus the most likely candidates for policy instruments will be emissions and output taxes and quotas.

In some cases, emissions and output taxes will be equivalent. For example, a tax per pound of carbon would have the same overall economic effect as an equivalent tax on gasoline because carbon emissions per gallon are currently invariant to gasoline production technology. By contrast, an emissions tax on carbon and an output tax on electricity would have different impacts because different generating technologies produce different levels of emissions. Despite there being no control technologies, imposition of carbon taxes would encourage substitution from higher-carbon fuels to lower-carbon ones. Uniform taxes on *energy* (e.g., dollars per Btu) should *not* be used. Uniform taxes on energy would provide no incentive to consumers and producers to substitute lower-carbon-emitting fuels for higher-emitting ones.

We also discussed the advantages and disadvantages of taxes versus quotas in the presence of uncertainty in Chapter 7. As you may recall, Weitzman (1974) showed that the choice of price-based or quantity-based instrument should depend on the slopes of the marginal cost and marginal benefit functions. Weitzman shows that the steeper (less elastic) the marginal benefit function and the flatter (more elastic) the marginal cost function, the greater the social losses from choosing the "wrong" tax level. If, as the model of Edmonds and Barnes (1991) shows, the marginal-cost-of-abatement curve is steep, losses from choosing the "wrong" tax will be reduced. Thus from an efficiency standpoint, taxes on carbon emissions would probably have the most advantages in terms of effectiveness.

Another benefit of carbon taxes over strict emissions quotas is that carbon taxes would raise revenues that could be used to reduce other taxes. The revenue potential from this tax "recycling" could help provide funds to countries in greater need of capital for investments in new, lower-carbon-emitting technologies; emissions taxes provide continued incentives for technological change so as to reduce the burden of the tax; and emissions taxes can be easily modified—either upward or downward—as scientific knowledge about the greenhouse effect and its consequences increases.

The principal disadvantage of taxes on carbon emissions is the uncertainty of the amount of abatement that would be achieved, owing to the uncertainty of least-cost emissions reductions. Furthermore, it is sometimes argued that emissions taxes can be regressive in that they can impose relatively larger costs on the poorer members of society. This would not be the case with a set of carbon quotas, which could guarantee a chosen level of emissions reductions. Of course, setting the quota level correctly could be difficult, as might verification that individual country quotas were being met.

Even though there may be efficiency reasons to prefer emissions and output taxes, there may be equity reasons for choosing emissions limits that are not tradable. With tradable permits, richer countries might be able to bid for a greater share of allowable emissions. As a result, poorer countries could find themselves worse off, with limited options for economic growth and increased income, because of a lack of sufficient capital for investments in lower-emissions technologies. There would also be the problem of initially allocating permits. The controversy would likely overshadow that experienced in the United States in negotiating the new Clean Air Act's allocations of permits for sulfur dioxide. Awarding quotas on the basis of past emissions ("grandfathering") would reward past inefficiencies. It would also penalize developing countries, whose overall emissions might be expected to increase as their economies grow.

As with international establishment of quotas, internationally set taxes could also present inequities. Because of the scope of the global climate change problem, cooperative international action will have to be taken to reduce carbon emissions effectively. However, there are significant differences in the existing structure of energy taxes between countries. Most European countries, for example, impose very high taxes on gasoline, while the United States imposes relatively low taxes. Equity concerns, however, would ultimately require consistency in the levels of taxes among countries so as to avoid the problem of low-tax countries' free-riding on higher-tax ones.

By 1994, about the only form of global climate change mitigation policy in use was carbon dioxide adders by some state utility commissioners, which were imposed on electric utilities.[25] In most cases, the adders recommended were based on the costs of carbon sequestration, usually in the form of planting trees. This method, though appealing because of its simplicity and political expediency, suffers from essentially the same flaws as basing taxes on control costs. The cost of sequestration will not necessarily represent an efficient level for a carbon tax, if efficiency is chosen as the primary goal, nor is there any reason for the cost of sequestration to represent the ideal level for equity reasons.

Addressing Uncertainty   Whether this generation's contributing to continued global climate change is fair or unfair to the future depends on its ultimate effects. In 1996, there was still a great deal of uncertainty associated with the pace, magnitude, and ultimate economic, environmental, and social impacts of global climate change. By 1996, no major policy initiatives, other than voluntary commitments to reduce international emissions of carbon dioxide stemming from the Rio de Janeiro Conference in 1993, had been imposed.

Many different policy alternatives are available to address and mitigate uncertainty. These are summarized in Table 21.3. Which of these is relevant to mitigating uncertainty over global climate change? First, it is doubtful that traditional insurance policies will be of much use. Private insurers who believe that there is the possibility of catastrophic losses will often refuse to provide insurance. A good example of this is earthquake insurance. In California, because the magnitude of damage from past earthquakes has been so large, private insurers were reluctant to

---

[25]We discussed the use of adders in Chapter 7. Ongoing deregulation of the electric industry will likely eliminate the use of such "adders" by public utility commissions.

TABLE 21.3 AVAILABLE POLICIES TO MITIGATE UNCERTAINTY

Category of Policy	Type of Uncertainty	Policy Actions
Traditional insurance	Diversifiable risks (floods, crop failure, fire, etc.)	Private insurance (life, casualty, homeowners, etc.) Social insurance
Consumption smoothing	Risk of catastrophic loss	Precautionary saving and investment
Precautionary investments	Uncertain damage or mitigation costs	Precautionary abatement (e.g., high emissions taxes) Precautionary adaptation (e.g., moving away from coastal flood zones)
		Investment in additional research and development (e.g., more sophisticated modeling, research into "clean" energy technologies)

Source: After Nordhaus (1994).

offer it to homeowners and businesses, and if they did offer it, the cost was prohibitive. Now the state of California requires any insurer who wishes to do business in the state to provide such insurance. Also, insurance companies have finite resources. Catastrophic claims can bankrupt private firms and even firms that insure insurance companies.

Consumption smoothing and precautionary investments both offer real possibilities for mitigating global climate change uncertainty, although the work of Nordhaus (1994) suggests that the latter offers more possibilities. Consumption smoothing often makes sense for risks that cannot themselves be reduced. For example, individual businesses cannot prevent overall business cycles such as recessions. For that reason, many businesses whose incomes are cyclical will hoard cash to "save for a rainy day." Automobile manufacturers, whose business is notoriously cyclical, often pursue this strategy.

In the case of global climate change, it is not at all clear what amount would have to be set aside, and what the money would be used for. A better solution appears to be precautionary investments. Nordhaus (1994) showed that high carbon taxes, coupled with revenue recycling, would provide benefits that extended beyond reducing the potential for catastrophic damages. Additional research also seems warranted, especially research into cleaner energy sources that are already becoming competitive, such as wind, fuel cells, and solar power. Research that can better model the global climate and thereby reduce the breadth of uncertainty over potential climate change scenarios also seems warranted. Such research may also reduce other environmental costs, providing society with additional benefits unrelated to climate change. And gradual adaptation will be less costly than needing to make a sudden adaptation. Thus to the extent that precautionary investment encourages such adaptation, it may have future benefits.

Finally, policies that encourage precautionary adaptation may provide benefits by reducing the costs of climate-related *moral hazard*. Moral hazard refers to individuals' engaging in riskier behavior than they otherwise would because they know they will not pay the full costs of their actions. For example, many individuals build their homes on beaches or in known floodplains, knowing that (at least in the United States) the government will pay the costs of rebuilding their home should a hurricane or flood destroy it. Eliminating this form of subsidy would discourage the practice and encourage adaptation to higher ground, reducing future damage.

A fourth policy approach seems to be quite common: "wait and see." (This response corresponds to Nordhaus's "wait, then act" scenario.) The rationale for this approach is that if global climate change turns out to be less of a problem than anticipated, the current generation will have avoided policies that would have imposed costs on itself for nothing. Such policies might have inadvertently made future generations worse off by draining capital from more productive investments for use in carbon abatement strategies. However, the arguments for precautionary investment sound reasonable, which argues for active policies today. The only difficulty with precautionary investment is that it may be cheaper to wait. For example, the costs of clean energy technologies, such as wind and solar power, continue to decline. Waiting several years until these technologies are more cost-competitive and then investing more heavily in them may be able to reduce future GHG emissions as much as investing today, and at a lower cost. The difficult question, of course, is how far will the cost of these technologies fall?

As we discussed in Chapter 14, there are legitimate reasons for society today to approach environmental externalities, including global climate change, from a risk-averse perspective. The most compelling one is fairness: the costs of global climate change, however realized, will almost certainly fall disproportionately on the people who are the least well off. If policy actions are taken today that can eliminate the possibility of "catastrophic" warming, we can also avoid a scenario that might overwhelm future society's resources and have irreversible consequences.

CHAPTER SUMMARY

While our understanding of the complex mechanisms that determine the earth's climate continues to advance, the ultimate impacts of those mechanisms over time and our future as a species remain elusive. As a consequence, policies that address global climate change will of necessity be developed in the presence of uncertainty. Responding to global climate change will not constitute setting a "correct" emissions tax or quota and leaving things there. Unlike most other pollutants, producers of GHGs and bearers of the costs of such emissions may be separated in time by decades or centuries. Therefore, policy instruments designed to combat global climate change, if indeed that is what such instruments ought to do, cannot be based solely on efficiency criteria.

Effective policies that address important equity issues will have to be developed by many nations working together. This will be difficult. Some nations will perceive that they have insufficient resources to divert to global climate change policies. Other nations may, for political reasons, wish to use GHG reductions as "bargaining chips," extracting from wealthier nations disproportionately large payments as inducements to reduce emissions. Still other nations may be insignificant producers of GHGs, yet face potential calamity should some of the predicted impacts come to pass. The future of these nations may lie at the mercy of many others. Thus the transboundary nature of global pollutants significantly complicates the development and, especially, the implementation of effective policies. Politicians, many only too eager to dither, will be provided ample excuses if other nations can be shown not to be "playing fair."

Despite this pessimism, there are likely to be actions that can and will occur. Energy efficiency improvements, which tend to reduce GHG emissions, continue to be developed for purely economic reasons. There are slow signs that countries are beginning to manage their forests more effectively and limit indiscriminate deforestation. The replacement of command-and-control economies with market-driven ones will improve economic welfare in many nations and likely reduce population growth and its related environmental strains. This trend is already being observed in many developing nations (Robey, Rustein, and Morris 1993). There also is precedent for international agreements to reduce or eliminate certain pollutants. The Montreal Protocol is proving effective in eliminating emissions of CFCs, which not only damage ozone but are also strong greenhouse gases. So even though considerable uncertainty will continue to exist as to the exact nature and scope of global climate change, economic trends may allow us collectively to address the inherent equity issues involved more effectively.

CHAPTER REVIEW

Policy Issues

- The current state of knowledge about global climate change is limited to the extent that there is a great degree of uncertainty as to the existence, timing, and magnitude of future impacts. The existence of uncertainty, however, does not imply that inaction is the preferable policy alternative. Rather, separate irreversible impacts associated with positive policy action and inaction must be weighed.
- Policymakers addressing global climate change should approach the issues involved from a risk-averse standpoint. A reasonable policy question, therefore, is the amount of climate change "insurance" to purchase.
- Policymakers must separate issues of intertemporal economic efficiency from those of intergenerational equity. Policies enacted today will also have distributional impacts on the current generation. Care must be taken not to justify specific nonefficiency actions using tools best suited to address economic efficiency.
- The most efficient policy instruments available are likely to be a global carbon tax or internationally tradable emissions permits. Both would raise significant

distributional issues between developed and developing countries. Noncooperative solutions, such as second-best tariffs, are almost certain to prove ineffective.

- Revenue recycling could provide significant benefits by reducing both environmental costs and economic distortions that arise from other taxes.

DISCUSSION QUESTIONS

1. One consequence of the increasing cost of CFCs has been the development of a well-established market for smuggled CFCs. Would you have predicted this as a consequence of the Montreal Protocol? What economic instruments could be used to combat such illegal activities that reduce the effectiveness of a CFC tax?

2. The Swedish economist Peter Bohm suggested the use of deposit refund system for CFCs. Under such a system, purchasers of some types of equipment using CFCs, such as refrigerators, would pay a fee that would be refunded only when the CFCs were removed eventually by a licensed CFC recycler. Evaluate the economics of this proposal. Would it avoid some of the problems arising from the smuggling operations described in question 1?

3. To what extent should the equity consequences of global climate change take precedence over the efficiency consequences?

4. Brown (1991) states that global climate change is not a problem for cost-benefit analysis, because its effects will last for centuries, that "rational" decision making cannot be made on the basis of arguments found in cost-benefit analyses, that discounting the costs of global climate change is inappropriate because it "imperils the future by undervaluing it," and that some things cannot be measured in monetary terms. Evaluate Brown's arguments. Assuming that all of his arguments are correct, how should alternative policies to combat global climate change (including do-nothing policies) be evaluated?

5. To the extent that effective global climate change policies will require international cooperation, how can nations with the potential to emit relatively large amounts of GHGs be encouraged not to? For example, how could these nations be discouraged from using their emissions as a form of worldwide "extortion"?

6. Suppose that a *worldwide* carbon tax is enacted. What should be done with the revenues collected? How should they be distributed most efficiently? How should they be distributed most equitably? Which basis for distribution of the revenues should be given priority? Why?

REFERENCES

Adams, R., C. Rosenweig, R. Peart, J. Ritchie, B. McCarl, J. Glyer, and R. Curry. 1990. "Global Climate Change and U.S. Agriculture." *Nature* 345(6272): 219–224.

Brown, P. 1991. "Why Climate Change Is Not a Cost/Benefit Problem." In *Global Climate Change: The Economic Costs of Mitigation and Adaptation*, ed. J. White. New York: Elsevier.

Bruce, J., H. Lee, and E. Haites. 1996. *Climate Change 1995: Economics and Social Dimensions.* New York: Cambridge University Press.

Burniaux, J., J. Martin, G. Nicoletti, and J. Martins. 1991. *The Costs of Policies to Reduce Global Emissions of CO_2: Initial Simulation Results with GREEN.* Working Paper No. 103. Paris: Economics and Statistics Department, Organization for Economic Cooperation and Development.

Cairncross, F. 1992. *Costing the Earth.* Boston: Harvard Business School Press.

Cline, W. 1992. *The Economics of Global Warming.* Washington, D.C.: Institute for International Economics,

Dixit, A., and R. Pindyck. 1994. *Investment Under Uncertainty.* Cambridge, Mass.: MIT Press.

Edmonds, J., and D. Barnes. 1991. *Use of the Edmonds-Reilly Model to Model Energy Sector Impacts of Greenhouse Gas Emissions Control Strategies.* Richland, Wash.: Pacific Northwest Laboratories.

Emsley, J. (ed.) 1996. *The Global Warming Debate.* London: European Science and Environment Forum.

Friis-Christensen, E., and K. Lassen. 1991. "Length of the Solar Cycle: An Indicator of Solar Activity Closely Associated with Climate Change." *Science* 254(5032): 698–700.

Hansen, J. 1988. "The Greenhouse Effect: Impacts on Current Global Temperature and Regional Heat Waves." Testimony before the Committee on Energy and Natural Resources, U.S. Senate, June 23.

Houghton, J., G. Jenkins, and J. Ephraums. 1990. *Climate Change: The IPPC Scientific Assessment.* Cambridge: Cambridge University Press.

Houghton, J., L. Filho, B. Callender, N. Harris, A. Kattenburg, and K. Maskell. 1996. *Climate Change 1995: The Science of Climate Change.* New York: Cambridge University Press.

Intergovernment Panel on Climate Change (IPCC). 1992. *1992 IPPC Supplement.* Cambridge: Cambridge University Press.

Jaeger, W. 1995. *Optimal Environmental Taxation.* Discussion Paper No. 10. Seattle: Institute for Economic Research, University of Washington.

Jorgensen, D., and P. Wilcoxen. 1991. "Reducing U.S. Carbon Dioxide Emissions: The Cost of Different Goals." In *Energy, Growth, and the Environment,* ed. J. Moroney. Greenwich, CT: JAI Press.

Just, R., D. Hueth, and A. Schmitz. 1982. *Applied Welfare Economics and Public Policy.* Upper Saddle River, N.J.: Prentice Hall.

Kerr, R. 1991. "Greenhouse Science Survives Skeptics." *Science* 256(5050): 1138–1140.

Kimball, B., J. Mauney, F. Nakayama, and S. Idso. 1993. "Effects of Elevated CO_2 and Climate Variables on Plants." *Journal of Soil and Water Conservation* 48(1): 9–14.

Lashof, D., and D. Ahuja. 1990. "Relative Contributions of Greenhouse Gas Emissions to Global Warming." *Nature* 344(6266): 529–531.

Lettenmaier, D., and D. Sheer 1991. "Climatic Sensitivity of California Water Resources." *Journal of Water Resource and Planning Management* 117(1): 108–135.

Manne, A., and R. Richels. 1992. *Buying Greenhouse Insurance: The Economic Costs of Carbon Dioxide Emissions Limits.* Cambridge, Mass.: MIT Press.

Nordhaus, W. 1991a. "The Cost of Slowing Climate Change: A Survey." *Energy Journal* 12(1): 37–65.

————. 1991b. "Economic Policies and the Greenhouse Effect." In *Global Warming: Economic Policy Responses,* ed. R. Dornbusch and J. Poterba. Cambridge, Mass.: MIT Press.

————. 1994. *Managing the Global Commons: The Economics of Climate Change.* Cambridge, Mass.: MIT Press.

Office of Technology Assessment (OTA). 1991. *Changing by Degrees: Steps to Reduce Greenhouse Gases.* Washington, D.C.: U.S. Government Printing Office.

Palmer, A., W. Mooz, T. Quinn, and K. Wolf. 1980. *Economic Implications of Regulating Chlorofluorocarbon Emissions from Non-Aerosol Applications.* Report No. R-2524-EPA. Los Angeles: Rand Corp.

Poterba, J. 1991. "Tax Policy to Combat Global Warming: On Designing a Carbon Tax." In *Global Warming: Economic Policy Responses,* ed. R. Dornbusch and J. Poterba. Cambridge, Mass.: MIT Press.

Ramanathan, V. 1988. "The Greenhouse Theory of Climate Change: A Test by an Inadvertent Global Experiment." *Science* 240: 293–299.

Rawls, J. 1971. *A Theory of Justice.* Cambridge, Mass.: Harvard University Press.

Robey, B., S. Rustein, and L. Morris. 1993. "The Fertility Decline in Developing Countries." *Scientific American* 269(6): 60–67.

Schelling, T. 1992. "Some Economics of Global Warming." *American Economic Review* 82(1): 1–14.

Sen, A. 1982. "Approaches to the Choice of Discount Rate for Social Benefit-Cost Analysis." In *Discounting for Time and Risk in Energy Policy,* ed. R. Lind. Baltimore: Johns Hopkins University Press.

Solow, A. 1991. "Is There a Global Warming Problem?" In *Global Warming: Economic Policy Responses,* ed. R. Dornbusch and J. Poterba. Cambridge, Mass.: MIT Press.

"Stormy Weather Ahead." *The Economist,* March 23, 1996, pp. 83–85.

Thomson, D. 1995. "The Seasons, Global Temperature, and Precession." *Science* 268: 59–67.

Watson, R., M. Zinyowera, and R. Moss. 1996. *Climate Change 1995: Impacts, Adaptations, and Mitigation of Climate Change.* New York: Cambridge University Press.

Weitzman, M. "Prices vs. Quantities." The Review of Economic Studies 41(3): 477–491.

Whalley, J., and R. Wigle. 1990. "The International Incidence of Carbon Taxes." Paper presented at the Conference on Economic Policy Responses to Global Warming, Rome.

CHAPTER 22

THE FUTURE OF ENVIRONMENTAL ECONOMICS AND POLICY

INTRODUCTION

Depending on your outlook, you may see the world mired in an inevitable spiral of increasing environmental degradation and misery or regard environmental improvements and solutions as hopeful signs that eventually we will provide a high-quality environment for every one and everything. For all of the environmental problems we have discussed in this book, whether a homeowner dumping trash in his neighbor's backyard or the excruciating complexity of global climate change, there is hope. Yet hope should not be confused with uncritical optimism. Many environmental problems, such as the safe disposal of nuclear wastes, still appear intractable. However, we believe that such intractability ultimately arises from a lack of clarity over the environmental goals to be achieved rather than the problems themselves.

THE ECONOMIC APPROACH TO ENVIRONMENTAL POLICY ISSUES

In Chapter 1, we discussed a sequence of steps necessary to develop effective environmental policies and the role of economists in that policy development. It seems appropriate to review those steps, having examined the economic concepts involved and the policy considerations associated with many environmental issues.

1. *Policymakers must understand economic concepts, such as supply and demand, and also understand the broader linkages between the economy and the environment.*

In Chapter 2, we saw that these linkages were quite real and that they can complicate the development of effective policies. Policymakers must seek to reduce the unintended consequences of their policies. Too often, policies undertaken with the best of intentions, to say nothing of those undertaken nefariously, fail to consider general equilibrium effects and as a result lead to unintended problems. Any emissions or output tax, say, may induce economic distortions. For example, despite the political maneuverings, President Clinton's proposed Btu tax would have affected all sectors of the economy. Whether those effects would have caused the doom and gloom predicted by the opponents of the tax is an open question. Nevertheless, if successful policies are to be developed, the overall impacts of any action must be addressed, if for nothing else than to refute the catastrophic claims of special-interest opponents.

Command-and-control policies, such as many of the regulations under the original Clean Air Act that we discussed first in Chapter 7, have the greatest potential for inducing unwanted distortions. Unlike policies that enhance the operation of markets, such institutional policies substitute for efficient markets. Even with the best of intentions, often it will be difficult for environmental regulators to substitute their specific judgments for market responses. Regulating the types of pollution control equipment, for example, may prevent the development of more efficient substitutes for which markets provide ample incentive.

This is not to say that command-and-control policies are never appropriate. In some situations, the power of government will be the most efficient tool to achieve desired results. Emergency restrictions on polluting behavior or complete bans on harvesting fisheries may be the best initial solutions to environmental "crises." And although an ideal world would never reach such crisis points, the pace of new information and technological change will almost surely exceed our ability to understand their impacts.

2. *Policymakers must understand economic concepts of scarcity, value, and efficiency and such often conflicting philosophical concepts as equity, fairness, rights, and justice.*

The economic approach to environmental policy does not preclude the inclusion of noneconomic values. Rather, it distinguishes those values from purely economic ones and develops policies that effectively separate economic from noneconomic goals.

Many of the criticisms of economic analysis, especially those levied against the mechanical implementation of cost-benefit analysis, fail to understand the proper role of economics and economists. Economics does not create values. Economics does not condemn children to be exposed to lead or consign endangered species to extinction. Critics of economic analysis often misunderstand its role: economics is a tool to provide information relevant to decisions and clarify the implications of value-based choices.

It is easy for economic concepts to become hopelessly entangled with noneconomic ones, as we saw in discussions of much U.S. environmental law, such as the

Endangered Species Act and Superfund in Chapter 9. The continuing debates over sustainability, which we reviewed in Chapter 19, result from overarching and conflicting definitions of that concept. Deciding that policies to promote sustainability are "bad" or "good" is meaningless until and unless the values embodied in the concept are clarified and the conflicts between values are addressed. The United States values individual rights and freedom but also enacts laws that constrain individual behavior. Other countries make different trade-offs. Economics has nothing to say about the ideal trade-off; it can merely illustrate the implications of any given trade-off.

Policymakers who fail to distinguish between alternative concepts and values will almost surely enact bad policies. They must be able to use existing value systems to determine economic values. The economic value of preserving old-growth forests depends on the willingness to pay for preservation, and will almost surely differ from a value based on the willingness to accept additional old-growth loss. But economics cannot say which is the "correct" basis for valuation.

3. Policymakers must determine the most important economic, environmental, and philosophical issues to be addressed for the environmental problem under consideration.

No environmental problem can be "solved" until there is clarity and agreement as to the underlying problems and the most appropriate type of solution. That was the message of Chapter 5. The health problems associated with lead poisoning in children were clear, but the relevant "safe" exposure level was not. Nor was there agreement among all of the affected parties as to the "right" of children not to be exposed to lead. The Clean Air Act clarified the issues by stressing the noneconomic aspects of the problem. As such, the administrator of the Environmental Protection Agency developed an appropriate policy. On the surface, such a policy may have appeared uneconomic and, indeed, from an economic efficiency standpoint may have been so. But economic efficiency was a secondary priority.

When environmental (and other) policymakers address difficult issues, often there will be multiple conflicting goals. Equity, efficiency, and rights considerations will have to be balanced. The 1994 Basel Convention (see Chapter 9), which banned the export of hazardous wastes from developed countries to third-world countries, may have "solved" one environmental problem but created others. What wastes should be considered "hazardous" is not clear. Nor is the trade-off between the environmental benefits of reducing third-world exposure to hazardous wastes and the potential environmental damage caused by lower economic growth and less wealth available for providing better water and sanitation facilities. Economics cannot value all of these trade-offs. However, the multiattribute approach we introduced in Chapter 10 is one way of examining and ranking trade-offs, once identified.

4. Policymakers must be familiar with the contents of the economist's "toolbox" and how those tools can be used to make necessary trade-offs and resource allocations among worthy goals.

The economist's toolbox contains several concepts of value, which we discussed in Chapter 3, including willingness to pay and willingness to accept. It also contains criteria for establishing "good" from "bad" actions, including the Kaldor-Hicks (potential Pareto) test and the Harberger criterion. The economist's toolbox also contains techniques that can be used to provide relevant information to decision makers, such as benefit-cost analysis.

No policy action can be deemed "valuable" until we agree on what that term means. There are different concepts of value, which encompass both economic concepts such as willingness to pay and willingness to accept and noneconomic concepts of morally superior actions. Legal concepts, such as the concept of "standing," can help determine the most relevant concept. The mugger may "value" the ability to beat and rob his victim, but society does not recognize that value as part of the decision calculus.

Environmental issues, such as the preservation of endangered species, will often embrace multiple concepts of value. There may be disagreements as to whether a willingness to pay or willingness to accept measure is appropriate because of disagreement over the initial allocation of property rights. Economists cannot settle these debates because they do not have the necessary tools. What they can provide, however, are estimates of the *consequences* of different decisions that may be made.

As we discussed in Chapter 21, for example, some economists have been criticized for recommending policies to address complex environmental issues such as global climate change. Critics may fault economists such as William Nordhaus for not addressing the rights of future generations and the obligations of the current generation in the "correct" manner. But as long as economists like Nordhaus make the scope and limitations of their analysis clear, such criticism will not be well founded.

Ultimately, the economist's toolbox will be needed for all environmental policies because resources are scarce. Society will always have to choose between worthy goals, just as individuals do. It is for clarifying choices that the economist's toolbox will be most useful.

5. *Policymakers must be able to measure and value trade-offs, either in monetary terms or in some other way.*

However values are defined, there must be ways of measuring and comparing them. Much of the debate over "sustainability" and "sustainable development" arises from definitions that are vague, contradictory, or both. We may all agree that sustainable development is "good," but that will be small comfort to policymakers who are unable to measure its attainment. That is why the development of specific measures of environmental and resource value that we discussed in Chapter 19 is important.

Here again, the economist's toolbox can be helpful. Economists have developed several empirical valuation techniques, all of which we discussed in Chapter 11. Hedonic price studies can use data from market transactions to infer the values individuals place on unpriced goods. Using hedonic pricing, we can determine the value of a view of the ocean by comparing price differences between similar houses with different views. Because many environmental goods will not be traded in markets, even indirectly, however, economists developed the contingent valuation method to survey individuals' preferences and thereby determine willingness-to-pay and willingness-to-accept measures of value. Contingent valuation studies have been used in diverse environmental policy questions, ranging from the value of recreation opportunities along scenic rivers to the damages suffered from the Exxon *Valdez* oil spill in Alaska's Prince William Sound.

Because many environmental issues concern risks to human health and well-being, many empirical techniques have been used to determine the statistical value of a life (see Chapter 12). None of these is perfect, and none can address fundamental ethical issues, such as the risks we are willing to impose on children. But they do recognize the trade-offs all of us make, whether by driving our cars faster to save time, building skyscrapers, or working deep in coal mines. All involve risks.

Policy debates over health and safety are often vocal and strident. Some of us may become alarmed by certain food additives, such as BST for cows and Alar sprayed on apples. We may debate the health risks of farm pesticides yet also enjoy the greater abundance of the produce they allow. Again, economists cannot say what is "right" or "just." But the empirical techniques they employ can clarify many of the trade-offs involved.

Trade-offs need not be measured monetarily, however. One significant problem of environmental policy is incommensurability—the "apples and oranges" problems that comparing alternative environmental goals can raise. Saving old-growth forests at the expense of endangered salmon raises questions as to how they can be compared. Yet for policymakers allocating scarce resources for environmental improvements, resolving such problems is crucial.

6. *Policymakers must understand the critical role of time because environmental problems (and the policies that address them) can have impacts for years, centuries, even forever.*

Asking someone to weigh the benefits to future generations against those for the current generation is difficult. Environmental policymakers confronting global climate change or species preservation must do just that. The role of discounting is crucial to developing policies that are economically efficient. Even environmental policies whose primary goals are not economic efficiency will require resources to be allocated efficiently.

In Chapter 13, we discussed the confusion over discounting. Comparing alternative policies using the wrong discount rates will misallocate resources. If done badly enough, it may reduce, rather than improve, environmental quality. Discounting is a fundamental concept of economic efficiency. Discount rates reflect the opportunity cost of capital—money invested in one project is unavailable for another. Contrary to popular belief, discounting is not "unfair" to future generations. The legacy of environmental problems arising from federal water resource development in the western United States (see Chapter 17), which was often justified on the basis of artificially low or zero discount rates, is a stark reminder.

Arguments over the appropriateness of discounting future benefits and costs arise because of confusion between efficiency and equity goals. The former require discounting; the latter preclude it. As we saw in Chapter 13, there are more appropriate ways of addressing equity goals than by artificially adjusting discount rates.

7. Policymakers must know how to deal with uncertainty and the unknowable and how to gauge how much risk is worth taking.

The future is constantly changing. All that we can know for certain about the future is that what we know now will be found to be wrong or will be supplanted by newer information. Environmental policymakers must confront this problem. They must balance different risks and make decisions with imperfect, and sometimes incorrect, information.

What is the appropriate policy to address global climate change, even assuming that we resolve all of the competing efficiency, equity, and rights issues? How can environmental policymakers make the "right" decisions, not knowing all of the intricacies about the earth's climate? The answer, as we discussed in Chapters 14 and 21, is that there are no uniquely correct answers.

Just as individuals must determine the right amount of life insurance to purchase, environmental policymakers will have to decide how much risk they should take. In some cases, the risks will be minimal or offset by other events. If global climate change turns out to be more severe than envisioned, investments today in wind and solar power will have bigger payoffs. Conversely, if global climate change turns out to be less severe than envisioned, investments in wind and solar power may have a lower payoff, but the state of the world will be wealthier.

Economists cannot tell policymakers the right amount of risk to take, but the economist's toolbox can provide methods of measuring and ranking risks. Techniques such as multiattribute analysis and stochastic dominance can use the foundations of expected utility theory to evaluate uncertain outcomes. Even simpler techniques, such as sensitivity analysis, can provide valuable information to policymakers and allow them to focus more effort on key uncertainties.

Uncertainty can also change the entire concept of value. As we saw in Chapter 14, willingness to pay in the case of uncertainty is no longer best approximated by expected consumers' surplus. Rather, it is best approximated by option price, which may be compared to buying a season's pass guaranteeing access to a park, whether or not you intend to visit.

The existence of uncertainty means that the answers to environmental policy questions will never be without risk, whether from the risk of doing too little and allowing an environmental problem to worsen or the risk of doing too much and forcing individuals to devote scarce resources where they are not of most use. The tools of economics, however, can clarify the trade-offs involved and highlight key risks.

THE FUTURE OF ENVIRONMENTAL ECONOMICS AND POLICY

Since the first Earth Day in 1969, many changes have taken place in the economies and the environments of all nations. What have we learned from these changes? First, there is little reason to fear the catastrophic collapse of societies postulated by the authors of *The Limits to Growth* in the 1970s. The substitution of competitive markets for rigidly regulated ones has provided new incentives to explore and develop energy and mineral resources. Reserves of many important commodities have been increased, through new discoveries or greater incentives to recycle products that were formerly treated as wastes. This is especially true in less developed countries, for whom "wastes" from the developed countries have been an important source of raw materials for industries.

The treatment of environmental problems has also changed greatly. Many nations are turning to market-enhancing solutions to combat environmental decay and abandoning command-and-control policies. Whether the development of clearer water rights in the Middle East or the use of tradable emissions allowances as part of the U.S. Clean Air Act, there is growing recognition that market-based solutions can, in many cases, achieve environmental goals more efficiently than government edicts.

Of course, there remains a critical role for regulation. Policies that have at their root the protection of certain rights, of humans or of nature, or policies designed to improve equity between different groups are often a consequence of market breakdowns. In many cases, the establishment of markets to address these issues will be either prohibitively costly (it is doubtful we could envision a market for the air we all breathe) or irrelevant (it is not clear how we could develop markets for the preservation of many endangered species and prohibit the continued operation of markets for others).

Many environmental issues also remain unresolved, especially transboundary issues. Global climate change may represent the "ultimate" transboundary issue, but there are numerous others. Pollution of waterways that straddle international borders, allocation of international resources, regional air pollutants that adversely affect nearby international neighbors, and even the use of scarcity as a "weapon" to subjugate others remain critical issues in many parts of the world.

Whereas economics can suggest efficient remedies, political processes and the establishment of moral guidelines are needed as the basis for policy development. This does not mean that every incident of transboundary pollution is an act of environmental imperialism, nor should its goal be the complete elimination of all transboundary pollutants. Like other environmental policy issues, transboundary issues must be addressed systematically. The additional challenge, however, lies in the existence of multiple political processes.

Whatever environmental problems policymakers encounter in the future, the approach should remain the same. First, define the relevant issues and the goals of any solutions. Second, examine the various policy alternatives and consider their consequences and the trade-offs they entail. That approach will never be easy, but it offers the best hope for addressing environmental problems before they become environmental crises.

REFERENCE

Meadows, D., D. Meadows, J. Randers, W. Behrens. 1972. *The Limits to Growth: A Report for the Club of Rome's Project on the Predicament of Mankind.* New York: Universe Books.

APPENDIX A

A BRIEF REVIEW OF THE CALCULUS OF ONE AND SEVERAL VARIABLES

This appendix is designed to serve as a brief review of calculus; it is not intended to replace a course on the subject. However, if your mathematical skills are a bit rusty, this appendix may provide some help to refresh your memory.

FUNCTIONS

We can begin with the general specification of a function. We can state that y is a function of a variable x if there is some relationship between y and x that defines, for each value of x, a corresponding value of y. Thus when we speak of the demand function for an environmental good, we simply mean that the willingness to pay for that good will be determined by one or more variables. In general, we can write a function y of n variables $x_1, x_2, \ldots, x_n$ as

$$y = f(x_1, x_2, \ldots, x_n)$$

The variables $x_1, x_2, \ldots, x_n$ are called the *independent* variables, and y is called the *dependent* variable. We also distinguish between the variables (which may vary) and the parameters of a function (which do not). Thus, the function

$$y = \alpha x^{\lambda}$$

has one variable, x, and two parameters, α and λ.

Functions may also be described as *continuous* or *discontinuous*. A continuous function is one that has no "breaks" in it. If you trace a function with a pencil without lifting the pencil off the paper, you are tracing a continuous function. For example, the function $y = x^2$ is continuous for all values of x.

Continuity is formally defined by the concept of the *limit of a function*. As the independent variable approaches some value x_0, the value that $f(x)$ approaches as x approaches x_0 is written

$$\lim_{x \to x_0} f(x)$$

For example, the limit of the function $y = x^2$ as x approaches 3 is 9. If the limit of the function as x approaches x_0 equals the value of the function at x_0, the function is said to be continuous. As we shall see in the next section, continuity is important when we wish to determine rates of change of functions.

FUNCTIONS OF ONE VARIABLE AND DERIVATIVES

In economics, we often wish to know the effect on the dependent variable of changes in the independent variable. For example, one issue discussed in Chapter 8 was the relationship between increasing income and willingness to pay for environmental goods. The ratio of change in the dependent variable to change in the independent variable is called the *slope*. Put in terms of the function $y = f(x)$, the slope will equal $\Delta y / \Delta x$, which we can write as

$$\frac{\Delta y}{\Delta x} = \frac{f(x_2) - f(x_1)}{x_2 - x_1} \tag{A.1}$$

At any point x_0, the slope of the function $f(x_0)$ can be determined by examining the line tangent to $f(x_0)$. This is shown in Figure A.1.

In Equation A.1, as the difference between x_2 and x_1 decreases, the slope of the function will more closely approximate the tangent line at x_0. We call the slope of the tangent line to a function at any point x_0 the *derivative* of the function $f(x)$. The derivative of the function equals the slope as the change in the independent variable x approaches 0 (that is, as $\Delta x \to 0$). (For a linear function $f(x) = ax + b$, the slope will be a constant and equal to a.) The first derivative tells us how the value of the function changes as the independent variable changes.

We use the notation dy/dx or $f'(x)$ to denote the derivative of the function $y = f(x)$. Thus we have

$$\frac{dy}{dx} = f'(x) = \lim_{\Delta x \to 0} \frac{f(x + \Delta x) - f(x)}{\Delta x} \tag{A.2}$$

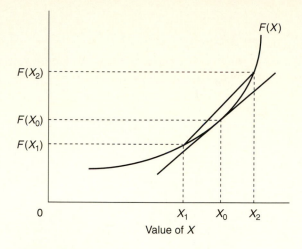

Figure A.1   Slope of a Nonlinear Function

Three Useful Rules of Differentiation

1. *The Chain Rule.* Let

$$y = f(x) = g(h(x))$$

where $h(x)$ and $g(x)$ are themselves functions of x. Then

$$\frac{dy}{dx} = g'(h(x))\,\frac{dh}{dx} \tag{A.3}$$

For example, suppose that

$$y = (a + bx^2)^c$$

Then

$$\frac{dy}{dx} = c(a + bx^2)^{c-1}2bx$$

2. *The Product Rule.* Let

$$y = f(x) = g(x)h(x)$$

Then

$$\frac{dy}{dx} = g'(x)h(x) + h'(x)g(x) \tag{A.4}$$

For example, suppose that

$$y = (a + bx^\delta)(cx^\beta)$$

Then

$$\frac{dy}{dx} = \delta bx^{\delta-1}(cx^\beta) + \beta(a + bx^\delta)(cx^{\beta-1})$$

3. *The Quotient Rule.* Let

$$y = f(x) = \frac{g(x)}{h(x)}$$

Then

$$\frac{dy}{dx} = \frac{g'(x)h(x) - h'(x)g(x)}{(h(x))^2} \qquad (A.5)$$

For example, suppose that

$$y = \frac{a + bx}{c + dx}$$

Then,

$$\frac{dy}{dx} = \frac{b(c + dx) - d(a + bx)}{(c + dx)^2} = \frac{bc - da}{(c + dx)^2}$$

Higher-Order Derivatives

The derivates just defined are often referred to as *first derivatives*. We can also define a function that is the derivative of the slope, or first derivative. This function indicates the change in the slope of the function as the independent variable changes and is generally referred to as the *second derivative*.

We can derive the notation for the second derivative as follows, noting that we can first write it as the derivative of the first derivative:

$$\frac{d}{dx}\left(\frac{dy}{dx}\right) = \frac{d^2y}{(dx)^2} = \frac{d^2y}{dx^2} \qquad (A.6)$$

For example, if $y = (a + bx)^2$, then

$$\frac{dy}{dx} = 2(a + bx)b$$

and

$$\frac{d^2y}{dx^2} = 2b^2$$

We can define higher-order derivatives in an analogous manner. Thus

$$\frac{d^3y}{dx^3} = \frac{d}{dx}\left(\frac{d^2y}{dx^2}\right)$$

and, in general,

$$\frac{d^n y}{dx^n} = \frac{d}{dx}\left(\frac{d^{n-1}y}{dx^{n-1}}\right) \tag{A.7}$$

The notion of continuity can also be applied to first and higher-order derivatives of functions. A continuous function that has continuous and well-defined derivatives of every order is *smooth* if there are no gaps or kinks in the function. This is important in economics because we will often want to determine maxima and minima of functions.

FUNCTIONS OF TWO OR MORE INDEPENDENT VARIABLES

Though we may be able to determine, say, individual willingness to pay for environmental goods as a function of one variable, such as income, often the willingness to pay for environmental goods will depend on many variables, including income, the price of substitutes, the price of the environmental good in question, and risk. As a result, empirical work will often deal with functions of two or more independent variables.

Consider the function $z = f(x,y)$, where both x and y are independent variables. With a function of two variables, the concept of slope is no longer unique. In fact, there are at least three ways of defining the slope of such a function. To see this, consider the example of an individual's willingness to pay for an improved view of the Grand Canyon, as defined by the function

$$z = (0.004)y^2 + (0.025)y - (0.1)x_v - (0.02)x_v^2 \tag{A.8}$$

where z = willingess to pay, y = the individual's total income, and x_v = the direct price of the view, as represented by the admission price to Grand Canyon National Park. Suppose that we wish to know the slope of this function holding the price x_v constant at x_{v0}. We can determine the slope by taking the derivative of the function $z(y, x_{v0})$. This is called the *partial derivative* of z with respect to x. Thus

$$\frac{\partial z}{\partial y} = \frac{dz}{dy}\bigg|_{\Delta x_v = 0} = f_y$$

For example, taking the first partial derivative of Equation A.8 with respect to y yields

$$\frac{\partial z}{\partial y} = 0.008y - 0.025$$

We can also hold y constant and take the derivative of z with respect to x_v. This is called the partial derivative of z with respect to x. From the example of Equation A.8, we have

$$\frac{\partial z}{\partial y} = \frac{dz}{dx_v}\bigg|_{\Delta y = 0} = f_{x_v} = -0.1 - 0.04x_v$$

Finally, we can determine the *total* change in z when *both* x and y change. This is called the *total differential* of the function z. The total differential can be thought of as the weighted sum of the individual partial derivatives.

From Equation A.2, for a function of one variable, we can write

$$dy = f'(x)\,dx \tag{A.9}$$

However, a partial derivative can be thought of as a single variable derivative when all of the other variables are held constant. Thus

$$dz\bigg|_{dy=0} = \frac{dz}{dx}\bigg|_{dy=0} dx = \frac{\partial z}{\partial x}\,dx \tag{A.10}$$

The total differential evaluates the total change dz when all of the independent variables change. It is expressed as the sum of the individual dz when each independent variable is allowed to change separately. Thus from Equation A.10, we have

$$dz = \frac{dz}{dx}\bigg|_{dy=0} dx + \frac{dz}{dy}\bigg|_{dx=0} dy = \frac{\partial z}{\partial x}\,dx + \frac{\partial z}{\partial y}\,dy \tag{A.11}$$

In the example of Equation A.8,

$$z = (0.004)y^2 + (0.025)y - (0.1)x_v - (0.02)x_v^2$$

Then

$$dz = (0.008y + 0.025)dy - (0.1 - 0.04x_v)dx$$

Once we have defined partial derivatives and the total differential for functions of two independent variables, the extension to n independent variables is straightforward. If

$$z = f(x_1, x_2, \ldots, x_n)$$

then the n partial derivatives $\partial z/\partial x_i$, $i = 1, n$, can be written

$$\frac{\partial z}{\partial x_1} = \frac{dz}{dx_1}\bigg|_{dx_2, \cdots,\, dx_n = 0} = f_{x_1}$$

$$\frac{\partial z}{\partial x_2} = \frac{dz}{dx_2}\bigg|_{dx_1, dx_3,\, \ldots,\, dx_n = 0} = f_{x_2}$$

.
.
.

$$\frac{\partial z}{\partial x_n} = \frac{dz}{dx_n}\bigg|_{dx_1, dx_2, \ldots, dx_{n-1}=0} = f_{x_n}$$

The total differential of z will be the n-variable generalization of Equation A.11:

$$dz = \frac{\partial z}{\partial x_1} dx_1 + \cdots + \frac{\partial z}{\partial x_n} dx_n \tag{A.12}$$

Second Partial Derivatives and Second Total Differentials

Just as we defined second and higher-order derivatives for functions of one variable, we can do the same for functions of two or more variables.

The second partial derivative of z with respect to x is therefore

$$\frac{\partial^2 z}{\partial x^2} = \frac{\partial}{\partial x}\left(\frac{\partial z}{\partial x}\right) = f_{xx} \tag{A.13}$$

The second *cross-partial* derivative of z with respect to x and y is

$$\frac{\partial^2 z}{\partial x \partial y} = \frac{\partial}{\partial x}\left(\frac{\partial z}{\partial y}\right) = f_{xy} = \frac{\partial}{\partial y}\left(\frac{\partial z}{\partial x}\right) = f_{yx} \tag{A.14}$$

Thus, the *order* of differentiation does not matter.

The second total differential can be written as follows:

$$d^2 z = d\left(\frac{\partial z}{\partial x_1} dx_1 + \cdots + \frac{\partial z}{\partial y} dy\right)$$

$$= \frac{\partial^2 z}{\partial x^2} dx\, dx + \frac{\partial^2 z}{\partial x \partial y} dx\, dy + \frac{\partial^2 z}{\partial y^2} dy\, dy + \frac{\partial^2 z}{\partial y \partial x} dy\, dx$$

$$= \frac{\partial^2 z}{\partial x^2} dx\, dx + 2\frac{\partial^2 z}{\partial x \partial y} dx\, dy + \frac{\partial^2 z}{\partial y^2} dy\, dy$$

which can also be written as follows:

$$d^2 z = f_{xx}(dx)^2 + 2f_{xy}dx\, dy + f_{yy}(dy)^2 \tag{A.15}$$

For example, consider again Equation A.8. Thus

$$z = (0.004)y^2 + (0.025)y - (0.1)x_v - (0.02)x_v^2$$

$$\frac{\partial z}{\partial y} = 0.008y - 0.025$$

$$\frac{\partial z}{\partial x_v} = -0.1 - 0.04x_v$$

$$\frac{\partial^2 z}{\partial y^2} = 0.008$$

$$\frac{\partial^2 z}{\partial x_v \partial y} = 0$$

$$\frac{\partial^2 z}{\partial x_v^2} = -0.04$$

$$\frac{\partial^2 z}{\partial y \partial x_v} = 0 = \frac{\partial^2 z}{\partial x_v \partial y}$$

$$dz = (0.08y - 0.025)dy + (-0.1 - 0.04x_v)dx_v$$

$$dz^2 = 0.008dy^2 + 2(0) - 0.04dx_v^2 = 0.008dy^2 - 0.04dx_v^2$$

MARGINAL FUNCTIONS OF ONE AND SEVERAL VARIABLES

In many cases, we will wish to determine the effect of changes in important variables, such as the cost of an input or the price of output, on an overall economic system. For example, we might wish to know how a change in the price of gasoline, in the form of an output tax, would affect the overall demand for gasoline and total emissions of carbon dioxide.

Suppose that we begin with a function of the total demand for gasoline,

$$Q_g = 250 + 100y - 15P_g - 0.15P_g^2 + 0.5P_{pt} \tag{A.16}$$

where Q_g is the number of gallons of gasoline demanded, P_g is the price in dollars per gallon, P_{pt} is the average price of public transit in dollars per mile, and y is household income in dollars. The partial marginal function is the change in the total function for a given change in one of the independent variables. The partial marginal function with respect to changes in the price of gasoline is given by the partial derivative of the total function with respect to price, holding income constant. Thus

$$\frac{\partial Q_g}{\partial P_g} = -15 - 0.3P_g < 0 \tag{A.17}$$

Notice that, as would be expected in this case, the marginal function is always less than zero. An increase in price will always reduce the quantity of gasoline demanded.

The Concept of Elasticity

Equation A.17 measures the absolute change in the quantity of gasoline demand-ed relative to changes in the price of gasoline. Often, however, we will want to determine relative changes in quantity with respect to one of the independent vari-ables. The measure economists use for such comparisons, which is related concept to the marginal function, is called an *elasticity*. An elasticity measures the *percent-age* change in one variable divided by the percentage change in another. It is thus a unitless measure.

The most common elasticity measures of demand are own-price, cross-price, and income. We can define the own-price elasticity as

$$\epsilon_{xx}^d = \frac{\%\Delta Q_x}{\%\Delta P_x}$$

Percentage change can be represented as the change from one point to another, divided by the average value of the range times 100. For example, the percentage change in the quantity of gasoline demanded from Q_1 to Q_2 gallons is given by

$$\%\Delta Q = \frac{Q_2 - Q_1}{(Q_1 + Q_2)/2}(100)$$

Similarly, the percentage change in price is given by

$$\%\Delta P = \frac{P_2 - P_1}{(P_1 + P_2)/2}(100)$$

Putting these together, we have what is called *arc elasticity*, which is elasticity mea-sured for a discrete change along the demand function:

$$\epsilon_{xx}^d = \frac{\dfrac{Q_2 - Q_1}{(Q_2 + Q_1)/2}(100)}{\dfrac{P_2 - P_1}{(P_2 + P_1)/2}(100)} = \left(\frac{Q_2 - Q_1}{P_2 - P_1}\right)\frac{\overline{P}}{\overline{Q}} \tag{A.18}$$

where $\overline{P}$ and $\overline{Q}$ refer to the average price and quantity demanded, respectively.

If we are evaluating changes at single points, however, the changes will be infinitesimal, and the average over the range can be replaced by the point values themselves. Writing Equation A.18 in differential notation, we have

$$\epsilon_{xx}^d = \frac{\partial Q_x}{\partial P_x}\frac{P_x}{Q_x} \tag{A.19}$$

If we assume that demand functions are downward-sloping, the own-price elastic-ity of demand will always be less than or equal to zero. Economists generally divide own-price elasticity into three categories: we say that demand is *elastic* if $\epsilon_{xx}^d < -1$, unitary elastic if $\epsilon_{xx}^d = -1$, and inelastic if $-1 < \epsilon_{xx}^d < 0$.

Cross-price elasticity and income elasticity are defined in a similar manner to own-price elasticity:

$$\epsilon_{xy}^d = \frac{\partial Q_x}{\partial P_y} \frac{P_y}{Q_x} \tag{A.20}$$

$$\epsilon_{xM}^d = \frac{\partial Q_x}{\partial y} \frac{P_y}{y} \tag{A.21}$$

where y equals income.

Estimates of demand elasticities are crucial to much applied environmental policy analysis work. For example, policymakers may wish to know how the tax on gasoline will affect overall expenditures on gasoline, to assess equity impacts. Alternatively, policymakers may wish to know how the tax will affect the demand for public transit and hence potential changes in levels of air pollution.

UNCONSTRAINED MAXIMIZATION AND MINIMIZATION

Often in economic problems, we will want to determine the best combination of goods or the best way to produce something. In environmental economics, for example, we will want to determine how individuals trade off different goods and services, including environmental goods. We will also want to determine how these trade-offs change as various parameters change. In the case of firms, we will want to know how they will respond to different sorts of policy instruments, such as emissions taxes or command-and-control regulations. Or we will want to determine so-called second-best solutions, where some environmental regulations must be taken as given and the problem is to determine societally optimal solutions subject to those given regulations.

A function is said to attain a local *maximum* at a point that is higher than any other nearby point and a local *minimum* at a point that is lower than any other nearby point. The process of determining maxima and minima is called *optimization*. For a given function $f(x)$, typically we would label the value of x that produces a maximum or minimum of $f(x)$, x^*. Thus we would write $y^* = f(x^*)$. This is shown in Figure A.2 for two different functions. In panel (a), the function $f(x)$ achieves a minimum at x_1^*, and in panel (b), function $g(x)$ attains a maximum at x_2^*. In both cases, the slope of the functions $f(x)$ and $g(x)$ have a slope of 0 at the critical points. It would seem, therefore, that one condition for a function to attain a local maximum or minimum is for the slope of the function to equal 0. In fact, this is one necessary condition. And because the first derivative of a function equals its slope at any point, we can write the first condition for a maximum or minimum as:

$$\frac{dy}{dx} = 0 \tag{A.22}$$

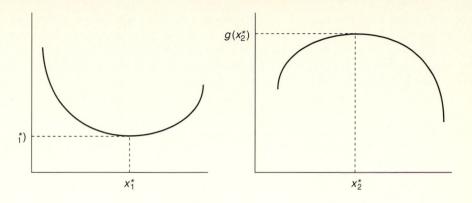

Figure A.2   Minimum and Maximum Points

Although this condition is *necessary*, it is not *sufficient*. To see why, consider the function $h(x)$ in Figure A.3. At x^*, the slope of $h(x)$ is zero, but $h(x^*)$ is neither a local maximum nor a local minimum. At point A, we say that the function $h(x)$ has an *inflection* point. An inflection point is a point that has a slope of zero along a function that is otherwise increasing or decreasing.

Because of the possibility of an inflection point, the first-order condition (A.22) is not sufficient to ensure a minimum or maximum of the function. We need some other means of distinguishing between a minimum or maximum and an inflection point. To do this, we can look at the behavior of the slope of the original function near the identified critical points. In panel (a) of Figure A.2, notice that the slope of the function is negative and increasing for values of x , x_1^* and positive

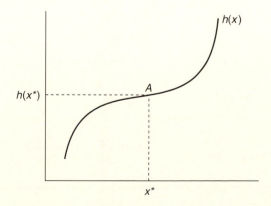

Figure A.3   An Inflection Point

and increasing for values of x . x_1^*. Thus the slope of the slope is always increasing in the vicinity of x_1^*. Conversely, in panel (b), the slope of $g(x)$ is positive and decreasing for values of $x < x_2^*$ and negative and decreasing for values of $x > x_2^*$. Thus the slope of the slope is always decreasing in the vicinity of x_2^*. However, at the inflection point shown in Figure A.3, the slope of the slope is zero.

These conditions can be translated into conditions on the *second* derivative of the function, which is the slope of the slope function or first derivative. In the case of a local *minimum* like Figure A.2(a), the second derivative will be *positive*:

$$\frac{d^2y}{dx^2} > 0 \tag{A.23}$$

Similarly, in the case of a local *maximum*, the second derivative will be *negative*:

$$\frac{d^2y}{dx^2} < 0 \tag{A.24}$$

Once the necessary first-order condition (A.22) is satisfied, the second-order conditions (A.23 and A.24) are *sufficient* to ensure a local maximum or minimum.

Consider two examples.

1. $y = 24x + 2(x + 5)^2$. The first-order condition is

$$\frac{dy}{dx} = 24 + 6(x + 5) = 54 + 6x = 0$$

$$\Rightarrow x^* = -9$$

The second-order condition is

$$\frac{d^2y}{dx^2} = 6 > 0$$

Therefore, $x^* = -9$ is a local minimum of the function $y = 24x + 2(x + 5)^2$.

2. $y = 15 + 10x - 1{,}000/x$. The first-order condition is

$$\frac{dy}{dx} = 10 - \frac{100}{x^2} = 0$$

$$x^* = \pm 10$$

The second-order condition is

$$\frac{d^2y}{dx^2} = \frac{2{,}000}{x^3}$$

The second-order condition is positive for $x^* = +10$ and negative for $x^* = -10$. Therefore, the function $y = 15 + 10x - 1{,}000/x$ attains a maximum at $x^* = -10$ and a minimum at $x^* = +10$.

FUNCTIONS OF SEVERAL VARIABLES

Finding minima and maxima of functions of several independent variables is analogous to finding them for one-variable functions. We begin with first-order conditions by writing out the total differential of the function $z = f(x, y)$. This is just Equation A.11.

$$dz = \frac{\partial z}{\partial x}dx + \frac{\partial z}{\partial y}dy = 0$$

For $dz = 0$, it must be the case that

$$dz = \frac{\partial z(x^*, y^*)}{\partial z}dx + \frac{\partial z(x^*, y^*)}{\partial y}dy \equiv 0$$

at the critical points described by (x^*, y^*) for all possible changes dx and dy; otherwise we could not be sure that $dz = 0$. (Because the equality must hold at the critical points, we use the identity symbol.) Thus it must be the case that

$$\frac{\partial z}{\partial x} = f_x = 0 \quad \text{and} \quad \frac{\partial z}{\partial y} = f_y = 0 \tag{A.25}$$

To convince yourself that these conditions are necessary, suppose that it was not true. Suppose that $(\partial z/\partial x) \neq 0$ and $(\partial z/\partial y) \neq 0$ with $dz = 0$ for some combination of dx and dy. Then it must be the case that for some other combination of dx and dy, $dz \neq 0$, since both terms on the right-hand side of Equation A.11 will be nonzero. Since this cannot be true for a minimum or maximum point, the necessary conditions in Equation A.25 must hold.

Like the first-order conditions for functions of one variable, the conditions in Equation A.25 are necessary but not sufficient for a minimum or maximum point. Sufficient conditions are to be found in the second-order terms. In the two-variable case, for example, if all first-order partial derivative are 0, the sufficient second-order condition for a maximum is for the second *total* differential to be less than 0:

$$d^2z = f_{xx}(dx)^2 + 2f_{xy}dx\,dy + f_{yy}(dy)^2 < 0 \tag{A.26}$$

for any combinations of dx and dy when both are not equal to 0. Similarly, if the first-order conditions are met, a sufficient condition for a minimum in the two-variable case is for the second total differential to be greater than 0:

$$d^2z = f_{xx}(dx)^2 + 2f_{xy}dx\,dy + f_{yy}(dy)^2 > 0 \tag{A.27}$$

The conditions in Equations A.26 and A.27 also imply three conditions for the signs of certain second partial and cross derivatives. For example, besides the condition in Equation A.27, for a minimum, assuming that dx and dy are not both zero, it must also be the case that

$$dx = 0 \Rightarrow dy \neq 0 \quad \text{and} \quad f_{xx} < 0$$

and

$$dy = 0 \Rightarrow dx \neq 0 \quad \text{and} \quad f_{yy} < 0$$

If we factor Equation A.27 by f_{xx} and add and subtract $(f_{xy}\,dy/f_{xx})^2$, we have

$$d^2z = f_{xx}\left\{(dx)^2 + 2\frac{f_{xy}\,dx\,dy}{f_{xx}} + \left(\frac{f_{xy}dy}{f_{xx}}\right)^2 - \left(\frac{f_{xy}dy}{f_{xx}}\right)^2 + \frac{f_{yy}(dy)^2}{f_{xx}}\right\} > 0$$

$$= f_{xx}\left\{\left(dx + \frac{f_{xy}dy}{f_{xx}}\right)^2 + \left(\frac{dy}{f_{xx}}\right)^2 [f_{xx}f_{yy} - (f_{xy})^2]\right\} > 0$$

Since it must be the case that $f_{xx} > 0$, the second term in the expression above must be positive. But this will be guaranteed only if

$$f_{xx}f_{yy} - (f_{xy})^2 > 0 \tag{A.28}$$

The condition in Equation A.28 will also hold for a maximum. We leave it as an exercise to show that with

$$d^2z < 0$$

$$dx = 0 \Rightarrow dy \neq 0 \text{ and } f_{xx} < 0$$

$$dy = 0 \Rightarrow dx \neq 0 \text{ and } f_{yy} < 0$$

$$f_{xx}f_{yy} - (f_{xy})^2 > 0$$

for a maximum. For those with an understanding of matrix algebra, the condition in Equation A.28 can be represented by the sign of the matrix of second partial derivatives:

$$\begin{vmatrix} f_{xx} & f_{xy} \\ f_{yx} & f_{yy} \end{vmatrix} > 0$$

This matrix is derived by totally differentiating the first-order conditions, which are functions of the independent variables x and y. Thus for $z = f(x, y)$, the first-order conditions are

$$f_x(x^*, y^*) \equiv 0$$

$$f_y(x^*, y^*) \equiv 0 \tag{A.29}$$

Again, the identity notation refers to the fact that the first-order conditions must always be true at the solution values (x^*, y^*).[1] Totally differentiating the first-order conditions yields

---

[1] See Silberberg (1978) for a more detailed exposition.

$$f_{xx}dx^* + f_{xy}dy^* \equiv 0$$
$$f_{yx}dx^* + f_{yy}dy^* \equiv 0 \qquad (A.30)$$

In matrix notation, this can be written as

$$\begin{vmatrix} f_{xx} & f_{xy} \\ f_{yx} & f_{yy} \end{vmatrix} \begin{vmatrix} dx^* \\ dy^* \end{vmatrix} = \begin{vmatrix} 0 \\ 0 \end{vmatrix} \qquad (A.31)$$

The n-variable extension of Equation A.31 is straightforward. For the function

$$z = f(x_1, x_2, \ldots, x_n)$$

the total differentiation of the first-order conditions will yield the $n \times n$ matrix

$$\begin{pmatrix} f_{x_1 x_1} & f_{x_1 x_2} & \cdots & f_{x_1 x_n} \\ f_{x_1 x_2} & f_{x_2 x_2} & \cdots & f_{x_2 x_n} \\ \vdots & \vdots & \ddots & \vdots \\ f_{x_n x_1} & f_{x_n x_2} & \cdots & f_{x_n x_n} \end{pmatrix} \begin{pmatrix} d^*_{x_1} \\ d^*_{x_2} \\ \vdots \\ d^*_{x_n} \end{pmatrix} = \begin{pmatrix} 0 \\ 0 \\ \vdots \\ 0 \end{pmatrix} \qquad (A.32)$$

The leftmost matrix is known as the *bordered hessian*. Conditions for maxima and minima are determined by the determinant of this matrix. For example, for a one-variable maximization, the 1×1 determinant condition will just be

$$|f_{xx}| < 0$$

We have already shown that for the two-variable case, it must be that

$$\begin{vmatrix} f_{xx} & f_{xy} \\ f_{yx} & f_{yy} \end{vmatrix} > 0$$

The signs of subsequently larger determinants will alternate. Thus the determinant in the 3×3 case will be negative, the 4×4 positive, and so on.[2]

REFERENCE

Silberburg, E. 1978. *The Structure of Economics*. New York: McGraw-Hill.

---

[2] See Silberberg (1978).

APPENDIX B

INTRODUCTION TO SELECTED ECONOMETRIC CONCEPTS

In this book, we have often used examples of empirical work designed to elicit willingness to pay for environmental amenities and small changes in environmental risk. Much of this work relies on econometric techniques, especially multiple regression. In this appendix, we provide a basic overview of estimation of linear models of behavior. Of course, this appendix is no substitute for an econometrics textbook, which should be consulted by readers who wish to develop a more thorough understanding of the subject.[1]

Suppose that we are trying to determine willingness to pay (WTP) for improvements in views at the Grand Canyon and to differentiate WTP by various demographic characteristics including education, income, and proximity to the Grand Canyon, among other variables. Using a sample of data collected from a contingent valuation survey of n individuals, we wish to estimate a model such as

$$Y_i = a + bE_i + cI_i + dD_i + \epsilon_i \qquad (B.1)$$

for individuals $i = 1, N$,

where Y_i = WTP for individual i
E_i = education level, in number of years of postelementary education
I_i = household income level for individual i

---

[1] See, for example, Kennedy (1992) or Johnston (1984).

D_i = distance from the Grand Canyon in miles

ϵ_i = a random-error term

The object of the econometrician is to estimate the coefficients a, b, c, and d that provide the "best" estimates of *WTP*. Unfortunately, it is not always clear what "best" means. And the best estimator in one circumstance might be an altogether unsuitable estimator for another.

THE LEAST-SQUARES ESTIMATOR

The most common criterion for determining the "best" estimator is to minimize the *sum of the squared residuals* ϵ_i, which represent the difference between the predicted value of the dependent variable, denoted $\hat{Y}$, and the observed value. This is shown in Figure B.1 for the relationship between *WTP* and income.

For this reason, this criterion is called the "least-squares" estimator. Once the constant terms a, b, c, and d are determined, it is then possible to estimate $\hat{Y}$. The residual term, e_i, is defined as

$$e_i = Y_i - \hat{Y} = Y_i - a - bE_i - cI_i - dD_i, \qquad i = 1, n \qquad (B.2)$$

The reason we wish to minimize the sum of the squared values of the residuals is that minimizing the sum of the residuals would fail to account for both positive and negative residuals. In Figure B.1, for example, the residuals associated with points 1, 4, 5, 8, and 9 are positive, while those associated with points 2, 3, 6, 7, and 10 are negative. Their sums would tend to cancel out. Since the square of any real number is positive, however, minimizing the sum of the squared residuals would result in a "good" fit to the data. Thus the choice problem is to minimize

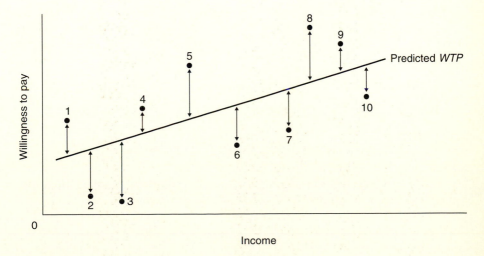

Figure B.1   Minimizing the Sum of Squared Residuals

$$\frac{\partial\left(\sum e_i^2\right)}{\partial a} = \frac{\partial\left(\sum e_i^2\right)}{\partial b} = \frac{\partial\left(\sum e_i^2\right)}{\partial c} = \frac{\partial\left(\sum e_i^2\right)}{\partial d} = 0 \tag{B.3}$$

The solution to the optimization problem in Equation B.3 requires that we take the partial derivatives of B.3 with respect to a, b, c, and d to determine the minimum. Thus we will wish to solve the following four equations for the parameters a, b, c, and d:[2]

$$\frac{\partial\sum e_i^2}{\partial a} = -2\sum(Y_i - a - bE_i - cI_i - dD_i) = 0 \tag{B.4}$$

$$\frac{\partial\sum e_i^2}{\partial b} = -2\sum E_i(Y_i - a - bE_i - cI_i - dD_i) = 0 \tag{B.5}$$

$$\frac{\partial\sum e_i^2}{\partial c} = -2\sum I_i(Y_i - a - bE_i - cI_i - dD_i) = 0 \tag{B.6}$$

$$\frac{\partial\sum e_i^2}{\partial d} = -2\sum D_i(Y_i - a - bE_i - cI_i - dD_i) = 0 \tag{B.7}$$

The solutions to these four equations will have several important properties. First, the regression line will pass through the point of the means $\overline{Y}, \overline{E}, \overline{I}$, and $\overline{D}$. This follows directly from Equation B.4, which on division by n (the number of observations) and rearrangement of terms gives

$$\overline{Y} = a + b\overline{E} + c\overline{I} + d\overline{D}$$

The second property concerns the residuals, e_i. These will have zero covariance with the sample values of the independent variables and also with the predicted $\hat{Y}$ values. It also turns out that for the class of linear unbiased estimators, the least-squares estimator wll have the lowest variance. That is, the least-squares estimator will most closely fit the sample data.

THE MULTIPLE CORRELATION COEFFICIENT

The four regression coefficients estimated by Equations B.4 through B.7 describe a "line" (really a hyperplane) in four dimensions that passes through the scatter-

---

[2]We leave the solution of these four equations as an exercise.

ing of points. The two-dimensional analogue of *WTP* versus income, shown in Figure B.1, shows the line fitted in X, Y space. When fitting a regression, we will want some measure of the "goodness" of fit. One such measure is called the *correlation coefficient*. With more than one independent variable, the correlation coefficient, R, is called the *multiple correlation coefficient*. It is defined as the explained sum of squares divided by the total sum of squares, *measured around their respective means*. Thus

$$R^2 = \frac{ESS}{TSS} \tag{B.8}$$

where $ESS = \Sigma \hat{Y}^2$ and $TSS = \Sigma Y^2$. The residual sum of squares, RSS, is defined as the total sum of squares less the explained sum of squares. Thus $RSS = TSS - ESS$, or

$$\sum \epsilon^2 = \sum Y^2 - \sum \hat{Y}^2 \tag{B.9}$$

It follows from Equations B.8 and B.9 that

$$R^2 = \frac{ESS}{TSS} = \frac{\sum \hat{Y}^2}{\sum Y^2} = 1 - \frac{\sum e^2}{\sum Y^2} \tag{B.10}^3$$

It follows from this that $0 \leq R^2 \leq 1$ as long as there is a constant term in the regression.[4]

Most of the time, reported R^2 values are adjusted for *degrees of freedom*—the number of "free" or independent observations used in calculating the value of a statistic. For example, with only two observations, *any* linear function with one independent variable and a constant term will fit the data perfectly, regardless of the independent variable chosen. (Draw a picture to convince yourself why.) Adding a third observation may destroy the perfect fit, but the fit is still likely to be good because there is only one observation to "explain." The more observations there are, the harder it will be for any random model to fit the observations well. That is why R^2 is often adjusted for degrees of freedom: the unadjusted R^2 can always be increased by simply adding another explananatory variable.

The adjusted R^2, which is often written $\overline{R}^2$, is defined as follows:

$$\overline{R}^2 = 1 - \frac{\sum e^2/(N - k)}{\sum Y^2/(N - 1)} \tag{B.11}$$

---

[3]In matrix notation, $R^2 = \hat{Y}'\hat{Y}/Y'Y$.
[4]Note that without a constant term, the regression is forced through the origin. As a result, such a regression line will not necessarily pass through the means of the data points, as Equation B.4 implies. In that situation, it is possible for the residual sum of squares to exceed the total sum of squares.

where N = total number of observations and k = number of independent variables. Combining Equations B.10 and B.11 yields an alternate expression for the adjusted $\overline{R}^2$:

$$\overline{R}^2 = 1 - \frac{N-1}{N-k}(1 - R^2) \tag{B.12}$$

The rationale for this adjustment is that k parameters have been used to fit the model from which the residual sum of squares is measured, while one parameter (the mean of the sample data) has been used to compute the total sum of squares $\sum Y^2$. Thus unlike the unadjusted R^2, $\overline{R}^2$ can decline if an added variable has very little explanatory power.

INFERENCE IN THE LEAST-SQUARES MODEL

As we stated at the start of this appendix, the least-squares model will provide the "best" fit of the sample data if several assumptions hold. Often least-squares estimates are referred to as "BLUE," which means that they are the *best linear unbiased estimates* of the independent-variable parameters. We will not prove that assertion, but it rests on several underlying assumptions about the sample data and the residual terms. The first assumption is that the sample data points are fixed over repeated sampling. For example, in the regression specified in Equation B.1, we assume that the observations on income over N individuals would be the same if we sampled the same N individuals numerous times. That just means that income is not a random variable.

A second assumption is that the residuals are uncorrelated with one another and have zero mean and constant variance. This means that the residual for one person is not correlated with the residual of another. For example, if the residuals increased as income increased, then the least-squares model would no longer be BLUE. Instead, the estimated-model parameters, such as the coefficient c on income, would likely be biased.

A third assumption is that the model is indeed linear. If willingness to pay actually included a complicated multiplicative function of income and distance, it might not be possible to use a linear model unless the model could be transformed into a linear form.[5]

Assuming that the least-squares assumptions hold, however, we will still want to know how significant the explanatory variables of a model are. To determine this, we need some basic statistical assumptions, which we will not attempt to prove.

First, we need to know the variance of the sample residuals, s^2. Two alternate estimators are

$$\frac{\sum e^2}{N} \quad \text{and} \quad \frac{\sum e^2}{N-k} \tag{B.13}$$

---

[5]Nonlinear models can often be transformed into linear ones. For example, if a model is specified as $y = x_1^a x_2^b$, we can transform it into a linear model by taking logarithms of both sides. Thus we can rewrite the model as $\ln(y) = a \cdot \ln(x_1) + b \cdot \ln(x_2)$. The transformed model is then *log-linear*. In Chapter 11, for example, we used a log-linear model to estimate a hedonic price model.

The latter is generally used for inference purposes, for reasons that will become apparent. The sample variable standard deviations are given by

$$s_{x_k} = \sqrt{\frac{\sum x_k^2}{N}} \quad k = 1, K \tag{B.14}$$

We further assume that the residuals are distributed normally with mean 0 and variance σ_ϵ^2; that is, $\epsilon \sim N(0, \sigma_\epsilon^2)$. If this holds, then it turns out that the coefficients of the least-squares model will also be distributed normally, such that

$$b_k \sim N\left(\beta_k, \frac{\sigma_\epsilon^2}{\sum x_k^2}\right) \tag{B.15}$$

where b_k refers to the estimated coefficient for the kth explanatory variable and β_k refers to the "true" (and unknown) value of the coefficient b_k.

Because we will not know the "true" variance σ_ϵ^2 of the sample residuals, Equation B.15 is not operational. To derive the sampling distribution, we replace σ_ϵ^2 with its sampling estimate s^2. It then turns out that

$$\frac{\sum e^2}{\sigma_\epsilon^2} \sim \chi^2(N - k) \tag{B.16}$$

where $\chi^2(N - k)$ is the *chi-square* distribution.

To derive inferences about the distributions of the parameter estimates b_k, we use the results from Equations B.15 and B.16. It turns out that the t distribution is given by the ratio of a standard normal variable (i.e., one with mean 0 and variance 1) to the square root of a χ^2 variable divided by its degrees of freedom. Thus, it follows from Equation B.15 that

$$\frac{b_k - \beta_k}{\sigma_\epsilon / \sqrt{\sum x_k^2}} \sim N(0,1) \tag{B.17}$$

so we have

$$t = \frac{(b_k - \beta_k)\sqrt{\sum x_k^2}}{\sigma_\epsilon} \div \frac{\sqrt{\sum e^2 / \sigma_\epsilon}}{\sqrt{N - k}}$$

or

$$t = \frac{(b_k - \beta_k)}{s / \sqrt{\sum x_k^2}} \sim t(N - k) \tag{B.18}$$

Replacing σ_ϵ^2 by its estimator s^2 shifts us from a normal distribution to the t distribution. As the sample size becomes large, however, the t distribution closely resembles the normal distribution. For sample sizes above 30 to 40 observations,

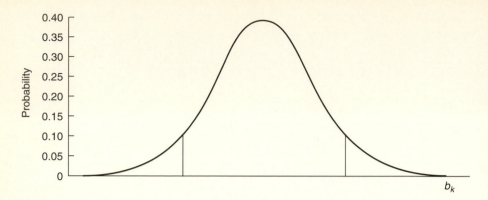

Figure B.2   Sampling Distribution of b_k under H_0: $\beta_k = \bar{\beta}_k$

little loss of accuracy will occur if it is assumed that $(b_k - \beta_k)/\sqrt{\sum x_k^2}$ is distributed as a standard normal variate.

Equation B.18 can be used as the basis for various standard inference procedures. A 95 percent *confidence interval* for β_k will be given by

$$b_k \pm \frac{t_{0.025}s}{\sqrt{\sum x_k^2}} \tag{B.19}$$

where $\sqrt{\sum x_k^2}$ is computed from the sample data, and b_k will be computed from equations similar to Equations B.4 through B.7,[6] s from Equation B.14, and $t_{0.025}$ from the 2.5 percent point of the t distribution with $N - k$ degrees of freedom. In general, a $100(1 - \delta)$ confidence interval for β is given by

$$b_k \pm \frac{t_{\delta/2}s}{\sqrt{\sum x_k^2}} \tag{B.20}$$

To test the null hypothesis that β_k has some specified value $\bar{\beta}_k$ (H_0: $\beta_k = \bar{\beta}_k$) against the alternative hypothesis that β_k has some value other than $\bar{\beta}_k$ (H_1: $\beta_k \neq \bar{\beta}_k$), we insert $\bar{\beta}_k$ into Equation B.18. If the null hypothesis is true, then

$$\frac{b_k - \bar{\beta}_k}{s/\sqrt{\sum x_k^2}} \sim t(N - k) \tag{B.21}$$

which provides the sampling distribution under the null hypothesis. This is shown in Figure B.2.

---

[6]In matrix notation, the vector of parameters $\mathbf{b} = (\mathbf{X}'\mathbf{X})^{-1}(\mathbf{X}'\mathbf{Y})$, where $\mathbf{X}$ = the $N \times K$ matrix of N observations of the K independent variables $(x_1, x_2, \ldots, x_k)$ and $\mathbf{Y}$ = the $N \times 1$ vector of dependent variable observations.

If the null hypothesis were true, then 95 percent of the sample values of b_k would lie within $t_{0.025}$ standard errors of $\bar{\beta}_k$. If the sample b_k is found in either tail of the distribution, either the null hypothesis is true but something unusual has happened, or the null hypothesis is false. In such cases, we usually choose the latter interpretation.

LIMITED DEPENDENT VARIABLES

Often in environmental economics models, data will be limited in some way. For example, in travel cost models, data are collected only for individuals who actually travel to a recreation site. For other individuals, whose willingness to pay is less than the cost of travel to the site, no data will be collected. Yet these nonvisiting individuals do comprise a portion of the demand curve for recreation, for if the cost were lower, they might then visit.

In other cases, such as contingent valuation models, economists will ask survey respondents series of yes-no questions to elicit ranges of willingess to pay. In such studies, the dependent variable is limited to just two possible values, yes and no. Thus, it would make little sense for predicted values of the dependent variable to be 0.28 yes or 1.1 no; they are simply yes or no. Economists generally use what are known as "maximum likelihood" techniques to estimate models with these sorts of dependent variables so as to avoid biased estimates of model parameters.

Censored or Truncated Regressions

Consider first the case where a variable can be observed only in a limited range, such as individuals with a sufficiently high *WTP* to be observed visiting the Grand Canyon. In this case, the model would be

$$y_i = \sum_{k=1}^{K} \beta_k X_k + e_i, \qquad \text{if } y_i \geq 0$$

$$= 0 \qquad\qquad \text{otherwise} \qquad\qquad \text{(B.22)}$$

Suppose that of the total of N observations, the last q observations of y are zero. Taking expectations of both sides of Equation B.22 gives

$$E(y_i, y_i \geq 0) = \sum_{k=1}^{K} \beta_k X_k + E(e_i, y_i \geq 0) \qquad \text{if } y_i \geq 0, \quad i = 1, N - q \qquad \text{(B.23)}$$

If the expectation of the conditional error term were zero, a least-squares regression on the $N - q$ observations would provide an unbiased estimator of β_k. Unfortunately, this is not the case, as is shown in Figure B.3.

In the figure, the dashed line reflects the "true" regression $y_i = \beta_1 + \beta_2 X_i$ on all N observations. However, since only $N - q$ observations are used, the actual

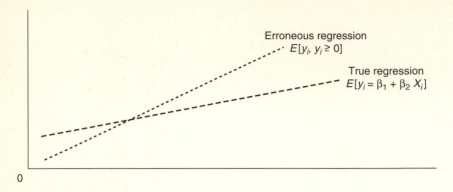

Figure B.3   The Effect of a Truncated Regression

regression values will be scattered about the dotted line y_i, $y_i \geq 0$. Thus a least-squares regression on the $N - q$ observations will be biased.

Dichotomous Dependent Variables

Next consider a case where an economist is attempting to model the determinants of *WTP* for improving visibility at the Grand Canyon. Using a contingent valuation study, the economist has sampled a number of individuals and questioned them about their *WTP* using a series of questions such as "Would you be willing to pay between $X and $Y to improve visibility at the Grand Canyon?"[7] In the survey, the dollar amounts $X and $Y are varied. Using the data collected and demographic data about the individuals surveyed, the economist develops a model that predicts the probability that an individual would be willing to pay a given amount to visit the Grand Canyon.

　　If a linear model were used to estimate the probability that a given individual would be willing to pay a particular amount, an immediate problem could arise, as shown in Figure B.4. In this figure, observations for a given payment level, X, are observed. Respondents will respond either yes or no to a given payment level, with yes corresponding to a probability of 1 and no corresponding to a probability of 0. If a linear model is used, predicted probability levels can lie outside the range [0, 1], which is impossible. Thus the line labeled "linear estimating line" will yield biased and possibly even nonsensical results.

　　What is needed instead of a linear model of probability is a model that ensures that all of the estimated probabilities lie between 0 and 1, as shown by the curve labled the "'True' probability estimator" in Figure B.4.

　　There are different ways to do this. The most popular way is through the use of a *logistic* function which creates the *logit* model.

---

[7]Chapter 11 discusses some of the technical issues associated with contingent valuation models. Here we abstract from those complexities in order to focus on the empirical techniques themselves.

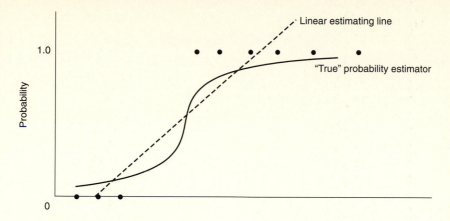

Figure B.4   The Linear Probability Model

The logistic function is given by $f(\theta) = \dfrac{e^{\theta}}{1 + e^{\theta}}$ and varies from 0 to 1 as $x\beta$ varies from $-\infty$ to $+\infty$. Suppose that θ is a linear combination of variables $x\beta$. We can then estimate the probability of being willing to pay a given amount as a function of $x\beta$. Thus

$$\text{prob}(WTP\ \$k) = \frac{e^{x\beta}}{1 + e^{x\beta}} \tag{B.24}$$

Using equation B.24, the probability of not being willing to pay the amount $\$k$ is given by

$$\text{prob}(\text{Not } WTP\ \$k) = 1 - \text{prob}(WTP\ \$k) = 1 - \frac{e^{x\beta}}{1 + e^{x\beta}} = \frac{1}{1 + e^{x\beta}} \tag{B.25}$$

Equations B.24 and B.25 imply that $\text{prob}(WTP\ \$k)/\text{prob}(\text{Not } WTP\ \$k) = e^{x\beta}$. Taking logarithms of both sides, we have

$$\ln\left[\frac{\text{prob}(WTP\ \$k)}{\text{prob}(\text{Not } WTP\ \$k)}\right] = x\beta \tag{B.26}$$

Equation B.26 is the logit model, which is short for "log-odds." The benefit of this model is that the log-odds can be estimated using least-squares techniques. It is a valuable addition to the economist's empirical toolkit.

REFERENCES

Johnson, J. 1984. *Econometric Methods*, 3rd ed. New York: McGraw-Hill.

Kennedy, P. 1992. *A Guide to Econometrics*, 3rd ed. Cambridge, MA: The MIT Press.

APPENDIX C

ENVIRONMENTAL INFORMATION AVAILABLE ON THE INTERNET

The Internet is a rapidly expanding system of interconnected computer networks. These provide users with access to thousands of sites and computers throughout the world. The Internet supports electronic mail and transfers of files, including text, graphics, video, and sound files. Think of the Internet as a gateway. You can travel to various sites and explore what they have to offer. Those sites themselves will often be gateways to still other sites, and so on in a sort of chain.

Until a few years ago, "navigating" the Internet was difficult because the computer commands required were not user-friendly. As more commercial on-line services became available, there was a need to improve the ability of novice users to gain access to Internet resources. To address these problems, a software program called Mosaic was developed. Mosaic provides users with access to the World Wide Web, which is sometimes just called the Web. The World Wide Web supports a type of computer linkage called *hypertext.* Hypertext allows users with a computer mouse to click on special words, phrases, or images, and step through to other Web sites. There are numerous Web browsers, each of which provides a convenient way of sorting through the various categories of information available, serving as what is known as a *search engine.* Most commercial on-line services provide access to the Web, and no doubt, access will become *de rigueur* in the future.

The Internet contains files of all types on almost every imaginable (and unimaginable) subject. A great deal of information about the environment and environmental economics is available, and more is added daily. Most Web sites are accessed using a uniform set of location codes. These *uniform resource locators,* or URLs, will point you to various resources. They all begin with *http://.* The addresses of many sites on the Web are then followed by *www* (for World Wide Web).

722

All sites can be connected to directly once you know their individual URLs. A few of the many sites you may find interesting include these:

1. United Nations Environment Programme (UNEP)
   http://www.unep.ch/
   This site contains links to the various environmental and natural resource programs conducted by the UN. For example, you can access the work of the Intergovernmental Panel on Climate Change (IPPC), which we discussed in Chapter 21. It also contains information on environmental programs in a variety of UN members.
2. Oak Ridge National Laboratories (ORNL) Environmental Science Division
   http://www.eso.ornl.gov/
   This site contains a great deal of information regarding environmental research programs and news conducted by ORNL. It also contains information on upcoming events, such as seminars. And it has a great many links to other environmental sites.
3. Econet
   http://www.econet.apc.org/econet/
   Econet brings together much information on ongoing environmental protection work and contains links to many other sites.
4. Resources for the Future (RFF)
   http://www.rff.org/
   At this site, you can explore current research under way at RFF, which specializes in the examination of environmental and natural resource issues.
5. EnviroLink Network
   http://www.envirolink/org/
   The EnviroLink Network is a vast database of information about environmental research, organizations, products, and activism. It is a great site to explore.
6. Environmental Research Laboratories
   http://www.erl.noaa.gov/
   The Environmental Research Laboratories perform research and technology development designed to improve our understanding of the earth's oceans and atmosphere and improve policies for environmental management.
7. United States Geological Survey (USGS)
   http://sun1.cr.usgs.gov/
   The Earth Resource Observation System (EROS) data center collects and processes data for NASA from LANDSAT satellites.
8. USGS Global Resource Information Database (GRID)
   http://grid2.cr.usgs.gov/grid/grid.html/
   GRID provides a wealth of technical data on the environment. It is designed especially for decision makers and environmental analysts.

Keep in mind that sites change countinuously. New ones are created all the time, and old ones sometimes vanish. If you have trouble finding any of the sites listed here, try searching one of the many available search engines for specific keywords, such as *environment*.

NAME INDEX

SUBJECT INDEX